EMPIRE BY LAW

Columbia Studies in International and Global History

COLUMBIA STUDIES IN INTERNATIONAL AND GLOBAL HISTORY

Cemil Aydin, Timothy Nunan, and Dominic Sachsenmaier, Series Editors

This series presents some of the finest and most innovative work coming out of the current landscapes of international and global historical scholarship. Grounded in empirical research, these titles transcend the usual area boundaries and address how history can help us understand contemporary problems, including poverty, inequality, power, political violence, and accountability beyond the nation-state. The series covers processes of flows, exchanges, and entanglements—and moments of blockage, friction, and fracture—not only between "the West" and "the Rest" but also among parts of what has variously been dubbed "the Third World" or "the Global South." Scholarship in international and global history remains indispensable for a better sense of current complex regional and global economic transformations. Such approaches are vital in understanding the making of our present world.

Andrew B. Liu, Owen Miller, and Meha Priyadarshini, eds., *Melancholy Borders: Mobility, Migration, and Exclusion in Global History*

Ebru Turan, *The Race for Universal Monarchy: Apocalypticism and the Ottoman–Habsburg Rivalry in the Sixteenth-Century Mediterranean*

Paul van Trigt, *Progress from the Margins: Human Rights and Disability Internationalism Since the 1960s*

Marian Füssel, trans. Brían Hanrahan, *The World in Flames: A Global History of the Seven Years' War*

Q. Edward Wang, *Staple to Superfood: A Global History of the Sweet Potato*

Pierre Singaravélou, trans. Stephen W. Sawyer, *Tianjin Cosmopolis: An Alternative History of Globalization*

James De Lorenzi, *Feasting on History: Ethiopia and the Orientalists*

Jie-Hyun Lim, trans. Megan Sungyoon, *Victimhood Nationalism: History and Memory in a Global Age*

Hale Eroğlu, *Muslim Transnationalism in Modern China: Debates on Hui Identity and Islamic Reform*

Sandrine Kott, *A World More Equal: An Internationalist Perspective on the Cold War*

Julia Hauser, *A Taste for Purity: An Entangled History of Vegetarianism*

Hayrettin Yücesoy, *Disenchanting the Caliphate: The Secular Discipline of Power in Abbasid Political Thought*

Anne Irfan, *Refuge and Resistance: Palestinians and the International Refugee System*

Michael Francis Laffan, *Under Empire: Muslim Lives and Loyalties Across the Indian Ocean World, 1775–1945*

Eva-Maria Muschik, *Building States: The United Nations, Development, and Decolonization, 1945–1965*

Jessica Namakkal, *Unsettling Utopia: The Making and Unmaking of French India*

Michael Christopher Low, *Imperial Mecca: Ottoman Arabia and the Indian Ocean Hajj*

Nicole CuUnjieng Aboitiz, *Asian Place, Filipino Nation: A Global Intellectual History of the Philippine Revolution, 1887–1912*

For a complete list of books in the series, please see the Columbia University Press website.

Empire by Law

THE OTTOMAN ORIGINS OF THE MANDATE SYSTEM IN THE MIDDLE EAST

Aimee M. Genell

Columbia University Press
New York

Columbia University Press
Publishers Since 1893
New York Chichester, West Sussex
cup.columbia.edu

Library of Congress Cataloging-in-Publication Data

Names: Genell, Aimee author
Title: Empire by law : the Ottoman origins of the mandate system in the Middle East / Aimee Genell.
Description: New York : Columbia University Press, [2026] | Series: Columbia studies in international and global history | Includes bibliographical references and index.
Identifiers: LCCN 2025051563 (print) | LCCN 2025051564 (ebook) | ISBN 9780231203340 hardback | ISBN 9780231203357 trade paperback | ISBN 9780231554992 ebook | ISBN 9780231566902 PDF
Subjects: LCSH: Turkey—Administrative and political divisions | Turkey—Politics and government—19th century | Turkey—Politics and government—1909–1918 | World War, 1914–1918—Territorial questions—Turkey | Sovereignty | Eastern question
Classification: LCC JS6952.A5 G46 2026 (print) | LCC JS6952.A5 (ebook) | DDC 320.9561–dc23/eng/20260421
LC record available at https://lccn.loc.gov/2025051563
LC ebook record available at https://lccn.loc.gov/2025051564

Printed and bound by CPI Group (UK) Ltd, Croydon, CR0 4YY

Cover design: Elliott S. Cairns.
Cover image: Photograph of a sign that says "Wilsonian Principles Article 12" in Ottoman Turkish, at Ezerum (Erzurum), September 25, 1919. Courtesy of the National Archives.

GPSR Authorized Representative: Easy Access System Europe, Mustamäe tee 50, 10621 Tallinn, Estonia, gpsr.requests@easproject.com

Contents

Acknowledgments

This project began as an analysis of how Ottoman sovereignty in Egypt shaped the British military occupation of the province between 1882 and 1914. The scope of the research subsequently expanded significantly to consider how Ottoman practices of administrative autonomy affected late imperial statecraft. As the boundaries of my work increased, so too did the number of people and institutions that supported me. I owe an enormous debt to everyone who helped me to develop my research and language skills and to sharpen my arguments, as well as to those who funded my research and writing over many years and in many places.

At Columbia University, a constellation of scholars, research projects, and arguments about international law and international institutions animated my own research—especially the Center for International History's seminars on military occupation, sovereignty, and humanitarianism. Mark Mazower's conversations and criticisms profoundly shaped my thinking and prompted me to consider what Europe looked like from the perspective of Istanbul. Susan Pedersen taught me more about the craft of history than anyone else. She pushed me to think critically about the overlap between imperial governance and international politics and stimulated my love of archival research. Christine Philliou has remained a mentor and friend and is responsible, in all the best ways, for animating my obsession with late Ottoman history. My discussions with Rashid Khalidi on autonomy as a persistent tool of great power politics in the

Middle East fundamentally shaped how I conceived of the Ottoman privileged provinces. Beth Baron taught me how to be generous with the scholarship of others. I owe a special thanks to Nader Sohrabi. One of the first Ottoman texts I read with him was the 1876 Ottoman constitution, which begins by stating that the empire is composed of "its present domains and territories, including the privileged provinces (*eyalet-i mümtaze*)." I asked, "What is a privileged province?" In so many ways, this book is the result of trying to answer that question. Sam Moyn, Marwa Elshakry, and John Fabian Witt all stimulated my thinking about international law and empire.

I had the good fortune to know and exchange ideas with a dazzling group of young scholars at Columbia. I thank especially my dear friend Jared Manasek, who was also responsible for my Ottoman conversion, as well as Leyla Amzi-Erdoğdular, Seth Anziska, Hannah Barker, Rosie Bsheer, Toby Harper, Shehab Ismail, Kaveh Niazi, Cenk Palaz, Eileen Ryan, Simon Stevens, Merve Tezcanlı, Mari Webel, Steven Wertheim, Natasha Wheatly, and Adrien Zakar. William McAlister provided incredible mentorship at the Mellon Interdisciplinary Graduate Program within Columbia's Institute for Social and Economic Research and Policy—the fellowship program altered my research and professional trajectories. I am indebted to my colleagues in the program, especially Claire Eddington, Abhishek Kaicker, Seema Golestaneh, James Chappel, and Tyler Williams.

I spent two years as a fellow at Yale's International Security Studies and am thankful for the time to expand the scope of my research. It was only through weekly seminar discussions that I fully realized the larger significance of this book's argument and that Egypt was but one of many privileged provinces in the Ottoman Empire. I am grateful for conversations with Adam Tooze, Alan Mikhail, Steffen Rimner, Paul Kennedy, Amanda Behm, Radhika Natarajan, Jeremy Friedman, and Jesse Tumblin.

I have had extensive help over the years with modern and Ottoman Turkish. I am grateful to the late Etem Erol, Yorgos Dedes, Mustafa Küçük at the Ottoman Archives, Bilal Yılmaz, and Ülkiye Çapa. Züleyha Mary Fikret cultivated my love for Ottoman and spent years reading Ottoman documents and newspapers with me, even after I left New York.

I would not have been able to write this book without generous research support from the National Endowment for the Humanities, Boston University's Center for the Humanities, the Pardee School of Global Studies at Boston University, the American Research Institute in Turkey,

International Security Studies at Yale, the American Council of Learned Societies, the Fulbright for Turkey, the Middle East Institute at Columbia, and the London School of Economics–Columbia Academic Exchange. I did most of my research in Turkey, the United States, and the United Kingdom and thank all the archivists and librarians who helped me find my way; their assistance proved invaluable. I thank the staffs of the Ottoman Archives—especially Mustafa Tekbaş—and the Atatürk Library in Istanbul; the National Archive, the Parliamentary Archives, and the British Library in London; Gavin McMahon at the Public Record Office of Northern Ireland in Belfast; Jane Hogan and Michael Harkness at the Sudan Archives at Durham University; and the staffs of the Hoover Institution at Stanford, Yale, and the Library of Congress. I could not have navigated the Ottoman Foreign Ministry records without Sinan Kuneralp's encyclopedic knowledge and assistance. I learned so much from our wonderful conversations over tea at the archives.

I have been fortunate to present my research at universities in the United States and abroad, and I appreciate those opportunities to test out my arguments. I am grateful to Lâle Can and Michael Christopher Low, who organized a workshop at the Graduate Center (CUNY) on international law in the Ottoman Empire that which resulted in several publications and paved the way for many enduring friendships. They not only brought together excellent junior and senior scholars but also put Ottoman international law on the map. Several scholars asked key questions at workshops, conferences, and talks that forced me to sharpen my arguments. I especially appreciate the tough questions from Laura Robson, Baki Tezcan, Edhem Eldem, and Mostafa Minawi. As I was finishing the manuscript, I had the great fortune to attend a workshop at the University of Salamanca, which forced me to reflect on the words I use to describe practices of autonomy throughout the book. It was organized by Arda Akinci and Kent Schull, who has always been the biggest cheerleader for junior scholars in the field.

I owe a great debt to the many scholars who have helped me to refine my arguments over the years—especially the Ottoman international law crew, including Will Smiley, Umut Özsu, Youssef Ben Ismail, Lâle Can, Cemil Aydın, Will Hanley, David Gutman, and Joshua White. So many colleagues made my research and writing intellectually rewarding, and I have been inspired by their work—especially Nora Barakat, Roy Bar Sadeh, Omar Cheta, Camille Cole, Bedross Der Matossian, Gábor Egry, Rüdiger Graf, Zoe Griffith, Vladimir Hamed-Troyansky, Scott Heerman,

Peter Holquist, Catalina Hunt, Ülkü İnal, Hasan Kayalı, Selim S. Kuru, Chuck Lipp, Molly McCullers, Elinor Morack, Orçun Okan, Marcus Payk, Uğur Peçe, Zozan Pehlivan, Ünver Rüstem, Nir Shafir, Elizabeth Williams, Murat Yıldız, and Seçil Yılmaz, among many others. Elizabeth Thompson and Mustafa Aksakal organized an NEH summer seminar in Georgetown on World War in the Middle East that transformed the final chapters of the book, my broader research trajectory, and what and how I teach. In addition to their enduring mentorship, I benefited immensely from conversations with coparticipants, especially Melanie Tanielian, Jonathan Wyrtzen, İpek Yosmaoğlu, Devi Mays, Yiğit Akın, Lerna Ekmekçioğlu, and Stacy D. Fahrenthold.

Christine Philliou's intellectual support at Berkeley and beyond fundamentally changed how I understand the late Ottoman Empire and the people who lived there. She organized a summer workshop in Crete on the Armistice press in Istanbul (1918–1923), where, together with Janet Klein, Carole Woodall, Lerna Ekmekçioğlu, Amy Mills, Zülyeha Mary Fikret, and Christan Zurbach, we read newspapers across the empire's languages during the critical years of state unmaking in Istanbul. More recently, she initiated another collaborative research project, funded by the NEH and called İstanΠόλις, which traces the Ottoman Greek communities in Istanbul from 1821 to 1923. I am thankful for her and my co-collaborators Firuzan Melike Sümertaş, Panagiotis Poulos, Ayşe Ozil, and Emily Neumeier, who helped me to realize the centrality of the Greek revolution and its aftermath to the story I tell.

I am thrilled to be part of the International and Global History series at Columbia University Press. Mathew Connelly and the late Adam McKeown, among my many mentors at Columbia University, started the series, and to me, it has always occupied a special place of experimentation and thinking through what is possible in international and global history. At a moment when there was very little written on the topic, Adam pushed me to scour the Ottoman Foreign Ministry archives for the international law story. I miss our many debates and conversations about international law in China and the Ottoman Empire. I am grateful to Cemil Aydın, the current series editor, whose scholarship has inspired me and who has supported my research since we first met. I am exceptionally lucky to have Caelyn Cobb as my editor and Alex Gupta as my assistant editor, both of whom have been patient and amazingly supportive. I would also like to thank Anita O'Brien, my heroic copy editor who rescued me from many mistakes, and Marisa Lastres, my phenomenal production editor. I am also grateful to the anonymous manuscript reviewers who provided thoughtful suggestions for strengthening my argument and improving the book overall.

I landed at the Pardee School of Global Studies at Boston University a few years ago and have been astonished by my brilliant colleagues and their intellectual generosity. It has been electrifying to be in an interdisciplinary department. In particular, I thank Jeremy Menchik, Quinn Slobodian, Andrei Mamolea, Betty Anderson, and Roberta Micallef, who have all read parts of my manuscript and offered invaluable feedback. William Grimes has been a fantastic mentor. Conversations with Alexander de la Paz and Shamiran Mako about international law and autonomy helped me think about the longue durée and afterlives of empire in the Middle East. Erik Goldstein and Mark Storella have vastly expanded my thinking about treaty making and nineteenth-century diplomatic practices. My wonderful dean, Scott Taylor, supported a critical trip to London and Istanbul to finalize research for this book. I cannot imagine navigating Boston University without my writing companion and dear friend Sanne Verschuren. At all the institutions where I have taught, I wish to thank my students, from whom I have learned much.

Dale Stahl has been a wonderful archive and travel companion across the Middle East and the UK. Our scholarly adventures included visits to dams on the Euphrates, Ottoman inscriptions in Cairo, and puffins in Yorkshire. Michael Christopher Low and I worked on different parts of the empire but faced similar puzzles about administrative privileges and exceptions. He has been a constant interlocuter and has helped me to see the broader significance of my arguments, often before they were apparent to me. Emily Greble has transformed how I think about legal history. I am thankful for her intellectual generosity and for showing me traces of the Ottoman past in Belgrade and in towns along the border of what had been autonomous Serbia. I am grateful to Emily and to my other friends and colleagues who read the manuscript in part or in its entirety and offered extensive criticism, especially Dominque Reill, Alison Frank Johnson, Chris Low, Mustafa Aksakal, Youssef Ben Ismail, and Will Smiley.

Above all, I am indebted to my family and friends. They supported me throughout my years in graduate school, the rough years of a shrinking history job market, and two health dramas that could have derailed everything. I especially thank David Weir, Dr. Clark Baxter, Kaspar Genell, Nazario and Zoey Irene Benvenuti, Sharon Lasker, Eric Oldmixen, Lia Avant, Shane and Julia Stratton, Emma Lewis, Jordan Mathews, Veronica Hoyo, Hector Bracho, and my marvelous cousin, Karen Weiss. In Atlanta, Jason and Alora Brock, Dustin Dalton, Mike Flint, Matt Cauthorn, and Daamin Foster taught me how to be calm under pressure and in absolute chaos. I had the excellent fortune to sit next to Oscar Aguirre-Mandujano in an Ottoman class at SOAS in London, which sparked one of the great friendships of my life.

Of all the cities in which I have lived, Boston has become my favorite, not least because it brought me close to my dear friend Alison Frank Johnson and her wonderful family. I met Dominque Reill waiting in line at the post office on my first day and her last day at Columbia. It is fitting that one of my most prized intellectual friendships should have blossomed within a bureaucratic institution. I thank my dearest friend Alida Lasker, who, along with Dr. Erica Mayer and Dr. Laura Dominici at Dana-Farber, saved my life, but was also responsible for convincing me to become an historian. I thank my brother, Sean Preciado Genell, the real writer in the family. My parents, Susan and John Genell, have always supported and encouraged me in all my intellectual and more eccentric endeavors, for which I am profoundly grateful. I dedicate this book to them, to Maddy, and to Michael Houk and Ziggy Paşa. My deepest thanks are reserved for the brilliant Michael, whom I have known since I was teenager and who has made life thrilling and wonderful. His support is immeasurable. There is no one else with whom I would rather hash out ideas, look at paintings, and walk the great cities.

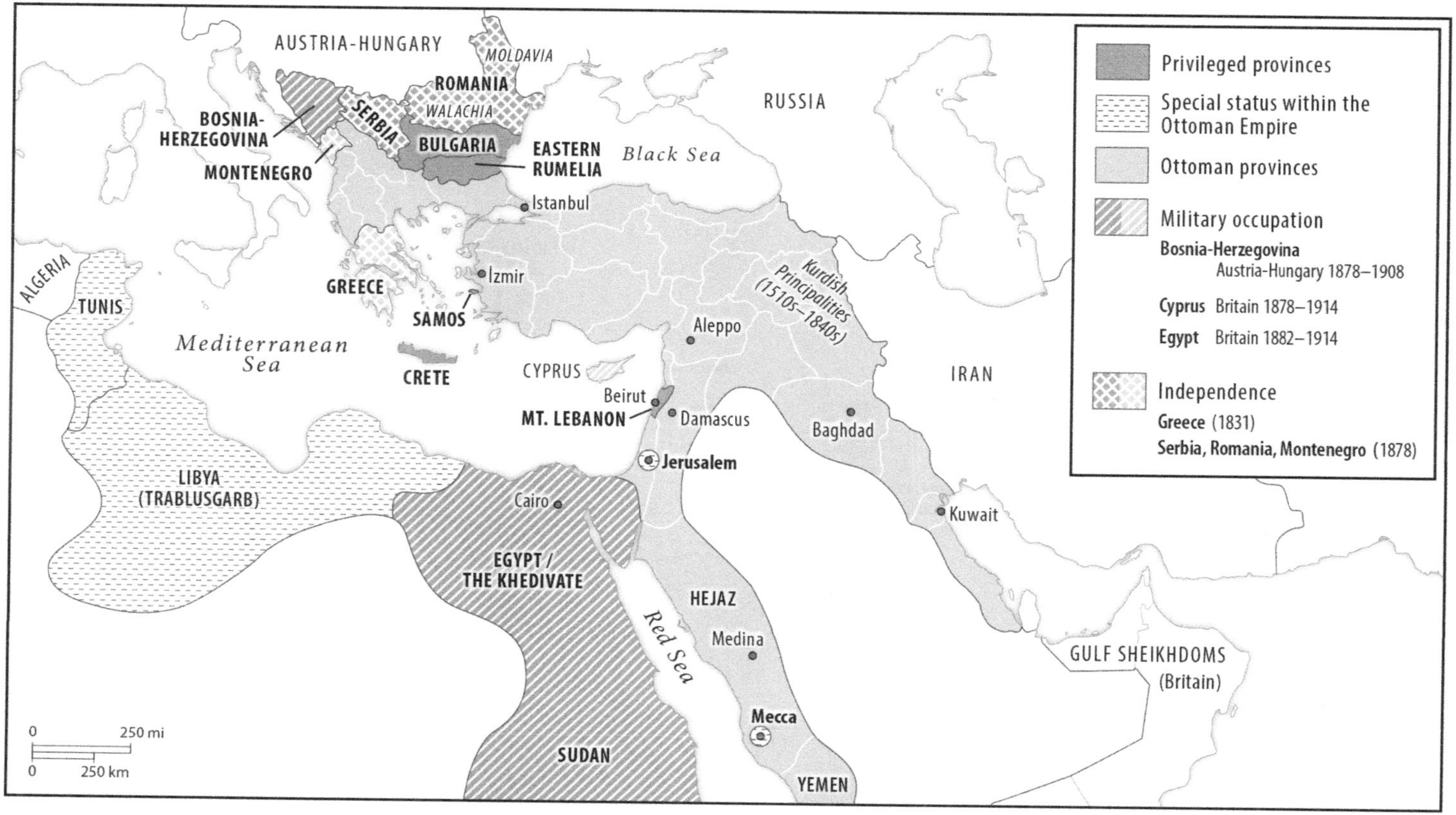

Figure 0.1 Privileged and autonomous provinces of the Ottoman Empire, 1830s–1878. (Map by Erin Greb.)

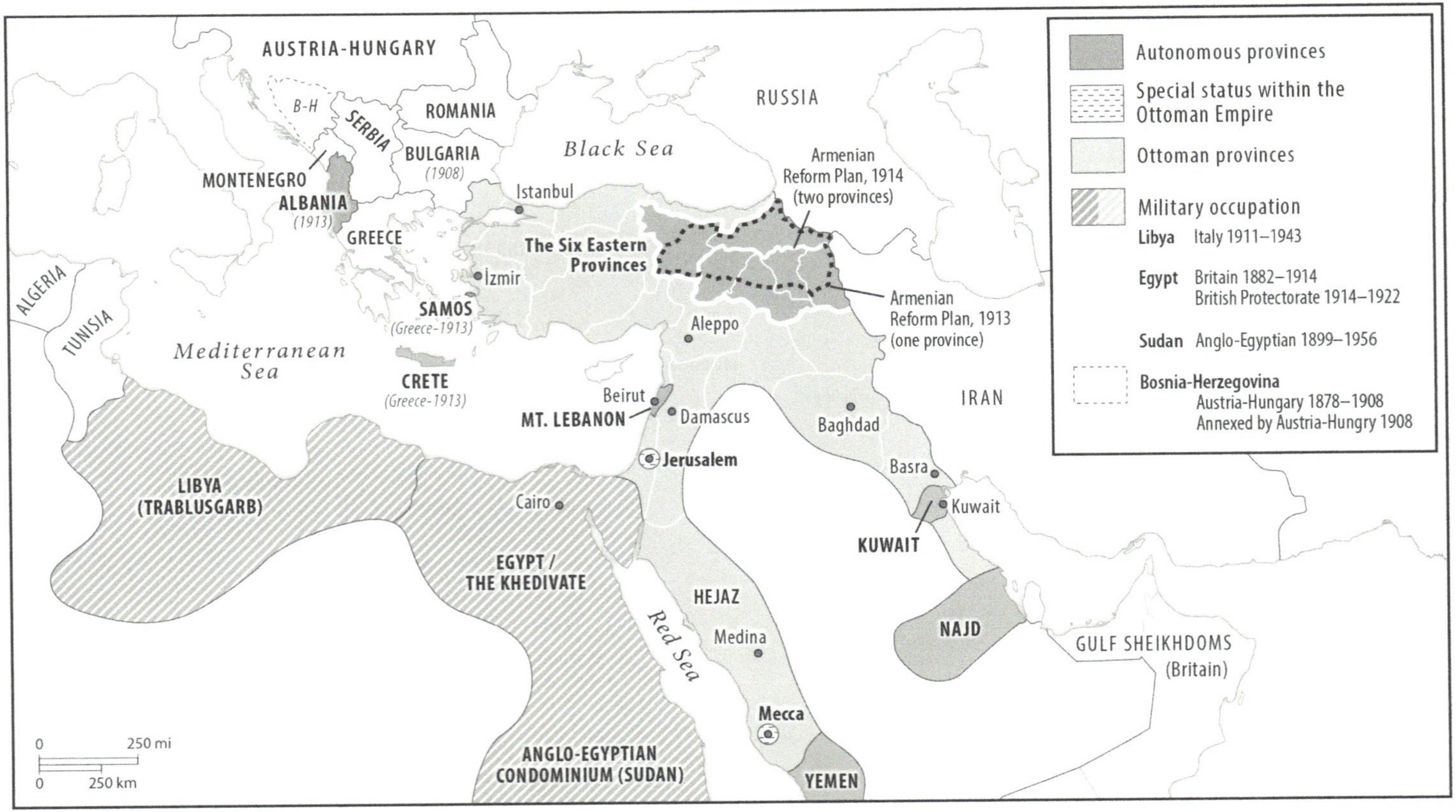

Figure 0.2 Privileged and autonomous provinces of the Ottoman Empire, 1878–1914. (Map by Erin Greb.)

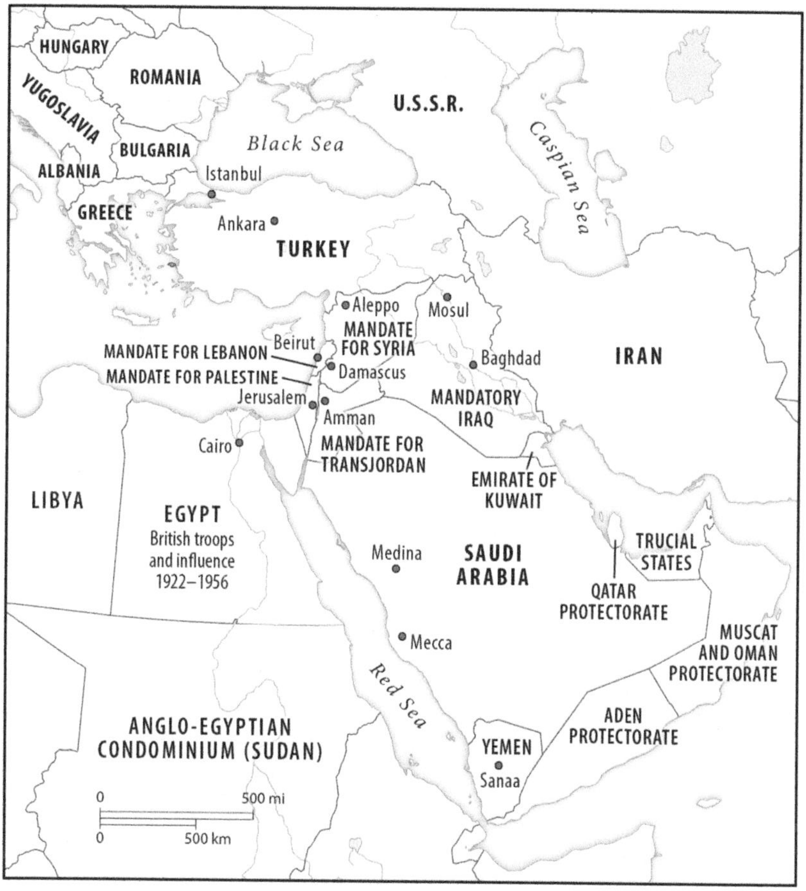

Figure 0.3 The post-Ottoman Middle East, from 1918 through the early 1930s. (Map by Erin Greb.)

EMPIRE BY LAW

Introduction

On January 30, 1919, the victors of the First World War overhauled the Middle Eastern political order at the Paris Peace Conference. Drawing on the racial and imperialist languages that had structured international politics in the nineteenth century, the Allied powers separated the occupied imperial and colonial territories of the vanquished Ottoman and German empires into one of three classes of mandates according to the inhabitants' supposed level of "civilization." Class A mandates were reserved for Ottoman subjects in the Arab provinces who had "reached a stage of development where their existence as independent nations can be provisionally recognized subject to the rendering of administrative advice and assistance by a Mandatory until such time as they are able to stand alone." The "less developed peoples" of Africa and the Pacific were placed in Class B and C mandates under direct European rule. From the moment of the mandates' inception, historians have interpreted them as a British and French imperialist compromise with Woodrow Wilson's anti-annexationist rhetoric and his support for self-determination and national sovereignty.[1]

Yet when reports about plans for the Allied partition of the empire began to appear in Ottoman newspapers in early months of 1919, imperial subjects offered a vastly different interpretation. Editors and intellectuals—recently released from wartime press restrictions—viewed the mandates as an explicit breach of Wilsonian principles.[2] While at first some writers saw the new system as an opportunity for much needed economic aid and political reforms, by the time of the Greek invasion of Anatolia in May 1919 the dominant voices insisted that mandates were little more than a new iteration of an old legal device, hatched to undercut Ottoman sovereignty.[3] To Ottoman lawyers, intellectuals, and journalists, the emerging Middle Eastern postwar order was not new; in fact, it had a clear Ottoman genealogy. They saw the mandates as a reconfiguration of a local system of administrative autonomy that the Ottoman government had developed in the Balkans and the Eastern Mediterranean to limit European imperialism and retain the benefits of Ottoman imperial sovereignty.[4]

Imperial subjects in Istanbul were not alone in recognizing the connection between Ottoman experiments with administrative autonomy and the post-1918 emerging mandate system. As one British statesman put it, the mandates were nothing more than the "kind of system which we have in practice been trying to work out in [Ottoman] Egypt."[5] Non-Ottoman Muslims, especially in the British Empire, vigorously protested the planned partition of the largest independent Muslim empire at the hands of the Allied powers and repudiated the Allied justifications for the mandates. The mandates were based on the principle of partition "in the guise of emancipatory measures," and that was familiar story.[6] Both the defeated empire that had controlled much of the Middle East before the war and the postwar empires that would control it afterward agreed: Britain and France's new empire in the name of self-determination was modeled on the system of Ottoman autonomous provinces.

Despite continuities, Ottomans in the Arab provinces experienced British and French colonial rule as a radical break with the imperial past. The new system severed the region's ties to the legal, economic, political, and social structures of the empire and ushered in a new era of direct colonial exploitation, the consequences of which are still unfolding today.[7] Yet, on the ground, the mandates' legal underpinnings were based on extraordinary continuities, particularly in terms of the detached relationship between sovereignty and political control. This book shows how the Ottomans developed a system of autonomous provinces in the nineteenth century, drawing on earlier institutions of autonomous governance, as a means of preserving imperial sovereignty in the increasingly competitive international legal order. It demonstrates how this system was internationalized in the form of League of Nations mandates for the Arab provinces. Though the Ottoman Empire drew its last breath in 1923, Ottoman-style autonomy lived on, reconfigured and inscribed into the postwar international legal order. Historians have detailed the disastrous consequences of the mandate system in the Middle East; this book reveals how that system was a direct consequence of Ottoman autonomy in the region.

Autonomy in the Late Ottoman Empire

In the nineteenth century, many Ottoman provinces enjoyed levels of administrative autonomy that were unparalleled not only within the Ottoman domains but in late nineteenth-century imperial systems more broadly. Spanning from the Ottoman Balkans to North Africa, the autonomous provinces included, among others, Serbia, Moldavia and Wallachia (today's Romania), Mount Lebanon, Egypt, Eastern Rumelia (part of Bulgaria), Tunis, Kuwait, and the Eastern Mediterranean islands of Samos and Crete. Throughout the nineteenth century, the "autonomous" or "privileged" provinces attracted the attention of international lawyers—Ottoman and European—who found them an intriguing legal puzzle.[8] Some lawyers saw autonomy as a possible solution to the clashing notions of sovereignty developing in the international system, one that might help to order an increasingly globalizing and nationalizing world. The Russian international lawyer Fedor Martens viewed Ottoman privileged provinces as a cheat—a compromise between competing European and local interests rather than a "radical solution" to the problem of international order. They were provisional, and they might become independent or remain under the domination of the Ottomans.[9] For most European observers, the autonomous provinces were simultaneously part of the Ottoman Empire and outside it. For Ottoman lawyers, they were absolutely part of the imperial constitutional order. For both sets of lawyers, it was the international legal status of each province and the corresponding question of sovereignty that mattered. Alongside exceptional forms of local administrative control, the privileged provinces were guaranteed in international law.

As legal entities, Ottoman privileged provinces raised important questions for diplomats, lawyers, nationalists, and activists about the nature of sovereignty in the late nineteenth century. For example, if the Ottoman sultan was legally the sovereign in the Principality of Bulgaria, why did locals have so much administrative control? How was power divided in a place like the Principality of Serbia, where Ottoman and Serbian garrisons and an Ottoman and Serbian government coexisted in the same cities? Why, after 1882, was local control in Egypt divided between a hereditary governor and British Foreign Office officials but legally under the sovereignty of the sultan in Istanbul? As they puzzled over these cross-Ottoman-European-local creations of the international order, European theorists of international law recognized that they had something in common, but like most historians today, they have also cast these same provinces as European colonial protectorates, Ottoman in name only.[10] Indeed, Ottoman autonomous provinces, which have not generally been counted as part of the imperial domains by European or Middle Eastern historians, are much more firmly rooted in national historiographies than in imperial ones.[11] Ottoman officials and the Treasury, however, regarded these privileged provinces as part and parcel of their imperial territories and enjoyed very practical and material benefits by preserving sovereignty. The transfer of administrative control to locals was a price worth what the Ottomans got in exchange. And for locals and European imperialists, it offered rewards to stave off threats. All in all, maintaining Ottoman sovereignty in these provinces produced unexpected consequences for Istanbul, Ottoman subjects, and the Great Powers. But how did these "privileged" provinces come into being, and why did they matter on the ground and for the evolution of the international legal order in the nineteenth century?

Autonomy, as a generalized concept of rule, had a long history throughout Ottoman lands. From the early days of the empire, Ottoman administration patterns varied across its Asian, European and African provinces, giving more or less discretion to local elites on how lands and peoples would be managed and taxed.[12] But starting with the Greek War of Independence in the 1821, a new form of autonomy appeared, one that bore the trace of European intervention in Ottoman affairs.[13] Increasingly, European powers compelled the sultan to grant special status to provinces as a result of military conflict or local rebellion, which was often preceded by European military intervention. Autonomy was no longer the result of imperial choices in coordination with local expectations; instead, it became a tool for preserving Ottoman sovereignty in the face of both local and European imperial pressure. The new provinces were created in areas of strategic importance and arenas of intense imperial competition in the Ottoman Balkans, North Africa, and Arab provinces. While there was continuity and borrowing from past administrative practices, the new provinces were legally and constitutionally distinct from their predecessors. As with Belgian neutrality in 1839, the Great Powers agreed to bracket off the autonomous provinces as "outside the sphere of European warfare and international jealousies," an arrangement that was codified in treaty law.[14] In some cases, like Egypt, the new autonomies had had a special status within the Ottoman Empire before the 1830s. Their new international status, embedded in international law, was not merely a formalization of on the ground practices but was fundamentally different.

Although there were antecedents, the first of the new provinces emerged out of regional disorders generated by the Greek War of Independence (1821–1832)—Moldavia and Wallachia, also known as the Danubian Principalities (today's Romania), Serbia, and the island of Samos (today part of Greece). Even Egypt, which gained autonomy in 1841, was a long-term consequence of the Greek rebellion.[15] Mount Lebanon and Crete achieved autonomy in 1861 and 1868, respectively, due to a combination of local unrest against the centralizing authority of the Tanzimat state and external European pressure.[16] By the 1870s, European Great Powers, especially Britain, regularly threatened the Ottomans with supporting the creation of more autonomous provinces whenever local imperial crises might expand into international questions—in Macedonia, Bosnia, the Persian Gulf, and beyond. In the lead-up to World War I, Britain and the European powers attempted to impose autonomous administrations in the "kaza of Kuwait" as well as the six eastern provinces, which European states designated as "Armenia."[17] Along the Mediterranean, the Black Sea, and the Persian Gulf, European imperialists and regional Ottoman power brokers pushed the state to increase the number and scope of privileged provinces, all in their continued push for increased influence.[18]

These provinces were not simply imposed on the Ottoman state; they were the product of local and international negotiation. Often with the support of European diplomats, representatives from the new "exceptional" or privileged provinces, the *eyalet-i mümtaze*, as the Ottoman bureaucracy categorized them, reached individual agreements with Istanbul. There was no single formula for gaining autonomy, nor any blueprint for what it would look like in practice in terms of taxation, law, or administration. Each model changed over time. Some of the privileged provinces were exempted from empire-wide policies, such as the introduction in 1864 of the new secular or *nizamiye* courts, a three-tiered system that was a key feature of legal reforms designed to harmonize Ottoman institutions with European models.[19] A handful of autonomous provinces had a hereditary prince, as in Serbia. Others had Christian governors appointed by Istanbul for limited term appointments, as in Mount Lebanon. Despite their differences, the exceptional provinces shared one important commonality: They remained legally part of the constitutional order of the empire. The sultan guaranteed the status of these provinces in an imperial edict (a *hatti-i hümayun* or a *ferman*), as did the "public law and system of Europe"—a nineteenth-century expression for international law. In many cases, Ottomans and Europeans worked out an organic charter (*règlement organique*) or fundamental statute that laid out how each province would be administered without much local input, except for that which the European powers claimed to represent. The status of such provinces was guaranteed in international law by treaty and in Ottoman administrative law—the *kanun*.

The treaty/ferman formula would emerge as the preferred method for solving Ottoman questions within the Eurocentric international order. The autonomous provinces were not just embedded in two legal systems—the Ottoman and the international—the treaties preserved the "territorial integrity" of the empire in international law. This is the key reason why so many European and Ottoman international lawyers focused on these provinces and the multivalent questions they engendered from the perspective of sovereignty.

This book demonstrates that the privileged provinces were central to the way that the late Ottoman Empire conceptualized its sovereignty in a world of expansionist European empires, where European states intervened in the domestic affairs of the state and pushed the Ottomans to the margins of the Europocentric international order. By the 1870s, imperial administrations viewed the autonomous provinces as a coherent category within the Ottoman domains, not just as an intermediate stop on the way out of the empire. For instance, the first article of the Ottoman Constitution of 1876 stated that the territory of the Ottoman Empire was indivisible and "comprised the present territory" and "the *eyalet-i mümtaze* (the privileged provinces) and no part could be detached from the whole."[20] In other words, autonomous provinces were recognized as a distinct constitutional category within the empire, not as an extraneous, soon-to-be-lost part. They constituted an Ottoman form of imperial rule, not a fig-leaf for European control.

Empire by Law does not just reconstitute how these privileged provinces were transformed into an administrative category; it also recovers how important this new systematization was seen to be, both within and beyond Istanbul. After the disasters of the Russo-Ottoman War (1877–78) and Ottoman territorial losses in the Balkans, the grand vizier created a special office, the Office of Autonomous and Privileged Provinces (Eyâlet-i Mümtaze Kalemi), to manage such territories and to better incorporate them into the regular administration of the empire.[21] Paradoxically, it was precisely because there were so many different types of negotiated settlements that fell into the category of "privileged provinces" that led to an administrative body to be created to treat them as a group and to develop a coherent plan to retain sovereignty over them all. European diplomats and international lawyers recognized this, commenting on Ottoman efforts to assert greater centralized control over the privileged provinces through this office.[22]

But what did autonomy actually do within the empire? One could tell a tragic story about Ottoman victimization at the hands of Europe, but autonomy actually satisfied a large number of interested parties, from the sultan in Istanbul to locals in the autonomous provinces, everyday Ottoman subjects, to the wider European diplomatic and legal system.

On the surface, autonomy was never seen as a positive within Istanbul circles. Sultan Abdülhamid II (r. 1876–1909) and later the leadership of the Committee of Union and Progress (CUP), the political party that dominated Ottoman policymaking from 1908 until 1918, understood autonomy as a limitation on sovereignty and an existential threat to the empire. To these political leaders, autonomy seemed little more than a thinly veiled stepping stone to independence, akin to the humiliation caused by the Capitulations (*imtiyazat*).[23] These fears drew on historical precedent, notably that in 1878, when three Ottoman "privileged provinces," Serbia, Montenegro, and Romania, had won independence with European intervention. Yet, despite this persistent anxiety, most Ottoman officials still viewed administrative autonomy and even permanent military occupation by European powers (such as the British occupation in Egypt or Austria-Hungary's occupation in Bosnia-Herzegovina) as preferable to losing a province to annexation or independence. Diplomatically and politically, autonomy helped the Ottoman center keep what it risked losing. In fact, by the late nineteenth century, Ottoman officials preemptively applied autonomy within the empire to save exposed territories from potential European interference. The holy cities of Mecca and Jerusalem were awarded a special administrative status for precisely this reason, as were Benghazi (part of what is today Libya) and Yemen.[24] Whereas initially autonomy emerged as a result of intervention, after almost a century of experience in autonomous politicking, the Ottomans redefined sensitive provinces as "privileged" before European intervention could become too much of a threat.[25]

This willingness to expand "autonomy" was also a result of the tangible benefits in the form of revenue streams the Ottoman state enjoyed from these setups. Privileged provinces, including Bulgaria, Cyprus, and Egypt, actually paid for their autonomy. In exchange for their special status, most of the exceptional provinces remitted an annual lump sum "tribute" to the imperial treasury. In 1840–1841 when Mehmed Ali, the governor of Egypt, first negotiated the province's privileged status through war, the imperial edict stipulated that in exchange for a hereditary governorship in Egypt, the province would continue to send a yearly tribute (*irsal-i hazine*) to Istanbul. Over the years, Mehmed Ali's successors bought more and more privileges from the sultan, including the Persian title, khediv (prince), and the right to succession via primogeniture. When the British invaded and occupied Egypt in 1882, the annual tribute was £T750,000.[26] Because the Egyptian tribute was pledged as collateral to secure loans and serviced the Ottoman debt, there is a tendency among historians to discount its financial importance. Tributes from other privileged provinces also serviced the debt. The Ottoman Public Debt Administration (*Düyun-ı Umumiye-i Osmanliye Varidat-ı Muhassasa İdaresi*), which was created in December 1881 to collect debt on behalf of European bondholders, was empowered to collect revenue from eight types of indirect taxes, including salt, stamps, alcoholic beverages, and tobacco, but also surplus revenue from the Bulgarian, Eastern Rumelian, and Cyprus tributes.[27]

The category of autonomy also appeased local subjects, who invoked their special status against Italian, Greek, Russian, French, and British imperial encroachment. From Moldavia and Wallachia to Mount Lebanon and Crete, locals were invested in defending their privileges by guarding the legal and administrative status quo.[28] In Mount Lebanon, for example, autonomy attracted merchant families and investments from elsewhere in the empire, as Beirut became a major urban and economic center. Taxes were spent locally, and elected provincial councils had actual power.[29] In Habsburg-occupied Bosnia Herzegovina, as much as in British-occupied Egypt, Muslims appealed to the sultan to intervene on their behalf and demanded particular rights from their occupiers. Muslim intellectuals also remained entrenched in religious debates unfolding in Istanbul.[30] The protected legal status of the exceptional provinces worked double-duty: They thwarted European interference in local administration while simultaneously safeguarding against the increasingly centralizing economic and political policies of the Ottoman state.

The discursive model of autonomy stimulated much excitement for other parts of the Ottoman Empire intrigued by the idea of decentralization. When a new wave of Ottoman leaders was brought to power during the Constitutional Revolution of 1908, one of the major debates among the empire's subjects concerned imperial organization. The question of autonomous provinces was critical to these debates. Liberals, Greeks, Arabs, Jews, Armenians, Kurds, and many Turks insisted that administrative decentralization and local autonomy offered a solution to reorganizing and strengthening the empire. Local power brokers too, like the sharif of Mecca, who would later plot the Arab Revolt during the First World War, tried to obtain more autonomy on the model of Egypt before 1914. To whomever controlled the state, Abdülhamid II or the Committee of Union and Progress, however, this was just the latest threat posed by the autonomous provinces model. Nevertheless, the influence of the autonomous provinces model cannot be discounted. They promised local control in worlds that were increasingly resistant to centralized imperial power.

The Ottomans were not the only ones to be thinking about the benefits and problems of autonomy structures. The British Foreign Office viewed autonomy as a way of protecting their own imperial interests in Ottoman lands against both the encroaching imperialism from France and Russia and the centrifugal nationalism in the Balkans and Egypt. Britain saw the Ottoman autonomous provinces as a useful model for continuing the long policy of devolving Ottoman control of its territory, without the responsibility, cost, and risks of outright "liberating" lands and supplanting the other empire. British officials often argued that deferring to Ottoman autonomy offered the best means to maintain British influence.

In sum, the discursive and administrative categories of the Ottoman privileged provinces proved a unique and effective solution to resolving myriad crises of sovereignty that comprised the nineteenth-century international order. It provided a porous relationship between Ottoman sovereignty and European incursion; it filled the coffers of the imperial treasury, ample recompense for the Treasury having been forced to develop the entire setup against its will; it opened up models of decentralization for everyday imperial subjects; it shifted possibilities for local and imperial loyalty; and it created an entire international law regime of negotiated imperialism under the umbrella of autonomy, a structure that would continue to inspire diplomats, especially after the Ottoman Empire disappeared.

Sovereignty and Autonomy: The Case of Ottoman Egypt

The first part of this book examines the emergence of the new privileged provinces and its application in Ottoman Egypt. Why focus on Egypt? The simple answer is that Egypt was one of the richest provinces of the empire, served an important legitimizing function for the Ottoman sultan and caliph, and experienced over fifty years of Ottoman-British autonomy politicking.[31] In 1841 Mehmed Ali Paşa wrested a hereditary governorship from the sultan. With the opening of the Suez Canal in 1869, European investment and political influence infiltrated every aspect of Egyptian administrative life. In 1882 Britain's permanent military occupation of Ottoman Egypt transformed a local rivalry between the sultan and his Egyptian governor into a major issue of international politics. Egypt remained one of the most important and protracted political questions between the Ottoman and European empires, from the 1830s through the end of the empire in 1923. Egypt, in many ways, is the prime case study to see how Ottoman autonomy was developed, shifted, and framed locally, within the Ottoman Empire and beyond.

Thus far, we have been trained to not see a relationship between the Ottoman imperial center and autonomous Egypt. Instead, our histories have focused on European efforts to break up Ottoman sovereignty throughout the Middle East and North Africa, with Egypt serving as the most important lynchpin in this strategy.[32] In part, this is an understandable consequence of investigating how encroaching British and French power structures pulled much of the Ottoman Mediterranean under their sway. It is also the result of national historiographies that trace a linear history of imperial resistance against the Ottomans, the British, the French, and the Italians.[33] Even historians of the late Ottoman Empire focus more on European encroachment than on Ottoman continued rule through autonomy by focusing on all that was "lost," instead of the mechanisms utilized to retain as much as they did until the empire fell apart with World War I.[34] To help correct these perspectives, recognizing how much Egyptian elites fostered Ottoman ties helps overturn past assumptions. Though our histories have not yet recognized it, the legal connection of autonomy mattered enormously to all, not just Istanbul administrators or British imperialists, but even Egyptians from high to low.

But the main reason that Egypt is the most productive case for unlocking the numerous promises that "autonomy" held as a legal-imperial designation in the late empire, is because of its clear and direct links to the making of the Middle East mandates. Egypt was where the British worked out a form of nonsovereign imperial administration. It was through the experience of occupation and dealing with the multifold problems engendered by Ottoman sovereignty in Egypt that the British learned that sovereignty could reside elsewhere—preferably in a local monarch—as long as an army of British advisors controlled economic policy. Many historians have viewed British practices of indirect rule in the Middle East after World War I as emanating from their experiences in the princely states in India or the Trucial States in the Gulf.[35] Like the princely states, the government of India recognized the Gulf sheikhdoms as independent princes or suzerains, but only within the British imperial order, not within the international system. This critical legal distinction separates the Ottoman autonomous regions, Egypt above all, from British experiments within their own imperial domains. The practice of ruling through Ottoman institutions in Egypt offered a distinct model of imperial administration that the British employed in the form of League of Nations mandates in the territories seized from the Ottoman Empire after the First World War. While Egypt itself was never a League mandate, though there was much talk in London and Paris that it could be, it provided the legal framework for the exercise of British rule in the postwar Middle East.

Empire by Law gives much attention to Egypt, but it is not a history of Ottoman Egypt. Instead, it uses analysis of Ottoman Egypt, along with the other autonomous provinces, to trace the emergence of the new legal-imperial designation and Ottoman constitutional category of autonomy in the nineteenth century through its reconfiguration in the twentieth-century Middle East. In so doing, this book reveals how the category of autonomy became recognized by Ottoman statesmen, international lawyers, European imperialists, and ordinary Ottoman subjects as a central tool of empire-making in the shifting international system. It spotlights how the Ottomans were prime players in the development of this system and were the most affected by how it developed.

"Autonomy Under Ottoman Rule"

Throughout the text, I have opted to use the words and expressions Ottomans and Europeans employed when writing and talking about the privileged provinces.[36] I alternate between privileged provinces, exceptional provinces, autonomy, administrative autonomy, and autonomous provinces, which reflects both Ottoman and European usage. There were several ways to express the meaning of autonomy in Ottoman Turkish, including *muhtariyet* and *serbestiyet*, and these expressions changed over the nineteenth and early twentieth centuries. In Ottoman government records, the post-1830 autonomous provinces—those provinces with a special status within the empire and within international law—were increasingly grouped together in the 1860s and 1870s as a constitutional category within the empire and referred to by bureaucrats and lawyers as the *eyalet-i mümtaze*—the exceptional provinces. They were distinct from the regular provinces of the empire governed by the Vilayet Law of 1864, which reorganized and standardized provincial administration.[37] The Office of Autonomous and Privileged Provinces managed the provinces and had a regulated status vis-à-vis the central state—an organization that was legible to European observers.

Beyond the official state categorization, from the 1860s the expressions "autonomous" (*muhtariyet-i idare*) and "exceptional administration" (*idare-i mümtaze*) appear frequently in newspapers, books, pamphlets, and government documents, often in reference to those territories that had exceptional status, like Serbia or Crete. The historian and bureaucrat Ahmed Cevdet Paşa used both *eyalet-i mümtaze* and *muhtariyet-i idare* when writing about the Balkans and Egypt. But on his special mission to Ottoman Albania in 1861, he wrote that the "sanjak of İşkodra was under an ancient and exceptional administration (*ez-kadim bir idare-i mümtaze tahtında olup*) and, although it was taken over to a certain extent, it was exempt (*müstesna*) from Tanzimat and reorganization."[38] Exceptional administration could be something that was both older than and distinct from the privileged provinces but also reflected an exemption from the imperial reforms. This link between privilege and exception was forged precisely in the midcentury era of centralization and bureaucratization. Ottoman lawyers, bureaucrats, and everyday subjects increasingly conflated different types of exception together as privileges (*imtiyazat*) and exceptions from the standard political or legal order. The state granted non-Muslim Ottoman subjects a variety of privileges (*imtiyazat-i mezhebiye*), including exemption from military service until 1908. Foreigners subject to the Capitulations, the unequal treaties governing the relationship between the Ottoman Empire and foreign subjects, were also privileged (*imtiyazlı*), as were the exceptional provinces, but so too were special provinces like Hejaz—home to Mecca and Medina—and Yemen, which were exempted from empire-wide policies.[39]

By the late nineteenth century, the privileged provinces were a battleground between European states, who threatened to extend the system of autonomy, and Ottoman bureaucrats, who furiously shored up imperial sovereignty against imperial and legal encroachments. It is no wonder that Sultan Abdülhamid II often used "otonomie" instead of *muhtariyet* or *eyalet-i mümtaze*, in exchanges with European ambassadors.[40] In a discussion with the British ambassador to Istanbul in 1881 in which the ambassador tried to convince the sultan to create an autonomous province in the six eastern provinces, Abdülhamid II announced: "I never enjoyed nor desired this word autonomy (*otonomie*)."[41] *Otonomie* was a European import, and *muhtariyet* was a feature of Ottoman administration. At the time, Gabriel Noradounghian, one of the two leading Ottoman international lawyers of the late empire, saw no problem using autonomy to describe Serbia's status within the empire after 1830.[42]

One of the larger arguments of this book is that the existence of the Ottoman privileged provinces held out the possibility for imperial subjects of gaining a similar status. Thus during the Second Constitutional period, especially between the outbreak of the Young Turk Revolution in 1908 and coup d'état in 1913, one of the key debates among political factions concerned imperial administration, which prompted a battle over the many meanings of autonomy. Ottoman centralizers insisted that administrative terms like "decentralization" (*adem-i merkeziyet*) and the "devolution of responsibility" (*tevsi-i mezuniyet*) were indistinguishable from autonomous administration and thus antithetical to creating a strong centralized state. In contrast, their opponents, who favored administrative decentralization, insisted that their ideas had nothing to do with privileged provinces and instead offered citizens a stake in the empire by devolving responsibility to the local. The meaning of autonomy was not always clear; it was in flux and a matter of debate.

European writers generally used autonomy or "privileged province" for the exceptional provinces, but they also used a series of terms borrowed from European feudal history to categorize the provinces, including vassal, tributary, and suzerainty. This was especially true among international lawyers. Henry Wheaton was typical: He wrote that the "Barbary states and the principalities of Wallachia and Moldavia, at all times; Egypt, under the Mamelukes, and more recently under Mehemet Ali; and Servia, since the peace of Bucharest, might be considered rather as vassal states than subject provinces."[43] Indeed, late nineteenth-century international lawyers developed the category of "semi-sovereignty" based on categorizing the privileged provinces vis-à-vis the Ottoman Empire and the international order—a category that profoundly shaped theories of state sovereignty in the lead-up to World War I and in the Middle East mandates after the war.[44] Semi-sovereignty and suzerainty were terms designed to reflect attenuated sovereignty in the Ottoman Empire, but they also had the effect of actively undermining sovereignty in those places. The corrosive effects of the idea of suzerainty on Ottoman sovereignty are clear in the transformation of how the idea was rendered in Ottoman. While Ottoman-Turkish has well over forty words and expressions to describe "sovereignty," there is not an easy equivalent for "suzerainty." In the nineteenth century, Ottoman international lawyers used the expression semi-sovereignty (*şibh-i sultanat*) and semi-independent (*nim müstakil devletler*), but "suzerainty" itself was always difficult to render. By the First World War, however, "suzerainty" increasingly appeared as protection (*himaye*). The Ottoman lawyer Ahmed Vahid explained "the states that govern the politics of such governments (suzerain states) and the relationship between these states and their subordinate governments is called *metbûiyet* (suzerainty)."[45]

As an 1878 article in the *Times of London* on the Balkans noted, "Autonomy is a somewhat elastic word. It may mean anything, or almost anything, from absolute independence to independent local administration."[46] That imprecision was dangerous for Ottoman reformers and for European international lawyers. The legal ambiguities surrounding the privileged provinces—guaranteed in international law and by internal laws—were precisely why Ottoman bureaucrats attempted to tame those provinces by making them more standard and concrete. Ottoman sovereignty puzzles attracted the attention of European international lawyers because they exposed larger problems of order within the system of Eurocentric international law.

There is tremendous value in thinking through how Ottomans understood, thought about, made claims about, assimilated and rejected, and sought opportunities and bargains within the framework of the privileged provinces. Too often, historical actors, but also historians, have discounted the significance of the autonomous provinces within late Ottoman statecraft. European lawyers, who acted in their own political interests, cast exceptional provinces like Egypt and Bulgaria as "sovereign in all but name," "de facto independent," "too anomalous to admit classification."[47] Historians, with critical exceptions, have largely reproduced the view of the European lawyers, almost always describing Ottoman sovereignty in these provinces as "nominal."[48] But what did "nominal sovereignty" mean in the nineteenth century world of competing empires, where sovereignty was always fragmented, marked by overlapping jurisdictions, and, in so many places around the globe, barely felt?[49] We rarely use this undermining language to describe European sovereignty vis-à-vis their empires. One would be hard pressed to find examples of historians, much less historical actors, discussing nominal British sovereignty, even though we know imperial power was projected unevenly across the empire. Instead, we treat British imperial variation as a theory of administration. Indirect rule, self-governing territories, protectorates, the Trucial States, and Indian princely states are all techniques of rule, not a reflection of weakened sovereignty.[50] The key difference, of course, was that those British arrangements were not under the same level of threat from rival empires, whereas the autonomous provinces were the parts of the empire most exposed to outside invaders. While the privileged provinces had unparalleled local administrative control, what distinguished them in a world of multiple sovereignty puzzles was that they were bracketed off and guaranteed by the international order. Taking Ottoman autonomy seriously rejects the enormous condescension with which the late empire has been understood in international history as an object to satisfy great power ambitions. This is important because no matter how weak imperial control might be, in the nineteenth century recognized sovereignty established in international law mattered and fundamentally shaped what was possible on the ground.

International Law and the Problem of Sovereignty in the Ottoman Empire

The privileged provinces are an essential part of the history of international law in the Ottoman Empire, and Europe more broadly. They help to explain how and why the empire opted to adopt international law as part of its diplomatic arsenal. While the empire had long made war and peace treaties and hashed out economic agreements with Europe, that relationship shifted fundamentally in the 1820s, coincident with rebellion in Ottoman Greece (1821–1832). European imposed autonomy entered the empire as a result of the decades-long crisis, in which the modern Ottoman Foreign Ministry was also forged. The settlement of the Greek crisis was not just territorial, with Greece obtaining recognized independence; it was also administrative.

An equally important experiment emerged from the crisis years, in which a series of Balkan provinces obtained internationally recognized autonomy under Ottoman sovereignty. For the first time, the empire's sovereignty was limited by treaty, but by the 1840 those treaties also guaranteed the "territorial integrity" of the empire. Ottoman lawyers seized on these treaties as an instrument of positive international law to defend the empire.[51] By the 1870s Ottoman officials regularly relied on international legal arguments in their dealings with Europe, Iran, and the wider world, and never more so than in attempts to outmaneuver European powers over colonial questions at the edges of the empire.[52]

This is also a story about international law in practice, rather than only in intellectual thought. Ottoman international lawyers were activists. They appealed to positive international law as a means to maintain territorial claims throughout the empire, especially in the autonomous provinces. If the majority of European international lawyers argued that the Ottomans were not fully part of the "family of nations" (*Avrupa ailesi*) for lack of a common culture born out of Christianity, Ottoman lawyers pointed to the massive corpus of shared treaty law between them. Positive international law, one of the main sources of international law, served as evidence of a mutual international legal culture resulting from years of diplomatic engagement—an argument that international lawyers and diplomats in Europe could not simply ignore.

Historians of Japan and China have shown how international law shaped domestic institutions.[53] Along with these countries, the Ottoman Empire was one of the vexing states in nineteenth- and early twentieth-century international legal theory—not always fully accepted as part of the family of nations making up international society, but unquestionably part of the international system.[54] For vast parts of the world in the nineteenth century, the central animating question was how to gain a seat at the table. For many states at the edges of the Eurocentric order that faced iterations of European and American intervention in politics, economy, and administration, international law offered a language and a pathway out of inequality and intervention.[55] This was the case for the Ottomans.

Organization of the Book

This book has two major findings that change the way we should think about the Ottoman Empire and European colonialism in the nineteenth and twentieth centuries. First, it argues that the unusual legal and administrative status of Ottoman autonomy—most clearly seen in the case of Egypt, but true throughout all the privileged provinces—was one of the driving catalysts that compelled the Ottomans to develop international law as a tool of defensive diplomacy. Against a historiography that casts the late Ottoman Empire as a "semicolonial" space kept around to satisfy the Great Powers' desire for "balance" in relation to one another, the book shows a dynamic Ottoman state that responded to the challenges posed by Europe in innovative and unexpected ways—most important, through recourse to international law. This research demonstrates that the late empire directly engaged with and contributed to processes that shaped the international order.

Second, using Ottoman Egypt as a case study, the book contends that Ottoman autonomous provinces set the groundwork for how postwar structures of nonsovereign European imperial incursion would be formulated. The exceptional provinces were places where the Ottoman and British Empires worked out a type of nonsovereign imperial administrative framework that predated and inspired the League of Nations mandate system.

In developing these arguments, the book is organized in three parts. Part I examines the emergence of the new privileged provinces as a transferrable administrative model around the empire and demonstrates how these impositions from outside were ultimately deeply productive for late Ottoman foreign policy and statecraft. Part II looks at how Great Power–imposed autonomy produced unexpected consequences at the local and imperial levels. Part III shows how the First World War prompted Ottoman subjects and the government as well as European powers, the British above all, to look back at the management of the Ottoman privileged provinces as a model for the new empire in Ottoman lands. Critically, Ottoman lawyers, backed by the Foreign Ministry and armed with treaties, international law textbooks, and arguments, suddenly vanished from the diplomatic scene. Their absence fundamentally transformed what autonomy looked like when it was reinscribed in the mandates.

The two chapters in part I each highlight a specific case study's contribution to this international legal process. Chapter 1 argues that the origins of the privileged or exceptional provinces can be traced back to administrative experiments in the Balkans during the Greek Revolt (1821–1832), and that those experiments were taken up as a solution to the Mehmed Ali crisis in 1840–1841. The treaty/ferman formula was worked out fully in Egypt and from there could be transferred elsewhere in the empire to solve a broad range of international issues. Chapter 2 considers how the empire responded to the problem of Great Power–negotiated autonomous provinces. It asserts that the exceptional provinces, which limited Ottoman sovereignty, spurred the empire to learn international law and integrate it into its diplomatic apparatus. At the same time, the state worked to incorporate those provinces through institutional building.

Part II then shifts the historical gaze away from how autonomous provinces were made to how they were lived, locally and internationally. Chapter 3 considers local, international, and imperial politicking in autonomous Egypt and shows how the structure of internationally guaranteed autonomy limited British action in Egypt. At the same time, Istanbul learned how to play in the European game of empire. It wasn't just Istanbul intellectuals and politicians who fought over the empire's administrative organization; power brokers across the Arabian Peninsula—from Yemen to Kuwait—negotiated for more autonomy within an Ottoman imperial framework. Chapter 4 looks at the case of autonomy in Kuwait and argues that the privileged provinces became the go-to solution for vastly different imperial problems.

Part III looks at how one hundred years of Ottoman–Great Power debates over sovereignty, autonomy, and international law paved the way for a new form of empire without sovereignty. Chapter 5 describes how the Ottoman government and intellectuals understood Woodrow Wilson's 14 Points as a promise to maintain the Ottoman Empire as a web of autonomous provinces—drawing on the *eyalet-ı mümtaze*, allowing many to use "Wilsonian principles," as ammunition for imperial continuity. The final chapter traces how Britain moved from supporting the idea that the Ottoman Empire would be organized as a series of autonomous provinces in 1915 to establishment of the mandate system. It argues that British internal debates on Egypt's future informed discussions that formulated the multitier system.

From the Greek Revolution in the 1820s to the creation of the mandate system in the Middle East in the 1920s, the Ottoman Empire was a site of experiments in political control and sovereignty, both within the empire and in the larger imperial order. The field of "law and empire" has in many ways been defined by the Ottoman and British Empires, yet no other study has put them together in this way. We have often looked at that history as one of failure and territorial losses—a series of Great Power slights that undermined a beleaguered empire on the margins of Europe. This work posits instead that a very active and inventive Ottoman state hashed out the "autonomous" compromise to stay afloat as a European power, despite ever increasing European incursions. The international legal, financial, and economic limitations on Ottoman sovereignty that shaped everyday life in the empire reflected an almost century-long tug-of-war between the Ottoman center, local elites, and European powers. The Ottomans were able to keep the autonomous provinces without the burdens of local governance—precisely the same approach the British would take in the exercise of power in the postwar Middle East, which was a direct product of Britain's longtime engagement with Ottoman international legal arguments about sovereignty. Excavating this history enables us to see how systems and hopes continued as long as they did before encountering the travesties that would obliterate so much.

PART ONE

Competing Visions of Autonomy and International Law

CHAPTER 1

The Emergence of the Privileged Provinces

On September 10, 1840, Ottoman, British, and Austrian soldiers and marines landed ten miles north of Beirut. For three days, thirty-three allied warships and steamers that were anchored in the bay bombarded coastal fortifications, destroying the remnants of a crusader fort that Saladin had conquered in 1187 as well as a fourteenth-century Mamluk tower. Observers noted that that fire coming from so many ships packed so tightly together was "terrible," the intensity of the barrage produced a "a galling fire."[1] Beirut "was besieged."[2] Connected to Marseilles, Istanbul, and Alexandria by steamship, Beirut had emerged as a vital Mediterranean port city. Along with Ottoman merchants, mostly Christian and Muslim, the seaside town was already inundated with European traders and consuls, a handful of whom had scrambled aboard allied ships with their worldly possessions in the hours before the attack.[3] Many of the town's structures, its warehouses and quarantine station, were severely damaged in the offensive. The purpose of the three-month naval and ground assault, which killed thousands of soldiers and civilians including women and children, wounded scores more, and captured over five thousand prisoners of war, was not to recover debt or indemnity nor to force open a new market. The allied military intervention, summoned by the Ottoman sultan, blockaded and bombarded eastern Mediterranean ports from Beirut to Alexandria in order to enforce international law.

Coercion through violence rested on a treaty hammered out in July between the Ottoman, British, Russian, Prussian, and Austrian foreign ministries to tame the ambitions of the Mehmed Ali Paşa, the Ottoman governor of Egypt. Since 1832 the governor and his son İbrahim had expanded family control beyond Egypt and occupied core territories in the Arab provinces, including Syria, Lebanon, Palestine, Adana, and the island of Crete, adding to their administration of Sudan and Hejaz, which shelters the holy cities of Mecca and Medina. Istanbul's efforts to reconquer the occupied territory failed, and the sultanate itself was under threat. The Convention on the Pacification of the Levant (July 15, 1840), or the Treaty of London as it was also known, offered a twofold solution to the renewed crisis. In exchange for Mehmed Ali's complete submission to the sultan and evacuation of territory under military occupation, the signatories offered the hereditary "administration" of Egypt, where "all of the treaties and laws of the Ottoman Empire" would be applied. The stated justification for this extraordinary settlement—European military assistance to crush an internal rebellion, while preserving the rebel's political office—was to maintain "the integrity and independence of the Ottoman Empire as a security for the Peace of Europe."[4] Ottoman sovereignty, like the neutrality of Belgium in 1839, was bracketed off and guaranteed by the system of European politics.[5]

Once the occupation was crushed by allied military intervention, Sultan Abdülmecid issued an imperial edict, a ferman of investiture, that conferred hereditary privileges (*imtiyaz-i veraset*) of administration on Mehmed Ali Paşa and his descendants in exchange for submission to the state.[6] The official state newspaper, *Takvim-i Vekayi* (Calendar of Events), reported from Istanbul the terms of the ferman, noting that "his highness will prove his submission by actions and will be reinstated in the government of Egypt" and that the people of Egypt were all subjects of the sultan (*ve Mısır ahalisi dahi teb'a-i saltanat-i seniyeden*).[7] Thus, alongside the Treaty of London, the sultan codified Egypt's new administrative status in imperial law.

These two legal instruments—the 1840 London Convention and the Abdülmecid's 1841 imperial ferman offering the privilege of hereditary administration—were designed to solve an acute political crisis yet produced far-reaching consequences that transformed Ottoman-European relations and the empire's status within the emergent Eurocentric international order. The Convention safeguarded the territorial integrity and independence of the Ottoman Empire by rooting it within the European system of treaties and law, but it did so on unequal terms. Embedded within the treaty, the European signatories imposed a condition determining how a portion of the Ottoman domains would be administered and required further that the sultan codify that arrangement in imperial law.[8] Critically, inequality did not mean exclusion from the international order.[9] Indeed, it was this legal administrative setup that formed the ground upon which the Ottoman Foreign Ministry would later claim equality in international relations and assert imperial sovereignty against an expansionist Europe. The formula had consequences for locals, too. Mehmed Ali and his successors in Egypt exploited the ambiguities of the new administrative arrangement and Egypt's relationship to Istanbul in order to extract more concessions from the imperial center and in the process reconfigured the meaning of sovereignty within the empire.

Egypt was not the first, and was far from the last, of what the Ottoman state would later call the exceptional or privileged provinces (*eyalet-i mümtaze*), but it was the critical case where the Great Powers and a much weaker Ottoman empire worked out a legal-administrative settlement that safeguarded Ottoman sovereignty in international law by treaty while erecting a special administrative status within the framework of imperial law. The first of the exceptional provinces emerged out of the decisions ending the multi-imperial crises stemming from Greek Revolution in the 1820s. While Greece gained independence and international legal recognition in 1832, Christian majority provinces in the Balkans, including of Serbia, Moldavia and Wallachia, and Samos, were transformed into autonomous provinces. Had it not been for Mehmed Ali's threat to the imperial order, those new autonomies might have remained a one-off solution to an international crisis in post-Vienna Europe. Instead, the emergency in Egypt laid the groundwork for an important reworking of imperial autonomy, one that would spark administrative and legal reform at home, and the adoption of international law as a tool of diplomacy to safeguard empire. What began as a provisional settlement in the Balkans—one that drew on a broad array of sources, including existing Ottoman administrative practices, and European understandings of those mechanisms—increasingly became a dependable solution to a variety of imperial crises that threatened the European-led international order. The treaty/ferman formula of preserving the "territorial integrity" of the empire in international law, together with a special administration embedded in the domestic legal order, governed Ottoman-European relations through the start of the First World War.

Ottoman Practices of Decentralization and Autonomy Before European Intervention

By 1841 a handful of provinces obtained internationally mandated administrative control within the governing framework of the Ottoman Empire. Administrative rights were secured through international agreement—a treaty, convention, agreement—but also through an imperial decree governing the internal affairs of the empire. Each of the privileged provinces had its administrative rights conformed in a sultanic decree—a ferman of investiture, a *hatt-ı hümayun, hatt-ı şerif, kanunname, nizam-ı memleket, irade, nızamname*, etc.[10] The new privileged provinces were not the exclusive creation of European powers imposed from outside, though that is how historians have generally viewed them. Instead, they began as an ad hoc experiment in the 1830s, negotiated between Istanbul and European powers during the imperial crisis stemming from the Greek Revolution.[11] The new provinces, unique in international law, were far less exceptional within the Ottoman imperial order. The diplomats who created them deliberately borrowed from existing Ottoman administrative arrangements and simultaneously responded to late eighteenth- and early nineteenth-century debates about the nature of sovereignty and administrative power within empire. The juxtaposition between tradition and innovation is one of the most important characteristics of the new autonomous arrangements created in the nineteenth century. Both the European powers and the Ottoman state shared an interest in presenting novel forms as continuations of older Ottoman practice.

Local administrative autonomy, provincial privileges, and decentralization were not new concepts within the empire in the early nineteenth century. Ottoman administrative patterns exhibited a range of governing arrangements. From the founding of the state in 1299, newly conquered lands retained features of their preconquest administrative and dynastic structures. Even in the fifteenth and sixteenth centuries, a period associated with a high degree of administrative centralization, borderlands far from Istanbul were controlled by local powerbrokers. The new nineteenth-century provinces were legally and administratively distinct from these early modern Ottoman autonomies—for one, they were the result of negotiation, not the result of imperial choice—nevertheless there were important continuities, and the early autonomies would provide a legitimizing genealogy for the new form. Egypt, Moldavia, and Wallachia all had special privileges in the early modern period, and that mattered for how Ottomans and Europeans would explain and justify their creation from the 1830s onward.

Long before Mehmed Ali acquired internationally guaranteed administrative privileges in 1840–1841, Egypt had an exceptional status within the Ottoman domains. In 1517 Sultan Selim I conquered the Cairo-based Mamluk Sultanate, which encompassed Egypt, Syria, and Hejaz, including Mecca and Medina. Initially, the Ottomans experimented with how Egypt would be absorbed into the empire. Selim offered to preserve the local power of the Mamluk sultanate in exchange for recognition of Ottoman sovereignty, an old strategy that helped drive early expansion. When those negotiations collapsed, Selim attacked Cairo and succeeded in crushing the Mamluks. At first, the Ottoman soldiers pillaged the city and attacked the governing elite, but following a series of rebellions, the state opted to preserve the existing Mamluk governing structures. The Ottoman law code of Egypt (*Kanunname-i Mısır*), promulgated in 1525, spelled out how the province would be administered and mixed local and imperial institutions with oversight from Istanbul.[12] The law code covered everything from the administration of the army and religious charitable endowments (*waqf*) to irrigation and land usage. Laws on finance, taxation, and custom duties remained on the books, while Mamluk ceremonies, governing practices, and officials were maintained, though over time these autochthonous structures were Ottomanized.[13] Egypt was so financially and strategically important to the central state that the sultan appointed a governor-general (*beylerbeyi*) who had near total local control and was responsible for securing the state's military and financial interests in Egypt. This basic administrative structure remained in place, with periodic changes and modifications, until Napoleon's occupation of Egypt (1798–1801) smashed the existing order.[14]

Egypt had long held a series of vital economic, military, and legitimizing roles within the empire. Egypt functioned as the empire's main supplier of agricultural products—Egyptian grain, lentils, sugar, cotton, and linen fueled the state.[15] Cairo was at the center of a dense trade network that linked markets across North Africa, the Red Sea, the Persian Gulf,

India, and the Eastern Mediterranean, selling everything from coffee, spices, and gold to slaves, and generating massive customs duties. So many goods came from Egypt that in the mid-eighteenth century, one of the two most important markets in Istanbul was renamed the Egyptian Spice Market (*Mısır Çarşısı*).[16] In the same period, Istanbul mandated that ships carrying rice, coffee, and other goods from Egypt must prioritize grain deliveries to the capital: "Ships arriving at the capital take on their full cargo, and no grain is given to ships bound for other ports."[17] Egypt's strategic location and its seven military units facilitated imperial expansion to Iraq, Libya, Tunis, Algeria, and Yemen and guaranteed the general security of the province and its lucrative trade networks.[18]

When the Ottomans annexed Egypt, the sultan acquired a new title, the Servant of the Two Holy Places (*Khadim al-Haramayn al-Sharifayn*)—Mecca and Medina. This privilege bestowed immense religious legitimacy on the sultan and would ultimately serve as the basis of the later Ottoman claim to the title of caliph. While historians have debated how significant the title of caliph was in this early period, the fact remains that the sultan was responsible for the security and provisioning of the annual pilgrimage to Mecca, the Hajj, and the upkeep of the Holy Places.[19] Every year, the Ottoman governor of Egypt organized the annual Hajj caravan from Cairo to Mecca, sending grain, soldiers, money, and gifts, including the *kiswa*, the embroidered cloth covering the Ka'ba and made anew each year in Cairo. This Mamluk-era ritual continued until the establishment of the Saudi state in the mid-1920s. In line with Mamluk administrative practices, the Ottomans preserved the local power structure in Mecca known as the Sharifate. The emirs of Mecca were selected from local Hashemite families descended from the prophet Muhammad. After 1517, and until the Arab Revolt in 1916, the sultan appointed new emirs, but the local rulers preserved their traditional autonomy, including exemption from conscription and the payment of imperial taxes.[20]

Egypt's wealth generated more tax revenue than any other single province in the empire. In the sixteenth century, Egypt became the first of several special provinces, called *salyaneli*, that functioned as a large tax-farm (*salyane* translates to "annual salary"). In *timar*, the system of land tenure and tax collection practiced in Anatolia and the Balkans, cavalry officers received tax revenues from assigned land grants in exchange for military service. In Egypt, by contrast, the governor remitted an annual lump-sum tax payment to the imperial treasury.[21] The governor presided over a provincial budget and treasury, which was swollen with revenues from taxes and customs duties. The treasury paid all the province's expenditures, including the governor's annual salary, as well as wages and pensions for military, bureaucratic, and religious offices, the upkeep of the Holy Cities and the Hajj caravan, the maintenance of public works such as dams, canals, and waterways, plus subsidies for Hejaz, Yemen, and Habeş (Ethiopia). The surplus was sent to Istanbul as an annual remittance, known as the *irsaliye-i hazine*.[22] The annual remittance was so vital to the imperial treasury that the sultan appointed skilled governors for short terms who had often served in other important provinces before coming to Egypt, and Egyptian governors regularly went on to become the grand vizier, the highest position in the empire after the sultan.

In addition to the annual remittance Egypt was required to send to the imperial treasury, Istanbul expected two other things from Egypt in exchange for local governing control. The first was recognition and submission to Ottoman sovereignty. The Egyptian mint issued coins in the sultan's name, and prayers were read in his honor during the Friday sermon, privileges that constituted sovereignty in Islamic empires that belonged to the ruler alone (*sahib-i sikke ve hutbe*—the possessor of the coin and sermon).[23] The governor had to accept imperial officials appointed from Istanbul, including a *defterdar* and *kadi*.[24] Second, Egypt was required to send the annual remittance (*irsaliye-i hazine*) to the imperial treasury. Third, the Ottoman army in Egypt—janissary garrisons—were obliged send a contingent of local troops to fight in imperial campaigns. As Michael Winter put it, as long as these objectives were met "Istanbul was satisfied, no matter how independent the local emirs in Egypt seemed."[25] This exchange—local control for recognition of Ottoman sovereignty and a hefty remittance to Istanbul—would remain the foundation of the relationship between Istanbul and Cairo to the end of the empire. When Egypt gained its internationally guaranteed privileged status in 1840–41, these three requirements were reinscribed in the imperial ferman that elucidated the relationship between Cairo and Istanbul. Europeans, Ottomans, and locals could thus all plausibly claim that autonomy in 1840–41 was merely a reconfiguration of what had proceeded it in the early modern period.

Egypt was exceptional within the empire, but in other ways it was entirely ordinary and served as a model for other provinces throughout the early modern period. The central state created more and more *salyane* provinces across Ottoman North Africa in Algeria (Cezayir-i Garb), Tunis, Libya (Trablus-i Garb), and Abyssinia (Habeş), and in the Ottoman Gulf in Yemen, Kuwait (Lahsa, al-Hasa), Baghdad, and Basra.[26] *Salyane* provinces had their own provincial budgets, and their governors possessed a high degree of local authority—in some cases powerful local families rather than governors appointed from Istanbul administered the province.[27] By the early seventeenth century, bureaucrats lumped Ottoman provinces into one of two categories based on how the state collected tax revenues. In 1607 Ayn Ali, who served as the treasurer of Egypt, produced a handbook for state officials that divided the empire into provinces like Rumeli and Anatolia, which were taxed directly (*has ile*), and those like Egypt, which submitted yearly payments to the capital.[28] Ottomans would scrutinize this division anew in the 1860s amid provincial reorganization when the distinction between the regular provinces and the exceptional provinces was once again codified by the state—it was no accident that Ayn Ali's treatise dividing the empire on the basis of tax remittances was republished in Istanbul in 1864, the same year as the Provincial Reform Law (*Vilayet Nizamnamesi*) was issued.[29]

In all the *salyâne* provinces, as in Egypt, local rulers recognized Ottoman sovereignty, sent annual remittances to the imperial treasury or were released entirely from taxes, and in other cases supplied local troops to military campaigns elsewhere in the empire.[30] In frontier provinces along the Iranian border, Sultan Süleyman (r. 1520–1566) granted Kurdish emirs an array of privileges, including hereditary rule over subprovinces (*sancak*) and tax exemptions in exchange for loyalty to the state, especially military aid—privileges that would continue through the early Tanzimat reforms.[31] The sultan, in short, provided local privileges only in exchange for a service essential to the functioning of the state.

In addition to the *salyane* provinces, the Ottoman state laid claim to several protected "tributary" principalities, located largely in southeastern Europe (Moldavia and Wallachia, Ragusa, Transylvania, several Aegean islands), and at the eastern edges of the empire in the Crimean Khanate.[32] In the case of the Christian majority provinces in the Balkans, inhabitants paid an annual tribute, called the *haraç* or *cizye* (the tax on people of the book), to the state treasury in exchange for imperial protection—in Ottoman documents they were called *haracgüzar*, or "one who pays tribute (gift)."[33] In contrast, the Crimean khans did not send a tax payment to Istanbul but received considerable subventions from the sultan and had far more control over relations with their neighbors than other provinces.[34] While many historians, have interpreted this relationship between the so-called tributaries and the Ottoman Empire to be one merely of protection rather than sovereignty, the reality is that submission to Istanbul and the annual tribute were manifestations of imperial power and recognition of Ottoman sovereignty.[35] According to early modern Ottoman theorists of empire, which were based in part on Hanafi interpretations of Islamic law, these "tributary" provinces were part of the empire and distinct from states such as Aceh, Kashgar, Morocco, and the Bornu Sultanate, which maintained relations with the Ottoman Empire within the framework of political protection and military alliance but were never part of the imperial domains.[36]

Local privileges were not a result of imperial weakness; they could be taken away as punishment. After exhibiting disloyalty to the sultan in a war between Russia and the Ottoman Empire in 1711, the *voyvoda* or governors in Moldavia and Wallachia were punished by Istanbul. In place the of the autochthonous noble families that had dominated administration in the provinces since imperial incorporation, Greek elites from Istanbul, known as Phanariots, were appointed directly by the sultan as the princes of the two principalities. This system persisted through the start of the Greek Revolution in 1821.[37]

While there were differences between the Christian majority provinces and the *salyane* provinces, not least how local privileges were justified by the state, it is nevertheless profitable to treat administrative autonomy in the early modern empire as a broad category with considerable variation rather than a rare exception. After 1525, Egypt offered a blueprint for imperial incorporation for other newly conquered parts of the empire. When the Ottomans set their sights on Wallachia and Moldavia (Eflak ve Boğdan voyvodalıklar), the former governor of Egypt and later grand vizier Koca Sinan argued that both provinces should be incorporated into the empire "in the way of the province of Egypt (*vilayet-i Mısriyye gibi*)."[38] Though historians view centralization as the hallmark of the era of Ottoman expansion, exceptions abounded, and those provinces and subprovinces with hereditary governors and local administrative control and other privileges were no less part of the empire.[39] The projection of state power was uneven, and the sultan depended on locals at vulnerable frontiers of the empire to serve as a fortification against neighbors to the west as much as to the east. As the Turkish legal historian Ekrem

Ekinci has argued, historians should take seriously one of the official names of the empire: the "well-protected domains" (*memalik-i mahrusa*), which "emphasized that the Ottoman lands were an empire consisting of many countries, kingdoms, principalities, and sultanates."[40] The empire was an amalgam of different polities, all absorbed and assimilated into the imperial machinery of the state on a case-by-case basis.

In the eighteenth century, administrative decentralization was the norm throughout the empire. From North Africa to the border of Iran in the east and as far north as the Balkans, local families, military commanders, and state officials exerted economic and military power in the provinces. Enriched in part through lifetime tax-farms, provincial powerbrokers exercised extensive local control and were responsible for everything from tax collection, security, and policing to managing public works.[41] At times, locals vied for regional supremacy or allied with each other to dominate markets and maintain wealth. Multiple times in Egypt during the eighteenth century, powerful magnates ignored imperial orders or withheld remittances. Critics of decentralization pointed to these powerful provincial notables as evidence of the dwindling state capacity and power. But decentralization enabled the state to remain adaptable in the face of new military and economic challenges from Europe.[42] Even though powerful Ottoman families and provincial officials had vast authority in Egypt, Syria, Greece, and beyond, as Arial Salzman and Ali Yacıoğlu have shown, provincial notables were integrated into the political and administrative order and carried out the functions of the government in partnership with the Ottoman state. Like Mehmed Ali in the nineteenth century, they might have resisted and challenged the central administration, but their local legitimacy depended on the sultan, and their local power was comprehensible only within an imperial idiom. Nevertheless, for Ottoman critics demanding military and administrative reform, the provincial magnates, periodic revolts, and resistance to efforts at centralization were seen as the root cause of economic difficulties and a roadblock to good governance.[43]

Administrative patterns were never static and fluctuated over time. They existed across a continuum of possibilities between centralization and local control. This early administrative history influenced how European and Ottoman diplomats and lawyers framed the new autonomies of the 1830s and beyond. While Ottoman commentators looked to earlier autonomies to explain the diversity of administrative arrangements as a longstanding feature of the empire's political order, Europeans—especially from the late eighteenth century—began to view autonomy as a derogation of central state sovereignty.

"The Wrecks and Fragments of the Ancient World"

For European observers, Ottoman provincial administration evidenced the flexibility of the early modern state and lent explanatory power to the empire's duration and vitality.[44] But this story changed dramatically in the eighteenth century, coincident with a string of military defeats against Russia and the Habsburg Empire, capped by Napoleon's three-year occupation of Egypt (1798–1801). The loss of the Crimean Khanate in 1774 in the wake of the Russo-Ottoman War (1768–1774) spurred a torrent of administrative critiques emanating from European writers as well as from Ottoman reformers, much of which centered on the problem of autonomy and imperial privileges in North African provinces including Egypt, the Balkans, and Crimea.[45] European critics categorized each of these territories as "vassal states" and "tributaries," separate from the regular governing structures of the empire. Both concepts were derived from feudal Europe, and neither reflected Ottoman understandings and practices of sovereignty.[46] Before the eighteenth century, European descriptions of the empire and its institutions distinguished between "regular" provinces (*eyalet*) and "tributaries," which demonstrated the legibility of Ottoman administrative and fiscal practices to outsiders. The division was descriptive and indicated how state revenues were generated or the type of governor in a province, not a mark of diminished sovereignty.[47] But after the Russo-Ottoman War of 1768–1774, European writers lumped together Egypt, the Crimean Khanate, and Wallachia and Moldavia as administrative oddities in the age of centralizing states. Exceptions to the regular system of provinces were now classified as feudal remnants, barely under central state control and distinct from the core provinces of the empire. Europe's feudal interpretation of Ottoman provincial administration played an important role in the framing and implementation of the new autonomies in the 1830s.[48]

The turning point was the Treaty of Küçük Kaynarca (1774). While the treaty most often appears in historical debates on the disputed claim that it gave Russia the right to intervene in the empire on behalf of the sultan's

Orthodox Christian subjects, a significant portion of it centered on the early modern autonomies. The treaty recognized the independence of the Crimean Khanate—less than a decade later Russia would annex the territory to its expanding empire. From an Ottoman perspective, the loss of a Muslim majority territory was a catastrophe that prompted an outpouring of reform literature centered on administration, which expressed a growing concern that Russia attacked the empire in precisely those provinces that had special status within the empire.[49] While Crimea exited the empire, the treaty restored Wallachia and Moldavia, which had been under Russian military occupation, to Ottoman sovereignty.[50] Between 1711 and 1856, over the course of seven wars with the Ottomans, Russia invaded and or occupied some part of Moldavia and Wallachia no fewer than six times. In each case, the army of occupation withdrew, and the provinces were restored to the Ottoman Empire. In 1774 the occupation ended with strings attached, including ten requirements that dictated how the provinces would be reassimilated into the empire. While these requirements were vague—they provided temporary tax relief, freedom to leave the provinces and guaranteed freedom of religious practice—Russia would insist that the articles related to Wallachia and Moldavia guaranteed local autonomy. For late eighteenth-century commentators, the loss of the Crimean Khanate and the new regulations governing Wallachia and Moldavia prompted a reexamination of the nature of Ottoman power in the autonomies at the frontiers of the state.[51]

By the late eighteenth century, European legal and political theorists didn't simply resuscitate feudal terms to describe Ottoman administrative practices; they used feudal analogies to undermine imperial sovereignty. At issue was the relationship between sovereignty and control—a subject that would govern Ottoman–European arguments on administration through the end of World War I. Egypt was now cast as an "independent" vassal state with medieval institutions untouched by centuries of Ottoman rule. Wallachia and Moldavia were ruled by "Christian sovereigns," and the empire's central provinces were "disorganized and scarcely yielding more than nominal obedience to the sultan."[52] In *A Survey of the Turkish Empire* (1797), the author argued that "with regard to the more distant provinces, they may be considered as connected with the Porte rather by treaty than as integral parts of the empire"—a sentiment that would only increase in the 1830s with the new codified autonomies. European commentators, in other words, used "vassal" and "tributary" to equate Ottoman governing strategies with outmoded feudal practices, which amounted to diminishing claims to sovereignty, and called into question the provinces' status vis-a-via Istanbul and Europe. Such texts were early iterations of European "Eastern Question" literature that cast the Ottoman state as both irredeemable and kept around to satisfy Great Power interests. But the crucial point is that European writers saw variation in Ottoman administrative practices increasingly as a problem, despite the clear fiscal and governing benefits they brought to the state.[53]

The European feudal interpretation of Ottoman administrative practices laid the groundwork for one of the most contentious and enduring debates between the Ottoman Empire and its rivals, which was a long and bitter struggle to define the meaning of sovereignty versus suzerainty within empire. Like vassal and tributary, European texts employed "suzerainty" in the eighteenth century primarily to describe the legal relationship and privileges in feudal Europe between a lord and vassal—a discussion that appeared in legal texts on customary law and in essays on "the science of government."[54] After 1774, European commentators applied feudal terms to recast Ottoman sovereignty as something less than fully sovereign and used them to explain the legal relationship between the sultan and Egypt, Crimea, and Wallachia and Moldavia. After the 1830s and the creation of the new Balkan autonomies, European lawyers and diplomats used "suzerainty" almost exclusively to refer to Ottoman autonomous provinces in treaties, international law textbooks, and diplomatic correspondence.[55] As Nobuyoshi Fujinami has shown through tracing the use of "suzerainty" in Ottoman-European treaties across the nineteenth century, the word first appeared in this legal context amid the Napoleonic Wars in the Treaty of Constantinople (1800) between Russia and the Ottomans. The treaty created the Septinsular Republic, a polity under the "suzerainty" of the Ottoman Empire and under Russian protection.[56] While that short-lived administrative experiment fell apart soon after it was inaugurated, the idea that the sultan had "suzerain" rather than "sovereign" rights in certain provinces proliferated in subsequent treaties between the Ottomans and European powers.[57]

One of the many problems with the feudal characterization of the autonomous provinces—both early modern and new—was that Ottoman patterns of land tenure, military protection, and taxation did not correlate with European practices of vassalage. While Ottoman-Turkish had well over forty different words and phrases that were commonly used to describe "sovereignty"—some were Turkic, others borrowed from Persian and Arabic, as well as the Quran and practices of power in earlier Islamic empires—there was not a clear equivalent for "suzerainty," which in the nineteenth century had to be explained and was only ever awkwardly approximated.[58] The same holds for the feudal category "vassal," where there was not an obvious Ottoman analog.[59] In contrast, "tribute" and "tribute paying" existed in Ottoman-Turkish, and they were applied to Egypt and Wallachia and Moldavia, but also to non-Muslim taxes. Such terms (*haraç, haracgüzar, baçgüzar, vergi, arz-ı harac, muahid*) were linked to state revenues and the protection of non-Muslims; they did not describe the legal relationship between a lord and vassal. The closest equivalent to tributary territories was *bilad-i haraciye*, "lands subject to the payment of *haraç*."[60] From the perspective of the Ottoman state, these territories were legible in fiscal terms.

This earlier administrative history came to matter for Ottomans as much as for European powers in the construction of the new provinces in the 1830s. Throughout the nineteenth century, and especially after the onset of the British occupation of Egypt in 1882, Ottoman bureaucrats and lawyers recast European negotiated autonomous provinces as variations of existing administrative norms that had been central to state practice in earlier periods. Similarly, European ideas and experiments surrounding the new autonomies were not treated as *sui generis*, or revolutionary in any way—coming as they did in the aftermath of Napoleon's occupation of Europe—but were instead portrayed as a formula sanctioned by previous Ottoman state practice. The idea of privileges from "ancient times" (*kadimden beri*) could and would be leveraged by both Ottoman bureaucrats and Europeans. While the new provinces were distinct from their early modern counterparts, it was convenient and strategic to link them together for all parties concerned. Nevertheless, the argument that the empire was less than fully sovereign in the autonomous provinces remained remarkably durable through the nineteenth century. Despite the incongruity between Ottoman understandings of sovereignty and European misinterpretations of imperial practices, Europe's feudal interpretation of Ottoman provincial administration in the late eighteenth century framed the implementation of the new autonomies in the 1830s.[61] Later in the century, European international lawyers would seize on the feudal characterization of imperial control to develop a theory of semi-sovereignty, an idea that would shape theories of state sovereignty well beyond the Ottoman Empire.[62]

The Greek Revolution and the Autonomous Principality Idea

The beginning of the Ottoman nineteenth century was not auspicious. The early 1800s were marked by decades of crisis and warfare—from Napoleon's invasion and occupation of Egypt to wars with Russia and the renewed military occupation of Wallachia and Moldavia.[63] In the same period, Ottoman provincial power brokers and strong governors across the empire resisted central state control and attempted to exert more independent military and financial power. Periodic uprisings among subjects and janissaries roiled across the Balkans and the Eastern Mediterranean. When Greek insurgents initiated a revolt in 1821—a rebellion that broke out in Moldavia and soon inflamed the southern Greek lands of the Morea and Istanbul—it appeared as just one more domestic crisis alongside others. No one could have anticipated that the revolution would end with the wholesale reorganization of the empire and its institutions, and a permanent reconfiguration of Ottoman–European relations.[64]

The Greek crisis began as a dispute within the empire but quickly drew European scrutiny and ultimately military intervention.[65] By the time the conflict ended in the early 1830s, the empire was transformed. The Greek Revolution and its settlement ushered in the Tanzimat—the era of imperial reforms, or "reorganization," designed to render Ottoman political and legal institutions legible to an increasingly interventionist Europe—and transformed the basis of Ottoman–European relations.[66] For the first time, European powers, led by Russia, demanded that the Ottoman sultan extend special administrations to parts of his empire. Within a ten-year period, the state was forced to pilot new administrative regimes in Ottoman Serbia, Wallachia and Moldavia, Samos, and Egypt, a turn of events that grew out of the search for a solution to the crisis that began in Greece.

One of the main outcomes of the Congress of Vienna was the agreement to prevent revolutionary claims and maintain the status quo. Two compelling logics drove European powers to intervene in Ottoman affairs, despite a distaste for nationalist revolution. First, French intervention in Spain in 1823 showed that temporary limits on sovereignty could help secure order.[67] Second, both the revolt and its suppression featured alarming levels of violence. Sultan Mahmud II had responded to the "Greek sedition" (*Rum fesadı*) with astonishing force. Greek insurgents had massacred Muslim subjects in Moldavia, and the state retaliated with ferocity. The elite Phanariot princes who administered Wallachia and Moldavia, along with the chief imperial dragoman and the dragoman of the fleet—positions also held by Phanariots—were blamed for the insurgency, stripped of office, and exiled or executed. The Greek Patriarch, Gregorios V, was deposed and hung from the door of the Patriarchate on Easter Sunday in 1821.[68] Orthodox churches were destroyed across the empire, from Istanbul to Sidon in Palestine.[69] State-directed, communal, and insurgent violence was inflected with religious justifications on all sides.[70] Across the Morea, scores of Greeks were enslaved.[71] Non-Greek Orthodox populations in the Balkans were under suspicion as potential rebels—a contingent of Serbian princes (*knez*) and priests were held hostage in Istanbul throughout much of the crisis.[72] Widely circulated reports of state-led violence prompted broad public support for the Greek cause across Europe and put enormous pressure on the Great Powers to intervene.

While the European response throughout the crisis was uneven, one idea was remarkably consistent among them: Any resolution to the crisis required that Greece should be given a special administrative status within the empire.[73] Far from viewing autonomy as a revolutionary solution to a revolutionary problem, European diplomats represented autonomous administration in Greece as merely an extension of what the sultan allowed elsewhere in the Balkans.

European powers also expected administrative restructuring to contribute to the peace. Russia's first solution to warfare between the Ottoman Empire and its subject population in Greece was a European-brokered administrative settlement. In 1823 the Russian foreign minister, Count Nesselrode, explained to the British ambassador in St. Petersburg that the Ottomans would never accept Greek independence and the Greeks would refuse to return to the normal order of things. Instead, he offered a third way. The Russian memoir proposed that "Continental Greece be divided into three Principalities (similar to those in the Danube)." Despite the fact that the territory making up much of what would become Greece never had a special status within the empire, the old autonomies—the principalities of Wallachia and Moldavia—served as the model. The proposal was clear that the "Porte should retain its sovereignty, although precluded from the appointment of Pachas or Governors, and should receive a fixed tribute."[74] The agreement, moreover, should be guaranteed by the powers of Europe by treaty. Initially, Austria and Britain balked at the proposal and worried that Russia wanted to create a patchwork of weak Christian principalities along the Ottoman border.[75] Despite disagreements among the powers on the future of Greece, the various plans hewed closely to first iteration proposed by Russia.[76] An 1826 agreement between Russia and Britain included a provision that would prevent either state from obtaining territory or influence in what Britain called the Greek "dependencies." Britain invited Prussia, Austria, and France to join them to guarantee the treaty in concert. The animating idea was to secure the special status of the new province(s) in the treaty, not the territorial integrity of the Ottoman Empire—that would come later.

Russia and Britain called the shots through the 1820s, and their solutions to the crisis drew on different aspects of Ottoman privilege in rethinking a new Ottoman imperial order. While specific elements of the plan changed over time, the broad strokes remained—a Christian principality with extensive local governing powers, which would remit an annual tribute to the central state. From a Russian perspective, a Greek principality under Ottoman sovereignty would weaken Ottoman control and open the provinces to Russian influence.[77] Autonomy was an appealing idea for the British, too, not least because it was not innovative and thus aligned with the conservative principles of the Concert of Europe. Until 1830, Russia, Britain, and France consistently adhered to the idea that Greece should be established as an Ottoman principality.[78]

The London Protocol (1829) reiterated the general elements contained in earlier iterations but expanded on the nature of government in Greece:

> Greece shall enjoy, under the suzerainty of the Porte, the internal administration best calculated to guarantee the religious and commercial liberty, as well as the prosperity and the repose, which it is desired to assure to it. With this view, that administration shall be assimilated, as much as possible, to monarchical forms, and shall be confided to a Christian Chief or Prince, whose authority shall be hereditary, in the order of primogeniture.[79]

The protocol introduced two innovations; the first was the insistence on "monarchical forms," in this case a Christian hereditary prince. In the same way that European powers drew on existing Ottoman administrative practices, the idea that a local hereditary prince could serve as an intermediary between provincial subjects and the sultan was deeply conservative and borrowed from Ottoman as much as imperial practices in Britain, Russia, and Central Europe.[80] The second innovation was more damaging to the Ottoman state: the shift in language from "sovereignty" to "suzerainty." in Greece. Much like late eighteenth-century European observations of Ottoman Egypt and Crimea, the language of suzerainty diminished central imperial control over the province. All these elements would find their way into the storehouse of imposed autonomies later in the nineteenth century—including as options for Egypt just a few years later.

From the beginning of the rebellion in 1821, Ottoman diplomatic relations with Europe were thrust into disarray—a disaster that would shape events through the end of the crisis.[81] As Christine Philliou has argued, diplomacy and everyday correspondence between Istanbul and the courts of Europe broke down alongside the destruction of the Phanariot network in 1821.[82] The removal of Phanariots from their critical diplomatic role as translators in 1821 rendered Ottoman diplomatic engagement with Europe episodic and was compounded by intermittent breaks in diplomatic relations with Russia, Britain, and France. The fact that the Ottoman diplomatic corps remained in various states of disorder from 1821 through 1832 meant that the Great Powers largely determined the final agreements and outcomes in Greece and the Balkans. Russia, Britain, and France were able to impose their vision of postrebellion Greece rather than negotiate with Istanbul.[83]

In many ways, the independence on offer to Greece in 1830 was not vastly different from what had been proposed in the tributary plans. Many, if not most, of the stipulations in the 1830 agreement were transposed in their entirety from earlier iterations. The great exception was that Ottoman sovereignty in Greece would be extinguished. But the nature of the independence extended to Greece in the early 1830s was limited by the powers that guaranteed it.[84] When Prince Leopold Saxe-Cobourg was offered the title of "Sovereign Prince of Greece"—a position he rejected for numerous reasons—the negotiations compelled the three powers to explain clearly that sovereignty resided in the prince, not in the people or territory.[85] Prince Otto of Bavaria finally accepted the crown in 1832 and arrived with 3,500 Bavarian troops for protection and to train the Greek Army.[86] The new kingdom was devastated by the war and required an infusion of cash and European loans to stay afloat—the vast majority of Ottoman Greek subjects opted to remain within the empire. In Greece, local political factions were dependent on support from Russia, Britain, and France, and their interests were secondary to foreign experts who governed. In sum, sovereignty in the first Ottoman successor state of the nineteenth century was severely constrained, politically, and financially, although in this case by Europe rather than by the sultan.

Nevertheless, the Greek case offers a compelling counterpoint to the autonomy agreements hashed out in the same period for Moldavia, Wallachia, and Serbia because sovereignty mattered, just as it did in the Ottoman Empire. Even if sovereignty in the Kingdom of Greece was heavily circumscribed and interference from European powers was the norm, the fact that Greece was no longer in an Ottoman orbit determined on the ground possibilities in terms of governance and political claims. In Greece, one leg of the imperial-local-international triad was removed. Istanbul was out of the equation. As a result, Greece was suddenly much less important as a problem of international politics. In contrast, it was the new autonomies that would overshadow nineteenth- and early twentieth-century relations between the Ottoman Empire and Europe.

Formalizing Autonomy in the Balkans: The Settlement of the 1830s in Serbia

The plans for Greece borrowed from European understandings of Ottoman administrative practice in the early modern "tributaries" that masked their novelty. In the 1820s, those plans were adapted for the Balkans—Wallachia, Moldavia, Serbia, and Samos—in ways that were far more enduring. These adaptations of the autonomy idea began to coalesce into a transferrable model of administration that would reappear across the empire. In the wake of revolution and warfare and under pressure from Russia, the Ottoman state used administrative autonomy to reincorporate rebellious and occupied lands and reorder its relations with its imperial subjects and with European powers.

Alongside the demand to establish a tributary province in Greece in the 1820s, Russia pursued a parallel campaign to codify autonomy in Moldavia, Wallachia, and Serbia—which, unlike the tributaries, prior to the nineteenth century never had a special administrative status within the Ottoman Empire. In April 1826, amid the Greek crisis, Russia issued an ultimatum demanding the evacuation of Ottoman troops from Wallachia and the restoration of the tributaries' "status" to what it was before the Greek uprising. The ultimatum insisted that the Serbian princes and priests held hostage in Istanbul be released, and that the sultan confirm the "privileges" promised earlier to Serbian subjects.[87] Russia's justification for expanding and codifying autonomy between the two empires rested on a corpus of bilateral treaties worked out between the Ottoman and Russian Empires from 1774 through the Napoleonic Wars. Russia claimed that administrative privileges across the Balkans were already guaranteed by Russo-Ottoman treaties, hammered out over a series of wars and peace negotiations in the eighteenth and early nineteenth centuries.[88]

The purpose of the 1826 ultimatum, and subsequent negotiations at Akkerman, was to implement the terms of the 1812 Treaty of Bucharest. That treaty ended the Russo-Ottoman War (1806–1817) on the eve of Napoleon's invasion and contained a series of vague administrative assurances for both the tributaries and Serbia, which Russia intended to enforce.[89] During contentious meetings held between August and September 1826 in Akkerman—in present-day Ukraine—Russia imposed an overly broad interpretation of past Russo-Ottoman treaties and expanded or wholly invented privileges where none had previously existed.

The Treaty of Bucharest, too, was stubbornly vague and did not specify particular administrative rights, beyond the right to collect taxes on behalf of the sultan.[90] Serbia had never been among the tributaries, nor did European commentators categorize it as "vassal" in eighteenth-century descriptions of the Ottoman domains, and yet it was singled out in the treaty as possessing "internal administration." In the clause related to Serbia, the French version of the treaty noted that the people of Serbia had "long been subservient and tributary" but offered no explanation for what "tributary" meant.[91] The same text in Ottoman Turkish did not use the word "tributary" and instead stated "the Serbian community (*Sırp milleti*) shall, as in previous times, be subjects of the Ottoman Empire and pay the *cizya* tax [the tax for non-Muslim subjects], in accordance with Islamic law."[92] Russian claims to Serbian autonomy were tied to an awkward construction that permitted the Serbian community "the administration of their internal affairs and the collection and delivery of their taxes and other designated payments."[93] When the treaty was negotiated in 1812, the sultan's Imperial Council rejected the clause for Serbia, noting that was incompatible with imperial sovereignty and would encourage Balkan peasants to migrate en masse to Serbia to escape regular taxation.[94] From an Ottoman perspective, Russia was clearly attempting to undermine imperial control in the Balkans through recasting Serbia as a "tributary province."

Unlike the earlier treaties, the Akkerman Convention of 1826 not only reconfirmed every vague Russo-Ottoman agreement concerning the tributaries and Serbia but also explicitly developed the meaning of administrative autonomy. The Convention recast all three territories as provinces with special "privileges." For both the tributaries and Serbia, Russian negotiators additionally compelled the state to issue separate imperial edicts (*hatt-i şerif*), which in the Ottoman sources are described as "agreements" (*sened*), that delineated the meaning of autonomy—these texts, issued by the state, were to form an "integral part" of the Convention.[95] Russia had reinvented Serbia as a Christian tributary state and gave autonomy an explicit set of parameters.

Russia thus drew on existing Ottoman imperial edicts to justify new practices. The model for the additional guarantees in Akkerman was Sultan Selim III's 1802 imperial ferman or edict (*hatt-i şerif*) for the tributaries, which he issued under intense pressure from Russia following Osman Pazvantoğlu's raid into Wallachia.[96] The meandering edict assured subjects of the benevolence of Ottoman rule, especially toward the impoverished peasants in Wallachia and Moldavia.[97] Reformist ideas suffused the text and focused on securing justice against oppression and curbing government corruption. Much of the ferman concerned the collection and kinds of taxes to be remitted to Istanbul, who could graze cattle where, and what happened to the property of Christian converts upon death. The sultan reminded subjects that their provinces functioned as the granary and timber supplier of the empire, and nothing should be withheld. In response to complaints about the frequent changing of the governors appointed from Istanbul, the sultan announced they would now serve a fixed seven-year term of service.[98] Apart from the term requirement, the 1802 edict, like the Russo-Ottoman treaties, resisted offering an explicit set of criteria or conditions for autonomy.[99] As in the case of Greece, Akkerman pitched a new administrative order, but it did so as a reconfiguration of something old. Over the course of the 1820s, Russia succeeded in compelling the Ottomans to accept a far broader and explicit interpretation of the meaning of autonomy in the Moldavia, Walachia, and Serbia, all while maintaining the pretense that these transformations in local governance were rooted in longstanding Ottoman practice.[100]

To limit Russian involvement in the Greek crisis, the Ottoman negotiators reluctantly agreed to the terms of Akkerman, but when British, French, and Russian ships sank the Ottoman fleet at the Battle of Navarino (1827), the newly codified Balkan privileges were off the table. Sultan Mahmud II (r. 1808–1839) cancelled the Akkerman Convention and closed the Bosporus to ships from the Black Sea. Russia retaliated, occupied Wallachia and Moldavia, and went to war to preserve Balkan rights.[101] The war declaration asserted two key claims: The first was that Russian was fighting to defend the "existing treaties" between the two empires. Second was a new and lasting idea in Ottoman-European relations that the empire's territory was inviolable and preserved in the system of law and treaties. Russo-Ottoman treaties guaranteeing Balkan privileges, the war declaration argued, had preserved "the integrity of its Frontiers, under the protection of the Law of Nations."[102] This was one of the first instances, but far from the last time, in which administrative autonomy and imperial privileges would be explicitly linked to preserving the territorial integrity of the empire in international law.[103]

By the end of the war, Russian administrative demands were much more explicit and laid out a vision of what autonomy would look like in the years following the crisis. The Treaty of Edirne (1829) demanded the Ottomans affirm the "ancient privileges of the Principalities of Moldavia and Wallachia," guarantee administrative rights to Serbia, and accept an autonomous principality in Greece according to the terms of the London Protocol (1829). A band of Christian autonomous principalities would form the border between the sultan's realm and Europe: "Such are the fundamental bases of a Peace which has happily terminated a bloody and obstinate War."[104] Moldavia and Wallachia were now "placed under the suzerainty" of the state, while Russia "shall preserve all the privileges and immunities which have been granted to them either by their Capitulations, or by the Treaties concluded between the two Empires, or by the *hatti-şerifs* (imperial edicts) promulgated at different times."[105] Neither the word nor the concept of "suzerainty" appeared in the Ottoman version of the treaty.[106] As in the Akkerman Convention, the powers agreed to a separate agreement that spelled out in unambiguous terms the organization of local bureaucracy in Moldavia and Wallachia. The governors (*voyvoda* or *hosposdar*) would now be elected for life instead of seven years and have full control over the administration of the provinces. The sultan's privileges very clearly meant noninterference in local governance.

For Serbia, Mahmud II was pressured to issue a new edict, which reconfirmed the existing Russo-Ottoman treaties and introduced verbatim whole parts of the imperial decree from 1826.[107] In short, Russia used the accumulation of Russo-Ottoman agreements from 1774 onward to secure a status that had previously been negotiated within Ottoman borders between the sultan and subjects. As Will Smiley has argued, it was precisely in this period that both empires worked out a regional system of Eurasian "international law," hashed out in war and peace negotiations over prisoners of war, that gradually expanded to "include other states."[108] Russia's great innovation in the Balkans was to internationalize the agreements between St. Petersburg and Istanbul.

The burdens Russia placed on the Ottoman Empire in the Treaty of Edirne (1829) informed the final negotiations on the status of Greece and shaped the settlement in the Balkans. As the legal reformer and historian Cevdet Paşa would later argue, "The independence of Greece had always been rejected by all powers; it was declared several times that Greece would be established as a privileged province (*eyalet-i mümtaze*) subject only to the Sublime State. The matter was declared repeatedly, and the only discussion was in determining its form."[109] That was until the about-face following the Treaty of Edirne. Although the European powers ultimately opted to grant Greece independence in 1830, the almost decades-long bargaining over the status of the territory—as a tribute-paying, autonomous, Christian tributary, principality under the "suzerainty" of the sultan—survived in the inventory of options for regulating the margins of the European legal order.

Elements from the plans for Greece reappeared in the negotiated settlements in the Balkans—an annual tribute, a local prince under Ottoman "suzerainty" (a sentiment only expressed in European languages and never in Ottoman), and control over internal administration. A proliferation of Russo-Ottoman treaties and agreements, together with Ottoman imperial edicts, delineated the relationship between the provinces and Istanbul. Even though Russian officials had compelled the empire through war to sign onto these legal texts, it did not mean that the sultan and his ministers played no role in shaping the new administrative order. Interested European states and locals, too, all exercised influence. Serbia offers a case in point.

The Serbian Emirate (*Sırp Emareti*)—as it was increasingly named in Ottoman texts—officially gained autonomy with Mahmud II's 1830 imperial ferman.[110] This ferman built on earlier privileges, including freedom of religion and the right to travel and trade freely throughout the Ottoman domains, by adding a wider array of privileges.[111]

From an Ottoman perspective, administrative privileges remained an award for submission to the state—just as they were in the early modern period. The imperial decree recognized hereditary succession in the family of Miloš Obrenović (Bey) and offered internal administration in exchange for obedience and an annual tribute remitted to Istanbul. Recognizing Miloš as the local Christian leader responsible for administering the Orthodox population was a reward for his refusal to support the Greek rebellion and for his assistance to the state during the 1828–29 Russo-Ottoman War.[112] Mahmud II argued that it was a maxim of his state to employ the most capable and skilled public servants to prevent oppression and arbitrary rule. He selected Miloš for "his aptitude for governing his nation, but above all his loyalty and devotion to my imperial person are well known."[113] Mahmud granted Miloš the title of knez of Serbia—a lifetime and hereditary office. Through this legal instrument, the insurgent military leader was transformed into a prince.

Miloš operated skillfully within an Ottoman idiom, obtained further privileges, and acted as a crucial intermediary between Istanbul and Belgrade. In December 1833 the sultan issued a third imperial ferman for Serbia that reiterated the privileges of 1829—control over local administration, an annual tribute, and Muslim removal—but laid out what amounted to dual Orthodox-Muslim administrative structure.[114] Muslims were now limited to residing in the main garrison towns throughout autonomous Serbia. In addition to Belgrade, five other towns, including Užice and Sokol, maintained sizable Muslim populations. Muslim officials maintained administrative and policing functions in the garrisons. Unlike the rest of Serbia, where Muslims were relegated to garrisons, Belgrade was established as a mixed city.[115] In a setup that mirrored the European Capitulations, Muslims subjects were administered by an Ottoman garrison commander (*muhafiz*) with the rank of paşa, who was assisted by a local council composed of Muslim notables and state officials, while Christians were administered by Miloš.[116] Locals were disarmed except for police officers, soldiers serving the paşa, and Christian officers under the command of the local prince. The prince collected taxes on behalf of the sultan and remitted an annual tribute to Istanbul.

What autonomy did to local, imperial, and international politics was not always clear, especially in this early era of administrative experimentation.

In a phenomenon that would be repeated across the privileged provinces at the local level, local elites and the governing authority often disagreed about what autonomy meant on the ground. In Serbia, Miloš controlled tax and customs revenues, monopolized trade, and owned some of the most productive lands. Local notables and merchants—who themselves had been enriched by Miloš at the expense of Muslims who were forced to abandon the rural areas for garrison towns—opposed his economic and administrative policies.[117] Throughout the 1830s, Serbian elites and rich peasants issued complaints against Miloš to local Ottoman officials and to Istanbul. They argued that that the prince was corrupt, abused his position and had exceeded the terms of his privileges, which has been bestowed on "the Serbian people," not the prince.[118] In February 1835, the opposition ultimately compelled Miloš not only to issue a French-style constitution to check his abuses of power, but also to debate what autonomy signified. Within a month, the Ottomans, Russians, and Austrians forced Miloš to rescind the constitution. It cut against the ideas animating restoration Europe and had exceeded the terms of autonomy guaranteed by the 1833 ferman.[119]

Formalized autonomy reorganized the relationship between local governors and Istanbul, and required constant negotiation. Amid the constitutional crisis in Serbia, Miloš requested an audience with the sultan to "personally express his gratitude for all the privileges (*imtiyazat*) and honors he had received."[120] He arrived in Istanbul via steamship from Varna and remained in the imperial capital for seventy-five days, where he encountered a city transformed by the early Tanzimat reforms. Miloš toured modern barracks, watched soldiers drill, visited government ministers at the Sublime Porte—the center of Ottoman state power, met with European ambassadors and consuls, and went to places in the city "worth seeing and visiting." Mahmud II received Miloš at Beylerbeyi Palace on the Bosporus. The sultan reminded his prince that the "peace and tranquility of all the subjects of my noble empire are my foremost concern" and that care should be taken to prevent further unrest in Serbia. It was Miloš's duty to punish officials and individuals for misconduct, and to ensure the province's security and prosperity—he received the Ottoman Order of Glory (*nişan-i iftihar*) for services rendered to the state.[121] The episode echoed earlier ceremonies of investiture for the princes of Moldavia and Wallachia—the most recent one was in 1834. Miloš received a robe of honor, and the medal was accompanied by a small portrait of the sultan ornamented with diamonds.[122]

Miloš commemorated the visit to Istanbul with a formal portrait. Dressed in a military uniform and adorned with European and Ottomans medals and honors, the prince bears a painting of Mahmud II on his chest and wears the same style of fez as the sultan—the *Mahmudiye* with its eruption of long black tassels. He is seated in the capitol with the Hagia Sophia dominating the background. The painting hung in his royal residence in Serbia—reportedly alongside a portrait of Mahmud II, Napoleon, and Russian tsars.[123] How should we understand Miloš's meeting with the sultan and his Ottoman portrait? While historians often cast the era of Serbian autonomy (1830–1878) as little more than a step in nationalist struggle for independence, the portrait tells a different story and reflects Miloš's position within the governing order of the state. He was dependent on the Mahmud II for his local legitimacy and authority. In the same way that provincial notables (*ayan*) in the eighteenth and early nineteenth centuries were reliant on the sultan's recognition to exercise local power, a similar process continued to play out between the sultan and his governors in the privileged provinces.[124] What was crucial for Miloš's position—but also for local elites, the imperial center, and the Great Powers—was the text of the *hatt-ı şerif.* The sultan's words laid the groundwork for political, legal, and economic claims within each of the privileged provinces.

Already in the 1830s, it was clear that the sultan's grants, in whatever form—a ferman, a *hatt-ı şerif,* a *kanunname*—determined what was possible. The power of these grants explains why the Ottomans, Russia, and Austria crushed the 1835 Serbian constitution as beyond the "terms of the ferman." While Serbia was not the most important imperial hotspot in the 1830s—that place was taken by Egypt—official autonomy brought European powers into its orbit. Between 1835 and 1839, Austria, Britain, Russia, and France opened consulates in Belgrade.[125] The powers agreed that Serbia's revolutionary impulse, and local complaints against Miloš, had to be managed through a more robust administrative order.

In December 1833, Mahmud II issued a new imperial decree addressed to the Muslim and Christian powerholders in Serbia.[126] Known as the "Turkish Constitution" (*Turski Ustav*), the new *hatt-ı şerif* laid out the most explicit picture to date of how administrative privileges would function in Serbia. It was, above all, an assertion of Ottoman sovereignty. As in the earlier edicts, privileges were a reward for the Serbian people's loyalty—though Miloš and his family were awarded the responsibility for the "internal political administration" of Serbia. The principality received a "privileged internal administration" (*imtiyazatlı bir idare-i dahiliye*) in exchange for continued submission to the state and an annual tribute remitted to Istanbul.

The 1838 regulations created detailed bureaucratic structures for the internal administration of the province. To ensure "proper administration of the people and the country" (*hüsn-i idaresi için zîr-i rey-i hükmünde olmak üzere*), Mahmud II gave Miloš the right to appoint ministers of the interior, finance, and justice. In each case, the duties reflected the global impulse to centralize and standardize state administrative practices—not least those unfolding in Tanzimat Istanbul. Policing and quarantine fell to the interior minister, who managed issues of public welfare, including repairing roads and maintaining post offices. Administration of public revenues, the budget, and tax collection was the preserve of the minister of finance. He encouraged trade, managed a land registry, and was responsible for exploiting the province's natural resources, including mines and forests. The minister of justice had a rather capacious role. In addition to overseeing the judiciary, the minister of justice certified judges and was responsible for overseeing the construction and management of prisons, hospitals, schools, and charitable institutions. A council of state (*meclis-i şura*), composed of notables, was entitled to offer consultation on administrative affairs and had the right the suggest laws, "on the condition that they do not infringe upon the legitimate rights of the sovereign."[127]

Alongside the separation of bureaucratic power, designed to impede corruption, the sultan guaranteed a broad set of individual rights, similar to those that would later be imbedded in the 1839 Hatt-ı Şerif of Gülhane, that assured equality among all Ottoman imperial subjects.[128] At the same time that he asserted that the inhabitants of Serbia were his imperial subjects, Mahmud II offered protection for "life, property, honor, and rank" and guaranteed free trade. He abolished forced labor and confiscation and the old system of taxation through military land grants (*timar*). No subjects could be deprived of their rights or face corporal punishment or exile without trial. To ensure these rights, there was a multitier system of courts, from the village level to a court of appeals. The edict elaborated a system of district (*kaza*), subdistrict (*nahiye*), and village (*köy*) administration.

Though Mahmud II proclaimed Ottoman sovereignty over Serbia, the edict allowed for the creation of a consular registry office with a local official to issue passports and to "manage Serbs' relations with foreign officials." Unlike the rest of the detailed edict, this role was vague and would eventually open questions about autonomous Serbia's capacity to engage in foreign relations—a serious concern that would recur in nearly all privileged provinces.[129] To further bind Serbia to Istanbul, the *hatt-ı şerif* created the position of Serbian agent (*kapıkethüdası*)—a Serbian official based in the imperial capital who acted as a conduit between Istanbul and Belgrade.[130] While the Serbian position was undoubtedly appropriated from the earlier Phanariot practice in Moldavia and Wallachia, it marks another instance in which an existing provincial institution was transformed through the new autonomy. For the imperial center, the agent was a manifestation of imperial sovereignty and part of the governing order, but for locals, the agent in Istanbul was increasingly an opportunity to expand the capacities of provincial privilege. The question of how the privileged provinces related to Europe and foreign relations was fraught through the early twentieth century.

One of the last details to sort out in the wake of the Greek crisis concerned the island of Samos. Locals, predominately Orthodox Christians, had fought against the empire in the 1820s but were also at odds with Athens. For strategic reasons, European Great Powers opted not to include this island of fewer than fifty thousand inhabitants in the new Greece. These negations took place in Istanbul and, as Christine Philliou has shown, represented the emergence of a reconfigured Ottoman Foreign Ministry that opted to use diplomacy and Great Power legal guarantees to secure the territorial domains of the empire.[131] Ottoman and European diplomats together agreed to give Samos administrative autonomy. Mahmud II issued an imperial decree containing yet another Organic Statute detailing how the island would be managed. In exchange for submission to the sultan, authority would rest in an elected council composed of local notables, presided over by a Christian prince appointed from Istanbul, who would be responsible for remitting an annual report. No Ottoman troops would be stationed on the island, and the inhabitants would pay an annual tribute.[132] Samos would remain among the least troubled of the new autonomies.

National historians have interpreted individual Organic Statutes as "constitutions," yet the reality is that the 1830s were not a constitutional moment. The Organic Statutes are best understood as administrations designed to contain political claims—an objective important to both the Ottomans and European powers. It is worth recalling that Russia imposed an Organic Statute on Poland at the precise moment that Russian Foreign

Ministry officials were hashing out the administrative order for Moldavia and Wallachia. The Kingdom of Poland's Organic Statute (1832) was used to crush autonomy in the wake of the 1830–31 uprising, not create it. It incorporated formerly constitutional Poland more fully into the Russian empire. From Russia's perspective, neither the Ottoman nor the Polish Organic Statutes were planned as liberal political experiments paving the way for representative government and democratic practices, though some Ottoman bureaucrats and many imperial subjects would later cast them in precisely these terms. Instead, for all the empires involved, they were calculated to neutralize and arrest revolutionary politics. How they worked on the ground is another story, which is explored in subsequent chapters.

The Ottoman Foreign Ministry's fear of losing the Balkan territories altogether curbed resistance to the agreements over Wallachia, Moldavia, Serbia, and Samos, but they were able to advocate for important concessions. The new autonomies were not just European-imposed experiments to meddle in the domestic affairs of the Ottoman Empire—Istanbul got something out of the reconstitution of Ottoman diplomatic practices carried out in the tumultuous 1820s. The Battle of Navarino (1827) and the destruction of the entire Egyptian fleet had demonstrated that the empire required something more than military power to deal with European incursions, and the solution was found in a new activist diplomacy that would increasingly adhere to European norms. The loss of Greece was a bitter humiliation, but autonomy offered an alternative to forfeiture of imperial possessions. The idea, first articulated by Russia in the 1820s, that international treaties protected Ottoman "territorial frontiers" would become formalized as part of the system and laws governing Ottoman relations with Europe.[133] The nascent Foreign Ministry, which would not be formalized until 1836, initially viewed the autonomies as a guarantee of continued Ottoman sovereignty. Only much later in the nineteenth century would bureaucrats come to regard them as a limitation on state power.

The Ottoman Foreign Ministry was clear that the new privileges in no way eroded state sovereignty. "The land comprising each of the Wallachia, Moldavia and Serbia and the territorial integrity of the State, subject to the Sultanate and subject to the sovereignty of the Sultanate and assuring them of the privileges granted to each of them under the sovereign's internal administration, which are now being extended and strengthened. That the Sublime will take the preservation of the special privileges and permits it has granted to these lands under the responsibility of the states that are its friends and will consider them as part of the general law of Europe and other articles of the regulations for the three countries."[134] But it was also clear that the settlement of the Greek crisis—especially in the new autonomies the new Foreign Ministry cautiously entered into—embedded the Ottoman Empire deep within the system of European politics, and this entrenchment was framed in terms of treaty law.

Greece was the first post-Ottoman state recognized by Europe and was seen as an experiment to neutralize an unstable European periphery. An equally important administrative experiment emerged out of the years of crisis and intervention in the Balkans. The autonomy plan developed for Greece had significant consequences for Ottoman relations with Europe and for domestic administrative arrangements within the empire. The model of formalized administrative autonomy worked out for Greece would be implemented, through Russian pressure, in Wallachia and Moldavia and in Serbia. The island of Samos, kept out of the boundaries of the new Greek state, likewise achieved a special administrative standing in 1832. Until the 1878 Treaty of Berlin granted independence to numerous Balkan states, statehood on the model of Greece remained the exception, whereas the autonomy compromise—fought out between the European powers and what would become the new Ottoman Foreign Ministry—became the new norm. Even after 1878, European powers compelled the Ottoman state to extend autonomy to several provinces, all of which were rooted in experimental models worked out in the Balkans in the 1820s and 1830s. Autonomy would remain the most common solution for Ottoman separatist provinces until the end of the Ottoman Empire in 1923. From a European perspective, autonomy was as much a tool for stabilizing Europe as it was a way of managing political claims among Ottoman subjects.

Egypt, Autonomy, and International Law

Amid the final negotiations over Greece and the Balkans, a far greater and unexpected catastrophe emerged in the heart of the Arab provinces. In 1831 the governor of Egypt, Mehmed Ali Paşa (1769–1849), launched an attack against the sultan's domains in Greater Syria that threatened the sultanate itself. The solution to the crisis in Egypt was plucked from the experiences and experiments in Greece and the Balkans in the 1820s and 1830s.

On November 3, 1831, Mehmed Ali dispatched his son İbrahim and nearly thirty thousand combined ground and naval forces to invade Ottoman Syria. The modernized army rolled through Lebanon and Syria, easily defeating Ottoman soldiers.[135] In the summer of 1832, the Egyptian army was in Anatolia and occupied fertile and mineral rich lands in Adana.[136] Now the son of the upstart governor of Egypt had claimed the territory. Mehmed II declared Mehmed Ali a rebel and sent his grand vizier, Reşid Mehmed Paşa, to take on İbrahim in Konya.[137] The two had fought together against Greek rebels and now faced each other on the battlefield. Reşid Mehmed Paşa was a dependable troubleshooter who was often dispatched to crush rebels in provincial hotspots. In addition to fighting in Greece, he helped bring down Ali Paşa of Yannina and subdued rebellions in Albania and Monastir. Just before arriving in Konya, he had put down a military insurrection in Bosnia, where locals demanded autonomy—the rebellion was initiated over outrage that the sultan had offered Serbia autonomy but not Bosnia.[138] On the plains north of Konya, İbrahim defeated and captured Reşid Mehmed Paşa, along with ten thousand Ottoman troops—a humiliating and dangerous setback for an empire already reeling from the shock of Greek crisis.[139]

İbrahim wanted to play the sovereignty game Ottoman style. He urged his father to mint coins and to have Friday prayers read in Mehmed Ali's name.[140] Rather than opting for Greek-style independence, however, Mehmed Ali favored Balkan autonomy. He wanted to secure his position in Egypt with a hereditary governorship, like the one given to Miloš Obrenović in Serbia. He ordered his son to stop his advance at Kütahya, just over two hundred miles from the capital. European powers responded haltingly at first. Russia and France assisted in discussions, but ultimately it was the sultan and his governor who brokered the uneasy truce in 1833. In exchange for submission to the state, the sultan rescinded his declaration declaring Mehmed Ali a rebel and reinstated him as governor of Egypt, Crete, and the Greater Syrian provinces of Jeddah, Sidon, Tripoli, Jerusalem, and Nablus that Mehmed Ali had initially requested. Even though Mehmed Ali wanted the governorship of all Syria, he accepted İbrahim's appointment as the governor of Damascus and Aleppo and the tax collector (*muhassil*) of Adana.[141] Mehmed Ali submitted and resumed payment of the annual tribute, which was increased to thirty thousand purses to reflect the expansion of territories under his control.[142] This deal brokered between Istanbul and Cairo was an internal agreement, not an enforceable international treaty, and from the start it seemed unlikely to hold. No governor, and certainly not a governing family, had ever been awarded so many important provinces. No matter how rebellious and how large the region they controlled, none of the eighteenth- and early nineteenth-century provincial magnates had come so close to rivaling Istanbul's own power. Even though the offer denied Mehmed Ali the hereditary governorship he had hoped for, it was still more than the sultan was likely to tolerate. One family in charge of both Greater Syria and Egypt represented a direct challenge to the legitimacy of the sultan. It was only a matter of time before relations exploded anew.

Mehmed Ali and İbrahim faced challenges in Egypt and Syria that soon led to renewed friction with the sultan. The formidable Egyptian army had not been paid, peasants resisted conscription, and locals throughout occupied Syria and Lebanon rebelled against Egypt's extractive labor policies and methods of taxation. In need of cash and concerned about the fragility of his status, Mehmed Ali launched a new round of attacks against the sultan in 1839. The Ottoman fleet was forced to surrender to Egypt, but the new foreign minister, Mustafa Reşid Paşa, had a plan to save Ottoman sovereignty. One of the main architects of Tanzimat—the legal, administrative, and fiscal reorganization of the empire—Mustafa Reşid had spent decades studying European law and diplomacy. He concocted a plan to use European power to contain the governor's ambitions.

Just as Mustafa Reşid hoped, Europe intervened decisively on behalf of the Ottoman Empire. On July 15, 1840, Britain, Russia, the Austria, Prussia, and the Ottoman Empire issued the Convention on the Pacification of the Levant.[143] The Ottoman negotiator, Mehmed Şekib Paşa—the first reform-era Ottoman ambassador to London—pushed for an agreement that would exclude Mehmed Ali's longstanding demand for a hereditary governorship, but he was overruled by Lord Palmerston. After negotiations, the Ottoman Foreign Ministry and the four European powers offered an ultimatum to Mehmed Ali Paşa, "in the interest of preserving peace in Europe." In exchange for evacuating the territory under occupation (Syria, Lebanon, Crete, Adana, Jeddah, and the Holy cities of Mecca and Medina), the Great Powers (including the Ottomans) would guarantee a hereditary governorship and unspecified local administrative rights in Egypt for Mehmed Ali Paşa, as well as the lifetime administration of Acre and other districts in southern Syria.[144] At the same time, the governor would continue to pay tribute, and all the "treaties and laws" of the Ottoman Empire would be in force "in the same manner as to every other part of the empire." Mehmed Ali was given ten days to comply to keep Egypt and Acre; if he waited twenty days, he would lose both.

Unlike in the Balkans, the Ottoman Foreign Ministry was fully involved in the negotiations over Egypt. While the Foreign Ministry would have preferred to not offer a hereditary governorship, the Ottomans obtained even more than they wanted from the deal. Mehmed Ali had threatened "the integrity of the Ottoman Empire (*tamamiyetiyle istiklal-i alisi*) and the independence of the Sultan's throne," and for this reason the powers of Europe had acted together to maintain "the Integrity and Independence of the Ottoman Empire as a security for the Peace of Europe."[145] This was the first of many times that the Great Powers would promise to guarantee the territorial domains of the Ottoman Empire in international law—that is, the first iteration of a principle that would define Ottoman–European relations until 1914. The 1856 Treaty of Paris was in some ways a modification of this exchange of territorial sovereignty for autonomy. It guaranteed the territorial integrity of the empire in exchange for imperial reforms recognizing all subjects, Muslim and non-Muslim, as equal before the law. In both cases, what mattered more than the subject matter of the agreement was a new method of enforcement: domestic law matched by international treaty.

The Convention on Pacification of the Levant (July 15, 1840), signed jointly by Britain, Russia, Prussia, Austria and the Ottoman Empire, offered Mehmed Ali hereditary administration of Egypt as well as lifetime administrative rights over part of Syria. In exchange, he was required to submit to the sultan within ten days. Added to this exchange was the now durable idea that the Ottoman Empire was part of the system of Europe and required Great Power territorial guarantees. Mehmed Ali's rebellion had threatened the independence and integrity of the state, which was now explicitly protected in a multilateral treaty.[146]

Mehmed Ali rejected the agreement and unleashed a fury of violence that arrived in the form of the allied fleet, cannons, ground troops, and a torrent of legal decrees.[147] In the name of the sultan, the allies hoisted the Ottoman flag over every captured and now ruined fort and flooded the coastal provinces with muskets, Arabic translations of the Treaty of London, and copies of the 1839 reform decree (*tanzimat-ı hayriye*) that announced the reorganization of imperial institutions and equal application of law for Muslims and non-Muslim subjects.[148] Reincorporating the occupied territories back into the imperial fold was carried out through force and the announcement of the new legal order within the empire. Egypt, too, was reconquered through law, though not as fully as Istanbul bureaucrats had desired.

Mehmed Ali's conditional surrender in late November and ultimate military defeat paved the way for imperial reincorporation. After wrangling with the European powers over Mehmed Ali's restoration as governor Egypt, Sultan Abdülmecid (r. 1839–1861) settled the matter and issued an imperial edict, a ferman of investiture that conferred hereditary privileges (*imtiyaz-i veraset*) of administration on Mehmed Ali Paşa and his descendants, in exchange for complete submission to the state.[149] As in the Balkans, the international guarantee for administrative autonomy in Egypt was stated generally in the treaty. It was up to the sultan and his ministers to work out the details. Autonomy was an opportunity to force Egypt back into the state—and one that coincided with broader imperial reforms.[150]

The end of the conflict was a complete disaster for Mehmed Ali's army and forced him to accept the terms laid out in the Convention. But, despite his initial resistance, those terms represented a massive personal success for Mehmed Ali and his heirs.[151] The terms of the Convention on the Pacification of the Levant, which were designed to appeal to the Egyptian governor, stood. In mid-February 1841 Sultan Abdülmecid issued a ferman of investiture that matched the agreement hashed out in international law. As the Convention required, it conferred hereditary rights of administration upon Mehmed Ali Paşa and his family.[152] The ferman stipulated that Mehmed Ali's successor had to be the eldest direct male descendent and that each new governor was required to go to Istanbul for a ceremony of investiture. The governing heirs would be equal to the rank of vizier. The 1839 Gülhane edict (*hatt-ı humayun*), which guaranteed equality among imperial subjects and banned tax-farming and corruption, would remain in force in Egypt. All locals would legally be Ottoman subjects. In continuation of the practice laid out in 1525, the governor would continue to send a yearly tribute to Istanbul. Taxes would be collected in the name of the sultan, and the governor would perform the customary duties historically associated with the governorship of Egypt and the Hajj, such as sending grain to pilgrims, and the *kiswa* (the black cloth covering the Kaʿba) from Cairo to Hijaz. The size of the Egyptian army was reduced to eighteen thousand, and the province was still required to send troops in times of war—as subsequent governors would do in the Crimean War (1856) and beyond.

This new iteration of autonomy was successful on the local, imperial, and international levels—that is, it satisfied Istanbul, Egypt, and the European Great Powers. Not only was Egypt's autonomy guaranteed by treaty in international law and by imperial edict, but the agreement remained tied to Great Power territorial protections. From the perspective of the reformed Ottoman Foreign Ministry, this was a great success and the beginnings of a foreign policy that would incline increasingly toward international law as the route to equality in international relations. The European territorial guarantee in the Convention had military bite. For European and Ottoman commentators in the late nineteenth century, as well as for late historians of the Middle East and European empire, Mehmed Ali's rebellion is often understood as an Ottoman catastrophe. The usual interpretation is that the Great Powers propped up a flagging empire, and that it was the moment that Egypt officially forever spun out of the Ottoman orbit. Instead, it should be viewed as a moment of opportunity for the Ottoman Empire. Autonomy in Egypt, as much as in the Balkans, was used to secure sovereignty in a world that was increasingly hostile to non-European states. At the local level, Mehmed Ali was finally assured of the security of his position, not just in an imperial edict, but in international law. Egypt would get to continue to administer itself locally, as it had. But from now on, the sultan could not threaten to take away administrative rights. One by one, the old, powerful provincial magnates were either crushed or incorporated into the state via the Tanzimat of the sword. In many ways, Mehmed Ali Paşa was the last of them and managed to escape that fate. It wasn't just Ottoman subjects and elites who benefited: From the perspective of the British Foreign Office, the agreements contained Mehmed Ali as much as the French and Russian interference in Ottoman affairs, while strengthening Istanbul.

The 1841 agreement with Egypt was not written in a vacuum but was based on established models of autonomy worked out in the Balkans. That model shaped the agreements governing Egypt's new legal relationship to the sultan and empire. It explicitly tied autonomy to European territorial guarantees securing the Ottoman domains. Autonomy was thus fused to international law and European territorial guarantees. This triad fundamentally structured Ottoman relations with Europe until 1914. At the same time, from 1841, the legal status of Egypt became a problem of

European politics and international law. Debates in the 1880s and later concerning the location of authority and the legitimacy of British rule in Egypt cannot be understood without reference to these events and to the legal texts and treaties generated in the 1840s. Throughout the period leading up to and including the British occupation, Ottoman and European diplomats and commentators drew upon these documents to make claims about Egypt vis-à-vis the "sovereign rights" of the Ottoman sultan in Egypt and those of the governor of Egypt.

Setting up Egypt as a privileged province in 1840–1841 appeased nearly everyone. For Britain, autonomy checked both local separatist and European interventionist politics. The sultan retained his rebellious provinces and had clarified a decade of uncertainty in Egypt, while Mehmed Ali remained within the Ottoman system.

A Model Province for the Empire and the International

Mehmed Ali's decade-long occupation of Ottoman Syria, together with the forceful reincorporation of the occupied territories through law in 1840, ushered in Tanzimat reforms and further unsettled the region. The nineteenth-century imperial reorganizations were meant to centralize state power at the expense of provincial power brokers, control unruly peripheries, and harmonize the empire's legal, political, and administrative institutions with European models. In some cases, reform meant more paved roads, local representative councils, and bilingual newspapers; in many others, Tanzimat arrived by the sword and was implemented through violence. Resistance took many forms: Landowners and provincial elites fought to protect their existing authority, peasants opposed new methods of taxation and conscription—as much as they resented rich landlords to whom they were indebted—and some Muslims and religious authorities resented that the reforms would be applied equally to Muslims and non-Muslims.[153] Tanzimat unsettled older patterns of patronage, disrupted the disbursement of old privileges, and challenged the established societal order in profound ways. Violent resistance to the government, and against those people who appeared to be enriched through Tanzimat, brought unwanted European attention—especially when those revolting were the empire's non-Muslim communities. While the empire managed to avert European inference in anti-Tanzimat rebellions in Bulgaria and

Bosnia, when violence broke out between Christian and Muslim communities in Lebanon in 1860, outside military intervention was swift.[154]

The first post-Egypt test was in Mount Lebanon, when violence erupted between Maronite and Druze mixed communities in northern Lebanon. In the nineteenth century, the population was composed largely of Muslim and Christian communities of various sects, comprising Sunni, Shi'a, and other groups of non-Orthodox Muslims—including a large population of Druze—as well as Maronite Catholics, Greek Orthodox, Protestants, and a small Jewish community. When fighting broke out between Maronites and Druze in the spring of 1860, it started as a peasant-landlord dispute. By the summer, what looked more like a civil war that pitted Christians against Muslims exploded across the mountain—largely sparing Beirut—and spread into neighboring Syria, culminating in massacres in the provincial capital of Damascus. Mixed villages were sacked and burned to the ground, thousands were injured and killed, and whole communities were left homeless as refugees.[155]

The Ottomans responded quickly and forced the warring Druze and Maronite communities to sign a peace treaty before Europe could organize a united response. Leading the charge was Fuad Paşa (1815–1869), one of the main architects of Tanzimat. Born into a religious family in Istanbul, Fuad Paşa went to medical school and learned French, eventually gaining an appointment in 1837 at the Translation Bureau (Tercüme Odası), the epicenter of Tanzimat activism. He was sent on diplomatic missions to London, Madrid, and St. Petersburg, where in 1848 he negotiated the settlement of Hungarian and Polish refugees in the Ottoman Empire. By the 1860s he was one of the Ottoman personalities best known to European audiences. He was appointed five times as foreign minister and twice as grand vizier. Before storming into Lebanon, he was sent on sensitive missions to Christian-majority provinces, including Moldavia and Wallachia and Bulgaria. In Egypt he conducted negotiations over the implementation of Tanzimat, renegotiated the terms of the Egyptian tribute, and later pushed to approve the Egyptian railway and Suez concessions.

Fuad Paşa was an imperial fixer and problem solver who believed that the path to establishing equality in international relations was to make Ottoman legal and administrative institutions legible to Europeans and that this meant guaranteeing equality between Muslims and non-Muslims in law and practice. He understood that the empire had to act rapidly to solve domestic conflicts before Europe could intervene. It was no surprise that in July 1860, the sultan appointed him "envoy extraordinaire" and dispatched him to Syria to restore order—a mission that was communicated to European ambassadors in Istanbul and to local consuls in the Syrian provinces.[156]

Fuad Paşa had full civil and military powers and brought the Tanzimat state to Damascus and Lebanon with a fury. He immediately arrested over 700 people and set up a special military tribunal to try perpetrators, publicly executing 167 people in Damascus and exiling scores more. Damascus was occupied by the army, and to further punish the inhabitants, the city was forced to produce 2,000 conscripts. Most of the incarcerated and condemned were Muslim tradesmen, but there were elites in the mix too. Ahmed Paşa, the governor of Damascus, was blamed for inaction and sentenced to death.[157] Fuad Paşa provided food and money to the growing Christian refugee population and instructed French priests and consuls in Damascus to stop providing these same services and even tried to repay the French for their aid.[158] He justified his actions as in the name of "civilization" and argued that he was bringing justice to imperial subjects under the state's "protection."[159] Swift justice in the name of the state was modern and in line with European standards. Despite these efforts to forestall intervention by resolving the conflict internally, French troops arrived in August to "restore order" and encamped outside Beirut. The British, afraid that France would use this incident as a chance to establish a permanent military occupation, demanded that an international commission be formed to examine the causes of violence and reconsider administrative reforms for Mount Lebanon. The commission set to work in October 1860, and its conversations would engage with the legal anatomy in new ways.

The international commission, which was established in Beirut and comprised Ottoman, British, French, Prussian, Habsburg, and Russian representatives, was charged with three tasks: to investigate the causes of violent events in Mount Lebanon and Damascus, to determine who was guilty of perpetrating acts of violence and who deserved punishment, and to agree on a settlement for "the future order and security in Syria." The British representative, Lord Dufferin, pushed a plan to completely reorganize Syria as a "decentralized" province—an idea that Fuad Paşa fully rejected.[160] The British plan, "Respecting Reorganization in Lebanon," argued that Syria would require a constant military presence, but in the spirit of local autonomy, it noted that troops should be raised and maintained locally and not be integrated into the Ottoman army: "At the same time that the future Administrator of the province is invested with this character of partial independence, the organization of its garrison ought to be placed on a footing somewhat different from the rest of the imperial army." This model directly contradicted Ottoman efforts to centralize the military by sending conscripts far from their home districts. The province's independence, Dufferin believed, should extend to financial matters. Outside of a fixed tribute payable to the imperial treasury, the "governor-general" should have wide budgetary discretion based on local considerations, so that the "resources of the country would become second only to those of Egypt."[161] The echoes of Egyptian autonomy were obvious—it was remarkable, too, that in the 1860s, Dufferin could cast Egypt as an unproblematic moneymaker for the state. He anticipated challenges to his proposal and knew it sounded like he was erecting another Egypt in Syria. But he still insisted, in contrast to Egypt, that the "new Pasha" would "still remain the Servant of the Sultan, not the Viceroy of the Province."[162]

The Ottoman government was completely unconvinced. Dufferin's plan sounded like the Great Power post-Greek autonomies in the Balkans and Egypt. They viewed the scheme as an attempt to turn Syria into a new autonomous province along the lines of Egypt, one that countered the ethos of Tanzimat and undermined state sovereignty. The acting Ottoman foreign minister, Ali Paşa, openly criticized the plan, noting that it "would involve nothing less than the erection of a Vice-royalty like Egypt and the Danubian Provinces." He also argued that the scheme expanded the scope of the European presence as stipulated by the European Commission and allowed for illegal intervention.[163] In a letter to Musurus Paşa, the British ambassador in London, he warned: "Lord Dufferin's project, covering the whole of Syria, and constituting a nearly separate state, will never be accepted by the Porte."[164] To allay these concerns, Lord Dufferin insisted that Britain would continue to support the "territorial integrity" of the Ottoman Empire.

The "nearly separate state" was Mehmed Ali's autonomous Egypt, but it also hinted at other autonomous provinces of the empire that were quickly becoming detached from central authority, especially the *Memleketeyn,* the principalities of Wallachia and Moldavia, and Serbia. The Ottoman government was all too familiar with the model of a strong local governor in command of an independent army and in control of the local economy, sending only tribute to the treasury. It was a model the Ottomans had perfected over several centuries that had worked, but in the age of centralizing states it went against the goals of the Tanzimat. The British plan reshaped Ottoman structures of autonomy to serve British interests. As Ali Paşa noted: "The plan in question tends to erect a new principle, quasi-independence subject to the direction of a European commission, in other words a Syria separate from the Ottoman domains."[165] The Ottoman government dismissed Dufferin's plan on the basis that it would create a strong province insulated from central imperial control.

The British ambassador in Istanbul, Henry Bulwer, shared Ali Paşa's skepticism. Bulwer worried that to treat Syria differently from the rest of the empire would undermine Britain's commitment to support "the territorial integrity" of the Ottoman Empire. He thought the best course of action was to treat Syria as a "model province to which the other provinces of the Empire can be assimilated." To his mind, reform in Syria and Lebanon should be linked to a much larger project of administrative reform in the Ottoman Empire. Bulwer noted:

> If I were charged with the reforms in Syria I would endeavor to make that province a model province for the rest of Turkey: I would endeavor so to constitute it that the Sultan's dominions at large might undergo the ameliorating influence; and I would guard as carefully as I could against propounding in it what could not safely be adopted elsewhere. Establish governors for ten years in the present state of the empire generally, and these governors will in fact become independent princes and Turkey without identity or unity will cease to be a European Power.[166]

The example of Egypt and the danger of both a hereditary governorship and provincial autonomy to Ottoman sovereignty clung to Bulwer's analysis. Egypt was still Ottoman, but the degree of local autonomy awarded to the province in 1840–41, a prize guaranteed by European powers and the Ottoman government, undermined the project of Tanzimat. Rather than reject Dufferin's plan outright, Bulwer argued that any provincial reform scheme should be developed with the entire empire in mind. What is especially curious is that Bulwer was in regular communication with Fuad Paşa about everything from the Suez Canal concession to the crisis in Lebanon and held meetings with him and the sultan. He supported Fuad and knew that he had been planning a general reorganization of the provincial system, which would be first tested out a few years later in a "model province" in Bulgaria.[167]

Despite losing support from the British ambassador in Istanbul, Dufferin's plan remained on the table as an option through the remainder of the international commission's negotiations. Ali Paşa rejected it outright in January 1861, and by the spring of that year the rest of Beirut Commission ditched it. Instead of integrating the mountain into a larger Syrian province, the commission opted to establish Mount Lebanon as an autonomous province under the sovereignty of the sultan—though aspects of Dufferin's plan remained in the final agreement. European diplomats, together with Fuad Paşa and other members of the Ottoman government in Istanbul, took the commission's recommendations and hammered out an agreement that was promulgated on June 9, 1861. The "Regulations and Protocols Relative to the Organization of Mount Lebanon," the *Règlement Organique*, created the *mutasarrifiyya*, as it was known until its demise in 1915, when another Ottoman provincial troubleshooter, Cemal Paşa, would bring his vision of the empire to Syria, backed by full military and civil powers.[168]

Mount Lebanon was established as an autonomous province within the empire. Like the *Règlement Organique* for the earlier Christian majority autonomous provinces in the Balkans, the regulations laid out the administrative order of the province and side-stepped political questions.[169] Mount Lebanon, which did not include prosperous Beirut, would be administered by a nonlocal Christian governor appointed by the sultan, in agreement with the Great Powers. The governor was directly responsible to the sultan and would serve a three-year term, which was extended to five years in 1864. As in the Dufferin plan, the governor would have broad local control over the subprovince. He was invested with "executive power" and was responsible for maintaining order, security, and tax collection. This meant maintaining a local police force, separate from the military.

The new system created a multiconfessional "administrative council," which was composed of two each of Maronites, Druze, Greek Orthodox, Greek Catholics, Shi'a, and Sunni representatives. It functioned as an advisory board and was responsible for assessing taxes and managing revenues and expenditures. The principle of representation was broadly applied—each administrative district had its own "local administrative council" that would meet annually to hear local complaints, provide tax information to the governor, and offer advisory opinions on local administrative issues. These districts should be further divided into zones—the regulations stipulated that each zone should be "insofar as possible of homogenous population." In addition to the administrative councils, the regulations created a system of judicial councils based on confessional identity.[170] The regulations echoed other Tanzimat principles articulated in 1839 and 1856, promised equality before the law, and abolished tax-farming. The imperial center reserved the right to collect taxes, but generally taxes would be spent locally, and only a surplus would become state revenues. All large-scale public works projects would be the responsibility of the imperial government.[171]

Mount Lebanon was not a cookie-cutter copy of the autonomous provinces created in the Balkans and Egypt in the 1830s and 1840s. None of the autonomies were identical in taxation, administration, or even law. In Lebanon, the confessional basis of the administrative and judicial councils was distinct—though each of the early autonomous provinces raised questions about administering Muslim and non-Muslim populations, where one population was dominant—and each autonomous province had some variation of an administrative counsel or advice-giving body of "notables from the country." A Christian governor was in no way innovative—Samos had one appointed by Istanbul who was given the title "prince," but the term was at first not limited and the office was dominated by Phanariot Greeks from Istanbul.[172] What distinguished Mount Lebanon was that Ottomans had a dominant role in the negotiations in Beirut and Istanbul. Ottoman officials had far more control over writing the final regulations for the province than the ones produced for Serbia and the Danubian Principalities. Fuad Paşa looked to the earlier autonomies in the Balkans, and especially Egypt, as negative models for Lebanon. Like Dufferin, he supported the idea of a strong governor with broad authority to make local decisions. He also agreed that the governor should serve a fixed term but insisted that he have no local or familial connections to Lebanon, to prevent the emergence of another hereditary governor as in Egypt. What put Mount Lebanon on equal footing with the autonomous provinces was that its special status was protected in international law by treaty and by the domestic legal order of the state. For Fuad Paşa, the fact that autonomy was negotiated at all with European powers was the problem, and one that desperately needed to be fixed. The regulations for Mount Lebanon paved the way for administrative reform throughout the empire—it was a preemptive move without interference from European powers.

In the aftermath of the Beirut Commission negotiations, Fuad Paşa designed and implemented an empire-wide system of provincial and legal reform. Since the 1850s he had urged the government to give provincial governors more authority to make and enforce decisions on their own, but it was European military and administrative intervention in Lebanon that provided the opportunity to act decisively. Lord Dufferin's vision of a large, autonomous Syria was a portent of what Europe could do to the empire, and over time Dufferin and the British Foreign Office would increasingly push administrative autonomy as the solution to vastly different imperial crises. Just three years after the regulations were promulgated for Lebanon, Fuad Paşa, together with Midhat Paşa, drew up administrative regulations for the empire. They first tested their scheme in Bulgaria in a newly created Danube province (Tuna).[173] After deeming the experiment in Tuna a success, starting in 1867 provincial reorganization was implemented throughout the imperial domains. The Vilayet Law (*Teşkil-i Vilayet Nizamnamesi*), which was promulgated on November 8, 1864, shared more than a few similarities with the regulations for Mount Lebanon. Governors were given far more local discretion and power—for Fuad, delegating authority to the provinces would take pressure off the central administration. The execution of imperial law fell to the governors, who had power over local police as well as financial and legal affairs. The entire empire was reorganized into a hierarchal and standardized system of provinces (*vilayet*), subprovinces (*sancak* or *liva*), administrative districts (*kaza*) all the way down to the level of towns (*kariye*), and rural settlements (*nahiye*). As in Lebanon, there were representative and administrative councils (*meclis-i idare*) at the top three tiers of the hierarchy. More important, the law implemented the three-tiered system of secular courts, known as *Nizamiye* courts, which were presided over by a judicial inspector and three Muslim and three non-Muslim members.[174] The new system of courts addressed imperial needs but also enabled the Ottomans to argue that law and courts were in accordance with European models. As we will see, this argument, used against European audiences, was about dismantling the Capitulations, the system of unequal treaties that prevented the Ottoman Empire from achieving equality with European empires.

Fuad Paşa announced the new legal and administrative system to European powers in 1867. Drawing on the civilization language both Fuad and Dufferin used to describe the inhabitants of Mount Lebanon, Fuad noted that the state had established a form of administration the corresponded to "the needs of the country, to the customs of the populations, and to the demands of the concept of civilization which presses upon the empire from all directions."[175] He viewed the new legal and administrative system as comprising centralizing and standardizing elements that would make the state more palpable in the provinces and more legible to European powers, who increasingly justified their intervention in Ottoman affairs with recourse to the language of "civilization." At the same time, the new provincial system, Fuad argued, possessed decentralizing elements that gave governors more latitude to make on-the-spot decisions that considered the specific interests of locals and would get imperial subjects in far-flung provinces to buy into the empire. Fuad's vision for the empire embraced both centralizing and decentralizing elements. This was a clear instance in which autonomy was productive for the Ottoman state, but it was also valuable for Dufferin, and by extension the British Foreign Office.

Conclusion: "We Are Laboring in the Interests of the World at Large"

From the 1840s, diplomats, imperial problem solvers like Fuad Paşa, joined in the 1880s by international lawyers, experimented with new administrative and political formations within empires that pushed the boundaries of the meaning of sovereignty. In the nineteenth century imperial sovereignty looked like a patchwork of differentiated legal and administrative spaces. Rights and privileges attached unevenly to different groups of subjects, provinces, or local elites, and state power was felt unevenly, especially in imperial frontiers and zones of overlapping authority.[176] In this period, the Ottoman Empire was among the principal sites of experiments in sovereignty and political control. The empire, however, was not simply acted upon by Great Powers, which is the usual story in the historiography of the Eastern Question. Instead, state officials negotiated with European powers, especially Britain, to define and redefine the meaning of sovereignty. International lawyers, geographers, Ottoman as well as European diplomats, and policymakers hashed out the various forms of autonomy, the meaning of the legal concepts of suzerainty versus sovereignty, autonomy versus self-governance, as well as the legal meaning of frontiers, borders, and protectorates.[177]

For the British, some measure of administrative autonomy within the Ottoman state guaranteed by the "public system of Europe" became the preferred Foreign Office solution for maintaining British interests in the Ottoman Empire, while at the same time managing Ottoman weakness in the international system and emerging nationalisms. Foreign Office officials viewed autonomy as an administrative bulwark against encroaching imperialisms and centrifugal nationalisms. British foreign secretaries, diplomats, and later lawyers seized on the autonomy idea as an administrative solution to political problems. Autonomy through decentralized imperial administration, they argued, was the best means to prevent annexation by other powers as well as to manage nationalist claims in the Balkans and Egypt. The British regularly drew on their own imperial structure to think through how autonomy would work. The relationship between the United Kingdom and the self-governing settler colonies was being renegotiated during the same period that the British turned their attention to the Ottomans. Arguments for closer union between the United Kingdom and the Dominions assumed a range of forms, privileging variously constitutional, federative, and economic or citizenship arrangements. As governor-general of Canada, Dufferin actively participated in this debate and was a partisan of "Greater Britain," a supporter of closer union between the UK and the white settler colonies.

Ottoman leadership understood that these legal maneuvers were damaging their sovereignty but viewed them as part of the interimperial negotiation needed to stay afloat as a European empire. The goal of Tanzimat was not so much centralization as stability through imperial incorporation. The Ottoman autonomous provinces were never easily separated from the general administration of the empire—the "regular" and what would increasingly be known as the "privileged" provinces (*eyalet-i mümtaze*) remained bound to each other. The more European powers tried to force autonomy on Ottoman locals in restive peripheries, the more pressure the state faced to regularize patterns of administration throughout the empire. From the start, Istanbul officials insisted that Egypt and the rest were "integral parts of the Ottoman Empire," even if they possessed exceptional privileges vis-à-vis other provinces. As we will see in the next chapter, after the territorial losses of 1878 and the start of the British occupation of Egypt in 1882, Ottoman lawyers would overhaul the system of autonomous provinces and insist they were part of the constitutional order of the state and a normal feature of empire. After 1882, Ottoman lawyers and intellectuals would argue in textbooks, newspaper articles, legal opinions, and law journals that the privileged provinces were analogous to the British settler colonies—especially South Africa and Canada.[178]

Importantly, concepts and frameworks for autonomy and self-governance remained in flux through the end of the Ottoman Empire, as did understandings of sovereignty. Despite Ottoman territorial losses in the Balkans in 1878, which resulted in independence for Serbia, Montenegro, and Romania, the nation-state had not yet properly emerged as the principal solution to imperial crises, and for many, systems of "self-governance" did not necessarily equate sovereignty—self-governance was possible within empire. Though the Treaty of Berlin appeared to signal the end of longstanding British support for maintaining the territorial integrity of the Ottoman Empire, on the contrary it marked more explicitly a growing Foreign Office policy favoring administrative autonomy within the Ottoman Empire, guaranteed by what was still termed the public system of Europe. Accordingly, the management of international relations was more often a question of balancing interests within empire. Autonomy schemes presented a particular theory of international relations, which overlapped significantly with a theory of empire that sought to strengthen imperial architecture through administrative decentralization.

Most important, the new autonomies were not just experiments imposed by European states eager to meddle in the domestic affairs of the Ottoman Empire. Istanbul got something out of each deal. Late in his life, the Tanzimat statesmen Ali Paşa explained that the driving purpose of Ottoman foreign policy was for Europe to recognize the empire's "right to exist and be admitted to the Concert of Europe." The Foreign Ministry had been successful in this objective, he argued, and had obtained European territorial guarantees securing the full extent of the imperial domains. The empire made concessions in exchange. Ali Paşa cast the autonomous provinces as part of that story, but just like the European powers who insisted that they had not invented anything new in Balkans, he argued that autonomy in the Balkans was longstanding: "Pressured by Europe, we gave these states *what they already possessed.* Their de facto autonomy was legalized under a new form; but we defined our rights irrevocably. Sometimes we gave in reluctantly to Europe's demands in order to avoid heavier sacrifices."[179]

CHAPTER 2

Taming Autonomy Through Law

Between 1875 and 1882 the Ottoman state confronted a series of crises that fundamentally shifted the meaning of autonomy within the empire. If, before the 1870s, European-imposed autonomy was a dangerous intrusion into Ottoman domestic affairs but one that could be managed through diplomacy and legal reform, by the 1880s autonomy posed an existential threat to the empire. It was precisely in the Balkan provinces and Egypt—the first sites of legal-administrative experimentation—that autonomy turned from a negotiated compromise between the Ottomans, their rivals, and locals into a menace that threatened to eviscerate the state.

In 1878, after three years of rebellion and warfare, the Balkan privileged provinces exited the empire as successor states. This "exit" was a net loss for the Ottomans, representing a two-fifths decrease in territory, a one-fifth decrease in population, and a massive influx of Muslim refugees fleeing their new Christian-Orthodox-oriented successor states. After 1878 the Ottoman Empire was smaller and poorer and had shifted its demographic balance, creating a Muslim majority state for the first time.[1] At the same time, the Ottoman Mediterranean was increasingly exposed to European imperial encroachments: Britain established a protectorate in Cyprus in 1878, while France signed a treaty of protection with locals in Tunis in 1881.[2] But the most devastating assault on the system of autonomous provinces worked out between the 1820s and 1840s was Britain's permanent military occupation of Ottoman Egypt, starting in 1882. These episodes showed in stark terms that autonomous administration could indeed be the midpoint of an arc from imperial province to independent state. The spate of military occupations at the empire's exposed edges demonstrated that local administrative rights not only diminished Ottoman political control by inviting European intervention but also significantly weakened sovereignty in the autonomies and throughout the empire. Imperial sovereignty was at risk, and autonomy was the problem.

The Balkan losses, together with the British invasion of Egypt, forced state bureaucrats to rethink the empire's approach to negotiated autonomy. Rather than write off the military occupations and autonomies as lost causes—as much of the historiography has viewed such cases—the state was ever more resolved to exert sovereignty in its vulnerable peripheries. After 1882 Egypt became central to the Foreign Ministry's strategy to shore up territorial claims and effective political control across the edges of the empire in North Africa and the Arabian Peninsula. Ottoman lawyers and Foreign Ministry officials turned to international law to weaponize state-consolidating efforts. While this project was first rooted in Tanzimat reforms, it became a distinctly Hamidian (1876–1909) legal project that should be seen alongside broader efforts to develop the empire and exert control over imperial peripheries.[3] The British occupation of Egypt, immediately following the loss of the privileged provinces in the Balkans, drove the state to formalize international law as part of its diplomatic apparatus. While international law had shaped Ottoman diplomacy much earlier, it was only in the 1880s that it was explicitly tied to the ways the empire countered European aggression. Ottoman activism around autonomy took a two-pronged approach. First, international lawyers vigorously defended the empire against European encroachment by insisting on the state's recognized sovereign rights in the autonomous provinces via the treaties and imperial decrees (fermans) that guaranteed local autonomy as well as imperial sovereignty—a strategy that, as we will see, was surprisingly successful until the onset of the Young Turk Revolution of 1908. Second, the same lawyers who protected the state at the diplomatic level worked to better incorporate Egypt and the remaining privileged provinces into the constitutional and administrative order of the empire. In both cases, the goal was to limit local authority and European interference while strengthening imperial sovereignty.

This chapter examines Ottoman institution building around international law and the formal use made of law as a weapon of the weak in the empire's struggles against Europe. In particular, it looks at the Foreign Ministry's Office of Legal Counsel, a new institution staffed by public and private international law experts who hashed out the legal arguments to preserve the state against an ever more hostile and expansive Europe. Focusing on the empire's leading international lawyers—Gabriel Noradounghian and İbrahim Hakkı (later Paşa)—this chapter shows how international law was not an intellectual project in the Ottoman Empire, but rather one focused on the practice of using it to strengthen the state against European incursions.[4] Because the line between international and domestic legal orders was pierced through a set of instruments that limited Ottoman sovereignty, the chapter also explores how Ottoman lawyers tamed European-imposed autonomy and reclaimed it as a longstanding feature of imperial administration. This legal work was part of a broader strategy to achieve parity with Europe and to reassert full imperial sovereignty. While the empire never managed to achieve sovereign equality with the Great Powers—few states succeeded in this venture, even European ones—the drive fundamentally transformed the state and its relations with European empires.[5] Though the fight against an ever more rapacious Europe was never resolved, the consequences were great. Autonomy, fused with international law, was generative of Ottoman institutions, administrative ideas, and broader political claims to sovereignty—claims that would become increasingly important for everyday imperial subjects.

The Road to Legal Positivism

Learning the science of international law was not a choice for the Ottoman Foreign Ministry. The incipient discipline, whose modern usage was forged in part out of disputes between the Ottoman and European empires, arrived in the imperial capital as a cudgel.[6] International law was not theoretical problem to debate among expert elites. Unlike their European counterparts, Ottoman lawyers didn't fret about the relevance of their profession to state practice and foreign policy—such abstractions had no role to play in an empire that faced the hard edge of European military, fiscal, and administrative power.[7] As we have seen, from the 1830s, the

Ottoman Empire was tied to Europe via a series of legal instruments that protected the "territorial integrity" of the state but did so in exchange for foreign powers having a say in how the parts of the empire would be governed. Because Ottoman incorporation into the post-Vienna system of European politics was executed through treaties, international law emerged as the dominant arena through which the state challenged its unequal position in the international order and asserted its sovereignty throughout the imperial domains—especially in the autonomous provinces.

Though international law offered opportunities to the state in its relations with Europe, its dominion was inescapable and ever present in the daily life of the empire. European states, by and large, could choose how and when to deploy international law arguments to justify policy in domestic and international relations.[8] International law in the Ottoman Empire, in contrast, was lived. It determined governing practices in the autonomous provinces, justified European military intervention, exempted foreign residents from domestic law and taxation, kept import rates disastrously low, permitted the extension of a system of foreign post offices, brought unfavorable loans, the influx of and concession hunters, and generally hindered the development and state centralization. Throughout most of the nineteenth century, international law, both public and private, was embedded in everyday politics and interactions between Ottomans and Europeans and fundamentally mediated the relationship between the empire's subjects and foreigners—in Istanbul, Cairo, Damascus, İzmir, Jerusalem, Baghdad, and wherever European merchants and counsels proliferated.[9]

The privileged provinces were just one of a fixed set of European-imposed restrictions on Ottoman governance that emerged out of the settlement of the Greek and Egyptian crises. In the 1830s the Ottoman state was forced to contend with additional legal barriers that hindered the full exercise of state sovereignty, including the reconfigured Capitulations—unequal treaties that exempted foreigners from local law—and a range of financial instruments. By the 1870s, Ottomans bundled together administrative, legal, and financial restrictions on the state's exercise of sovereignty as part of the same problem, which they argued was a result of the empire's unequal status in European politics. Like the privileged provinces, legal and financial limitations on sovereignty grew increasingly onerous over the course of the nineteenth century, and Ottomans viewed them as not only obstructing reform but also impeding the state's capacity to project power evenly throughout the empire. As the international lawyer Mehmed Cemil (Bilsel) would later argue, the principles underlying these policies "restrict the sovereignty of the state."[10] While the main concern of this chapter is to demonstrate how the privileged provinces spurred the state to build institutions around international law, it is impossible to separate that project from the concurrent effort to abolish the Capitulations. Crises in the privileged provinces were the direct catalyst for the formalization and bureaucratization of international law as the main mechanism of Ottoman foreign policy, but once created, the Ottoman diplomatic machine attacked all limitations on its sovereignty (administrative, legal, and financial) at every opportunity.[11]

Restrictions on Ottoman sovereignty made it enormously difficult to separate questions related to public international law—the body of law and practices that govern the relationship between states—and private international law—the law governing legal jurisdiction between private citizens, which touches on issues of personal status, citizenship, nationality, and identity documentation.[12] This was especially true for the nineteenth Capitulations, and nowhere more so than in the privileged provinces.[13]

In the same period that the Great Powers determined how parts of the Balkans and Egypt would be managed, the early modern agreements known as the Capitulations were drastically reengineered from a privilege that facilitated trade between Muslim and non-Muslim empires, into unequal treaties that justified the empire's precarious position at the legal edges of the international order.[14] In the early modern period, successive sultans conferred privileges to European sovereigns that offered protection to their merchants traveling and trading in the Ottoman domains—unilateral grants that expired with the death of the sultan.[15] "Protected foreigners" (*müstemen*) could not be enslaved, their property could not be seized as booty, and they were not subject to the *haraç*—the tax non-Muslims paid to the empire in exchange for protection and acceptance of Ottoman rule. European consular officials obtained the legal authority to arbitrate civil and criminal disputes between members of their particular community, though foreigners could opt to bring a case to Ottoman *sharia* courts. As Maurits van den Boogert has demonstrated, even in the late eighteenth century foreigners were not separate from Ottoman legal system but instead were subject to it.[16] That rapidly changed in the first half of the nineteenth century, however, when the Capitulations provided foreigners with extraterritorial rights and jurisdiction. Foreigners residing and traveling in the empire were exempt from Ottoman law and courts and were protected against search and seizure and conscription. Foreign governments operated their own post offices throughout the empire.[17] While originally called *ahdname*, treaty or privilege, by the late nineteenth century the Capitulations were referred to simply as privileges or *imtiyazat*—a word with the same Arabic root as *mümtez*, as in the *eyalet-i mümtaze*, meaning to distinguish or to grant a special privilege.[18]

Until the first half of the nineteenth century, neither Ottoman officials nor states with capitulatory privileges viewed the Capitulations as a derogation of sovereignty.[19] It was only when they were reworked into permanent treaties that the Capitulations were a mark of inequality in international relations, a process that began in 1774 and was increasingly standard by the late 1830s. As the French international lawyer Paul Pradier-Fodéré explained, the alchemy that transfigured temporary privileges, "revocable at the discretion of the government that had granted them," into international law happened when foreign powers embedded the text of the old capitulations in new international treaties: "Foreign powers thus transformed the concessions that Turkey had granted them temporarily into treaties."[20] Pradier-Fodéré, whose works were often positively cited in Ottoman international legal treatises and legal opinions, offered an interpretation that accorded with late Ottoman understandings of the Capitulations and explains how, in particular, Ottoman lawyers invoked positive international law as a viable means to protect the imperial domains.[21] İbrahim Hakkı Paşa, one of the empire's leading international lawyers, insisted that the original Capitulations were not subject to international law because they were never bilateral treaties and were merely privileges. In reference to the 1740 French Capitulations—which France claimed provided the legal basis for their extraterritorial rights in the nineteenth century—he argued: "These capitulations are in the form of an imperial edict (*ferman*), with only one side speaking. It is well known that in treaties (*muahedelerde*), commitments are made by both parties. They are signed by both rulers. However, in this case, only one ruler is speaking . . . but nothing is said on behalf of the other party. For example, what treatment will we receive in France? There is no ruling on this matter! This is the nature of the Capitulations."[22] No clearer example existed that the Capitulations were not treaties than the empire's dense treaty relationship with Europe. These were states that not only traded with each other but went to war, formed alliances, and hammered out peace treaties, but the Capitulations were only part of that story insofar as they prompted trade; they were not legal frameworks governing the relationship between Ottomans and non-Ottoman foreigners.

For İbrahim Hakkı Paşa, it was only in the late eighteenth century, starting with the Treaty of Küçük Kaynarca (1774), when Europeans began to embed the Capitulations into bilateral treaties, that they began to take on their current pernicious form: "The Treaty of Kaynarca opened painful wounds in the body of the state and brought about many unfortunate issues for the state. Until this date, Russian subjects had no privileges. According to this treaty, Russian subjects would receive most-favored nation status (*en ziyade nail müsaade millet*), equivalent to that of the other nations, and would also benefit from the privileges of the other nations. Likewise, Russia's right to protect (*hakk-ı himayesi)* its subjects was confirmed."[23] In the critical period between 1774 and the 1830s, Russia's foreign privileges were reinscribed in trade agreements and peace treaties, including the Treaty Edirne (1828)—discussed in chapter 1—which strengthened Russian claims for autonomy in Serbia and Wallachia and Moldavia.

From the Napoleonic Wars through the settlement of the Greek crisis, European powers with existing privileges began to insert the old Capitulations into new peace treaties and trade agreements with the Ottomans. For instance, the 1809 Anglo-Ottoman Treaty, which ended conflict between the empires, noted that the Capitulations of 1675's "other privileges" would be reinstated, as though the two empires had never been at war.[24] In addition, the powers signed a secret defensive alliance that promised to ensure "the integrity of the territories of the Empire" should Britain make peace with Russia first, the concern being the status of Moldavia and Wallachia, under Russian military occupation (1806–1812). The 1838 Treaty of Baltılimanı—the Anglo-Ottoman commercial treaty that abolished Ottoman monopolies and flooded the empire with British goods—started with the declaration that all "rights, privileges, and immunities which have been conferred on the subjects or ships of Great Britain by the existing Capitulations and Treaties, are confirmed now and forever."[25] The treaty contained a fifteen-page list of all the articles British merchants were allowed to import across the Ottoman domains, which included everything from Venetian fezzes and playing cards to capers and caviar, as well as manufactured goods and raw materials. A shorter, five-page list contained the items Ottomans could export to

Britain—mostly agricultural products and small-scale manufactured goods like carpets and textiles. Much like the reconfiguration of the older autonomies into the new privileged provinces in the 1830s, European governments imposed overly broad interpretations of earlier capitulatory privileges to claim legal immunity throughout the Ottoman domains.

The transition from privilege to unequal treaty, and thus from an imperial prerogative to the subject of public and private international law, wasn't simply standardizing old practices with new legal instruments. There was also a burst of new Capitulations in the same period, including to Sardinia (1825), the United States (1830), Belgium (1838), Portugal (1843), as well as trade agreements offering most favored nation status to Mexico (1862)—extracted during the French occupation and the Second Mexican Empire under Maximillian. İbrahim Hakkı complained bitterly that these states were given privileges. He maintained that the American text was particularly pernicious and undercut state sovereignty. What most puzzled him was that the state should have signed a treaty in the first place, given America's weak position within the international order in 1830:

> A government newly established, having been separated from the British Empire, 20,000 kilometers away from us cannot be expected to have entered into such an unreasonable agreement out of necessity. If this agreement were made today, there might be some reason for it. At present, America is a great power, possessing a large navy and having defeated Spain. Although its colonies are far away, it is still a state to be reckoned with. However, at the time of the treaty, none of these reasons existed; in short, this treaty is unreasonable.[26]

Why did the empire offer concessions when it was not obligated to do so? İbrahim Hakkı reminded his readers that, at the time, the state hesitated to expand the number of states with capitulatory rights not because "privileges restricted the sovereignty of the state," but rather because the state was not sure which states could be trusted as friends.[27] There were two critical underlying arguments. The first was that the Ottoman Empire did not think it was giving anything way—certainly not its sovereignty. More galling was the fact that small and weak states attempted to obtain and abuse privileges—an argument that perhaps says more about Ottoman attitudes toward military power and empire in 1910, when the piece was published, than it does about the structure of international politics in the

1830s. Second, it also tells us much about Ottoman understandings of international order. İbrahim Hakkı insisted that the state was happy to establish and maintain relations with every other recognized state, but only on the basis of legal equality, guaranteed by international law:

> Today, we do not grant these privileges to governments that request Capitulations. For example, Japan sought to conclude such an agreement, but we did not do so. What reason could there be for granting such privileges? In our country, the principles of international law are in force, and they can maintain relations with us within the framework of these principles. There is no obligation for the state to grant excessive privileges for its own sake. For example, the governments of China, Japan, and Liberia want to establish relations with us. Very well, let them come, let them stay in our country within the framework of international law, let them be subject to Ottoman jurisdiction in all matters.[28]

The real problem with the Capitulations as treaties was that they cut against the empire's position as one of the states that mattered in nineteenth-century international politics. For İbrahim Hakkı, the state's status within the international order changed dramatically with the Treaty of Paris (1856) concluding the Crimean War. The Crimean War (1853–1856) was one of the few wars the Ottomans successfully executed against Russia over the course of the eighteenth and nineteenth centuries, and, far more important, its outcomes shaped Ottoman approaches to warfare and peacemaking through the collapse of the state.[29] Ottoman justification for war was pitched as an explicit defense of sovereignty: "The state can no longer tolerate or endure the existing state of things, as well as the prolonged occupation of the Principalities (Wallachia and Moldavia), which are integral parts of its empire; the Ottoman cabinet, with the fixed and laudable intention of defending the sacred rights of sovereignty and the independence of its government, will resort to just reprisals against a violation of treaties which it looks upon as a casus belli."[30] Even before the Treaty of Paris was negotiated and signed, the Ottoman Foreign Ministry claimed that treaty law protected and guaranteed imperial sovereignty, which was enshrined in the earlier autonomy agreements.

Britain justified its intervention on behalf of the Ottoman Empire in similar terms, arguing that that Russia had invaded and "assailed"

Ottoman independence, and that Britain was acting in the interest of the "independence of the states of Europe." In April 1854, Britain, the Habsburg Empire, France, and Prussia affirmed their commitment to ending the Russian occupation of Moldavia and Wallachia and to maintaining the "territorial integrity of the Ottoman empire"—a phrase that appeared increasingly with the agreements worked out for the autonomous provinces and would be duplicated through subsequent peace treaties. In December, the Allies vowed to collectively guarantee "the privileges accorded by the sultans" in the principalities and Serbia. The lumping together of Great Power territorial guarantees and imperial privileges, issued by the sultan, was prefigured by the negotiations over the status of Greece and the Balkan territories that gained autonomy in the 1830s, but it also anticipated the major articles of the Treaty of Paris concluding the Crimean War in 1856. Article 7 invited the Ottoman Empire "to participate in the advantages of the public law and system (concert) of Europe" and guaranteed the empire's territorial integrity and independence. While the Ottoman Foreign Ministry viewed that article as a major achievement, Article 9 immediately undercut the full exercise of Ottoman sovereignty. Nonintervention in Ottoman affairs was contingent on the empire's agreement to "ameliorate the condition of the Christian populations" of the empire, text that Ottoman negotiators unsuccessfully opposed. As İbrahim Hakkı put it, the treaty was signed "by the great powers of the time: the Ottoman Empire, Russia, Austria, Prussia, England, France, and the Sardinian states, which were not considered great powers at the time but were at war with Russia."[31]

In all his writings—legal, historical, and administrative—İbrahim Hakkı Paşa carefully demonstrated the long legal history of European–Ottoman relations and the proliferation of legal documents that established this relationship. Like other Ottoman lawyers, İbrahim Hakkı was a legal positivist and ardently subscribed to the idea that the source of international law was state practice, and that practice was embedded in treaties of war and peace. Yet, incredibly, he set that history aside to insist that something distinct happened in 1856:

> Until that time, our position in Europe was not the same as it was after the Treaty of Paris. From a legal standpoint, Europeans are now united like a family. There are certain general rules that determine the relations within this family. These rules do not apply to

> those outside the European family—for example, certain Eastern governments (*şark-ı hükumetleri*) today—but such governments do benefit from these general rules to some extent. These are rules pertaining to humanity. They are not part of the family, so they cannot be naturally rejected. Humanity prevents this. However, a government outside the family cannot benefit from the other rules that Europeans apply to each other. They are told: your customs, your position, your status, and your civilization are different. . . .
>
> The Ottoman Empire was excluded from the general principles established by the European family and European states. However, the Paris Treaty put an end to such an exception. There is an article in that treaty—the seventh article—which confirms the territorial integrity and supreme independence of the Ottoman Empire with the joint guarantee of the European powers and declares that the Ottoman Empire is a party to the general laws of Europe and is entitled to participate in its political organization. According to this article, the Sublime State is also considered to be one of the states belonging to the European family, that is, the community of nations. Whatever rules are in force among them shall be applied in the Sublime State.
>
> The inclusion of such a clause in the treaty necessitated that the previous situation be considered an exception. From then on, the Ministry of Foreign Affairs was established, and it sought to apply these rules in every respect, and the state at that time sought to achieve the natural consequences of this established rule. Ali Paşa issued a statement to the congress, saying: "Since you have accepted us, we will also benefit from European public law. Remove from us anything that is contrary to this law. In Europe, there is no such thing as the right of consuls to judicial immunity."[32]

This was a hierarchical vision of international relations, but one that included the Ottoman Empire inside the "family of nations." European lawyers agreed. Johann Caspar Bluntschli, the Swiss international lawyer, argued that the Ottomans were excluded from the "European community of states," but it was still "impossible to avoid concluding international treaties." The year 1856 changed everything: "But it was not until the Paris Peace Congress of 1856 that Turkey was accepted as a legitimate member of the European community of states, thereby confirming the universal human character of international law." Later in the century, some international lawyers debated whether the treaty did in fact bring the Ottomans into the family of nations and the Concert of Europe.[33] Despite those later debates, the reality is that accepting the Ottoman Empire into the concert of Europe utterly transformed the types of arguments Ottoman lawyers could and would make from 1856 onward and how European lawyers and diplomats responded to them. The Treaty of Paris, Hakkı Paşa argued, should have protected the state from foreign interference of all kinds, including "in the internal administration" (*saltanat-ı seniyelerinin idare-i dahiliyesi*).[34]

But the enduring gap between the rhetoric of equality promised in 1856 and the continuation of European-imposed restrictions on Ottoman sovereignty proved to be an obstinate source of tension between empires and among Ottoman and European international lawyers. The Capitulations, periodic military interventions on behalf of Ottoman Christians, Great Power guaranteed autonomous provinces, and, later in the nineteenth century, permanent military occupations of Ottoman territory in Tunis, Egypt, Bosnia, and Cyprus, as well as the Ottoman Public Debt Administration, all pointed to the fact that the Ottomans had not actually achieved sovereign equality with Europe in 1856—an issue that was clear in the process of negotiating the peace after the Crimea. And as İbrahim Hakkı noted, Ali Paşa, the grand vizier and chief Ottoman representative at Paris, repeatedly argued that the Capitulations and other limitations on Ottoman sovereignty were at odds with the empire's new status as a member of the European concert.[35] European representatives offered a vague promise to revisit the issue after the peace had been settled, but they never seriously returned to the question, despite the near constant efforts to do so by the Foreign Ministry.[36]

Because the Ottoman relationship with Europe was mediated through treaties, Ottoman lawyers became strict legal positivists, in advance of some of their European colleagues. International law also mattered on a day-to-day basis in a way that simply did not pertain in Europe but was very similar for countries who were recognized in international relations as independent but whose sovereignty was circumscribed in much the same way. Istanbul had far more in common with Latin America, Iran, Japan, and China—what Houchang Chehabi, and David Motadel have termed "unconquered states."[37] Ottoman bureaucrats and intellectuals bundled limitations on sovereignty together derisively as part of the same general problem that prevented the empire from achieving equality in international relations and limited the state's ability to project centralized power.[38] Indeed, when İbrahim Hakkı Paşa negotiated the status of Kuwait as an autonomous subprovince with Britain in 1913, he demanded higher customs duties on British imports, the dismantling of European postal system, and the abrogation of the Capitulations.[39]

İbrahim Hakkı Paşa didn't just theorize the boundaries of international law, he implemented his ideas through diplomatic practice. It was the crises between 1878 and 1882 that brought international law to the center of Ottoman diplomacy.

Autonomy Crises

Between 1856 and 1875, the Ottoman Empire was relatively stable from an international perspective. Internally, however, the empire used tremendous violence to extend the power of the central state. Tanzimat by the sword stimulated resistance across the state, and the 1860s were marked by resistance—sometimes resulting in Great Power intervention, as in Mount Lebanon in 1860–61, and other times not, as in Arabian Penninusla.[40] In the aftermath of an anti-Tanzimat rebellion, Crete gained Lebanon-style autonomy, complete with its own Organic Regulations.[41] As the empire intensified the project of centralization under the rubric of reform and reorganization, many of the autonomies were exempted and pulled further away from the reach of the central administration. Moldavia and Wallachia combined into a single autonomous province to form the United Principalities, Egypt was increasingly embedded in the world of European concession hunters, while Serbia expelled the Ottoman Muslim population from garrison towns in 1862.[42] A new anti-Tanzimat rebellion in the Balkans, which would precipitate war with Russia, altered the uneasy management of autonomy within empire.

The road to war began with a rebellion in Herzegovina in 1875. From the start, European powers clamored for administrative reform and additional protections for non-Muslim subjects as a solution to the crisis, which was pitched as a matter of European security. In February and March, while putting down the rebellion, the government granted local reforms for Bosnia-Herzegovina and reissued the Provincial Law of 1864, with its centralizing and decentralizing elements.[43] The Ottoman Foreign Ministry argued that a standardized administration offered the best protection against corruption and equal treatment under the law. In April, the rebellion expanded from Bosnia and Herzegovina to Bulgaria, and in July, Serbia and Montenegro—where locals had been vying for an autonomy deal. All the provinces in rebellion declared war against the Ottoman state. In a proposal for a conference in Istanbul to settle the matter, the British foreign minister, Lord Derby, recommended that Bosnia-Herzegovina receive a "system of local or administrative autonomy." Predicting Ottoman pushback, Derby noted that autonomous Bosnia would not have the monarchical and hereditary governorships awarded to Serbia and Wallachia and Moldavia: "there is to be no question of the creation of a tributary State."[44] Bosnia would look like Mount Lebanon and Crete, not Egypt and Serbia. The Ottomans reluctantly agreed to these terms for a conference, only because Britain insisted on preserving "the independence and the territorial integrity of the Ottoman Empire" and a return to the status quo in Serbia and Montenegro.[45] Ottoman officials, including locals based in Bosnia, rejected autonomy for the province.[46]

In contrast, the Russia proposals—supported by the Habsburgs and Germans—deviated wildly from what had emerged as the British model of autonomy. When the European powers met in Istanbul in December 1876, they pushed for an array of humiliating interventions that gutted Ottoman sovereignty in the Balkans.[47] The first proposal placed the administration of Bosnia-Herzegovina and the Bulgarian provinces under foreign control—executive, judicial, and military powers would be in the hands of the occupying power. The Ottoman foreign minister, Mehmed Esad Safvet Paşa, bluntly refused, arguing that it was tantamount to "forfeiting the independence of the state."[48] Subsequent proposals were not much better. On December 21 the Great Powers hammered out an agreement to give Bosnia-Herzegovina and eastern and western Bulgaria autonomy, but under conditions much altered from earlier nineteenth-century models. Each province would have a European-appointed governor, and an international commission of foreign inspectors would act as the enforcement mechanism, rather than relying solely on legal guarantees through international treaty and imperial law. Two days later, Abdülhamid II (r. 1876–1909), proclaimed the first Ottoman Constitution. The first article encapsulated the Ottoman Foreign Ministry arguments: "The Ottoman Empire comprises the present territory and the privileged provinces (*eyalet-i mümtaze*). It forms an indivisible whole, from which no portion can be detached under any pretext whatever."[49] The Ottomans flatly refused an international commission and European-appointed governors—they countered with an offer to establish three internal commissions, "freely elected by the people," composed of Ottoman Muslims and non-Muslims for western and eastern Bulgaria, and Bosnia-Herzegovina.[50] No consensus was reached, and the meeting dissolved in late January 1876, paving the way for an expanded war with Russia.

When Russia declared war on the Ottoman Empire in 1877, the Ottoman Foreign Ministry responded by arguing that it was Russia who was destabilizing the European order by ignoring the Treaty of Paris: "History will take note of this astounding fact, that in this age of enlightenment, of civilization, and of justice, a great Power has carried into a neighboring State fire and sword, because that State demanded that international engagements, that international law, the independence of internal administration, and, above all, the honor and dignity of its Sovereign, should be respected in her case, as it respected them in that of other States."[51]

The Russo-Ottoman War (1877–78) was a catastrophe. The war ended with massive territorial losses, military occupations across the empire, and a huge demographic shift in the population.[52] For the first time in its history, the empire was majority Muslim. In March 1878, after decisively winning the war, the Russians forced a brutal peace on the empire, known as the Treaty of San Stefano. Not only did they recognize the autonomous provinces in the Balkans as independent principalities, but Bulgaria was established as an independent principality stretching from Albania in the west to the Black Sea in the east the Danube in the north, and covering much of Ottoman Macedonia. Bulgaria had no special status within the constitutional order of the empire, autochthonous prince or governing elite, or history of special privileges—this was a Russian innovation as revolutionary as the erecting of the monarchial principle in Greece in the 1820s. In the lead-up the war, Midhat Paşa had warned that Russia wanted to create "small autonomic states" to weaken the empire; with San Stefano, his prediction appeared right.[53] Britain and the other Great Powers refused to leave so much in Russian hands and insisted on a meeting of the Great Powers, justifying it on the basis that new territorial order that Russia contemplated cut against the Treaty of Paris (1856), which had guaranteed to the territorial integrity of the Ottoman Empire.

The Congress of Berlin, hosted by Bismarck in the summer of 1878, generated entirely new questions about how autonomy would operate in the empire. Tanzimat bureaucrats were able to manage autonomy as long as "the independence and territorial integrity of the Ottoman Empire" was also upheld by the European powers. That changed with the Treaty of Berlin. The Great Powers opted to give independence to autonomous Serbia, Romania (Moldavia and Wallachia), and Montenegro. Instead of autonomy for Bosnia-Herzegovina, Austria-Hungary initiated what would become a permanent military occupation of the province, annexing it in 1908. Bulgaria, where the first experiments with provincial reorganization and reform had flourished and succeeded, was divided into two provinces. The new Principality of Bulgaria was established as a "tributary" on the model of Serbia, and "Eastern Rumelia" was created as a "privileged province" complete with its own regulations on the model of Mount Lebanon.[54] Britain permanently occupied Cyprus—an agreement that was made possible only by Britain agreeing to recognize a future French military protectorate in Tunis. Berlin threatened to create more autonomous provinces and targeted the eastern provinces of the empire bordering Russia and Iran for administrative reform—the zone had a mixed population of Muslim Kurds and Armenians. From an Ottoman perspective, Article 61, "Improvements and Reforms in Favor of Armenians, Protection Against Circassians and Kurds," looked like the administrative reforms in favor of Christians in the Balkans.[55]

The Ottomans faced a new problem: Berlin had restricted their negotiating power. Two legal instruments introduced in 1878 would change the ways that autonomy would operate within the Ottoman Empire and allow for more legal British intervention into autonomous provinces. First was the Cyprus Convention, a defensive military alliance concluded between the British and Ottomans in June 1878 and hashed out in the desperate months between San Stefano and before Berlin, when the state was in urgent need of a Great Power backer to roll back Russian gains. The Convention guaranteed British military support against future Russian encroachments in the eastern parts of the Ottoman Empire in exchange for provincial reform in the East "for the protection of Christians and other subjects of the Porte in these territories." The British wanted an eastern Mediterranean military base, but the vaguely worded agreement provided more legal grounds to intervene unilaterally in Ottoman affairs.[56]

Article 61 shifted the international framework for thinking about Ottoman autonomous provinces. It called for administrative reform in the eastern provinces, on the grounds of protecting Armenian Christians against Muslim attacks, and the British Foreign Office claimed the right to intervene when these minority groups were considered to be under threat.[57] Sultan Abdülhamid was determined to prevent European intervention in the empire on the basis of pro-Christian reforms. To this end, the state immediately focused on shoring up Ottoman sovereignty at its most vulnerable points, which meant the eastern provinces of the empire singled out by Berlin for reform.[58] Before Berlin, the state would have followed British advice and entertained a Lebanon-style autonomous province in Eastern Anatolia; now it was to be prevented at all costs.

For the Ottomans, autonomy was no longer something that could be passively tolerated or easily tamed to work for the state—it had to be attacked and assimilated far more aggressively. But for the British, administrative autonomy continued to be a preferred solution to solve political problems in the empire. Lord Dufferin, who was among the negotiators for the Organic Regulations in Mount Lebanon, was appointed British ambassador to the Ottoman Empire in the spring of 1881. His mission: resolve problems related to the Treaty of Berlin and the imperial reordering of 1878. Dufferin's chief duty was to convince the Foreign Ministry and the palace, as well as the other European ambassadors in Istanbul, to agree to implement administrative reforms in the six eastern provinces.[59]

Berlin initiated a crisis of governance that would remake state institutions and revise Ottoman approaches to international law and diplomacy. Much like the Tanzimat bureaucrats, saving the empire remained central to Ottoman foreign policy, but the means had to change. The new sultan, Abdülhamid II, and his ministers were determined to prevent further territorial losses, and to put an end to European interference in the administrative affairs of the empire.[60] When Lord Dufferin arrived in Istanbul with an autonomy scheme for "Armenia," it was the sultan rather than his ministers who argued that Europe had no legal claim to impose reform on the state and refused to entertain schemes that would limit the reach of the imperial center in Eastern Anatolia.[61]

In the fall of 1880, the British Embassy in Istanbul pushed for administrative reform in eastern provinces, and the European powers issued a collective note in response demanding that the Ottomans comply with Article 61 of the Treaty of Berlin. There were numerous Foreign Office dispatches addressing this idea specifically. Repeated throughout was the idea that "Armenia may be managed with something like the Lebanon scheme," but with the governor given "more independence."[62] The British prime minister, William Gladstone, directly ordered Dufferin to find a trustworthy and reasonably competent Ottoman functionary to serve as a governor-general of Armenia. He acknowledged the tense situation of shifting concepts of autonomy and "hinted, as means of procuring this, at the small value we set upon our nominal, sole, and illegal title (preferably to the Treaty of Paris) to interfere between the Sultan and his Asiatic subjects generally."[63] In other words, the cost of British support for Ottoman territorial integrity would be that the Ottomans consent to their "administrative reforms" in Eastern Anatolia.

As ambassador to the Ottoman Empire, Dufferin promptly set to work bringing the Lebanon plan to life in Eastern Anatolia, requesting that the Ottomans send a high commissioner "like Fuad Paşa," who would be equipped with full military and administrative authority to govern Eastern Anatolia until broader imperial reforms could be adopted. The governor-general, Dufferin insisted, needed to exercise rule independent from Istanbul, including control over a reorganized gendarmerie charged with restoring order, and control over provincial resources and infrastructure. In particular, Britain's reform project in Anatolia pushed the idea that someone like Fuad Paşa—the reformer in Mount Lebanon—should be sent to Eastern Anatolia. Toward the end of the summer 1881, Dufferin seized on the idea of sending Ahmed Muhtar Paşa, the famous Ottoman general stationed at Kars during the 1878–79 war with Russia. As we will see in the next chapter, Muhtar Paşa himself would eventually be appointed to Cairo as the Egyptian high commissioner for the Ottoman government, serving for over thirty years in office. Dufferin's advocacy of Muhtar Paşa displayed British Foreign Office preference for a local strongman who was also well-known in Europe and a major figure in Ottoman diplomacy.

Abdülhamid pushed back against British demands for autonomy in the six eastern provinces. He argued that the British were trying to provide Armenian Christians in Eastern Anatolia with administrative autonomy (*otonomie*).[64] The British were not endowed with any special rights to interfere in Ottoman domains on the basis of the Cyprus Convention or the Treaty of Berlin. The latter, he insisted, dealt very with specific territories and had outlined the categories of autonomy in concrete terms. These terms included limited self-governance (for Serbia, Montenegro, and Romania), autonomy (for Eastern Rumelia), protection (for Tunis), and Austrian military occupation (for Bosnia-Herzegovina).

Whereas Ottoman leadership now had concrete proof that European-engineered administrative schemes would undermine state sovereignty, the British continued to understand autonomy as a way to preserve imperial structures in the face of local violence and Great Power interference. They had fundamentally different frameworks for the past and future of autonomy. Dufferin arrived in Istanbul in 1881 and attempted to convince Abdülhamid that the British had no desire to create another autonomous province in Eastern Anatolia, even though everything the Foreign Office did before his arrival indicated otherwise. He tried to persuade the sultan that though it was the Christians who had attracted attention in Europe, administrative reform was not for the benefit of Christians alone, but rather for all the inhabitants of "Armenia."[65] In one of his first meetings with Abdülhamid, Dufferin stated in clear terms that the British wanted basic reforms to balance the threat of Russia: "Regarding the Armenians neither 'autonomy' nor exceptional treatment (*muamele-yi istisnai*) would be permissible. . . . The Armenians who are wise, know that they are bound eternally to the Ottoman state. Because they know their freedom, nation, and religion (*hürriyet, milliyet, ve mezhep*) would be lost if their administration were to pass to Russia."[66] His argument to the sultan was that autonomy enabled nationalism to coexist with imperial loyalty. Dufferin's earlier ideas on autonomy for Syria were not all that different: Autonomy was a pragmatic device to curtail Great Power interference, manage separatist tendencies, and check the power of the Ottoman state—all in support British interests in the Middle East.

Abdülhamid saw through the ruse. The sultan realized that Dufferin's "basic reforms" were another autonomy plan in disguise. Dufferin might have tried to change the language, but Abdülhamid understood that his plans for Eastern Anatolia would undermine Ottoman sovereignty in the region and grant Armenians a form of autonomy that Christian provinces throughout the empire had attained in the Balkans and Mount Lebanon, and he refused to accept reforms carried out on these terms: "The Armenians there are treated better than the rest of the population because the consuls protect them. However, if there were a clear problem, and if and when the Sublime Port embarked upon solving this question, the solution would not be carried out by means of autonomy. I would not be pleased by this word 'autonomy' and I would not want it. His Majesty does not accept autonomy in respect to his confirmed and clear imperial rights."[67]

Abdülhamid argued further that the European consuls in Eastern Anatolia had exaggerated the severity of problems in the eastern provinces and that Armenians were working with them to undermine Ottoman reform efforts. The consular reports, which were filled with detailed descriptions of lawlessness and violence, had a direct effect on European public opinion (*efkar-i amm*) but, he claimed, they were only stories. Europe clamored for reforms and an immediate response to these by dispatching "a clever governor known to Europe to establish law and order."[68] The sultan contended that the problem with this idea was that though it might satisfy Europe, the sultan and his ministers were still left to consider which theories of reform would best suit local conditions.[69] Abdülhamid accused Europe of wanting the appearance of reform without actually resolving on-the-ground problems.

In addition to attempting to persuade the palace to engage Britain on reform in Eastern Anatolia, Dufferin tried to enlist the other European powers to apply pressure on Abdülhamid. Just two months after Dufferin arrived in Istanbul, the German ambassador told him that he was not authorized by his government to support any "scheme of reform" and asked what was behind Britain's revived demands for reform in Eastern Anatolia: "He then asked me what was the motive underlying England's policy in Asia Minor. It could not be merely humanitarian, because no country was really actuated by impulses of that description." After insisting that England's interests were in fact humanitarian, Dufferin responded, noting "quite apart from these considerations, we were convinced that the best guarantee for the peace of Europe was the reformation of the internal administration of the Ottoman government." As always, his main concern was international relations. When the German ambassador insisted that surely the settlement of Armenia posed no threat to the peace of Europe, Dufferin revealed his underlying ambitions, claiming the Armenian settlement was linked to the "general question of Turkish reorganization." He continued:

> And as for autonomy, I had convinced myself that it would be impossible to endow the members of the Armenian community with rights or privileges which were not equally extended to the rest of their provincial fellow-subjects; and that I thought we could not make a graver mistake than to allow phrases such as "autonomy," "constitution," or the like, to creep into our programme, as they would at once excite the jealousy of the Porte against whatever plans of reform we might propose. On the contrary we should represent ourselves as urging administrative rather than Constitutional

reforms; otherwise the Sultan would take alarm, and would imagine that we were either bent upon the further dismemberment of his Empire, or on a democratic revolution; whereas we should try to persuade him that by following our advice he would be adopting the course most conducive to the establishment of his authority and the consolidation of his Empire.[70]

Dufferin was trying to sell a plan for European peace premised on broad imperial reforms in the Ottoman Empire. Decentralization in Ottoman imperial administration would balance British interests with the requirements of international security and European rivalry in the Ottoman Empire. Instead of creating an autonomous province or provinces in Eastern Anatolia, which would have a formal juridical status within the Ottoman Empire and would require European agreement to be formed, the British were trying to achieve their own interests through simple administrative reforms. The sultan may not have been able to resist British imperial manipulation, but he was not fooled by it. His close attention to legal terminology—"autonomy," "constitution," "democratic"—demonstrated both a deep understanding of and serious concern about the legal implications in these various entities. To name something in law, especially in an international treaty, provided Europeans with the legal justification to intervene in Ottoman affairs. Abdülhamid consistently called attention to the vagueness of Article 61 and continued to argue that under no circumstances did it endow Europe with a positive right to interfere in the Ottoman Empire.

From an international legal perspective, the treaty was ambiguous and did not specify the type of administrative reform required in the eastern provinces. The sultan maintained that imperial administrative practices were always complex and legally differentiated across the space. Good governance should fit the habits of the people:

The source of reform that will be considered hence should be appropriate to the manners, customs, and ideas (*ahlak ve adet ve efkar*) of the inhabitants. Before considering these, nothing will not be done blindly; otherwise the desired benefits will not be obtained and may result in harm. Moreover, the administrative framework that will be established, either one of the centralized or decentralized methods (*esas-i idare dahi ya merkeziyet ya da mütevessi-yi idare usullerinden biri*)

> will require a foundation. Practically, it cannot be denied that either method of administration under discussion would bring good order. But this administration, whichever form will be selected, will be adapted to the habits and the custom's province, whether good or bad. Between theory and practice, one often finds discrepancy.[71]

Abdülhamid dismissed Dufferin's suggestions for Eastern Anatolia, but in terms that would have been familiar to European imperialists. In contrast to Ali and Fuad's critique of Dufferin's plan for Lebanon, Abdülhamid drew on the culturist vocabulary employed by his European counterparts in discussion of their own imperial dilemmas. The "manners, customs, and ideas" of the inhabitants should determine the best form of imperial administration—not ideas from Europe about Ottoman administration.[72] Abdülhamid directed the conversation away from a broad critique of Ottoman administrative practices to a discussion of a discrete imperial problem in the periphery. He distinguished himself from midcentury Tanzimat reformers and criticized their attachment to French *département*-style administration and model provinces for an empire-wide reorganization: "With respect to the situation in Anatolia, as is known, until the time of my grandfather Sultan Mahmud Han, the method of administration was the *derebeylik*. But Sultan Mahmud Han, by abrogating this system, enacted new laws related to reform and it was even reorganized repeatedly at later times."[73] In other words, imperial administration in Eastern Anatolia was a persistent problem and one that had not yet been solved by importing solutions that may have worked in one part of the empire. For Abdülhamid, the problem with the Tanzimat was not administrative centralization, but that a French model of state administration had been imported wholesale without considering local conditions throughout the vast empire. A one-size-fits-all scheme for the empire diminished imperial flexibility—a point that the British above all would have understood. Abdülhamid recast the Ottoman Empire as a European empire. By treating Eastern Anatolia as an imperial problem analogous to the problems European empires experienced in their own peripheries, he attempted to halt British efforts to introduce broad reforms for the entire empire. But the British invasion of Egypt in the summer of 1882 overwhelmed any further discussions between the Dufferin and Abdülhamid on administrative reform in Eastern Anatolia. Dufferin instead turned his attention to reforming autonomy in Egypt.

Britain's military invasion and occupation of Egypt in 1882, which will be examined in the next chapter, made it clear to the state that it required new tools to combat Europe in the age of expansionist empires.

The Ottoman Office of Legal Counsel

The loss of the Balkan provinces, together with the occupation of Egypt, facilitated the empire's turn to international law as a tool to manage European imposed limitations on Ottoman sovereignty. This turn was manifested through both learning international law as a tool of diplomacy and harmonizing domestic legal institutions to be legible to Europeans who claimed that the Ottoman state lacked the capacity to treat their subjects fairly in a court of law. Between the 1860s and 1880s, new and reformed legal institutions and codification projects proliferated in Istanbul and the provinces—including the introduction of a three-tiered system of secular courts, codification of the Islamic jurisprudence in the Ottoman Civil Code (*mecelle*), and the establishment of the Imperial Law School, which included international law as a required subject of study.[74]

The most important weapon against European intervention in Ottoman affairs was the establishment of the Office of Legal Counsel (*Hukuk Müşavirliği İstişare Odası*). In the spring of 1883, the Ottoman Foreign Ministry established the new office to manage questions related to international law. From the office's creation until its reconfiguration within the Turkish Foreign Ministry in the 1920s, Foreign Ministry legal advisors (*hukuk müşavirleri*) generated thousands of legal opinions in response to a wide range of problems, from issues of personal status to matters of high diplomacy. Staffed initially by European and later Ottoman lawyers, legal advisors provided much of the raw legal material and arguments for Ottoman diplomatic engagement with Europe. The Office of Legal Counsel systematized the longstanding Ottoman practice of hiring European lawyers for assistance in public and private legal matters, but it was pressure from territorial losses in the Balkans and the British military occupation of Egypt that added urgency to the creation of a special department dedicated to international law. In the absence of military strength, territory recently lost or endangered on the battlefield could be preserved through law.

Foreign ministries across Europe absorbed international legal experts into their diplomatic arsenals in the 1880s and 1890s and similarly created new offices to deal with international law, but the Ottoman Empire was the first to formalize a legalistic approach to foreign policy. For much of the period between the reign of Abdülhamid II and the Balkan Wars, Ottoman international lawyers appealed to positive international law, particularly treaty law, as a viable means to protect the imperial domains. While European Foreign Ministries harnessed international law to justify imperial expansion, the Ottoman state relied on international law as a defensive strategy against Europe and as a tool to consolidate power within the empire.[75] Simply put, international law mattered more for a weak empire at the margins of the international order.

After the Crimean War, the Ottoman Foreign Ministry intermittently called on European legal experts who resided in the empire for support on a broad range of foreign policy questions.[76] In the period leading up to the establishment of the Office of Legal Counsel, the Foreign Ministry employed a handful of European subjects as occasional legal advisors, which was not a permanent bureaucratic position. The need for international legal expertise was ever more pressing, particularly as the Ottoman relationship to Europe was defined in terms of treaty obligations. In the 1860s, the state could not depend on Ottoman subjects for its legal work—there were not even enough foreign-trained lawyers.[77] Instead the Foreign Ministry relied on European legal consultants, which laid the groundwork for the Office of Legal Counsel.

During this period, most of the European lawyers hired by the Foreign Ministry obtained their expertise working within the European consular court system in the Ottoman Empire. They were part of the great network of European lawyers circulating through consular courts in North Africa and the Eastern Mediterranean.[78] For instance, William Parnis, a British-Maltese subject, worked at the Supreme British Consular Court in Istanbul before acting as a legal advisor starting in the 1860s. He also served as a legal consultant for the Ottoman Empire during the Congress of Berlin in 1878 and worked as a legal advisor for the Foreign Ministry until his death in 1883. Similarly, Carl Gescher (Şarl Geşir), a German subject, worked as a legal advisor within the Office of Legal Counsel until he was appointed by the German government to the Mixed Courts in Egypt in 1894.

It was the disasters of the Russo-Ottoman War in 1877–78 that prompted the Foreign Ministry and Sultan Abdülhamid II to institutionalize this ad hoc approach. On the heels of the Berlin calamity, France occupied Tunis in 1881, quickly followed by the British occupation of

Egypt in 1882. All these events unfolded against the intensification and expansion of colonial empires, which European powers increasingly justified through appealing to international law and legalized through formalizing the rules of imperial expansion.[79] The international context is critical for understanding not only why the Ottoman state formally adopted international law as tool of diplomacy, but also why the state officials thought they needed an office dedicated to international law.

In 1883 the Foreign Ministry established the Office of Legal Counsel (Hukuk Müşavirliği Istişare Odası) and created the position of legal advisor (*hukuk müşaviri*).[80] The special department was intended to deal more systematically with questions related to international law but was also a Hamidian institution and part of the project to extend Ottoman control more firmly throughout the empire, to reduce the influence of European powers in the empire, and to assert equality with the powers of Europe.[81] Much like the improvisational approach of the 1860s and 1870s, the Ottoman Foreign Ministry appointed European legal experts who had already provided legal counsel. While it is not entirely clear from the archival record, it appears that Carl Gescher and Gabriel Noradounghian were among the first legal advisors appointed to the formalized Office of Legal Counsel. Gescher's Ottoman employment record notes that he was appointed to service within the office on April 19, 1883—the same day as the Ottoman subject Noradounghian.[82] Though European lawyers originally occupied the position of legal advisor, Ottoman subjects eventually took over these posts entirely.

From its inception in the 1880s through its demise in the early 1920s, the Office of Legal Counsel was more often than not staffed by a first and second legal advisor, posts that where generally held by one Armenian and one Muslim Ottoman subject, as well as a handful of directors (*müdir*) and legal assistants (*muavin*).[83] This structure was not permanently fixed, and there was some flexibility within the organization of the office. For example, for several years leading up to the Young Turk Revolution, there were three rather than two legal advisors. The number of directors and legal assistants also swelled and contracted over time.[84] Most of the directors and legal assistants, and later the legal advisors themselves, were graduates of the Imperial Law School and the Law Faculty at the Darülfünun—the main European-style university of the empire.[85] After the Hamidian era (1876–1909), the first and second legal advisors worked their way up to the posting from within the Office of Legal Counsel. Though legal advisors might have studied law in Europe as well, the fact that the Foreign Ministry had a trained body of international lawyers on which it could rely indicates the expansion of legal education in general and the development of international law in the Ottoman Empire in particular.[86]

The Hamidian era was the high point of the Office of Legal Counsel. During that period, the office shifted from a being a domain of European international law experts, who had cut their teeth in the Capitulation Courts, to an office staffed entirely by Ottoman subjects who were trained and professionalized as international lawyers. When the Foreign Ministry first recognized the diplomatic need for international legal expertise in the 1860s and 1870s, the Ottoman state did not have a qualified group of international lawyers upon whom it could rely for legal advice. But by the mid-1890s, the Foreign Ministry no longer required European lawyers for the functioning of the office. The Hamidian period is also noteworthy for the fact that the empire's most authoritative international law experts occupied the post of legal advisor for much of the period: Gabriel Noradounghian (Kapriel Noradunkyan) and İbrahim Hakkı Bey (later Paşa).

Almost immediately after the Foreign Ministry formalized the Office of Legal Counsel, the Grand Vizier Said Paşa (Küçük) appointed Noradounghian, an Ottoman-Armenian, to the post of legal advisor. According to Noradounghian's secretary, the Foreign Ministry wanted to limited European influence within the office, and when Parnis Efendi died in 1883, Said Paşa proposed Noradounghian for the job.[87] Knowledge of European languages, especially French and English, was critically important for the post. Noradounghian studied law in Paris and, in addition to French, Ottoman Turkish, and Armenian, knew English and Italian—a linguistic profile that was not unusual for the staff at the Office of Legal Counsel. Like İbrahim Hakkı Paşa, he taught law at the Mekteb-i Hukuk before entering the Foreign Ministry.[88] For nearly ten years, Noradounghian worked alongside Carl Gescher, producing legal opinions on questions of public and private international law.[89] The advisors authored a wide assortment of legal opinions for the Foreign Ministry, covering everything from issues related to the laws of war, to Ottoman territorial claims, to Egypt and Sudan. Alfred returned to Germany in 1889, and Carl left Istanbul for the Mixed Courts of Egypt in the early 1890s.[90] Abdülhamid II personally appointed İbrahim Hakkı Paşa to take his place in 1895.[91]

Hakkı Paşa had a long and varied career in the Ottoman civil service during the Hamidian and Young Turk period. In the early 1880s he worked in the palace (*mabeyn*) for Abdülhamid as a translator. He also taught international law at the Law Faculty in Istanbul.[92] During the CUP period, İbrahim Hakkı obtained several ministerial posts. Noradounghian and İbrahim Hakkı had much in common and were later appointed to the highest bureaucratic positions within the empire—a point that underlines the significance of this posting within the Ottoman administration. Hakkı Paşa was briefly grand vizier, while Noradounghian served as the minister of foreign affairs from the summer of 1912 through the Bab-ı Ali Coup in January 1913. Before that, they were dedicated to the cause of preserving the empire. Both lawyers evangelized the benefits of international law for the Ottoman state through publishing and teaching. The chief legal advisor played a major role in late Ottoman political affairs, even after leaving the office. The two most authoritative international law experts in the empire, Noradounghian and Hakkı Bey directed the office through 1908 and the Second Constitutional Revolution. Together they represented the Ottoman Empire abroad at international conferences and policed the boundaries of the empire through recourse to international law arguments—especially treaty law.

These lawyers developed expertise in private and public international law. The Capitulations demanded Ottoman engagement with questions of personal status, while the autonomous provinces compelled lawyers to regulate the line between domestic and international law.[93] They scrutinized relations between the exceptional provinces and European empires. Whenever a local governor exceeded his privileges, the lawyers drafted opinions to assert the proper order. Legal opinions were transformed into diplomatic cables that made their way into European foreign ministries. In short, much of the work done to tame autonomy was carried out by Foreign Ministry lawyers in the Office of Legal Counsel. Incredibly, this strategy worked well through 1908, and Europeans responded favorably to Ottoman demands. But the constant recourse to asserting Ottoman sovereign rights based on treaty law slowly hollowed out the meaning of sovereignty—a point the Ankara government would later be quick to capitalize on at Lausanne.

Both lawyers preached the gospel of international law through their publications and teaching. In addition to generating legal opinions for diplomatic use, each wrote extensively on positive international law. Noradounghian wrote in French, and his work was widely available and cited by European readers. In contrast, Hakkı Paşa wrote in Ottoman Turkish, and while he was a well-known figure in Europe and the United

States—in Ottoman documents this idea was expressed in a recurring phrase "*Avprupa'da malum bir zat*" (a person known in Europe)—the content of his ideas was not broadly understood among European audiences.[94] Already in the 1850s there emerged a distinction between how the Ottoman Foreign Ministry cast legal arguments at home in the empire, versus aboard to European audiences. A brief examination of Noradounghian's and Hakkı Paşa's main legal publications will demonstrate that that this division persisted well into the twentieth century.

Noradounghian's four-volume "compendium of international treaties," *Recueil d'Actes Internationaux*, was a collection of treaties and international legislation to which the Ottoman Empire was a signatory. Emphasizing the Ottoman role in adding to the modern international legal foundations of Europe, he insisted that any treaty collection is "a whole philosophy of history."[95] He explained that the various European treaty compendia in French and German emerged out of diplomatic use for ambassadors, reflected state practice, and were thus the key source of international law. He noted that the Ottoman Empire "played a considerable role" in the history of the European world. In laying out his justification for why the world needed yet another collection of treaties that could be found in any of the standard collections issued by Russia, France, Austria, or Britain, he squarely attacked European limitations on Ottoman sovereignty, especially the Capitulations.[96]

Noradounghian argued that that Ottoman Empire, "more than any other country," needed a complete compendium, "given that for the state, treaties, especially ancient ones, have an importance and value that they would not have, at least to the same degree, for other states." European translations of Ottoman legal texts and treaties were flawed, often wrong, or deliberately misleading:

> It would be superfluous to dwell on the importance of studying treaties for statesmen, diplomats, historians, publicists, and generally anyone who wishes to base their historical knowledge as much as possible on authentic and official documents. A collection of treaties is, in itself, a whole philosophy of history. For each of them either summarizes the political conclusions of an era, characterizes the relations between peoples, or marks the starting point of a new phase in those relations. They are like milestones on the road traveled either by a single nation or by a group of states. At the same time as

> they are the skeleton of history, they serve as a basis for diplomacy and international law. Therefore, despite their apparent dryness, their study is of the utmost interest and of multiple and undeniable usefulness.[97]

What Europeans required, as much as the Ottoman state, was a set of treaties translated into French from the original Ottoman Turkish. Noradounghian insisted that his work was "aimed at practical use," to make the confusing legal landscape in Ottoman lands more legible to Europeans. His compendium was well reviewed and broadly used across Europe and in the Eastern Mediterranean. While his purpose in assembling this text was clearly an attack on European limits on Ottoman sovereignty, it supplied the itinerant network of consular court lawyers with much needed translations of important Ottoman legal texts.

Among Noradounghian's legal opinions and published work, there is little to no discussion of Islam, its role in imperial statecraft, or its place in the construction of international legal order. In contrast, İbrahim Hakkı Paşa's Ottoman Turkish international textbooks, treaties, and histories claimed a role for the Islamic Law of Nations, or *siyar,* in especially his books written for the Law Faculty. His *History of International Law* traced the foundations of international law to ancient and Roman law, then moved through Islamic law en route to establishing to the Treaty of Westphalia in 1648.[98] He argued that the limitations on warfare in the Quran and Hadith anticipated many of the *jus ad bellum* and *jus in bello* restrictions hashed out in the nineteenth-century codification of the laws of war.[99] From declarations of war to the legal protections afforded to non-Muslims, Islam, he argued, was far more civilized in its treatment of prisoners of war than were European states. Despite Hakkı Paşa's exploration of *siyar* and placing it firmly in the development of the global history of international law, he made it very clear to his students that contemporary international law emerged more directly from the long history of war, peace, and commerce between Europe and the Ottoman Empire. Nevertheless, it was in this same period that international law became part of the standard curriculum at the School for Civil Service and the Imperial Law School, which trained a generation of bureaucrats, lawyers, and intellectuals.[100] Textbooks produced for both schools presented Ottoman approaches to international law as originating in Islamic practices of warfare.

In a vein similar to other Ottoman international law textbooks published between the 1880s and 1908, before the Second Constitutional Revolution, Hakkı Paşa's *History of International Law* was bound chronologically by the dates of important international treaties, major wars, and historical events. He analyzed the meaning of the Treaty of Paris (1856) at length and underlined the fact that the treaty had reiterated legal equality in the Ottoman Empire between Muslims and non-Muslims. Instead of using the phrase "family of nations," he wrote that the empire joined the "European association of states."[101] He also addressed the problem of European intervention in Ottoman affairs but did so more obliquely than Noradounghian. He focused on how parts of the empire had obtained administrative autonomy through rebellion (*isyan*) and European intervention. He then explained precisely how provinces such as Serbia and Egypt gained autonomy by a decree from the sultan and by international treaty. He substantiated many of his claims by referencing other well-known European international lawyers—especially those who had criticized the Capitulations. In other texts he explained the differences between natural and positive law and cast international law as "a science" in much the same way that his counterparts in Europe did, as a civilizer of international relations. He was particularly interested in elucidating schemes for European peace and stability. For example, he analyzed Bentham's and Kant's ideas for perpetual peace.[102] In another text, he criticized European treatment of the Ottomans simply by noting what the law should do: "Foreign relations are based on reciprocity between states. It should not be forgotten that the fact that a state must comply with the laws regulated by another state will undoubtedly violate the states' right to independence."[103]

Hakkı Paşa's and Noradounghian's legal ideas overlapped significantly, arrived at the same key points, and were animated by uniform aims. They wanted to establish equality with Europe states, end the Capitulations, and limit the capacity of the autonomous provinces to do damage to the empire—aims that were shared with the sultan, across the Foreign Ministry and the wider bureaucracy. Despite Hakkı Paşa's use of Islamic law and Islam in his analysis of the history of international law, such arguments would never be shown to a European audience—a fact that is reflected in the library of the Office of Legal Counsel. Among the many books there, not a single text related to the Islamic Law Nations was included, apart from İbrahim Hakkı's own works. Instead, the library was packed with European and Ottoman international law textbooks, treaties, international agreements, as well as texts related to imperial problems and colonial questions. Several volumes dealt with Ottoman autonomous provinces in Egypt, Eastern-Rumelia, Bulgaria, and Crete, including texts that criticized European policies toward the unprotected fringes of the empire.[104]

İbrahim Hakkı and Gabriel Noradounghian did far more than the intellectual work of institution building: They managed the arguments that animated the day-to-day diplomatic relations of the empire. Together, they authored scores of legal opinions on public and private international law and played a key role in both limiting the autonomy in the privileged provinces and policing the capacities of local rulers.[105]

For example, the Foreign Ministry submitted legal questions to the İstişare Odası for commentary and sought legal advice in order to reassert Ottoman sovereignty in Egypt. The issues the Ottoman government submitted to the lawyers on Egypt concerned every aspect of Egyptian affairs outside of internal administration and made certain everything was done in accordance with the fermans and international treaties guaranteeing Egypt's status as an Ottoman province.[106] Consequently, the lawyers produced opinions on the Egyptian debt and tribute as well as on European diplomatic exchanges related to Egypt, and British attempts to sever the administration of Egypt from Sudan after 1899.

Nearly five months into the British occupation of Ottoman Egypt, the British government announced plans for the reorganization of institutions. Among the many administrative changes proposed was the broad expansion of khedival authority at the expense of Istanbul. In particular, the British argued that the khedive's rights should be extended to include the capacity to make trade agreements with European powers and to contract foreign loans without the permission of the Sultan. The British particularly wished to get around the tobacco regie. Individual European powers large and small began signing treaties of commerce with the Egyptian Ministry of Foreign Affairs. Predictably, the Ottoman government sent copies of these commerce conventions and customs agreements to the İstişare Odası for commentary.[107]

In addition to producing legal analysis critical of British policy in Egypt, the legal advisors wrote opinions in support of the possibility of coordinating Ottoman and Egyptian policy with regard to the Capitulations and questions of nationality. For instance, among the opinions related to Egypt, a number dealt with Ottoman subjects claiming European privileges—ostensibly to enjoy the benefits of the Capitulations.[108]

In one such example, the Egyptian Foreign Ministry maintained that an alarming number of Greek Ottoman subjects resident in Egypt were claiming Greek nationality in order to evade taxation. In this case, the İstişare Odaş ı advised that appeals to the Egyptian government follow Ottoman policy concerning the procedure for changing nationality.[109]

At times, the legal advisors supported British policy in Egypt—or, more precisely, found no immediate legal challenge. In what may seem like an incredible example, the analysis of the 1904 Entente between Britain and France, which historians cast as the moment France recognized the British occupation of Egypt, suggested no immediate legal action other than obtaining a declaration from Britain further recognizing Ottoman rights in Egypt.[110] The Ottoman Foreign Ministry's use of international law arguments against British policy should not be seen as a last-ditch effort to assert Ottoman claims to sovereignty in Egypt. Precisely because Egypt's sovereignty and administration were guaranteed by the "political system of Europe," any changes in Egypt's international legal status vis-à-vis Istanbul required European agreement.[111]

Containing Autonomy

At the same time that the Foreign Ministry developed expertise in international law to be deployed at the diplomatic level, the state also worked to better incorporate Egypt and the remaining privileged provinces into the constitutional and administrative order of the empire. İbrahim Hakkı Paşa and Gabriel Noradounghian played a major role in this project, alongside other state officials who worked to tame autonomy by claiming it as a constitutional category within the empire. Much like the state's attitude toward international law, institution building around autonomy as an Ottoman form of governance was at first ad hoc, but by the 1880s it was formalized and embedded in state practice.

When the European-imposed autonomies first emerged in the 1830s, the state did not have a system to distinguish between them and other provinces. There was no clear difference between "regular" and "autonomous" provinces, though there were clear requirements for the administration and collection of taxes and administration of justice in each. But with administrative reform, which started in the 1860s, the category emerged between "regular" and "privileged" provinces.[112] The emergence of differentiation can be seen in the annual statistical yearbooks that very much functioned as an "imperial self-portrait."[113] Starting in 1847, the empire published state yearbooks, or *salnames*. These texts, like İbrahim Hakkı's textbooks, were designed exclusively for Ottoman readers and bureaucratic usage. They contained administrative, demographic, and economic statistics for the entire empire. Earlier, Serbia, Egypt, and the other European imposed autonomies were treated as any other province and were not grouped or categorized as distinct in any way, apart from the fact that there was less centrally available imperial knowledge about them. In 1864 and 1867 the Provincial Reform Laws (*Vilayet Nizamnamesi*) abandoned the old system of provincial organization and created a new organizational hierarchy in each province, along lines not dissimilar to the French administrative system by *département*. In this same year, for the first time, autonomous provinces were grouped together as distinct classification.[114] By 1881 the annual *salname* categorized the provinces as the "privileged" provinces (*eyalet-i mümtaze*).

Starting in 1873, Grégoire Aristarchi Bey, an Ottoman lawyer and Greek subject, began publishing *Législation ottoman*.[115] It was a compendium of Ottoman laws and decrees translated into French with the purpose of making the empire and its complex legal landscape legible for non-Ottomans, but it was also critical for imperial subjects who did not know Ottoman Turkish, especially non-Muslims.[116] *Législation ottoman* contained French translations that reflected the project of Ottoman legal reform—such as the Ottoman civil code, the Mecelle, and *Düstur*, a collection of penal, civil, and commercial laws. In addition to explaining the legal privileges of non-Muslim religious communities as well as foreigners, the collection included laws and regulations related to the privileged provinces. The first volume states that "the existence of several tributary principalities within the empire" justified creating a special classification for the legal instruments that established the provinces' "privileges and other exceptional rights" guaranteeing their "internal administrative independence." Aristarchi Bey included all the fermans and regulations for Moldavia and Romania, Serbia, Montenegro—which did not have juridical autonomy in 1873 when the first volume was published—the Khedivate, Samos and Tunis, as well as Mount Lebanon and Crete. What is striking is that he placed Mount Lebanon and Crete in the category of "privileged province" and the cast the rest as "tributary principalities"—a position that the central government would not have agreed with. The editor had to explain how the privileged province functioned vis-à-vis the empire:

> Like individuals—such as religious communities—principalities enjoy certain rights or privileges. There are certain provinces which, either because of their exceptional position or because of very special circumstances, are entitled to enjoy a privileged political and judicial administration, which is therefore different from that of other provinces. This is the case in Lebanon, which, as a result of international agreements, is governed by a special administrative and judicial organization. Similarly, since 1869, the island of Candia (Crete) has been governed as a privileged vilayet, with special administrative and judicial institutions.[117]

In the 1870s, imperial subjects were hashing out the distinction between regular and privileged provinces, before the category was embedded in the Ottoman Constitution of 1876 as a constitutional category. As we have seen, the first article of the 1876 Ottoman Constitution stated that the territory of the Ottoman Empire was indivisible and included "the present territory and the privileged provinces (*eyalet-i mümtaze*)."[118] Article 7 offers an extensive list of the sultan's "sacred rights," including the right to name and dismiss officials, assign rank, orders, and titles, and "the execution of appointments in accordance with the requirements of the privileged provinces."[119] It affirmed the sultan's position as *sahib-i sikke ve hutbe*—the possessor of the coin and sermon, the attributes of sovereignty in the Islamic world. He also claimed the power to conclude treaties with foreign powers, make declarations of war and peace, and implement religious and legal rulings. Sovereignty resided in the sultan. These two article bound the privileged provinces to imperial sovereignty through law.

Abdülhamid II issued the constitution in December 1876, just as the Great Powers of Europe gathered in Istanbul to solve the rebellion in the Balkans. Days before the official newspaper published the constitution, the empires of Europe had demanded special privileges for non-Muslims and administrative autonomy for Bosnia, Herzegovina, and Bulgaria.[120] The constitution was implemented, in part, as a bulwark against European intervention in Ottoman affairs and an explicit assault on European-imposed autonomies. Though it was suspended in 1878 during the Russo-Ottoman War and remained so until 1908, it nevertheless established the privileged provinces on a constitutional basis. At the same time, it reflected the fact that the privileged provinces had already become a legible category in administrative and political debates.

Alongside the project of institutionalizing international law, the grand vizier created another special office, the Office of Autonomous and Privileged Provinces (*Eyalet-i Mümtaze ve Muhtare Kalemi*). The first mention of the office appeared in the imperial yearbook, *salname*, of 1881, but it is possible it was established as early as 1879, after the Berlin Conference.[121] Housed within the Office of the Grand Vizier, the new agency managed relations and correspondence between Istanbul and the privileged provinces. Provincial reform in the 1860s put pressure on the state to make sense of the bewildering number of exceptional provinces, each with their own deals with the sultan and their own laws and regulations. As we have seen, the provinces' administrative orders were determined by treaties and imperial privileges, which required complex management. It was a problem of imperial organization. Though distinct from the administration of regular provinces, the goal was to better incorporate the privileged provinces into the administration of the empire and to insulate them from European interference. If the constitution claimed the privileged provinces as part of the imperial order—against Great Power intervention—the Office of Privileged Provinces had the effect of standardizing and concretizing the category for bureaucrats and imperial subjects across the empire.

The last Ottoman official to head the Office of Autonomous and Privileged Provinces, İbnülemin Mahmud Kemal İnal—the great chronicler of late Ottoman bureaucrat poets, calligraphers, and grand viziers—explained its significance through analogy: The office was Istanbul's equivalent to a European colonial office (*diğer devletlerde"müstemleket nezareti"*).[122] It is worth thinking through what İbnülemin Mahmud Kemal might have meant by the provocative statement, by looking at what the office actually did. With a few crucial exceptions, it has not received extensive treatment from historians.[123] We might assume that this reflects the office's lack of importance to the state, but as İbnülemin Mahmud Kemal himself noted, it was "politically more important" while being "less prestigious" than other posts in the grand vizier's office. Moreover, any historian who has worked on Bulgaria and Eastern Rumelia after 1878, Lebanon after 1861, Crete after 1868, Egypt after 1841, Samos after 1831, Cyprus and Bosnia after 1878; or Libya (Benghazi and Tripoli) has worked in files that were created or managed by this office.

Egypt, Crete, and Bulgaria (both the Principality of Bulgaria and Eastern Rumelia) generated an enormous amount of paperwork as recurring imperial hotspots. This idea is reflected in the volume of records produced by the office for provinces. A survey of records held by the office at the Ottoman archives supports this argument, with those on Mount Lebanon in the thousands, there are over twenty thousand for Egypt and Bulgaria, and even more for Eastern Rumelia. The office generated a massive paper trail in each province and required training more staff to deal with the influx of correspondence between Istanbul and provincial capitals, which in some provinces, like Eastern Rumelia, was conducted in French rather than Ottoman Turkish.[124] Paradoxically, it was precisely because there were so many different types of negotiated settlements that fell into the category of "privileged provinces" that led to the creation of an administrative body to treat them as a group and to develop a coherent plan to retain sovereignty over them all.[125]

When the office was established in the 1880s, those provinces that had gained privileges before 1878 were transferred to it—including the older archive. For Egypt, the Office of Privileged Provinces managed all the records dating back to 1841, when the province first gained its special status.[126] Because Egypt was so important from the perspective of international politics, the sultan dispatched an Ottoman high commissioner to Egypt (Mısır Fevkalade Komiseri) and maintained an Egyptian agent (*kapıkethüdası*) in Istanbul, along with a bevy of spies. Bulgaria too had these offices.[127] Taking the example of Egypt alone, and only after the onset of the British occupation of Egypt in 1882, the volume of documents and the variety of issues they cover are staggering. In addition to spying on the Khedive, the local governor, and his ministers, the high commissioner, as we will see in the next chapter, reported on political activities among Egyptians, recruited students for schools in Istanbul, including the Sultan's School for Tribes, and offered detailed reports for the sultan on British actions in Egypt.[128]

European diplomats and international lawyers recognized the emergence of the Office of Privileged Provinces and understood the project for what it actually was. Ottoman efforts to assert greater centralized control over the privileged provinces through this office, a process that was apparent to outside observers.[129] The Russian lawyer Fedor Martens acknowledged that after 1878, the Ottoman state attempted to better incorporate the autonomous provinces into the regular administration of the empire.

He noted that the Ottoman bureaucracy created a special office, the "Office of Privileged Provinces," to limit the range of independence of provinces in "the Levant, Samos, Candia (Crete) and Eastern Rumelia."[130]

The work of incorporating the autonomous provinces into the regular administration of the empire fell to the international lawyers as well, and not just their policing of the legal capacities of autonomous princes. İbrahim Hakkı Paşa authored the main textbook on administrative law used at the imperial law school. Published in 1891, the text opens with an author's statement, noting that the popularity of the first edition, along with the significance of administration to the state practice, warranted the republication of and expansion of the book. Based on İbrahim Hakkı's lectures at the Law Faculty, the text asserted that "every state, as a political entity, is inherently endowed with fundamental rights." In the Ottoman case, those rights were rooted in "imperial decrees and edicts," as well as "ancient national customs and practices" and "laws and regulations issued by the state and the rules adopted by the administration to clarify them." Administrative law, the author argued, clarified the rules necessary for the "administration and preservation of the public interest" by defining the rights and duties between the administrative body and the people. Chapter 1 described how the core functions of the central state were organized and managed—it outlined the responsibilities of the various ministries and deliberative bodies at the center. İbrahim Hakkı compared these practices with both the pre-Tanzimat empire and European empires, noting how decentralized Britain was against France.[131]

The second chapter moved from the core of the empire to the provinces, and it is here that İbrahim Hakkı worked to embed the privileged provinces within the constitutional order of the state. The first paragraph began by listing the autonomies and restating their connection to the central administrative order: "Under the protection and sovereignty of the Ottoman Empire, and with autonomy (*muhtariyet*) in internal administration and partial privileges in foreign affairs—the Emirate of Bulgaria, the Khedivate, and the privileged provinces, including the Emirate of Samos, and Bosnia and Herzegovina administered temporarily under Austria and Cyprus under Britain—are all imperial lands divided administratively into provinces, districts, and subdistricts."[132]

After explaining how provincial administration operated since the 1860s in much of the empire—the governor, the provincial councils, and administrative divisions (*vilayet*, *liva*, *kaza*, *nahiye*)—İbrahim Hakkı turned to analysis of each of the privileged and autonomous provinces. Like Aristarchi Bey's *Législation ottoman*, he detailed the conditions of "autonomy and privilege" in imperial law and by treaty. In eight subchapters—Bulgaria, Tunis, Egypt, Tunis, Eastern Rumelia, Samos, Crete, and Mount Lebanon—İbrahim Hakkı described, analyzed, and explained the dense set of legal instruments that determined administration in each territory. For Egypt, for instance, he listed and examined each of the fermans and treaties that limited the local within the imperial and international. The project was one of standardizing what was in reality unwieldy. He noted, because they are "institutions established according to local requirements, a certain degree of variation is evident." Much of his analysis was directed toward concretizing Ottoman claims to sovereignty in the privileged provinces by domesticating and bringing into the imperial order what Europeans tried so hard to push out.[133]

As in the first chapter with the imperial center, İbrahim Hakkı compared Ottoman provincial administration to pre-Tanzimat and European practices. He claimed that the Ottoman Empire had long maintained flexible administrative arrangements throughout its vast domains. Autonomy and administrative exceptions were not new.[134]

In addition to reclaiming autonomy as a feature of past Ottoman administrative practices, Hakkı Paşa treated the privileged provinces as part of a global imperial norm. He categorized these provinces as an administrative variant, like British settler colonies including Canada and South Africa—a remarkably durable comparison in late Ottoman legal thought, one that did not appear in late Ottoman international law textbooks, law journals and newspaper editorials.[135]

Conclusion: An Empire of Lawyers

While İbrahim Hakkı Paşa and Gabriel Noradounghian played a crucial role in protecting state sovereignty through institution building and diplomacy, they made an equally important contribution to the popularization of international law arguments among Ottoman elites and intellectuals. Hakkı Paşa had done more than anyone to incorporate the privileged provinces into the constitutional order of the state as a matter of administrative law. Alongside Noradounghian, their publications disseminated the core principles of Ottoman international law to subjects. Scores of students studied directly with Hakkı Paşa, and scores more were trained in international and administrative law using his textbooks.

The Young Turk Revolution pulled Noradounghian and Hakkı Paşa out of the Office of Legal Counsel and into other important administrative offices. As soon as Abdülhamid II reinstated the constitution, a proliferation of political parties emerged, most of which were accompanied by a newspaper to publicize the party platform and policies.[136] These were edited by an astonishing number of graduates from the Imperial Law School and the Civil Service School.[137] In the second constitutional era, both lawyers supported publication of *Journal of Legal Studies and Comparative Law*, acting as board members and writing articles on pressing issues such as the Capitulations and imperial administration.[138] The journal covered a broad range of topics and drew out the similarities between Ottoman and European imperial practices.

One of the most striking features of the daily press in Istanbul during the Second Constitutional period was the high degree of literacy around questions of international law. The fact that Ottoman sovereignty was constrained though international law in the form of the treaties regulating the autonomies, the Capitulations, and the Public Debt Administration meant that imperial subjects were particularly attuned to the problem of law in the empire. Moreover, Ottoman subjects lived and felt these restrictions daily. But it was not obvious that daily newspapers should debate the problem of Ottoman sovereignty in international law.

At the end of World War I, the major intellectuals of the Ottoman-Turkish press, with very few exceptions, were trained at the Imperial Law School and would have been familiar with the works and arguments of both Noradounghian and Hakkı Paşa. One could open almost any Istanbul newspaper between 1908 and 1922—written in all the languages of the empire—and easily find editorials dissecting the unequal treatment of the Ottoman Empire at the hands of Europe, as well as robust debates about imperial administration. This was the legacy of Gabriel Noradounghian and İbrahim Hakkı Paşa.

Nineteenth-century European interventions in the Ottoman Empire were framed in humanitarian terms and were often made on behalf of Christian subjects in the aftermath of rebellion or domestic disputes. Concert diplomacy solved these crises, which more often than not rose to the level of international politics, by insisting on administrative and legal reforms in exchange for the evacuation of foreign troops. Far from being ineffectual or weak, as depicted in earlier scholarship, Ottoman lawyers and bureaucrats tackled encroachments into their sovereign realm with experimentation and compromise. From 1878 until 1908, this legal strategy worked. No imperial territory was lost. But the question should not be whether Ottoman diplomatic strategy was successful, as a single metric to assess state practice. A more productive question to consider is what the negotiated autonomies did to the state and its institutions. This chapter has shown the unpredictable consequences of the privileged provinces on state institutional development; the next will consider what Ottoman sovereignty did on the ground, with equally surprising outcomes. As will be seen in the next two chapters, the discursive model of autonomy stimulated much excitement for other parts of the Ottoman Empire intrigued by the idea of decentralization.

PART TWO
Autonomy on the Ground

CHAPTER 3

Ottoman Sovereignty in Egypt

On July 11, 1882, the first day of the bombardment of Alexandria, the British Foreign Office produced a justification for the intervention that summed up Egypt's constitutional and international legal status: "The position of Egypt is a peculiar one. Although it is a province of the Ottoman Empire, its relations with the Porte are the subject of international agreement."[1] International lawyers writing in the wake the British occupation of Egypt agreed. The province was exceptional within the domestic order of the Ottoman Empire, and at the same time unique in international politics. Britain's occupation of Egypt added a third layer of legal complexity to the mix. From the beginning of the military occupation in 1882 through the end of the Ottoman Empire in 1923, Egypt was one of the most pressing international legal puzzles of the era and was featured in major international law textbooks and journals as an "anomaly," an "exception," "curious," and a "peculiarity."[2] John Westlake, the Whewell Chair of International Law at Cambridge, tried to explain why Egypt's already extraordinary legal status became more troubling with British boots on the ground. While the sultan retained sovereignty over Egypt, the khedive had broad administrative powers, and yet the "practical authority," Westlake noted, was "in the hands of Great Britain under an occupation which began in 1882, and the case is too anomalous to admit classification."[3] Before 1882, European international lawyers had written about autonomy in Egypt as a feature of Ottoman imperial administration. But now lawyers increasingly cast Ottoman sovereignty in Egypt, and within the Ottoman autonomous provinces more broadly, as a dangerous legal fiction, one that tempted powerful states to disregard the rules of international order. Separating legal sovereignty from administrative control created ambiguities that had the potential to upend international politics. Legal sovereignty, many argued, should reflect actual power relations.[4]

It wasn't just European international lawyers who were troubled by the gap between legal sovereignty and political control in Egypt. If the lawyers were concerned about what Egypt might do to the international order, European politicians fought over how Egypt should be governed, and by whom. After 1882 the "Egyptian question"—the myriad administrative, financial, and legal questions posed by autonomy in Egypt that first arose during the era of Mehmed Ali—generated a storm of commentary in speeches, books, and articles across Europe and the Middle East that did not abate until the Ottoman Empire was dead and buried.[5] British Foreign and Colonial Office officials, journalists, and later historians described Egypt as "nominally Ottoman" and British "in all but name." According to these interpretations, the sultan was no more than a paper sovereign, a "shadow of authority." He possessed the trappings of Islamic sovereignty in Egypt—he had the right to issue coinage, and prayers were read in his name during the Friday sermon, rights that constituted sovereignty in the early Islamic empires and were captured in the title (*sahib-i sikke ve hutbe*)—but the province had ceased to be meaningfully Ottoman coincident with occupation.[6] Alfred Milner, a British colonial administrator, called Egypt under occupation the "veiled protectorate" and argued that the province was a political anomaly that had effectively become a British colony without the advantage of Colonial Office oversight.[7] Milner's critique, which emanated from the British Colonial Office, was an argument for annexation and regularizing the status of Egypt vis-à-vis London, but was so powerful that it has set the terms for the historical debate and largely determined our understanding of how Ottoman sovereignty in Egypt functioned during the occupation.

Yet, the European preoccupation with Egypt's international legal status reveals more about changing theories of international relations, ideas and practices of sovereignty, and imperialist claims than the function of politics on the ground. The relentless insistence that the sultan's sovereignty was "theoretical" and thereby illusory betrayed an escalating anxiety, especially from a British perspective, that Ottoman sovereignty in Egypt did in fact matter. Despite the immense power imbalance between the British Foreign Office, Istanbul bureaucrats, and local Egyptian officials in Cairo and Istanbul, the fact that European states had recognized the sultan's sovereignty throughout the imperial domains by treaty—and explicitly in Egypt through the agreements that formalized autonomy—fundamentally shaped what was possible under military occupation.[8]

At the precise moment that historians mark Egypt as outside of the Ottoman legal and political penumbra in 1882, the empire embarked on a multifaceted campaign to bind the province more tightly to the imperial center through law and the construction of imperial institutions in Istanbul. As we have seen, Great Power–imposed autonomy altered the Ottoman Empire's central institutions and drove the Foreign Ministry to deploy international law as a weapon of the weak in its relations with Europe. Autonomy worked in equally dramatic but no less predictable ways at the provincial level. Far from being merely "symbolic," Ottoman sovereignty determined everyday legal and economic possibilities and shaped political claims in Egypt from the 1880s through the early 1920s, but perhaps not in the ways we might expect. Egypt's legal status as an Ottoman province did not prevent Britain's invasion and transformative military occupation of the province, but it did constrain Britain in other ways—from compelling the War Office in 1882 to treat Egyptian solders as legally recognized prisoners of war, protected by the laws of war, to preventing annexation when war broke out between the British and Ottoman Empires in 1914. Every British policy, plan, and vision for governance under occupation hit against the fact of Egypt's internationally guaranteed autonomy, and the inexorable band of Ottoman Foreign Ministry officials and lawyers who insisted on Ottoman legal rights to sovereignty in Egypt.[9] At the same time, autonomy under occupation benefited a surprising array of actors in Cairo. Egyptian elites and nationalists, the khedive and his ministers, European lenders, concession hunters and laborer organizers, the occupiers themselves, rebellious Ottoman subjects, and ultimately even the sultan all profited in different ways from the ambiguity of administrative autonomy under occupation.[10] This chapter looks at what Ottoman sovereignty did on the ground in Egypt.

Egypt was an object of international politics for all the reasons historians have explained: its central place in the new imperialism of the 1800s and the Anglo-French rivalry in the Mediterranean, its geostrategic location, the Suez Canal as a critical waterway for trade and communication, not least with Britain's Indian Ocean empire, and the emergence of anticolonial nationalism. But what historians have paid less attention to are the ways in which international law and Ottoman imperial institutions shaped political and economic possibilities on the ground. Britain's invasion and occupation of Egypt fundamentally transformed the practice and meanings of autonomy in the Ottoman Empire. Occupied Egypt became one of the world's great arenas for working out an array of questions related to the practices and contested meanings of sovereignty in an age of expansionist empires. Egypt's status as legally Ottoman generated political and economic experimentation. Autonomy under occupation enabled so much of what made the Egyptian story in the late nineteenth century both unique and common. Local elites across the empire depended on European capital and expertise for development. Predacious lending practices and concessions undermined, but did not cede sovereignty. Maintaining Ottoman sovereignty offered flexibility without the burden of governing. In the new theories of international relations that exploded in the late nineteenth century to explain the rapid expansion of formal empire, Egypt was the central case study. In treatises on protectorates, condominium, and semi-sovereignty, Egypt featured prominently in the debates. Finally, the period of autonomy under occupation was critical for learning on the part of a series of actors. While practices and theories of sovereignty hardened in the years before 1914, another lesson also emerged, one where sovereignty and control could be divided at little risk to the global capitalist order. This story matters not just for Egypt and the Ottoman Empire, but because we often get a story about British practices of indirect rule with little concern for the ways in which the people who experienced domination responded.

Autonomy Under Occupation

On July 11, 1882, British ships bombarded coastal fortifications in the port city of Alexandria. For nearly a year, an experiment in constitutional politics had been underway in Egypt, led by Colonel Ahmad 'Urabi, the former Egyptian Minister of War, which, among other things, challenged European political influence and financial control of the Ottoman province. Within two months of the bombardment, General Wolseley, the commander of British troops in Egypt, apprehended 'Urabi, whom Sultan Abdülhamid had declared a rebel and enemy to all. 'Urabi's capture signaled the end of constitutional politics in Egypt and set into motion the over thirty-year military occupation of the province, which transformed the meaning of autonomy in Egypt.

Between the start of the Egyptian crisis in February 1881 and the riots at Alexandria in June of 1882, the key event precipitating British intervention in Egypt, European and Ottoman foreign ministries debated the best means to "restore order and the status quo in Egypt." Three issues dominated international discussions: the status of the sultan's sovereignty in Egypt, Egypt's adherence to external obligations, and the preservation of the khedive's privileges, secured in the fermans.[11] All the interested parties (Britain, France, the Ottoman Empire, locals, and the Khedive) made arguments about what should be done in Egypt by drawing on legal texts generated in the 1840 and 1841, all for their own ends.

On January 8, 1882, Britain and France issued a "Joint-Note" declaring their support for the khedive, "on the terms laid down by the Sultan's firmans, and officially recognized by the two Governments, as alone able to guarantee for the present and the future good order and general prosperity in Egypt, in which England and France are equally interested." The Ottoman government protested the Anglo-French action on the grounds that the sultan had the exclusive right to communicate with his governor, noting that "Egypt forms an integral part of the possessions of His Imperial Majesty the Sultan." The Ottoman Foreign Ministry interpreted the Joint-Note as an infringement on the sultan's rights of sovereignty in Egypt. Mahmud Esad Paşa, the Ottoman ambassador in Paris, reported that "the collective note submitted to the Khedive was directed not only against the interior disorders, but principally against all interference from the Porte."[12] Colonel 'Urabi himself sent a letter directly to Abdülhamid and begged him to intervene to prevent Egypt from turning into a new Tunis, an Ottoman autonomous administration, over which France had declared protectorate in 1881. Britain and France, he argued, were plotting to break up the Muslim world:

> The states of France and England are trying extraordinarily to occupy the regions of Egypt and to attract harm to the Exalted State. By exerting their complete effort on this issue, they are acting dishonestly, lighting the specter of intrigue as much as possible, with

power and effort in the Arab and non-Arab lands and will be able to provoke and incite divisions within the community of Islam. . . . With this memorandum [the Joint-Note], they proclaimed our separation from our exalted state and hereafter we would be subject to these two states.[13]

Abdülhamid II too, was certain the Joint-Note meant a transformation of Egypt's legal status. Because of the major territorial losses in the Balkans in 1878 and the French protectorate over Ottoman Tunis—but also the turn to international law—the Ottoman Foreign Ministry embarked on a campaign to obtain written recognition of Ottoman sovereignty in Egypt. Ottoman diplomats sought reaffirmation from all the European capitals that Egypt formed an "integral part of the imperial possessions of the Sultan."[14]

Asim Paşa asked his ambassadors in Berlin, St. Petersburg, and Vienna to communicate the Joint-Note to the respective European foreign ministries. The three states responded nearly identically. The Russian Ministry of Foreign Affairs disapproved of the Joint-Note and affirmed that Egypt was "recognized by the treaties as a part of the Ottoman Empire," saying that the Joint-Note should have been addressed directly to the "suzerain court." Furthermore, if any sort of intervention became necessary, it would be an "international question of Europe."[15]

At first glance it would seem the Ottoman diplomatic strategy was successful—each of the major continental European countries had affirmed that Egypt was indeed part of the Ottoman Empire. The problem was with the expression "suzerain power." The Ottoman Foreign Ministry instructed ambassadors to protest against this expression in place of "sovereign power." Asim Paşa argued that the relationship of the Ottoman Empire to Egypt was not a question between "suzerain and vassal, but one between sovereign and subject."[16] A flood of letters followed the Ottoman protest. British ambassadors in Paris, Vienna, Berlin, Rome, and Istanbul wrote to the Foreign Office in London requesting the British position on which term to use. The debate about the difference between "suzerain" and "sovereign" even found its way into the House of Commons.[17] Lord Granville, the British foreign minister, wrote to the permanent undersecretary at the Foreign Office, Lord Tenterden, seeking legal advice and asked simply: "Is the Sultan Sovereign or Suzerain of Egypt?" Tenterden responded that the sultan was indeed sovereign of Egypt, and to underline the point he described the legal relationship between the sultan and another part of the imperial realm, citing the 1878 Treaty of Berlin: "I have no doubt that the Sultan is Sovereign of Egypt. The Sultan is Suzerain of Bulgaria. Bulgaria constituted an autonomous and tributary Principality under the suzerainty of His Imperial Majesty the Sultan. The expression 'suzerainty' is often used loosely to mean allegiance. I should say that a good proof of the distinction is that the Sultan can (and does) depose the Khedive. He cannot depose the Prince of Bulgaria."[18] Granville accepted Tenterden's legal analysis and forwarded the memo to his ambassadors. Eventually the other European foreign ministries agreed with the British position. In one case, the Habsburg foreign minister blamed the inadvertent use of "suzerain" on a faulty translation.

For the Ottomans, it was clear that European powers, especially Britain and France, were attempting to attenuate the legal relationship between the Ottoman center and Egypt. Before 1878, the difference between "sovereignty" and "suzerainty" did not seem to trouble the Ottoman Foreign Ministry—correspondence written in French referred interchangeably to the sultan as the suzerain or sovereign. That changed in 1882.

On July 11, 1882, Britain bombarded the fortifications at Alexandria to restore order. The precipitating cause of the intervention was violence against Europeans in Alexandria in June. Britain acting alone in Egypt, without the support and consent of Europe, was not easily surmounted. The British government never declared war and instead classed the intervention as a police action in support of the khedive and the protection of the sultan's sovereign rights against 'Urabi. The secretary of the Admiralty sent instructions into the field to "avoid the use of the word 'neutrality' for we are not at war, but supporting the Viceroy against rebels." On July 16, 1882, the War Office explained to Admiral Seymour the purpose of the mission: "The object of employment of force on shore is police protection of the place, and it is essential for political reasons to avoid appearance of military occupation."[19]

Over a month into the war, another round of telegrams went between the War Office and Cabinet about whether the Laws of War should be applied to the Egyptian belligerents. The Cabinet decided yes but noted that Britain was still not at war and forwarded the following message for wider distribution: "Though occasion has not arisen for settling question of belligerent rights, you are authorized to treat rebels according to recognized rules of civilized warfare, including exchange of prisoners."[20]

Ottoman–British diplomacy during the war was dominated by British efforts to compel the sultan to issue a proclamation denouncing 'Urabi as a rebel and a statement of explicit support of the khedive. From the start, Musurus Paşa, the Ottoman ambassador in London, argued that the Ottoman government had to send troops to Egypt. He cautioned that without an Ottoman military presence there, the province would slip into the hands of the British. Two weeks after the bombardment, he urged the imperial government to make haste: "In the meantime it is important that the imperial government not lose time. The presence in Egypt of an imperial Army, sufficient at the same time imposing, is of the highest importance for maintaining the effective (*réel*) sovereignty of the Sublime Porte: 'Beati possidentes' (Blessed are the possessors)."[21]

Abdülhamid II issued a decree in support of the khedive and against 'Urabi's rebellion. But at the same time he dispatched a letter to 'Urabi, translated into Arabic and justifying the Ottoman proclamation of rebellion. He blamed the Egyptian crisis on 'Urabi, claiming that 'Urabi wished to become khedive, and that Britain wanted to take possession of Egypt along with the khedive. Abdülhamid insisted that Egypt was an integral part of the Ottoman Empire. His letter claimed that the proclamation in support of the khedive and against 'Urabi was necessary for the protection of his sovereignty rights and for the protection of the Muslims (*mülkmün ve Müslümanların muhafazası*): "In this case, your movement wholly exceeds your rights. Egypt is part of the Ottoman domains. Egypt does not belong under anyone's protection apart from my royal person and all who are inhabitants of the aforementioned province are required to submit to my imperial throne whether by custom or by the şeriat [Islamic Law]." But the real substance of the letter was the justification for why the sultan had to proscribe 'Urabi's movement a rebellion:

> I have endured this [Urabi's rebellion], with the purpose and intention to prevent disunion among the Muslims. Now, if you continue in this way, your dangerous enterprises will have more than serious consequences to the domains of Egypt and for the Muslims. This situation will cause Egypt to fall into the possession of another state, and it will be taken from the protection of the throne of our exalted state. You are required to come to this side, outwardly and manifestly obeying and conforming to my imperial edicts. If you do not submit to this sovereign command, your rebellion will be become known in

that case, because it is obligatory to protect Muslims and my domains, and it would be necessary to proscribe publicly your revolt among the people and they will keep a distance from you.[22]

During the summer, plans for the future administration of Egypt began to take shape. For the Gladstone Cabinet, the next step was to reestablish the authority of the khedive and decide the future of Egyptian administration. "The Settlement of Egypt" would have to address four key issues: sovereignty, local institutions, the Suez, Canal and international engagements.[23] Gladstone thought that the last two issues were matters to discuss with the powers but assumed that England could begin to deal with the first two problems alone. He thought with the sultan continuing to claim the tribute and homage of the khedive, he should not be able to raise troops in Egypt and should no longer be able to appoint "local sovereigns," that is, the khedive. He requested that a committee be formed to "to examine the conditions of the Balkan and Rumanian suzerainties" in order to determine, among other things, "the conduct of the foreign relations of Egypt." In other words, Gladstone wanted to limit the sultan's legal right to interfere in Egypt by diminishing his legal capacity there, and to turn Egypt into Serbia.

Foreign Office legal advisors regarded "suzerainty" as a much weaker legal bond than sovereignty. Gladstone and his Cabinet were in the end unable to carry out this particular change in Egypt's legal relationship with the Ottoman Empire, but the Cabinet still managed to achieve the desired effect. From the capture of 'Urabi in 1882 until Britain's declaration of protection in Egypt in 1914, British official documents referred to the sultan as the legal "suzerain" of Egypt rather than the sovereign. European governments soon followed suit. The Ottoman Empire continued to use words and phrases meaning sovereign or sovereignty to express the relationship between Istanbul and Egypt in internal documents. In diplomatic and personal correspondence conducted in French, Ottoman diplomats and ambassadors employed the words "souverain" and "souveraineté" rather than "suzerain" and "suzeraineté" to describe the legal bonds between Egypt and Istanbul, though this pattern began to change just before World War I.

On February 6, 1883, nearly five months into the British occupation of Ottoman Egypt, Parliament published a blue book outlining official occupation policy and plans for the "reorganization" of the province.[24]

Three months earlier, the Cabinet commissioned Lord Dufferin, the British ambassador to Istanbul and autonomy crusader, to produce a scheme for the future administration of Egypt. He proposed far-reaching institutional changes that radically expanded khedival authority and limited Ottoman and European rights and privileges in the province.

Dufferin revived the main features of his early plans for Lebanon and Eastern Anatolia. Autonomy from the Ottoman imperial center, coupled with a strong independent governor, were key elements in his proposal. Immediately after the seizure of 'Urabi, the Cabinet decided that the sultan's sovereignty in Egypt would be maintained, but with new restrictions on his power. The foreign secretary wrote to Dufferin, "We shall maintain the Sultan's sovereignty, and his tribute, but we shall have to limit some of his power of doing mischief—such as his power of borrowing troops, and deposing the Khedive."[25] This statement is significant because nothing in the Dufferin plan for Egypt dealt directly with altering the legal status of Egypt vis-à-vis the Ottoman Empire. Instead, Dufferin created a series of buffers to reduce Ottoman claims to interfere in the province by expanding khedival authority. The local governor would be even stronger and more independent from Istanbul than before the occupation. Moreover, a strong khedive backed by British advisors would have the obviously advantage of limiting European interference in the province. Dufferin also proposed to reduce European privileges by abolishing the Capitulations and subjecting foreign residents to taxation.

The British occupation of Egypt was a clear defeat for the Ottoman Empire, yet the immediate Ottoman response to Dufferin's reorganization plan for Egypt was relief. Though the sultan's privileges were circumscribed in the new administrative plan, Dufferin did not attempt to explicitly alter the legal relationship between Cairo and Istanbul, and of course he could not do so without consent from the European powers.

Abdülhamid worried that the Foreign Office planned to establish a protectorate in Egypt within the British imperial system.[26] The sultan was convinced that the British sent their ambassador to Cairo as the new governor-general for the province. His ambassador in London warned repeatedly that someone of Dufferin's stature should not be sent to Cairo.[27] His fears were inflamed by the fact that Dufferin brought his entire family with him to Cairo, rather than leaving them as guests of the sultan in Istanbul, as requested. One of Abdülhamid's informants (*jurnalcı*) in Cairo met with Dufferin just as his reorganization scheme was to be published.

The informer reassured the sultan on every point. He noted that Dufferin "was attempting to put into order a basic reform for Egypt" and that this reordering would "defend the law of the exalted sultanate."[28]

Abdülhamid saw European autonomy schemes for what they were, efforts to diminish Ottoman sovereignty, without outright annexation. Such sentiments are expressed in an undated report produced for the sultan: "It is clear that England—God forbid!—is striving to dissolve the Ottoman Empire into statelets. It amounts not to autonomy, but to anatomy, by creating for example, an Albanian Albania, an Armenia in the Armenian inhabited places, an Arab government in all the places inhabited by Arabs, and a Turkey in the Turkish-inhabited areas."[29]

The British occupation transformed autonomy. It was now more dangerous to the state, and it was clear that the idea of suzerainty had to be attacked. The Foreign Ministry worked in new ways to bring Egypt into the empire.

Istanbul in Cairo

In December 1885 Abdülhamid II dispatched Gazi Ahmed Muhtar Paşa, the decorated military commander and Ottoman high official, to Cairo to negotiate the withdrawal of British troops from Egypt. Though negotiations collapsed, Muhtar Paşa remained in Cairo as the Ottoman high commissioner to Egypt (Mısır Fevkalade Komiseri) until the beginning of the second constitutional period. With few exceptions, Muhtar Paşa's time in Egypt, a near quarter century, has been understood as either a period of exile, having ostensibly fallen out of favor with the sultan, or otherwise insignificant to his early military and later political career as a member of the upper house of the Ottoman Parliament and his brief stint as grand vizier.[30] At best, historians have viewed Muhtar Paşa as a hallow vestige of Ottoman sovereignty in Egypt and a nuisance to the British diplomatic agents, particularly Lord Cromer.[31] Yet by the time Muhtar Paşa arrived in Cairo, he had had extensive administrative experience throughout the empire as a military commander and governor. He was dispatched almost exclusively to provincial hotspots with the mission to put down rebellion, extend the reach of the state, or prevent European intervention in Ottoman affairs. Between the late 1860s and 1885, he was on the ground during critical moments in Yemen, Bosnia-Herzegovina, Erzurum, Crete, and Monastir.

Rather than treat Muhtar Paşa's time in Egypt as separate from his earlier administrative experiences, this chapter contends that he was dispatched to Egypt precisely because it was a hot spot within the empire. Egypt in the 1880s was the arena in which the Ottomans faced the most the serious confrontation with Europe since the loss of Balkan provinces in 1878. Muhtar Paşa was seen as a strong governor who might successfully end the British occupation, and short of that, mitigate the effects of the British occupation within the empire and within Ottoman relations with Europe. While the first aim failed, his presence in Egypt was nevertheless important to maintaining Ottoman legal claims to Egypt, but also for interpreting British imperial ambitions in Egypt and beyond.

During his tenure in Cairo, Muhtar Paşa generated an extensive body of policy recommendations for Sultan Abdülhamid II. Experiencing the "Scramble for Africa" firsthand, he advised the sultan to engage European powers directly and to lay claim to Ottoman territorial rights in North Africa and the Red Sea coast. Muhtar Paşa, along with other high officials, especially Musurus Paşa, the longtime Ottoman ambassador to London, claimed that Sudan was the key to reestablishing Ottoman hegemony in Egypt. Muhtar Paşa acted as Abdülhamid's "man on the spot" and provided the palace with crucial information that allowed the Ottoman government to participate, with varying degrees of success, in the European game of empire. Despite the British occupation, Egypt remained a major concern for Abdülhamid and other high officials in Istanbul. Ottoman insistence on maintaining sovereign rights in Egypt mattered; indeed, it shaped British administrative practices and justifications on the ground in Cairo and determined how Britain laid claim to Sudan in the 1890s.

"I Am a Peacemaker Everywhere"

By the time Muhtar Paşa arrived in Cairo in 1885, he had engaged in or devised various reform and reorganization schemes for restive Ottoman provinces.[32] In many ways, he was at the forefront of implementing Tanzimat by the sword. After graduating from the *Mekteb-i Harbiye* in Istanbul, his first postings were in the Balkans, though perhaps his first significant appointment was as a staff officer in the Reform Force (*Fırka-yı İslahiye*) dispatched to Kozan (Sis) in the mid-1860s. The Reform Force was tasked with pacifying the *derebeys* around Mount Kozan, forcibly settling Turkmen tribes, and establishing direct Ottoman control over the territory in the reorganized *sancak* of Kozan.[33]

Ahmed Muhtar continued to participate in major state centralization projects. After another period in the Balkans, he was sent to Yemen with the purpose of incorporating the province into the regular administration of the empire. Concluding what appeared to be a successful military campaign in the early 1870s, Muhtar Paşa was appointed as governor and military commander (1871–1873) of the newly reorganized vilayet of Yemen. Here again he attempted to extend Tanzimat policies to the Red Sea and to bring the local "lords" under centralized state control.[34] In this position, Muhtar Paşa observed and was increasingly concerned about European, especially British, activities in the Red Sea—concerns that he brought to Egypt and broadcast back to Istanbul. Yemen appears to have been critical, too, for contributing to the shaping of Muhtar Paşa's theory of imperial disorder. Excessive European influence in imperial peripheries affected local outbreaks of rebellion. Finally, with Yemen, Ahmed Muhtar Paşa's reputation was cemented as a strong and effective reforming governor who could be depended on for the "restoration of tranquility and public order" (*iade-i sükûn ve asayiş*), as well as to extend, as much as possible, the effective control of the Ottoman state into imperial hot spots and peripheries. In the lead-up to his appointment in Cairo, Muhtar Paşa occupied a series of posts that combined military and governing responsibilities in Erzurum (1874–75), Crete (1877), and Monastir (1879–80). In each case, his assignment coincided with local uprisings.[35]

If Ahmed Muhtar Paşa was such an effective tool of Ottoman centralization and able to quell rebellion, why would Abdülhamid send him to Egypt, a province that, even before the British occupation, had autonomous control over its internal affairs since 1841? What looks at first like exile might be explained by examining Muhtar Paşa's reputation in Europe and beyond. Muhtar Paşa knew Europe and was known by European diplomats and high officials. British Foreign Office agents regularly compared him favorably to Mehmed Fuad Paşa, one of the key reformers of the Tanzimat. In 1867 Muhtar Paşa, along with the then *Şehzade* (a prince in the royal household), Abdülhamid, accompanied Sultan Abdülaziz on his trip to European capitals. He also received military honors from multiple European courts. Indeed, following the Russo-Ottoman War of 1877–78, he was a distinguished figure whose past administrative and military experiences were visible even to audiences in the United

States. In 1879 *The New York Times* printed his obituary upon the mistaken intelligence that Albanians had murdered him in Montenegro. The extraordinarily detailed memorial, which reads like a copy of Muhtar Paşa's official employment record, noted that his death "deprives the Turkish Government of one its most skillful and promising servants."[36] In Cairo, when Muhtar Paşa first met Sir Drummond-Wolff, the official with whom he attempted to negotiate the withdrawal of British troops from Egypt, his reputation as the conqueror of Yemen had preceded him. Sir Drummond-Wolff noted that he had heard of him as "the peacemaker of Yemen." Muhtar Paşa replied, "I am a peacemaker everywhere."[37]

Beyond the fact that Muhtar Paşa had a good reputation as a strong governor among European officials, he was also the subject of a protracted dispute between the Ottoman and British governments on the best method of imperial administration in Eastern Anatolia. As noted in the previous chapter, the new British ambassador to Istanbul, Lord Dufferin, arrived in Istanbul with the mission to implement administrative reforms in the eastern provinces in accordance with Article 61 of the Treaty of Berlin (1878). The Foreign Office insisted that he find an experienced Ottoman functionary to serve as governor-general of a reorganized "Armenia." Dufferin pushed for Ahmed Muhtar Paşa almost immediately upon arrival. Again, he insisted in meetings with Abdülhamid that whoever was sent to Eastern Anatolia, it had to be "a person well-known by Europe" (*Avrupaca ma'ruf bir zat*), an expression that filled the Ottoman versions of these meetings. Abdülhamid refused Dufferin's insistence that a new administrative regime should be implemented in Eastern Anatolia. Despite the fact that the Egyptian crisis was expanding rapidly during this period, Dufferin continued to push Abdülhamid to agree to appoint someone "like Muhtar Paşa" as governor of a reorganized "Armenia."

Ahmed Gazi's Cairo appointment to Cairo was the source of debate between the British and Ottoman Empires. The Foreign Office ordered Ambassador Dufferin to Egypt to "reorganize the province" in the fall of 1882. His plan for Egypt was, and still is, largely regarded as Lord Cromer's blueprint for the occupation. From the beginning of the Egyptian Crisis, Abdülhamid and his advisors were determined to preserve Egypt as an Ottoman province and were worried about turning the population of Egypt against Istanbul—a point that is not well articulated in the historiography. From the onset of occupation, various officials within the Ottoman government looked to Sudan as a possible arena from which to reestablish Ottoman control over Egypt. The Mahdist revolt in Sudan appeared to provide a possible pretext as it offered the opportunity to negotiate the withdrawal of British troops from Egypt.

When Muhtar Paşa arrived in Egypt to negotiate the end of the occupation, he was given instructions to restore public order in Sudan, to reorganize the Egyptian army, and to establish the security of the frontiers of Egypt (*Mısır hududunun husul-i emniyeti*). In many ways, he adhered to these instructions throughout his long tenure in Cairo. During the entire period, he sent innumerable telegrams, dispatches, and memoranda directly to the palace, much of which was read by Abdülhamid himself. He wrote about a variety of issues—sending Egyptian students to the Tribal School (*Aşiret Mektebi*) in Istanbul, the security of the Suez Canal, attitudes toward the Ottoman government in the Egyptian press—but a substantial portion of his dispatches concerned ways to shore up Ottoman sovereignty in Egypt. He sent detailed observations of Lord Cromer's policies and Britain's plans for Egypt more broadly. He noted episodes when the khedive exceeded his capacities according to the fermans regulating Egypt's status as an autonomous province. But perhaps more than anything, Muhtar Paşa became an astute observer of the unfolding "Scramble for Africa" and analyzed the various tools and justifications the European powers invented to rationalize the vast seizure of territory throughout the continent.

As the Ottoman high commissioner in Egypt, Muhtar Paşa's most significant policy recommendations were linked to maintaining Ottoman sovereignty in Egypt by pressing claims first in Sudan and later fortifying the Ottoman positions along the boundaries of Egypt—particularly in Libya and the Arabian Peninsula. Until the early twentieth century, Sudan was viewed as the path to end the British occupation, but also to ensconce Egypt more firmly within the Ottoman Empire. Upon arrival, Muhtar Paşa, like Musurus in London, warned the sultan that the ongoing British evacuation of Egyptian garrisons would be detrimental to Ottoman territorial claims in Sudan. If the Ottoman state relinquished its rights, it would lose part of the tribute from those territories, but also prestige in Europe. Moreover, the territory would be available for European conquest.

Muhtar Paşa's arrival and continued presence in Egypt, especially after the collapse of British-Ottoman negotiations over the withdrawal of troops, was broadly commented on and the subject of varying levels of concern for the khedival regime as much as the occupying power. For the

British, Cromer above all, Muhtar Paşa represented the limits of the occupation and regarded him as an interfering intriguer sent by Abdülhamid. For the khedive, especially Abbas Hilmi II, Muhtar Paşa had been a useful tool to balance against British claims to control Egyptian administration. At the same time, he thought Muhtar had to be treated carefully, as he had undoubtedly been sent to Cairo to diminish the khedive's authority and bring Egypt into the regular administration of the empire. Abbas II's description of Muhtar's time in Cairo is revealing. Abbas wrote in his memoirs that though Muhtar might be better known for his political career after the Young Turk Revolution, his time in Egypt was potentially more significant. He noted, "But his actions in Istanbul were not to be compared with those which he took in our interest as a diplomat on the spot, who, above all, considered Egypt as a post of observation for British schemes."[38]

The Idea of Sudan in the Ottoman and British Empires, 1882–1898

From the beginning of the British occupation of Egypt, Abdülhamid and the Ottoman Foreign Ministry looked to Sudan as a possible arena to reestablish control over Egypt. The Foreign Ministry and ambassadors looked for ways to get troops or an Ottoman High Commissioner on the ground in Cairo. The Mahdist revolt in Sudan appeared to provide a possible pretext.

Ottoman territorial claims to Sudan date initially from the conquest of Egypt (1517) and consisted largely of Red Sea ports, notably Sawakin and Massawa. In the modern period, Ottoman territorial rights in Sudan stemmed from the early phase of Mehmed Ali's expansionist campaigns.[39] Following the long and costly but ultimately successful Wahabi campaign (1811–1818), Mehmed Ali turned toward Sudan.[40] He launched a short but violent campaign to the south (1820–1822) and expanded the boundaries of Egypt into present-day Sudan, doubling the size of his empire.[41] The administrative regime established by the Paşa was called the "Turkiya" in Sudan.[42] It remained intact until the 1870s, when broad discontent mounted against the policies of the khedive, 'Ismail, including his appointments of European governors to the province—even at one point General Gordon.[43]

Muhammad Ahmed, a Sufi sheikh from Northern Sudan, proclaimed himself the "Mahdi" in June 1881, and he and his followers (*Ansar*) started a broad revolt against the Turkiya, synchronous with the revolt against the khedive by the 'Urabists.[44] When Britain invaded Egypt in the summer of 1882, Sudan almost immediately became a pressing policy question. While Lord Dufferin left it largely untouched in his "reorganization" scheme for Egypt, a portion of his time in Cairo was spent dealing with security questions at Egypt's southern boundary.[45] The Mahdist revolt continued to gain strength, and, following a major British defeat in December 1883, the Foreign Office ordered the evacuation of Sudan, with the exception of Red Sea ports and Khartoum. General Gordon was dispatched to Khartoum to oversee this process and was later captured and killed when the Mahdi and his followers succeeded in sacking the capital in 1885. The Mahdist state governed in place of the Turkiya until the "reconquest of Sudan" in 1898.[46]

During the early years of the occupation, Istanbul was anxious to sign an agreement with Britain on the withdrawal of troops from Egypt and to end the occupation, and the Foreign Ministry sought ways to pressure Britain into agreement. Even before Dufferin published his scheme for the reorganization of Egypt in February 1883, the Ottoman Foreign Ministry linked events in Sudan to a possible agreement with Britain. As the Ottoman ambassador in London, Musurus Paşa, stated, "The questions of Sudan and Egypt are tied."[47]

Just after the first major British defeat against the Mahdi in 1883, Musurus Paşa wrote a lengthy letter to the Foreign Ministry in Istanbul concerning the state of affairs in Egypt. He began by denouncing Britain's military intervention in Egypt as the "most serious breach of the Sublime Porte's rights of sovereignty" and a "flagrant infraction of existing treaties in international law." He expressed his concern that Britain's actions in Egypt, "this humiliation," would lead the other European powers to act similarly elsewhere in the empire. He noted that the Foreign Office claimed it would wind down the occupation as soon as the "maintenance of order and tranquility there had been assured" according to Lord Dufferin's reorganization plan. The cholera epidemic in 1883 had been the first cause to delay the British evacuation, but now security concerns in Sudan threatened to swell the number of British troops stationed in Egypt. The real occasion for Musurus Paşa's letter to the foreign minister was the Sudan question.

The news of General Gordon's mission to Khartoum and Britain's planned evacuation of the Egyptian garrisons in Sudan presented a danger to the Ottomans but also offered an opportunity. The significance British public opinion and Parliament appeared to attach to Gordon's assignment alarmed Musurus. He argued that the Foreign Ministry should seize the opportunity to assert Ottoman rights in Sudan. There were two alternatives if the sultan did nothing. Either Britain would reestablish Egyptian authority in Sudan and claim the territory for itself, or, alternatively, it would abandon Sudan to the Mahdi, who would become a rival Muslim potentate of a large state. In either case, the Ottomans would lose more ground against the British:

> In this state of things, it is important, especially these days with the sudden emergence of the Sudan question, that the Sublime Porte show keen interest in this new issue, and make it known to the British government in terms courteous and kind, by virtue of its status as a sovereign power, it can not consent to the abandonment of Sudan, which has always been an integral part of Egypt from time immemorial, and from the settlement of the Egyptian Question in 1841, it has had an obligation to defend the integrity of Egypt and to assist the Khedive's government militarily in suppressing rebellion. If the Sublime Porte appears indifferent and does not manifest its firm intention to insist upon concrete intervention in Egyptian affairs, in the presence of current circumstances, one of two things will happen. The British government would be obliged to send a new army composed of English and Indian troops to the Sudan, and, claiming, after the victory, the abstention of the Sublime Porte and having made great sacrifices in men and money, would organize the province as they wish, which they would definitively detach from Egypt; and then the Sublime Porte, at the same time that it would be potentially deprived of its rights of sovereignty over the Sudan, it would allow the Egyptian government to claim a reduction on the current tribute.[48]

If Britain was allowed to manage the rebellion in Sudan on its own, nonintervention not only would jeopardize Ottoman claims to Sudan but would also have the potential to weaken Ottoman sovereign ties to Egypt. The Egyptian tribute was not insignificant.[49] More than its practical value, which should not be underestimated, the tribute was a concrete legal attachment between Egypt and Istanbul. Legal connections like the tribute, but also the ferman of investiture, everything guaranteed by the "treaties and the fermans," were precisely the things that Musurus, Abdülhamid, and the legal advisors at the Ottoman Foreign Ministry were so keen to maintain. The Egyptian tribute was not just a symbol of the caliph's legitimacy for Abdülhamid's Muslim subjects; it was a legal means to Ottoman intervention in Egyptian affairs—and one that Europeans, Britain especially, would be called on to recognize.[50] Ottoman territorial claims to Sudan could not be abandoned to the British—to do so would counter a broader Ottoman strategy for dealing with Europe. The relentless Ottoman appeal to international law, "the existing treaties," and "sovereign rights" should be seen as strategy of a weak power in an international system dominated by expansionist European powers, but also in terms of the Ottomans' particular experience with Europe in legal terms. For the better part of a century, Europeans had already used legal standards to justify intervention in Ottoman internal affairs.

If the British did not conquer and seize Sudan for themselves, Musurus imagined a second option that would end again with the Ottoman forfeiture of rights and loss of international standing. He continued:

> Or the British government will retreat from the garrisons in Sudan and from Egyptian authority, leaving this province to the will of the so-called Mahdi, and following an agreement with the latter will limit itself to the defense of Egypt proper; and in this case, not only will the Sublime Porte suffer in fact the same deprivation of its rights of sovereignty, but the so-called Mahdi, who with the moral support of England will become a monarch of a great state including besides Kordofan, Darfur, and the other equatorial provinces, all the parts of Sudan annexed to Egypt, he would appear in the eyes of Muslims surrounded by the prestige of success, and will become an invader more audacious than Mehmed Ali and a dangerous element for the internal peace of the Empire in Arabia, in Syria, and in Mesopotamia, provinces inhabited by Arab tribes.[51]

To leave Sudan to the British, Musurus warned, would be another blow to the Sultan in the Arab provinces, directly on the heels of the British occupation of Egypt.

It is striking that Musurus cast the Mahdi as a potential rival to Ottoman prestige and power in the form of Mehmed Ali.[52] If nothing else, it underscored the late Ottoman preoccupation with Egypt as the supreme negative model province in the Empire—a province lost to centralized imperial control at the hands of powerful governor supported by Europe. At the same time, and contrary to the dominant view of Ottoman interests, or lack thereof, in the "Scramble for Africa," Musurus's assumptions about British imperial practices demonstrated a keen awareness of European, especially British, modes of strategic control and incorporation.[53] Abandoning Egyptian territorial rights, and by extension Ottoman sovereign rights, would in effect increase British control of Sudan. In Musurus's estimation, one very good way for the British to maintain security in Egypt while extending influence throughout Sudan would be to recognize the Mahdi as a quasi-independent ruler.[54]

Musurus urged the Foreign Ministry to come to an agreement with Britain and suggested it send an Ottoman imperial commissioner along with troops to Egypt. The Ottoman commissioner, he recommended, should work with the Egyptian government on the best means to pacify the rebellion in Sudan, and it should be carried out by the Ottoman and Egyptian armies. Second, drawing on the same language Britain used in its promises to end the occupation, he stated, "After the prestige of the khedive has been restored in the eyes of the people and his authority reaffirmed, the imperial (Ottoman) army will evacuate Egypt."[55] Musurus advised that the proposal to the British should emphasize how the "legal and legitimate cooperation of the Sovereign Powers could only be advantageous to the British Government, who would not only be spared the expense of sending new envoys to Egypt, but would also find a suitable occasion to recall its troops currently in Egypt."[56] Finally, while the British might want to make a monarch out of the Mahdi, the Ottoman solution to rebellion was not that far off. Musurus argued that the Ottoman commissioner could also work out an agreement with the "so-called Mahdi, who His Imperial Majesty would deign, in his position of Caliph and sovereign, to confer, under certain conditions, the hereditary government of Kordofan, of Darfur and other adjacent provinces."[57]

The Ottomans had no illusions that they could "effectively" govern Sudan from Istanbul, but neither did Britain from London or even Cairo. If Britain could offer "independence" to the Mahdi, the Ottomans should too. Whatever happened in Sudan, it should occur under the penumbra of the sultan, even if meant the most unpalatable solution—a hereditary governorship for a rebel. During the Hamidian period and beyond, the Ottomans had well-founded fears that the British considered establishing a rival caliphate to Istanbul in either Egypt or the Hijaz, so it is doubtful whether the Mahdi would fit the bill, but the last thing the Hamidian state wanted was a strong, quasi-independent Muslim ruler on the Red Sea unattached to the sultan.[58] Nonetheless, for the Ottomans, pacifying the rebellion in Sudan was not a question of who should control Islam; rather it was a question of who should control Egypt—and for Musurus, legal claims to Sudan for much of the 1880s and 1890s appeared to be the key.[59]

Sudan also figured into British calculations at the start of the occupation. The Mahdist revolt was initially a question of security but soon became a question of administration—not that the two were mutually exclusive.[60] Just after the fall of Khartoum in 1885, Evelyn Baring, later Lord Cromer, and the Foreign Office began an exchange on the future of Sudan. Cromer pushed the Foreign Office to consider Britain's ultimate political objectives in Sudan. He wished to receive clarification if the withdrawal from Khartoum had been a political as well as a military decision—did the British plan to establish a "settled form of government at Khartoum or not"? He assumed not and argued that there were only two alternatives to consider: Britain should either come to terms with the Sultan and allow the deployment of Ottoman troops to "effect the pacification of the Soudan" or leave "Khartoum in the possession of the Mahdi." If, however, the government decided to establish a settled government in parts of Sudan, which would require taking back Khartoum, Cromer suggested four possibilities. The first was that the British could again come to terms with the Sultan and leave Ottoman troops to manage the territory, or the territory could be given to Italy. Alternatively, and in line with Musurus's Paşa's suspicions, the British might "establish a quasi-independent ruler who would be subsidized by Egypt or by England." Last, he suggested that Britain could administer the territory "in some form or another."[61]

The "subsidized ruler" idea, according to Cromer, had originally been Gordon's plan and had appeared to be the best possible solution, but that solution was complicated now with the success of the Mahdi. Cromer noted, "Under the present circumstances I am far from confident that the policy of setting up a subsidized and quasi-independent ruler at Khartoum will result in the creation of a stable and settled form of government, unless, indeed a foreign military force be placed at the disposal of a new ruler . . . such a force must, so far as I can judge, be either Turkish or English." He ultimately rejected this idea for lack of a suitable candidate to balance against the Mahdi, and ignoring the Italian and Ottoman options left the British option:

> Thus we may either annex the country outright; or we may establish an Englishman as a quasi-independent ruler or as a Governor-General under the Khedive, with the accompaniment, which I should consider necessary, of an English force, or at all events of a force officered by Englishmen, to keep him in his place; or perhaps a Company might be formed somewhat on the model of the old East India Company. But all of these plans virtually rest on the same foundation. Under all of them England would virtually take a hand in the government of the Soudan.[62]

Cromer's vision for Sudan as a quasi-corporate body administered from afar by the Foreign Office was rather close to what the Condominium became—that is, an administration with a British governor-general under the khedive, with a separate Sudan civil service. The animating issue for Cromer though, like Musurus, was Egypt, not Sudan. If Britain established a government in Khartoum, Cromer argued, it would lead to a reconsideration of the British position in Egypt. "It is very probable that our occupation of Egypt will, in any case, be a long one. If we are to become responsible for the government of the Soudan I think we may at once, for all practical purposes, abandon any hope of getting away from Egypt at all. Under these circumstances it would become a very open question whether it would be advisable to continue the present system of government in Egypt."[63] British control of Sudan would force a reexamination of the policy of occupation, and that meant "regularizing" the status of Egypt—in other words, incorporating it into the British Empire. At the end of his lengthy note to the Foreign Office, Cromer retreated entirely from this vision and argued instead that the Sudan must be left either to the sultan or the Mahdi, indeed, "abandoned to anarchy." He thought, given the circumstances, London should come to terms with Istanbul and consider allowing the Ottomans to send a detachment of troops, because he would rather "the permanent occupation by British troops of Egypt without the Soudan, than the occupation of Egypt with the Sudan." Cromer did not want permanent responsibility for Egypt and Sudan.

Between 1885, when Britain effectively initiated the abandonment of Egyptian garrisons in Sudan, and the decision to "recover" the lost territory of the khedive in 1895, the Ottoman government repeatedly attempted to come to an agreement with Britain on the Egyptian question. When Salisbury became prime minister and secretary of foreign affairs during the Home Rule Crisis in Ireland in 1885, one of the first things he did as foreign secretary was to dispatch Sir Henry Drummond Wolff to Istanbul to negotiate a "settlement on the Egyptian Question." The negotiations lasted three years and took place in Istanbul, Cairo, and London. Muhtar Paşa was appointed as the Ottoman high commissioner opposite Drummond Wolff and arrived in Cairo at the end of the year in 1885. He remained in the position until 1908 and was a source of constant frustration to Cromer throughout the years of the occupation. The agreement that was worked out for the evacuation of British troops from Egypt was never signed—in part because it provided Britain with what was in effect a standing right to intervene in Egypt, a *droit de surveillance.* At the same time, the agreement reiterated the validity of the "existing treaties and fermans" regulating Egypt's legal status as an Ottoman province with all the attendant European privileges.[64]

Musurus Paşa persistently pressed London to recognize Ottoman rights in Sudan and to send Ottoman troops, fearing that abandoning the Egyptian garrisons there would lead to a European scramble for Ottoman territory in Africa.[65] His concerns were borne out almost immediately when Italy occupied the Red Sea port of Massawa in 1885. The Egyptian government was also apprehensive about surrendering any territory over which the sultan had legal claims. Cromer noted, "The attitude of the Egyptian Government is that they cannot cede territory which belongs to the Porte. . . . The possession of Massawah itself is not an important Egyptian interest, but it is important that the Khedive not get into trouble with the Porte."[66] During this period, the Foreign Office alternated between recognizing parts of Sudan as Ottoman territory and parts as *terra nullius,* depending on their interests and needs. London's flexibility with regard to Sudan came to a halt when French, Belgian, and British imperial claims clashed in Sudan on the Upper Nile.[67] In 1895 the British government authorized Lord Kitchener as commander of the Egyptian army to "reconquer" territories lost to the khedive by rebellion. The extraordinarily brutal war began the following year and ended with the defeat of the khalifa at Omdurman on September 2, 1898.[68]

The Anglo-Egyptian Administration Agreement

On January 19, 1899, Cromer and Butrus Ghali, then Egyptian foreign minister, signed the "Agreement between Her Britannic Majesty's Government and the Government of His Highness the Khedive of Egypt, relative to the future administration of Sudan."[69] In keeping with British patterns in Egypt, the convention was presented as an administrative solution to a political problem, in this case chronic rebellion. Most accounts of the idea and creation of the Condominium argue that an Egyptian political façade was required to satisfy the European powers as well as the khedive and the Egyptian government.[70] The Condominium, like the permanent occupation of Egypt, was a political anomaly. In the case of Sudan, Britain supplied the fiction of co-dominion, but the partners were unequal, and all the attributes of sovereignty were controlled by Britain, through the British governor-general of Sudan. Without discounting the veracity of these descriptions, the Ottoman Empire has more often than not been sidelined as one of the animating problems in the equation. Even Cromer, who could be counted on to disparage Ottoman governance at every turn, acknowledged that the Ottoman legal factor presented an obstacle, but one that could be spun into an opportunity:

> British statesmen were continually harassed by a Nemesis in the shape of the *magna vis veritas*, which was forever striving to shatter the rickety political edifice constructed at the time of the occupation on no surer foundations than diplomatic opportunism. At every turn of the political wheel, fact clashed with theory. Nevertheless, in the year 1889, of which period I am now writing, Ottoman supremacy in the Soudan, whether in the person of the Sultan or to the Khedive, presented a sufficient character of solidity to necessitate its recognition as a practical fact. It could not be treated as a mere diplomatic wraith. However much it tended at times to evaporate into a phantom, its shape was still sufficiently distinguishable through the political mist to enable the outline of a kingly crown to be

> clearly traced. Hence the necessity arose of cloaking the reality of fact with some more or less transparent veil of theory.[71]

During the Sudan campaign, the Foreign Office, along with Cromer, considered various possibilities for administering Sudan, but, as earlier, they wished to maintain British flexibility. The imperial confrontation with France over Fashoda, which immediately followed Omdurman, added to the urgency of defining the British position in Sudan, however vaguely:

> What therefore, is the political status of the country to be? Annexation by England would, of course, solve all the difficulties of which I am now treating. But I understand that, for many obvious political and financial reasons, we do not wish to annex. On the other hand, the recognition of the Soudan as a portion of the Ottoman Domains in no way distinct from the rest of Egypt, would perpetuate all the international difficulties and obstruction of which, during the last 15 years, we have had such an unfortunate experience in dealing with Egyptian affairs. Under these circumstances we have to find a compromise between the two extremes. Such a compromise may, I think, be found; but it is to be remembered that we shall be creating a status hitherto unknown in the law of Europe, and that, therefore—more especially in view of the extreme complications of the come of the details—it is no easy matter to put down on paper any arrangement which may confidently be predicted to be workable in practice, and perfectly capable of defense in all of its parts by valid and logical argument. I think the arrangement had better take the form of a convention, or agreement, with the Egyptian government.[72]

For Cromer, the Condominium idea was a compromise between annexation, accompanied by direct British sovereignty, and an administration built on model of the Egypt, where sovereignty and administration were divided. The problem with Egypt was what Cromer called the "incubus of internationalism," that is, the Capitulations and other European privileges, which he constantly protested. Cromer wanted the flexibility of occupation without the Capitulations. To achieve this, he and Ian McIlwraith, the British judicial advisor of the Egyptian government, devised the administrative agreement. They were certain that France and the Ottomans would challenge it because one could argue, as French lawyers and Ottoman diplomats eventually did, that the agreement between Britain and the khedive would infringe on the imperial fermans. There were two problems. The first was that the fermans stipulated that the khedive only had the right to carry out commercial and customs conventions and absolutely did not have the juridical capacity to make political treaties with foreign powers.[73] Second, Abbas Hilmi's ferman of investiture (1892) added a new stipulation to the existing treaties and fermans: "The Khedive shall not, on any pretext or motive, abandon to others, in whole or in part, the privileges accorded to Egypt, which are entrusted to him and which pertain to the inherent rights of the Sovereign Power, nor any portion of the territory."[74] In other words, the khedive could not sell, cede, or abandon any territory under the Sultan's domain—an addition that should be understood in the context of the European scramble for territory in Africa and an Ottoman guard against the abandonment of Egyptian garrisons in Sudan.

Cromer and McIlwraith readied a twofold response to the problems generated by the fermans. Cromer argued:

> In the first place, it may be said that the convention is no treaty properly so-called; that in signing it the Khedive will not perform any act of external sovereignty; that he will merely be exercising his acknowledged right of making arrangements for the internal administration of the territory accorded to him by the firmans; and that the fact of the Egyptian flag continuing, in concert with the British, to fly everywhere in the Sudan, shows that the suzerainty of the Sultan is, in part at all events, still recognized in that country. This argument is, however, in my opinion weak, for the more we dwell on whatever fragment of the Sultan's suzerainty which will remain, the more difficult will be to differentiate the Soudan from the rest of the Ottoman domains in respect to the treatment of Europeans and other subjects. I prefer therefore to take our stand boldly.[75]

Cromer thought they might get around the fermans by making Sudan a matter of internal Egyptian administration, which would accord with Egypt's status as an autonomous province. But this solution would allow the extension of Ottoman institutions into Sudan, and Cromer wished to establish British dominance there, without European or Ottoman interference: "If the political status of Soudan were to be assimilated in all respects to that of Egypt, the necessary consequence would be that the administration of the country would be burdened by the introduction of the Capitulations, and in fact, by all the cumbersome paraphernalia of internationalism, which had done so much to retard Egyptian Progress."[76]

The first public indication of British plans for Sudan arrived with Cromer's speech on January 4, 1899, to a group of sheikhs at Omdurman. Cromer pointed out the British and Egyptian (Ottoman) flag flying together and announced that "this is an indication that for the future you will be governed by the Queen of the England and the Khedive of Egypt. The sole Representative in the Soudan of both the British and the Egyptian Governments will be the Sirdar, in whom both Her Majesty the Queen and His Highness the Khedive have the fullest confidence. No attempt will be made to govern the country from Cairo, still less from London."[77] Even before the speech at Omdurman, Ian McIlwraith had drawn up the administrative agreement that became known as the Condominium.[78]

The agreement "relative to the future administration of Sudan" argued that Britain and Egypt, in a joint military and financial effort, had jointly reconquered territory in rebellion against the khedive. Britain accrued rights in Sudan by right of conquest "to share in the presentment and future working and development of the said system of administration and legislation." The agreement was composed of twelve articles and became the basis of administration for Sudan, with minor changes, until 1956. Sudan was to be decentralized from Egyptian administration—the "backwards and unsettled" conditions of large parts of the territory required a distinct system of governance—with a British governor-general, the sirdar, at its head.[79] Though the governor-general was appointed by the khedive and could theoretically be removed by him, the post was given broad sovereign powers—although in practice this would have required a successful Egyptian national revolt against the British, or the Ottoman reconquest of the province from the British invaders. Article V stipulated that "no Egyptian Law, Decree, Ministerial Arreté" shall be promulgated in the Sudan, unless at the discretion of the sirdar. Articles VI–VIII covered issues related to "internationalism." No privileges would be extended to the Europeans, but they would be free to live and trade there. The jurisdiction of the Mixed Courts, too, would not apply in Sudan. Article X stated that no "Consuls, vice-Consuls, Consular agents" would be accredited and allowed to live in Sudan without British permission. The document concluded with articles banning the import of slaves and a weak promise to fulfill the Brussels Act of 1890 regarding the import of and sale of firearms, munitions, and alcohol. McIlwraith's basic law and framework was entirely administrative and was silent on the question of sovereignty.

The Sultan's high commissioner in Egypt, Ahmad Muhtar Paşa, followed events in Sudan closely throughout the reconquest campaign and kept Istanbul well informed of British plans.[80] Muhtar alerted the Porte of Cromer's speech to the notables at Omdurman, but Abdülhamid was nevertheless surprised by the announcement of the Condominium.[81] The day before the announcement, the khedive, Abbas Hilmi II, wanted to inform the sultan about the joint British-Egyptian administration in Sudan. Abbas told Cromer that he was anxious to reveal something but did not want to send the actual text for fear of repercussions against him. Salisbury was entirely against informing Istanbul and argued that such a move would open the door to Ottoman interference, which was precisely what the Foreign Office had hoped to avoid.[82] In the end, it was Muhtar Paşa who telegrammed Abdülhamid and informed him that the khedive had signed a political agreement with London, contravening the fermans.[83]

Abdülhamid's first response was to blame the khedive. He sent a note to the British ambassador in Istanbul, Sir Nicolas O'Connor, reiterating his understanding that Britain respected his sovereign rights in Sudan and the fermans:

> Soudan, in which a rebellion had broken out, was attached to Egypt, and formed part of the Ottoman Empire, and the British troops, being in temporary occupation, had very naturally put down the rebellion in cooperation with the Egyptian forces. England had repeatedly given assurances, both previous to the occupation and subsequently, that she would respect the integrity of the Ottoman Empire, and observe and protect the sovereign rights of the Sultan in Egypt. . . . His Majesty was convinced that if the Khedive had acted in a matter contrary to the tenor of the fermans, which were perfectly clear, England would not approve of such acts, and would unite with the Turkish government in inducing His Highness to abandon his irregular and illegal attitude. His Majesty felt sure that England would not approve the Khedive's actions, since it was with

> the Sultan that a Convention was to be concluded about Egypt, and therefore it was also with the Sultan that a Convention ought to be concluded about Sudan.[84]

Just as Cromer, McIlwraith, and Salisbury expected, the Ottomans charged that the khedive had exceeded his capacity as a representative of the sultan and the only the Ottoman government could sign political agreements concerning Egypt, and by extension Sudan.

Salisbury met with Ottoman ambassador in London, Antopulos Paşa, who also lodged a complaint against the Condominium. Salisbury admitted that the sultan's rights to the Sudan was an "intricate question," but he was not prepared to offer anything. He argued that the agreement concerned administration and was "adopted purely for the purpose of maintaining good order and good government in the provinces." The claim to administer Sudan, he argued, was by "right of conquest." The Mahdi and his followers, "an enemy far more hostile to the Sultan, both in his spiritual and temporal character," invaded Sudan and exercised "dominion" in it for over thirteen years.[85] The sultan had never done anything to take back the territory and had left it to "British and Egyptian" to defeat the rebellion, "These military events led to and justified the occupation of the country by the British and the Egyptian forces, and conferred upon them the sanction required for the power which they were now exercising."[86] Salisbury's justification for the occupation and administration of Sudan had far-reaching implications. How could the khedive act in his own capacity in Sudan? If the Mahdi exercised "dominion" in the provinces of Sudan for only thirteen years, what did this mean about the British position in Egypt?

The Ottoman ambassador in London again met with Salisbury, as Abdülhamid continued to be disturbed by the fact that Britain and Egypt claimed Sudan by conquest. Istanbul wanted further assurances that Britain recognized Ottoman rights there. Salisbury again claimed that Britain was in Sudan on the basis of conquest, not recovery of the Padışah's rights. But the problem returned to the capacity of the khedive as the sultan's agent:

> Anthopoulo Pasha replied that we did it with an ally, and that that ally was the Khedive, the Vizier and *mandataire* of the Sultan. I entirely denied that the Khedive could be looked upon in that light,

> or that his action could be judged on those principles. Mehemet Ali, from whom his rights were derived, certainly never would have admitted that he was a *mandataire* of the Sultan. It is true that he was not independent, but neither was he dependent. With respect to a certain circumscribed portion of his action, the result of all the transactions which had taken place during the last sixty years was to make the Khedive independent, but outside that inner circle there still remained unaffected the general sovereignty of the Sultan. In his alliance with Great Britain he had acted within the area of his independent rights. . . . There was no ground in international law for saying that when, mainly by the action of a third party, such as Great Britain, the Khalifa was driven out of the territory that he had conquered, that the rights of the Sultan, which had been extinguished thirteen years ago, revived in force for his benefit, though he had taken no part whatever in recovering them from the dominion of the Khalifa.[87]

Ottoman attachments to Egypt were far more important in the eyes of the sultan than those to Sudan, but the Condominium was viewed as a dangerous precedent. It had pushed the boundaries of the fermans and admitted that the khedive had a greater functional range in international relations. Salisbury's attitude toward the capacities of the khedive was deeply alarming to Istanbul, particularly with regard to Egyptian autonomy. If the khedive was as legally independent as Salisbury claimed, the whole structure of the British occupation, which preserved Ottoman sovereignty, might come to an end. In this context, rather suddenly the sultan and his ambassadors backed off questions related to Ottoman sovereignty in Sudan in London, though they did not let the matter drop, and focused on shoring up Ottoman claims adjacent to Egypt's frontier.[88]

The confusion stemming from any analysis of the Condominium as an administrative apparatus is that Salisbury and the Foreign Office presented competing theories of conquest and recovery to justify the acquisition of Sudan to different audiences. For the French and European powers, the rights of the sultan were paramount. For the Egyptian government, the Anglo-Egyptian army had secured the rights of khedive, which had never been "abandoned." But for the Ottomans, the Foreign Office favored the theory of conquest.

Sovereignty Problems: The Condominium in International Law

The debate among international lawyers on the Condominium mirrored the diplomatic debate and concentrated on the method of Anglo-Egyptian territorial acquisition of Sudan. Whereas European and American lawyers had taken up Egypt as a vexing problem of international law in the late nineteenth century—one lawyer wrote, "Egypt is the classic territory of international law"—the Anglo-Egyptian Condominium in Sudan produced a far narrower debate among them.[89] The Condominium found its place in the treatises and textbooks, but it inspired much less confusion and fewer disagreements among lawyers than had Egypt and other Ottoman provinces under permanent European military occupation from the late 1870s onward. Among American and British lawyers in particular, the Condominium appeared in discussions of colonial territorial acquisition; it was one of a number of instruments to extend imperial claims, along with so-called effective occupation, protectorates, spheres of influence, the doctrine of hinterland, and buffer zones.[90] A small but vocal group of French international lawyers, however, cast the Anglo-Egyptian Condominium as a problem of international order. These publicists highlighted and critiqued two issues stemming from the Anglo-Egyptian agreement on Sudan. First, they argued that Britain supplied two incompatible theories of territorial acquisition: *terra nullius* and reconquest—the recapture of territory temporally lost to rebellion. Related to the method of conquest, and they argued that defining Sudan's international legal status as British, Egyptian, or Ottoman mattered, and that to avoid the question, as Britain had thus far, posed serious risks for international relations as well as the "science" of international law.[91] While the French critiques of the Condominium need to be set in the context of the Fashoda incident, these arguments, along with those of the French and Ottoman governments, helped to revive old debates about Britain's ambiguous position in Egypt.

At best, then, the Anglo-Egyptian Condominium appeared in international legal treaties and textbooks as a category of shared or co-sovereignty. But more often than not, international lawyers characterized it as a diplomatic convenience invented during the European colonial partition of Africa. For instance, John Westlake wrote about Sudan from the perspective of the destabilizing effects of "spheres of influence" on international relations: "Colonial protectorates differ so little from annexations, especially in the responsibilities which they involve, that they could not satisfy the haste which characterized the latter part of the nineteenth century for the provisional appropriation of territories in advance of anything resembling occupation. A more shadowy form of earmarking was therefore invented, in what are called spheres of influence or interest."[92] Westlake noted that spheres of influence were weak agreements between states, and "the most significant diplomatic incident connected with this question" was the Fashoda incident. Lassa Oppenheim's first edition of *International Law: A Treatise* scarcely mentioned the Anglo-Egyptian Condominium. He noted, "Egypt and Tunis are half-sovereign, the one under Turkish suzerainty, the other under French protectorate. . . . The Soudan has an exceptional position; being under the *condominium* of Great Britain and Egypt, a footing of its own within the Family of Nations the Soudan certainly has not."[93] Despite the fact that the Condominium appeared to shock European diplomats more than international lawyers, there was a small group of predominantly French lawyers who attacked its legal basis and argued that Britain's invention threatened international relations and the field of international law.

Immediately after the announcement that Sudan would be administered jointly by Britain and Egypt, Franz Despagnet, a French lawyer and member since 1891 of the Institut du Droit International, argued that Britain's new position in Sudan was nothing more than a rearguard action to hold Egypt more firmly in its grasp, without regularizing the legal position of Egypt vis-à-vis the British. Sudan was inevitably linked to the Egyptian question. While the convention of 1899 would "jolt international jurists and overthrow all of their concepts," it would hardly surprise the diplomats, he argued.[94] The agreement was "out of harmony with the rights of Turkey and Europe" and was the result of longstanding British policy in Egypt, which Europe had failed to check "thanks to the passive complicity, or rather the powerlessness of the Great Powers, paralyzed by their divisions and greed." Sudan brought Britain's indistinct position in Egypt into sharp relief. The reconquest forced Britain to clarify once more its intentions in Egypt, particularly in the period between the battle of Omdurman and the convention of January 1899, when rumors spun round British plans for Egypt. Salisbury declared that Britain had no intention of establishing a protectorate in Egypt, which for Despagnet merely showed Britain's aversion to clarifying their position in Egypt:

"We know what ambiguity surrounds the word protectorate, especially in England. For the English, this expression often refers to what is meant elsewhere by 'colonial protectorate.'"[95]

For Despagnet, Egypt fit the definition of a protectorate, but Britain was unwilling to change the legal status of Egypt out of fear of "provoking the protestations of Europe." The international treaties and the fermans regulating Egypt's relationship with Europe and the Ottoman Empire made it impossible for Britain to incorporate Egypt into the empire. The only way around the treaties and the fermans was to hold Sudan jointly with Egypt, forestalling the British evacuation of the latter. In other words, the Condominium might provide the justification for Britain's permanent military occupation.

For Despagnet, as well as for other French commentators and politicians, it was by way of Sudan that Britain would cement its position in Egypt without European consent. After the much-publicized program of reform in Egypt, unrest in Sudan offered a "continual pretext" for the British to maintain the occupation. Despagnet argued that Britain's dual theory of reconquest and conquest was unsupportable in international law. He said that Britain's voluntary desertion of Egyptian garrisons was an attempt to transform the territories of Sudan attached to Egypt into *terra nullius* by way of abandonment. Despite the fact that the Ottoman grand vizier, Said Paşa, claimed Ottoman territorial rights surrounding the Nile at the Berlin West Africa conference, European diplomats agreed that "the region in question was no longer recognized by the Sovereign."[96] Yet, once Kitchener's Sudan campaign resumed in 1896, Britain resorted to the theory that "sovereignty was never juridically effaced" in Sudan and that they were merely, with the help of the Egyptians, reestablishing the khedive's authority in rebellious provinces.

Despagnet argued that the Anglo-Egyptian Agreement of 1899 shocked "so profoundly the principles of the most elementary law of nations universally recognized by civilized nations" because the khedive did not have the contractual capacity to accede to the agreement with Britain. Whichever way Egypt was categorized in international law textbooks and treaties at the time—a vassal or tributary state, or privileged or autonomous province of the Ottoman Empire—the result was the same: "There is no doubt-that Egypt has a position such that it is absolutely without capacity to accept conventions such as the one she signed with England because of her subordination to the Sublime Porte, which is recognized by the great powers." That is, Egypt's legal status as an Ottoman province precluded the khedive from signing political treaties—an argument that Ottoman legal advisors aggressively insisted on since the beginning of the occupation. Despagnet went further and argued that the Condominium contradicted British policy toward the Ottoman Empire more broadly by abrogating the treaties promising to maintain the territorial integrity of the empire: "Each word in the treaty of 1899 contains however an abandonment of territorial sovereignty to the benefit of England."[97]

In addition to Ottoman rights, the Agreement of 1899 trampled European rights in Sudan. By preventing the Capitulations, mixed courts, and European consular agents from operating in Sudan, Britain unilaterally rescinded European privileges in Ottoman territory. This is precisely why the method of conquest mattered so much to French jurists when critiquing British legal justifications for the Condominium. If the territory were actually liberated from rebels, all the rights and privileges accorded to Europeans by the Capitulations in Egypt and the Ottoman Empire more broadly would logically extend into Sudan. The only plausible explanation for preventing their implementation was if Britain claimed title to Sudan by conquest. Despagnet concludes by imploring Europe and the Ottoman Empire to demand their rights in Sudan, which Britain has so openly usurped with the Condominium.

Georges Blanchard was even more pointed in his critique of the Condominium as a destabilizing force in international relations. He posed two interrelated questions. The first was by what means had Sudan been territorially acquired—was it "a country without a master, a *res nullius*, or as an integral part of Egypt, temporarily occupied by a victorious rebel?" As with Despagnet, whether by conquest or reconquest, the means mattered very much and determined the legality of the Anglo-Egyptian Condominium and also had far reaching implications for Britain's position in Egypt. Second, Blanchard asked what Sudan's international status was: "Is it an Egyptian province, an autonomous province of the Ottoman Empire or an independent state? What are the links that attach it to England, to Egypt, and to Turkey?"[98] Rather than demanding that Europeans and Ottomans claim their trodden rights, Blanchard attempted to find a legal theory to explain the Condominium.

He quickly disposed of the first question. It was impossible for a territory to be *terra nullius* and under military occupation or in the throes of rebellion. If Britain justified the seizure of Sudan by right of conquest, it would make "a clean break with the institutions that preceded the Mahdist insurrection." According to Blanchard, this was the most practical solution because it would enable Britain to reject the Egyptian and Ottoman claims to the territory and thereby avoid the problem of extending European privileges or "internationalism" to Sudan.[99] If, in the second case, Britain claimed to recover lost territory, the old institutions, "the ancient state of things," would need to be restored. In other words, the territory would be recognized as Egyptian, and by extension Ottoman, as the khedive acted in the legal capacity of the sultan governor—"the exercise of the benefits of the right of sovereignty would gather anew on the head of the Sultan, represented by the Khedive."[100]

Britain chose the former theory of conquest, and the "internal situation" in Sudan was defined by shared British and Egyptian sovereignty. Without discussing the inequality of the members in this shared administrative partnership, Blanchard noted that from the perspective of international law, the internal administrative question mattered less than Sudan's external situation. He sought the right legal theory to justify the condominium, noting that the Sudan's external status could be defined in only three ways: Sudan is an Egyptian province placed under the official protectorate of Great Britain, or, like Egypt, it is an autonomous Ottoman province, or, finally, it is an independent state.[101]

Blanchard immediately disposed of the first possibility. "The Sudan cannot be an Egyptian province placed under the protectorate of Great Britain, because the suzerainty of the Sultan and a British protectorate could not coexist."[102] In this case, Ottoman sovereignty, here termed suzerainty, in Egypt precludes the possibility that Sudan is an Egyptian province under British protection.[103] If Sudan is legally part of Egypt, "it is endowed with a special administration and continues to be one of the provinces of the Sultan; and yet from the point of view of public law, it is precisely the existence of this suzerainty of the Porte that renders impractical the idea at hand"—that is the idea that Sudan is a British protectorate. Despite the complexity and variability of the Ottoman Empire from an internal constitutional perspective, there had never been a protectorate over Ottoman territory that remained Ottoman: "Europe, which has already found many ingenious methods to snatch the Sultan's authority over some provinces, while claiming to respect the integrity of his empire, has yet to resort to this state of affairs."[104] Consequently, notwithstanding European intervention in Ottoman internal affairs in the form of permanent military occupations (like Egypt, Bosnia, and Cyprus) or imposed decentralized administrative regimes (like Samos, Mount Lebanon, Egypt, or Crete), no European power had maintained an internationally recognized protectorate over Ottoman territory that did not then cease to be Ottoman. Tunis, for instance, was internationally recognized as a protectorate, whereas Egypt was not and was never categorized as such until 1914.[105]

> It (Sudan) is indeed here a protectorate of modern form and not a vassal link which is understood in ancient feudal organizations, and which can be found again presently over certain parts of Ottoman territory. Bulgaria, the island of Samos, Egypt (although for the latter the question is debatable) forms thus the vassal states of Turkey in the feudal sense of the word, and in exchange for this title each year they pay a tribute in recognition of the Sultan's suzerainty. If it were the same in Sudan, the solution to the problem would not offer any difficulties: the king of England would be a vassal of the Sultan for his Sudanese possessions.[106]

For Blanchard, territory was defined in international law not by its internal administrative organization, which has no real bearing on its international relations, but by its external relations. This point is critical for understanding why Egypt, and the Ottoman Empire especially, occupied such an exaggerated place in European international legal thought.[107] Europe constrained the empire's external affairs through various types of legal, financial, economic, and administrative limitations, and, as noted throughout these chapters, the late Ottoman state's internal and external affairs could hardly be separated.[108] But at the same time, Europe guaranteed the empire's territorial integrity by treaty, and international law became the language of Ottoman diplomacy and was used to assert and maintain its territorial claims. The point here is that Blanchard recognized that Egypt was not a British protectorate, despite Alfred Milner's and Lord Cromer's best efforts, and as such Britain could not establish a protectorate over another sovereign's territory because it was "not possible for the Khedive to be the vassal and ward of two monarchs."

Blanchard considered if Sudan might be characterized as a separate autonomous Ottoman province. In this case, the sultan would hand over the internal administration of the province to two equal chiefs—the khedive and Great Britain. The situation would be analogous to the relationship between the central Ottoman state and the provinces under permanent military occupation. Thus "it would no longer be a question here of a line of vassalage, but a simple administrative mandate given collectively to two persons." Blanchard cited the examples of the British administration of Cyprus and the Habsburg administration of Bosnia-Herzegovina. The problem with this solution was that Britain and Egypt would be required to request that the sultan establish such a regime. Blanchard doubted it would be possible to find the right inducement as the sultan jealously guarded his territory. "Moreover, would the Sultan, who theoretically controls without limits the right to modify the administration of the provinces of his empire, might he be compelled to transform the political regime of the Sudan by his own authority? It is doubted because Europe intervenes on every point of administration in the entirety of the Empire."[109] In the end, it was too dangerous for the Ottomans from the perspective of greater European intervention, and it was too dangerous for the British and the Egyptians from the perspective of Ottoman interference in Egyptian affairs.

The last option that Blanchard suggested was that Sudan should be an independent state placed under the joint protection of Egypt and Great Britain. He resolved the obvious problem, that the khedive had no legal capacity to engage in foreign treaties, by arguing the khedive did not accede to the Condominium in his capacity as khedive but rather acted as an individual person. In short, the Anglo-Egyptian army conquered Sudan, "a land without a master," and there the Anglo-Egyptian Condominium was established over the independent state of Sudan, to be jointly administered by the queen and the khedive acting in his capacity as an individual.

Blanchard's driving argument was that Egypt's legal status as an Ottoman province administered by Britain limited and determined how the Anglo-Egyptian Condominium could be framed, at least in terms that fit international legal categories and not just in terms of flimsy legal justifications applied to annexation. Blanchard shared Despagnet's concerns: The system of international law had to conform to certain realities or risked producing international anarchy.

Jules Cocheris, a French lawyer who characterized Egypt as the "classic territory of international law," similarly argued that Egypt and Sudan's juridical and administrative nonalignment posed a serious threat to the stability of Europe and Africa. For Cocheris, Egypt's juridical position was one of the most important problems of nineteenth-century international law, and widespread confusion about its international status had the potential to erode the foundations of the discipline—a problem to which the publicists themselves contributed and that the politicians exploited. Cocheris began his text with the simple statement: "Egypt is a province of the Ottoman Empire," to which he juxtaposed its complex administrative realities:

> No country is possessed of an international status by all appearances, so complicated. Imagine a state tied to Turkey by the fermans, to Europe by the treaties, to Great Britain by force . . . a state governed by a khedive of whose powers are paralyzed by the tutelage of an omnipotent British mentor, from an Ottoman high commissioner and the European consuls-general, he can choose, by his discretion, his ministers and his collaborators; a state of which the interests are defended by a Power who has not received this mission, neither title nor mandate and who treats on its behalf with third parties . . . a state whose finances are at the mercy of the commissioners of the debt; justice is enchained by multiple shackles: the Capitulations, mixed courts, indigenous courts . . . a state where all the administrations, the domains, the railroad, the telegraph, post, customs, ports, lighthouses, canals, roads, police, education, highways are directed by foreigners . . . a state declared as semisovereign, vassal, tributary, protected, autonomous, privileged province, regular province, many would neutralize it, others would internationalize it, but which for now will not enjoy any freedom in the exercise of its executive, legislative, regulatory, judicial powers.[110]

The problem was not just that the juridical status of Egypt and Sudan did not correspond to administrative realities; rather, European political interests and imperial claims had created political anarchy and chaos there. The disorder that resulted had the potential to erode of one the key foundations of the sources of international law: international treaties and conventions, which we have seen was the main tool of Ottoman diplomatic wrangling with European states. In positive international law, publicists of the time, and today, considered international treaties to be one of main sources of the law, but also its force. For Cocheris, it was essential to recognize the force of international treaties, or to change them if they no longer fit existing conditions, but to allow political calculations to suspend or ignore international conventions and treaties jeopardized the project of international law.[111]

International lawyers were responsible for much of the confusion surrounding Egypt's international legal status as they incorrectly categorized the province as "semisovereign" (*mi-souverain*). As a positivist, Cocheris cast semi-sovereignty as "regrettable in all regards, irrational and antijuridical."[112] For him, and for most positivist international lawyers, sovereignty was indivisible and was defined by independence of a state vis-à-vis foreign state—an attribute that Egypt did not possess. Egypt was instead a province of the Ottoman Empire, "in possession of a certain amount of administrative autonomy which is fixed and limited by the fermans." Cocheris's analysis of Sudan stemmed from Egypt's juridical position as an Ottoman province.

Like Despagnet and Blanchard, Cocheris agreed that the Anglo-Egyptian agreement over Sudan was meaningless in law and abrogated the rights of Europeans in Egypt as well as the rights of the sultan. The Condominium, by preventing the extension of European consuls, the mixed courts, and Capitulations, "dispossessed" Europeans of their "acquired rights." Moreover, the khedive was not endowed with any special right to carry out an international convention with Britain. Citing Abbas Hilmi's ferman of investiture, he noted that the khedive had only been authorized to sign commercial and customs conventions, but not political conventions, "which would infringe upon the territorial sovereignty of the Sultan, who is the primary chief." The Condominium also cut against Britain's repeated recognition of the territorial integrity of the Ottoman Empire.[113] This argument was precisely the one crafted by Ottoman Foreign Office lawyers in their legal opinions for their ambassadors in Europe.

For Cocheris, the real problem was that Britain refused to play a fair game. Politicians like Salisbury and Cromer invoked international law, or the sultan's territorial rights, whenever it suited their interests, and ignored these same laws and rights when it did not. When France established a protectorate in Tunis, the state was forced to engage in protracted negotiations with all the powers concerning the Capitulations and other European privileges.[114] Britain seized Sudan on the precarious and incompatible legal theory of conquest and recovery and unilaterally denied these same European privileges on the grounds of conquest.

For the French lawyers, the more serious implication of the critique of the Condominium was that British diplomats and politicians used international law to justify territorial expansion—conquest and reconquest—but at the same time they ignored international treaties and agreements governing Egypt's relationship with the Ottoman Empire and the European powers. They were demonstrably concerned about the effects of employing legal justifications in the service of furthering imperial claims. Ignoring the existing European rights and the treaties and fermans that guaranteed Egypt's international legal status diminished the significance of international law as a science. If longstanding treaties and rights could be trampled on so explicitly and without protest, what was the value of international law? In other words, once the diplomats had recourse to the langue of international law to justify Great Power politics, what was left of the project? Again, this was precisely the same argument emanating from Ottoman Foreign Ministry lawyers.[115]

Sovereignty questions in Egypt remained an enduring concern of international lawyers in the late nineteenth century. As we have seen, Britain, leading the way, pushed the other Great Powers to recognize the sultan's "suzerainty" rather than "sovereignty" in Egypt. This categorization was reflected by European international lawyers who claimed that Egypt, as well as the other privileged provinces," were "semisovereign."[116] Before 1878, Moldavia and Wallachia and Serbia were placed alongside Egypt as examples of "suzerain" provinces. In the 1846 edition of *Elements of International Law*, just a few years after Egypt gained autonomy, the American jurist Henry Wheaton categorized Wallachia and Moldavia, Serbia, and Egypt as "semi-sovereign or dependent states" under the suzerainty of the Ottoman sultan.[117]

Semi-sovereignty (*mi-souverain* in French, *Halbsouverän* in German, and later *şibh-i sultanat* in Ottoman-Turkish) emerged as a new category in international law, and it was one that was dominated almost exclusively by the Ottoman privileged provinces.[118] Earlier in the nineteenth century, special administrative arrangements were not broadly understood as a diminishment of Ottoman sovereignty. As we saw in chapter 1, autonomy was cast as a feature of Ottoman administration, and after 1774 as a reflection of outmoded "feudal" forms of governance. Many European international lawyers would explicitly make this claim, but in the 1840s, semi-sovereignty purportedly did not "impair the sovereignty" of the suzerain power. As Wheaton noted, "all of the laws of the Ottoman empire were applicable to Egypt in the same manner as other parts of the empire," and "that the military and naval force maintained by him should always be considered as maintained for the service of the state."[119]

Until the mid-nineteenth century, semi-sovereignty mattered in terms of the internal workings of the Ottoman state, and only a question in international relations insofar as European powers had guaranteed their status by treaty.[120] Other midcentury international lawyers categorized a range of territories outside of the Ottoman Empire as semisovereign, counting small territories and principalities guaranteed by the Concert of Europe, including the Free City of Krakow, the principalities of Monaco, San Marino, and Andorra, but also German principalities and Native American "nations" vis-à-vis the United States. Semi-sovereignty was not sovereignty at all.

While the midcentury story was one of ambiguity, by the 1880s semi-sovereignty and the assortment of feudal terms were applied almost exclusively to Ottoman autonomous provinces and among European lawyers meant less than sovereign—though Ottoman lawyers and the Foreign Ministry fought back. Attempting to explain the sovereignty puzzles arising out places like Egypt, Tunis, Bulgaria, Serbia and Romania before 1878, Crete, and others required a new category in international law. It was precisely because the Ottoman Empire was inside the Eurocentric international order but at the edges that forced lawyers to produce a new theorization. The key issue was the division between sovereignty and control.

Late nineteenth-century publicists became increasingly rigid when defining the proper subjects of international law and sovereignty in international relations. Lassa Oppenheim's 1905 treatise on international law and his 1908 article "The Science of International Law" are representative texts of the "highest stage" of legal positivism. These texts, along with other early twentieth-century legal treaties, viewed the proper subjects of international law as those states that had complete sovereign control over international and external relations. In such texts there is far less uncertainly about states like the Ottoman Empire and China—the old "semisovereign" category in classic nineteenth-century international law texts. Accordingly, the novelty of a territory held in condominium was viewed as one of many inventions to manage European expansion in Africa, particularly among British and American lawyers. While lawyers readily admitted the Anglo-Egyptian Condominium defied the existing categories in international law, they were less bothered by it than by Britain's permanent military occupation of Egypt.

In 1920, just as the empire was on the precipice of vanishing from the map altogether, an American international lawyer, Edwin de Witt

Dickenson, published one of the last nineteenth-century-style international textbooks. In it, he argued that the idea of suzerainty and other feudal terms were only revived to explain Ottoman sovereignty in the autonomous provinces:

> The conception of suzerainty had its origin in feudalism, where it was used to describe a well-defined relation between lord and vassal. The great historical example of its application to the relations between separate states was furnished by the Holy Roman Empire, which ended in 1806. The term was revived in the nineteenth century to describe the relation between Turkey and its provinces during the period of their gradual emancipation. . . . Egypt, from 1840 to 1914, and Crete, from 1898 to 1912, were recognized as autonomous under the suzerainty of the Sultan. In fact, each enjoyed a very limited international capacity, and in each case the international status was further complicated by the protection of other states. The term "suzerainty" has been little used elsewhere than in connection with the moribund Empire of the Near East.[121]

Ottoman sovereignty was not only damaged and antiquated—a relic from another era—autonomy was a steppingstone to independence. Historians of Europe, as much as historians of the late Ottoman Empire, cast European-imposed autonomous provinces as the halfway house between empire and independence—and of course had tangible cases to draw on between 1878 and 1923. At the same time, privileged provinces have barely counted as Ottoman within national historiographies.[122] Yet from an Ottoman perspective, European-imposed autonomy, while resisted and challenged by the Foreign Ministry, was ultimately domesticated and assimilated into the constitutional and administrative order of the empire.[123] Ottoman privileged provinces were deeply productive within late imperial statecraft. From the 1830s to 1860s, Great Power territorial guarantees were understood as a safeguard to protect the "territorial integrity" of the empire. All autonomies were not the same, and it was easier for the state to make concessions to European powers over Montenegro than it was over Egypt. As Ali and Fuad Paşa later wrote, a concession at the edges of the empire that was not particularly important economically was strategically always preferable to a territorial loss.[124] Autonomy solved the multiple crises of sovereignty that encompassed the nineteenth-century international order. It absorbed the damage of European interventions in internal affairs, and it created, under its penumbra, an entire international law regime of negotiated imperialism.

Conclusion: "In Avoiding a Legal Scylla, We Run Some Risk of Falling Into a Diplomatic Charybdis"

The announcement of the joint Anglo-Egyptian Condominium over Sudan led to extensive international debate on Egypt's constitutional relationship to the British Empire.[125] These debates unfolded in London in the press and in Parliament, but also among international lawyers and foreign diplomats. At issue was the separation of sovereignty from authority in Egypt. Analysis of legal discussions concerning the Condominium demonstrates how Egypt created constitutional problems within the British Empire, as well as for the Ottoman Empire. In Istanbul, the announcement was cause for the Ottoman state to assert more direct control over the provinces of Bingazi and Trablusgarp (Libya), fearing that the last Ottoman outpost in North Africa would come under European occupation.

Despite French and Ottoman protests, the Condominium endured as the basic organizing structure for Sudan until independence in 1956. In 1904 the British and French antagonisms over Egypt, which had been heightened by Fashoda and the creation of the Condominium, were worked out in the *entente cordiale*. France recognized Britain's irregular position in Egypt in exchange for British recognition of the French position in Morocco, among other things. For many, 1904 represented the end of the Egyptian question in international politics. Yet the *entente cordiale* was an agreement on shared strategic interests and did not change the legal status of Egypt or Sudan. Like the colonial agreements that John Westlake worried about concerning "spheres of influence" and "interests," the *entente cordiale* was a diplomatic instrument. Despite the fact that the agreement endured between Britain and France, from a legal perspective it was rather weak. The fact that it was a diplomatic instrument and did not have immediate implications in terms of Ottoman sovereignty brought some relief to the Ottomans.

In response, the Ottoman legal advisors at the Bab-ı Ali's Office of Legal Consul suggested no immediate legal action because British "declared that it had no intention of altering the political status of Egypt."

The ambassador should obtain further assurances from Britain that the sultan's rights in Egypt and Sudan would continue to be recognized.[126] As long as the fermans and treaties guaranteeing Egypt's position remained unchanged by the *entente*, there was no need for any immediate political action on the Ottoman side.

Ottoman diplomacy was still guided by international law, with the single idea of maintaining the territorial extent of the empire. The Hamidian era policy of appealing to international law and existing treaties to secure the Ottoman position in Europe would start to come undone with the Young Turk Revolution. While the guiding Ottoman foreign policy goal continued to be maintaining the empire at all costs, the annexation of Bosnia-Herzegovina and Bulgaria's declaration of independence in 1908 caused a serious re-evaluation of Ottoman diplomatic strategy. The Office of Legal Counsel, which was originally staffed in the 1880s by Europeans who were gradually replaced with Ottoman subjects, hired another European, Léon Ostrorog, as the chief legal advisor in 1908, who looked to Japan as a model of regeneration.[127] International law continued to be an important tool for Ottoman diplomacy, but maintaining sovereign rights alone was no longer enough. Ottoman foreign policy under the Young Turks focused on ways to close the gap between internal and external affairs by attacking European derogations of Ottoman sovereignty. In the lead-up to World War I, it was clearly understood that paper sovereignty counted for much less against force.[128]

Just before World War I, one international lawyer came around to the Condominium. While other lawyers had termed it "monstrous" and beyond the existing "frameworks of international public law," Grégoire Sarkissian wrote, "But the political status has subsisted for fifteen years. It has proven to be viable and it possesses elements of life. Should the law of nations not account for this finding, and expand its horizon, and to take to heart this mode of government which was established by the Convention of January 19?"[129] Sarkissian's realist view of international relations, accepting British conquest and the legal fiction of co-sovereignty in Sudan, was representative of a hardening of attitude toward sovereignty and force.

CHAPTER 4

Egypt on the Gulf

On February 15, 1913, İbrahim Hakkı Paşa, the one-time chief legal advisor to the Ottoman Foreign Ministry, arrived at Charing Cross Station on the evening train from Paris. He left Istanbul amid war and traveled to France, crisscrossing former Ottoman territories with whom the Sublime State was locked in a battle for control over the Macedonian provinces. He was greeted on that cold night by staff from the Ottoman Embassy and taken directly to Claridge's Hotel—a favorite among European heads of state and later exiled monarchs.[1] Rumors swirled in Istanbul and London that Hakkı Paşa was in town to resume the stalled-out peace talks concluding what would become the first of two Balkan Wars. Negotiations had been suspended in January following the coup d'état in the Ottoman capital. The territorial settlement across the Balkans was left up in the air, and the former imperial capital of Edirne was under siege by the Bulgarian and Serbian Second Armies. One British editorial conjectured that İbrahim Hakkı would most certainly be joined by Gabriel Noradounghian, a leading international law expert and the former minister of foreign affairs, whose compendium of Ottoman treaties was well known among European diplomats and lawyers.[2] Other newspapers alleged that the presence of the former grand vizier in London could only mean that he was there to fight to keep Albania within the empire as an autonomous province. All the speculators had it wrong.

İbrahim Hakkı Paşa was in London to negotiate the legal status of Kuwait vis-à-vis the Ottoman and British Empires.

Amid imperial crises that spanned the empire from Libya to the western Arab provinces and the Balkans, the empire's most distinguished international lawyer was busy hashing out a compromise with the British Foreign Office over a quiet port town on the western shores of the Ottoman Gulf. After nearly four months of negotiating, İbrahim Hakkı Paşa consented to give Kuwait, an Ottoman subprovince of Basra, administrative autonomy and to recognize Sheikh Mubarak al-Sabah as the hereditary *kaymakam* (district governor) of the territory. In exchange, the British agreed to recognize Kuwait as part of the Ottoman imperial domains. For many observers, the parallels to autonomous Egypt were as obvious as they were astonishing. As in Egypt, a local power broker was let loose in the sovereignty market. Mubarak succeeded at this because he played the Ottomans and British off each other and generated crises and conflicts that threatened to spill out into the world of European imperial politics. While in Egypt, Ottoman governors amassed unprecedented prestige and power through the actions of Mehmed Ali, who threatened the sovereignty of the Ottoman Empire itself, in Kuwait Ottoman and British imperial powers allowed a man who murdered his way to power to become the nominal master of the disputed territory.

In many ways, Egypt and Kuwait had nothing in common. At the outset of the British occupation, Egypt sustained a population of 6.7 million inhabitants, whereas Kuwait at the turn of century had a population of barely 35,000, which was an almost twofold increase since the 1860s.[3] Egypt was not only one of the richest provinces of the empire but was constantly at the center of high imperial politics. In contrast, Kuwait scarcely felt the presence of the central state until the 1870s. But in other ways they had much in common: They both were seen as sites of extraordinary potential wealth of the evolving transport-dense global capitalist project. Britain eyed Kuwait as a deep-water port in the Gulf that could rival Ottoman Basra in Iraq. Kuwait, too, figured prominently in Ottoman visions of increased trade and development in the Gulf. But the reality was that the subprovince was an imperial backwater that made money on pearl diving, shipbuilding, and Mubarak's privately owned date farms in Basra. Kuwait didn't even pay taxes until 1902, and few seemed to care. This was hardly Egyptian cotton and the Suez Canal. Yet, incredibly, the Ottomans and British drew upon Egypt as a model to satisfy both empires and get the locals to play along. For the Ottomans, as always, that meant holding onto imperial territory and securing European legal recognition of sovereignty—an old calculus that was starting to become more automatic in the years before the war. For the British, it meant neutralizing Ottoman interference within their own domains and papering over their own tenuous legal claims.

By the early twentieth century, the Ottoman-British autonomy experiment in Egypt became a diplomatic, political, and legal impulse. It was used as a go-to solution in Egypt as it was in Kuwait, and in an array of vastly different local political questions. In the years leading up to the First World War, autonomy emerged as the answer to a host of problems in conflicts between the Ottomans and European powers, especially Britain. Between 1878 and 1914, over a dozen well-known local crises in the empire were solved through extending some form of administrative autonomy.[4] It wasn't only the imperialist powers that gained something or learned from this compromise; the Ottoman government started using administrative autonomy domestically. Moreover, the empire's own subjects drew upon the example of autonomy worked out in Egypt to make claims about the future organization of the state. Kuwait is a perfect example to see the Egypt model in action, not because it was the first or only time this knot of interests was resolved using the Ottoman autonomy model. It is the perfect test case because it clarifies how much all parts of imperial brokering system within the Middle East saw autonomy compromises as a way to satisfy all interests at once: Ottoman, British, and local. These have been treated thus far as a "typical" British means of layered imperial structures. By showing how Ottoman, local, and British the Kuwait autonomy story is, we can move beyond it to abstract and see how many other Ottoman autonomy histories between 1878–1914 were, like Kuwait's, actually just reinterpretations of the Egypt model.

The goal of this chapter is to see the Egypt model in play, and to do this the bulk of the chapter will focus on the making of the autonomous district (*kaza*) of Kuwait in 1913, before discussing how what we see in Kuwait happened to one extent or another throughout Ottoman lands. Focusing on the period of the Second Constitutional Revolution (1908–1913), I argue that the empire was increasingly interconnected at the precise moment that we think of it as failing and breaking up before the storm of the First World War. In the critical and dramatic years before that war, the Ottoman Empire was being remade on the model of Egypt.

Ottoman rule arrived in Arabia in the sixteenth century by land and by sea, pushing its way in against regional and overseas empires.[5] Ottoman oversight spread slowly and unevenly across the area's Bedouin-dominated desert planes and dunes. Ottoman imperial power, if it was felt at all, was intermittent and concentrated in larger settlements and in rich ports that lined the coast from the Red Sea to the Gulf, like Jeddah, Aden, Doha, and Basra. Linked to the Indian Ocean trade through the networks of Sunni, Shia, and Jewish merchants, the eastern provinces of Arabia (al-Hasa, Kuwait, Bahrein) interested the world inasmuch as the pearls, dates, metal, and textiles on offer could entice. Otherwise, these lands were known as relatively unimportant subprovinces to Ottoman Iraq, a territory encompassing Mosul in the north, centrally located Baghdad, and Basra in the south.

Kuwait is located strategically on the northwestern coast of the Persian Gulf, adjacent to the Shatt al-Arab, the river where the Tigris and Euphrates meet and empty into the Gulf. In many ways the lands known now as Kuwait acted as the maritime border between Iraq and Iran. The Kuwaiti sheikdom was established in the early eighteenth century, and though it began as little more than a small fort on the Gulf coast, it quickly grew thanks to its role in advancing trade with overland caravan networks from Aleppo and Baghdad. As ships got bigger and heavier, Kuwait's importance expanded, too, as it boasts one of the best deep-water ports in the Gulf. Infrastructure is important, but most of Kuwait's wealth was not officially made; it was a hub for smuggling rather than for state projects. Its proximity to Basra, which was more tightly controlled, made it an ideal place to avoid the high Ottoman tariffs.[6] In essence, before the end of the nineteenth century, Kuwait prospered mostly because of how faint its connections to Istanbul were. It was Ottoman to an extent, but the looseness of the bond is what made Kuwait grow.

To date, the development of Ottoman Kuwait has been seen more as a family drama than a global one. In most versions of the story, the emergence of Kuwait is seen as the product of a scheming tribal family, the al-Sabah, who in the nineteenth and early twentieth centuries played the Ottomans and British against each other to solidify an independent state on the edge of both empires. There can be little doubt that local maneuverings had much to do with Kuwait's status within the empire, but the reality is far more complicated and more Ottoman-oriented than heretofore understood.

To understand how Kuwait became the pressing international legal question that brought İbrahim Hakkı Paşa to Claridge's Hotel in February 1913, it is necessary to chart all the work Ottoman administrators did to consolidate imperial control over the province in the late nineteenth century, all the local wrangling that thwarted it, and all the inroads the British tried to create to take advantage of the situation. In essence, Ibrahim Hakkı went to London because he had another Egypt fiasco on his hands. Except unlike Egypt, Kuwait had never been a global hotspot. How it became a flashpoint of international politics strangely enough begins with Ottoman efforts to foreground Kuwait within its imperial domains at the same time as protecting it from being internationalized. Though the al-Sabah family had dominated regional politics in the maritime lands between Iran and Iraq since the mid-eighteenth century, they only become global players capable of setting the Ottomans and British against each other with Midhat Paşa's "reconquest" of Ottoman Arabia in the early 1870s.

Ahmed Şefik Midhat Paşa (1822–1883) embodied the drive to "reconquest" Ottoman Arabia. Born in Istanbul to a religious family and shaped by a medrese education, Midhat was a *hafiz*, meaning he had memorized and could recite the Quran, by age ten. His father, who was from Ruse (Bulgaria), was posted as a religious judge in Vidin and Lofča (Bulgarian towns). Midhat's sense of "home" within Ottoman society was thus always imperial, never circumscribed by the metropole. He entered the imperial service in the mid-1830s and soon distinguished himself. Among his first appointments were secretarial postings in the Arab and Anatolian provinces, where he threw himself into projects for provincial reform and stamping out brigandage. Much like "the conqueror of Yemen," Ahmed Muhtar Paşa, mentioned in chapter 3, by the 1860s Midhat Paşa was frequently sent to hot spots around the empire—usually in the midst rebellion—to sort out what needed sorting. In essence he was one of the Ottomans' "imperial fixers." Mostly his tasks consisted of addressing grievances and implementing imperial reforms. What made him good at his job was that he promoted imperial norms while tailoring them to different local contexts. He was so good, in fact, that his star kept rising within imperial administration; he had important governorships in in Bulgaria, Iraq, and Syria, twice serve as grand vizier, and was generally regarded the leader of the constitutional movement in the empire.[7]

The reason for Midhat Paşa's success is easy to trace: Wherever he went in the empire, paved roads, electric lights, tramways, telegraph lines, model farms, and libraries followed in his wake.[8] His vision for a resurgent empire against an encroaching Europe was tied to his approach to imperial reorganization. First, he emphasized local economic development and imperial infrastructure as the best way to secure loyalty. In the Danube province (Tuna, today part of Bulgaria and Serbia), where he was posted just before Iraq, Midhat founded agricultural credit cooperatives that provided low-interest loans to peasants. In Baghdad, he argued that local discontent was caused by corrupt taxation and land tenure practices. Accordingly, he reduced the tax burden and implemented the Land Law of 1858, which required owners to register their land with the state. Within a relatively short span of time following Midhat's arrival, peasants were given title to land they cultivated without charge.[9]

Land was not the only thing Midhat thought needed fixing. He also replicated waterway initiatives he had instituted while working in the Balkans. Just as Ottoman steamer service networks had been expanded in the Danube under his supervision, now the Euphrates saw ever more puffs of smoke moving along its horizon. As Midhat had done in the Balkans, in Ottoman Iraq he saw the best way to strengthen Ottoman sovereignty against European incursion by increasing Ottoman-supervised trade with Europe and thereby increasing local, provincial wealth.

Wealth was one way to consolidate empire. Another was to promote subject loyalty. This Midhat believed was attainable through empire-sponsored educational initiatives. Just as he had done in the Danube province and would later do in Syria, in Iraq he established bilingual newspapers, libraries, military and secular schools. These schools did not service just one community; he pushed for the founding of many, including schools catering to Muslims and non-Muslims, again just as he had done in the Danube.[10]

Midhat Paşa's Ottoman stabilization plan on every level was geared to benefit the local in order to elucidate the importance of the imperial. He consistently argued that delegating governing responsibility to the provinces would strengthen the empire internally and act as a powerful bulwark against Europe. Like the imagined wealth and prosperity linked to infrastructure, local responsibility would give subjects a direct stake in the empire. To this end, he helped draft the 1864 Vilayet Law with Fuad Paşa, which created a hierarchical system of provinces throughout the empire.

Each vilayet was subdivided into smaller and smaller administrative units, from the *sancak*, to the *kaza*, to *nahiye* or villages, with each having a corresponding direct representative.[11] The law delegated enormous amounts of power to the *vali*, or provincial governor. It also permitted the creation of local counsels (composed of an equal number of Muslims and non-Muslims, at the province, sancak, kaza, and village levels). In theory, these counsels had control over where and how a portion of local tax revenue would be spent.

In many ways, what Midhat was trying to do in Ottoman Iraq was exactly what he had done in the Danube: consolidate state power through investment by enticing local buy-in through autonomy. But while pushing for good government in the rich Danube territories made sense because of a fear of wealth that would be lost, Iraq, especially its maritime regions, attracted his attention not for fear of losing a past treasure trove. Instead, he was appointed governor of the Baghdad province in 1869 to strengthen ties with "loose" territories because of the new promise and challenge they could represent.

Kuwait ticked all the boxes in Midhat's vision of a reformed empire. A natural deep-water harbor on the Persian Gulf that was linked to prosperous trade networks in Basra, Iran, the Indian Ocean, and the overland caravan routes solved a number of problems. An Ottoman port at Kuwait Harbor would generate much needed revenue. The Suez Canal, which had just opened in 1869, ensured a much higher volume of ships from the Red Sea and the Indian Ocean, which crisscrossed the Gulf between Iran and the Ottoman Empire and increased the value of Iraqi grain and dates. At the same time, Kuwait fit perfectly with the type of decentralized rule Midhat envisioned in the 1864 Vilayet Law. Local power would ensure loyalty at the fringes of the state. But most important, restamping Ottoman sovereignty on a territory that was once counted as a part of the imperial domains was part of an assertive strategy to shore up territorial claims across the empire, especially at the vulnerable edges in the age of increased imperialism.[12]

Midhat set his sights on bringing al-Hasa (al-Ahsa) and Kuwait back into the Ottoman fold because of where these lands lay: on the edges of the empire where British ambitions in the Gulf were growing. Midhat's job was to thwart British obtrusion as much as it was to Ottomanize Iraq. On paper, his plans seemed like they would do the job, that he could "fix" Iraq quickly within the multilayered centralizing impulses of the Ottoman state. But on the ground, something happened that no one had expected. Just as had been the case in Ottoman Egypt, local elites manipulated Ottoman reform efforts to create more power for themselves. And no family in the region did so more surprisingly than the Kuwaiti al-Sabah family.

In preparation to retake al-Hasa, Midhat approached the al-Sabah family, who had acted as local sheikhs and power brokers in the area since the eighteenth century, with a variety of inducements to throw their weight behind the Ottomans.[13] But this was much more than a strategic partnership to take back al-Hasa. From his experiences in the Balkans and the intelligence he had about Kuwaiti politics, Midhat knew that local cooperation could not be assumed; it needed to be forced. He compelled the al-Sabah family to deal with the state directly by seizing their date farms in Basra, which was one of the family's most prized sources of income.[14] The al-Sabah responded by insisting that they were long-time loyal subjects of the sultan and that Kuwait was part of the imperial domains. The family cleverly repackaged initial resistance to Ottoman reform initiatives (which included new custom duties) as methods used to placate local resistance, not as a form of elite resistance engineered by themselves. Midhat then did what he did everywhere and fit outlying Kuwait into his empire-wide scheme for provincial reorganization. He declared that Kuwait was a kaza attached to Basra, and codified sheikh Abdullah al-Sabah as the kaymakam of Kuwait. Claiming that he only wished to "protect" the district, he required no taxes to be paid into imperial coffers, and there would be no Ottoman customs official posted at the harbor. In return, all the usual trappings of Ottoman sovereignty were instituted in the district: An Ottoman flag flew over the kaymakam's dwelling, mosques invoked the name of the sultan at Friday prayers, and the kaymakan gave letters of appointment from the sultan to be distributed to new state officials.[15] Abdullah al-Sabah demonstrated loyalty to the state and provided troops to retake al-Hasa in 1871, as well as in subsequent conflicts in Basra and Qatar. In exchange for their military service, Midhat exempted the family date farm in Basra from taxes in perpetuity.[16]

From Kuwaiti Incorporation to Regional Crisis

Midhat's Ottoman plans for reform were animated by ideas about modernization, the needs of the imperial center, and global competition, which he tried to tailor to what the center thought the local needed. But what a center sees as the local needs and what locals themselves push for are not the same. Few cases could embody this point better than the Kuwaiti ruling family headed by gunrunners who had very different ideas of what best profited their local environment.

Until the mid-1890s, this strategy worked well. The compromise was institutionalized from above with just enough local control thrown in that everyone felt they could profit. Within just a quarter of a century Kuwait—the port and hinterland—entered a period of sustained economic and demographic growth. The town built on the harbor expanded well beyond its second fortified wall, its population nearly doubled in size, and trade increased thanks to Suez steamer traffic that bought American and European demand for the gemstones and luxury goods Kuwaiti merchants advertised.[17] Ever richer and more diverse merchants from India, Yemen, East Africa, and the Gulf endowed Kuwait with mosques and fountains.[18] It seemed to have worked as Midhat had envisioned. Then local politics showed just how reliant Ottoman power was on "local sovereignty" playing along as planned when in 1896 the Kuwaiti al-Sabah family was taken over by a new leader who refused to follow the rules in a way that only using the "Egypt model" could hope to control.

The source of this shift in Ottoman-Kuwait relations was someone Midhat had met toward the beginning of his Iraqi posting, Mubarak al-Sabah (1884–1915). From the little that is known about Mubarak's early life, there was little cause for Midhat to foretell Mubarak would destroy the balance he worked so hard to build. Mubarak was one of many sons, not the first or last; like his brothers, he was trained in military affairs and Islamic science. Starting with the Ottoman campaign in al-Hasa in 1871, he led local troops in Ottoman campaigns through the region to tame local factions. When he wasn't fighting on behalf of the empire, Mubarak was dispatched to the hinterland to manage tribal disputes, where he cultivated and maintained local Bedouin support. As expected, his older brother, Muhammad, inherited the Ottoman title of kaymakam and took control over the family sheikdom when his father died in 1891. Mubarak's role within the sheikdom was assumed to continue much as it had, just as Kuwait's role within the Ottoman Empire would.

This changed in 1896 when Mubarak led a palace coup, murdering his brothers in order to wrest the family's power into his own hands. The reasons are the same as in so many such situations—siblings checking each other's powers, alliances, lines in the sand. The consequences are what are important: Within a day the roles of Ottoman kaymakam and local sheikh were taken suddenly and without the slow protocols Ottoman practices preferred.[19] To legitimize his claims as kaymakam to the Ottoman state, Mubarak bribed and corrupted local and regional administrators and institutions to shift power toward himself. In Istanbul, the fallout was felt intensely, with other al-Sabah family members demanding that he be stripped of the title he killed so many in order to seize. They also brought suit in the Ottoman *nizamiye* (secular) and sharia courts to press their legal claim to family properties in Basra.[20] Midhat's 1870s fix of a balanced Ottoman-local sovereignty solution in the lands around Kuwait were unmoored by Mubarak's 1890s ambitions.

Once in power, Mubarak proved not just less predictable than his father; he was less accommodating to Ottoman stewardship as well. On one hand he operated within the administrative framework that Midhat had established in the 1870s. He managed his distant sovereign through recourse to imperial idioms—accepting honors, medals, and titles. But there was a constant push and pull, and Mubarak often rejected manifestations of state power that had any political or economic teeth. In 1899 he imposed local customs duties at the harbor on all goods, including those imported from neighboring Ottoman Basra—these duties swelled Mubarak's coffers, not Istanbul's. The Naval Ministry in turn sent an Ottoman harbor master, whom Mubarak simply blocked from assuming office.[21] The following year, like Colonel Ahmed Arabi in Egypt, the sultan offered Mubarak the title "paşa" and honors in exchange for a written testament to his submission to the state. Mubarak acceded to this request—why not? It was an extra title with no added imperial infringements. He also built a mosque in honor of Abdülhamid II near the port, which was completed in 1908.

Ottoman sovereignty in Kuwait for Mubarak was a perfectly tolerable thing if it was limited to a ceremonial facade, but it had a few strings attached. When required to aid in the slow incorporation of the kaza into the centralized imperial fold, Mubarak did not shy from frustrating Ottomans' plans. His political strategies were easy to read for all: consolidate his position, expand his power, either by working with the Ottomans or by backing Ottoman rivals in central Arabia. That is not to say that Ottoman sovereignty in Kuwait didn't matter. It did. As in Egypt, Ottoman sovereignty determined power relations on the ground and shaped justifications to rule. It gave the power broker—in this case the sheikh, in others the khedive, the prince, the Christian governor—local authority and legitimacy to collect taxes, demand corvée labor, and regulate markets. Falling under the penumbra of the Ottomans also provided a powerful tool for the sheikh against a rival empire.[22] Nevertheless, Mubarak was a wildcard who had rendered Midhat's solution vulnerable to the British.

"Kuwait Is Ottoman Territory"

How did a power broker at the furthest reaches of the state upset the balance of the empire? Why didn't the Ottomans simply depose Mubarak al-Sabah or resort to less savory ends that had worked in Arabia in the past? The answer is that Mubarak, just like the Egyptians governors before him, cultivated and eventually won British support. He did not become a British pawn in Ottoman clothing. Instead, he played both sides off each other. As one Ottoman statesman put it in 1911, he followed "a double-faced policy."[23]

Just as he kept his obligations to the sultan at a minimum, he similarly used his status as an Ottoman kaymakam to limit British interference in Kuwait. Until the First World War, for Mubarak, Kuwait staying in the Ottoman Empire brought far more benefits than "independence" under British control, and being under "British protection" brought more of autonomy that Ottoman Kuwaiti demanded.

Ever since the opening of the Suez Canal, British colonial administrators had been eager to curb Ottoman expansion and centralization in the Gulf; British India relied on a Red Sea and Suez subservient to the empire's trade and security needs. Ottoman consolidation in the Gulf, especially around the ports, threatened that. When Mubarak threw Kuwait into a new "no-man's land" of coup and court cases, the time seemed ripe to put a British oar in. Mubarak made the first move. He sought out a meeting with the British Resident in Bushehr—a branch of the Government of India and the locus of British power in the Gulf. Rumor had it that the sheikh wanted to put Kuwait under British protection on the model of "Bahrein and Trucial Chiefs." British officials were astonishingly well aware of the al-Sabah local drama, from the family lawsuits, to the bribes Mubarak paid to Ottoman officials, to the money to be gained through securing the Ottoman title. Mubarak's spectacular seizure of power prompted a blistering debate between the Foreign Office and the Government of India. British lawyers and colonial officials clashed over Kuwait's legal status—was the port Ottoman? Or was Mubarak an "independent Arab Chief" who could be treated like the sheikhs in Aden and the Trucial States? When Mubarak explicitly asked for the same deal the British had offered the Trucial States, the Foreign Office refused. Perhaps to Mubarak's disappointment, British officials replied that such a deal was impossible as Kuwait was part of the Ottoman domains.[24]

But the story did not end there. The British were not the only imperial rivals who envisioned Kuwait harbor as a moneymaker. Plans soon emerged for Kuwait as the terminus of two different European financed railway schemes, each of which would connect far-flung provinces to this new Suez on the Gulf. Even before Sultan Abdülhamid II granted a concession to the German-owned Anatolian Railway Company for the Baghdad Railway in the fall of 1899, Kuwait harbor was the terminus most imagined for the project. The threat of a rival railway to British shipping in the Gulf prompted the Foreign Office to finally allow the Government of India to proceed with hammering out a secret protection agreement with Mubarak.

Secret agreements serve many purposes; they create a plan of action without any securities in that plan's future. On January 23, 1899, a low-level British official carried out this vague diplomacy between Kuwait and the British Empire; each signed a contract that that no other empire would bother to recognize. Mubarak agreed "not to cede, see, lease, mortgage, or give occupation or for any other purpose, any portion of his territory to the Government or subjects of any other power without the previous consent of Her Majesty's Government."[25] In return, Britain provided a cash payment of 15,000 rupees and offered "good offices of the British government towards you, your heirs, and successors."[26] Mubarak wanted more than the British were willing to offer: He wanted a written declaration and a "definite promise of protection" as well as the explicit assurance that his legal claim to the family estates in Basra would be safeguarded.[27] But in internal correspondence, the British were clear.[28] What they offered Mubarak was not a protectorate, it was nothing more than a placeholder to cover the what-ifs of global capitalism where predatory concession hunters and plans for infrastructural projects abounded. As one Indian Office civil servant framed the problem, "We don't want Koweit [*sic*], but we don't want anyone else to have it."[29] The agreement would supply the legal rationale for a future British claim to Kuwait should any other power try to absorb it into its orbit.

While the British and Mubarak tried to keep the agreement secret, Istanbul learned of Mubarak's perfidy almost immediately, and soon after, when German engineers and surveyors descended on Kuwait harbor, the British ambassador was forced to admit that the empire had an agreement with Mubarak that would prevent them from agreeing to the Baghdad railway extending to Kuwait. In 1902 the Ottomans and the British agreed to recognize the "status quo" in Kuwait. The British would not declare a protectorate, and the Ottomans would stop sending troops and other methods of establishing "effective control" over the territory. But this didn't stop Britain and the Ottoman Empire from engaging in a furtive battle over the control of Kuwait. The Ottomans sent troops, a harbor master, quarantine officials, telegraph lines, medals, and titles to Mubarak. The British worked to undermine Ottoman claims to sovereignty in Kuwait by flooding the harbor with British vessels, extending the Government of India Residency system to Kuwait, sending an official representative, and erecting a quarantine station. British officials even tried to redesign the Ottoman flag that flew over Mubarak's palace and created Kuwaiti "nationality" documents, printed in English and Arabic for use on Kuwaiti boats. Colonial officials didn't trust that Mubarak would really go all-in with them instead of an Ottoman-Kuwait plan, so they made the new flag and nationality certificates of their own initiative, providing all the emblems of separation before the separation had actually occurred.[30]

Mubarak, like the khedives of Egypt, gained much from the Ottoman-British clash over sovereignty in Kuwait. The 1899 protection agreement with the British, together with the uneasy truce between London and Istanbul in 1902, unleashed Mubarak. He bought a car and a yacht. He transformed the simple stone structure that had been the kaymakam's residence into a proper palace.[31] According to Ottoman reports, Mubarak ran Martini rifles through the port, which made their way into the personal arsenal of Bedouins across the peninsula. The same reports argued that he inflamed regional rivalries and encouraged brigandage. The deputy from Baghdad cast him as a thug and thief who robbed everyone.[32] To fund his military adventures, Mubarak imposed new taxes on everything from the pilgrimage to Mecca, to housing construction and pearling.[33] He demanded the British support his property rights in Basra, while at the same time refusing to take on Ottoman nationality to secure those same rights. The dormancy of the Ottoman-British legal tug-of-war over Kuwait created much of the vacuum that allowed Mubarak's ambitions to run wild.

That legal battle was reignited in early 1911. The direct impetus appears to have come from a series of biting articles published in a widely read Istanbul paper that disparaged British policy in the Gulf. Much had changed in the Ottoman Empire between 1902 and 1911: A new generation of leaders had taken over the state. In July 1908 a military coup led by the Committee of Union and Progress (CUP) forced Sultan Abdülhamid II to reinstate the Ottoman Constitution of 1876. Early euphoria gave way to bitter political debates in the capital and provinces on the meaning of the constitution, the rule of law, and how best to save the empire in the face of an increasingly hostile Europe. By 1911, the constitutional experiment was fractured. Abdülhamid II had been forced to abdicate, and the CUP was in control of the government, though it faced a splintered but growing opposition. The ruling party believed that imperial regeneration could only be achieved through centralization and making state power palpable evenly throughout the imperial domains. This meant rolling roll back the very privileges and administrative exceptions that had helped Ottoman Kuwait flourish and British power-grabs lie dormant. While Britain feigned support for the new constitutional regime, the reality was that the CUP's determination to extend the reach of the state made the colonial government uneasy. The series of articles that sparked a new legal battle over Kuwait were directly in line with CUP attacks against prior Ottoman practices of extending authority, in order to shore it up. In short, the articles, entitled the "Iraq Letters," accused prior Ottoman practices of helping the British to destroy Ottoman sovereignty in the Gulf.

The "Iraq Letters" attacking Ottoman–British collusion in the Gulf were not the work of underground yellow journalism. Instead, they appeared in *Tanin*, the semiofficial newspaper of the ruling CUP party, and their author was none other than the Istanbul-trained international lawyer and Ottoman deputy from Baghdad, Babanzade İsmail Hakkı.[34] Babanzade's letters created such a stir because of how grounded they were in "witnessing" the ills of autonomy. Their content was based on his 1908 inspection tour of Iraq and the Gulf, and throughout he showed how Britain undermined Ottoman sovereignty at every opportunity.[35] Whether through steamship concessions, control of telegraph lines, or the postal service, Babanzade emphasized how little room there was for effective

Ottoman imperial governance because of British companies' control of the region's major infrastructure. Kuwait's "particular" triad of power brokers emblematized much of what he saw as Britain's successful whittling down of Ottoman power in the Gulf. As he put it:

> There is no writer on international law who could define the political position of Kuwait. Officially it is a kaza, and the sheikh, Mubarak al-Sabah, bears a purely Ottoman title, that of paşa, and he flies an Ottoman flag as a sign of allegiance. But there is, nevertheless, a doubt about his position in practice. Until seven or eight years ago Kuwait had been Ottoman without any doubt; but pressure was brought to bear upon it by a jealous chief, who took refuge with the English. . . . Kuwait is from our point of view, Ottoman territory without any doubt. . . . How can the expressions "Ottoman sovereignty" and "English Harbor" be reconciled?[36]

The question was a rhetorical one, of course. Babanzade's "Iraq Letters" argued once and for all that compromises like Kuwait could not continue as they had. "Ottoman sovereignty" could not reign within an "English Harbor." And Mubarak needed to be put in his place for helping to put this in action in the first place. Babanzade ended one of his articles asking, "Are these acts of brigandage to remain forever unpunished? Is a petty sheikh to have an authority which not even the greatest emperors possess in our time?" The answer to all this was a clear "No." Things had to change.

Babanzade's article fomented a broader debate in the Istanbul press about the compatibility of sovereignty and administrative autonomy in the Gulf.[37] Hüseyin Cahid (Yalçın), the editor-in-chief of *Tanin* and mouthpiece of CUP policy, condemned Britain for weakening international law by undermining treaties with the Ottomans.[38] He insisted that autonomy and imperial sovereignty were in no way irreconcilable, what was irreconcilable was how the British were trying to work around it. Quoting extensively from Lord Curzon's *Persia and the Persian Question* (1892), Hüseyin Cahid showed how the architect of Britain's aggressive policy in the Gulf had explicitly recognized Ottoman sovereignty in Kuwait.[39] Moreover, he emphasized that "Kuwait's attainment of certain privileges and exceptions is no proof that Ottoman sovereignty over Kuwait has expired. There are places in all parts of the imperial domains that are privileged, and their exceptional position has never meant the lapse of Ottoman sovereignty. . . . By treaty and by law, Kuwait is Ottoman territory."[40] What was wrong in all this wasn't Kuwait's administrative autonomy nor Ottoman rights to claim sovereignty over these lands, it was the corruption of this system promoted through Britain and Mubarak's secret treaty. It wasn't just *Tanin* that weighed in on the debate, the liberal opposition papers, too, denounced British policy in Kuwait. What has the solution? For Hüseyin Cahid, it was lawfulness and respect for treaties on the part of Britain. For Babanzade and others, the only way to resolve Britain's underhanded imperialism was to bring the full weight of state to the periphery.

The articles in *Tanin* whipped up Ottoman concern over the Gulf, and the Iraqi province more broadly, but they also triggered a British response. When the Foreign Office first learned about the articles in early 1911, British official and commercial representatives in Istanbul were quick to meet with the grand vizier, İbrahim Hakki Paşa, to understand the state's official position. Articles appeared almost immediately in the *Times of London* refuting Babanzade and casting doubt on Ottoman sovereignty in the Kuwait and the Gulf.[41] Internally, the British viewed the CUP as dangerous because it wanted to make Ottoman sovereignty concrete and unquestionable. To nip these ambitions in the bud, British officials manufactured new criteria for sovereignty. In the same way that the CUP wanted Ottoman sovereignty to have the teeth of state policing power, the British began to argue that this was precisely what was missing from the Ottoman claim to Kuwait: "Turkey can point to no real act of sovereignty in Koweit [*sic*], e.g., levying of taxes or direct administration in any form," and thus Ottoman claims were as "preposterous" as were any land claims built on sixteenth-century titles without twentieth-century lived governance.[42]

Reminiscent of the "Principle of Effective Occupation" hashed out at the Berlin Conference of 1884–85 that set as legal precedent that the empire would only be respected if it governed "effectively," the British response to the "Iraq Letters" reversed earlier stances on the geopolitical situation of Kuwait. Before, Ottoman sovereignty over Kuwait went unquestioned because it was part of the empire. Now, the British tried to shift understandings of Kuwait as "colonial," thereby opening up the possibilities of incursion if not "run" effectively. In short, as Kuwait did not have direct Ottoman administration, it was not Ottoman.

In a strange twist, both the CUP and the British seemed to agree that Kuwait could not continue "above and between" empires. But which way would the issue be resolved? Full Ottoman centralization or British protectorate? The task of renegotiating the "Kuwait question" fell to İbrahim Hakkı Paşa, the famed international lawyer with whom this chapter began. As we know, İbrahim Hakki was not just the longtime chief legal advisor at the Foreign Ministry, he was also one of the principal architects of the entire system of Ottoman statecraft that had engineered the Egypt solution of imperial autonomy. The same lawyer who wrote hundreds of legal opinions that outlined a strategy to assert Ottoman sovereignty against British encroachments in Egypt, Sudan, and Hejaz was now tasked as the principal Ottoman negotiator in what led up to the 1913 "Anglo-Ottoman Convention" determining Kuwait's legal status.[43]

When he arrived in London in 1913, İbrahim Hakkı Paşa had one goal. With new territorial losses in the Libya and the Balkans, he had to reinforce Ottoman sovereignty and prevent more ground from being lost at the edges of the empire.[44] Despite the fact that the empire was at its weakest point internationally since the Mehmed Ali episode in 1840–41, Hakkı Paşa showed up at the British Foreign Office with big asks. Not only did he request a binding agreement in which Britain would recognize Ottoman sovereignty in Kuwait, he also requested correctives for much of what the "Iraq Letters" had denounced. Among his polite demands: a raise in Ottoman customs duties from 12 to 15 percent, the complete dismantling of the European postal system within the Ottoman Empire, and the abolition of the Capitulations. Even though most considered the Ottoman Empire at its knees in 1913, Hakkı Paşa showed up in London like Bismarck at Versailles. This was precisely why the CUP, which had just overthrown the elected government in Istanbul, chose him to negotiate with Britain. Like Fuad, Midhat, and Ahmed Muhtar, İbrahim Hakkı not only knew how to play the European international law game; he had helped to craft it. He expected that Britain would claim to have to defer to the other powers and couldn't possibly commit to any of his demands that would alter the legal "status quo" between states. But he also realized that this would make recognizing Kuwait as Ottoman, without fundamentally altering the order of things locally, a relatively easy feat to give instead.

The gambit worked. Reports were written, lawyers were asked to weigh in on the idea, and British officials sputtered on about how impossible it was to even begin to imagine that the Capitulations, "those ancient laws," could be abolished. Throughout the negotiations, the Finance Office was prepared for talks to fail and for İbrahim Hakkı to be recalled from the London. But the CUP government in Istanbul did no such thing. Hakkı kept pushing, and to preserve Ottoman *amour-propre*, the Kuwait question seemed a small thing to relent on to avoid bigger rifts on the international scene.

By late March 1913, the Foreign Office and İbrahim Hakkı Paşa had worked out a draft declaration on Kuwait and Persian Gulf, along with various railway and steamship concessions in Anatolia and the Arabian Peninsula. They secretly discussed expanding Egypt's borrowing power. In essence, the "Kuwait question" was resolved by imposing the same autonomy model the two powers had hashed out in Egypt.

There were two stumbling blocks for closing the Anglo–Ottoman Convention with an Egypt solution, and they hinged on words and titles. The first problem was around the age-old question of how to define "sovereignty." Britain was willing to concede that the sultan was the "suzerain" power in Kuwait, but not the "sovereign power." As we have seen, Ottoman lawyers were extremely well versed in the difference between these terms and pushed for European recognition of Ottoman "sovereign rights" throughout the empire—often successfully. In earlier days, Foreign Office lawyers were willing to go along with this usage, and their own lawyers conceded that the Ottomans were right to argue that "suzerainty" implied a diminution of "sovereignty." A suzerain power was less than fully sovereign. The Foreign Office, however, refused to recognize Ottoman "sovereignty" in Kuwait.[45] The first draft of the agreement read, "Great Britain and Turkey recognize Koweit [*sic*], as defined in Article 4 of this agreement, as the autonomous sheikhdom under the suzerainty of Turkey." To this, İbrahim Hakkı remained intractable; he would not accept anything less than sovereignty. After another month of haggling, the draft declaration was changed to "the territory of Kuwait, as delimited in Articles 5 and 7 of this convention, constituted an autonomous kaza of the Ottoman Empire."[46] The solution was twofold: If the British refused to use the word sovereignty, the Ottomans would refuse the words suzerain and "sheikhdom," as they implied a diminished sovereign link to the center. Both words would be dropped and replaced with the malleable and magical word "autonomy."[47]

The second big stumbling block in the negotiations involved how Britain would sell Ottoman autonomy to Mubarak. İbrahim Hakkı Paşa insisted that Kuwait should have an Ottoman high commissioner (*fevkalade*), just like Ahmed Muhtar Paşa in Egypt. The British didn't push back very hard on this demand. From an Ottoman perspective, the high commissioner was far more than a symbol of Ottoman sovereignty. He was the man on the spot. A high commissioner kept tabs on locals, supplied critical information to the palace and Foreign Ministry, and could be counted on to smooth out problems to keep local power brokers in check. For the Ottomans, the high commissioner was as much of a physical manifestation of the state as a telegraph office or a railway station. The British accepted the idea of an Ottoman representative in Kuwait but insisted that the position would have to be reduced from a high commissioner to an "Ottoman agent."

It was the local Kuwait triad of this dispute that caused problems in this issue, not the British or the Ottomans. Mubarak understood that any official Ottoman presence in Kuwait would limit the free hand he had carved out for himself since 1902. British diplomatic reports explained that "Mubarak accepted Ottoman supremacy but on the question of a Turkish agent in Koweit [*sic*] he expressed with the utmost strength and vehemence his absolute refusal to permit it." At the heart of it, Mubarak, sickened by illness and seeing how international accords were threatening to upset the cozy arrangement he had helped create, accused the British of selling him out. It wasn't "Ottoman autonomy," per se, that he minded. He'd been playing that game for a while, and it didn't cost him much. The shift he refused to accept was the posting of an Ottoman high commissioner. He explained to any British official who would listen that the only reason he had signed a protective agreement with the British in the first place was "expressly as a defense against this contingency." The British kept Mubarak's refusal to accept an Ottoman agent from İbrahim Hakkı. Ultimately, the Foreign Office deferred to Ottoman over local wishes, and Mubarak's resistance was ignored. Empires ended the matters as they saw fit; local maneuvers had to work within imperial bounds.

On July 29, 1913, Lord Grey and İbrahim Hakkı Paşa finally signed the Anglo-Ottoman Agreement on the Persian Gulf. Kuwait became an internationally recognized autonomous kaza of the Ottoman Empire.[48] Autonomy now was less fluid, less secret, less flexible than Mubarak had liked it. Instead, it was directly modeled on what the Ottomans and British had done in Egypt. Like the khedives, Istanbul would extend complete local administrative rights to the sheikh, without any interference from the imperial center. The al-Sabah's reign within Ottoman strictures was made hereditary. The family estates in Basra were recognized as private property and would be protected under Ottoman law. British special agreements in Kuwait were upheld. Ottoman high commissioners were introduced. Kuwait continued to work much as first Midhat and then Mubarak had planned, with the one big difference: Now all these compromises and concessions were not piecemeal, secret, or "above and between" empires. Instead they were hammered into internal agreement and law, just as Egypt had been.

How to Govern an Empire: Autonomy During the Second Constitutional Era

During the Second Constitutional era, the Ottoman state repeatedly offered some form of autonomy to provincial rebels to suspend disorder and stave off direct European intervention. Despite their deserved reputation as uncompromising centralizers, the Committee of Union and Progress presided over the largest extension of administrative autonomy in the empire since the Treaty of Berlin in 1878—in Kuwait, Yemen, Libya, the six eastern provinces (Armenia), and Najd, while the liberal opposition offered "privileged administration" to Albania. Each of these cases was forced by circumstances of war, rebellion, and the threat of intervention. In some, autonomy was a stop-gap measure to preserve Ottoman sovereignty against nationalist and European imperialist claims, but every instance demonstrated that it was part of the inventory of Ottoman administrative options. Moreover, it was not only the peripheral magnates who agitated for autonomy. In the new era of constitutionalism, everyday imperial subjects made the case for extending different forms of autonomy to the provinces. While some historians have understood agitation for autonomy in the Ottoman world in nationalist terms, the reality is far more complex. Autonomy had become a tool of Ottoman governance—one that was available to state officials, just as it was to provincial power brokers and imperial subjects.

This is important to remember for many reasons. First, understanding the motives and missions of the CUP remains difficult if the decentralizing, autonomy model of Ottoman statecraft is not foregrounded. When the Young Turk Revolution erupted in July 1908, the most enduring and contentious issue between political factions concerned imperial administration and how best to strengthen the empire against internal crises and external foes. There were two main administrative options on the table. The first, supported by the CUP, was centralization. As in Kuwait, the state had to be felt everywhere. "Union" (*ittihad*) meant terminating all forms of privilege that drew legal, political, or administrative distinctions between subjects.

Publicly, the CUP denounced autonomy in all its forms. For Unionists, decentralization, federalism, and devolution of authority evoked the privileged provinces and European restrictions on Ottoman sovereignty. Members of the CUP, their party publications, and political programs insisted that the main purpose of the organization was to protect the "complete sovereignty and independence of the state" (*tamami-i mülkiyenin muhafazası*).[49] Centralization and internal development were the only means to preserve the "territorial integrity" of the empire in the international arena. The era of relying on great power territorial guarantees had passed. The prevalence of the autonomy system was precisely why the CUP modeled itself as a revolution against dominant and existing patterns of Ottoman governance.[50]

The other reason why the CUP painted itself as revolutionary was that it was not the only political option in 1908. There was an opposition, made up primarily of liberal-oriented statesmen and lawyers who supported decentralization (*adem-i merkeziyet*) and wanted to expand the autonomy solution. Culminating in the Freedom and Accord Party (Hürriyet ve İtilaf Fırkası) in 1911, this group was composed largely of the different minority religious and ethnic groups of the empire, as well as ethnic Turks, who argued that administrative decentralization would cultivate a true sense of imperial belonging, strengthen the state, and forestall separatist movements.[51] There was no single agreed on vision for administrative autonomy in the Second Constitutional period—some liberals invoked the privileged provinces as a model for imperial reorganization, but many others explicitly disavowed that association. But no matter what side of the debate Ottomans found themselves on, the privileged provinces based on Egypt were a lightning rod as each side hashed out the virtues and harms of autonomy.

Even before the 1908 Revolution, the major fault line dividing the various groups in opposition to Abdülhamid II was drawn starkly along administrative lines and the method for initiating a constitutional revolution.[52] At the Congress of Ottoman Liberals held in Paris in 1902, two clear factions emerged. One side was led by Prince Sabahaddin—a

European-trained sociologist and Abdülhamid II's nephew—who favored administrative decentralization, including extending autonomy to the six eastern provinces, and British intervention to effect regime change at home. Sabahaddin looked to the British Empire as a model of imperial organization and governance and argued that imperial unity could be forged only through accommodating religious and ethnic difference. On the other side, Ahmed Rıza led what would emerge as the CUP and argued in favor of centralization and internal development while flatly rejecting Great Power intervention—revolution had to be stimulated from within. Sabahaddin established the Society for Private Initiative and Decentralization (Teşebbüs-i Şahsi ve Adem-i Merkeziyet Cemiyeti) to promote his ideas and would play a leading role in the opposition to the CUP through the end of the empire.[53] These early fault lines became even more entrenched with the outbreak of revolution.[54]

It is almost impossible to understand the rancor with which the CUP and the various iterations of the opposition fought over the methods of imperial administration between 1908 and 1913 without recognizing how the existing option of autonomy weighed on the debates. Hüseyn Cahid—the owner of *Tanin* (The Clarion), which functioned as the CUP's main press organ—and Sabahaddin and his supporters clashed over the meaning and implications of centralization versus decentralization, and it was the words that mattered. By 1908, autonomous administration (*idare-i mümtaze*) meant something very specific, and no matter how much opposition figures insisted their decentralizing schemes were distinct from the privileged provinces, CUP writers accused the liberal opposition of acting as handmaidens to Great Power intervention and imperial dissolution.

In a series of dueling newspaper editorials in September 1908, following a speech by Sabahaddin that announced his political program, Ali Kemal—a member of the liberal opposition—drew a sharp line between autonomy and decentralization.[55] He noted, "Decentralization (*adem-i merkeziyet*) is one thing, autonomy (*muhtariyet*) is another."[56] To emphasize the distinction, Ali Kemal included the French word alongside the Ottoman and insisted that anyone with the slightest knowledge of administrative procedure would understand the distinction. Ali Kemal believed that the British Empire offered the best model of administrative organization for the Ottomans. "Private initiative" and the "devolution of responsibility" (*tevsi-i mezuniyet*), which transferred governing power from London to the far-flung provinces, were the secret to British strength and wealth.[57]

He noted that when "the nationalist faction, which they called imperialist," tried to exert more central control over the settler colonies—Canada, South Africa, Australia, and New Zealand—it backfired: "What does decentralization have to do with this issue? Canada and Australia already have full administrative autonomy; centralization cannot be applied to decentralization!"[58]

Despite his insistence that autonomy and decentralization were distinct ideas, invoking the relationship between the British settler colonies and London and casting them as autonomous provinces would not have been lost on Ottoman readers. The comparison between the settler colonies and the Ottoman autonomous provinces remained durable. Ali Kemal claimed further that the Ottomans already tested these ideas under Midhat Paşa's administrative experiments in Bulgaria and Baghdad—they were not a foreign import, but part of the existing range of imperial practices. Midhat Paşa was the "shining example of decentralization" at work: "Did he ask the center to spend more than five thousand piastres, to build roads and schools, or even to operate those trams and steamboats?"[59] The central government delegated local governing powers to Midhat Paşa, and he not only incorporated Ottoman Iraq into the central state, he addressed the needs of locals, improved infrastructure, and increased provincial wealth.[60]

Like Ali Kemal, Sabahaddin argued that Ottoman centralizers had confused the meaning of decentralization with autonomy. In his speeches and writings, he repeatedly made the point that "decentralization is not autonomy."[61] He stressed that the only way to save the empire was through "sincere unity between Muslims and our Christian citizens" and that "none of the elements constituting the Ottoman Empire, regardless of race or sect, such as Greeks, Armenians, Bulgarians, etc., should pursue administrative autonomy or political independence."[62] Centralization crushed enterprise and private initiative (*şahs-i teşebbüs*). In contrast, decentralization would connect "Ottomans to the Ottoman state" and suppress "nationalistic rivalries," expand national trade, act as a bulwark against foreign powers, and cultivate "global friendship." Citizens in the capital and villagers in the provinces should understand where and how their taxes are spent. In short, decentralization offered a stake in local and imperial politics to all Ottomans, as well as legitimacy to the new constitutional government, and could mitigate differences of geography, ethnicity, and language.[63]

Hüseyn Cahid was completely unconvinced and relentlessly attacked Ali Kemal and Prince Sabahaddin in the pages of *Tanin*. He too focused on words and their misinterpretation. Hüseyn Cahid had no problem with the devolution of authority (*tevsi-i mezuniyet*), since it was already embedded in the constitution—Article 108 assured that provincial administration would be implemented according to the principle of devolution, which reflected Midhat Paşa's provincial reforms and established local administrative councils at the provincial, sancak, and kaza levels.[64] The problem was the idea of decentralization, which "must necessarily imply greater authority than that outlined in the constitution"—why else include it in the party program?[65] He argued that the "term 'decentralization' has been specifically included in the program to be understood as a form of autonomous administration."[66] In other words, Sabahaddin Bey renounced administrative autonomy to distinguish his political program from those citizens making precisely this demand, but also to make it more agreeable to people who would otherwise reject autonomy. Decentralization was a Trojan horse for autonomy—something Sabahaddin's supporters would recognize, especially autonomist parties and groups.[67]

The debate between the CUP and the liberal opposition on administration never abated, as every parliamentary discussion on provincial administration reignited the fight. By far the most dramatic episode occurred during the brief period when the CUP was in the opposition and the Freedom and Accord Party controlled the government (July 1912–January 1913). Since 1909, the Albanian provinces (İşkodra, Yanya, Kosova, Monastır) had been in revolt against the CUP, clamoring not for independence but for autonomy within the empire.[68] Albanian demands shifted during the revolution but centered on questions of language and education policy, military service, and the recognition of local customary law.[69] The leading political figure of the Albanian autonomist movement was İsmail Kemal Bey (1844–1919).[70] He was a loyal state bureaucrat who had served as governor of Beirut (1891–92) and thus had firsthand knowledge of differences between Beirut and neighboring Mount Lebanon, governed by the Organic Regulations. He participated in the 1902 Ottoman Congress of Liberals and sided with Sabahaddin and broadly supported autonomy for different ethnic groups in the empire. Throughout the Second Constitutional era, İsmail Kemal Bey argued that the privileged provinces functioned as a model and offered an empire wide solution to the centrifugal problem of nationalism.[71] In

1911 he was one of the authors of the Albanian autonomy decree, known as the Gerche Memorandum or the Red Book. Among other things, he demanded recognition of Albanian ethnicity, proportional representation in parliament, local Albanian schools and language instructions, amnesty for rebels, and the return of weapons, and that Albanian soldiers serve in Albanian provinces during peacetime.[72] While the rebellion roiled on, Albanians again demanded autonomy and submitted a fourteen-point program to execute their vision. On August 10, 1912, the Liberal Party, under the leadership of Ahmed Muhtar Paşa—the old Ottoman high commissioner of Egypt—accepted twelve of the fourteen points put forward by the rebels.

Just after the government agreed to Albanian demands, Hüseyn Cahid wrote a scorching editorial against the government and the problem of autonomy within the empire. Once the liberals agreed to special privileges in the Albanian provinces, it would be impossible to withhold the same offer for "Syria, Iraq, Kurdistan, Armenia, and the Aegean Islands." Differential rights and privileges attached to people or provinces cut against the CUP's efforts to create political unity by ensuring every citizen enjoyed the same "political rights" and respected "the same law." Extending privileges to people and provinces based on ethnicity eroded the empire's purpose. If every imperial domain could "organize itself according to its race (*ırk*)" where each territory has "their own language, their own laws, and their own armies," what would remain of Ottoman unity? Decentralization undercut the possibly of creating a strong government and threatened to eviscerate the state:

> It could be said that since the Ottomans are composed of different races, let them have administrative autonomy (*muhtariyet-i idareye*) based on the principle of decentralization (*adem-i merkeziyet*), what harm would that do? If we had forgotten the evidence of history, we might have been somewhat deceived by this argument. However, until now, every piece of land that has been taken from the homeland started out as a privileged administration or autonomous province (*idare-i mümtaze, vilayet-i muhtara*) and eventually gained independence and separated from us. Therefore, extending the privileges granted to Albania to other regions and applying the principle of decentralization would be tantamount to tearing our country apart with our own hands.[73]

Hüseyn Cahid was now explicit. Decentralization, provincial privileges, autonomous administration, and special privileges encouraged separatist impulses and would allow nationalism to obliterate the empire. This was not simply a matter of policy differences between political parties. The Freedom and Accord Party was trying to destroy not just Committee of Union and Progress, "but the homeland and the country, the Turkish sultanate and the Ottoman government." This intense bitterness toward the liberals and the abiding suspicion that decentralization was indistinguishable from autonomy, and thus a steppingstone to independence and imperial dissolution, was emblematic of CUP attitudes toward any form of privilege for people or provinces.

After the start of the First Balkan War in October 1912, Albanian demands shifted from autonomy within the empire to independence. Like so many other ethnic and religious minorities in the empire who resented the CUP's centralization policies, İsmail Kemal Bey argued that Albanians had understood "union" as the association of nationalities to strengthen the empire by "guaranteeing to each its national existence," but the CUP "only thought of uniting all the different races by forcing them to deny their origin." He authored the Albanian declaration of independence and acted as the state's first prime minister.[74] Albania declared its independence on November 28, 1912, the day before the government offered it privileged administration (*idare-i mümtaze*).[75]

These were not simply debates about Ottoman citizens knowing where their tax dollars would be spent and having a stake in local politics. From the start of the Second Constitutional era, autonomy was a battleground between empires and imperial subjects. Over three consecutive days in October 1908, just three months after Abdülhamid II reinstated the constitution, three privileged provinces, all managed by the Office of Autonomous and Special Provinces, exited the empire. On October 5 Autonomous Bulgaria declared its independence, Austria-Hungary annexed Bosnia and Herzegovina—which was under military occupation since 1878 but recast as a privileged province after Berlin—and autonomous Crete declared union (*enosis*) with Greece.[76] Unionists and many liberals, though not all, opposed these declarations and fought against them through economic boycott, public protest, and resorting to the now well-worn route of diplomatic complaint grounded in international law.[77] Despite the treaty guarantees and fermans that bound each of the provinces to the empire, the European powers opted not to intervene in defense of broken treaties.[78]

Autonomous Crete offers a case in point. The "Creten Question" roiled the capital and sparked waves of protests in Istanbul and the wider empire.[79] Newspaper editorials, public speeches, and parliamentary debates demanded urgent protections for Muslim subjects in Crete, refused to accept territorial separation, and insisted on the terms of Crete's special status. Crete's status as a privileged province, guaranteed by treaty in international law and in imperial edicts, drove part of the debate and fueled public outrage against the separatists in Crete and against the guaranteeing European powers.[80] In the spring of 1909, none other İbrahim Hakkı Paşa debated the matter in parliament. He insisted that that the government's policy remained as it was at the beginning of the crisis, which was to preserve of the international and domestic ensuring agreements Crete's status: "Crete is a special province under the sovereignty of His Majesty the Sultan. The Sublime State has accepted this administrative autonomy and does not intend to take Crete. The rights of the Muslim population in Crete will be fully preserved and are fully guaranteed by the states." The fact that the Great Powers did not adhere to the agreements governing Crete's status, while the Ottoman had done so, produced intense anger across the empire, and not only among Muslims. Pamphlets and editorials recounted Crete's recent history and insisted that "the overwhelming desire of the majority of the population was summed up in their own words as "autonomy under Ottoman rule" (*Osmanlı idaresi altında muhtariyet*).[81]

The Office of Privileged Provinces, too, anticipated Crete's return to the imperial fold. A memorandum on reorganization of the office in 1908 explained that as the unjust annexation of Bosnia and Herzegovina to Austria and the recognition of Bulgaria reduced staffing, there was simply less work. But "as the state's sovereignty over the island of Crete is soon to be secured by divine grace, the administrative work will become even more important and the correspondence will increase, so it will be necessary to employ a few more clerks for this purpose."[82]

The debates in the imperial capital over centralization and decentralization were mirrored in CUP critiques emanating from the Arab provinces. Indeed, some of the most stubborn clashes between the central government and the Arab provinces during the Second Constitutional era centered on the rights of local to determine—or at least have a say in—economic, educational, and legal policies in a way that conformed to needs of the province. From Jerusalem's criticism of Zionist immigration to Ottoman Palestine, to Baghdad's rage against British concessions for steamship navigation on the Tigris and Euphrates and Syrian criticism against the CUP's language policies, provincial leaders wanted a say in determining how they were governed. In each case, the critique contended that the central government couldn't fully comprehend nor counter the manifold iterations of European intervention in the provinces. Only locals, who were better informed, could create the necessary bulwark to increasingly nefarious forms of economic and political interference.[83] In Mount Lebanon, subjects were further divided over the how to approach new constitutional regime. Many worried that the Organic Regulations (*Règlement Organique*), which guaranteed Lebanon's special administrative status, could be dismantled by centralizing bureaucrats in Istanbul and result in the loss of local privilege.[84] Shakib Arslan, the Druze prince and Islamist, argued that it was Mount Lebanon's special status as an autonomous province that opened the door to European intrigue and intervention.[85]

It wasn't just Ottoman liberals, Greeks, Arabs, Jews, Armenians, Kurds, and Turks who insisted that administrative decentralization and local autonomy could both reorganize and strengthen the empire. Local power brokers beyond Mubarak, including the sharif of Mecca, who later plotted the Arab Revolt during the First World War, vied for autonomy within an imperial framework on the model of Egypt. Even before the Young Turk Revolution, Ottoman officials preemptively offered autonomy to save exposed territories from potential European interference. The holy cities of Mecca and Jerusalem obtained special administrative status for precisely this reason.[86] While autonomy initially emerged out of armed military intervention, after almost a century of experience with autonomous politicking, the Ottomans began defining sensitive provinces as "privileged" before European intervention could do even more damage. Autonomy, in other words, promised local control in worlds that were increasingly resistant toward centralized imperial power.

Despite the fact that the CUP tried to centralize state power, the reality was that it lacked the capacity and money to fully carry out this vision. Even though complete sovereignty, without restrictions, was its driving domestic and foreign objective, the CUP was also exceedingly practical and relied on methods that had worked to shore up Ottoman sovereignty, and it was only in the First World War that it took the opportunity to crush autonomy in all its forms. In Yemen, it was the CUP, and not the liberals or local rebels, who preemptively extended autonomy to save exposed territories from potential European interference and to prevent territorial loses. The Daan Agreement, which recognized Imam Yahya as an autonomous ruler in Ottoman Yemen, was arguably far more successful.[87] In 1911, Imam Yahya was recognized as "dependent ruler" and given autonomy over some districts in Yemen based on religious sect and was paid a stipend by government. Autonomy in this instance, was designed to neutralize Yemen from outside interference. Yemen would later be distinguished as the last imperial land to officially bid farewell to the empire. That imperial divorce didn't happen between Mustafa Kemal and Imam Yahya until 1924.[88]

In another spectacular case of preemptive autonomy, İbrahim Hakkı Paşa offered Abd al-Aziz ibn Saud—the future king and founder of Saudi Arabia—autonomy in an effort to prevent further British meddling in the Gulf. Central Arabia had never been under direct Ottoman administration, and yet in May 1914 İbrahim Hakkı hammered out a deal, enshrined in an imperial ferman giving Ibn Saud hereditary governorship of Nejd in exchange for loyalty to the sultan—expressed in Ottoman flags, post offices, and military advisors. The only requirement of submission was that Ibn Saud "was not allowed to correspond with or interfere with foreign affairs, nor sign international treaties, or to grant concessions to foreigners."[89]

Notwithstanding Ottoman attempts to thwart European intervention through preemption, the years immediately preceding the First World War dealt a series of blows to the project of negotiated autonomy within empire, which would have tragic consequences in wartime. First, Italy's unprovoked invasion of Ottoman Libya (*Trablusgarp*) in 1911, as well as their use of banned weapons in "civilized warfare," prompted intellectuals, government officials, and lawyers to reconsider the value of international law to defend the Ottoman domains. It was not just that the war was illegal or that the Italians had violated the laws of war in the Tripolitania Campaign. Rather, it was the fact that European powers, especially Britain, chose to ignore such flagrant violations of the laws of war, which had only recently been formally codified in 1899 and 1907 Hague Conventions. European silence on Italian violations of the laws of war, despite vigorous Ottoman protest, prompted the Ottoman Foreign Ministry to reevaluate the centrality of international law in its diplomatic dealings with Europe.[90]

Even though the mood in the capital had shifted away from international law as the best means to save the state, autonomy remained on the table. The war in the Balkans (1912–1913) forced the Ottoman Foreign Ministry to negotiate. After the Italian declaration of annexation, the grand vizier, Mehmed Said Paşa, proposed that the Libya could remain under the sovereignty of the sultan but would be given autonomy on the model of Egypt; the khedive could act as the hereditary governor of both provinces. The proposal fell flat. Two days before the Ottomans were forced to sign the Treaty of Lausanne on October 18, 1912, which concluded the war and proclaimed Italian sovereignty over Libya, the sultan issued a ferman proclaiming that the sultan granted Libya complete autonomy (*tam muhtariyet*).[91]

The Armenian Reform Agreement

Autonomy remained a tool of great power domination, and in this case it would have catastrophic consequences for Ottoman Armenians. On February 8, 1914, amid the twin crises of Libya and the Balkan Wars—Russia, with European support, crafted and compelled the Ottoman state to agree to the reorganization of the six eastern provinces (*vilayet-i sitte*) as two autonomous provinces—each with a European inspector general and a high degree of local control.[92] Since 1878, reform in the six eastern provinces had been an episodic question among European ambassadors in Istanbul, bursting onto the diplomatic scene during flashpoints of violence, including the massacres of the 1890s, and in the aftermath of the counterrevolution in Adana in 1909.[93] The recent wars and territorial losses provided the opportunity for Russia to press the CUP anew to implement reforms.

André Mandelstam fully crafted the first iteration of the Reform Agreement. He was a Russian diplomat and translator (*dragoman*) who had trained at the University of St. Petersburg in international law under Fedor Martens.[94] Mandelstam served the Russian Embassy in Istanbul from 1898 to 1914.[95] He not only knew the capital well, but also the empire, its institutions and laws, and legal restrictions on sovereignty—his dissertation was on the codification of international private law, and he published a book on the Capitulations in 1911.[96] Mandelstam's 1913 plan was astonishingly broad and shows clearly how European powers deliberately repurposed existing autonomy agreements to extend the system of autonomy, which inevitably resulted in a further limitation of Ottoman sovereignty. Ever fastidious about the sources of law, he recorded all the documents and precedents he used to draft the agreement. The first iteration of the Armenian Reform Agreement was based directly on Organic Regulations (*Règlement Organique*) for Lebanon (1861 and 1864), the 1913 Draft Law on Provincial Administration, and drafts of reform plans for the eastern provinces. He also examined the regulations for Crete and Eastern Rumelia.

Mandelstam claimed his reform agreement was based on the model of Mount Lebanon, but like the earlier autonomous provinces, the plan had unique features particular to it while borrowing from earlier iterations of the *eyalet-i mümtaze*. He proposed a single autonomous province that would cover nearly half the territory of Anatolia.[97] As in Mount Lebanon, the governor would be appointed by the sultan for a five-year term with the "consent of the powers." But in distinction to Lebanon, the governor should be a "Christian Ottoman subject, or, preferably, a European." The governor had extraordinary executive and military powers and would be responsible for appointing all administrative officials, including judges. An advisory council composed of the administrators, religious leaders, and European technocrats would assist the governor, alongside three Muslim and three Christian local advisors. A provincial assembly, which had budgetary and legislative powers, was required to submit laws to the sultan for approval.[98] Mandelstam went far beyond the other regulations, and local administrators, police, gendarmes, and judges would be equally divided between Muslims and Christians. As in the autonomy plans for Albania, soldiers would be recruited exclusively from the province and remain there in peacetime. Only "sedentary inhabitants shall enjoy the rights of suffrage and eligibility," and no Muslim refugees (*muhacir*) should be settled in the province.[99] Mandelstam's plan aligned with critiques of the CUP emanating from the edges of the empire. All petitions and court pleas could be written in the language of choice, while all laws, state publications, and court judgments would be issued in Ottoman Turkish, Armenian, and Kurdish. Each "nation" had the right to establish private schools, where the language of instruction would be in the "national language." While the Armenian Constitution of 1863 would be formally recognized, a new Règlement Organique would be drawn up for the province.[100]

Critically, and in distinction to most earlier agreements, the Ottomans were not part of the crafting of the new administrative order. When Mandelstam first presented the text to state officials, he was told the CUP was in the processing of drafting new provincial regulations to reform the entire empire, instead of for the six provinces alone. Like Hüseyn Cahid's arguments against Albanian autonomy, there would be a single set of laws and administrative regulations for a single state.

From June to July 1913, an "Armenian Reform Commission," composed of dragomans rather than ambassadors, met to debate the program in Yeniköy at the summer residence of Austro-Hungarian Embassy—an imposing mansion on the Bosporus. The German dragoman was especially critical: Mandelstam's project went "beyond the status of Lebanon" and, if implemented, "would turn half of Anatolia into an Armenia that would retain only a weak link with Turkey through the sovereignty of the Sultan." Like Hüseyn Cahid, he thought that once autonomy was applied to the eastern provinces, it would be impossible to stop there; the plan would "effectively lead to the beginning of the partition of Turkey."[101] Against this criticism, Mandelstam argued that his program was no different from earlier experiments with special administrative status. He insisted that "the well-known precedents of Eastern Rumelia, Crete, and Mount Lebanon, where the appointment of a governor-general with the consent of the Powers had not been deemed incompatible with the sovereignty of the Sultan." The German and Austro-Hungarian dragomans countered that the Russian draft deprived the state of "rights essential to sovereignty."[102] Even though Mandelstam had drawn on the existing privileged provinces, the German dragoman found that "such autonomy would necessarily lead to the complete separation of Armenia from the Ottoman Empire."[103] Mandelstam complained bitterly that the German dragoman was preoccupied with "safeguarding imperial sovereignty," instead of dealing with how to implement reforms.[104]

Ultimately, Mandelstam's plan crashed against Ottoman intransigence and increasingly strained relations between Russia and Germany and Austria-Hungary. The final agreement, signed February 8, 1914, was massively condensed and bore little relationship to Mandelstam's vision of autonomy. While the final agreement created two provinces directed by European inspectors, they had none of the robust local governing power imputed to the single governor in the 1913 plan. The Russian chargé d'affaires was direct: "It must certainly be admitted that the document of

January 26 does not grant the Armenians the extensive rights of self-government that the initial Russian project sought to guarantee them." Like the 1820 agreement on autonomy in Serbia and the Danubian Principalities, this was a Russo-Ottoman legal instrument. Said Halim Paşa, the grand vizier, managed to secure a more favorable deal for the Ottoman state, but one that nevertheless extended the system of European-imposed autonomies that the state tried desperately to circumvent.

Mandelstam's reform plans are important for several reasons. They show a far more dangerous vision of what autonomy within empire could do, one that was explicitly designed to undercut Ottoman sovereignty. In co-crafting the earlier autonomies with the Ottomans, European powers generally used autonomy to bracket off territory within the system of European law and politics. The first Mandelstam plan represented what the CUP most feared and confirmed its worst suspicions: Autonomy inflamed separatist impulses, and this was by Great Power design. The fact that the 1914 plan was dramatically curtailed could not be disaggregated from the ideas animating the first plan. As many genocide scholars have argued, the agreement was a crucial factor in the state treating Armenian subjects in the six eastern provinces as a fifth column once the war started. The Armenian Reform Agreement would never be implemented. The European inspectors—a Dutch colonial administrator and Norwegian military officer—arrived in Istanbul but, interrupted by the outbreak of war, never made it their respective provinces.[105]

Conclusion: The Autonomy Reflex

The Egypt autonomy model was not just a diplomatic reflex between empires; it was a system. From the 1860s through the First World War, Ottoman bureaucrats and lawyers looked to Egypt as an administrative model to solve imperial crises preemptively outside of the penumbra of Great Power legal guaranties. The Kuwait story is striking beyond trying to understand how the local history of an Ottoman subprovince became so pivotal geopolitically throughout the twentieth century. What makes Kuwait distinctive in the world of the late empire is not the fact that it was a unique singular case, but instead how astonishingly normal it was. Kuwait was just one of several instances in the Mediterranean, Gulf, Red Sea, and Black Sea regions where the Ottomans and Europe—especially

Britain—returned to an autonomy model based on Egypt to resolve international, imperial, and local disputes. Most important for the Ottoman state, autonomy preserved imperial sovereignty. Autonomy would remain a key battleground between the Ottoman and European empires, between imperial subjects, provincial power brokers, and the government.

PART THREE

The Making of the Mandate System

CHAPTER 5

Woodrow Wilson in the Ottoman Empire

On October 19, 1918, Ahmed İzzet Paşa, the new grand vizier, announced to the Ottoman Parliament that the imperial government accepted Woodrow Wilson's 14 Points as the foundation of the peace and the postwar order.[1] Ahmed İzzet argued that peace according to Wilsonian principles (*Wilson prensipleri*) would provide Ottoman equality in international relations, assure "national sovereignty" (*hakimiyet-i milliye*), and at the same time preserve the empire by extending administrative autonomy to the Arab provinces. Though silent about the future status of non-Muslim Ottoman subjects, İzzet Paşa promised that the world of Islam would remain united: "In order to maintain the connection between the Caliphate and the Sultanate we will work to solve the question of the Arab provinces by ensuring an autonomy (*muhtariyet*) that is in accordance with national desires and wishes."[2] That same day, the Post and Telegraph Directorate instructed local press offices throughout the empire to publicize İzzet Paşa's peace program based on Wilsonian principles—which included full sovereignty, "justice in international relations," as well as minority rights protection—and to underline the point that the government would grant administrative autonomy for the Arab provinces.[3]

Yet, as we have seen in previous chapters, reorganizing the empire along decentralized lines cut against longstanding administrative policies backed by Sultan Abdülhamid II (r. 1876–1909) and the Committee of

Union and Progress. Indeed, incorporating the autonomous provinces into the regular administration of the empire was an Ottoman war aim and one that was ruthlessly pursued throughout the First World War. The Unionists canceled the contentious Armenian Reform Agreement in December 1914, which would have reorganized the six eastern provinces into two autonomous provinces. In July 1915 the state revoked Mount Lebanon's privileged status as an autonomous province, and in August Cemal Paşa, the wartime governor of Syria, executed Syrian dissidents who had favored decentralized administration before the war.[4] How, then, might one explain the official Ottoman shift toward decentralized administration?

Historians have largely maintained that Wilson's twelfth point contained the principle of partition.[5] While that may have been the American president's intention, it is hard to explain why the Ottoman government, which fought a war to achieve sovereign equality with Europe as an empire, would embrace Wilson so wholeheartedly. Erez Manela has argued that Wilson's support for the rights of small nations, self-determination, and the promise of peace without annexations briefly offered anticolonial nationalists a discourse of legitimacy.[6] But what did "Wilsonianism" offer to a defeated empire with numerous provinces under European military occupation? The few analyses that consider broad support for Wilson throughout the Ottoman Empire during the armistice period accord with Manela's story—that is, that "Wilsonian principles" supported the establishment of a Turkish national state.[7] There were Ottomans who understood Wilson's Article 12 as a promise for independence, whether Turkish, Arab, Greek, Armenian, Kurdish, or Lebanese.[8] But in the early days and months of the Armistice, many Ottomans interpreted "Wilsonian principles" as a promise for the continuity of imperial rule in Anatolia and the Arab provinces—what in a few short years would become independent Turkey and the Class A mandates under the League of Nations—Palestine, Transjordan, Iraq, Syria, and Lebanon. This chapter argues that "Wilsonian principles," Article 12 above all, supplied the wartime and immediate postwar governments, as well as Ottoman intellectuals, with ammunition to make a case for imperial continuity.

The imperial interpretation of Wilson matters for two reasons. First, histories of the end of World War I in the Middle East generally assume that the Ottoman government and its subjects knew the empire was a dead letter once the Armistice was signed aboard the HMS *Agamemnon* in

Lemnos Bay on October 30, 1918. In the aftermath of genocide, famine, war-profiteering, the European military occupation of the great Islamic cities of Baghdad, Jerusalem, and Damascus, and the loss of Mecca to Faisal's Sharifian army, the six-hundred-year-old empire suffered a crisis of legitimacy from which it could never hope to recover.[9] Certainly, the Allied Powers thought this was case. Nevertheless, the Ottoman government, and many of its subjects, desperately tried to save the empire from partition into the early 1920s, and they looked to the empire's own administrative practices for a solution. In particular, they embraced the *eyalet-i mümtaze*, the privileged provinces, as a model for the postwar empire. The future composition of the Ottoman Empire was up for grabs in 1918 and remained so until the signing of the Treaty of Lausanne in 1923.[10] Throughout the Armistice period (1918–1923), or the *mütareke*, as it was known in Ottoman Turkish, there was far more flexibility about the future boundaries of the state than is often admitted in the historiographical debate. We risk reading the Turkish state backward in time, when in fact the route to statehood was halting and ultimately pragmatic, as options to hold on to the empire were foreclosed by external intervention. In the end, the Turkish state was what remained of the empire, largely but not entirely within the Armistice lines of 1918.

Second, it was not just Ottoman statesmen, lawyers, and intellectuals who looked to the constitutional history of the empire for a new model of imperial administration in the aftermath of the First World War. British postwar planners also considered the Ottoman autonomous provinces as a model for managing the post-Ottoman Middle East. The mandates system of the League of Nations, which granted the former Arab provinces provisional recognition of their independence under British and French trusteeship, has overwhelmingly been seen as an imperialist compromise with Woodrow Wilson's anti-annexationist rhetoric and his support for national self-determination.[11] British and French mandatory powers accepted the façade of independence to satisfy the Americans, but in reality the new system provided a cover of legitimacy for the extension of empire as usual into the Middle East. There is no question that the extension of British and French colonial rule in the area was a radical break with the Ottoman past, but at the same time there were remarkable continuities, particularly in terms of British thinking about the function of Ottoman autonomous provinces in international relations before the war. As we will see in this chapter and the next, the system of autonomous provinces worked out by the Ottomans and European powers throughout the nineteenth century was internationalized in the form of the League of Nations mandates for the Arab provinces.

Despite the fact that the Ottoman and British governments had very different ideas about what the postwar order in the Middle East should look like, they drew on the same administrative practices to justify their respective postwar empires. As we have seen, autonomy as a legal-imperial designation had a specific meaning in an Ottoman administrative context, and it was mobilized by the Ottoman and British governments, as well as Ottoman subject nationalities, in order to make claims about postwar order.[12] Wilsonian rhetoric did not offer anything that was radically new to Ottoman or British wartime planners—in fact, Wilson appeared to refer to an old debate, both between empires as well as among Ottoman subjects.

Cemal Paşa, the Demise of the Privileged Provinces, and a Revolution in International Law

From the start of the war, the Ottoman government explicitly articulated its war aims. More than anything, the cabinet, under Enver Paşa, sought to achieve imperial security through centralized administrative control, by asserting full sovereignty in international and domestic affairs, which meant, quite simply, terminating European limits on the full exercise of Ottoman sovereignty.[13] Ottoman efforts to achieve sovereign equality with European empires took various forms during the war, but each hammered away at the legal, economic, and administrative constraints imposed by Europe and enshrined in treaty during the course of the nineteenth century. In practical legal terms this meant abrogating international mechanisms that had limited Ottoman sovereignty, notably the Capitulations and the internationally guaranteed privileged provinces.[14]

After obtaining the secret military alliance with Germany in August 1914, the government unilaterally abrogated the Capitulations, a move that was announced in September and went into effect on October 1, 1914.[15] The Ottoman Foreign Ministry circulated a note to each of the capitulatory powers that stated that the Capitulations, which, "restricting the sovereignty of Turkey in her relations with certain powers," had been annulled, and any other legal, economic, and administrative "privileges and immunities," linked to the unequal treaties, were also repealed.

The Foreign Ministry framed the argument in terms of equality and international law and announced that the "Imperial Government has adopted as the basis of its relations with the other powers the general principles of international law."[16] The next day, newspapers in Istanbul and provincial capitals enthusiastically celebrated the end of the unequal treaties, as a declaration of Ottoman independence. One pamphlet announced that the "scourge of the Capitulations has been lifted" and that the "nation and the state are now independent" (*Millet ve devlet şimdi istiklal buluyor*).[17] Across the empire, people held spontaneous celebrations and parades and gave speeches to commemorate the eclipse of a system of legal humiliation.

Ending the Capitulations was an assertion of sovereignty. Two days later, the Ottoman ambassador in Berlin during the July Crisis, Mahmud Muhtar Paşa (Katırcıoğlu), argued that the war was an opportunity that would determine the fate of the empire. Neutrality was not an option—it would "prevent us from taking advantage of the unique occasion which presents itself to the Ottoman Empire for the first time in many centuries to rebuild and secure its future as a Great Power. Can we continue to accept the humiliating situation that we have submitted to in Egypt and the fact that the [Aegean] islands, which we still claim, serve as military bases for other navies—insulting us in our own waters? . . . the fate of the Ottoman Empire will depend on the outcome of this war."[18] For Mahmud Muhtar Paşa, the Foreign Ministry, and the CUP leadership more broadly, sovereignty without control was no longer an option.

After this immensely popular measure, the wartime government then moved to fully centralize imperial administration by revoking the internationally guaranteed status of the remaining *eyalet-i mümtaze*. On December 16, 1914, the CUP canceled the Armenian Reform Agreement, which would have reorganized the six eastern provinces into two large autonomous provinces on the model of the autonomous provinces, notably Mount Lebanon.[19] As chapter 4 demonstrated, the Unionists understood the Armenian Agreement as they had come to see other European-imposed autonomous provinces in the empire, as a Great Power weapon to dissolve the empire into a series of European client states.

No one would do more to attack exceptional privileges than the wartime governor of Syria, Cemal Paşa. In his postwar memoir—published in German, Ottoman Turkish, and English on the eve of his assassination in Tiblisi (Tiflis) by members of the Armenian Revolutionary Federation—he bitterly attacked the Reform Agreement and framed his defense of wartime policies against Ottoman Armenians, in terms of the corrosive effects of political decentralization and autonomy on the Ottoman Empire:

> "Political decentralization" (*siyasi adem-i merkeziyet*) meant granting internal autonomy (*muhtariyet-i dahiliye*) to the various elements living in their respective regions and attempting to administer them all under the name of the "Ottoman Empire." If there had not been external enemies—who wholeheartedly desired the dissolution of the Ottoman Empire and resorted to all kinds of intrigues to achieve this—the Committee of Union and Progress would not have hesitated for a minute to accept this principle, of which Prince Sabahaddin Bey was a fervent advocate. However, with the French eyeing Syria, the British wanting to claim Mesopotamia and the entire Arabian peninsula, the Russians waiting for a favorable opportunity to seize the eastern Anatolian provinces, the Bulgarians, Serbs, and Greeks wanting to divide Macedonia, and the Austrians and Italians wishing to seize Albania, and the Greeks, who never gave up wanting to take the Aegean islands—would these (nations) encounter any difficulties, I wonder, gradually absorbing the provinces one by one if they were established on the principle of "political decentralization?"[20]

Autonomy in Cemal Paşa's view, and in the view of many CUP officials, opened the empire to nationalist intrigue and foreign intervention. It was far too dangerous a policy in a multiethnic empire with imperialists at the gate. Moreover, decentralization could not appease nationalists—they would still want to exit the empire. Writing from the perspective of the early 1920s, he noted that Habsburg policies of decentralization did not prevent the "Czecho-Slovaks, Croats, and Slovenes" from breaking away. Cemal Paşa reinforced his arguments against autonomy by looking at how the practice had functioned in the years before the war. He continued:

> It is impossible to imagine a broader form of administrative autonomy than the autonomy granted to the island of Crete, but have we been able to dissuade the Cretans from their desire to join Greece? The island of Cyprus enjoyed a very exceptional existence under the provisional British occupation, but did not the island's governing council repeatedly demand incorporation into Greece every year? Were we able to prevent Bulgaria's annexation of Eastern Rumelia,

> which enjoyed a high degree of administrative autonomy? Did the British have any difficulty occupying Egypt—one of the most important examples of exceptional provinces? Did the British refrain from claiming Kuwait, which had been a dependency of the Ottoman Caliphate for centuries, because Sheikh Mubarak al-Sabah accepted British protection?[21]

Like Hüseyin Cahid at *Tanin*, Cemal Paşa collapsed decentralization with administrative autonomy and pointed to the privileged provinces as durable proof that they were incompatible with empire and the rights of sovereignty. Autonomy was the first step toward qualified political independence under European political oversight.

As the governor and military commander of Syria between 1914 and 1917, Cemal Paşa cracked down on Arabs who advocated autonomy before the war—especially members of the Ottoman Party for Administrative Decentralization.[22] Taking advantage of the ambiguities of Britain's occupation, Muslim and Christian reformers from across Greater Syria established the political party in Cairo in 1913. That summer, the Decentralization Party, also known as the Decentralization Committee, joined with several other Arab societies and clubs in Paris to adopt a series of proposed resolutions to reform the Arab provinces.[23] Many of the animating ideas concerned the use of Arabic in local schools, courts, and in the writing of petitions destined for state bureaucrats—all of which were communicated to Istanbul, the British Foreign Office, and the French Foreign Ministry. Sending their own delegate to Paris, the CUP negotiated with the Arab representatives and supported many of their demands, especially around the use of Arabic. But the resolution that drew the ire of the CUP at the time, and Cemal Paşa in 1914, was point 3: "It is important to establish in each of the Syrian and Arab vilayets a decentralized administration (*régime décentralisateur/idarat al-lamarkaziya*), appropriate to its needs and capabilities."[24] That resolution hung over Cemal Paşa's mission to Syria.[25]

When war broke out between the Entente and the Ottoman Empire, enemy foreigners were subject to deportation across the empire, including consular officials. The French consul in Beirut, Georges-Picot—who would late negotiate the Sykes-Picot agreement with Mark Sykes on behalf of France—abandoned the city along with a trove of documents implicating locals in anti-CUP activity. The collection of intelligence reports, political tracts, and official documents, demonstrated that members of Arab clubs and political organizations, especially the Decentralization Party, had met with British and French officials in Cairo, and elsewhere across the empire. For Cemal, the texts confirmed CUP suspicions that Arab support for administrative decentralization was nothing more than a plot to undermine the state.[26] In 1916, he had the texts published in Istanbul—in Ottoman, Arabic, and French—to demonstrate the duplicity of Arab political organizations, clubs, and literary societies. Alongside the consulate documents, he included coerced confessions and political programs and pamphlets that were generated in the years before 1914.[27]

Among the letters between Arab and French consular officials was an intelligence report detailing the activities and meetings of the Decentralization Committee in Cairo. Written in March 1913—before the Arab Congress in Paris—the document claimed that "Muslim and Christian Syrians—especially those residing in Egypt" preferred that "Syria be governed by a Muslim prince as an autonomous principality." While there were debates among the members of Decentralization Party, there was broad agreement that the future principality should be placed under foreign protection (*himaye-i ecnebiye*) of either France or Britain. The search for a prince was focused on the khedival family. For Cemal, autonomous Egypt—and the earlier principalities—functioned as template for rebellious subjects to gain local control at the expense of the imperial government and invited foreign intervention.[28]

Another seized text—entitled the "Aspirations of the Christians of Syria" and signed by prominent Christians, including Yusuf al-Hani and Khalil Zeine—contained all the CUP's critiques and fears about autonomy. The petition requested the French seizure of Syria, "granting full autonomy to the province of Beirut under the de facto protection and supervision of France," and the incorporation of the vilayet of Beirut and Mount Lebanon, which is to be "under the suzerainty of France."[29] For Cemal, the evidence vindicated the CUP's arguments against autonomy. Arab claims that decentralization better represented local concerns over administration and how taxes were spent were a "deception," designed to undermine the CUP's actual reforms. Arab demands for administrative reform and local autonomy were nothing short of "revolutionary" plots to claim independence and break up the empire. Autonomy was incompatible with imperial sovereignty.

While Cemal derided the Arab decentralists as separatists, many of the seized documents reveal more about the fault lines of prewar political debates, and the struggle over which party was responsible for the many foreign policy failures leading up to the war. In a pamphlet addressed to "oppressed Ottoman nation," the author accused the CUP of destroying the state through mismanagement:

> For us, there are no Arabs, Turks, or Kurds; we are all children of this soil. A handful of tyrants have seized the government and are wreaking havoc. . . . They have surrendered Bosnia and Herzegovina, and Eastern Rumelia. Their leader and accomplice, Hakkı Paşa, sold the province of Tripoli, Benghazi, and its dependencies. . . . They sold the country and granted Yemen independence (*istiklal*). . . . Now they are beginning to negotiate the cession of Iraq piece by piece; they recognize England's sovereign rights (*hukuk-i mülkiye*) over Muscat, Bahrain, and Qatar. They have detached Kuwait from the empire. They have granted the English the right to oversee the Persian Gulf and privileges equivalent to the cession of Basra . . . Syria, and Anatolia. Our goal is that no privileges (*imtiyazat*) should be granted to foreigners that would endanger our country, that not even an inch of our country should be sold to foreigners, and that if the government needs to sell land, it should sell only to us, and grant our country decentralized administration (*adem-i merkeziyet-i idare vermesi*). With this, we want nothing more than to remain forever Ottoman under the banner of the Caliphate and the Ottoman Empire. Otherwise, what happened to the Muslims in Rumelia will happen to our wives and children too. This is not a rebellion against the state. It is simply to protect our land, our property, and our homeland. . . . We will rise up with the sword, demand our rights with force, and free our country from the band of tyrants.[30]

The pamphlet offered a blunt critique of Ottoman foreign policy in the years between 1908 and 1914. As we saw in the previous chapter, the CUP oversaw the most significant expansion of autonomy in decades—both in concert with the Great Powers, as in Kuwait, and preemptively, as in Yemen. From the jab against İbrahim Hakkı Paşa for negotiating with Britain over the legal status of territories in the Gulf to offering foreigners concessions and privileges in Iraq, and not fighting to retain autonomous Bulgaria and Bosnia, the argument was clear. Through corruption and incompetence, the CUP did more to undermine state sovereignty than

Arab decentralists did. In a reversal of CUP arguments, decentralization was not autonomy—that is what the state gave away in Yemen and Kuwait. Instead, decentralization offered locals a stake in the empire. The CUP haggled with the Great Powers when they should have bargained with their own subjects. As Mostafa Minowi has argued, what many Arab elites wanted was "an explicit, publicly acknowledged share in defining what it meant to be an Ottoman citizen."[31] For Cemal, the pamphlet was a call to mutiny and rebellion.

Cemal Paşa used the documents to justify the court martial, conviction, and execution of Arab decentralists—prominent politicians, intellectuals, and lawyers—in Beirut and in Damascus in 1915 and 1916, which earned him the name among Arabs as "the Butcher" (*al-Saffah*).[32] For Cemal, the seized documents, together with decentralist political programs, amounted to a plot to transform the political order of the Middle East—and it was the existing model of the imposed autonomies that would be used to execute the scheme. The accused were tried for treason in the military court. The rebels, the indictment argued, planned to "establish the Caliphate in Egypt under British protection and to transform the Khedive into the Caliph."[33] In addition, Ottoman Palestine—from the border of Egypt to Haifa—would be established as a British protectorate, while the areas from Haifa to Alexandria would fall under French protection (*himaye*). An "independent Muslim principality in Syria" would be established (*Suriye'de müstakil bir Müslüman prensliği vücuda getirmek*), but the final contours of the state were up for debate—some factions wanted to annex Mount Lebanon, or to place Syria directly under French occupation (*işgali altına aldırmak*). What is striking is the degree to which, for Cemal, the existing model of autonomy, together with practices of European military occupation, could be used to break apart the empire.[34]

Cemal Paşa's acts of state violence against prominent Ottoman subjects were part of the broader CUP project to bind the Arab provinces more closely to the imperial center by eradicating all forms of privilege and exception, which meant crushing the last of the Great Power guaranteed autonomies. Canceling the Armenian Reform Agreement was one thing—it had not yet been implemented and was deeply unpopular among Ottoman Muslims in the aftermath of the Balkan Wars—but abrogating Mount Lebanon's special status as an internationally guaranteed privileged province was quite another. In the same way that it was extremely challenging for Britain to justify absorbing Egypt into the empire as a protectorate in December 1914, as we will see in the following chapter, incorporating Mount Lebanon into the regular constitutional order of the Ottoman Empire posed several domestic difficulties. Locals in Mount Lebanon jealously guarded their special status as Ottoman privileged province and exercised wide control over local affairs, taxation, and infrastructure. They argued that nothing could be done to change the legal status of either province without consensus from all the states that created the provinces in the first place, including the Ottoman Empire.

Talaat, Cemal, and the governor of neighboring Beirut province, Bekir Sami Bey, were concerned about inflaming public opinion in the province, which had close ties to France and a large Maronite Christian population. Initially Bekir Sami Bey proposed that Mount Lebanon be absorbed into the regular system of imperial administration, and that the protocols governing the province guaranteed by Europe be abolished, while at the same time maintaining all the privileges that the province had enjoyed since the 1860s. The Ottoman state would guarantee Mount Lebanon's special status, rather than the powers of Europe.[35] Here the CUP was borrowing from their own tactics of extending autonomy to restive provinces in order to stave off European intervention, as in Yemen and Kuwait. When Cemal Paşa arrived in Syria, he immediately paved the way for annexing Mount Lebanon to the regular system of Ottoman administration. He declared martial law and sent a battalion to occupy the province. A few months later he removed the governor, Ohannes Paşa, an Armenian Catholic, from his post—he was the last nonlocal Christian governor appointed from Istanbul per the protocols governing Mount Lebanon.

On July 11, 1915, the CUP revoked Lebanon's autonomous status and reincorporated the territory into the empire as a regular subprovince (*liva*).[36] It was the last privileged province still in the empire—though the government did not recognize Britain's protectorate in Egypt. Cemal Paşa replaced Ohannes Paşa with Ali Münir Bey, a Muslim Unionist, cutting against the *Règlement Organique* requiring a Christian governor. When Ali Münir announced that Lebanon's status had been annulled, he framed the decision in terms of Ottoman war aims as an assertion of state sovereignty. He declared that "after overcoming all foreign intervention, the state will act in this province with full independence in accordance with the rights of sovereignty."[37]

It fell to İbrahim Hakkı Paşa, still the state's leading international law expert, to justify this legal revolution to his allies. Now serving in the critical role as the wartime ambassador to Berlin, he formally declared the termination of the internationally guaranteed autonomous regime in Mount Lebanon, along with a radically new interpretation of international law.[38] Before the First World War, state bureaucrats relied on international law, especially Great Power territorial guarantees, to maintain imperial sovereignty. The dense treaty relationship between the empire and Europe was designed to protect the state. As one of the chief architects of that order, it was perhaps fitting that İbrahim Hakkı Paşa should be the agent of its destruction. He announced that the German-Ottoman alliance of August 1914 put the empire on equal footing with the states of Europe, the empire "entered the group of European powers with all the rights and prerogatives of a completely independent government," and as a result the Imperial Government announced that it no longer recognized restrictions imposed by the Treaty of Paris (1856) and the Treaty of Berlin (1878).

İbrahim Hakkı Paşa enumerated European violations of Ottoman territorial integrity and singled out administrative autonomy as a particularly pernicious device used to undermine Ottoman sovereignty. The French had intervened militarily to "demand a new system of administration" in Mount Lebanon, contrary to the Treaty of 1856, which prohibited intervention in Ottoman internal affairs. Russia had similarly undermined Ottoman sovereignty in the Balkans by flooding the region with guns, soldiers, and military officers. It too had demanded "the establishment of a new internal administration in some Ottoman provinces":

> The same clauses did not prevent France from occupying Tunis and establishing its protectorate over this dependent Ottoman territory; nor the British occupation of Egypt, which installed a system of a disguised protectorate and carried out a series of encroachments against Ottoman sovereignty in southern Yemen, in Nejd, in Kuwait, in Qatar as well as in the Persian Gulf. These same clauses did not prevent the four governments currently at war with Turkey, to modify by force, the existing state of things in Crete and to force the creation of a novel situation in flagrant contradiction with the integrity that the Powers engaged themselves to respect.[39]

İbrahmin Hakkı Paşa argued that the European powers had so often violated the positive articles of these treaties, which recognized "the independence and the territorial integrity of the Ottoman Empire," that the government now considered them "null and void and completely without any contractual value." He noted that the imperial government had "scrupulously executed the onerous clauses," but the clauses that were favorable to the Ottoman Empire "remained a dead letter" as European governments actively obstructed administrative and economic reforms in the empire. Moreover, the treaties of 1856 and 1878 were fundamentally at odds with the principle of state sovereignty. They carried "stipulations that regulated the interior organization of the state, which established differences between the various provinces of the empire and imposed thereby positive obligations incompatible with territorial sovereignty, which profoundly affected the independence of the imperial government."[40]

Despite the fact that the Ottoman government denounced the treaties of 1856 and 1878, Hakkı Paşa noted, the empire would "not fail to take advantage of the principles of international law in order to enforce its rights to its advantage by the aforementioned treaties and which have hitherto been ignored." Through this disavowal, "the letter concluded noting that the government no longer recognized the autonomous regime in Lebanon imposed by Europe."[41]

İkdam, an Istanbul daily, published the entirety of the diplomatic note to the German and Austro-Hungarian ambassadors—taking up over half the front page—together with an editorial note praising the government for disavowing "unjust treaties" that have been an emblem of "oppression and violence within the legal system." For the editors, the diplomatic note was an assertion of imperial strength and vitality. As İbrahim Hakkı argued, it was not international law that was the problem. It was the fact that the empire had been brought into the system of international law on unjust and sovereignty eviscerating terms: "Until now, there have been two types of international law: one derived from natural law, to which European states adhered. The second was international law applied only when Turks were involved."[42]

The article asserted that İbrahim Hakkı Paşa's letter not only "erased" the unequal of the treaties of 1856 and 1878 but it was also "revenge" (*intikam*) for the disasters of the Ottoman-Russo War (1877–78). The government was "giving the Allies a lesson in international law":

> The arguments presented by the Sublime Porte are so solid, clear, and harmonious that no one—not even Martens, the Russian

> professor of international law—can refute them. Indeed, even Europe's most impartial and authoritative international law professors and advisors (*muallim ve müşavirleri*) could not conceal the extent to which the legal principles applied against us were unjust. Even Mandelstam, who sought to succeed Ignatiev with his intrigues against our state and nation, stated that the ancient treaties (1856 and 1878) were unjust.[43]

The degree to which Ottoman newspapers engaged with questions of international law is striking—as was the fact that a general reader could be assumed to know both Martens, who had written about the privileged provinces as a problem of international order, and Mandelstam. Ignatiev had negotiated the Treaty of San Stefano (1878) leading to Berlin and generally held an aggressive view toward the Ottoman Empire and plotted its demise. As we saw in chapter 4, Mandelstam wrote the first and second drafts of the Armenian Reform Agreement.[44] The editorial and the digs at Russian lawyers all reflected the transformation of international law in Ottoman foreign and domestic policy.

The Ottoman Foreign Ministry aggressively used the events of the war to establish full control over its internal administration, and to assert sovereign equality in international relations. The abrogation of the Capitulations on September 8, 1914, should be seen together with the cancellation of the Armenian Reform Agreement and Mount Lebanon's autonomy as part of the same project to reposition the role of international law within Ottoman foreign policy. If international law had been a weapon of the weak during the Hamidian era (1876–1909), with the First World War, the CUP transformed it into a weapon of the strong. The state's willingness to abandon the constraints of treaty law was a radical transformation, but it was long in the making. İbrahim Paşa's diplomatic note was not wrong. The Great Powers persistently failed to uphold their end of the bargain, and at keys points during the Second Constitutional era, they opted not uphold the terms of international agreements. The refusal to address Crete, Bosnia, and Herzegovina in 1908, followed by Italy's illegal war and seizure and Libya and the Balkan Wars, demonstrated that sovereignty was about force—not adhering to law to international legal norms. It is a lesson that would destroy the empire with catastrophic consequences for so many Ottoman subjects in wartime.

The Wartime Revival of the Privileged Provinces

In a stunning reversal, the CUP government suddenly turned toward administrative decentralization as a potential legal solution to save the empire from dissolution. By the fall of 1917, the government's hard-line centralization policies became increasingly difficult to sustain. Political dissatisfaction with Cemal Paşa's polices in Syria, along with years of mobilization, the corrupt system of war taxation and requisitioning—as well as the famine that would claim nearly 500,000 lives between 1915 and 1918, and which Ottoman subjects largely blamed on the Ottoman government—all culminated to undermine Ottoman legitimacy in the Arab provinces.[45] Added to this, the politicization of Islam between the Allied and Central powers had reached a fever pitch—Britain countered the Ottoman declaration of Jihad (1914) with the Arab Revolt of 1916.[46] Moreover, it appeared that Britain was winning this battle by taking control of the great Umayyad and Abbasid cities. By March 1917 Britain conquered and occupied Baghdad, and on December 11 Jerusalem fell to British forces under General Allenby's command. The Balfour Declaration, which promised a Jewish home in Ottoman Palestine, had been made public on November 9.[47] Soon thereafter, the Bolsheviks published imperial Russia's secret treaties with the Allies, including the Sykes-Picot Agreement, which were quickly translated into English and published in the *Manchester Guardian* on November 26 and 28.[48]

Amid these challenges, Cemal Paşa, in consultation with Talaat, initiated discussions with Emir Faisal, the leader of the Arab Revolt, to bring the rebels back into the imperial fold. Talaat thought it would possible to retain the Arab provinces through diplomacy by offering administrative autonomy to Faisal in exchange for abandoning the British.[49] While that offer didn't come to fruition, it signaled that the centralizing government was now considering autonomy to keep the empire intact. Along these lines, the Foreign Ministry initiated an investigation into the administrative history and effects of autonomy in Egypt and Ottoman territories in the Arabian Peninsula.[50] Legal advisors (*hukuk müşavirleri*) at the Office of Legal Counsel in the Foreign Ministry had long viewed autonomous provinces as a weapon that allowed European powers to intervene in the internal affairs of the Ottoman Empire. They argued that autonomy inexorably weakened Ottoman territorial claims and paved the way for either provincial independence or increased European interference.

Nevertheless, the Foreign Ministry commissioned several studies on pressing strategic questions related to international law. Along with a treatise on the future of the Straits, the Foreign Ministry published a series of texts that dealt directly with the historical problem of autonomy in the Ottoman Empire. The first concerned the legal status of the Arabian Peninsula vis-à-vis the Ottoman state, and the second, entitled "The Egyptian Question," considered Ottoman legal claims to Egypt and Sudan.[51]

While the war brought new urgency to the question of Ottoman sovereignty in the Gulf, Foreign Ministry lawyers had prepared a series of legal opinions for İbrahim Hakkı Paşa's negotiations with Britain over Kuwait.[52] For the Arabian Peninsula, the Foreign Ministry produced a series of short histories on Basra and the Shatt al-Arab, Kuwait, Najd, Dubai, Muscat, Qatar, Hadramout, Aden, and Bahrain.[53] These reports, and the subsequent published volumes, included details on conquest and imperial incorporation, local privileges, as well as the precise legal relationship between each location and the imperial center. In some cases, like Muscat, the authors noted candidly that the territory had never been part of the Ottoman domains: "Moreover, the Bab-ı Ali does not possess any documents in its archives concerning the incorporation of this region into the empire by right of conquest or by any other means."[54] Nineteenth-century international legal terms linked to the acquisition of territory in colonial territories, "right of conquest" and "effective occupation," filled the texts, while also noting each region's administrative autonomy. More than anything, the histories provided an account of the Ottoman-British contest over the Arabian Peninsula during the nineteenth and early twentieth centuries. Each underlined how Britain had exercised dominated the region through a series of informal protectorates. Kuwait generated the most consideration, with significant attention to the Ottoman-British negotiations over the legal status of the territory between 1911 and 1913.[55] In the various reports on Kuwait, British-imposed autonomy was viewed as a tool of empire to wrest the territory from effective Ottoman control.

The Foreign Ministry treated the problem of autonomy in Egypt similarly. Ragıb Raif Bey (Köseraif) and Rauf Ahmed, consuls for the British and French Embassies, respectively, wrote a short history of the Egyptian question in international relations between the period of Mehmed Ali and 1917, with a section on the British "conquest" of Sudan.[56] A substantial part of the report was dedicated to how Egypt became an *eyalet-i mümtaze*.

Though the imperial fermans had provided Mehmed Ali and his heirs with the right to internal provincial administration, the international treaties guaranteeing autonomy in Egypt laid the groundwork for perpetual European intervention in the province.[57] The report criticized autonomy as a form of imperial administration but also considered Egypt's future vis-à-vis the Ottoman Empire. Raif and Rauf examined this question from the perspective of the various fermans and treaties guaranteeing Egypt's international status. At the end of the study, they surveyed Egypt's status from the viewpoint of the key European international law textbooks and treaties.[58] The authors determined that the Ottoman Empire had an absolute legal right to Egypt, but that the legal status of the province should remain autonomous. They did not recommend that the Foreign Ministry recognize the British protectorate in Egypt, established in December 1914. Rather, they argued that given the high degree of European penetration, as well as Egyptian demands for autonomy, the best position for the Ottoman Empire was to maintain the status quo in Egypt: "The administrative system that has developed and flourished over a century has naturally given rise to an exceptional province (*vilayet-i mümtaze*), and we believe that the current legal instruments are appropriate to the on the ground realities."[59] Appended to the drafts for the volume was a map entitled "Egypt and Its Dependencies," which traced the territorial evolution of Egypt from Mehmed Ali in 1841 through agreements leading up to World War I, including the British occupation of Egypt. The map reflects the ways in which the fermans and international legal agreements determined the territory (see figure 5.3).[60]

The wartime government, in short, considered the possibility of extending administrative decentralization throughout the empire in the fall 1917—just before Wilson issued the 14 Points. Circumstances of the war forced a radical break with Unionist ideas about how the empire could be strengthened in the postwar period as a strong centralized state. But as we saw in chapter 4, the CUP was pragmatic and made concessions, and it had cut more autonomy deals than Abdülhamid II. Critically, the CUP's new way of thinking was not revolutionary. Its hesitant embrace of decentralization in 1917 was the opposite of Bolshevism. By finding a solution to partition within the constitutional history of the empire, the CUP, and later postwar governments, could claim that they were operating within an Ottoman idiom; moreover, it was one that the imperial subjects well understood.

The Ottoman Interpretation of Woodrow Wilson

When Woodrow Wilson's issued his 14 Points to the American Congress on January 8, 1918, as an expression of American war aims, it was met in Istanbul with a shrug. At that time, all attention in the capital was focused on the peace negotiations at Brest-Litovsk, the second round of which opened on January 9. With İbrahim Hakkı Paşa at the helm, the Ottoman government expected a major win in the form of regaining territory lost to Russia in 1878.[61] The Istanbul press, under military censorship, interpreted Wilson's speech with skepticism and treated it as little more than Allied war propaganda.[62]

For commentators in the capital, Allied peace proposals refused to acknowledge the fact the Central Powers had the upper hand with Russia out of the war. The Columbia University–trained journalist Ahmed Emin (Yalman) dismissed the 14 Points as a panicked American effort to counter the Central Powers negotiations with Russia. It was the "possibility of a separate peace treaty that has caused America to change its position." Wilson's conciliatory language that promised a peace without victors was merely an appeal to Russians and Germans. He criticized Wilson for demanding territorial changes in the Central Powers' empires—why should Germany and the Habsburgs give up land for his vague ideas? "Why should we relinquish our rights over part of our territory? Our enemies took up arms because they could not achieve what they call their war aims through peaceful means." Allied peace plans were fanciful: "While continuing our peace negotiations with the Russian delegates at Brest-Litovsk, we will simply shrug off (*omuz silkemekle*) the Allies' old and familiar proposals."[63]

By and large, newspaper editors conflated Wilson's 14 Points with Lloyd George's war aims speech from January 5, 1918.[64] Two days after Wilson's speech, Ahmed Emin again wrote a scathing analysis of Lloyd George's war aims speech at Caxton Hall to the British Trade Union Congress. Allied proposals were "tricks and stratagems to gain time." He argued that "self-determination" was nothing more than an Allied pretense to obtain German and Ottoman colonies:

> The final part of Lloyd George's statement takes a dangerous turn. He insists that it is necessary to apply the principle of self-determination

to the German colonies (*Milletlerin mukadderatlarını bizzat tayin etmeleri esasının Alman müstemlekelerine de tatbikine lazım gösteriyor*). It is an honorable thing for both the British prime minister and his government that he should care so much for the African natives in the German colonies, that he attaches a high degree of importance to establishing a method of administration that will fully guarantee their civil rights! Indeed, England has always shown excessive respect for the rights of African natives. The most striking example of this is bringing natives to northern Europe, packed in steamships, without knowing what they will suffer, and giving them the opportunity to sacrifice their own lives in the name of civilization, humanity, the rights of small nations, and other beautiful and good things. As for Ireland, India, and Egypt, these nations will naturally be excluded from self-determination. Since, for some reason, the people in these countries do not understand their own interests—keeping them under British rule by force is the foremost humanitarian duty for England![65]

Ahmed Emin's wartime writing was deeply critical of Allied policy, especially around questions of sovereignty and empire, but by December of 1918 he was a member of the Istanbul-based Wilsonian Principles League—a pattern that was broadly reflected in the government and among intellectuals in the capital. Ottoman indifference and outright hostility to Wilson remained until the fall of 1918, when suddenly it seemed his ideas might offer a solution to maintain the empire. The collapse of the Macedonian Front and Allenby's "breakthrough" at Nablus in Palestine, both in September 1918, signaled Ottoman defeat. In early October, disparate factions within and outside of the government attempted to contact the Americans to sue for peace along the lines of Wilson's 14 Points. This group included Talaat Paşa's wartime Cabinet, the Sultan Vahideddin, as well as a group of exiled CUP high officials who has fallen out of favor with Talaat and Enver.[66] It wasn't just high officials who had Wilson fever. As in Europe and Asia, Ottomans across the political spectrum appealed to "Wilsonian Principles" as the blueprint for the postwar order.

For Ottomans, it was not just the name "Wilson" that was important, but the specific article related to the Ottoman Empire—Article 12. If we look elsewhere in 1919, in Beijing, in Rome, in Fiume, people appealed to Wilsonian principles, broadly construed: the rights of small nations,

Figure 5.1 Soldiers in Erzurum, in Eastern Anatolia, holding a sign that reads "Wilsonian Principles: Article 12," written in Ottoman Turkish. (Library of Congress/ Official U.S. Army photographs, 1919, /5669 (F) [P&P]/#67342. Army "A sign advocating the 12th Article of Wilson's, at Ezerum (Erzurum). Sept. 25, 1919.")

"consent of the governed," and self-determination.[67] In contrast, in the images and journalistic accounts we have describing Ottoman enthusiasm for Wilson, Article 12 was what was relentlessly important: "XII. The Turkish portion of the present Ottoman Empire should be assured a secure sovereignty, but the other nationalities which are now under Turkish rule should be assured an undoubted security of life and an absolutely unmolested opportunity of autonomous development."[68] For Ottomans, including those advocating succession from the empire, Article 12 appeared to refer to the old debate between the Ottoman and European empires, as well as an old debate between Ottoman subjects and whoever controlled the state. And it was the idea of "autonomy" that appeared to hold so much potential (see figures 5.1 and 5.2).

By the spring of 1918, more and more officials began supporting a new vision of the empire, one that provided administrative autonomy to the Arab provinces in the Levant and the Arabian Peninsula. Indeed, between the onset of the Armistice in October 1918 and the signing of the Treaty of Sèvres in August 1920, government officials envisioned saving the empire by extending administrative decentralization throughout the imperial domains. The same people who had worked to restrict autonomy within the government, now embarked on an empire-wide campaign to transform the empire into a series of autonomous provinces. Ottoman peace proposals were consistent across the board, and each adhered to a particular Ottoman understanding of Wilson's twelfth point—assured sovereignty for the Turkish parts of the empire with autonomous administration for the non-Turkish provinces. Sultan Vahideddin's proposal even went so far as to provide autonomy in "Hejaz, Syria, Palestine and Mesopotamia under the suzerainty of the Sultan after the model of Egypt before the war."[69]

After receiving no response from the Americans, and against the prospect of continued war, the war cabinet resigned on October 8. Talaat, Enver, and Cemal escaped from the capital aboard a Russian submarine headed toward Odessa. A few days later Ahmed İzzet Paşa (Furgaç), a CUP general, formed a new cabinet and assumed the posts of foreign minister and grand vizier. Like Talaat, he attempted to sue for peace according to "Wilsonian principles," but he tapped the British rather than the Americans.[70]

The Ottoman government began negotiations for the Armistice with British General Townshend, a prisoner of war who had surrendered in 1915 during the Mesopotamian Campaign at the disastrous siege of Kut al-Amara and had been held in Istanbul for the remainder of the war.[71] Townshend met variously with İzzet Paşa and Rauf Bey (Orbay), the new minister of the Marine, in order to consider the initial Ottoman armistice terms. They arrived at six conditions dealing with prisoners of war, the Straits and other strategic issues, but the second point concerned imperial administration. Townshend argued that the Ottoman government should agree to implement "autonomous rule in Mesopotamia and Syria under the Sovereignty of the Sultan."[72] Rauf Bey agreed noting that "the Turkish government is ready to give autonomy to the territories under the sovereignty of the Sultan occupied by the Allies; England is to defend this system of government."[73] These points, nearly identical to those circulated in early October, became the basis from which the Ottoman delegation to Mudros would negotiate the armistice.

After spending the war attempting to extinguish the possibility of future autonomous provinces, the Foreign Ministry's best defense of the empire against partition was Wilson's promise of assured "Turkish sovereignty" and "autonomy" for the non-Turkish parts of the empire. The Foreign Ministry understood Wilson's autonomy in terms of how such provinces had functioned previously in the history of the empire. In preparation for the Armistice negotiations, the Foreign Ministry called on its legal advisors to consider how the empire might extend the system of autonomy into the Arab provinces, without diminishing Ottoman gains in international relations during the war.[74] One of the legal advisors at the Office of Legal Counsel, Mehmed Münir Bey (Ertegün), produced a lengthy analysis of Wilson's 14 Points and attempted to square Wilson's idea of "autonomous development" for the non-Turkish peoples with rebuilding the empire. Critically, there was no direct discussion of the autonomy for Greeks, Armenians, or Kurds. While the new government supported the idea of minority rights for non-Muslims, administrative autonomy was reserved for the Arab provinces.

Mehmed Münir was a key figure in establishing the new Foreign Ministry in the Turkish Republic. He joined the Office of Legal Counsel at the ministry in early 1913 and was a negotiator at Brest-Litovsk. During the Armistice period, he was a member of the Ottoman Committee to Study Peace in preparation for the Paris Peace Conference and provided legal advice regarding the Treaty of Sevres. In 1920 he abandoned the Istanbul government and joined the Ankara government as legal advisor to the Foreign Ministry. In addition to several other important early Republican negotiations, he was at Lausanne and later worked to keep Mosul within the boundaries of the Republic.[75]

Mehmed Münir reflected on the history and conditions of autonomous provinces in the Ottoman Empire and considered how a system of administrative decentralization might create a strong state that would be protected against European interference. Throughout the legal opinion, he insisted that autonomy could not function the way it had prior to the war. Autonomy had to be employed in such a way as to strengthen imperial architecture despite the condition of decentralized administration.[76] He noted that the Ottoman government accepted "Wilson's conditions":

> In localities that are inhabited by people of Turkish origin, the Ottoman government accepts absolute sovereignty without conditions. However, it is desired to establish a form of administration that will provide the possibility of autonomous development to the various

> nations under Turkish sovereignty, together with those places currently occupied like Iraq, Syria and Arabia. In short, it is necessary to put on record that Ottoman sovereignty should be confirmed—free from conditions like the Capitulations—and that the method of administration will not injure the development of the various nations.[77]

Even though the imperial government accepted Wilson's conditions, Mehmed Münir asserted that the old restrictions on sovereignty like the Capitulations had to be abandoned. The legal opinion examined various types of decentralized administration and found that, with the exception "of federal states like North America," decentralization was a political novelty, though one that could have some benefits from the point of view of creating local infrastructure like roads, lighting and waterworks.

Mehmed Münir went on to consider how autonomy had functioned "regarding the legal history of our administration" and compared the methods and problems of administration related to Egypt, Mount Lebanon, Samos, and Eastern Rumelia. For him, Egypt was the worst possible model for autonomy within the Ottoman Empire. He noted, "Its administration is restricted by family inheritance, and all the internal affairs of the state, including finance and local law, are legislated independent of the Ottoman sovereign. The province is allowed to conduct commercial treaties but is restricted from carrying out international treaties of a political nature. It sent a tribute to the Ottoman state, and the size of its army is restricted." The fact that Egypt had a hereditary governorship made it extraordinarily difficult for the central state to exert control. Mount Lebanon and Samos and Eastern Rumelia were not much better, he argued, but they had governors (*vali*) who could be removed more easily and who served for fixed terms. The real problem with the autonomous provinces was that "local political tendencies" produced a centrifugal force away from the concerns of the state, and this led to international pressure and intervention. No matter how well the Ottomans administered their Empire, localism would open the door to Europe. Despite the Ottoman government's longstanding desire to centralize administration, Mehmed Münir argued that in order to satisfy Wilson, the empire would accept autonomy and "whichever form of intervention resulted."[78]

Armed with Münir Paşa's legal opinion, the Ottoman delegation to negotiate the Armistice arrived in Mudros on October 25 and within five days worked out the terms of the Armistice. The Armistice demanded the surrender and evacuation of garrisons in Hejaz, Asir, Yemen, Syria, and Mesopotamia as well as the withdrawal of troops from Cilicia. Questions related to administration would be left to the Peace Conference.[79] Despite the blow offered by the Armistice, which mentioned neither autonomy nor Ottoman sovereignty in the Arab provinces, Ottoman officials continued to argue for a settlement in accordance with Wilson's principles.

It was during this period that İzzet Paşa announced to the Ottoman Parliament that the government would pursue peace according to Wilsonian principles. If the Allied victors applied the ideas embedded in the 14 Points, it would not only save the empire, it would enable the state to finally achieve sovereign equality: "If for the first time in international relations, the principles of justice and fairness are accepted and applied, our country will be protected from the ambitions of foreign powers, and the foundations of renewal and reform will be secured."[80] Limiting European interference in Ottoman affairs would also make autonomy far less dangerous. While nearly all the deputies approved the grand vizier's proposal to do so, the announcement occasioned a discussion on the future constitution of the empire. The Armenian deputy from Aleppo, Artin Boşgezenyen, expressed concern that the only known model for administrative autonomy along national lines was the Habsburg Empire, which itself struggled to maintain its existence.[81] Another deputy countered that Arab autonomy would not lead to partition and appealed to Islam as the true bond between "the Arab and Turkish nations."[82] The tension between nation and empire expressed within the Ottoman Parliament occurred on a far larger scale during the Paris Peace Conference and the Armistice more broadly. Publicists seized on key phrases within Wilson's twelfth point to further national and imperial ambitions. The battle for public opinion in Paris concerning the future of the Ottoman Empire was waged on particular understandings of what constituted the "Turkish portion" of the empire and the meaning of "autonomous development."

While government officials tried to save the empire through a constitutional solution rooted in the empire's administrative history, on the model of Egypt and Mount Lebanon before the war, Istanbul intellectuals focused on practical ways of creating a strong independent state. But like the Ottoman government, the goal by and large was to save the state from partition. During the Armistice, with very few exceptions, the majority of Ottoman Turkish newspaper editors were trained at the Imperial Law

School of the Darülfünun. Each would have been trained as a matter of course in Islamic legal theory, administrative law, as well as international law—these writers were not just intellectuals but trained lawyers with knowledge of Ottoman administrative law and international law.

Between the Ottoman wartime and Allied occupation censorship regimes (between June 11, 1918, with the end of military censorship, and the formal occupation of Istanbul on March 16, 1920), the press expanded and flourished after years of tight CUP regulation.[83] Several themes emerged, but one of the most vigorous early debates in the Ottoman Turkish press was how best to secure the future of the Ottoman domains. The subject that most divided intellectuals was not what kind of state should be built, but rather what means were necessary to achieve a stable political domestic and international order. It was in this context, amid mania for Wilson and preparation for the Paris Peace Conference, that editors of the major Istanbul papers established the Wilsonian Principles Society.

Broadly speaking, the Wilsonian Principles Society supported the establishment of a liberal domestic and international order, Ottoman equality in international relations, economic development, and a political reform agenda to create a viable state free from European intervention. The organization was founded, according to its creators, to openly debate and discuss ideas about to secure the future of the state. The founders—Halide Edib (Adıvar), Dr. Celaleddin Muhtar (Özden), Ali Kemal, and Refik Halit (Karay)—as well as its members had at times contrary political ideas.[84] While the Wilsonian Principles Society has at times been seen as a coherent political bloc that agitated for American intervention in the Ottoman Empire in order to create an independent Turkish state, or an American mandate in Turkey, the reality is that its members held divergent points of view and the views of specific editors shifted dramatically with the fate of the empire. The society came about in a moment of confusion and uncertainty about the future of the state. While many of its members were liberals and former members of the of the prewar Freedom and Accord Party (*Hürriyet ve İtilaf Fırkası*), others, like Yunus Nadi (Abalıoğlu), editor of *Yeni Gün* and later *Cumhurriyet*, would quickly become the mouthpieces of Mustafa Kemal's regime in Ankara.

Once Talaat Paşa's government resigned against looming defeat in October 1918, the CUP became an immediate object of derision and was roundly criticized in the press for the disasters of the war, corruption, and war profiteering.[85] Prewar political constellations and battles reemerged, and there were old scores to be settled.[86] One of the major debates that resurfaced was on imperial administration—the old centralization versus decentralization debate—and the place and privileges of non-Muslims within the newly reconfigured empire. The immediate context for these debates was the fact that the government self-proclaimed commitment to extending autonomy to the Arab provinces in October 1918.

The government's uncertainty about how exactly to implement autonomy throughout the empire was reflected in debates in the press. Intellectuals and newspaper editors proposed various schemes for the reorganization of the postwar order, including a political union of all Ottoman nations, an Arab Turkish federation, a "United States of Ottoman nationalities," as well as the devolution of authority to the local level outside of any kind of national or religious framework. While the idea of the nation-state was on the table, even the most fervent Turkish nationalists were reluctant to advocate total dissolution of the empire until much later than is generally noted in the historiography. By and large, in the early days of the Armistice, the press supported the government's plan to extend administrative autonomy to the Arab provinces. But every projected state model was accompanied by the same warning: No matter how well organized the internal constitutional order of the state might be, it would mean little if the empire's international position was not radically improved and if all the prewar European-imposed limitations on Ottoman sovereignty were not permanently abolished. In other words, obtaining equality in international relations was a prerequisite for a strong postwar state—a longstanding Hamidian era and CUP foreign policy goal—and the international order itself depended on maintaining the Ottoman state.

In November 1918 Prince Sabahaddin, whom we met in chapter 4, together with exiled CUP members in Geneva, issued a widely publicized declaration following a congress that examined "Wilsonian principals" and their application to the Ottoman Empire.[87] The revolutionary era crusader for decentralization (*adem-i merkeziyet*) continued to push for the devolution of responsibility (*tevsi-i mezuniyet*) but now explicitly linked decentralization to autonomy. The congress argued that Wilson's ideas would provide the foundation for a stable and lasting Ottoman federation: "It is only this condition that they could themselves choose the form of autonomy according to which they desire to live in the future under the protection of an Ottoman federalism." The congress viewed federation as a new iteration of the millet system: "Ottoman federalism, besides, would only be a natural evolution of the ancient tradition which conceded to the Christian peoples of the Empire freedom and ecclesiastical autonomy." Written before the Paris Peace Conference and the announcement of the mandates system, the authors could not imagine that states would replace empire in the new order. They were certain that the people of "Syria and Mesopotamia" would prefer remaining in the empire than wishing to be attached "to some other sovereign" and welcomed Poland as independent state, only because it had existed as such before partition.[88] Prince Sabahaddin's ideas, along with the liberal opposition, were revived in the aftermath of the disasters of the First World War.

That same month, in Istanbul, Sati al-Husri wrote a two-part article in *Vakit* on Prince Sabahaddin and administrative decentralization, entitled "Sabahaddin Bey: His Ideas and Opponents."[89] Historians have looked at Sati al-Husri as the classic case of the shift from Ottomanism to Arabism. An Ottoman constitutionalist and educator before the war, al-Husri was deeply committed to, and a theorist of, Ottomanism. Like other Ottoman reformers in the constitutional era, he was committed to preserving the state. But by 1921, he was in mandate Iraq serving as the director-general of education and had shifted his thinking from Ottomanism toward theorizing pan-Arab nationalism on the basis of language and common history instead of on the basis of ethnicity and religion. Between the general Armistice and June 1919, when Sati al-Husri left Istanbul for the emerging Arab government in Damascus, Arabs and Turks appealed to him to either go to Syria or stay in Istanbul.[90]

In his November 1918 editorials in *Vakit*, Sati al-Husri said nothing about Emir Faisal, nor the fall of Damascus. Instead, he remained committed to the Ottoman state and offered ideas for reorganizing the empire. He argued that the CUP leaders and political clubs who had maligned Sabahaddin in the years before the war had radically misconstrued his ideas. He noted that according to the CUP, "to accept decentralization . . . meant to be content with the fragmentation of the homeland. Because this type of administration would give autonomy to localities, it meant that within a period of time, autonomy would end with the complete separation. Thanks to the power and organization of the CUP—this opinion spread to every part of the country. And in the minds of the youth, it has become an article of faith."[91]

According to Sati al-Husri, the CUP's blind opposition to decentralization triggered a series of crises—particularly in Yemen, Albania, and

Syria—all of which weakened the empire in the years leading up to the war. In the aftermath of the wars in Libya and the Balkans, the CUP's belief in centralization was briefly shaken—even for writers at *Tanin* (CUP) and *Yeni Turan* (pan-Turkist journal): "Some of the people regretted that they insisted upon centralization, they said that they favored centralization only for the Balkans . . . right away everyone admitted that it was necessary to progress towards decentralization. . . . Even the ones who most strongly opposed the Albanian reform now discussed the necessity of giving wide-ranging autonomy to the Arab provinces (*Arabistan*) as much as is given to Hungary (in the Habsburg Empire)."[92]

After the CUP seized power in 1913, it attached "more importance to Arab claims." But, as Sati Bey put it, they could not save themselves from "their old mentality" and ultimately pursued a policy of centralization in the Arab provinces that was beyond the old "status-quo." The old tolerances in the provinces were brought to an end—even Arabic instructors were viewed as traitors by provincial officials. He was also deeply critical of Cemal Paşa's decision to execute Arabs who sought decentralization before the war—they were "persecuted and executed for their ideas."[93]

Despite the disasters of CUP policies in the Arab provinces, Sati al-Husri was not ready to abandon the empire. Instead, he proposed returning to Sabahaddin's proposals for administrative decentralization (*adem-i merkeziyet-i idare*) as an alternative to CUP centralization policies. He argued that prewar understandings of these ideas were skewed by the CUP, which had hoped only to discredit them. Sabahaddin had advocated imperial reorganization and the distribution of power to the provinces, where local councils and administrators could better implement finance, public works, and education policies: "I have no doubt that it is necessary to put in place a new form of administration for Turkey . . . the ideas of this program will bring great benefit (to the country)." When Sati Bey finally left Istanbul for Damascus, Ahmed Emin (Yalman) wrote in *Vakit* that "Syria has been severed from us."[94]

Not everyone agreed that administrative decentralization would save the Ottoman Empire, but even Turkist intellectuals who later supplied the early Republic with nationalist ideas and helped build the new order after October 1923 were not yet fully committed to the complete dissolution of empire in 1918. Even before it was clear that the war was lost, intellectuals began to consider the future of the state. In March 1918 Ziya Gökalp, who is widely seen as one of the most important theorists of Turkish nationalism, argued in an article entitled "Nationalism and Internationalism" that Arabs and Turks should have "cultural independence" and control over internal political affairs, but that ultimately it was too dangerous for each state to exist without the other. The only way to combat the rapaciousness of European imperialism, which had now set its sights on the Arab lands, was to form a confederation or political union between Turks and Arabs.[95]

Halide Edib too, who was one of the founding members of the Wilsonian Principles Society and would later play an important role in constructing the new state in Ankara, advocated for an Arab government in Syria but was similarly concerned about viability of independent states. She had spent part of the war in Syria working for Cemal Paşa in schools and at the orphanage Aintoura, where Armenian children, survivors of the genocide, were forcibly converted to Islam and assimilated. Her editorial "Turks in Syria" recounts her experiences in wartime famine-plagued Lebanon and at Aintoura.[96] She argued that a "rusty" (*paslı*) administration had failed to prevent death and the blockade—although she did defend Cemal Paşa's treatment of the Arabs intellectuals and leaders who wanted autonomy as a wartime necessity. We might expect that Halide Edib, who had supported pan-Turkism and Turkish nationalism before the war, to be perfectly happy with the death of empire. But even she is not entirely clear: "Syria doesn't want a Turkish administration (*idare*) anymore and certainly those who do, it is only out of personal advantage and political greed. . . . I wish with my entire heart that you are able to establish your own Arab government (*hükumet*), which has at least partial national independence in line with Wilsonian principles."[97] While on one hand it seems that she supported Arab independence, on the other, if we read this text alongside other Ottoman interpretations of Wilsonian principles as a promise of autonomy, it is much less clear.

While the period between the fall of Talaat Paşa's government and the beginning of the Paris Peace Conference was dominated by debates on how to implement İzzet Paşa's decentralization policy, there was increasing tension between the idea of nation and empire that would explode at the Paris Peace Conference. At Paris, publicists seized on key phrases within Wilson's twelfth point to further national and imperial ambitions. This, combined with Supreme Allied Council's decision to create mandates in the Arab provinces, reframed debates on the future of the empire in Istanbul. Ottoman intellectuals and bureaucrats continued to embrace "Wilsonian principles" as a pragmatic way to maintain or reconfigure the empire, but the meaning of "Wilsonian principles" shifted, as did expectations for what Ottoman sovereignty might look like.

Ottoman petitioners, as much as Entente delegates, drew heavily on population statistics to buttress territorial claims in the Ottoman domains. Representing Greece at the Paris Peace Conference, Eleftherios Venizelos, relied on Article 12 to argue that extensive parts of the Ottoman Empire, including Istanbul, should fall under either direct Greek control or be established as Greek autonomous province:

> The article already cited from the programme of President Wilson governs also the solution of the problem of Asia Minor: Ottoman sovereignty must, from now onwards, be limited to the interior of the country, where the Turkish element is predominant.

Venizelos, a lawyer and former Ottoman subject from autonomous Crete, argued that the principle of self-determination should extend to populations granted autonomy within the reconstituted Ottoman state. Instead of living in an autonomous province, they should be allowed to join "an already existing state of the same nationality."[98] Istanbul newspaper editors turned to population statistics and the language of minority (*akalliyet*) and majority (*ekseriyet*) in greater frequency soon after Venizelos presented Greek demands to the Peace Conference on February 3, 1919.

In late January 1919 the Allied Victors decided to not to return German colonial territory nor the Arab provinces of the Ottoman Empire that were under military occupation. Instead, territories under Allied occupation would be held by the occupying powers as mandates guaranteed by the new League of Nations. While the final system took time to work out, Britain and France would take control of the Arab provinces as Mandates. For much of 1919, there was a debate among the Europeans and Americans about imposing an American mandate on a new Armenia as well as the rump Ottoman state. Some Ottoman writers viewed the mandates as nothing more than a cover for the formal extension of European empire into the Middle East. Other political commentators understood the mandate idea as an internationally guaranteed state development project and clamored for an American mandate as a way to preserve the

Figure 5.2 Soldiers in Erzincan holding a banner that reads "Long Live Article 12!" in French. (LOC/Official U.S. Army photographs, 1919 /LOT 5669 (F) [P&P]/#67324/. Army "View of the courthouse and sign advocating the 12th Article of Wilson's, at Erzinjan (Erzincan), Sept. 23, 1919.")

empire—including the most prominent members of the Wilsonian Principles Society, Halide Edib (Adıvar) and Ahmed Emin (Yalman).

Several Ottoman intellectuals immediately saw the mandates for what they would become—an extension of European empire. After reading about plan for Arab mandates, Ahmed Reşid Paşa (Rey), the former interior minister and governor of Monastir, Aleppo, and Aydın—all prewar hotspots from the perspective of national questions—appealed to Wilson directly. Ahmed Reşid cast "Wilsonian principles" as directly in line with the prewar Freedom and Accord Party (*Hürriyet ve İtilaf Fırkası*), which favored decentralization. Referring to the longstanding debate among factions within the early Committee of Union and Progress, he noted that Ottoman liberals had welcomed Wilson's promise of autonomous administration in Article 12, as it accorded with decentralized administrative ideas among Ottoman Liberals before the war: "The liberal Turkish party, whom I have the honor to represent, having for a very long time, had as their own idea, the liberation of the ancient Empire into a Confederation."[99] The mandates, in contrast, cut against Wilsonian principles. Mandates abrogated the internal and external sovereignty promised by Article 12, violated the armistice, and provided a legal justification for European imperial annexation of Ottoman territory.[100]

In an anonymous article entitled "Mandate, Protectorate, Independence" in *Büyük Mecmua*, a journal owned and edited by the liberal journalists Zakeriya and Sabiha Sertel, the author warned that mandates would obliterate actual independence, no matter how well guarded. The author asked why any state would freely surrender its freedom. After all, "Following the defeat no Bulgarian would retreat from independence. No Bulgarian would say 'we cannot administer ourselves; we need a protectorate.'" The author further maintained that the mandates would inevitably erode economic and political sovereignty.[101]

In a pamphlet issued by the "League for the Defense of Ottoman Rights," the authors argued that the empire would accept foreign support in the form of aid and expertise but rejected any accompanying loss of sovereignty as "at odds with Point 12 of Mr. Wilson's program." The League warned that "if the Peace Conference decided to divide the territories of the Near East inhabited by Muslim peoples, who have never been subjected to domination and who have always governed themselves, and if the Peace Conference, with the label 'mandate,' wants to place those territories under the domination of foreign nations, they must impose this decision on the people by blood and fire." The Ottoman Empire would ensure the rights of non-Muslim minorities but "would never consent to alienate its independence nor yield a bit of its national patrimony either to a foreign power or to one of the ethnic minorities in its midst." The League for the Defense of Ottoman Rights appealed to Wilson's 14 Points in order to claim secure sovereignty for the Ottoman state, whereas "autonomous development" would be nothing more than minority rights protected by the Constitution.[102]

Some intellectuals viewed the mandate idea as a pragmatic expedient to save the state and to prevent partition. The idea could be used to legitimize demands for very practical forms of aid and expertise—in agriculture and education. Even before the Supreme Allied Council publicly announced that the German colonies and Ottoman Arab provinces would become League mandates in late January 1919, writers were already debating the merits and dangers of American or European administrative and financial oversight in the Ottoman Empire. Indeed, the Wilsonian Principles Society petition to Wilson in December 1918 requested American financial assistance, expertise, and advisors for the Ministries of Finance, Justice, Agriculture, Public Works, Education, and Industry and Commerce. The petition preserved Ottoman sovereignty under American "guidance and instruction . . . for a minimum period of 15 years or a maximum period of 25 years."[103]

In December 1918 Ahmed Emin (Yalman)—whom we met earlier writing about David Lloyd George and self-determination—defended the idea of inviting American experts to aid in the administration of the Ottoman Empire. He argued that American aid was necessary to establish a strong and independent state and would be distinct from European empire as usual: "We reject the idea of a protectorate or trusteeship. However, in order to truly accept state's needs, we require help from experts."[104] He had studied political science at Columbia University under the internationalist James T. Shotwell and the journalist Talcott Williams. For Ahmed Emin, the only way to save the empire was through development via an infusion of foreign financial aid and Western expertise.

Ahmed Emin continued to agitate for an American mandate along these practical lines, but, like other members of the Wilsonian Principles Society, his views of what the state might look like changed over time, particularly after the Greek invasion of İzmir in May 1919. In August he submitted a report to the King-Crane Commission in which he insisted that only a settlement based on Wilsonian principles would preserve peace: "An artificial settlement, in contradiction to the spirit of the Wilsonian principles and the ethical aims of the League of Nations would result in new series of conflicts in the continuation of the old chaos in a new form." But good government, which he hoped an American mandate might provide, did not mean "only justice, good roads, and better economic opportunities . . . the idea of good government must include . . . preparation for citizenship in form of universal education, good sanitary condition, a struggle for social betterment and a rising standard of living." Like the writer of the anonymous article in *Büyük Mecmua* noted earlier, Ahmed Emin saw British and French mandates as a cover for empire and argued that there should be a single mandate, under the United States, for Anatolia and the Arab provinces. He noted, "As a matter of fact, the question of a single mandate for Turkey for the good of the population itself, has not even been raised in Paris. There is only talk of several mandates, which would only serve to disguise the annexations of imperialistic powers and would mean a partition and exploitation for the benefit of the aliens."

Despite the fact that Ahmed Emin wanted to preserve some connection to the Arab provinces, he advocated population exchange for Greeks residing on the Aegean coast and Muslims in Macedonia. He argued that the Armenian Patriarchate should be relocated to the Armenian Republic, whatever form that state might take, and that Armenians who did not wish to remain and become "Turkish citizens" should be transferred to the new state. Ottoman Muslims would maintain a link with Turkey, and the protégé system, which indexed European intervention in Ottoman affairs, would be replaced with true citizenship: "Citizenship in the Near East must be given at last a real and loyal meaning. The Arabs should be given opportunity to run their own affairs autonomously. The only effective solution would be to extend them the supervision of the same mandatory power. The Kurds should be trained for self-government in the areas where they are segregated."[105] Even though Ahmed Emin began to view the trajectories of the Arab provinces and "Turkey" as distinct, he wasn't quite ready to ditch empire for the state. His vision for citizenship and imperial belonging had radically narrowed.

Ottoman journalists and intellectuals continued to appeal to Wilsonian Principles as the foundation for the postwar order through the San Remo Conference, which allotted the Arab mandates to Britain and France and the Treaty of Sevres and formalized the partition of the empire. Years later, Ahmed Emin remarked that newspaper editors in Istanbul continued to invoke Article 12 to put pressure on Americans: "The Turkish papers of patriotic tendencies, agreed among themselves to publish every day, on the first page with as much emphasis as possible, Wilson's twelfth point. The idea was to remind America of their moral responsibility and to urge them to defend their principles, which had been used by their European allies merely as bait for a quick armistice."[106]

An examination of debates within the Istanbul press shows a far greater inclination to remake the empire rather than make the state—a point that Mustafa Kemal fixated on in his critique of the Istanbul press, which he derisively labeled the "Armistice press" (*mütereke basını*). In his speech of October 1927—the foundational text of official historiography on the establishment of the Turkish Republic—Mustafa Kemal attacked the press in the capital as traitorous, but he singled out the Wilsonian Principles Society as a

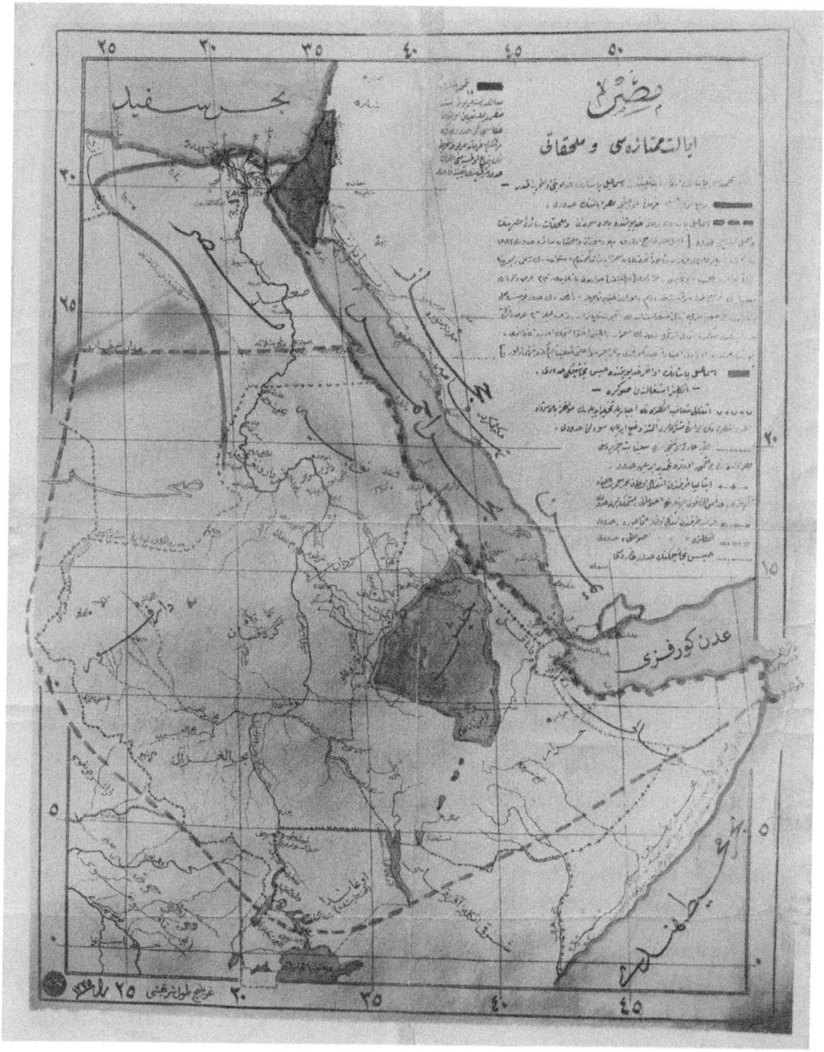

Figure 5.3 Autonomous Egypt and its dependencies, 1916. Ottoman Archives (Başbakalık Osmanlı Arşivleri) HR.HMŞ.IŞO/233/2 [Hijri 1335/1916].

particular enemy of the Turkish nation. He argued that the society refused to recognize that foundations of the Ottoman state had been shattered by the war. The only option that remained for a sovereign and independent government was to create a "new Turkish State."[107] The great error that Ottoman Wilsonians made was to imagine that the empire could be preserved against the inevitability of the state. The members of the Wilsonian Principles

Society who wrote memoirs after the war largely disavowed or downplayed the significance of the organization.[108] But it shows that even though Mustafa Kemal's position won out during the tumultuous years between 1918 and 1923, it was not at all clear how the future state might be configured.

Conclusion: Autonomy, the Last Gasp of Empire

It is not entirely clear what Wilson meant by the expression "autonomous development" in Article 12. On one hand, there is little doubt that the Inquiry, Woodrow Wilson's band of academics and geographers who helped draft the 14 Points and later joined the American delegation to Paris, planned for the partition of the Ottoman Empire. In preliminary suggestions for Wilson's speech on the terms of the peace, the Inquiry parroted the old European attacks against the Ottoman misrule:

> It is necessary to free the subject races of the Turkish Empire from oppression and misrule. This implies at the very least autonomy for Armenia and the protection of Palestine, Syria, Mesopotamia, and Arabia by the civilized nations . . . this will appear on the surface to be a drastic solution of the Turkish problem, but it is one which the military situation enables us to accomplish, and it can hardly be doubted that no principle of justice requires the return of occupied portions of Turkey to the German-Turkish alliance. The cancellation of Turkey's debt is the one final way to abolish German political and commercial penetration. It is also the one method by which Turkey can be given a new start, considerably reduced in size, without power to misgovern alien races, and therefore free to concentrate upon the needs of her own population.[109]

None of the members of the Inquiry specialized in the history, affairs, or languages of the Ottoman Empire, and unlike their counterparts in Britain and France, they had virtually no experience with Near East diplomacy. Despite this fact, the Inquiry was made astonishingly well aware of Ottoman autonomous provinces, which, if nothing else, suggests the relative transparency of Ottoman administration. The Inquiry's immense collection of "Special Reports on Countries, Peoples, and Regions" for the Ottoman Empire were dominated by discussions of how autonomous provinces had functioned prior to the war and to what extent the empire might be reorganized as a series of autonomous provinces.

American Protestant missionaries, geographers, and archeologists who lived or spent time in the Ottoman Empire authored the bulk of the special reports for the Inquiry.[110] Unlike the British or Ottoman analyses produced during the war and in its immediate aftermath, the Americans paid particular attention to religious autonomy, and several proposed extending the existing system of autonomous provinces, but only to the "non-Turkish" and especially Christian populations of the empire. For example, William Peet, treasurer for the American Board of Missions, sent a report to the Inquiry explaining that Ottoman non-Muslims had a long history of maintaining separate religious communities. He argued that religious autonomy had inspired constitutionalism among Christians within the empire and that they would be prepared to govern themselves. He noted that Ottoman Christians, particularly Armenians, had "become accustomed to self-governance, skilled in the drafting of legislative documents, and that they already have a valuable preparation for the duties that may be devolved upon them, should their territory become an autonomous state."[111] The main concern of this and similar such Inquiry reports that advocated the decentralized administration was to secure a future for Armenians within the Ottoman Empire.

Representatives of the various potential successor nations of the Ottoman Empire, along with the Ottoman government, appealed to Wilson's twelfth point in order to support overlapping territorial and political claims. Throughout the period of the Paris Peace Conference, such competing political claims were marked by a distinct tension between nation and empire. Establishing national majorities and national minorities within the Ottoman domains produced an abundance of warring population statistics, but these numbers were not necessarily always aimed at constructing a national state. A number of possible political configurations were imagined. Whether a Greater Greece or a Turkish Arab empire or a Turkish state in Anatolia, the final shape of the Middle East was not decided until well after the end of the war. The future composition of the Ottoman state was up for grabs in 1918 and arguably remained so until the Treaty of Lausanne in 1923. Throughout the Armistice period, both the government in occupied Istanbul and the government in Ankara were more flexible about the future boundaries of the state than is often admitted by the historiographical debate. While Turkish, Armenian, Greek,

Kurdish, and Arab nationalists appealed to Wilson to claim a stake in the future organization of the Ottoman domains, the Ottoman wartime and successive postwar governments invoked Wilson's twelfth point as an argument for maintaining the empire. Whatever Wilson meant by Article 12, a broad range of nationalists and imperialists inside and outside of the Ottoman Empire appropriated his language for their own ends. Each of them drew on prewar debates about imperial administration and sovereignty, as well as the longer history of autonomy and foreign intervention in the empire. As long as the Middle East remained legally unsettled, the autonomy idea remained a viable option for the future organization of the state. But as France and Britain legalized their political claim to the Arab provinces as mandates, and as Mustafa Kemal's resistance fought Greek soldiers in Anatolia, Ottoman subjects' political futures radically narrowed.

CHAPTER 6

Mandate Variations

On December 18, 1914, five months into the First World War, Britain ended the occupation and incorporated Egypt into the empire as a protectorate. The Ottoman entry into the war against the Allies in November provided the Foreign Office the opportunity to resolve Egypt's anomalous international legal status as a de jure Ottoman territory under British administration. The declaration of protection severed the legal relationship between the Ottoman Empire and Egypt and ended nearly four hundred years of Ottoman sovereignty in the province. By breaking this legal tie, Britain terminated the treaties and fermans that had guaranteed Egypt's status as an autonomous Ottoman province in international law since the era of Mehmed Ali.

From the Declaration of Protection in 1914 through the interwar years, legal and political commentators, colonial administrators, and bureaucrats wrote broadly about the meaning of the end of Ottoman sovereignty in Egypt—Ottomans and Europeans.[1] While there was extensive commentary about the British declaration of protection in Egypt at the time, for the most part the transfer from Ottoman to British sovereignty does not make up a significant part of the historiographical debate. Egypt's wartime story generally begins in 1915 with the Hussein-McMahon Correspondence, the establishment of the Arab Bureau, and the beginnings of the Arab Revolt—a chronology that separates the Ottoman past from Egypt and the modern Middle East.

Yet the international legal status of Egypt mattered in international politics in 1914 as much as it had since 1840. It threatened to bring the Ottomans into the war against Britain long before they were prepared. Germany and Britain also used Egypt to incentivize the Ottomans for their own ends in the war. British internal debates on the future of Egypt between the July Crisis and the declaration of protection also mirrored debates that would occur at the end of the war about how to deal with Ottoman territories under British military occupation in 1918. Egypt and Cyprus were the first Ottoman territories to be incorporated into the British Empire by protection and annexation, respectively. Egypt provided a potential model for thinking about British imperial control in the Middle East after the war. British internal debates on the virtues of annexation versus protection in conjunction with Egyptian demands for autonomy in 1914 were an important testing ground for thinking about the location of formal sovereignty in relation to imperial control.

Egypt and the Ottoman Entry in World War I

Between the July Crisis and the British declaration of protection in December 1914, the Egyptian question played a significant but underappreciated role in the unfolding war. Even though Egypt had been under effective occupation by Britain for nearly thirty years, Ottoman sovereignty in Egypt threatened to bring the Ottoman and British Empires into direct conflict. In the early days of the war, Britain pledged to preserve Egypt's political status to induce the Ottoman Empire to demobilize and remain neutral in the war against the Central Powers. At the same time, for the German Foreign Office, Egypt was an ideal site for Ottoman intervention.[2] The Ottoman government's immediate goal was to obtain an alliance while delaying involvement in the war indefinitely.[3] Enver Paşa, the Ottoman minister of war, proposed a secret defensive alliance with Germany, which was signed in early August. The empire needed time to mobilize and maintained a state of neutrality until November. During that period, rumors that the British planned to convert Egypt into a protectorate, coupled with patrols on the Suez and other measures taken to protect Egypt against Germany, threatened to be construed as acts of war.

The Ottoman Empire had four main goals in entering the First World War: to attain a European alliance, to reestablish direct control over the autonomous provinces of the empire, to regain territory recently lost in the Italian and Balkan Wars, and to revoke the Capitulations and other European privileges.[4] Though varied, each point was directed toward the same end: to remake a strong state independent of European restrictions. The Ottoman Cabinet, in other words, wished to close the gap between internal and external affairs by ending all European restrictions on Ottoman sovereignty. Ending the Capitulations was viewed as the path to gain control over the economy, while centralizing administration and ending the special status of the autonomous provinces were seen as the route to internal security and more efficient imperial control. These considerations are worth mentioning as they explain a fairly radical shift in Ottoman attitudes toward Britain, although this shift had been in the making for some time. Ottoman diplomacy, which long relied on British territorial guarantees and international treaties, viewed British territorial promises as completely bankrupt by 1914. While the Ottomans still maintained the goal of preserving the territorial extent of the empire, it would mean nothing if imperial security and administrative control remained in British and European hands.

From August 1914 it was clear that Ottoman sovereignty in Egypt had the potential to disrupt the Ottoman policy of nonintervention or delay. A few days after Britain declared war on Germany, Sir Edward Grey, the British foreign secretary, asked the embassy in Istanbul to assure the Ottoman government that Britain had no intention of changing Egypt's political status. "If Turkey remains neutral and Egypt remains quiet, and should no unforeseen circumstances arise, His Majesty's government do not propose to alter the status of Egypt. A report has reached me that it is being alleged that the annexation of Egypt is under consideration by His Majesty's Government. You should emphatically contradict this to the Turkish Government, and say that we have no intention of hurting Turkey."[5]

The occasion for Britain's halfhearted guarantee stemmed from the desire to prevent Ottoman engagement in the war but also from recent events in Cairo. The day before the government of Egypt, prompted by British advisors, had published a lengthy resolution intended to protect Egypt during the war. The measures were justified on the basis that the presence of the British army of occupation opened Egypt to a potential German attack.[6] The resolution prompted protest from the khedive, who wrote to his ministers in Cairo that "the Grand Vizier points out that Egypt has declared war on Germany." The consul-general of Germany did not want to leave Egypt either, as he considered it "neutral and not in a state of war."[7] During this same period, the German Foreign Office, and Kaiser Wilhelm in particular, pressured the Ottomans to enter the war and specifically to intervene in Egypt as a condition of the alliance.[8] The "Egyptian Campaign" was not meant to serve a real military objective but was designed to tie down Britain in Egypt and, as part of the Ottoman Jihad, to foment revolution against British, French, and Russian rule throughout their empires. Striking a balance between German and British demands, in Berlin the Ottoman government argued that it needed more time to mobilize for a successful campaign, while also assuring the Allied camp that the empire would maintain a policy of strict neutrality.

On August 10 Said Halim Paşa, the grand vizier, wrote to the German and Habsburg ambassadors in Istanbul and requested that Egypt be placed outside of the sphere of warfare, effectively neutralized during the conflict.[9] He noted Britain's resolution to protect Egypt during the war and their concern that Germany might launch an attack against Britain in Egypt. Said Halim argued that even if an attack were directed exclusively against British forces, it would nevertheless harm the Ottoman Empire. "In view of the cordial relations that exist between Germany, Austria-Hungry, and Turkey, the Sublime Porte remains convinced that at no point should Germany and Austria attack Ottoman territory under the khedivate, despite the presence of British troops in this domain. In consequence, I beg Your Excellency to send me assurance that Egyptian territory will not be the object of any kind of aggression on the part of the imperial forces of Germany and Austria."[10]

On one hand, Said Halim's bid to keep Egypt out of the war at this stage was part of the larger Ottoman plan to maintain the alliance with Germany under armed neutrality. At the same time, the proposal should be understood both as an effort to maintain Ottoman claims to Egypt along the lines of the war aims discussed, as well as recognition of the fact that Egypt's legal position could drag the Empire into a state of war. Amid rumors that Britain was planning to declare a protectorate in Egypt, Berlin continued to push Enver and Said Halim to enter the war by attacking the British in Egypt.[11] Late in August the German ambassador, Hans Frieiherr von Wangenheim, argued that Britain violated Ottoman rights in Egypt by detaining hundreds of German and Austrian reservists and by removing essential parts from German ships at Port Said. "By these acts, the British government seized the rights of sovereignty over Egyptian territory; the Government of Egypt however, in tolerating this conduct, has rendered itself culpable of flagrant violations of its right as a neutral state."[12] Germany appealed to longstanding Ottoman legal arguments defending their sovereign rights in Egypt and attempted to use the ostensible abrogation of Ottoman sovereignty in Egypt as a pretext for war. The Ottomans had a right to invade Egypt on the grounds that Britain had usurped Ottoman dominion. Enver and Said Halim responded again with delay and argued that the Ottoman state required more military support and more preparation to carry out a successful attack in Egypt.[13]

In the middle of September, two days after the Ottoman Empire announced the abolition of the Capitulations, Wangenheim sent Said Halim formal assurances that Germany recognized Egypt as "an integral part of the Ottoman Empire" and that the territory of the sultan would not be attacked by German imperial forces.[14] The note was in direct response to the Ottoman plea in August to keep Egypt out of the war sent in the midst of increased German pressure to launch an Ottoman attack there. Neither Berlin nor Vienna would strike Egypt, but the way was paved for the Ottomans to do so. The German Foreign Ministry again appealed to Ottoman legal claims in Egypt in order to draw the empire into war. The grand vizier and the war minister continued to prevaricate and delay. Enver again argued that the Ottomans were not prepared to strike Egypt and expressed a preference for a campaign in the Caucasus. Said Halim was not prepared to abandon Ottoman claims to Egypt and recognized that going to war against Britain, especially in Egypt, might prejudice postwar outcomes.[15] Launching a campaign against Britain in Egypt would mean striking Ottoman territory populated by de jure Ottoman subjects. The Ottoman dilemma in Egypt would parallel that forced by Britain once the two empires were at war, when Britain would find itself in control of a territory inhabited by enemy subjects. Nevertheless, despite German Foreign Office pressure to carry out the "Egypt campaign," when the Ottomans finally entered the war at the end of October they attacked Russia at Black Sea ports and Odessa, not Britain at Suez.

Throughout the fall of 1914, Britain demanded strict neutrality from the Ottoman Empire in exchange for maintaining the political status of Egypt.[16] The Foreign Office, too, tied any postwar decisions in the Near East to this condition, noting that Britain would continue to guarantee the territorial integrity of the Ottoman Empire in return for nonintervention and demobilization. Yet the old Foreign Office promises to preserve the empire against territorial losses and foreign encroachments lost much appeal after the recent defeats in North Africa and the Balkans. Ottoman officials were increasingly distrustful of European, and especially British, promises to guarantee the territorial extent of the empire and viewed the reassertion of Ottoman sovereignty in financial and administrative matters as the best way to achieve this objective, rather than through older methods of diplomacy and British support.[17] The Ottoman ambassador in Berlin was Mahmud Muhtar Paşa (Katırcıoğlu).[18] He rejected the British promise to continue to recognize Ottoman rights in Egypt out of hand, noting that "it is obvious that only the semblance of our sovereignty exists in Egypt, moreover our territory has been so often violated that the promise of our territorial integrity cannot generate any appeal which would offset the enormous benefits we could make by joining Germany. The British proposal, if it occurred, does not seem to be anything than the continuation of the state of vassalage and dependence on England and its allies."[19] Joining the Allied side might extend the life of the empire on paper, but without economic and administrative control, the state itself threatened to become another Egypt, where only the façade of sovereign control existed.

In another letter, Mahmud Muhtar Paşa advocated ending the state of armed neutrality and urged Said Halim to join the war on the side of the Central Powers. As with Egypt, he argued that Allied promises to maintain the territorial integrity of the empire were empty words, as each of the Powers had strategic and economic interests in the empire, which could only be fulfilled through Ottoman partition: Britain wished to dominate the space between the Persian Gulf and the Eastern Mediterranean, Russia wanted the Straits and Istanbul, while France continued to desire Syria and Lebanon. Neutrality would lead to the final dismemberment of the Ottoman Empire: "Yet, if Mesopotamia, Arabia, Syria and the Straits along with neighboring regions were not part of Turkey, one could well remain indifferent to the result of the current European struggle and remain neutral. . . . Can we continue to accept the humiliating situation that we have submitted to in Egypt and the fact that in the (Aegean) islands, which we still claim, serve as military bases for other navies—insulting us in our own waters? . . . the fate of the Ottoman Empire will depend on the outcome of this war."[20]

Ottoman officials saw themselves locked in an existential battle with Europe and viewed the war as a chance to reassert sovereignty internally as well as in international affairs.[21] Allied economic and strategic interests in the empire, along with the fact that these same powers controlled the very institutions that constrained Ottoman sovereignty—the Capitulations, the Ottoman Debt Administration, internationally guaranteed autonomous provinces, and permanent military occupation—proved that the Allied powers could not be counted on to secure the future of the empire. The only way to rejuvenate the state was to end European restrictions on Ottoman administrative control, and that required siding with Germany and the Central Powers in the war. The Ottoman Cabinet was not yet ready to sacrifice the empire for the nation, but the longstanding Foreign Office guarantees to maintain the political status of Egypt and the territorial integrity of the empire was no longer sufficient to sustain Ottoman neutrality. The Ottoman decision to abandon these timeworn international instruments, especially British territorial guarantees, which Ottoman diplomacy had relied on since the mid-nineteenth century, was a calculated risk against the alternative: nominal sovereignty and complete European control of the economy, administration, and security of the empire. The negative example of Egypt loomed over the Ottoman entry into the war at the end of October.

To Annex or Protect? Egypt and the British Foreign Office, 1914–1917

In 1914 Britain's position in Egypt was practically strong from a military and administrative perspective. From a legal perspective, however, it remained very weak. The ambiguity of Egypt's international position, an asset through the occupation, became increasingly unsustainable in the context of the European political crisis. War provided Whitehall with an opening to finally "regularize" the relationship between the British Empire and Egypt. As one future Egyptian high commissioner wrote, "hostile action by Turkey would provide an opportunity to clear up the legal situation and import some measure of definition and logic into our position in Egypt."[22] While the Foreign Office attempted to buy Ottoman neutrality with promises of maintaining Egypt's political status and the future territorial integrity of the Empire, a debate emerged between the acting consul-general in Cairo and the Foreign Office in London about the future of Egypt. Though London was hesitant to change Egypt's political status, the future of Egypt in the event of war with the Ottoman Empire was a pressing matter as all Egyptian subjects would become enemy subjects. The

Foreign Office only really entertained two possibilities: annexation or protection.[23] Maintaining the status quo, continued Ottoman sovereignty in Egypt, would be out of the question on security grounds, as all Egyptians were legally Ottoman subjects. In either case, the Foreign Office would alter the international legal status of Egypt and align Egypt more closely with the British Empire—whether as a protectorate or as a colony.[24]

For many in the Foreign Office, there was little substantive difference between annexation and protection. Yet, whichever policy the Britain pursued, there were two significant obstacles to end the occupation and to terminate Ottoman sovereignty in Egypt. The first and most persistent problem for the British was Egyptian support. To legitimize breaking with the Ottomans, the British needed broad public support, especially from the Egyptian ministers.[25] The second impediment to ending Ottoman sovereignty in Egypt was the European Powers. While France and Russia might be counted on with the right inducements to recognize changes in Egypt's political status, the Central Powers would not. As noted, both Germany and the Habsburg Empire formally reiterated their recognition of Egypt as an Ottoman province during September. There was another danger, too. If Germany were to win the war, the Ottoman claim to Egypt might be bolstered—a concern that the Foreign Office and members of the Egyptian government shared.

There were several practical and political considerations related to bringing Egyptians and the Central Powers on board with British plans to sever Ottoman ties to Egypt. Changing Egypt's political status produced a range of questions about the future of Ottoman institutions in Egypt, including the khedivate, the Capitulations, the Egyptian tribute to Istanbul, as well as the fermans and international legal instruments that had guaranteed Egyptian autonomy within the Ottoman Empire—questions that would not be resolved until Egyptian "independence" in 1922 and the Treaty of Lausanne in 1923.[26] The underlying tension in British internal debates was the question of what would replace Ottoman sovereignty in Egypt and how the British-Egyptian relationship would be defined in legal terms. The Egyptian question in 1914 also foreshadowed to a remarkable degree internal debates at the end of the war about the future of former Ottoman provinces under British control at the time of the armistice, particularly in terms of following a policy of annexation or protection. Changing Egypt's political status would not end cleanly in 1914 and would remain a subject of international politics through the mid-1920s.

Between August and December 1914, when Britain finally proclaimed the declaration of protection, Foreign Office officials in Cairo and London searched for the right theory and justification to support terminating Ottoman sovereignty in Egypt.[27] At the outset, Kitchener, and to a large degree Egyptian ministers, led the drive to end Ottoman sovereignty in Egypt with a declaration of protectorate while London urged caution and delay. Officials in Cairo first seriously considered the protectorate option in mid-August following the rumored sale of the *Göben* and *Breslau* to the Ottoman Empire. Cairo charged ahead with substantive plans despite the fact that Grey did not think that the sale indicated that the Ottomans would abandon neutrality or that Egypt was at risk from an Ottoman attack.[28] Milne Cheetham, acting consul-general in Cairo, reported that rumors of war with the Ottoman Empire had greatly agitated Egyptian ministers. Complicating matters was the fact that the khedive was visiting Istanbul when the war broke out, and Hussein Rushdi Paşa, the president of the Egyptian Council of Ministers, was acting as regent in his absence. Rushdi and Adli Paşa (Yeken), who at the time was Egyptian foreign minister, were the two key Egyptian figures with whom British agents in Cairo attempted to strike a bargain for the protectorate, along with Prince Hussein, Abbas's uncle. Cheetham was a step ahead of the Foreign Office in London and suggested that Egypt might be legally separated from the Ottoman Empire via a policy of protection if the British could provide an incentive for Egyptian ministers to support the policy. His proposals were animated by discussions with Rushdi, who argued that the ministers could not stay in office in the case of war with the "suzerain power." Rushdi proposed, too, that the Egyptian ministers might support a protectorate if it were "accompanied by the announcement of arrangement with His Majesty's Government granting to Egypt a measure of self-government in local matters compatible with general control by Great Britain."[29]

While officials in London looked for a solution that would not limit possibilities in the future, British administrators and advisors in Cairo supported relinquishing some amount of internal administrative control for tighter British external control of Egypt. Cheetham soon proposed a scheme that would provide Egypt with more autonomy. He noted, "If the fiction of Ottoman suzerainty were then maintained, Egyptians, and above all Egyptian officials would be placed in a position of divided allegiance, and their cooperation with us be thus seriously affected." The only plausible solution was to sunder the legal ties between Istanbul and Cairo and, in exchange, to provide Egyptian elites with more administrative control for their support. Cheetham continued, "If it were considered possible to accompany the declaration of protectorate by a statement to the effect that the progress of Egypt towards internal self-governance would not be retarded, but rather accelerated, by such a protectorate, I am firmly convinced that the majority of enlightened Egyptians would receive the declaration not only with acquiescence, but even with favor."[30] Cheetham insisted that even as Egyptians would secure the full status and advantages of British subjects under a protectorate, "the principle of an Egyptian national entity" should remain intact.[31]

In late August Ronald Storrs, the Oriental secretary in Cairo, reported on public opinion in Egypt and contended that though there was some support for Germany in Egypt, it emanated from the usual "Turks, Circassians, lawyers, students and extremist journalists," who represented Germany "as having befriended Islam without acquiring one acre of Muslim territory." This faction circulated all manner of rumors stating that if Germany should win the war, Britain would be expelled from Egypt and the province returned to regular Ottoman administration. But Storrs also argued that providing Egyptians with some form of greater autonomy or quasi-independence could mitigate the problem of Ottoman loyalty in Egypt:

> Unmistakable hints have been received from the most responsible circles, that a formal change of regime, leaving the position of the occupation unimpaired without wounding Egyptian *amour-propre* and "sense of nationality," would be far from unwelcome. It is pointed out that a transference of the temporal suzerainty from the Sultan to His Majesty the King, accompanied by guaranteed "autonomy" (for England must not show herself less generous than the Turks) or "independence" with subsequent abolition of the Capitulations, would go far towards disembarrassing the conscientious from the incubus of Ottoman loyalty, localizing aspirations, and diminishing almost to a vanishing point the attraction and influence of Pan-Islam.[32]

In other words, Storrs believed that it would be possible to transfer sovereignty from the sultan to the British king and maintain the status quo of the occupation, so long as some measure of autonomy could be promised to Egyptian ministers and to Cairine elites.[33] At this early stage, when it was still quite unclear which way the Ottoman Empire would go in the war, the main concern of officials in Cairo was how to acquire and maintain support from Egyptian ministers and notables in order to maintain civil government.

Throughout August and early September, Rushdi continued to offer Egyptian support for a protectorate in exchange for autonomy. In conveying these messages to the Foreign Office, Cheetham was cautious to note that he did not support giving away too much and would not offer anything that would jeopardize the benefits and "progress" of the occupation, but at the same time he pushed officials in London to recognize the importance of gaining Egyptian support for ending Ottoman sovereignty in Egypt:

> This proposition, as put before me, was equivalent to a plea for autonomy of a nature to endanger the progress which had been made in Egypt, and I have been very careful not to give the slightest encouragement to it. I should however, take the opportunity to state, for your information, that it is now apparent that a certain section of the politicians have been discussing possibilities of the kind described among themselves, though no allusion has been made to the subject in the press. It is clear that a large number of prominent Egyptians would look with complacency on a severance of the connection with the Ottoman Empire, though they would desire at the same time some satisfaction of moderate nationalist aspirations.[34]

At this stage Cheetham was less concerned about defining the terms of Egyptian autonomy and how to satisfy "modest nationalist aspirations" than he was about inducing elites to break with the Ottomans. Like Storrs, he viewed Ottoman loyalty in Egypt as a potentially serious impediment to changing the legal status of Egypt in the event of war with the Ottoman Empire.

The Foreign Office's initial call for calm and caution in Cairo began to shift toward thinking about changing the political status of Egypt. By the second week of September, Cheetham drafted a proclamation of protection for Egypt but without articulating what would happen to Ottoman sovereignty in Egypt. Was it to be forfeited by breaking neutrality or merely suspended? The draft proclamation simply stated that due to war between the British and Ottoman Empires, the British would protect Egypt and the khedival dynasty because "Egypt is liable to attack no less than British territory, and rights of autonomy won on the battlefield by [the] founder of the Khedival dynasty, as well as the reforms of the last thirty years are in danger."[35] Cheetham's appeal to Mehmed Ali was an attempt to satisfy Egyptian opinion and was attuned to earlier advice to the Foreign Office, which is to say, any declaration of protection had to be accompanied by a statement assuring "the progress of Egypt towards internal self-government." But it left open the question of the meaning and content of the "rights of autonomy won on the battlefield." Mehmed Ali and subsequent khedives' rights of autonomy were derived precisely from the international guarantees of 1840 and subsequent fermans, which granted the family of Mehmed Ali hereditary "administration of the Pashalic of Egypt." The logic of appealing to these rights was clear from a British perspective—they were administrative rights, not sovereign rights. Yet by avoiding the question of sovereignty in Egypt, while at the same time appealing to Mehmed Ali, Cheetham underscored the legal precariousness of the British position.[36]

Grey provisionally supported Cheetham's draft declaration but emphasized that nothing should be done to change the status quo in Egypt unless the Ottomans ended neutrality and broke definitively with the Allied powers. Grey pointed out, too, that the Capitulations and other privileges would have to be maintained to satisfy European opinion. There was one other unresolved difficulty that required settling in the event of war with the Ottomans, namely, what to do with the present khedive. Abbas Hilmi II was in Istanbul at his palace on the Asian side of the Bosporus when the war broke out.[37] He had just escaped an assassination attempt and was recovering in the Ottoman capital.[38] The Foreign Office had a long troubled past with Abbas, and his presence in Istanbul when the war broke out provided an opportunity to sideline him in Egyptian affairs.[39] Cheetham and British advisors in Cairo also found it easier to work with Rushdi, Adli, and the rest of the Council of Ministers in the khedive's absence and were convinced that Abbas would obstruct the protectorate—if it were indeed needed.[40] At the same time, the Egyptian ministers were initially anxious for Abbas to return to Cairo in order to protect Egypt's political status. It was after all in the person of the khedive to whom the hereditary rights of administration accrued. Abbas, too, wanted to return to Cairo in order to secure his position but was prevented from doing so by the British ambassador in Istanbul, a point that he wrote very bitterly about at the end of the war:

At the time, Turkey was not the enemy of Egypt, it was not my enemy, it had suzerainty over Egypt; in contrast, the English intervention in my country had no legal basis nor any legitimate justification, while I, Abbas II, was not committed by any single legal act or convention to involve myself in a conflict that did not concern me at all. I was, as I say, still bound by firmans which for over a century had confirmed the suzerainty of the Sultan of Turkey over Egypt; in addition, it was a suzerainty which had recognized our autonomy and left us free to govern ourselves at our will.[41]

While Abbas wrote after the war in exile, from the perspective of a deposed monarch, his critique of British actions preventing him from returning to Cairo in 1914 is striking—if only for the fact that his argument rested entirely on the international and Ottoman legal instruments guaranteeing Egypt's autonomous political status. The very ambiguity of Egypt's position between Ottoman sovereignty and British administration left room for the khedive, as well as his ministers, to assert claims about protecting their legal privileges as well as who would control Egypt's future in the absence of Ottoman sovereignty. Abbas's legal argument against the British was reanimated in debates among Egyptian and British officials between 1918 and 1923. While much attention has been directed to the effects of Wilson's ideas of self-determination on Egyptian nationalism after the war, along with wartime depredations and requisitions, the old international and Ottoman legal claims from 1840 and 1841 continued to matter in shaping Egypt's political future well beyond 1919. The point is that in 1914, war between the Ottoman and British Empires threatened the autonomy of Egypt and all privileges Egyptian ministers and elites had accumulated under that system, even under the occupation.

Just as British agents in Cairo understood that a bargain had to be made with the Egyptian ministers to secure public support for the protectorate and for cutting ties with the Ottomans, Rushdi Paşa and the Egyptian ministers were intent on using Egypt's political status to extract concessions from their British occupiers. At the outset of the war, their main concern was that Britain would simply annex Egypt. As a result, the ministers worked in various ways to prevent this outcome, while maintaining the claim to Egypt's autonomy. When the Egyptian government passed a proclamation for the protection of Egypt in the war with Germany, again under heavy pressure from Britain, Rushdi immediately telegrammed

Abbas in Istanbul justifying the ministers' actions.[42] The ministers were anxious that if they did not issue the proclamation, Britain would do so without the Egyptian Cabinet's consent. Either way, Egypt would be exposed to attack from Germany. But by issuing the proclamation in the name of the government of Egypt, the ministers had maintained their legal personality. Claiming that they delayed the proclamation as long as possible, Rushdi noted that "it seems to me that to safeguard the interests of our political status with regard to England, it is better that they [the British] act with our consent that if they act on their own authority."[43] Rushdi sent a series of messages to Abbas to this effect, explaining that the ministers and he had attempted to safeguard "our political status quo." He argued that if Britain should win the war, they would undoubtedly modify the political status of Egypt. The only way to mitigate the effect of this change would be to cooperate as much as possible with British wishes for "the form and conditions of this modification will be more or less harsh depending on how Egypt has behaved towards them."[44] Abbas only sporadically received communications from Cairo and was informed of events in Egypt largely by the grand vizier in Istanbul. These delays and lost messages caused Abbas to believe, rightly in the end, that the British intended to depose him.[45]

Abbas later accused Rushdi of selling out to the British by allowing the protectorate and the khedive's deposition. Yet in 1914 the question of the future of Egypt in the event of war between the British and Ottoman Empires was nowhere more existential than in Egypt itself. In early September, Rushdi wrote to Abbas's advisor at Çubuklu Palace in Istanbul asking what to do in the event the Ottomans abandoned neutrality. He believed correctly that Britain would only consider two options—annexation, and the corresponding complete loss of Egyptian legal personality, or protectorate, which would afford the chance to extract an explicit recognition of administrative autonomy from the British: "If, during His Highness's absence, Turkey enters the war on the side of Germany, we would here be at a total loss, without guide or compass. England may want either purely and simply to annex Egypt or to make a deal with Egypt promising autonomy in order to gain the support of the country. With regard to the former my decision is already taken: I will consider my mandate to have ended and I will simply retire to private life. But what to do in the latter case?"[46] For Abbas, Rushdi, and the ministers, the threat of war with the Ottomans posed the risk of abolishing the international treaties and fermans that guaranteed Egypt's political status, but also their own status and privileges that they sought to preserve and extend. The only solution to their predicament was to extract a promise from Britain to secure Egypt's future autonomy in exchange for cooperation with a future protectorate.

By late September, the Foreign Office proceeded under the assumption that war with the Ottomans would entail the simultaneous announcement of a declaration of war and a declaration of protection that would "terminate Turkish suzerainty." Grey proposed that Prince Hussein Kamil, Abbas's uncle, should assume the khedivate.[47] Along with the declaration of protection, Cheetham drafted a document that would become the blueprint for the protectorate. It explained the British decision for the protectorate and how the protectorate would function, noting first that Hussein had been selected "to occupy the Khedival throne free from all the rights of suzerainty or other rights heretofore claimed by the Sultan or by his Government." The text further explained that though the Capitulations were "no longer in harmony with the development of the country," they would remain in place until the end of the war. In this first draft, the paragraph that caused the most trouble related not to foreign relations, as might be expected, which were to revert to British control, but rather to internal administration.[48] Rushdi Paşa continued to argue that the protectorate would never be acceptable without an agreement of some form of limited self-government for Egypt in the future.

On the eve of the Ottoman entry into the war, Rushdi met with Cheetham to discuss the paragraph on internal administration. Rushdi argued that the British might win support for the protectorate from the ministers and elites if it included an explicit statement promising "a larger measure of self-government for Egypt." He threatened to resign from office without such a statement, claiming he would be unable to control the reaction in Cairo to the declaration of protection. Cheetham noted Rushdi's fears that "religious feeling in favor of Turkey would create a situation in which it would be impossible to control without a promise of increased rights of self-government."[49] As a result, Cheetham proposed to the Foreign Office that they add the phrase: "The clearer definition of Great Britain's position in the country will accelerate progress towards self-government." In the original version of the document, clarifying Britain's position in Egypt would "remove misunderstandings which in the past retarded the progress of reform."[50] In either case, Prince Hussein, like Rushdi, drew on British anxieties about the appeal of Pan-Islam by arguing that a promise of self-government for Egyptians would outweigh an ostensibly more obvious allegiance to the sultan-caliph.

As soon as it was clear that the Ottoman Empire had attacked Russia in the Black Sea, Grey proposed that Britain issue a proclamation of protectorate within two days, pending Prince Hussein's willingness to assume the khedivate. Cheetham, somewhat distraught, wrote that due to religious feeling in Egypt, agitated by the prospect of war against the caliph, Hussein was inclined to refuse the position. Prince Hussein argued that he "could not accept the khedivate without a grant or promise of autonomy to Egypt under British suzerainty." Cheetham did not think that Rushdi and Prince Hussein were acting in concert but rather that both possessed "the idea of necessity of some form of compensation to Egypt to break with Turkey."[51] He suggested that the declaration of protection be delayed given Hussein's unwillingness to assume office. Grey agreed: "You will of course postpone the declaration if protectorate until rupture with Turkey is complete, for this would alter status of Egypt, but there is no reason for postponing martial law."[52]

When Britain declared war on the Ottoman Empire on November 5, 1914, the general commanding officer in Egypt, John Maxwell, announced the state of war in Cairo and proclaimed that Great Britain would undertake responsibility for the defense of Egypt. He went further, stating, "Great Britain is now fighting both to protect the rights and liberties of Egypt which were originally won upon the battlefield by Mohammad Ali and to secure to her the continuation of peace and prosperity, which she has enjoyed during thirty years of British occupation." The text was almost exactly Cheetham's original draft declaration of protection from September, with a subtle shift in language and meaning. The "rights of autonomy won on the battlefield" by Mehmed Ali was changed to "the rights and liberties" of Egypt. Autonomy in an Ottoman, and especially in an Egyptian, context had a specific administrative meaning with particular attached privileges. Though "rights and liberties" were far more ambiguous than autonomy, at the outset of the war, the reference to Mehmed Ali made it appear that Britain had committed itself to protect Egypt's autonomy and special international legal status. For the British, it was a risky bargain to thwart Egypt allegiance to the Ottoman Empire. The deal may have paid off in 1914, but when the British defaulted on the promise to uphold rights derived from Mehmed Ali in 1919, Egypt would explode in protest.

On the same day that Maxwell issued his statement on Mehmed Ali, Enver Paşa declared the Ottoman Empire would protect all Muslims and that it was obliged to put an end to the disorders in Egypt and to bring the territory back under the rule of caliph. He attacked the British idea of liberating nationalities as a war aim and added that if Britain stood by its rhetoric, it should at long last release Egypt from British control. The Wafd would draw on this legalistic language at the end of the war when making clams for independence in Cairo and Paris.[53]

After the declaration of war and martial law, British officials in Cairo worked to find ways to bring Prince Hussein on board with the protectorate. For Cheetham and Storrs, the problem was balancing Foreign Office objectives with Egyptian public opinion. Grey worried about yielding too much and prejudicing the future administration of Egypt, whereas Hussein demanded concessions for risking a break with Istanbul and the Caliphate. It was in this context that the decision was made to exchange the title of khedive—prince—with that of sultan—ruler, sovereign.[54] Storrs proposed the change based on Hussein's professed desire to transform Egypt into a kingdom analogous to those in the Balkans, with an Egyptian monarch.[55] He argued that the title's benefits lie in its elasticity. The title "sultan of Egypt and the Sudan" would satisfy Egyptian public opinion but would also emphasize Egypt's preeminence among the Muslim powers of North Africa, a clear asset in the war against the Ottoman Empire.[56] Such influence would balance "the political effect of possible French acquisitions in Syria" or any other "any subsequent creation of rival potentates by hostile powers." Most important, he wrote, "The honor would cost Great Britain nothing whatever. But I venture to assert that its possible effect in the near future of the Eastern Mediterranean might be beneficial and far-reaching."[57]

While Storrs and Cheetham worked to bring Hussein around, the Foreign Office in London suddenly switched course and insisted instead on annexation, or, in other words, direct incorporation of Egypt into the British Empire as a colony.[58] Grey wrote that the British government "think the most effective step would be to declare annexation of Egypt, thus getting rid of all of the difficulties about succession to Khedive, and giving Egyptians at once the status of British subjects."[59] Grey mandated again that the Capitulations and Mixed courts remain unchanged in order to appease the other European powers—above all France. He sent a draft annexation Order in Council to Cairo on November 17. The order justified the policy of annexation on the grounds that the British military occupation, which itself had been implemented for the security and good governance of Egypt, was now under threat and due to war between the British and Ottoman Empires. To preserve the progress and order of the occupation, Britain declared, "It is necessary that the suzerainty of His Imperial Majesty the Sultan of Turkey over Egypt should be annulled, and that Egypt should cease to form a part of the Ottoman Dominions. . . . From and after the date hereof, Egypt is annexed to and forms part of His Majesty's Dominions."[60]

British officials in Cairo were stunned by the Foreign Office's new plan and found annexation to be out of touch with the situation on the ground. Cheetham understood that it would dismantle the entire apparatus of occupation and argued that Britain would lose all the benefits of the system in place since 1882. Grey argued that the plan for the protectorate was worked out before the Ottomans and British were at war. Now that the two empires were belligerent, he thought the protectorate would in fact make things more ambiguous. In the first place, Prince Hussein would not accept the khedivate while the yet to be deposed khedive Abbas resided in an enemy capital. "Egyptian subjects would cease to be Ottoman subjects, i.e., subjects of a large Moslem empire, and would be relegated the ambiguous position as protected subjects in a relatively small country. Our other Moslem subjects in other parts of the world would also probably consider that we had placed the Egyptians on a footing inferior to that which they had occupied under Turkish suzerainty."[61] London worried, too, that the uncertainty of the situation helped support Ottoman designs on Egypt. Grey emphasized that from the perspective of international relations it mattered little whether Egypt were annexed or under protection, particularly as the Capitulations and Mixed Tribunals would remain in place until further discussion with France.

The fact that Grey did not see a world of difference between annexation and protection prompted Cheetham to outline in rather stark terms the benefits of the system of occupation, which he argued could be maintained to a greater degree under protection rather than if Egypt were incorporated into the empire as a Crown Colony. Moreover, Rushdi and ministers were in discussion with Prince Hussein about "an arrangement with us for inclusion in the British Empire without the loss of Egyptian individuality." Cheetham noted that Cairo was calm following the declaration of martial law and that Maxwell's statement "in reference to the preservation of rights won by Mehmed Ali" did much to appease Egyptians, even the nationalists and "extremists." Annexation would disturb the relative calm that prevailed in Cairo, and the ministers would almost certainly resign. Cheetham again argued that the ministers were the only force in Cairo who could control the so-called religious element. He implored Grey to consider the effect of annexation "as contrasted with creation of Mahommedan nation under our protection, on Mohammedan feeling generally, and especially in the Arab world." Beyond the effect of the annexation on Muslims, the real problem with annexation was that it would mean more accountability for the British while creating greater dissatisfaction among Egyptians:

> I would add that the existing system of governing through native hands is not the most efficient form of government, but it is understood here and provides an excuse for administrative shortcomings which would disappear with annexation. Annexation must involve a more direct responsibility for Great Britain, for a higher standard of government, and for stricter protection of foreign interests. This would ultimately be attained, but only by free displacement of native officials. Although increased efficiency might be appreciated, an influential class of malcontents would be created.[62]

Alongside the concerns of officials in Cairo, France, too, worried that the British annexation of Egypt would backfire in various ways and places. The minister of foreign affairs, Théophile Declassé, thought that annexation would give the impression that Britain was already enjoying the territorial spoils of war—particularly after the annexation of Cyprus on November 2. He thought that the Germans and Ottoman would use it against the Allies and that it would alienate public opinion in France. He insisted that all territorial questions should be deferred until the end of the war and argued "that a protectorate is better suited than annexation to preservation of the internal situation of Egypt."[63] To appease Europeans, Britain already planned to maintain the tribute, which contributed to paying off the Ottoman debt, the Capitulations, and Consular and Mixed Courts until the end of the war. This despite the fact that the war "will theoretically put an end to the treaty on which capitulatory rights of the

Powers in Egypt depend, and the consular courts of that Power would then have no legal basis." Martial law would allow for all "necessary jurisdiction," but Grey also thought that it would be practical to maintain some consular jurisdiction to pacify European opinion

Arguments emanating from Cairo, along with Kitchener's support for protection over annexation, brought Foreign Office opinion around. Grey was prepared to accept the protectorate if it would preserve the "internal situation" in Egypt. He authorized the policy with the understanding that Cheetham ask Hussein to accept the khedivate, "intimating that if he refuses the alternative is annexation."[64] Until the actual declaration of protection, Grey emphasized repeatedly that nothing should be done that would limit British control of Egypt later. Accordingly, he was especially concerned with the wording of texts ending Ottoman sovereignty and creating the Egyptian sultanate. He wished to "guard against words which might be quoted afterwards to imply that the new Sultan was to be in practice the independent ruler and Governor of Egypt."[65] Grey was troubled that the British were giving far too much away to appease Egyptian opinion, and that these compromises were getting in the way of achieving the British aim in Egypt, which was to maintain the control they had during the occupation: "We are afraid the cumulative effect of all the concessions wanted by Prince Hussein will be to prejudice British control and make it less than heretofore; whereas our object is to substitute a British protectorate for Turkish suzerainty, retaining the British control exercised before."[66] Though there were outstanding questions related to succession and nationality, Grey approved a draft declaration of protection that in one blow terminated Ottoman sovereignty, deposed the khedive Abbas Hilmi, and appointed Hussein as the sultan of Egypt.

Hussein finally accepted the sultanate, but with the reservation that the protectorate approved by Grey be disaggregated into three separate statements: the termination of Ottoman sovereignty and the establishment of British protection, the deposition of Abbas Hilmi II with Hussein's appointment as sultan, and finally a statement explaining the terms of the protectorate. Cheetham noted that the order in which Britain severed the link between the Ottoman Empire and Egypt was of profound significance "because the feeling that the Sultan of Turkey still represents the legal authority remains strong, whereas once that authority is declared null and void Hussain would be justified in recognizing a new situation."[67] In other words, Hussein could not accept the sultanate without first changing the legal status of Egypt. Last, Cheetham assured Grey that Hussein, the regent, and ministers were all in favor of the protectorate, "which they anticipate and understand would tighten our control of administration, while giving them, as they have had hitherto, a reasonable voice in local affairs." This was the British model of how autonomy should work in Ottoman lands.

On December 18, Britain proclaimed a British protectorate in Egypt, which announced the protectorate and the termination of Ottoman sovereignty over Egypt.[68] The next day Abbas Hilmi II, the last khedive, was deposed, and Hussein Kamil was offered the title of sultan as the "eldest living Prince of the family of Mohammad Ali." The offer of the sultanate to Hussein was accompanied by a text addressed as a letter to Prince Hussein that justified the protectorate and the transfer from Ottoman "suzerainty" in Egypt to Britain under protection. From a legal perspective, the statement provided very little in terms of explaining what would replace the system of occupation in Egypt. "The future form of government" remained to be worked out, but it would be "freed from all rights of suzerainty or other rights heretofore claimed by the Ottoman Government." The document did not cancel the fermans—it would have been difficult to justify such a move since the family of Mehmed Ali derived their administrative and hereditary rights from these imperial commands—but it did lift some restrictions imposed by them, including the size of the Egyptian army and the ability of the now sultan to issue honors in his name. Elements of Cheetham's draft declaration of protection from September were reproduced in the statement to Hussein, including the argument that clarifying Britain's position in Egypt would "accelerate progress towards self-government," and that Britain would continue to "associate the governed in the task of Government," as during the occupation. The only explicit statement on governance under protection concerned foreign relations, which would now explicitly be conducted through the new British high commissioner of Egypt, that post replacing the consul-general.[69] For Europe, as promised, the Capitulations would remain in place until the end of the war. The letter concluded by noting that though the protectorate meant that Egypt was free from obedience to Istanbul, Britain was not motivated by hostility toward the Caliphate and that loyalty to the caliph was completely independent of political ties between Egypt and the Ottoman Empire.

The British legal advisor in Egypt, Macolm McIlwraith, summarized the legal revolution in Egypt succinctly: "Such were the brief announcements which by a stroke of a the pen, put an end to the complicated international status of Egypt, built up—as between the Porte and Europe—by a long succession of treaties in the course of the last five centuries, and—as between the Porte and Egypt—by a series of diplomatic conventions and Imperial firmans from 1840 onwards."[70] Though they tried, the Foreign Office protectorate could not "with the stroke a pen" undo all the international treaties and imperial edicts guaranteeing Egypt's international status. Claims, especially by Egyptians, would continue to be made based on Egypt's legal status well after the conclusion of the war and would not be resolved until Egyptian "independence" in 1922 and the Treaty of Lausanne in 1923.

Ottoman Autonomy and British Wartime Planning

The legal status and question of sovereignty in Egypt in 1914 prompted Britain to think more broadly about the empire's position in the Middle East. While the CUP government was forced to consider decentralization in the last years of the war, British wartime planners imagined this possibility for the Ottoman lands from the start. Throughout the First World War, the British Foreign, India, and War Offices devised various schemes for securing British interests in the Near East after the war—the most prominent were the seemingly incompatible promises offered by the Hussein–McMahon correspondence, the Sykes–Picot Agreement, and the Balfour Declaration. For many British imperial historians, the Ottoman entry into World War I on the side of the Central Powers was a moment of rupture and signaled a radical reconfiguration of British policy in the Near East.[71] The longstanding British policy of maintaining the territorial integrity of the Ottoman Empire against rival empires was replaced by contemplating direct control of the Ottoman territory in Greater Syria and Arabia. While Britain and France eventually partitioned the Arab provinces at the end of the war, and only assuredly after the Treaty of Lausanne, British wartime planning oscillated between direct and indirect administrative schemes for securing dominance in the Ottoman domains. Even after British thinking shifted definitively to considering what would replace Ottoman sovereignty in the Arab provinces, debates on the best method of incorporation wavered between direct annexation and more indirect methods of imperial control, debates that echoed those regarding the decision to incorporate Egypt into the British Empire as a protectorate.[72]

From the start of the war, British officials were set on keeping on Egypt. As Lord Milner put it, "Unless we lose the war, Egypt will in future be as much a part of the British Empire as India or Nigeria, whether we proceed to annexation or, as I personally think better, we content ourselves with a form of protectorate."[73] The future of the rest of Ottoman domains was less certain.

The Foreign Office's continued attachment to administrative autonomy as a solution to Ottoman weakness in the international arena was most clearly expressed in a statement on British territorial interests in the Ottoman Empire. Just over two weeks before the Allied landing at Gallipoli, Prime Minister Herbert Asquith appointed a special committee to consider "British desiderata in Turkey and Asia." Maurice de Bunsen, the undersecretary of state at the Foreign Office, headed the committee. Mark Sykes acted as Kitchener's personal representative, and other members were drawn from the Foreign, Colonial, India, and War Offices.[74] The de Bunsen Committee met for a month and a half and produced a lengthy report that it submitted to the War Council on June 30, 1915.[75] Though the British government never explicitly endorsed the report, the committee's territorial claims became the basis of Sykes–Picot (Sazanov) agreement, which included consolidating the British position in the Eastern Mediterranean and the Persian Gulf.[76] Beyond outlining British territorial desiderata in the Ottoman Empire, the de Bunsen Committee report was significant for presenting possible methods of extending British imperial interests, on one hand, while further attenuating Ottoman administrative control, on the other (see figures 6.1a and 6.1b).

The problem for the de Bunsen Committee was how to maintain British control over Palestine and Mesopotamia without undermining the postwar order. As in the late nineteenth century, European intervention and territorial advances into core Ottoman provinces could not be justified in terms of conquest and required legal invention. The problem remained one of international order, and the committee identified the solution in clear, legally defined boundaries rather than rely on a weaker system of protection. Ottoman space was not *terra nullius* in international relations, and finding a way to control the territory required international agreement:

> It has seemed to the Committee that any attempt to set up a system of protectorates would be destined to break down, for the rivalry of the Powers would force each of them to extend their protectorates to the limits of their neighbor's spheres, and there would be a clash and confusion of different systems of protectorate administrations with one another and with an obstructive central Turkish government. Nor would any scheme of internationalization seem practicable: it is a desperate remedy at best, and to extend it to large areas in Asiatic Turkey would be to invite disaster. In short, there must either be clearly defined territories, recognized as separate units, some independent, some belonging to European Powers, or the Ottoman Empire must continue, subject to certain necessary limitations.[77]

The committee wanted to avoid a complete territorial scramble that would prolong the war and alienate Muslims by destroying "the political power of Islam." It considered four possible options for the Ottoman Empire. The first option was partition through annexation, but the three other options maintained Ottoman sovereignty in "Asia" and included establishing a system of spheres of European influence, maintaining the status quo, and finally—the preferred method—enlarging the system of Ottoman autonomous provinces with territorial losses in Istanbul and Basra. According to the committee, all but the last option had the potential to lead to warfare among the Allies or were unsupportable from the perspective of expense and imperial defense. The autonomy option maintained the Ottoman Empire, with certain territorial adjustments, "as an independent state, but the form of government to be modified by decentralization on federal lines."[78]

The de Bunsen Committee argued that Europe had already engineered a system to balance European competition and supposed Ottoman misrule: "The Powers of Europe have consistently endeavored to ameliorate the evils of Turkish rule by securing or attempting to secure, some form of local administration in harmony with the local conditions in the Lebanon, Armenia, Samos, and Macedonia. Thus the idea of decentralization is no novelty to the various inhabitants of Turkey."[79] In one committee meeting, Mark Sykes argued that the "devolutionary scheme," the extension of Ottoman autonomous provinces, "must be accompanied by a revision of the Turkish Constitution which would have the effect of turning the Turkish Empire into a Federation. It was, in effect, the scheme favored by the Opposition or Liberal party in Turkey, who had always wished to

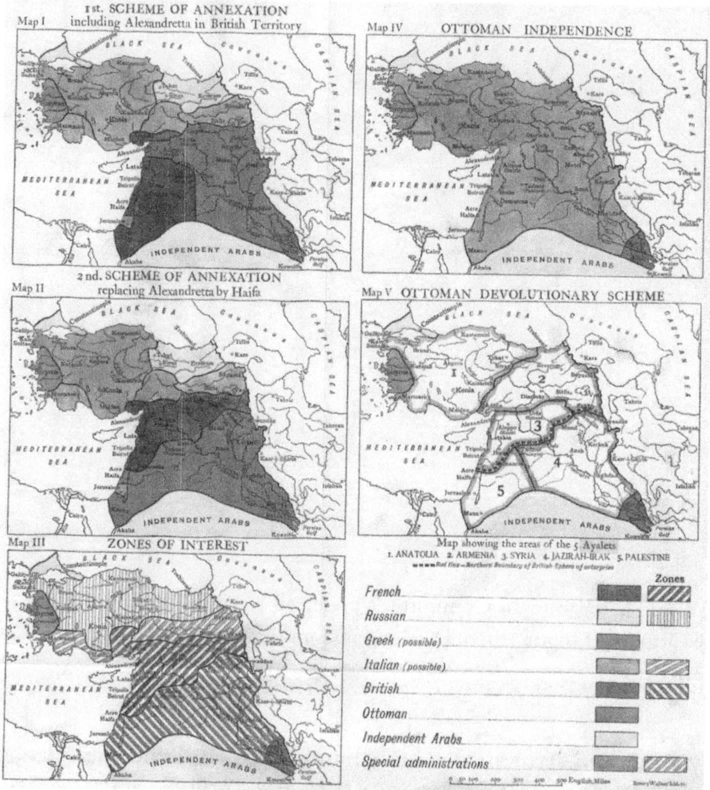

Figure 6.1a The de Bunsen Committee maps, reflecting various possible British administrative schemes for the Ottoman Empire after the war (1915). De Bunsen Committee, National Archives, UK War Office/106/6286, 1915.

free themselves of the CUP. It would more or less, divide Asiatic Turkey into national areas. There would be a Turkish area, Armenian and Arab area, each of which would have a National Assembly."[80] Sykes's appeal to the Ottoman "Liberal Party" as an effective tool against the Committee of Union and Progress was broadly shared among key Foreign Office figures during much of the war. As we saw in previous chapters, in the prewar period, the Liberal Party, which was known by various names during the Second Constitutional era, including the Liberal Entente and the Freedom and Accord Party (*Hürriyet ve İtilaf Fırkası*), favored the reorganization of the empire along decentralized lines.[81]

European-imposed autonomy in the Ottoman Empire, the de Bunsen Committee argued, would solve the problem of European competition,

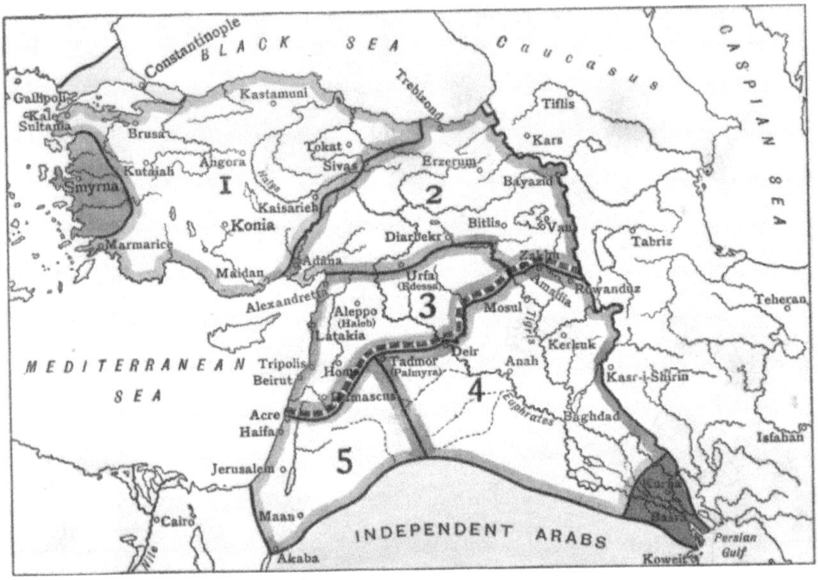

Figure 6.1b The de Bunsen Committee's preferred territorial reorganization scheme for the Ottoman Empire (1915). De Bunsen Committee, National Archives, UK War Office/106/6286, 1915.

satisfy Arab and Armenian national ambitions, and end the "dangers of centralization" favored by the Committee of Union and Progress. The autonomy plan consisted of creating five large provinces, including a Turkish province in Anatolia, a large Armenia with space for an autonomous Kurdistan, plus three large Arab provinces including an enlarged Palestine, a somewhat reduced Syria, and Iraq. Part or all of Basra province was to be under direct British control, and, like the other de Bunsen schemes, Arabia was to be independent in accordance with existing British promises. Flexibility was the greatest asset of de Bunsen's "Ottoman devolutionary scheme." It did not overcommit Britain to radically expanding the empire through multiple territorial annexations with corresponding military obligations. Second, the plan could fail without endangering British strategic and imperial concerns in the Eastern Mediterranean and Persian Gulf. The report noted that there were at least two satisfactory options in the event of a decentralized Ottoman Empire coming undone: "There is always a good chance of there arising several autonomous states, Turkey proper in Anatolia, an Armenian and an Arab federation, under a nominal suzerainty of the Sultan." Britain could always declare the autonomous provinces of Palestine and Jazirah-Iraq as "independent states under our protection, or annex them, or declare them to be our sphere of influence in a divided Ottoman Empire, according to circumstances."[82]

While the de Bunsen Committee plan may be best known as the first articulation of British territorial desiderata in the Ottoman Empire and a prelude to Sykes–Picot, it was equally important in terms of continuities in British thinking about managing the Ottoman Empire. While the "Ottoman devolutionary scheme" never came to pass, in 1915 it was the preferred way to establish imperial control without dealing with the problem of sovereignty. The Ottomans could effectively continue to run their empire in the service of British imperial and strategic interests. A weak state situated between the Eastern Mediterranean, the Persian Gulf, Russia, and a quasi-independent Arabia would check the power of France and Russia and provide Britain with maximum flexibility without the burden of military and administrative commitments. According to the report, resorting to administrative autonomy for the Ottoman Empire would also satisfy local nationalisms, particularly among Arabs and Armenians, just as nationalist claims in the Balkans had been managed throughout the nineteenth century via the creation of autonomous provinces and later Ottoman successor states.[83] More troubling were reports arriving in the India Office that the Germany, together with its Ottoman allies, planned to "extend autonomy for Syria and Arabia with a view of reconciling Arabs."[84] This was, of course, precisely when CUP thinking shifted in this direction.

From the "Illegal Protectorate" to Independence?

In the aftermath of the annexation-protectorate debate, Egypt played a significant role in wartime British planning about the new Middle East.[85] Between Cairo and London, various plans were made and remade, but most imagined Egypt at the center of Britain's "new Middle East Empire." The 1914 annexation-protection debate between London and Cairo was revived in the spring of 1917 with the illness and death of Sultan Hussein. In a reversal, it was the Foreign Office that maintained the position that annexation would not secure anything more for the British, while General Reginald Wingate, the British high commissioner in Cairo, argued that Britain's position in Egypt needed to be placed on more secure footing, advocating Egypt's annexation as a colony. At this stage in the war, it was the Ottoman Empire that troubled British officials in London and Cairo rather than rising nationalist sentiment in Egypt, which was ascribed to a small but vocal "Turkish clique." Wingate noted:

> It seems to me that a great deal will depend on the future of Turkey. If this Ottoman Empire is still to continue in more or less independent position in the world with a Sultan at its head who will be the Caliph of Islam, and if that re-established Ottoman Empire is not to be allied heart and soul with the British Empire, then I foresee considerable difficulties ahead for Egypt. No one knows better than you how intimately connected Egypt and Turkey are, especially amongst the higher classes, by race and religion, and the latter of course bulks more largely than the former and is the mainstay of the influence of the classes over the masses in this country. There is as you know, no *vox populi* in Egypt and it is a case throughout of "the tail wagging the dog"; in other words it is the small and noisy Turkish pasha clique, who are largely imbued with Nationalistic ideas, who can generally secure the adhesion of the Fellaheen to their views through the influence of religion.

The idea that the Ottomans posed a greater threat than Egyptian nationalism to British efforts to secure imperial interests in Egypt and the Middle East shaped British thinking until the end of the war. The Ottomans and later Turkish Republicans did indeed continue to pose legal problems to the new British Empire until the Treaty of Lausanne in 1923, but it was the extent of Egyptian mobilization against the British protectorate that most threatened British control over Egypt.

Two days after the armistice, a group of prominent Egyptians met with General Wingate to request permission to send an Egyptian delegation to Paris. Led by Sa'd Zaghlul, the Wafd—the "Delegation"—stated that Egypt wanted "full independence." The British government refused Zaghlul's "programme of complete autonomy," but at that stage, the Foreign Office did not yet think that the Egyptians saw themselves as one of the "liberated countries" that had been one of the rationales for the war. Rather, London was focused on keeping Egyptian questions out of the Paris Peace Conference, particularly any discussion of Egypt's legal status, and insisted that Egypt was "an imperial and not an international question." The Foreign Office argued that if the Ottomans were weakened politically, it would be possible to manage Egyptian demands for autonomy that had been promised in 1914. Yet as the Paris Peace Conference approached, Egyptian demands for independence only increased. The "illegal protectorate" was widely denounced and members of the Wafd began appealing directly to Woodrow Wilson and Georges Clemenceau to attend the peace conference.

On January 20, 1919, Zaghlul sent Clemenceau a memorandum on "Egyptian National Claims." In addition to appealing to Wilson and national self-determination, he argued that British legal claims to Egypt were unjustified based on Egypt's guaranteed international status. Much like Ottoman lawyers and diplomats throughout the occupation, Zaghlul invoked Egypt's status as an autonomous province guaranteed in international law by treaty. He did so to argue that Ottoman sovereignty could only be transferred to the Egyptians. He refuted Great Britain's title to Egypt by recapitulating the history of the "Egyptian question" in international relations from Mehmed Ali through the protectorate:

> Before the events of 1882 led to the English occupation, Egypt was a country under the Ottoman suzerainty, but possessing under the Government of the Khedives, who succeeded to the throne according to dynastic order of succession, complete autonomy. The Turkish suzerainty came to nothing more than the payment of an annual tribute, some limitation on the military establishment, and the observance of any treaties signed by the Sublime Porte. This complete autonomy was obtained by the Egyptians on the field of battle, and at the price of their blood. It needed nothing less than the intervention of Europe to stop the victorious march of Mohammed Aly, and to compel him to accept autonomy in place of the independence which was the aim pursued. The Convention of London of the 15th of July, 1840, followed by the Hatte Cherif of the 13th February, 1841, constituted the Charter of Egypt. Thus the recognition of the rights of the latter was not by Turkey alone, but also by the Great Powers, whose intervention guaranteed this complete deliverance. Is it conceivable that the rights thus acquired can be lost because interior troubles, exaggerated at will, had for a moment caused anxiety to a few European residents?[86]

In addition to invoking the treaties and fermans, Zaghlul drew directly on General Maxwell's language in 1914 that Britain was fighting to protect the rights of Egypt "won upon the battlefield by Mohammad Ali." Zaghlul cast doubt on the legality of the occupation itself, noting that the juridical meaning of "occupation" was itself unclear and that "the public law even omits to mention it as being a means or regulating the relations that may exist between two countries." He denounced the 1904 *Entente Cordiale* between Britain and France as nothing more than an agreement between two countries, noting that the agreement could not intrude on "the rights of Egyptians" or on their recognized "autonomy."[87] Zaghlul underlined the fact that the protectorate was a wartime measure and the mechanism alone could not negate Egypt's acknowledged political status. He claimed Egyptian independence was already recognized on the basis of Wilsonian principles as the "natural indefeasible right of nations," and because Egypt was now free of "Turkish suzerainty," it could finally proclaim "full sovereignty justified by her moral and material conditions." Criticizing Prince Faisal's presence at Paris, he argued, too, that it was not possible to treat Hejaz or other parts of Arabia differently from Egypt: "It seems to us that when Europe considers that the Hedjaz, which was but yesterday a Turkish province, has a right to independence, she cannot but treat Egypt, infinitely more developed and, in addition, autonomous, on the same footing of equality."[88] Finally, in keeping with his legalist arguments, Zaghlul pledged that Egypt would continue to recognize the rights of foreigners and to pay its debt.

These themes—the rights of Mehmed Ali and the civilizational superiority of Egypt over Hejaz and other Ottoman provinces—were repeated in several other letters and petitions sent by the Wafd around Paris, London, and Cairo. For instance, following riots and strikes against the protectorate, General Allenby replaced Wingate as high commissioner of Egypt. The Wafd sent Allenby a letter that stated that Egypt had a stronger to claim to independence than any other part of the Ottoman Empire, on the basis of its internationally guaranteed legal status, its civilization, and the fact that Egypt had supported Britain during the war: "During the time the Egyptians were reading with astonishment the news concerning the Delegations of other countries: the Hedjaz, Armenia, Syria, and the Lebanon etc., which yesterday still Turkish provinces, were for the most part in war against the allies, while Egypt richer, more civilized, and enjoying already an autonomy guaranteed by international treaty, had aided in the conquest of these same countries."[89]

On March 7, 1919, Zaghlul and key members of the Wafd were arrested for their activities against the British protectorate and deported to Malta. Massive protests and a general strike in Cairo followed almost immediately. Nationalist pressure in Egypt was felt in Paris, too.

Since 1914, international recognition of Britain's protectorate in Egypt had been protracted and incomplete at best. The United States never recognized the protectorate, and Russia's acceptance of Egypt's changed legal status no longer mattered as the Bolsheviks were outside of European diplomacy at the start of the Paris Peace Conference. While Britain managed to avoid discussion of Egypt's legal status with Europe and the United States, events in Egypt forced Britain to deal with recognition of the protectorate. Allenby pressured the Foreign Office to obtain wide international recognition of the protectorate, especially from the United States. On April 4, 1919, Allenby wrote to Arthur Balfour, "I would reiterate the great importance of obtaining an early announcement that our protectorate is recognized by the Powers."[90] After years of Foreign Office pressure, the United States responded to Allenby's request against growing unrest in Egypt, which was a massive blow to the Wafd. In the end, all the treaties imposed by the Allies on Germany, Austria, Hungary, and Bulgaria included provisions to recognize the British Protectorate in Egypt and to renounce their Capitulatory rights there. The first and second treaties (Sèvres and Lausanne) were slightly different from the other European treaties and forced the Ottomans, and later the Republicans, to relinquish all rights and titles over Egypt and the Sudan and to surrender all claims on the Egyptian tribute.

Recognition of Britain's protectorate in Egypt did not quell the revolution in Egypt. In May 1919 the British government announced that a special mission headed by Lord Milner would be sent to Egypt to "inquire into the causes of the late disorders in Egypt and to report on the current situation in the country and the form of constitution which under the protectorate would be best to promote peace, the progressive development of self-governing institutions, and protection of foreign interests." The Milner Mission consisted of a group of British colonial experts and the principal legal advisor at the Foreign Office, Sir Cecil Hurst.[91] The mission arrived in December 1919 and returned to London in March 1920.[92]

The Wafd boycotted the mission, which was also met with another waves of strikes.

The Milner Mission's internal discussions revolved around the meaning of the protectorate and what it had done for British interests in Egypt. The members of the mission discussed the meaning of the term "protectorate" at length. Rennell Rodd argued that it was the word itself that had offended Egyptians, as the same word was used in Arabic to "indicate the protection accorded under traditional usage by western Powers to subjects of the old Turkish Empire." He noted that the word "thus implies a diminution of sovereignty to Egyptians and has an unwelcome suggestiveness for them, as implying foreign intervention."[93] Similarly, General Owen Thomas interviewed local elites and reported that the Arabic word for protectorate, *himaye*, was the same word applied to protected foreign subjects in Egypt. He concluded that the "complete independence" that Egyptians demanded could be "satisfied with a little more than a shadow of independence with but very little substance."[94]

For Milner, the mission should not bother with terms but identify "how much authority" Britain should exercise in Egypt, and that meant thinking clearly about what to control versus what could be left alone. Second, he thought it was important to decide if the British could come to an agreement with Egyptians or if Britain should be "obliged simply to arrogate to ourselves such powers as we may deem necessary without their consent." He explained:

> The "veiled protectorate" had defiantly come to an end. It was perhaps the best system possible. But it was necessarily temporary—the wonder is that it lasted so long—the veil could not be maintained for forever and the veil has gone. Something has to be substituted for it, having a more definite and open character. I do not ignore the fact that, whatever the formal relations between Great Britain and Egypt, the reality will always be something different. But we cannot very well go on any longer without any formal relations at all, beyond the phrase 'Protectorate.' "[95]

Milner argued that, when possible, Britain should exercise control, in whatever branch of administration. Without "assuming executive authority," he noted, "the indirect method of effecting our object by guidance and advice is preferable to the direct method of doing all of the work ourselves or by direct orders." He thought that too much had been made of the word *protectorate*, but that it could not be abandoned altogether because it excluded all foreign influence from Egypt and at the same time was recognized in the peace treaties. He noted: "It is quite possible that what we mean by 'Protectorate' is not really incompatible with what they mean by 'independence.'" He argued that the protectorate could remain in place, but that Britain could work out a bilateral arrangement with Fuad, who had become sultan of Egypt in 1917 following the death of Hussein:

> My own idea of the form . . . is that of a contract (I will not call it a treaty) by which we should undertake to guarantee an agreed constitution for Egypt against foreign intervention and internal disorder, and Egypt, in return for this guarantee, would acknowledge our right to keep an army of occupation and to retain certain posts in the administration, and the control of the Sudan. All these could be based on obligations we should be undertaking for the defense of Egypt and for the maintenance of the constitution, including any provisions it might contain for the protection of foreigners. I do not see why it should not be possible to have such an understanding with the Egyptians without abandoning the Protectorate, which we have so far only defined as implying the control of Egypt's foreign relations, which control would be explicitly recognized in this contract. As between us and the rest of the world our position would rest on the declaration of 1914, and its acknowledgement by the Great Powers, and the Peace Treaties. But as between us and the Egyptians it would rest on a bi-lateral agreement, not inconsistent with but *in foro demestico*, taking the place of these various sets. I conceive that it is not beyond the skill of the draftsmen, who have invented in the last twelve months—"Mandates" and such like—to construct a document which would embody these ideas.[96]

Milner's plan for what would replace the so-called veiled protectorate, his expression for the British occupation of Egypt, was an idealized version of the occupation.[97] Lord Cromer, the British counsel general in Egypt between 1883 and 1907, and others, including Milner in the 1890s, had long argued against "internationalism" in Egypt. For much of the occupation, British Foreign Office officials complained that European and Ottoman interference in Egypt had obstructed British efforts at reform.

For Milner, a form of "independence" could be found to satisfy Egyptians while maximizing British interests and limiting European interference in British administrative practices. Upon returning to London, he recommended full sovereignty for Egypt over its internal government, including the right to conclude treaties with foreign nations. In return, Egypt should acknowledge the right of Great Britain to maintain capitulatory rights with some modifications. He argued that Britain should have rights to military bases to prevent "foreign intervention" in Egypt. Milner also thought Britain should negotiate with Zaghlul and the Wafd.

The British cabinet found Milner's suggestions unacceptable. Britain had finally obtained Egypt, and now Milner wished Britain to relinquish any sovereign claims to the territory. Subsequent negotiations between Egypt and Britain failed to produce a treaty that was satisfactory to nationalists. After a long stalemate, Allenby, without cabinet support, unilaterally declared Egyptian independence on February 28, 1922. Egypt was proclaimed a sovereign and independent state but subject to four reservations: Britain would control the security of communications and defense; minorities and foreign interests would be protected, including the preservation of the Capitulations; and finally, Sudan would not be affected by the declaration of independence and would remain jointly under British and Egyptian control. Britain's short-lived "sultan" became a king with the establishment of the constitutional monarchy and new constitution promulgated in April 1923. Egyptian independence looked rather like Milner's idealized version of occupation, especially since Britain's permanent military presence would continue as a "veiled protectorate."

The Ottoman Factor

On December 12, 1922, İsmet Paşa (İnönü), the Ankara's government representative at the Lausanne peace proceedings, gave, by all accounts, an unexpected and lengthy speech on the history of minority rights protection in the Ottoman Empire. Supplemented with extensive quotes from Michelet's *History of France*, assorted European international law textbooks, British diplomatic documents, and memoirs, İsmet argued that Islamic jurisprudence had dictated that "the rights of minorities, which it is sought to assure in the 20th century under the guarantee of the League of Nations, were spontaneously accorded to the non-Muslim elements of the Ottoman Empire." Starting in the late eighteenth century, he continued, European states took advantage of these privileges and supported "national communities ready for revolt" who were protected by the Great Powers "not restrained by international law."[98] The real problem with such "privileges," he claimed, was that they eroded sovereignty and opened the door to foreign intervention leading to violence and international instability. The only way to guarantee the rights of minorities, he argued, was not for the emergent Turkey to sign on to the new minority rights treaties, which had been applied in the expanded and new Versailles states of Eastern Europe, but rather through a liberal domestic law code that would protect all communities equally without distinction. İsmet insisted that the emergent state didn't need the sort of international oversight that new and expanded states in Eastern Europe were obliged to embrace at Paris because, quite simply, the Ottomans had invented minority rights.

At the Paris Peace Conference in 1919, European peacemakers justified the minority rights treaties as a reconfiguration of models worked out in Ottoman lands over the course of the nineteenth century.[99] International lawyers, bureaucrats, and intellectuals in Istanbul agreed that the emergent new minority rights discourse was rooted in their own imperial practices, but they understood this history rather differently from the diplomats gathered in France. In the last days of the war, before the idea of minority rights protection gripped Paris, and certainly before it became of the three major issues debated at Lausanne—including the Capitulations and the status of Mosul—Istanbul intellectuals and elites across ethnic and religious lines fought bitterly over the status of prewar rights and privileges accorded to non-Muslim subjects and Europeans residing in the empire. International lawyers at the Ottoman Foreign Ministry churned out legal opinions on the problem of special legal privileges for religious and ethnic minorities. At the same time, Ottoman parliamentarians deliberated on the history of special administrative and legal rights within the empire.

When the first Allied ships anchored in the Bosporus in November 1918, initiating the unofficial occupation of the imperial capital, the major newspapers in the capital—Ottoman Turkish, Greek, Karamanlidika, Ladino, Arabic, Kurdish, and Armenian—engaged in fierce debates over the status of non-Muslims.[100] The prevalence of the "minority question," as it would later come to be known, in internal government documents, parliamentary debates, and the Istanbul press was tied to the debates on the future of the state, which initially, for many subjects, was imagined as an imperial one. Arguments about minorities were entangled with an understanding of how Ottoman institutions and domestic legal structures had operated from the 1830s through the First World War—especially those imposed by European states that had limited state sovereignty. Throughout the Armistice period (1918–1923), lawyers and publicists in Istanbul and later in Ankara generated policy papers, legal opinions, speeches, and editorials on the place of "exceptional" or "autonomous provinces" (*eyalet-i mümtaze*), non-Muslim "privileges" (*imtiyazlar*) within the future state, and the function of the Capitulations.[101]

While the postwar Ottoman state based in Istanbul initially committed itself to reorganizing the empire as a series of autonomous provinces, and even considered reviving privileges for non-Muslims, after the Treaty of Sèvres (1920) there was broad resistance, especially among Muslims, to anything that looked like internationally imposed limitations on territorial sovereignty and domestic legal institutions. Autonomy, non-Muslim privileges, and the Capitulations were all lumped together as old tools of European imperialism used to eviscerate Ottoman sovereignty.[102] By the middle of 1920, Ottoman commentators understood legal privileges for particular groups—whether in the form of special administrative rights for the provinces, for non-Muslim Ottomans, or for foreigners in the form of the Capitulations—as potentially lethal to the state sovereignty and an invitation to European intervention in the domestic order of the state. At Lausanne, these critiques were manifested in the rejection of minority rights treaties guaranteed by the League of Nations, and the refusal to accept Allied efforts to create autonomous provinces for Armenians and Kurds in what would become Turkey.[103] İsmet Paşa and the Turkish delegation at Lausanne flatly rejected Allied-imposed limits on sovereignty that resembled older forms of European interference in Ottoman affairs. From the state's perspective, administrative autonomy, minority rights protections, and legal privileges for foreigners were off the table.

This story reveals a deep shift in longstanding Ottoman approaches to negotiating with Europe that had been anchored in pragmatism and accommodation with international legal norms for much of the nineteenth and early twentieth centuries. The bundling and rejection of any form of legal privilege and the abandonment of international law as a tool to ameliorate the international status of the empire within Europe were a striking reversal from past practices. In earlier disputes, the empire negotiated and begrudgingly accommodated European demands for domestic reform, or the granting of administrative or legal rights to imperial subjects (almost always non-Muslim), as long as the agreement was agreed to by treaty and thus enshrined in the "law and system of Europe."[104] The Ottomans who forged the Republic gave up on international law as the savior of empire and abandoned the old practice of preserving state sovereignty by treaty. Instead, sovereignty was a right claimed through force and violence. This episode matters because it explains the enduring resistance to special privileges and administrative rights in the Republic of Turkey, but it also reflects an important moment in the Ottoman history, where domestic legal institutions were disaggregated from international legal constraints and force was elevated over the burdens of law.

International Law at Lausanne

Ismet Inönü's impromptu speech on the history of European intervention Ottoman affairs—and many others just like it over the course of the Peace Conference that drew substantially on international legal questions—was authored, at least in part, by Mehmed Münir Bey (Ertegün). He arrived at Lausanne as the chief legal advisor for the emergent Turkish state and, throughout the conference, worked behind the scenes, assisting İsmet Paşa and the Turkish delegation on the most contentious legal issues of the proceedings, including the Capitulations, the status of Mosul, and the legal position of non-Muslims in the future state. Indeed, between 1918 and the late 1920s, Mehmed Münir would lead or assist negotiations related to nearly every legal aspect of the dissolution of the empire and the forging of the Republic—from the Capitulations and the Ottoman debt to the treatment of minorities and the final borders of state.[105]

Even though Mehmet Münir Bey provided the legal substance to defend the state against Europe's efforts to restore prewar limits on sovereignty, he does not figure prominently in stories about the Peace Conference. In Imre Kelèn and Alajos Desző's political caricatures from Lausanne, he appears to be the especially serious member among the Turkish delegation. He looks anxious and gaunt and was depicted clutching documents or hovering over maps.[106] But apart from these cartoons and a handful of photographs that portray a correspondingly grave face and somber demeanor, Mehmed Münir is a footnote in the drama—despite the crushing volume of legal work he performed to dismantle the empire and usher in the state.

Lausanne was far from Mehmed Münir's first experience dealing with fraught legal questions concerning European attempts to restrict Ottoman sovereignty. In fact, his early career was defined by these problems. During the war, he served as one of the chief legal advisors to the Office of Legal, a role to which he would return in Ankara in 1924, but for a radically reconfigured Foreign Ministry, one released from the spectacular and manifold pressures faced by the late empire. Trained in international law at the Imperial Law School in Istanbul, he entered the Foreign Ministry as a legal assistant in 1909 and was promoted to legal advisor in early 1913, amid the chaos surrounding the Balkan Wars and the Bab-ı Coup. He took charge of the legal work of the empire at the precise moment that international law was most discredited in the eyes of Istanbul elites, and certainly by the Committee of Union and Progress.

During the war, Mehmed Münir wrote several legal opinions that justified the CUP's war aims. He authored or commented on numerous legal opinions that defended episodes such as the abolition of the Capitulations in 1914, as well as the termination of Mount Lebanon's privileged status in 1915. Aiding İbrahim Hakkı Paşa, he acted as a legal advisor for negotiations at Brest-Litovsk in 1917 and early 1918. From an Ottoman perspective, this treaty was a success and fulfilled one of the empire's war aims: restoration of lost lands. Russia ceded Kars, Batum, and Ardahan to the empire—all of which had been under Russian occupation since the Russo-Ottoman War (1877–78).[107] But, as we will see, Mehmed Münir did not merely issue legal opinions that conformed to the CUP vision of a postwar centralized empire.

The Ottoman Invention of Minority Rights

The Ottoman exit from the war in late October 1918 ushered in a new round of legal uncertainty for the empire. Almost immediately, prewar debates erupted between political factions—especially the CUP and the Ottoman liberals who had been forced out of governing in 1913. Ottomans grappled with the difficult question of how to rebuild the empire and remake the body politic in the aftermath of total war and, at the same time, struggled with devising ways to limit European interference in Ottoman affairs. As long as it was possible to imagine imperial continuity, many intellectuals anticipated a return to the ethnic and religious diversity of the prewar Ottoman world. But as the Allied occupation became more entrenched, and as hopeful expectations for the Paris Peace Conference shattered, Ottoman bureaucrats and intellectuals abandoned any commitment to special rights for non-Muslims, followed by the complete surrender of the imperial order in favor of a Muslim-majority state.

These debates swirled in backroom conversations among high officials and unfolded publicly in the press and parliament during the early days of the Allied occupation of the capital. Ottoman newspaper editors continued to cast Europe as an existential threat as far as the empire's external relations, but also in terms of its domestic politics. They argued that the long history of European military and legal intervention on behalf of Ottoman Christians had to end in order to build a strong postwar order. In the same way that the old prewar political battle lines between partisans of centralized versus decentralized imperial administration reappeared in 1918, so too did Second Constitutional era debates on the problem of privileges and special legal protections for non-Muslims. Accompanying political analyses on the viability of reorganized empire, editors debated the rights of non-Muslims as Ottoman citizens. It was in these particularly thorny disagreements that the question of minority rights arose and was later tied to that emergent rights discourse at the Paris Peace Conference.[108]

It wasn't just liberals who were committed to rebuilding the multiethnic empire that asserted the Ottomans invented minority rights. Once the treaties hammered out in Paris were publicized in Istanbul, Ottoman editors and politicians argued that minority rights were already embedded in the "constitutional" order of the empire and nothing further was required. Cemal Paşa's commentary was typical: "I wonder if it is not the greatest model of the principle of 'rights of minorities,' which today the American president Wilson has tried to get recognized by the civilized world, then the privilege granted by the great Ottoman sultan in the fifteenth century?"[109] In other words, the new minority rights treaties were derived from Ottoman practices, but as İsmet Paşa later pointed out, that meant they were odds with new conceptions of state sovereignty. While Ottomans celebrated Wilson early on as providing the blueprint for equality in international relations and offering a way to save the empire, by the summer of 1919 there was increasingly palpable disdain toward Wilson in government commentaries and newspapers, and never more so than in his attempt to take credit for inventing minority rights.

What is important here is that there was initially an open debate about how to solve the problem of European intervention in Ottoman affairs while maintaining the multiconfessional basis of the empire. But these arguments morphed into a kind of stock repeated answer to reject minority rights in the Republic. İsmet Paşa's speech on minority rights was representative of an argument that would be made repeatedly at Lausanne and beyond, and used later to deny the genocide: The Ottomans invented minority rights protection. As such, robust safeguards for minorities were embedded in the domestic legal order and did not require international oversight.

The Sovereign State

Just as the first Allied ships anchored in the Bosporus, liberals were ascendant in the new political landscape. After the CUP dissolved itself and the leadership fled Istanbul in the fall of 1918, Mehmed Münir remained at his post and continued to issue legal opinions for the postwar liberal government. As we saw in chapter 5, he wrote an opinion that served as the blueprint for reorganizing the Ottoman Empire as a series of autonomous provinces, without the privileges once attached to such provinces, in accordance with prewar ideas shared by members of the Freedom and Accord Party. That legal opinion, which laid claim to all Arab lands currently under European military occupation, functioned as the basis for the Ottoman memoranda to the Paris Peace Conference in 1919.[110] Just like Brest-Litovsk, much of the legal work of diplomacy fell to Mehmed Münir in preparation for Paris.

The logic that connected Mehmed Münir's diverse legal opinions was the problem of sovereignty and the perpetual threat of European intervention in Ottoman affairs. In each of these opinions, Münir Bey disavowed an older Ottoman approach to diplomacy and international law that sought to increase Ottoman control over internal and external affairs but ultimately accommodated European-imposed limitations on sovereignty, such as the Capitulations, the Public Debt Administration, and the internationally guaranteed autonomous provinces (Egypt, Mt. Lebanon Eastern Rumelia, and Crete). Instead, he rejected any limitation on sovereignty. Sovereignty was singular and could not be divided, a radical departure from Ottoman views in the nineteenth century. He argued that the Ottoman state and now emergent Turkey should "not fail to take advantage of the principles of international law in order to enforce its rights."[111] While never explicit, the implications were clear. The only reason the Ottomans were back at the negotiating table at Lausanne was that force worked. It mattered more than the Foreign Ministry's old attachment to international law and empty European treaties that had promised to preserve the "territorial integrity of the Ottoman Empire."

Mehmed Münir was not alone in this view. During the Armistice period, Ottoman lawyers and intellectuals across a broad political spectrum—those favoring a revived Ottoman Empire composed of autonomous provinces, a Turco-Arab Federation, or a Turkish nation-state—argued that "privileges" of any sort had to be replaced with a unitary form of citizenship and administration. In early 1920, Mehmed Münir joined İzzet and Salih Paşa's mission to end the differences between the Ottoman governments in Istanbul and Ankara. Like so many other Ottomans that year, he abandoned the empire and ditched the sultan in favor of the nationalists, offering his legal services to the Ankara government.

İsmet Paşa's rejection of minority rights protection at Lausanne was matched by an equally vehement dismissal of Allied attempts to create autonomous Kurdish and Armenian zones within in postwar state—arguments that Mehmet Münir helped craft. Gabriel Noradounghian—the chief legal advisor to the Foreign Ministry—arrived at Lausanne representing Armenian interests within the Republic.[112] In one of the more dramatic episodes at Lausanne, Noradounghian requested a meeting with İsmet Paşa to discuss establishing an autonomous homeland for Armenians in the new Turkey.[113] İsmet, unsurprisingly, rejected the request.

Before arriving at Lausanne, Noradounghian worked in exile, campaigning on behalf of an independent Armenia allotted by the Treaty of Sevres. He met with other lawyers and gave interviews to French newspapers, but also to emerging internationalists. In September 1922 he met with Erik Colban, a Norwegian international lawyer who was the first director of the Minorities Section at the League of Nations, representing the National Armenian Delegation.[114] Noradounghian wanted to lay out a plan for minority rights protection and insisted such protections could only work if the state also gave Armenians autonomy within Turkey: "As to the Armenian problem, M. Noradounghian said that minorities protection would, of course, be no real help unless a national home for the Armenians were created. The Armenians as a minority in the Ottoman Empire would have a much better standing if they had to support them the Government of an independent Armenian State." Colban wrote in a handwritten marginal note in French that "I think that to the contrary that would be a danger for the Armenians, because the Turks would see it as a sign and a threat of having their national territory be divided again."[115] Because the wartime "massacres and deportations were a means of extermination" that had attracted the attention of the "civilized world," Noradounghian provided Colban with list of Kemalist tactics adopted to achieve the same ends. He noted that requisitioning continued against non-Muslims. He complained they were overtaxed and compelled to repay loans in gold instead of paper currency. Unlawful arrests, the refusal to issue passports, and general surveillance of non-Muslims were prevalent. The "Kemalist tactics" achieved the same end as violence had in wartime: Non-Muslims were "terrorized" into leaving the country.

The second document Noradounghian submitted to Colban, and the Minorities Section by extension of his position, was a piece entitled "Examination of the Issue of Minority Rights." The paper examined the new minority rights regimes in Bulgaria, Greece, and Poland and specific laws created to protect minority rights, especially equality before the law. Noradounghian noted protections for minority languages and their use as well as religious, charitable, social, and educational institutions. He argued that this bundle of rights was the precise right that the Ankara government should provide to non-Muslims remaining in Turkey. He wondered what had happened to the existing "Religious Privileges" of non-Muslim communities." Noradounghian noted that "European diplomacy never failed to insist to the Ottoman Government's need to grant and guarantee a special status to the (religious) Communities." He then referred to the Imperial edits of 1839 and 1856, as well as Article 62 of the Treaty of Berlin (1876), which had promised reform in the Eastern provinces of the empire. Yet, he argued, "Today, the Government of Angora wants to eliminate all the special legislation of Privileges for which no commitment has been stipulated and replace it with the rights of Minorities inserted in the Treaties of the Entente." To European states it appeared that Ankara was making a concession, by accepting minority rights, but in reality, it was dismantling the ancient rights "ab antique" that had protected Ottoman non-Muslims.

We do not know if Mehmed Münir and Gabriel Noradounghian met with each other, but they certainly knew that the other was at Lausanne. Mehmed Münir was the heir to the legal world Noradounghian had created with İbrahim Hakkı Paşa. All the accommodations with European states and the arguments marshaled during the Hamidian era to preserve imperial sovereignty served as the foundation of Mehmed Münir's education in international law and his career as a Foreign Ministry lawyer. His legal opinions on the problems of the Capitulations, autonomous provinces, and non-Muslim privileges were shaped by reading the legal archive, library, and treaty collections that Noradounghian and İbrahim Hakkı had created.

Not only did the Allied powers demand international supervision beyond the terms of the Minority Treaties already hashed out at Paris, they also demanded other privileges for non-Muslims, including exemption from military service and taxation. Unsurprisingly, the Ankara delegation rejected these proposals as incompatible with territorial sovereignty. In an interview with Falih Rifki Bey, Mustafa Kemal expressed concern that Britain would establish an autonomous Kurdish region in Mosul, which would inevitably encourage Kurds in the emergent state of Turkey to demand their own autonomous province. While worried about the provisions for an autonomous Kurdistan in the Sevres treaty, Mustafa Kemal was looking further back to how the privileged or autonomous provinces had functioned in the late empire, and he argued that autonomy was merely a stepping stone to independence.[116]

Europeans saw the same continuities but simply tried to invent new words and colonial forms to describe them: In the days leading up to the opening of the Lausanne conference, the Allied delegations agreed that the Capitulations must be retained but noted that although the actual word "Capitulations" should be used as little as possible and perhaps replaced, the substance of them would remain as they were before 1914. The British idea of creating new words for old legal forms that had disadvantaged the Ottoman state before the war was widespread during the Armistice years. For instance, in Egypt, several members of the Milner Mission, dispatched to Cairo 1919 to investigate the revolution, noted that Egyptians bristled at the word "protectorate" (*himaye*) because the same word was used to "indicate the protection accorded under traditional usage by western Powers to subjects of the old Turkish Empire . . . thus implies a diminution of sovereignty to Egyptians and has an unwelcome suggestiveness for them, as implying foreign intervention."[117] This idea was manifested further at Lausanne in discussions about creating autonomous provinces for Armenians and Kurds in the emergent Turkey, where "autonomy" would now instead be a "national home," à la the Balfour Declaration. Curzon argued that "the suggestion of a national home implied no intention to attack the sovereignty of Turkey, to create an *imperium in imperio* or a state within a state, or to set up 'an autonomous regime.'"[118] But of course everyone, especially the Ankara delegation, saw it that way.

Conclusion: Sovereignty Without Restrictions

In 1935 Ahmed Reşid, a professor of comparative constitutional law at Istanbul University and a former legal advisor to the Ottoman Foreign Ministry, insisted that the minority rights treaties appended to the treaties concluding the First World War, including those enshrined in Lausanne (1923), had a clear Ottoman genealogy.[119] In the aftermath of the First World War, he retired from politics and dedicated himself to teaching law, but he never lost sight of those old Ottoman preoccupations with shoring up a fragile sovereignty against a rapacious Europe. During the interwar years, he wrote extensively for Turkish and European audiences on the Capitulations and minority rights.[120] In the gloom of the 1930s, when the minority rights treaties were on the brink of failure, he argued that they were not the spontaneous creation of Woodrow Wilson and the diplomats at Paris to solve the problem of nation in place of empire: The "international protection of minorities was not imagined, so to speak, from the outset; it was not developed all at once; it is not, finally, the invention of the only victorious Powers of the Great War, acting in this matter under the direction of Wilson." Minority rights were Ottoman. He pointed out that though Turkey signed onto the minority rights regime dictated by Lausanne, the minority articles were qualitatively different from those in Europe because they protected religious minorities and not ethnic and linguistic minorities. Ultimately, he argued, the Turkish state was fortunate. So many of the new Versailles states failed to manage to assimilate their minorities into postimperial states because they lacked robust domestic legal institutions to protect all citizens equally without distinction.

The occupation of autonomous Egypt had a lasting effect on British imperial policy in the Middle East after the First World War. William

Roger Lewis argued that the British Empire was revived and reinvented in the Middle East after the war. Yet the reinvention of the empire that Lewis posits began in Egypt prior to the outbreak of the war. British officials in the Foreign Office had learned much from the occupation and over time developed a model of rule that was distinct from formal political control. Sovereignty could reside elsewhere, preferably in a local monarch, as long as an army of British advisors controlled foreign and economic policy. The British-Ottoman diplomatic relationship, but also the consolidation of positivist international law and the global territorialization of sovereignty between the 1880s and the end of the First World War, had a decisive influence on that model. The practice of ruling through Ottoman institutions, along with justifications for the occupation that highlighted international stability and the development of self-government, offered a distinct model of imperial administration that the British employed in the form of League of Nations mandates in the territories seized from the Ottoman Empire after the First World War.

During the protectorate experiment in Egypt, the Foreign Office learned something very important about formal sovereignty. The protectorate lasted briefly, but debates about it continued in London and Cairo from 1914 through the mid-1920s. During the war, these debates led to rather frank discussions concerning the past and future of British power in Egypt and the Middle East. The protectorate was a wartime exigency and one that deviated from the Foreign Office's usual anti-annexationist position in Ottoman territories, preferring a range of options to manage Ottoman weakness, from creating "autonomous" provinces to permanent military occupation. By the end of the war, many officials viewed the protectorate as a misstep, particularly as Egyptian nationalists, in demanding independence, continued to appeal to Egypt's special status in international law. Independence in 1922 was in many ways a return to the occupation, where formal sovereignty could reside in Egypt, as it had in the Ottoman sultan during the occupation, while Britain administered core functions of the state. On one hand, the protectorate in Egypt did not appear to be a radical departure from British policy during the occupation—and in fact the Foreign Office did much to emphasize the continuities between policies of occupation and protection. The practical problem for the Foreign Office was clear: Once Britain was at war with the Ottoman Empire, "all Egyptians being Ottoman subjects would suddenly find themselves technically enemy subjects in the eyes of Great

Britain and allies." Yet the fact remained that unilaterally ending Ottoman sovereignty in Egypt without the consent of European powers would produce short- and long-term problems for the British. The Capitulations and other immunities guaranteed to foreign residents in Egypt were kept in place to appease Allied opinion, which was successful. Beyond potential problems with Britain's allies, the Central Powers clearly refused to recognize the protectorate, as did the United States. The largest problem for the British, however, was the local Egyptian population and the Ottoman Empire. Foreign Office officials in London and Cairo were deeply concerned about Egyptian compliance with the protectorate, as well as the actions of the deposed khedive and his potential protectors in Istanbul throughout the war.

The debate on annexation versus protection did not die in 1914. Rather, it was revived in 1917 and again between 1919 and 1922. The British declaration of protection in Egypt should be seen alongside the other competing wartime agreements in terms of its role in shaping the post-Ottoman imperial order in the Middle East. While protection may have been a wartime contingency, British policy in Egypt during the war was not just the result of the wartime promises of greater autonomy for Egyptians. Rather the British wartime administration of Egypt needs to be placed in the longue durée of the occupation and Egyptian autonomy under Ottoman rule. The model of British rule in Egypt, exemplified by a princely, later monarchical alliance, an army of British advisors controlling key state functions, and formal sovereignty outside of the British imperial system, was the key contender for export throughout the Middle East.

Conclusion

The Problem of Sovereignty in the Middle East

In 1910 the Egyptian magnate Abbas Halim Paşa commissioned an imposing art nouveau building in Istanbul's most fashionable neighborhood, Pera. The residence was called Mısır Apartmanı (Egypt Apartments) and was ringed with Egyptian lotus capitals and stylized palm fronds. Abbas Halim was a grandson of Mehmed Ali Paşa and, like many members of the khedival family, lived between Cairo and Istanbul. When Mısır Apartmanı was built, Pera was the part of the capital where European power was most palpable. It was a short walk away from the major European embassies, the French Capitulation court, Galatasaray High School (*Mekteb-i Sultani*)—a French-style lycée that trained the empire's future bureaucrats—and the elegant Tokatlian Hotel, were Ottoman journalists and intellectuals gathered and whose Republican era guests included Leon Trotsky, Mustafa Kemal, and Agatha Christie's Hercule Poirot. Mısır Apartmanı was surrounded by cafés, department stores, restaurants, brothels, and night clubs, all bearing signs in Ottoman Turkish, Armenian, Greek, and French, and whose patrons spoke an even more diverse array of languages.

In some ways, Mısır Apartmanı was a fitting final home for Mehmed Akif Ersoy when he returned to Istanbul in 1936, after eleven years of exile in Cairo. At that time, the area was still vibrant and crowded with foreigners, spies, and refugees, but much had changed. The last independent Muslim empire had been crushed, the Caliphate abolished, the capital moved to Ankara. The city was demographically far more Muslim and Turkish than it had ever been in its history. Mehmed Akif Ersoy, who died in the Mısır Apartmanı on December 27, 1936, experienced the transition from empire to Republic in a way that was typical of a particular class of late Ottoman intellectuals. During the Second Constitutional era (1908–1918), he founded and edited a newspaper, *Sırat-ı Müstakim*, later *Sebilürreşad* (The Straight Path), in which he engaged in the major debates on constitutionalism and religious reform. He translated the works of Muhammad 'Abduh—the leading Muslim reformer and the grand mufti of Egypt—from Arabic into Ottoman Turkish and published the first of seven volumes of poetry.[1] At the beginning of the First World War, the government dispatched him to Berlin as a member of the Special Organization (*Teşkilat-i Mahsusa*)—the Ottoman paramilitary and intelligence-gathering organization—where he attempted to recruit Allied Muslim prisoners of war. In 1915 he joined Eşref Kuşçubası on a mission to Nejd (today in central Saudi Arabia) to strengthen Ottoman ties to the Rashidis and the Ibn Sauds—powerful local rulers in central Arabia—and as a counterweight to the incipient British-backed Arab Revolt initiated by Ottoman subject Hussein bin Ali, the Sharif of Mecca.[2]

When the volatile period of the Armistice commenced in late October 1918, Ersoy criticized the disastrous wartime policies of the Committee of Union and Progress, but, like many elites, he nevertheless expected the empire would survive the catastrophe. He was deeply alarmed by Allied threats to sever the Arab provinces from the imperial domains and wrote critically against such flagrant imperialism. Along with scores of other intellectuals and parliamentarians, he abandoned the sultan's government in early 1920 and was smuggled out of Allied occupied İstanbul so that he could join the opposition government in Ankara. Even though he was born in Istanbul and grew up in the Fatih district of the city, he entered the Grand National Assembly in Ankara as a deputy first for Biga, then Kastamonu—Anatolian provinces. He was an important Muslim intellectual voice in support of the nationalists, but always with an understanding that he fought on behalf of Muslim unity, not just Turkish interests. In a particularly vitriolic sermon, he condemned the Treaty of Sèvres (1920) as the final step in a long history of European aggression against Muslims and cast non-Muslim Ottomans as a dangerous fifth column ready to seize the privileges Europeans had once taken for themselves.[3] In the midst of war with Greece, with multiple provinces under Allied military occupation and power divided between Istanbul and Ankara, the National Assembly adopted Ersoy's poem *İstiklal Marşı* (Independence March) as the new national anthem in March 1921, over two years before the Republic was declared and the empire was officially a dead letter.[4]

As long as the war with Greece raged on and the Allies occupied Istanbul, it was possible to set aside substantive differences about what the post-Ottoman state would look like and instead commit to vague principles, the most important of which was complete sovereignty without conditions.[5] After all, from 1918 to 1923, everything, including territorial boundaries, appeared to be in flux. But once the negotiations at Lausanne got under way, competing visions for the state were harder to manage. Ersoy joined the faction that opposed Mustafa Kemal, which soon lost spectacularly. The Caliphate was abolished in 1924. By 1925 *Sebilürreşad* was banned, and Ersoy was out of a job and lost his pension.[6] The following year, like so many other former Ottoman subjects, he abandoned the state and retreated to the old lands of the empire, now under varying forms of European control. For eleven years, Ersoy lived in self-imposed exile in Cairo as a guest of the Egyptian royal family. During those years he taught and worked on a translation, or rendering, of the Qur'an into Ottoman Turkish.[7] He returned to Istanbul quietly in 1936 seeking medical assistance, again under the patronage of the Egyptian Abbas Halim, which is how he came to die inside the Mısır Apartmanı.

The kind of links between Cairo and Istanbul suggested by Ersoy's friendship with (and reliance on) Abbas Halim remained as unexceptional in the 1930s as they would have been in the 1830s. Although Egypt had been under British military occupation since 1882, the khedive, his family, and other local elites all summered in Istanbul, not London. Though legally autonomous within the Ottoman constitutional order, Egypt was part of the Ottoman sovereign domains and remained so until the end of the empire. That link had consequences that have been consistently underestimated by historians focusing only on Egypt's path to independence or its economic exploitation by European empire. Despite the rivalry between the rebellious governor and the sultan, the Kavalalı dynasty (*hanedan*) was firmly integrated into the political and social structures of the late Ottoman state. The khedival family members depended on the sultan for their own local legitimacy and strove to win over those Ottoman elites who viewed them as upstarts. As if to overcome the newness of their position, Egyptian princes and princesses sought marriages with members of the Ottoman palace and high political and military officials. They were a philanthropic family and funded the arts in both cities. They supported prominent Ottoman musicians, poets, and intellectuals, including Halil Halid, who wrote searing critiques of especially British imperialism directed against Muslims.[8] It is thus not at all anomalous that Abbas Halim would use his Egyptian fortune to invest in one of the grandest residential buildings in Istanbul.

Indeed, the Kavalalı dynasty left a distinct architectural imprint on Istanbul even beyond the Mısır Apartmanı. As Ahmet Hamed Tanpinar noted in his nostalgic essay, "Five Cities," Istanbul was transformed by wealthy families from the Eastern Mediterranean who moved there to live within "an Islamic milieu" (*bir İslam çevresinde*). Much of Istanbul's prosperity, he claimed, came from Egypt: "The flow of money increased, particularly after the Tanzimat. Above all, an important part of Egypt's wealth, which was being exploited through European methods, was pouring into Istanbul during the eras of Abdülmecid, Abdülaziz and Abdülhamid."[9] He argued that the guilds and markets, the "real backbone of the city" (*bu çarşılar şehrin asıl belkemiği idi*), supplied affluent families with handmade crafts that enabled the empire to survive despite the influx of cheap European goods and the predatory nature of the Capitulations. The Kavalalı dynasty built seaside mansions (*yalı*) on the European and Asian shores of the Bosporus, and, in the tradition of Islamic architectural patronage, they constructed hospitals and orphanages as well as religious schools (*medrese*) and restored Sufi lodges (*tekke*) throughout the imperial capital.[10] The Kavalalı built so many extravagant buildings in Istanbul that Ahmed Cevdet Paşa—the Tanzimat statesman who lead the effort to codify Islamic Law into a standard civil code for the empire—called them "Egyptian riff-raff" (*Mısır döküntüleri*) and worried that they corrupted the morals of other subjects through their lavish spending and ostentatious consumption.[11] This form of architectural patronage would surprise no one if it had occurred in the sixteenth century, when Egypt's yearly remittance to the state exceeded that of any other province. Instead, these structures were built during the period of Egyptian autonomy and the British occupation, when, by most historical accounts, Egypt had long ceased to be Ottoman in any meaningful way.[12] The Mısır Apartmanı is not an architectural curiosity but a reflection of ongoing economic, cultural, and even political ties between Cairo and Istanbul—ties that defined lives and policies well into the twentieth century.

The Mısır Apartmanı and other Kavalalı structures show that notwithstanding European efforts to demarcate the boundaries between Egypt and other Ottoman provinces and European colonial possessions in Africa, Egypt was bound to the Ottoman imperial center first through sovereignty. This legal connection mattered. It enabled and sustained flows of money, people, and ideas between the two cities during the last years of the empire. From the khedival family to North African pilgrims to Azhari Islamic reformers and tobacco smugglers, a series of formal and informal networks connected the sultan's subjects across the empire.

The networks and movement between Istanbul and Cairo connected the governor's family, Egyptian and Istanbul elites, and the artists and architects who lived from their patronage, but it was not limited to people who lived in or designed palaces, *yalıs*, or the Mısır Apartmanı. Starting in the mid-nineteenth century, the Eastern Mediterranean linked a series of port cities stretching from Salonika in the north down through Izmir, Beirut, and Alexandria in the south. Ottoman, Armenian, Greek, and Italian workers circulated through labor and radical political networks.[13] During the period of Sultan Abdülhamid II (r. 1876–1909), strict press laws prompted a number of Ottoman constitutionalists to seek exile in Egypt, where paradoxically they could publish more freely under the protection of the Capitulations. Cairo served as a center for revolutionary planning and publishing in the years leading up to the Young Turk Revolution (1908) and the Second Constitutional era. Muslim scholars corresponded and traveled between the two great rival centers of Islamic learning in the period: Al-Azhar University in Cairo and the *medreses* of the Süleymaniye mosque complex in Istanbul. Even with the arrival of steamships, Cairo, along with Bagdad and Damascus, remained one of the main overland caravan routes for the annual pilgrimage to Mecca, the Hajj, and served as an important legitimizing function for the Ottoman sultan and caliph.[14]

Egypt's international legal status as an Ottoman province during the British military occupation shaped high politics and international diplomacy and profoundly affected the everyday lives of Egyptians, who found themselves in court, engaged in commerce, or on the move. As in other provinces of the empire, autonomous Egypt was perforated by European financial and legal institutions, which circumscribed the authority of the Ottoman state and the local authority of the khedives. Along with preserving Egypt's legal status within the Ottoman Empire, British occupational policy dictated that Ottoman institutions in Egypt remained in force, including the Capitulations, the Mixed Courts, and the Commission of the Public Debt (*Caisse de la Dette Publique*).[15] Preserving Ottoman institutions in Egypt had direct and significant consequences on Egyptian administration and governance. On one hand, Ottoman sovereignty in Egypt constrained British administration on a day-to-day basis, but it also set the terms for claim-making among diverse groups, including Egyptian nationalists and Ottoman diplomats and lawyers. Throughout the occupation, the persistent legal connection between Egypt and the Ottoman Empire hampered British hegemony and always threatened to pull Egypt more fully into an Ottoman orbit. Indeed, until December 1914, fully two months after the Ottoman Empire entered the war against the Allied powers, Egyptians were legally Ottoman subjects.

Post-Ottoman historical geography is littered with the material detritus of empire. The built environment bears the traces of lives and possibilities that have long been extinguished by the logic of national states and territorialized sovereignty. In Istanbul, reminders of Armenian, Greek, Ladino, and Bulgarian-speaking subjects can be found in abandoned schools, churches, and synagogues, as well as textually over entryways in the old European quarter and in the Balat and Fener quarters—home to the Greek Orthodox patriarchate. Remnants of Europe's unequal treatment of the Ottoman state are abundantly visible, too, by way of scattered Capitulation court buildings, the still functioning European hospitals, the former American missionary college, the old foreign-owned Ottoman Bank, the Tobacco Régie, and the Ottoman Public Debt Administration—a building that is pronounced in city's western skyline, otherwise dominated by the great imperial mosques. Though the Turkish Republic replaced the Arabic alphabet with a modified Latin script, Ottoman Turkish and Arabic calligraphy are everywhere present on fountains, mosques, and palaces, as well as on ferry terminals, train stations, and the façades of functioning buildings—the central post office in Istanbul still bears the inscription "Ministry of Post and Telegraph" in stylized Kufic script (*posta ve telegraf nezareti*). And so the Egyptian buildings on *Istiklal*, the khedival palaces dotting the Bosporus, the summer residences on the Princes' Islands in the Sea of Marmara, and the Sufi lodge in Üsküdar all make up part of the visible Ottoman past.

After a period of near constant warfare from 1911 to 1922, many of the old connections between Egypt and Istanbul persisted; others were forever lost. Armenians who had survived the genocide settled largely outside the boundaries of the new Republic, especially in Egypt, Lebanon, and France. Like so many Armenian intellectuals, Hovsep Aznavur, the architect whom Abbas Hilmi had hired to design the Mısır Apartmanı, moved to Cairo. Similarly, a number of Islamic scholars left the Republic for Cairo when the new nationalist regime introduced state policies designed to circumscribe the religious establishment, including the abolition of the Caliphate and the Office of the *Şeyhülislam*, the prohibition of Sufi orders and lodges, and the forced closure of religious schools such as the *medreses* at the Sülmaniye mosque, which was transformed into a library.[16] The Capitulations remained in Egypt until the mid-1930s, but by the early 1920s the fluidity of individual legal personality, which characterized the occupation period, ground to a halt—it was impossible for Egyptians to claim Turkish citizenship and vice-versa. All the legal ties between the Ottoman state and Egypt were formally severed upon the ratification of the Treaty of Lausanne (1923), though occupation-era ideas persisted in British imperial practices in Egypt and their new Middle East empire.

Dissolving the imperial relationship between Cairo and Istanbul changed how local actors in both places made arguments about the state and its place in the international order. Egyptian nationalists could no longer appeal to the sultan-caliph for protection or intervention, while Turkish nationalists now linked sovereignty to territorial control, which was a true revolution in Ottoman international legal thought. The new states of Egypt and Turkey had a deep investment in forgetting the imperial past, as each took up separate programs of making the state national over the first half of the twentieth century. The imperial world that shaped everyday possibilities—where one lived, where one worked, paid taxes, and was buried—vanished in a brutal but slow-burning cataclysm that started with the Italian invasion of Libya in 1911. Some of those ideas lived on in the post-Ottoman world, but their imperial origins have remained obscure.

Imperial historians have argued that the British Empire reinvented itself in the Middle East following World War I and the collapse of the Ottoman Empire. The year 1919 is treated as the decisive break with the Ottoman past in the Arab Near East, when British and French colonial rule replaced Ottoman rule. The postwar order in the Middle East has largely been interpreted as the result of conflicting wartime promises, as well as the influence of Woodrow Wilson's anti-imperialist ideas and his support for national self-determination. Indeed, most histories of the League of Nations Mandates System, which granted the Arab provinces provisional recognition of independence under British and French trusteeship, have understood this conditional "independence" to be little more than an imperial compromise with Wilsonian rhetoric. In other words, the British and French mandatory powers accepted the façade of independence in order to satisfy the Americans, but in reality the new system provided a cover of legitimacy for the extension of empire as usual into the Middle East. If anything, the system of autonomous provinces worked out by the Ottomans and Europe was internationalized in the form of the League of Nations mandates for the Arab provinces.

The occupation of Egypt had a lasting impact on British imperial policy in the Middle East after World War I, but also on Egypt and the Republic of Turkey. British officials in the Foreign Office learned much from the occupation and over time developed a model of rule that was distinct from formal political control. Sovereignty could reside elsewhere, preferably in a local monarch, as long as an army of British advisors controlled foreign and economic policy. A number of accidents and issues particular to the period shaped the model, especially the British–Ottoman diplomatic relationship, but also the consolidation of positivist international law and the global territorialization of sovereignty between the 1880s and the end of World War I. Ruling through Ottoman institutions, along with justifications for the occupation, such as international stability and the development of self-government, offered a new model of imperial administration that the British employed in the form of League of Nations mandates in the territories seized from the Ottoman Empire after World War I.

The most consequential legacy of Ottoman autonomy in the postwar Middle East was the form of damaged sovereignty embedded within each of the Class A mandates. Britain and France disavowed the capacity of self-governance among former Ottoman subjects—despite the fact that they had voted in local and imperial elections, joined political and literary clubs, hashed out ideas about governance and international law in newspaper editorials, and demanded constitutional rule. While the mandatories attempted to the thwart this political inheritance, they upheld the legacy of administrative autonomy. Like the privileged provinces, the mandates were administrated in drastically different ways. What bound them together was their guarantor, the new League of Nations. Their status was guaranteed in international law by treaty, along with individual mandates for each territory. Britain especially viewed the mandates as they had autonomy, as an instrument to manage political claims with administrative solutions. Formal sovereignty need not rest with the mandatory power to achieve control.

In 1923 Quincy Wright, the American international lawyer, found ten separate theories to answer the critical question "where does sovereignty of the mandated areas reside?" Drawing on the ghost of nineteenth-century semi-sovereignty, Wright acknowledged that the separation of control and sovereignty was usually transitory and found in those types of territories that defied modern international law: "confederacies, federations, protectorates, spheres of influence, suzerainties, self-governing dominions."[17] The mandates, like their Ottoman precursors, were anomalous, difficult to categorize, and confounded international legal theory—a legacy that haunted all the territories controlled by Britain and France after the war, including places like Egypt that were left outside the system.

Even after independence and the Treaty of Lausanne, where the Ottoman/Republican state relinquished legal claims to Egypt and Sudan, problems related to Ottoman sovereignty in Egypt persisted through a series of measures in the 1930s stemming from the Anglo-Egyptian Treaty of Alliance in 1936. The treaty opened the way to the Montreux conference on April 12–May 8, 1937, which set the date to abolish the Capitulations—twenty-three years after the Ottomans had done so, and a full fourteen years after the Ottoman state had ceased to exist. Iraq also invited Egypt to join the League of Nations in February 1937, and the Republic of Turkey, itself a new member to the League, proposed that an extraordinary session should be held for the purpose. On May 26, 1937, the Assembly of the League of Nation's unanimously recommended Egypt as a League member. As one legal commentator noted, "Thus culminated the long progression of events which began with the establishment of Egypt's special status within the Ottoman Empire in the middle of the nineteenth century."[18]

The year 1919 was not a moment of rupture for the Ottoman Empire either. From the mid-nineteenth century onward, the Ottoman state understood sovereignty in terms of international legal recognition and was convinced that it mattered more than actual political control. The real rupture for the Ottoman state came in 1922, when Ottoman leadership decisively chose to ditch the empire in favor of the nation. The new state opted for uncompromising sovereignty—won through war—over the autonomy option. In his famous October 1927 speech, Mustafa Kemal, made the point succinctly: "Sovereignty is never transferred for some theoretical reason, or through debate or talk. Sovereignty is seized with strength and power and violence. The Sons of Osman seized the Turkish people's sovereignty by force and held this power they usurped for six centuries. And now the Turkish nation, through rebellion (*isyan*)—after warning these invaders to know their limits—has taken its sovereignty into its own hands."[19]

This story tells us that postwar challenges in the Middle East were not just a passive legacy built on top of the ruble of the Ottoman past. Instead, the international legal, financial, and economic limitations on Ottoman sovereignty that shaped everyday life in the empire reflected an almost century-long tug-of-war between the Ottoman and European powers, where a very active and inventive Ottoman state hashed out the "autonomous" compromise to demand recognition as a Great Power equal to its European neighbors, despite ever-increasing European incursions. The final death knell of the Ottoman state was not the realization of Article 12 under the auspices of mandate system, it was the abandonment of empire by the strongest remaining forces of the Ottoman leadership in favor of the Turkish national state. But those former Ottoman subjects left outside of the new Turkey found not local control, but rather a new iteration of European empire without responsibility.

The Ottomans got to keep Egypt without the burdens of governance, precisely the same approach the British would take in the exercise of power in the postwar Middle East, in the form of a client-state relationship that characterized British control in postwar Egypt, Iraq, and Transjordan—to a large degree in the Arabian Peninsula, and to a lesser extent in Palestine—which was a direct product of Britain's longtime engagement with Ottoman international legal arguments about the sovereignty. Outside of the Balkans, Turkey became one of the few properly independent states in the post-Ottoman Middle East, and one with an existing bureaucracy and state institutions.[20] At the same time, nominal sovereignty held less meaning in a world where political power increasingly resided in states rather than empires. The Ottoman attachment to the territorial integrity of the empire gave way to the Turkish Republic's slogan emblazoned still today on the wall of the Grand National Assembly: "Sovereignty belongs to the nation without limits and without conditions."[21] Permanent European military occupations of Ottoman territory, the Capitulations, and other derogations of Ottoman sovereignty were rejected by Turkish Republicans as incompatible with the territorialized state in the new global order established after World War I.

Notes

Archival Sources and Abbreviations

TURKEY

Başbakanlık Osmanlı Arşivi (Ottoman Archives, BOA), Istanbul, Turkey

A.DVN.MKL	Sadaret Divan-ı Hümayun Kalemi Mukavele Kısmı Belgeleri
A.MKT.MHM	Sedaret Mektubi Kalemi Mühimme Kalemi (Odası) Belgeleri
A.MTZ.04	Eyalet-i Mümtaze Kalemi Odası'nın kirislerinin çürümüs ve pervazlarının ayrılmıs oldugundan kesf ve muayene edilmesi
A.MTZ.05	Babıali Evrak Odası Eyalet-i Mümtaze ve Muhtare Kalemi-Mısır
BEO	Bab-ı Ali Evrak Odası
DH.EUM.5.Şb	Dahiliye Nezareti Emniyet-i Umumiye Beşinci Şübe
DH.İD	Dahiliye Nezareti İdare Evrakı
DH.MKT	Dahiliye Nezareti Mektubi
DH.SAİD.d	Dahiliye Nezareti Sicill-i Ahval Komisyonu Defterleri
HAT	Hatt-ı Hümayun Tasnifi
HR.HMŞ.İ ŞO	Hariciye Nezareti Hukuk Müşavirliği İstişare Odası Evrakı
HR.SFR.3	Hariciye Nezareti Sefaretler Evrakı (Londra)
HRT.h	Haritalar

İ.DH	İrade, Dahiliye
İ.HR	İrade, Hariciye
MV	Meclis-i Vükela Mazbataları
ŞD	Şura-yı Devlet
Y.A.HUS	Yıldız Sadaret Hususi Maruzat Evrakı
Y.A.RES	Yıldız Sadaret Resmi Maruzat Evrakı
Y.EE	Yıldız Esas Evrakı
Y.MTV	Yıldız Mütenevvi Maruzat Evrakı
Y.PRK.BŞK	Yıldız Perakende Evrakı, Mabeyn Başkitabeti
Y.PRK.EŞA	Yıldız Perakende Evrakı, Elçilik ve Şehbenderlikler Tahriratı
Y.PRK.HR	Yıldız Perakende Evrakı, Hariciye Nezareti Maruzatı
Y.PRK.TKM	Yıldız Tasnifi Perakende Evrakı, Tahrirat-ı Ecnebiye ve Mabeyn Mütercimliği

UNITED KINGDOM

Bodleian Library, Oxford

- Milner Papers; Maurice de Bunsen Papers; Asquith Papers; Bryce Papers

British Library, London (BL)

- India Office Records

Middle East Center, St. Antony's Oxford (MEC)

- Milne Cheetham Papers

National Archives, London (NA)

- Cabinet (CAB)
- Foreign Office (FO)
- War Office (WO)
- Granville Papers; Cromer Papers; Grey Papers; Kitchener Papers

Parliamentary Archives, London (PA)

- Lloyd George Papers

Public Record Office of Northern Ireland, Belfast (PRONI)

- Lord Dufferin Papers

Sudan Archives, University of Durham (SAD)

- Abbas Hilmi II Papers (HIL); Sir Reginald Wingate Papers

UNITED STATES

Library of Congress (LC)

- Tasker Howard Bliss Papers; James G. Harbord Papers; Woodrow Wilson Papers
- U.S. American Commission to Negotiate Peace Records, 1898–1919 (The Inquiry)

Stanford University, Hoover Institution Archives

- Hidayet Dağdeviren Collection

Yale University

- Colonel House Papers; Inquiry Papers

Introduction

1. The literature on the mandate system was particularly dense during the 1920s and 1930s and has recently become the subject of several new studies. For older literature, see George Louis Beer, *African Questions at the Paris Peace Conference* (New York: Macmillan, 1923); and Quincy Wright, *Mandates Under the League of* Nations (Chicago: University of Chicago Press, 1930), chap. 2. For more recent literature, see Susan Pedersen, *The Guardians: The League of Nations and the Crisis of Empire* (New York: Oxford University Press, 2015); and Antony Anghie, *Imperialism, Sovereignty and the Making of International Law* (Cambridge: Cambridge University Press, 2004). Mark Mazower has emphasized the genealogy of the mandate system in British imperial thought in his *No Enchanted Palace: The End of Empire and the Ideological Origins of the United Nations* (Princeton: Princeton University Press, 2013), chap. 1.
2. Military censorship was lifted on June 11, 1918. While the unofficial occupation of Istanbul, starting November 13, 1918, placed limitations on the press, they were not as stringent as those during the formal occupation of Istanbul beginning on March 16, 1920. See Orhan Koloğlu, *Osmanlı'da son Tartışmalar: Mondros'tan Mudanya'ya* (Istanbul: Doğan Kitap, 2008); Erol Baykal, *The Ottoman Press, 1908–1923* (Leiden: Brill, 2019); Ahmet Emin, *Turkey in My Time: Turkey in the First World War* (New Haven: Yale University Press, 1930); and Nur Bilge Criss, *İstanbul Under Allied Occupation 1918–1923* (Leiden: Brill, 1999).
3. [No author], "Manda, Himaye, İstiklal" [Mandate, protectorate, independence], *Büyük Mecmua*, 19 Haziran 1335 (June 19, 1919), 148; and Ahmed Selahaddin, "Himaye ve Vekâlet Cereyanları" [The Movements for protection and trusteeship], *Vakit*, 31 Mayıs 1335 (May 31, 1919). Debates on the meaning of the mandates in Istanbul reached a fever pitch in June 1919, when the

Ottoman delegation presented to the peace conference its memorandum outlining the state's desiderata, which included a plan to reorganize the empire as a series of autonomous provinces on the "model of Egypt before the war." See chapter 5 for a discussion of mandates in the early Armistice press. Even before the mandates were decided at Paris in January 1919, Ottomans debated accepting various forms of intervention in exchange for financial and agricultural expertise. See Ahmed Emin (Yalman), "Bir İzah" [An Explanation], *Vakit*, 7 kanun-i evvel 1335 (December 7, 1918).

4. Ahmet Selahaddin Bey "Mandaların Mahiyet-i Hukukiyesi" [The Mandate's legal reality], *Vakit*, 2 Haziran (June 2, 1919).

5. League of Nations Archives, hereafter LNA/R13, 1/1970/1970, Milner to Cecil, 2 Nov. 1919, quoted in Pedersen, *The Guardians*, 34.

6. Central Asian Islamic Society, "Muslim Protest" (London: Central Asian Islamic Society, [1919]), 5. Tasker Howard Bliss Papers, Manuscript Division, Library of Congress, MSS13037/Box 354, "Arab State, December 1918–October 1919." The pamphlet was translated from English into Ottoman Turkish and expanded as *Müslüman Protestosu* (London: Cemiyet-i Merkeziye-yi İslamiyesi, [1919]). See also Cemil Aydın, *The Idea of the Muslim World: A Global Intellectual History* (Cambridge, Mass.: Harvard University Press, 2017), 123.

7. Arabs had been citizens with political rights, which Britain and France annulled through the brutal extension of imperial rule into Ottoman lands. The postwar settlement organized the current state system in the region on a supposed national basis, without a corresponding right to political self-determination. See Elizabeth Thompson, *How the West Stole Democracy from the Arabs: The Syrian Arab Congress of 1920 and the Destruction of Its Historic Liberal-Islamic Alliance* (New York: Atlantic Monthly Press, 2020).

8. Fedor Fedorovich Martens, *Traité de droit international* (Paris: Chevalier-Marescq, 1883–1887), 331; Aimee M. Genell, "Ottoman Autonomous Provinces and the Problem of 'Semi-Sovereignty' in International Law," *Journal of Balkan and Near Eastern Studies* 18, no. 6 (2016): 533–49; Ekrem Buğra Ekinci, "Osmanlı İdaresinde Adem-i Merkeziyet ve İmtiyazlı Eyâletler," *Türk Hukuk Tarihi Araştırmaları* 6 (2008): 30–33. I offer a detailed explanation of Ottoman terms and expressions for autonomy and privilege below.

9. In 1892 Alfred Milner called Egypt, which had been under British military occupation since 1882, the "veiled protectorate" and argued that Egypt was a political anomaly that had effectively become a British colony without the advantage of Colonial Office oversight. Milner's critique only represented the opinion of annexationists in the Colonial Office but was so powerful that it has set the terms for the historical debate. Historians have largely treated occupied Egypt as a British colony in all but name, paying little to no attention to the

interests and motives of the sovereign in Istanbul or to those of the Foreign Office officials, who successfully resisted Colonial Office demands to annex Egypt. See Alfred Milner, *England in Egypt* (London: E. Arnold, 1894).

10. Until recently there were only a handful of significant articles in English and Turkish devoted to the Ottoman response to the British occupation of Egypt: Süleyman Kızıltoprak, *Mısır'da Ingiliz Işğali: Osmanlı'nın Diplomasi Savaşi (1882–1887)* [The British occupation of Egypt: The Ottoman war of diplomacy] (Istanbul: Tarih Vakfi Yayinlari, 2010); Ayhan Ceylan, *Osmanlı Taşra İdarî Tarzı Olarak Eyâlet-i Mümtâze ve Mısır Uygulaması* (Istanbul: Kitabevi, 2014); Selim Deringil, "The Ottoman Response to the Egyptian Crisis of 1881–82," *Middle Eastern Studies* 24, no. 1 (January 1988), and "Gazi Ahmed Mukhtar Pasha and the British Occupation of Egypt," *Al-Abhath*, vol. 34 (1986); Oded Peri, "Ottoman Symbolism in British-Occupied Egypt, 1882–1909," *Middle Eastern Studies* 41, no. 1 (January 2005): 103–20; Ekmeleddin İhsanoğlu, *Mısır'da Türkler ve Kültürel Mirasları* (Istanbul: Islam Tarih ve Kültür Araştırma Merkezi, 2006); Doğa Özturk, "Remembering" Egypt's Ottoman Past: Ottoman Consciousness in Egypt, 1841–1914" (PhD dissertation, Ohio State University, 2020).

11. See chapter 1. In the early modern period, autonomy indicated methods of imperial incorporation, as well as the flexibility of Ottoman rule with respect to its periphery. Administrative structures of conquered lands often remained in place but were often Ottomanized over time, as in the case of Mamluk Egypt. In Ottoman North Africa, the Gulf, and frontier provinces along the Iranian border, provincial governors and lords exercised a high degree of local autonomy, from Ragusa in today's Croatia to the Crimean Khanate. See Gábor Kármán and Lovro Kunčević, eds., *The European Tributary States of the Ottoman Empire in the Sixteenth and Seventeenth Century* (Leiden: Brill, 2013), chap. 1; and İlber Ortaylı, *Türkiye Teşkilat ve İdare Tarihi* (Ankara: Cedit Neşriyat, 2012).

12. Autonomy experiments abounded during the era of Napoleonic Wars, and some of the ideas tested across Europe were revived during the Greek crisis (1821–1832). Christine Philliou, "The Ottoman Empire's Absent Nineteenth Century: Autonomous Subjects," in *Untold Histories of the Middle East: Recovering Voices from the 19th and 20th Centuries*, ed. Amy Singer et al. (London: SOAS/Routledge, 2010); Konstantina Zanou, *Transnational Patriotism in the Mediterranean, 1800–1850: Stammering the Nation* (Oxford: Oxford University Press, 2019); and Aliki D. Nikiforu, ed., *Constitutional Charters of the Ionian Islands* (Athens: Hellenic Parliament Foundation, 2012).

13. See chapter 1.

14. National Archives, UK (hereafter NA)/FO/78/3454, Turkey (Egypt), Lord Dufferin's Special Mission, Dufferin to Granville, November 11, 1882.

15. Ussama Makdisi, *The Culture of Sectarianism: Community, History, and Violence in Nineteenth-Century Ottoman Lebanon* (Berkley: University of California Press, 2000).

16. The Armenian Reform Agreement of February 1914 created two large autonomous provinces "on the model of Mount Lebanon," with each to be overseen by a European inspector. World War I prevented the implementation of that program. See Peter Holquist, "The Politics and Practice of the Russian Occupation of Armenia, 1915–February 1917," in *A Question of Genocide*, ed. Ronald Grigor Suny, Fatma Müge Göçek, and Norman M. Naimark (Oxford: Oxford University Press, 2011); and Ronald Grigor Suny, *"They Can Live in the Desert but Nowhere Else:" A History of the Armenian Genocide* (Princeton: Princeton University Press, 2015).

17. See chapter 4.

18. Avi Rubin, *Ottoman Nizamiye Courts: Law and Modernity* (New York: Palgrave Macmillan, 2011); and Rubin, "Modernity as Code: The Ottoman Empire and the Global Movement of Codification," *Journal of Economic and Social History of the Orient* 59 (2016): 828–56.

19. The Ottomans and Europeans implemented organic regulations in the Danubian Principalities, Serbia, Mount Lebanon, and Crete. Other autonomous provinces, such as Egypt, received *fermans* of investiture, or edicts that created the administrative framework for the province. A ferman covered a wide range of imperial documents that bore the sultan's seal. There was a hierarchy among sultan-issued documents. For example, a *hatt-ı hümayun* was issued in the sultan's own hand. Mübahat S. Kütükoğlu, *Osmanlı Belgelerinin Dili (Diplomatik)* (Istanbul: Türk Tarih Kurumu Yayınları, 1998), 99–103, 172–88.

20. "Birinci madde: Devlet-i Osmaniye memalik ve kıtaat-ı hazırayı ve eyalet-i mümtaze-yi muhtevi ve yek vücud olmakla hiçbir zamanda hiçbir sebebile tefrik kabul etmez." *Kanun-i Esasi* (Istanbul: Matbaa-i Amire, 1292/1876). The expression *eyalet-i mümtaze* was translated as "autonomous province" (τὰς προνομιούχους Ἐπαρχίας) in the official Greek version of the First Ottoman Constitution of 1876, and as *al-ilayat al-mumtaza* in the Arabic edition. Stanford University, Hoover Institution Archives, Hidayet Dağdeviren Collection, Box 22/9, *Tarjamat al-khatt al-sharif al-sultani wal-qanun al-asasi* (Istanbul: Al-Jawa'ib Press, 1293/1876); θωμανικόν Σύνταγμα Ανακηρυχθέν τη 7 Ζιλχιτζέ 1293 (11/23 Δεκέμβριος 1876)]. Johann Strauss has examined the 1876 Constitution across the empire's languages and shown meaningful differences between languages. Strauss, "A Constitution for a Multilingual Empire: Translations of the *Kanun-i Esasi* and Other Official Texts into Minority Languages," in *The First Ottoman Experiment in Democracy*, ed. Christoph Herzog and Malek Sharif (Würzburg: Ergon in Kommission, 2010).

21. E. Eşrefoğlu, "Mümtaze Kalemi ve Bulgaristan Belgeleri," *Güneydoğu Avrupa Araştırmaları Dergisi* (1978); Carter Findley, *Bureaucratic Reform in the Ottoman Empire: The Sublime Porte, 1789–1922* (Princeton: Princeton University Press, 1980), 244, 305, 393.

22. Genell, "Autonomous Provinces," 540.

23. The Capitulations were a series of bilateral treaties between the Ottoman Empire and European powers that extended special privileges and immunities to foreigners residing and trading within Ottoman domains. The institution began in the sixteenth century. They were originally reciprocal agreements and were not initially "regarded as a derogation of sovereignty," yet by the nineteenth century the term took on a more pejorative meaning and suggested the attenuation of state sovereignty by effectively extending extraterritorial rights to foreigners within the Ottoman Empire. Will Hanley, *Identifying with Nationality: Europeans, Ottomans, and Egyptians in Alexandria* (New York: Columbia University Press. 2017), 11–13; M. van den Boogert, *The Capitulations and the Ottoman Legal System: Qadis, Consuls and Beraths in the 18th Century* (Leiden: Brill, 2005), 1–15; and Feroz Ahmad, "Ottoman Perceptions of the Capitulations 1800–1914," *Journal of Islamic Studies* 11, no. 1 (2000): 2–4.

24. For Jerusalem, see Butrus Abu Maneh, "The Rise of the Sanjak of Jerusalem in the Late 19th Century," in *The Palestinians and the Middle East Conflict*, ed. Gabriel Ben-Dor (Ramat Gan: Turtledove Press, 1978); and Alexander Schölch, *Palestine in Transformation, 1856–1882: Studies in Social, Economic and Political Development* (Washington, D.C.: Institute for Palestine Studies, 1993). For Mecca, see Michael Christopher Low, *Imperial Mecca: Ottoman Arabia and the Indian Ocean Hajj* (New York: Columbia University Press, 2020). For the creation of the *Mutasarrifate* in Benghazi, see Michel F. le Gall, "Pashas, Bedouins and Notables: Ottoman Administration in Tripoli and Benghazi 1881–1902," PhD diss., Princeton University, 1986; and Matthew H. Ellis *Desert Borderland: The Making of Modern Egypt and Libya* (Stanford: Stanford University Press, 2018). For Yemen, see John Willis, *Unmaking North and South: Cartographies of the Yemeni Past* (New York: Columbia University Press, 2013); and Caesar E. Farah, *The Sultan's Yemen: 19th-Century Challenges to Ottoman Rule* (London: Tauris, 2002).

25. Thomas Kuehn has shown that Ottoman policymakers in Istanbul and Yemen debated the options for bringing Imam Yahya and the Zaidis under imperial control and looked explicitly at the Anglo-Egyptian Condominium in Sudan, the Indian princely states, and Aden Protectorate as viable models. The final agreement was an amalgamated version of these ideas with existing models of Ottoman autonomy. Imam Yahya was recognized as "dependent ruler" and given autonomy over some districts in Yemen based on sect. Instead of remitting tribute to Istanbul, like Egypt, he was paid a stipend by the government.

Autonomy was designed to neutralize Yemen from outside interference, but, like Kuwait, the model was distinct from nineteenth-century autonomous provinces. See Thomas Kuehn, *Empire, Islam, and Politics of Difference Ottoman Rule in Yemen, 1849–1919* (Leiden: Brill, 2011).

26. The Egyptian tribute serviced the Ottoman debt. Abbas Hilmi II's ferman of investiture stipulated the tribute amount. See Gabriel Noradounghian [Noradunkyan], *Recueil d'actes internationaux de l'Empire ottoman* (Paris: F. Pichon, 1897–1903), 4, no. 967; "Firman Impérial d'investiture de Abbas Hilmi Pacha comme Khédive d'Egypte et Iradé Impérial relatif à la Péninsule du Sinaï," Government of Egypt, *Recueil de firmans impériaux ottomans addresses aux valis et aux khedives d'Égypte* (Cairo: L'institut Français d'archéologie orientale du Caire, 1934), pp. 340–42, no. 1060, 27 Shaban 1309 [March 27, 1892]. After the loss of the Red Sea ports Zeyla and Massawa, the tribute was reduced to around £T665,000 annually and remained at this rate for the duration of the occupation. NA/ FO 141/822/ Egypt and Soudan, "Minuet by Cecil Hurst on Egyptian Tribute Loans"; Suraiya Faroqhi, *An Economic and Social History of the Ottoman Empire*, vol. 2: *1600–1914* (Cambridge: Cambridge University Press, 2006); Diana Markides, *The Cyprus Tribute and the Geopolitics of the Levant, 1875–1960* (Cham, Switzerland: Palgrave Macmillan, 2019).

27. Murat Birdal, *The Political Economy of Ottoman Public: Insolvency and European Financial Control in the Late Nineteenth Century* (London: Tauris, 2010); Faroqhi, *Economic and Social History*, vol. 2; Markides, *Cyprus Tribute*; Hüseyin Al, "Debt and the Public Debt Administration," in *Encyclopedia of the Ottoman Empire*, ed. Gábor Ágoston and Bruce Masters (New York: Facts on File, 2009).

28. Vladislav Lilić has recently examined how Serbia's autonomous status during the period of autonomy (1830–1878) played out on the ground and in terms of international politics. Lilić, "Empire of States: Law and International Order in Ottoman Europe, c. 1830-1912" (PhD diss., Graduate School of Vanderbilt University, 2024).

29. The ways in which locals sought to protect their political and economic privileges within the exceptional provinces are perhaps best developed in the historiography on Mount Lebanon. See Engin Akarlı, *The Long Peace: Ottoman Lebanon, 1861–1920* (Berkeley: University of California Press, 1993); Jens Hanssen, *Fin-de-siècle Beirut: The Making of an Ottoman Provincial Capital* (Oxford: Oxford University Press, 2005); and Kristen Alff, "Levantine Joint-Stock Companies, Trans-Mediterranean Partnerships, and Nineteenth-Century Capitalist Development," *Comparative Studies in Society and History* 60, no. 1 (2018): 150–77. On the Eastern Mediterranean islands, see Elektra Kostopoulou, "The 'Muslim Millet' of Autonomous Crete" (PhD diss., Boğaziçi University, Istanbul, 2009), and "The Island That Wasn't: Autonomous Crete (1898–1912) and Experiments of Federalization," *Journal of Balkan*

and Near Eastern Studies 18, no. 6 (2016): 550–66; For Cyprus, see Marc Aymes, *A Provincial History of the Ottoman Empire: Cyprus and the Eastern Mediterranean in the Nineteenth Century* (London: Routledge, 2013).

30. Emily Greble, *Muslims and the Making of Modern Europe* (Oxford: Oxford University Press, 2021), chap. 3; Leyla Amzi-Erdoğdular, "Alternative Muslim Modernities: Bosnian Intellectuals in the Ottoman and Habsburg Empires," *Comparative Studies in Society and History*, 59, no. 4 (2017): 912–43, and *The Afterlife of Ottoman Europe Muslims in Habsburg Bosnia Herzegovina* (Stanford: Stanford University Press, 2023), 137–47.

31. Cairo was one of the main overland caravan routes for the annual pilgrimage to Mecca, the Hajj, and remained so during the steamship era. Venetia Porter, ed., *Hajj: Journey to the Heart of Islam* (Cambridge, Mass.: Harvard University Press, 2012).

32. The classic texts on the subject are John Gallagher and Ronald Robinson, *Africa and the Victorians: The Official Mind of Imperialism* (London: Palgrave Macmillan, 1978); David Landes, *Bankers and Pashas: International Finance and Economic Imperialism in Egypt* (Cambridge, Mass.: Harvard University Press, 1980); M. S. Anderson, *The Eastern Question 1774–1923: A Study in International Relations* (London: St. Martin's Press, 1966); and J.A.R. Marriott, *The Eastern Question* (Oxford: Oxford University Press, 1940).

33. The texts that shaped the field are Alexander Schlöch, *Egypt for the Egyptians!: The Socio-Political Crisis in Egypt, 1878–1882* (Oxford: Oxford University Press, 1981); Afaf Lutfi al-Sayyid Marsot, *Egypt and Cromer: A Study in Anglo-Egyptian Relations* (London: John Murry, 1968); Robert Tignor, *Modernization and British Colonial Rule in Egypt, 1882–1914* (Princeton: Princeton University Press, 1966); Juan Cole, *Colonialism and Revolution in the Middle East: Social and Cultural Origins of Egypt's 'Urabi Movement* (Princeton: Princeton University Press, 1992); and Timothy Mitchell, *Colonizing Egypt* (Berkeley: University of California Press, 1988).

34. Despite the dense material and intellectual connections between Istanbul and Cairo, which were obvious to contemporaries, Egypt strangely does not figure prominently in late Ottoman historiography. Until very recently, even the era of Mehmed Ali Paşa was examined outside of the Ottoman imperial framework. For Ottomanists, Egypt after 1882 is one of the lost lands, and another glaring example of the unequal treatment of the Ottoman Empire at European hands. After the beginning of the British occupation, the province is generally cast as an Ottoman province only in name. Khaled Fahmy of course is the great exception. Historical accounts of late Ottoman and British-occupied Egypt have been dominated by nationalist concerns and have projected the nation-state backward in time. Ottoman-Egyptian historians, especially Khaled Fahmy, Jane Hathaway, and Ehud Tolendo, have sought to

redress these arguments by putting Egypt back in the Ottoman imperial context, but such analyses more often than not end with the British occupation in 1882. Similarly, Alan Mikhail's environmental history of early modern Egypt makes a compelling case that Egypt was the most prosperous Ottoman province and central to functioning of the Ottoman Empire. Yet, he too argues that Mehmed Ali's reforms made the state and effectively torpedoed Egypt out of an Ottoman orbit into statehood. See Alan Mikhail, *Nature and Empire in Ottoman Egypt: An Environmental History* (Cambridge: Cambridge University Press, 2011); Khaled Fahmy, *All the Pasha's Men: Mehmed Ali, His Army and the Making of Modern Egypt* (Cairo: AUC Press, 2002); Jane Hathaway, *The Politics of Households in Ottoman Egypt: The Rise of Qazdağlıs* (Cambridge: Cambridge University Press, 1997); and Ehud Toledano, *State and Society in Mid-Nineteenth Century Egypt* (Cambridge: Cambridge University Press, 1990).

35. The British-Ottoman contest in the Gulf originated with the Ottoman reconquest of parts of Arabian Peninsula in the early 1870s. As James Onley and others have argued, Britain formalized its treaty relationship with Aden and the Trucial States as a direct result of Ottoman efforts to bring the peninsula under Ottoman dominion. The government of India, which ran the system of protected states in the Gulf through Indian, Persian, and Arab agents, scrambled to sign exclusive agreements with Bahrain, the Trucial States, and Aden in the late 1880s and 1890s in order to prevent Ottoman expansion and consolidation in the Gulf. See James Onley, *The Arabian Frontier of the British Raj: Merchants, Rulers, and the British in the Nineteenth-Century Gulf* (Oxford: Oxford University Press, 2008); Susan Pedersen, "Getting Out of Iraq—in 1932: The League of Nations and the Road to Normative Statehood," *American Historical Review* 115, no. 4 (2010): 975–1000; and Robert Tignor, "The 'Indianization' of the Egyptian Administration Under British Rule," *American Historical Review* 68, no. 3 (April 1963): 636–61.

36. "Osmanlı idaresi altında muhtariyet," *Girit Meselesi: Nasıl Hal Edilmeli?* (Dersaadet: Tanin Matbaası, 1326/1910]).

37. "Vilâyet Nizamnâmesi," *Düstur: I. Tertib*, 1:608. Nora Barakat pushes readers to reconsider changes in imperial governance during this precise period, especially the provincial reform and related imperial legislation. She shows that Ottoman *Bedouin* used new legal and administrative devices and were invested in the state. Barakat, *Bedouin Bureaucrats: Mobility and Property in the Ottoman Empire* (Stanford: Stanford University Press, 2023), chap. 2.

38. "Balada arz olunduğu üzere İkodra Sancağı ez-kadim bir idare-i mümtaze tahtında olup muahharan bir dereceye kadar ele alınmış ise de tanzimat ve tensikatan müstesna kalmıştır." Ahmed Cevdet's Report on İskodra, *Osmanlı Arşiv Belgelerinde Arnavutluk* (Istanbul: TC Başbakalık Devlet Arşivleri Genel Müdürlüğü, 2008), 225.

39. Low, *Imperial Mecca*, chap. 1; Ekrem Buğra Ekinci, "Osmanlı İdaresinde Adem-i Merkeziyet ve İmtiyazlı Eyâletler," *Türk Hukuk Tarihi Araştırmaları* 6 (2008): 7–84; Nobuyoshi Fujinami, "Between Sovereignty and Suzerainty: History of the Ottoman Privileged Provinces," in *A World History of Suzerainty: A Modern History of East and West Asia and Translated Concepts*, ed. Takashi Okamoto (Tokyo: Toyo Bunko, 2019).

40. Sultan İkinci Abdülhamid Han, *Devlet ve Memleket Görüşlerim*, ed. A. Atilla Çetin (Istanbul: Çamlıca, 2011), 2:40–47.

41. Başbakanlık Osmanlı Arşivi (hereafter BOA), Y.PRK.TŞF 1/46 30, Ramazan 30, 1298 (August 26, 1881).

42. "Hatti Chérif, concernant l'autonomie serbe." Noradounghian, *Recueil d'actes* 2, no. 63:197–200.

43. Dependency and independent regency could be added to the list, among others. Henry Wheaton, *History of the Law of Nations in Europe and America* (New York: Gould, Banks, 1845), 555; Charles Stubbs, *The Rights and Duties of Suzerain and Vassal States* (London: Pewtress, 1882); Sir Robert Phillimore, *Commentaries Upon International Law* (Philadelphia: T. & J. W. Johnson, 1854–1857), 113–14.

44. John Westlake, *International Law* (Cambridge: Cambridge University Press, 1904–1907), 1:26–27, uses suzerain, vassal, tributary, and semi-sovereignty to describe the privileged provinces; Frederick Edwin Smith, *International Law* (Toronto: G. N. Morang, 1901), 31.

45. Ahmed Vahid, *Bahriye zabitanına mahsus hukuk-i umumiye-i düvel* (Istanbul Matbaa-i Bahriye, 1912), 23. This shift can be seen comparing the Ottoman and English translations of the same text. In Ottoman, the expression "Fransa'nın fi'li himaye murakabesi altında olarak" is rendered as "which is to be under the actual suzerainty of France." Cemal Paşa, *Hatırat: 1913–1919* (Dersaadet: [Ahmed İhsan ve Şürekası Matbaası], 1339/1922), 209; Djemal Pasha, *Memoirs of a Turkish Statesman, 1913–1919* (London: Hutchinson, 1922), 231. Lâle Can and Chris Low have transformed how Ottoman historians approach the question and ideas of protection; Lâle Can, *Spiritual Subjects: Central Asian Pilgrims and the Ottoman Hajj at the End of Empire* (Stanford: Stanford University Press, 2020), chap. 2; Low, *Imperial Mecca*, chap. 2.

46. *The Times of London*, no. 29160, January 24, 1878.

47. Westlake, *International Law*, 26–27.

48. Youssef Ben Ismail has traced this precise idea in French-Ottoman debates over the sovereign status of Tunis and shows that European writers cast Ottoman sovereignty in the province as entirely fictional, in "Uncertain Histories: The Archive of Sovereignty in Ottoman Tunis," *Journal of the Ottoman and Turkish Studies Association* 11, no. 1 (2024): 123–53. The idea that the autonomous provinces were nominally Ottoman is prevalent in the historiography

on Serbia, Romania, Bulgaria, Egypt, Tunis, and Crete. For instance, Egypt is rarely discussed as an Ottoman province after the beginning of the British occupation in 1882, and few scholarly works have used Ottoman archival sources for this period. There are recent and important exceptions to this trend, however: Each insists that late Ottoman Egypt cannot be understood without the Ottoman political context. See, especially Hanley, *Identifying with Nationality*; Adam Mestyan, *Arab Patriotism: The Ideology and Culture of Power in Late Ottoman Egypt* (Princeton: Princeton University Press, 2017); Mestyan, *Modern Arab Kingship: Remaking the Ottoman Political Order in the Interwar Middle East* (Princeton: Princeton University Press, 2023); Matthew H. Ellis, *Desert Borderland: The Making of Modern Egypt and Libya* (Stanford: Stanford University Press, 2018); and Khaled Fahmy, *In Quest of Justice: Islamic Law and Forensic Medicine in Modern Egypt* (Berkeley: University of California Press, 2018), 15–21.

49. Lauren Benton, *A Search for Sovereignty: Law and Geography in European Empires, 1400–1900* (Cambridge: Cambridge University Press, 2009).

50. Eric Beverley, *Hyderabad, British India, and the World: Muslim Networks and Minor Sovereignty, c.1850–1950* (Cambridge: Cambridge University Press, 2015).

51. Genell, "Autonomous Provinces."

52. Michael Christopher Low, "Ottoman Infrastructures of the Saudi Hydro-State: The Technopolitics of Pilgrimage and Potable Water in the Hijaz," *Comparative Studies in Society and History* 57, no. 4 (2015): 942–74; Mostafa Minawi, "Telegraphs and Territoriality in Ottoman Africa and Arabia During the Age of High Imperialism," *Journal of Balkan and Near Eastern Studies* 18, no. 6 (2016): 567–87.

53. Turan Kayaoğlu, *Legal Imperialism: Sovereignty and Extraterritoriality in Japan, the Ottoman Empire, and China* (Cambridge: Cambridge University Press, 2010); Cemil Aydın, *The Politics of Anti-Westernism in Asia: Visions of World Order in Pan-Islamic and Pan-Asian Thought on Anti-Westernism in Asia and Middle East* (New York: Columbia University Press, 2007); Adam M. McKeown, *Melancholy Order: Asian Migration and the Globalization of Borders* (New York: Columbia University Press, 2008); Mohammad Shahabuddin, "The 'Standard of Civilization' in International Law: Intellectual Perspectives from Pre-War Japan," *Leiden Journal of International Law* 32, no. 1 (2019): 13–32; John Stern, *The Japanese Interpretation of the "Law of Nations," 1854–1874* (Princeton: Princeton University Press, 1979); Lydia Liu, *Clash of Empires: The Invention of China in Modern World Making* (Cambridge: Harvard University Press, 2004).

54. Umut Özsu, analyzing Ottoman attitudes toward the Capitulations, notes that "there is as yet nothing that would warrant recognition as a comprehensive body of scholarship pertaining to the Ottoman's engagement with what we would now characterize as international law." Özsu, "Ottoman Empire," in *The Oxford Handbook of the History of International Law*, ed. Bardo Fassbender

and Anne Peters (Oxford: Oxford University Press, 2012), 430. While that has changed over the past decade, it remains true that historians have undertheorized the edges of the Eurocentric international order in the nineteenth and early twentieth centuries. Gerrit Gong's text is now outdated; he nevertheless introduced a powerful idea into the history of international law. Understanding the idea that "civilization" was one of the main organizing principles in international relations during the nineteenth century enables historians of the non-Christian, non-European world to explain the transformation of domestic legal institutions to be legible to Europeans. Ntina Tzouvala has reinscribed the significance of civilization to the study of the history of international law. See Gerrit Gong, *The Standard of Civilization in International Society* (Oxford: Clarendon, 1984); Ntina Tzouvala, *Capitalism as Civilisation: A History of International Law* (Cambridge: Cambridge University Press, 2020); Antony Anghie, *Imperialism, Sovereignty, and the Making of International Law* (Cambridge: Cambridge University Press, 2005); Balakrishnan Rajagopal, *International Law from Below: Development, Social Movements and Third World Resistance* (Cambridge: Cambridge University Press, 2003); and Richard S. Horowitz, "International Law and State Transformation in China, Siam, and the Ottoman Empire During the Nineteenth Century," *Journal of World History* 15, no. 4 (2004): 445–86.

55. Arnulf Becker Lorca has argued that international law was shaped by actors at the edges of the international order as much as it was by lawyers in Europe. More recently, historians of international law in Latin America have focused on the practices of international law rather than ideas that animated the field. See especially Andrei Mamolea, "Escaping Washington's Tutelage: Latin America, the League of Nations, and International Law," *Journal of Global History* (January 2026): 1–20, and "Rogue State: The US and International Law, 1880-1945" (forthcoming); Arnulf Becker Lorca, *Mestizo International Law: A Global Intellectual History 1842–1933* (Cambridge: Cambridge University Press, 2015); Juan Pablo Scarfi, *The Hidden History of International Law in the Americas* (New York: Oxford University Press, 2017); Edward Corredera, *Odious Debt: Bankruptcy, International Law, and the Making of Latin America* (Oxford: Oxford University Press, 2024); and Allison Powers, *Arbitrating Empire: United States Expansion and the Transformation of International Law* (Oxford: Oxford University Press, 2024).

1. The Emergence of the Privileged Provinces

1. British National Archives, hereafter NA/FO 406/4/no. 257, enclosure 1, "Mr. Wood to Viscount Ponsby, September 13, 1840," enclosure 2,

"Mr. Consul Moore to Viscount Ponsby, September 16, 1840," enclosure 4, "Captain Walker to Viscount Ponsby, September 19, 1840"; Daniel Panzac, "International and Domestic Maritime Trade in the Ottoman Empire During the 18th Century," *International Journal for Middle Eastern Studies* 24, no. 2 (May 1992): 195–96; Jens Hanssen, *Fin de Siècle Beirut: The Making of an Ottoman Provincial Capital* (Oxford: Oxford University Press, 2005), 28–35; Charles Issawi, "British Trade and the Rise of Beirut, 1830–1860," *International Journal of Middle East Studies* 8, no. 1 (January 1977): 91–101; Leila Tarazi Fawaz, *Merchants and Migrants in Nineteenth-Century Beirut* (Cambridge: Harvard University Press, 1983), 49–51.

2. Mehmed Cemil (Bilsel), "Mısır Meselesi," *İlm-i Hukuk ve Mukayese-i Kavanin Mecmuası* 5 (31 Temmuz 1325/1909): 328.

3. A. B. Cunningham, *The Early Correspondence of Richard Wood, 1831–1841* (Cambridge: Cambridge University Press, 1966); Letitia W. Ufford, *The Pasha: How Mehemet Ali Defied the West, 1839–1841* (Jefferson, NC: McFarland, 2007).

4. *Muahedat Mecmuası* ([Istanbul]: Hakikat Matbaası, 1294–1298 [1877–1881]), 4:209–15; Gabriel Noradounghian, *Recueil d'Actes Internationaux de l'Empire Ottoman* (Paris: F. Pichon, 1897–1903), 2:303–12; Edward Hertslet, *The Map of Europe by Treaty* 2, (London: Butterworths, 1875), 2:1008–15.

5. Belgium broke away from the Netherlands in 1830, which the latter refused to recognize. The Treaty of London (1839)—signed by all the great powers as well as Belgium and the Netherlands—recognized Belgian independence and guaranteed the state's neutrality within the system of Europe. As in Egypt, the great power territorial guarantee was meant to preserve order. As Isabel Hull argues, the "Treaty of London was a cornerstone of European international law. It was part of the international system developed in the wake of the Napoleonic Wars to regularize and contain state relations and conflict through law." Isabel Hull, *A Scrap of Paper: Breaking and Making International Law During the Great War* (Ithaca: Cornell University Press, 2014), 17.

6. Başbakanlık Osmanlı Arşivi (hereafter BOA), A.DVNS.MSR.MHM.d MMM/no. 15, Evahir-i Zilhicce 1256 (February 12, 1841); Government of Egypt, *Recueil de firmans impériaux ottomans addresses aux valis et aux khedives d'Égypte* (Cairo: L'institut Français d'archéologie, 1934).

7. *Takvim-i Vekayi*, nos. 216 and 217 (Jan. 26, 1841; Feb. 16, 1841).

8. "Territorial integrity," the cornerstone of the United Nations Charter, enshrined in Article II, has a striking if underexplored history in the nineteenth century, particularly as this idea appeared in Ottoman-European diplomatic discourse. Limitations on sovereignty abounded in the nineteenth-century system of international relations. Historians continue to use colonial language to describe the Ottoman relationship to Europe—the Capitulations, unfavorable loans, extractive practices—but these are in parallel to the

experiences of other independent states, what historians H. E. Chehabi and David Motadel have recently called "unconquered states," in *Unconquered States: Non-European Powers in the Imperial Age* (Oxford: Oxford University Press, 2025), introduction.

9. This would have far-reaching implications for the development of the Foreign Ministry and domestic legal institutions. Ottoman sovereignty was guaranteed by the Great Powers in international law by treaty as a matter of European security, alongside Mehmed Ali's hereditary governorship, the details of which were fixed within the constitutional order of the state through the ferman.

10. On the specific genre of the *hatt-ı hümayun* see Mübahat S. Kütükoğlu, *Osmanlı Belgelerinin Dili (Diplomatik)* (Istanbul: Türk Tarih Kurumu Yayınları, 1998), 172–88.

11. Davide Rodogno, *Against Massacre: Humanitarian Interventions in the Ottoman Empire, 1815–1914* (Princeton: Princeton University Press, 2012).

12. For the significance of the *kanununname* and Ottoman provincial law codes, see Heather Ferguson, *The Proper Order of Things Language, Power, and Law in Ottoman Administrative Discourses* (Stanford: Stanford University Press, 2018), chap. 2. For the text of the *Kanunname-i Mısır*, see Ömer Lütfi Barkan, *XV ve XVIinci Asırlarda Osmanlı İmparatorluğunda Zirai, Ekonominin Hukuki ve Mali Esasları* (Istanbul: Istanbul Üniversitesi, 1943), 355–87. Kanunî Sultan Sülyeman (Süleyman the Lawgiver, known in the West as "the Magnificent") sent his grand vizier, İbrahim Paşa, to Egypt to restore order. He issued the *Kanunname-i Mısır* in April 1525. On the importance of irrigation in this text, see Alan Mikhail, *Nature and Empire in Ottoman Egypt: An Environmental History* (Cambridge: Cambridge University Press, 2011), 7–12; Halil İnalcık, "Kanunname," in *Encyclopaedia of Islam*, 2nd ed., 4:562–66 (Leiden: Brill, 1975); Halil İnalcık, "Osmanlı Hukukuna Giriş: Örfi-Sultani Hukuk ve Fatih'in Kanunları," *Ankara Üniversitesi Siyasal Bilgiler Fakültesi Dergisi* 8, no. 2 (1958): 102–26.

13. Jane Hathaway, *The Politics of Households in Ottoman Egypt: The Rise of Qazdağlıs* (Cambridge: Cambridge University Press, 1997); Michael Winter, *Egyptian Society Under Ottoman Rule 1517–1798* (London: Routledge, 1992), 12–16.

14. Winter, 31–38, 16–20.

15. Mikhail, *Nature and Empire*, 7–10; Halil İnalcik, *An Economic and Social History of the Ottoman Empire* (Cambridge: Cambridge University Press, 1994), 1:56, 84; Nelly Hanna, *Making Big Money in 1600: The Life and Times of Isma'il Abu Taqiyya* (Syracuse: Syracuse University Press, 1998).

16. Edhem Eldem, *French Trade in Istanbul in the Eighteenth Century* (Leiden: Brill, 1999), 71.

17. BOA, E. SMHD, I, 12287/ 20 August 1753; reproduced in *Osmanlı Belgelerinde Mısır* (Istanbul: Osmanlı Arşivi Daire Başkanlığ ı, 2012), 64–68.

18. Winter, *Egyptian Society*, 36.

19. There is an extensive debate among historians about how important the title was and at what points in the empire's history. See Hakan Karateke, "Legitimizing the Ottoman Sultanate: A Framework for Historical Analysis," in *Legitimizing the Order: The Ottoman Rhetoric of State Power*, ed. Karateke (Leiden: Brill, 2005); Hüseyin Yılmaz, *Caliphate Redefined: The Mystical Turn in Ottoman Political Thought* (Princeton: Princeton University Press, 2019). For the late empire, see Cemil Aydın, *The Idea of the Muslim World: A Global Intellectual History* (Cambridge, Mass.: Harvard University Press, 2019); and Michael Christopher Low, *Imperial Mecca: Ottoman Arabia and the Indian Ocean Hajj* (New York: Columbia University Press, 2020).

20. İsmail Hakkı Uzunçarş ılı, *Mekke-i Mükerreme Emirleri* (Ankara: Türk Tarih Kurumu, 2013), 16–30. For Mamluk and early modern Ottoman practices, see Suraiya Faroqhi, *Pilgrims and Sultans: The Hajj Under the Ottomans* (London: Tauris, 1994), 154–58; William Ochsenwald, *Religion, Society, and the State in Arabia: The Hijaz Under Ottoman Control, 1840–1908* (Columbus: Ohio State University, 1984), 18–19; and Low, *Imperial Mecca*.

21. Halil İnalcik, *The Ottoman Empire: The Classical Age, 1300–1600* (London: Phoenix Press, 1973), 105; Jane Hathaway with Karl K. Babir, *The Arab Lands Under Ottoman Rule, 1516–1800* (Edinburgh: Pearson, Longman Press, 2008), 49–50; Winter, *Egyptian Society*, 16–17; Ekrem Buğra Ekinci, "Osmanlı İdaresinde Adem-i Merkeziyet ve İmtiyazlı Eyâletler," *Türk Hukuk Tarihi Araştırmaları* 6 (2008): 30–33.

22. İnalcik, *An Economic and Social History*, 84; Stanford Shaw, *The Financial and Administrative Development of Ottoman Egypt 1517–1798* (Princeton: Princeton University Press, 1962), 283–312. Among other things, the Egyptian governor was required to send agricultural goods to the palace and ammunition to the imperial armory.

23. Şevket Pamuk, *A Monetary History of the Ottoman* Empire (Cambridge: Cambridge University Press, 2000), 16; Cornell H. Fleisher, *Bureaucrat and Intellectual in the Ottoman Empire: The Historian Mustafa Ali, 1541–1600* (Princeton: Princeton University Press, 1986), 279–83.

24. Halil İnalcık, *The Ottoman Empire in the Classical Age* (London: Phoenix Press, 1973), 104–7.

25. Winter, *Egyptian Society*, 20; Youssef Ben Ismail, "Sovereignty Across Empires: France, the Ottoman Empire, and the Imperial Struggle Over Tunis (ca. 1830–1920)," PhD diss., Harvard University Graduate School of Arts and Sciences, 2021, chap. 2.

26. Colin Imber, *The Ottoman Empire* (London: Palgrave, 2009), 167; Gábor Agoston, "A Flexible Empire: Authority and Its Limits on the Ottoman Frontiers," in *Ottoman Borderlands: Issues, Personalities and Political Changes*, ed. K. Karpat (Madison: University of Wisconsin Press, 2003), 16–17; İnalcik, *An Economic and Social History*, 84–88; Ekinci, "Osmanlı İdaresinde," 30; Youssef Ben Ismail, "Sovereignty Across Empires"; Atilla Çetin, "Garp Ocakları," *Türk Diyanet Vakfı Islam Ansiklopedisi*.

27. Mehmet İnbaşi, "XVIII. Yüzyılda Bitlis sancağ ı ve İdareciler," *Ankara Üniversitesi Türkiyat Araştırmaları Enstitüsü Dergisi* 33 (2007): 243–26; Agoston, "A Flexible Empire," 18–23.

28. The handbook was republished in 1864 in Istanbul at the precise time of reorganization of Lebanon and the provincial reform. Ayn Ali briefly served as the *defterdar*, or treasurer, of Egypt. Mehmet İpşirli, "Ayn Ali Efendi," TDV *İslâm Ansiklopedisi* (Istanbul: TDV İslâm Araştırmaları Merkezi, 1991); Douglas A. Howard, "A Phenomenology of Empire: Ayn Ali on the Ottoman Provinces," in *Ottoman War and Peace*, Frank Castiglione, Ethan Menchinger, and Veysel Şimşek, eds., (Leiden: Brill, 2019), 175; Douglas A. Howard, "From Manual to Literature: Two Texts on the Ottoman Timar System," *Acta Orientalia Academiae Scientiarum Hungaricae* 61, no. 1/2 (March 2008): 87–99; D. A. Howard, "The Historical Development of the Ottoman Imperial Registry (Defter-i Hakanî): Mid-Fifteenth to Mid-Seventeenth Centuries," *Ar.Ott.* 11 (1988), s. 227.1607; and Ayn Ali, *Kavanin-i Al-i Osman der hülası-yı mezamin-i defter-i divan* [The laws of the Ottoman Dynasty, comprising a summary of the contents of the Council registers] ([Istanbul]: Tasvir-i Efkar Gazetehanesi, 1280 [1864]). Several historical dictionaries note that the early modern state categorized provinces that were excepted from the general rules of taxation and control as "exceptional provinces" (*müstesna eyaletler*), but I have struggled to find this expression in use in archival documents, manuscripts, and later printed sources. Nevertheless, it is clear that early modern commentators divided the empire into two broad categories, which would influence how modernizing reformers in the nineteenth century wrote about the administration—an expression that would be reconfigured in EI2, VII "Eyalet," 756; Mehmet Zeki Pakalin, "Müstesna Eyaletler," *Osmanlı Tarih Deyimleri Ve Terimleri Sözlüğ ü*, 2:632–33; Ekinci, "Osmanlı İdaresinde," 33; and Cevdet Türkay, "Osmanlı İmparatorluğu'nda 'Vergi,'" *Türk Tarihi Dergisi* 39 (Nisan 2000): 64.

29. Ayn Ali, *Kavanin-i Al-i Osman*.

30. Colin Imber, *Ebu's-suud: The Islamic Legal Tradition* (Edinburgh: Edinburgh University Press, 1997), chap. 3.

31. Baki Tezcan, "The Development of the Use of 'Kurdistan' as a Geographical Description and the Incorporation of this Region Into the Ottoman Empire

in the 16th Century," in *The Great Ottoman-Turkish Civilisation*, ed. Kemal Çicek et al. (Ankara: Yeni Yürkiye, 2000), 3:540–53. On the transformation of "vassals," see Tezcan, *The Second Empire: Political and Social Transformation in the Early Modern World* (Cambridge: Cambridge University Press, 2010), especially chap. 3. Nilay Özok-Gündoğan has powerfully recast provincial autonomy in the eastern provinces of the empire as a form of Kurdish hereditary nobility that persisted well into the nineteenth century. Özok-Gündoğan, *The Kurdish Nobility in the Ottoman Empire: Loyalty, Autonomy and Privilege* (Edinburgh: Edinburgh University Press, 2022).

32. Gábor Kármán and Lovro Kunčević, *The European Tributary States of the Ottoman Empire in the Sixteenth and Seventeenth Century* (Leiden: Brill, 2013), looks at Moldavia and Wallachia, the Crimean Khanate, Transylvania, Ragusa, and Cossack Ukraine. See especially Viorel Panaite's contribution, "The Legal Status of Wallachia and Moldavia in Relation to the Ottoman Porte." For North African provinces Algeria, Tripoli, and Tunis see Joshua M. White, *Piracy and Law in the Ottoman Mediterranean* (Stanford: Stanford University Press, 2018); Giancarlo Casale, *The Ottoman Age of Exploration* (Oxford: Oxford University Press, 2010); and Ayhan Ceylan, *Osmanlı Taşra İdarî Tarzı Olarak Eyâlet-i Mümtâze ve Mısır Uygulaması* (Istanbul: Kitabevi, 2014).

33. Panaite, "The Legal Status," 43. See also Panaite, *Ottoman Law of War and Peace: The Ottoman Empire and Its Tribute-Payers from the North of the Danube* (Leiden: Brill, 2019).

34. Natalia Królikowska, "Sovereignty and Subordination in Crimean-Ottoman Relations (Sixteenth–Eighteenth Centuries)," in *The European Tributary States*, 43–65; Alan Fisher, *Between Russians, Ottomans and Turks: Crimea and Crimean Tatars* (Istanbul: Analecta Isisiana, 1998); Halil İnalcik, "Yeni vesikalar göre Kırım Hanlığ ının Osmanlı tabiliğine girmesi ve Ahidnamesi meselesi," *Belleten* 8 (1944): 185–229; Brian Davies, *Warfare, State and Society on the Black Sea Steppe, 1500–1700* (New York: Routledge, 2007).

35. Panaite, "The Legal Status," 21; Uzunçarlı, *Osmanlı Tarihi*, vol. 4, part 2, 41–77; Ariel Salzmann, *Tocqueville in the Ottoman Empire: Rival Paths to the Modern State* (Leiden: Brill, 2003), 46.

36. Ekinci "Osmanlı İdaresinde," 12; Panaite, "The Legal Status," 21; Catalina Hunt, "The Romanian Lands in the Sixteenth Century: Their Juridical Status According to Ottoman Law," in *Enjeux politiques, économiques et militaires en mer Noire* (Brăila: Musée de Braïla-Editions Istros, 2007).

37. Christine Philliou, "Communities on the Verge: Unraveling the Phanariot Ascendancy in Ottoman Governance," *Comparative Studies in Society and History* 51, no. 1 (January 2009): 151–81; and Philliou, *Biography of an Empire: Governing Ottomans in the Age of Revolution* (Berkeley: University of California Press, 2011).

38. Sándor Papp, "The System of Autonomous Muslim and Christian Communities, Churches, and States in the Ottoman Empire," in *The European Tributary States*, 387–88; Cevdet Paşa, *Tarih-i Cevdet* (Istanbul, 1309), 8:24–28. In Ottoman Turkish, Wallachia and Moldavia are rendered as *Eflak ve Boğdan voyvodalıklar*—the governorships of Wallachia (*Eflak*) and Moldavia (*Boğdan*)—or *Memleketeyn*, the two principalities (literally the two countries). In European languages, Wallachia and Moldavia are often referred to as the Danubian Principalities (*Donaufürstentümer*), which may be an approximation of *Memleketeyn*.

39. Agoston argues in "A Flexible Empire," 16–17, that the dominance of the imperial centralization during the so-called classical age has been massively overdrawn, and that the empire was far more pragmatic and flexible in the borderlands than in the timar system applied throughout Anatolia, the Balkans, and the northern fringes of the Arab provinces. See also Lâle Can and Aimee M. Genell, "On Empire and Exception: Genealogies of Sovereignty in the Ottoman World," *Comparative Studies of South Asia, Africa and the Middle East* 40, no. 3, (2020): 468–73.

40. Ekinci, "Osmanlı İdaresinde," 5. As Panaite has put it in *Ottoman Law of War and Peace*, 338–39, all these provinces were part of what he terms the "Pax Ottomanica system." The Ottoman domain, like many of its diverse neighbors, was a composite empire, and relations between the state and its provinces were not static but changed over time. See W. G. Runciman, "Empire as a Topic in Comparative Sociology," and Karen Barkey and Rudi Batzell, "Comparisons Across Empires: The Critical Social Structures of the Ottomans, Russians and Habsburgs During the Seventeenth Century," both in *Tributary Empires in Global History*, ed. Peter Fibiger Bang and C. A. Bayly (Basingstoke: Palgrave Macmillan, 2011); Dariusz Kołodziejczyk, "What Is Inside and What Is Outside? Tributary States in Ottoman Politics," in *The European Tributary States of the Ottoman Empire in the Sixteenth and Seventeenth Century* (Leiden: Brill, 2013).

41. Hathaway, *Arab Lands Under Ottoman Rule*, 82; Salzmann, *Tocqueville*.

42. Choon Hwee Koh, *The Sublime Post: How the Ottoman Imperial Post Became a Public Service* (New Haven: Yale University Press, 2024), 3.

43. For instance, when the government appointed Phanariot Greeks to the *voyvoda*, or prince, to the governorship of Wallachia and Moldavia in the early eighteenth century, in place of local elites.

44. "The Ottoman empire in Europe, Asia, and Africa, consists of a vast variety of populations, the wrecks and fragments of the ancient world. These heterogeneous materials have never been completely blended into one nation." Henry Wheaton, *History of the Law of Nations in Europe and America* (New York: Gould, Banks, 1845), 555.

45. Cemal Kafadar, "The Question of Ottoman Decline," *Harvard Middle Eastern and Islamic Review* 4, no. 1–2 (1997–1998): 30–75; Cornell Fleischer, *Bureaucrat and Intellectual in the Ottoman Empire: The Historian Mustafa Ali (1541–1600* (Princeton: Princeton University Press, 1986); Hathaway, *Arab Lands Under Ottoman Rule*, chaps. 5 and 6.

46. Thomas Thornton, *The Present State of Turkey* (London, 1809), 2:298–307; Halil İnalcık, "Power Relationships Between Russia, the Crimea and the Ottoman Empire as Reflected in Titulature," in *Passé turco-tatar, présent soviétique: Études offertes à Alexandre Bennigsen*, ed. Chantal Lemercier-Quelquejay et al. (Paris, 1986), 208–21; Painite, *Ottoman Law of War and Peace*, 18.

47. For instance, in a British map from 1680, the "tributaries" listed included Wallachia, Moldavia, and the Crimean Khanate, but also the Sharifate of Mecca, Algeria, Tunis, and Libya. In contrast, Egypt and Budin (Buda, which included Hungary and Serbia) were categorized as "governments," that is, provinces. Palmira Brummett, *Mapping the Ottomans: Sovereignty, Territory, and Identity in the Early Modern Mediterranean* (Cambridge: Cambridge University Press, 2015); "The empire of the Great Turk in Europe, Asia, & Africa: divided into all its beglerbeglicz or governments in which are also distinguished the states that are tributary to him," https://www.loc.gov/resource/g7430.ct004270/?r=0.508,0.133,0.421,0.242,0.

48. Kathleen Davis, *Periodization and Sovereignty: How Ideas of Feudalism Govern the Politics of Time* (Philadelphia: University of Pennsylvania Press, 2008); Hent Kalmo and Quentin Skinner, eds., *Sovereignty in Fragments: The Past, Present and Future of a Contested Concept* (Cambridge: University Press, 2010).

49. Nihat Celik, "The Ottomans and International Law: The Russian Annexation of the Crimean Khanate in 1783 in the Light of the Documents from the Ottoman Archives," *Journal of Islamic Law* 5, no. 1 (2024).

50. BOA, Düvel-i Ecnebiye Defterleri collection, 83/1 p. 62; Noradounghian, *Recueil d'Actes*, 1897, 1, no. 36, 319–34; Virginia Aksan, *Ottoman Wars 1700–1870: An Empire Besieged* (London: Routledge, 2007), 158–60; Roderic H. Davison, "Russian Skill and Turkish Imbecility: The Treaty of Kuchuk Kainardji Reconsidered," *Slavic Review* 35, no. 3 (1976): 463–83; Will Smiley, *From Slaves to Prisoners of War: The Ottoman Empire, Russia, and International Law* (Oxford: Oxford University Press, 2018), 64–65.

51. Natalia Królikowska, "Sovereignty and Subordination"; Aksan, *Ottoman Wars*, 159–60.

52. William Eton, *A Survey of the Turkish Empire* (London: Cadell and Davies, 1809); Christian sovereigns on p. 106. The first edition was published in 1797; the fourth edition had an added chapter on Napoleon in Egypt and Catherine

in Crimea. See preface to the fourth edition and especially chapter 8, "On the State of the Turkish Provinces," 275.

53. Eton.

54. Francois Ragueau, *Glossaire du droit François* (Paris: Chez Jean et Michel Guignard, 1704); Panaite, *Ottoman Law of War and Peace*, 344–45.

55. Baron de Tott, *Memoires sur les Turcs et les Tartares* (Amsterdam: [s.n.], 1785); Emer de Vattel, *Le droit des gens, ou, Principes de la loi naturelle: appliqués à la conduite & aux affaires des nations & des souverains* (Leiden: Aux depens de la Compagnie, 1758); *Histoire de l'empire Ottoman, depuis son origine; Tableau général de l'Empire othoman, divisé en deux parties, dont l'une comprend la législation mahométane; l'autre l'histoire de l'Empire Othoman.*

56. Thus, though the Septinsular Republic was short-lived, it would be revived as a possible model for experiments in autonomy in the 1820s. Nobuyoshi Fujinami, "Between Sovereignty and Suzerainty: History of the Ottoman Privileged Provinces," in *A World History of Suzerainty: A Modern History of East and West Asia and Translated Concepts*, ed. Takashi Okamoto (Tokyo: Toyo Bunko, 2019)," 45; Aliki D. Nikiforou et al., eds., *Constitutional Charters of the Ionian Islands* (Athens: Hellenic Parliament Foundation, 2012), 539–601.

57. Brummet, *Mapping the Ottomans*, 79; Fujinami, "Between Sovereignty and Suzerainty."

58. Ottoman writers rendered suzerainty by simply retaining the word in Latin characters, as semi-sovereignty (*şibh-i sultanat*) or semi-independent states (*nim müstakil devletler*).

59. Halil İnalcık, "The Ottoman State: Economy and Society, 1300–1600," in *An Economic and Social History of the Ottoman Empire*, ed. Halil İnalcık and Donald Quataert (Cambridge: Cambridge University Press, 1994); Bruce McGowan, *Economic Life in Ottoman Europe: Taxation, Trade and the Struggle for Land, 1600–1800* (Cambridge: Cambridge University Press, 1981).

60. Aksan, *Ottoman Wars*, 384.

61. It was precisely provinces with special administrative status at the edges of the empire that were exposed to repeated instances of European intervention and occupation.

62. Davis, *Periodization and Sovereignty*; Kalmo and Skinner, eds., *Sovereignty in Fragments.*

63. Between 1711 and 1856, over the course of seven wars with the Ottomans, Russia invaded and/or occupied some part of Moldavia and Wallachia no fewer than six times. In each case, the army of occupation withdrew and the Principalities were restored to the Ottoman Empire. Smiley, *From Slaves to Prisoners of War*; Aksan, *Ottoman Wars.*

64. H. Şükrü Ilıcak, *"Those Infidel Greeks:" The Greek War of Independence Through Ottoman Archival Documents* (Leiden: Brill, 2021).

65. Maurizio Isabella, *Southern Europe in the Age of Revolutions* (Princeton: Princeton University Press, 2023); Mark Mazower, *The Greek Revolution: 1821 and the Making of Modern Europe* (New York: Penguin, 2021); Giannis S. Koliopoulos, *The Greek Revolution and the Violent Birth of Nationalism* (Princeton: Princeton University Press, 2025); Ozan Ozavcı *Dangerous Gifts: Imperialism, Security, and Civil Wars in the Levant, 1798–1864* (Oxford University Press, 2021); Aliki D. Nikiforu, ed., *Constitutional Charters of the Ionian Islands* (Athens: Hellenic Parliament Foundation, 2012); *Cezayir-i Seb'a-i Muctemi'a Cumhuri.* For a local perspective on this period, see Konstantina Zanou, *Transnational Patriotism in the Mediterranean, 1800–1850: Stammering the Nation* (Oxford: Oxford University Press, 2019).

66. Philliou, *Biography of an Empire.*

67. Rodogno, *Against Massacre*; Isabella, *Southern Europe.*

68. Philliou, *Biography of an Empire*, 72–23.

69. A letter from the grand vizier's office to the governor of Sidon, in Lebanon today, on the demolition of churches in Palestine stated: "Since the demolition of the non-ancient, newly built monasteries and of the ancient churches that are detrimental to Muslims is permissible by religion, you are ordered by an imperial edict—pursuant to the issued fatwa—to destroy both the old and new churches."

70. Mazower, *The Greek Revolution*, chap. 9.

71. Smiley, *From Slaves to Prisoners of War*, 176–84; Hakan Erdem, "'Do Not Think of the Greeks as Agricultural Labourers': Ottoman Responses to the Greek War of Independence," in *Citizenship and the Nation-State in Greece and Turkey*, ed. Faruk Birtek and Thalia Dragonas (London: Routledge, 2004).

72. Ilıcak, "*Those Infidel Greeks*," nos. 573, 314.

73. The British Foreign Office initially pursued a policy of strict neutrality, despite British support for the rebels, and had to issue a decree that prohibited British subjects from joining the conflict under the Greek flag. Hertslet, *Map of Europe* 1, no. 125:731; Mazower, "The Making of a European Cause," in *The Greek Revolution.*

74. NA/George Canning Papers/FO 800/230, no. 1, "Abstract of Proceedings in the Greek Question, Up to the Period of the Duke of Wellington's Mission to St. Petersburgh in 1826."

75. Alexander Bitis, *Russia and the Eastern Question: Army, Government and Society, 1815–1833* (Oxford: Oxford University Press, 2012), 163; C. W. Crawley, *The Question of Greek Independence: A Study of British Policy in the Near East, 1821–1833* (Cambridge: Cambridge University Press, 1973); H.W.V. Temperley, *The Foreign Policy of Canning, 1822–1827* (London: G. Bell, 1925), 330.

76. Hertslet, *Map of Europe*, vol. 1.

77. Bitis, *Russia and the Eastern Question*, 463.

78. NA FO/78/209, Canning to Palmerston, March 7, 1832.

79. BOA, A.Am.d. 79/2 [1245]; Hertslet, *Map of Europe*, vol. 2, no. 142, protocol of conference between Great Britain, France, and Russia, relative to the continental and insular boundaries of Greece, London, March 22, 1829.

80. Lauren Benton, *The Search for Sovereignty: Law and Geography in European Empires, 1400–1900* (Cambridge: Cambridge University Press, 2009); Eric Beverly, *Hyderabad, British India, and the World Muslim Networks and Minor Sovereignty, c. 1850–1950* (Cambridge: Cambridge University Press, 2015).

81. Findley, *Bureaucratic Reform*, chap. 4; Philliou, *Biography of an Empire*; Ömer Kürkçüoglu, "The Adoption and Use of Permanent Diplomacy," in *Ottoman Diplomacy: Conventional or Unconventional?*, ed. A. Nuri Yurdusev (New York: Palgrave Macmillan, 2004).

82. Philliou, *Biography of an Empire*, chaps. 4–5; Findley, *Bureaucratic Reform*, chap. 4.

83. Philliou, *Biography of an Empire*, 109–17.

84. Thomas Gallant, *Modern Greece: From the War of Independence to the Present* (London: Bloomsbury, 2016).

85. "Sovereignty of Greece," 1830; Crawley, *Greek Independence*.

86. Gallant, *Modern Greece*, 55–60.

87. BOA, HAT/45727 27 Şaban 1241 (April 5, 1826)); Selim Aslantaş, "Osmanli-Rus İliskilerinden bir Kesit: 1826 Akkerman Andlasmasi'nin Muzakereleri," *Uluslararası İlişkiler* 9, no. 36 (Winter 2013): 150, 124–31.

88. Virginia Aksan, "Ottoman Military and Social Transformations, 1826–1828" in *Empires and Autonomy: Moments in the History of Globalization*, ed. Stephen Streeter, John Weaver, and William D. Coleman (Vancouver: University of British Columbia Press, 2009); Aslantaş, "Osmanli-Rus İliskilerinden bir Kesit," 150.

89. F. Ismail, "The Making of the Treaty of Bucharest, 1811–1812," *Middle Eastern Studies* 15, no. 2 (May 1979): 163–92; *Muahadet Mecmuası* 4:S. 49–57; Noradounghian, *Recueil d'Actes*, 1:86–92.

90. Article V "confirmed" the "treaties and conventions concerning the privileges (*imtiyazat*) of Moldavia and Wallachia" but did not elucidate the content of these rights. *Muahadet Mecmuası*. 4:S. 49–57; Noradounghian, *Recueil d'Actes*, 1:86–92. For an English translation, see J. C. Hurewitz, *The Middle East and North Africa in World Politics* (New Haven: Yale University Press, 1975), 193–97.

91. *Muahadet Mecmuası*, 4:S. 49–57; Noradounghian, *Recueil d'Actes*, 1:446. For an English translation, see Hurewitz, *The Middle East and North Africa*, October 7, 1826, no. 131,Convention between Russia and Turkey, explanatory of the Treaty of Bucharest. Signed at Ackermann, September 25/October 7, 1826.

92. "Sırp milleti mukaddemki devirde olduğu veçhile Devlet-i Aliyye-i Osmaniyye'ye cizye-güzar reayası olup haklarında bir mukteza-yı şer'iye." *Muahadet Mecmusi*, 4:53–54.

93. The Ottoman text was not far off from the French in this case: "Devlet-i Aliyye'nin bazı cezair-i bahr-i sefid'de ve mevkiler-i sairede olan reayasına nail oldukları fevaid-i misillü millet-i mezkûreye dahi müsaade ve asar-ı şefikane-i Aliyye'sine mazhar olmalarına müsaade birle onlara kıyasen umur-ı dahiliyelerinin kendi taraflarından idaresi ve vergilerinin ve vech-i maktuenle de tahsis kendi ve bıdarından kabz ve teslimi misillü millet-i mezkurenin taraf-ı Devlet-i Aliyye'den olacak istid'alarını Devlet-i Aliyye Sırp milleti ile tanzim eyleye." The state "permitted them to manage their internal affairs and collect and deliver their own taxes and levies." *Muahadet Mecmusi*, 4:53–54; "en leur laissant à eux-mêmes le soin de l'administration intérieure du pays, et en recevant immédiatement d'eux le montant des impôts modérés qu'elle lèvera sur eux et en prenant à cet effet des mesures de concert avec ce people." Noradounghian, *Recueil d'Actes*, no. 30, 2:86–92.

94. F. Ismail, "The Making of the Treaty of Bucharest, 1811–1812," *Middle Eastern Studies* 15, no. 2 (May 1979): 182.

95. Noradounghian, no. 39, "Séned relatif aux Principautés de Moldavie et de Valachie"; no. 40, "Séned relatif à la Serbie," 2:121–26.

96. Fred Anscombe, "The Balkan Revolutionary Age," *Journal of Modern History* 84, no. 3 (September 2012): 572–606; Ali Yaycıoğlu, *Partners of the Empire: The Crisis of the Ottoman Order in the Age of Revolutions* (Stanford: Stanford University Press).

97. Ahmed Lûtfî Efendi, *Vak'anüvîs Ahmed Lûtfî Efendi Tarihi* 1, no. 14 (Istanbul: Yapı Kredi, 1999): 262–74; Noradounghian, *Recueil d'Actes*, no. 18, 2:55–67.

98. Viktor Taki argues that the 1802 *hatt-i şerif* was the first instance of Russia's "direct involvement in the internal poltical and administrative organization of Moldavia and Wallachia," mostly from the point of view of fixing the terms of the *voyvoda* (hosposdar) to seven years. For the Russian perspective, see chap. 1, pp. 38–39; Anscombe, "The Balkan Revolutionary Age"; Ali Yacıoğlu on Panvanzoğlu; Noradounghian, *Recueil d'Actes*; Efendi, *Vak'anüvîs Ahmed Lûtfî Efendi Tarİhİati*, 262–74.

99. Noradounghian published the French version of the text, which used the expression "tributary," as in "as long as they (local governing officials) fulfill their obligations as subjects and tributaries, they will experience only clemency and mercy." Lutfi's version in Ottoman does not capture the idea of tributary and instead refers to offices and governing roles in the two provinces. Noradounghian, *Recueil d'Actes*; Efendi, *Vak'anüvîs Ahmed Lûtfî Efendi Tarihi*.

100. Bitis, *Russia and the Eastern Question*, chap. 2; Hertslet, *Map of Europe*.

101. Smiley, *From Slaves to Prisoners of War*, chapters 7 and 8. Hertslet, *Map of Europe*, 2:779.
102. Hertslet, *Map of Europe*, 2:779.
103. Smiley, *From Slaves to Prisoners of War.*
104. Hertslet, *Map of Europe*, 2, no. 147, "Manifesto of the Emperor of Russia on the Conclusion of Peace with Turkey," October 1, 1829, 835–36.
105. Hertslet, 2, no. 145, "Treaty of Adrianople," 813–35; *Muahadet Mecmuası*, 4:70–80; Noradounghian, *Recueil d'Actes*, nos. 53–54, 2:166–77.
106. *Muahadet Mecmuası*, 4:70–80; Noradounghian, "Séned relatif aux Principautés de Moldavie et de Valachie," 2:39; "Séned relatif à la Serbie," 2:40, 121–26.
107. *Muahadet Mecmuası*, 4:70–80; Noradounghian, *Recueil d'Actes*, 2:40.
108. Smiley, *From Slaves to Prisoners of War*, 238. A move that reflects what Smiley has demonstrated was a regional system of international law between the Eurasian empires. Virginia Aksan, "Ottoman Military and Social Transformations, 1826–1828" in *Empires and Autonomy: Moments in the History of Globalization*, ed. Stephen Streeter, John Weaver, and William D. Coleman (Vancouver: University of British Columbia Press, 2009); Selim Aslantaş, "Osmanli-Rus İliskilerinden bir Kesit: 1826 Akkerman Andlasmasi'nin Muzakereleri," *Uluslararası İlişkiler* 9, no. 36 (Winter 2013): 150.
109. Ahmed Cedvet Paşa, *Tarih-i Cevdet* (Dersaadet: Matbaa-yi Osmaniye, 1309/1893), 11:203–16. "Bu vakte kadar Yunanistan'ın istiklali la-ferdisi hep devletlerce merdud olup mücerred Devlet-i Aliyye'ye tabi olmak üzere bir eyâlet-i mümtaze şekline konulması bil-defaat ilân olunmuş ve bahs ancak şeklinin tayini hakkında câri olup Edirne musâlahasında dahi daha ileriye gidilmeyerek Londra kararnamesinin kabulü şart kılınmış iken bağteten devlet-i müttefika beyninde Yunanistan'ın istiklaline karar verilmiştir."
110. For the reception of the ferman in Belgrade, see Marko Attila Hoare, *Serbia: A Modern History* (Oxford: Oxford University Press, 2024), chap. 3.
111. Hertslet, *Map of Europe*, 2:832–34; Noradounghian; Muhadet Mecmuası, 4:56.
112. In exchange for ending the rebellion, the governor of Belgrade, Maraşlı Ali, awarded Miloš the exclusive right to collect taxes in the Smederevo sanjak. See Hoare, *Serbia*, 60–61; Leopold von Ranke, *Die serbische Revolution* (Hamburg: Bei F. Perthes, 1829), chaps. 8–12; von Ranke, *Serbien und die Türkei im neuzehnten Jahrhundert* (Leipzig: Duncker & Humblot, 1879), chaps. 19–24; and Ayhan Ceylan, "Sırbistan'ın İdare-i Dâhiliyesine Dâir Kanunnâme: 1838 Türk Anayasası (Turski Ustav)," *Türk Hukuk Tarih Araştırmaları* 28 (2019): 10.
113. Hertslet, *Map of Europe*, 2:246–50; Noradounghian, *Recueil d'Actes*, Noradounghian, "Hatti Chérif concernant l'autonomie serbe" (August 29, 1830 /

Rebi-ul-ewel 1246) 2:197–200; BOA, YEE. 41/139 (evahir-i rebiülahir 1246/ 1830). The various imperial fermans from 1830 to 1838 were reproduced in the rare Ottoman Turkish text that covered Miloš and the era of Serbian autonomy. Raşid Belgradi wrote bitterly about the mobility and residency controls for Muslims in Serbia and was deeply suspicious of Miloš. He eventually fled Belgrade for Istanbul in the 1860s. Raşid Belgradi, *Tarih-i Vak'a-i Hayretnümâ-i Belgrad ve Sırbistân* [Chronicle of the astonishing events in Belgrade and Serbia] (Istanbul: Tatyos Divitçiyan Matbaası, 1291 [1874]), 1:232–51; Börekçi, 187.

114. Hertslet, *Map of Europe*, 2:146–50; Noradounghian, *Recueil d'Actes*, 2, no. 63, "Hatti Chérif, Ceoncernant l'autonomie serbe" (August 29, 1830/Rebi-ul-ewel 1246).

115. From 1815, Miloš pressured Muslims officials and civilians to move in to garrison towns. Muslim "abandoned land" enriched the notables and wealthy peasants who surrounded Miloš. Hoare, *Serbia*, 62; Selim Aslantaş, "Sırp Knezliği'nde İktidar Mücâdelesi: '1838 Türk Anayasası'nın (Turski Ustav)' İlanı, Büyük Güçler ve Osmanlı Devleti," *Cumhuriyet Tarihi Araştırmaları Dergisi* 9, no. 17 (Spring 2013): 5.

116. Ayetekin, 592. As Ayetekin notes, this was before the creation of Tanzimat councils in 1838 to administer taxes after the abolition of tax farming. Autonomous Serbia was not subject to Tanzimat, so this council did not function in the same way as Tanzimat councils. But it is tempting to think about the degree to which autonomous provinces provided templates for administrative experiments conducted elsewhere in the empire.

117. For a new interpretation of the period of Serbian autonomy and Miloš, see Vlada Lilić, "Empire of States: Law and International Order in Ottoman Europe, c. 1830–1912," PhD diss., Vanderbilt University, 2024; Aslantaş, "Sırp Knezliği'nde," 5.

118. BOA, HAT. 1117/44874 A. [29 Zilhicce 1250/1835]; Aslantaş, "Sırp Knezliği'nde," 12–15.

119. On the Sretenje Constitution, see Tanja Cerevicki, "1835–1838 Yılları Arasında Sırp Knezliği'nde Anayasa Hareketleri," *Ankara Üniversitesi Osmanlı Tarihi Araştırma ve Uygulama Merkezi Dergisi* 53 (Spring 2-23): 1–25; Ayhan Ceylan, "Sırbistan'ın İdare-i Dâhiliyesine Dâir Kanunnâme: 1838 Türk Anayasası (Turski Ustav)," *Türk Hukuk Tarih Araştırmaları* 28 (Istanbul, 2019): 18–19.

120. BOA, HAT. 1121/44925 C [29 Safar 1251/1835]. The Ottoman governor of Vidin, Hüseyin Paşa, pressured Miloš to do so. Ahmed Lütfi Efendi, *Vak'anüvis Ahmed Lûtfî Efendi Tarihi* (Istanbul: Yapı Kredi Yayınları, 1999), vol. 5, pp. 829–31, 856–57.

121. BOA, A.DVNS.NMH.d. 11/174 [10 Cemâziyelevvel 1251/1835]; Ahmed Lütfi, *Vak'anüvis*, 856–57. Reforming bureaucrats already spoke the language of corruption, and misconduct as an affront to the state. Cengiz Kırlı, *Yolsuzluğun İcadı: 1840 Ceza Kanunu, İktidar ve Bürokrasi* (Istanbul: Verita, 2014); Ayşe Özkan, *Miloş'tan Milan'a Sırp Bağ ımsızlığ ı* (1830–1878) (Istanbul: Kültür Sanat Yayıncılık, 2011), 45–46.

122. Alison Terndrup argues that Miloš's visit was modeled in part on the 1834 ceremony of investiture for the princes of Moldavia and Wallachia in Istanbul. Terndrup, *Image of the Modern Ottoman Sultan* (Leiden: Brill, 2025). For a description of the investiture ceremony with Phanariot princes before the Greek revolution, see Philliou, *Biography of an Empire*, 21–24.

123. Terndrup, *Image*, 145–47; Miloš Jagodić, "Library of the Ministry of Foreign Affairs of the Principality of Serbia in 1846," *Istraživanja* 26 (2015), 107.

124. Emily Neumeier has demonstrated how "*ayan* architecture" in the provinces reflected the sovereign power of the imperial center. While her main case study is Tepedelenli Ali Paşa, she insists that it is crucial to compare his architectural patronage to other ayan to see a wider phenomenon. Neumeier, *Architectural Revolution on the Ottoman Frontier: Greece and Albania in the Age of Ali Pasha* (University Park: Penn State University Press, 2025), 11–17. Khalid Fahmy makes similar argument about Mehmed Ali Paşa's relationship to the Ottoman political order in *All the Pasha's Men: Mehmed Ali, His Army and the Making of Modern Egypt* (Cairo: The American University in Cairo Press, 1997).

125. Lilić, "Empire of States," chap. 1; Aslantaş, "Sırp Knezliği'nde," 10–14; Hoare, *Serbia*, 94; Tanja Cerevicki, "1835–1838 Yılları Arasında Sırp Knezliği'nde Anayasa Hareketleri," *Ankara Üniversitesi Osmanlı Tarihi Araştırma ve Uygulama Merkezi Dergisi* 53 (Spring 2023): 16; Ceylan, "Sırbistan'ın," 19.

126. Döndü Düşmez, "Tanzimat Devrinde Kapı Kethüdalığ ı Müessesesi Hakkında Temel Bilgiler," Selçuk Üniversitesi Türkiyat Araştırmaları Dergisi, 28 (December 2010), 387–90; Youssef Ben Ismail, "Sovereignty Across Empires: France, the Ottoman Empire, and the Imperial Struggle over Tunis (ca. 1830–1920)" (PhD diss., Harvard University, 2021), chap. 2; BOA, YEE. 41/45. From 1835, Yusuf Muhlis Paşa was the *muhafiz* of Belgrade and later served as the governor of Rumelia (1840–1843). In the Russo-Ottoman War, he was the commander of Varna (Bulgaria) during the Russian siege and capture of the garrison. He was taken as a prisoner of war and blamed for the Ottoman defeat. İbnü'l-Emin Mahmud Kemal İnal, *Son Asır Türk Şairleri*. C. II. (Istanbul: Milli Eğitim Basıevi, 1969), 2:969–73.

127. BOA, YEE. 45 "şu şartla ki sahib-i mülk olan Devlet-i Aliyyemin istihkakat-ı meşrua-yi hükümdaranesine asla dokunmamak."

128. Leonidas Moiras argues that the Hatt-ı Şerif of Gülhane, or the Tanzimat Ferman, was rooted in the language and rights outlined in the 1838 Turkish Constitution for Serbia. Moiras, "The Balkan-Wide Dimension of 1838 'Turski Ustav,'" *Srpske Studije* 11 (February 2020): 47–50. In contrast to this argument, see Butrus Abu-Manneh, "The Islamic Roots of the Gülhane Rescript," in *Studies on Islam and the Ottoman Empire in the Nineteenth Century* (Istanbul: Isis, 2001).

129. See chapter 2. The *hatt-ı hümayun* uses the word *kançılarya*, which means chancellery or registry office of a consulate. The title given to the new role was *prestavnik*, meaning steward or representative. YEE, "Emaret için bir kançılarya tahsisiyle kethüdan prestavnik marifetiyle idare olunup pasaport itası ve Sırplının ecanib memurlarıyla olan muamelatının idaresi işbu prestavnik ta'bir olunan memurun zimmetine tarafından ihale kılınmak."

130. A *kapıkethüdası*, also rendered *kapıkahya*, was a capacious term and an enduring office within the empire. The term can be translated as agent, gatekeeper, representative, official, or steward. Philliou, *Biography*, 21; Ceylan, "Sırbistan'ın, 10; Mehmet Canatar, "Kethüda," *İslâm Ansiklopedisi* (Istanbul: Türkiye Diyanet Vakfı, 1998–2016), vol. 25; Findley, *Bureaucratic Reform*, 180–81, 195.

131. FO 78/208; FO 195/102/115; FO 371/145/64; Philliou, *Biography of an Empire*, 111–17.

132. *Corps de droit ottoman; recueil des codes, lois, règlements, ordonnances et actes les plus importants du droit intérieur, et d'études sur le droit coutumier de l'Empire ottoman*, 114–16.

133. See the Russian War Declaration in 1824, Hertslet, *Map of Europe*, no. 138, 2:779.

134. BOA, A.AMD. 80/35 [1246 Z. 29] 1831.

135. Mehmed Ali's expansionist campaigns began soon after he was appointed governor of Egypt. His first campaign was in Hijaz against the Wahabis, who had taken over the Holy Cities (1811–1818). After Hijaz, he expanded the "Egyptian empire" into Sudan during a short but violent campaign (1820–1822). He then shifted toward Syrian provinces in the 1830s. Khaled Fahmy, *All the Pasha's Men: Mehmed Ali, His Army and the Making of Modern Egypt* (Cairo: The American University in Cairo Press, 1997); Heather Sharkey, *Living with Colonialism: Nationalism and Culture in the Anglo-Egyptian Sudan* (Berkeley: University of California Press, 2003); Hassan Ahmed Ibrahim, "The Egyptian Empire, 1805–1885," *The Cambridge History of Egypt*, vol. 2 (Cambridge: Cambridge University Press, 1998).

136. Khaled Fahmy, "The Era of Muhammad 'Ali Pasha, 1805–1848," in *The Cambridge History of Egypt*, ed. M. W. Daly (Cambridge: Cambridge University Press, 1998), 66–67.

137. BOA, İ.MTZ(05) 3/68 Ca. 3 1256.

138. Aksan, *Ottoman Wars*, chap. 9.

139. Aksan, 373.

140. İbrahim wanted his father to claim the title *sahib-i sikke ve hutbe*—the possessor of the coin and sermon. Fahmy, "The Era of Muhammad 'Ali Pasha," 167.

141. BOA, İ.MTZ(05) 3/68 Ca. 3 1256.

142. Aksan, *Ottoman Wars*, 374.

143. On July 15, 1840, Britain, Austria, Prussia, and Russia concluded a convention with the Ottoman Empire for settlement of the "Egyptian question." France was not initially a party to the convention. For the text of the "Convention for the Pacification of the Levant," see Hertslet, *Map of Europe* 2, no. 192: 1021–23, and Noradounghian, *Recueil d'Actes*. The story of Mehmed Ali and the London Convention appears in nearly all the classic international law textbooks of the nineteenth century. See, for example, Henry Wheaton, *Elements of International Law* (Boston: Little, Brown, 1855).

144. BOA İ.MTZ.(05) 5/133 L. 21, 1256; BOA İ.MTZ.(05) 6/168 Z., 29 1256; BOA İ.MTZ.(05) 6/174 Z. 29, 1256; BOA İ.MTZ.(05) 6/177 Z., 29 1256.

145. Hertslet, *Map of Europe* 2, no. 192:1009–10; Noradounghian, *Recueil d'Actes*; *Muahedat Mecmuası*, 4:242–58.

146. Hertslet, *Map of Europe* 2, no. 192:1009–10; Noradounghian, *Recueil d'Actes*; *Muahedat Mecmuası*, 4:242–58.

147. The governor was deposed and declared a rebel. Part 2, 1840, NA/FO/406/ no. 199, September 10, 1840, Ponsby to Palmerston (September 16, 1840).

148. Grégoire Aristarchi, *Législation ottomane* (Istanbul, 1873–1888); Ozan, *Dangerous Gifts*, 199–298; Mehmet Ö. Alkan, *Modern Türkiye'de Siyasi Düş ünce*, vol. 1 (Istanbul: İletişim Press, 2001); Butrus Abu-Manneh, "The Islamic Roots of the Gülhane Rescript," *Die Welt des Islams* 34, no. 2 (November 1994.

149. BOA, MMM, no. 15, Evâhir-i Z. 1256 (February 12, 1841), 11–12. See Government of Egypt, *Recueil de firmans impériaux ottomans addresses aux valis et aux khedives d'Égypte* (Cairo: L'institut Français d'archéologie, 1934).

150. *Takvim-i Vekayi*, no. 216 [1256-12-24] and no. 217 [1256-12-04].

151. Fahmy, "The Era of Muhammad 'Ali," 175–76.

152. BOA, MMM, no. 15, Evâhir-i Z. 1256 (February 12, 1841).

153. Ussama Makdisi, *Age of Coexistence: The Ecumenical Frame and the Making of the Modern Arab World* (Berkeley: University of California Press, 2021).

154. For a political history of events in the 1840s and 1860s in Lebanon and Damascus, see Leila Tarazi Fawaz, *An Occasion for War: Civil Conflict in Lebanon and Damascus in 1860* (Berkeley: University of California, 1994); Kamal Salibi, *A House of Many Mansions: The History of Lebanon Reconsidered* (Berkeley: University of California Press, 1990); Meltem Toksöz, *Nomads, Migrants*

and Cotton in the Eastern Mediterranean: The Making of the Adana-Mersin Region (Leiden: Brill, 2011); and Yonca Köksal, "Coercion and Mediation: Centralization and Sedentarization of Tribes in the Ottoman Empire," *Middle Eastern Studies* 42, no. 3 (May 2006): 469–91.

155. Fawaz estimates in *An Occasion for War*, 226, that eleven thousand people died in Mount Lebanon and another twelve thousand in Damascus. Ussama Makdisi estimates that at least two thousand villages were destroyed. Makdisi, *The Culture of Sectarianism: Community, History, and Violence in Nineteenth-Century Ottoman Lebanon* (Berkeley: University of California Press, 2000), 118.

156. Mehmed Fuad Paşa (Keçizade) is perhaps best known, along with Ali Paşa, as the major champion of the Tanzimat reforms. Soon after working in Lebanon, he authored the *Teşkil-i Vilayet Nizamnamesi* (Vilayet Law) in 1864 along with Midhat Paşa. See R. H. Davison, *Reform in the Ottoman Empire, 1856–1876* (Princeton: Princeton University Press, 1963); Mehmed Süreyya, *Sicil-i Osmani* (Istanbul, 1996), 2:539–40; R. H. Davison, "Fuad Pasha, Kecedji-zade Mehmed," in *Encyclopedia of Islam*, 2d ed.

157. On Ahmed Paşa, see Makdisi, *Culture of Sectarianism*, 144–51; Fawaz, *Occasion*, 138.

158. Fawaz, *Occasion*, chap. 6.

159. Makdisi, *Culture of Sectarianism*, 148–49.

160. For Dufferin's activities as the British member of the Beirut Commission, see especially Fruma Zachs, "'Novice' or 'Heaven-born' Diplomat? Lord Dufferin's Plan for a 'Province of Syria': Beirut, 1860–61," *Middle East Studies* 36, no. 3 (July 2000): 160–76; Fawaz, *Occasion*; Makdisi, *Culture of Sectarianism*.

161. Enclosure 8, no. 240. NA/FO/406/10, enclosure 8, no. 240, Dufferin to Bulwer, November 2, 1860. This became article 4 of Dufferin's Memorandum on the Administration of Syria.

162. Dufferin's actual scheme was a memorandum with seventeen articles. The first asserted the "integrity of the Ottoman Empire." See BOA, HR.SFR(3), 56/4/10, "Mémorandum de Lord Dufferin contenant les principes d'après lesquels serait dirigé la future administration de la Syrie."

163. BOA, HR.SFR(3), 56/4/8, Ali to Musurus, January 16, 1861. Mehmed Emin Ali Paşa (1815–1871) was deputized as foreign minister during Fuad's absence in Lebanon. He served as grand vizier five times and had earlier been the Ottoman ambassador to London. Along with Fuad, Ali was the face of Tanzimat reforms. İbnülemin Mahmut Kemal İnal, *Osmanlı Devrinde Son Sadrıazamlar*, 1:4–58; Davison, *Reform in the Ottoman Empire*; Stanford Shaw, *History of the Ottoman Empire and Modern Turkey*, vol. 2: *Reform and Revolution* (Cambridge: Cambridge University Press, 1977).

164. BOA, HR.SFR(3), 56/4/8. Kostaki Musurus Paşa was the longest-serving Ottoman ambassador to Britain and still held the post during the Egyptian

Crisis. He was from a Phanariot Greek family in Istanbul and acted as the Ottoman ambassador in London from March 1851 to November 1885. See Philliou, *Biography of an Empire*, 148–51; Sinan Kuneralp, "Bir Osmanlı Diplomati: Kostaki Musurus Paşa 1807–1891," *Belleten* (Türk Tarih Kurumu) 34, no. 135 (1970); Mehmed Süreyya, *Sicil-i Osmani*, vol. 6 (Tarih Vakfı, 1996).

165. BOA, HR.SFR(3), 11-13, Ali to Musurus, January 22, 1861.

166. NA/PRO 30/22/89, Bulwer to Lord John, January 9, 1861.

167. Based on the fact that Fuad later authored the 1864 Vilayet Law, modeled in part on the *Règlement Organique* for Lebanon, it appears that Bulwer supported Fuad's measures. See Roderic Davison, "Provincial Government: Midhat Paşa and the Vilayet System of 1864 and 1867," in *Reform in the Ottoman Empire, 1856–1876* (Princeton: Princeton University Press, 1963).

168. In Ottoman-Turkish from 1861, Mount Lebanon was known as the Mount Lebanon Mutasarrifate (*Cebel-i Lübnan Mutasarrıflığı*). A *mutasarrıf* was a governor of a *sancak* or subprovince. The commission debated what to call the local governor and rejected several options, including emir (prince). For the English translation of the 1861 Règlement, see Hurewitz, *The Middle East and North Africa*, 346–49. The powers expanded the Règlement in 1864; the text can be found in Thomas Erskine Holland, *The European Concert in the Eastern Question: A Collection of Treaties and Other Public Acts* (Oxford: Clarendon, 1885), 206–18. For further analysis of the Règlement of 1861 and 1864, see Noradounghian, *Recueil d'Actes*, 3:144–49; *Düstur*, vol. 4 (1878): 695–701. For an analysis of how the *mutasarrifiyya* operated on the ground, see Engin Akarlı, *The Long Peace*.

169. See chapter 1.

170. J. C. Hurewitz, *The Middle East and North Africa*, 347, 348. Mixed communities would have an appointed *sheikh* who would only be responsible for his "co-religionists."

171. For the text of the 1861 Regulations, see Hurewitz, 346–49. The powers expanded the regulations in 1864. The text can be found in Thomas Erskine Holland, *The European Concert in the Eastern Question: A Collection of Treaties and Other Public Acts* (Oxford: Clarendon, 1885), 206–18; and Aristarchi, *Législation ottoman*, 204–10. For further analysis of both sets of regulations, see Akarlı, *The Long Peace*; Noradounghian, *Recueil d'Actes*, 3:144–49; *Düstur*, vol. 4 (1878): 695–701.

172. Aristachi, *Législation ottoman*, 2:145–46.

173. Milen V. Petrov, "Tanzimat for the Countryside: Midhat Pasa and the Vilayet of Danube, 1864–1868," PhD diss., Princeton University, 2006. To what degree Bulwer knew of Fuad's exact plans is not clear. Based on the fact that Fuad later authored the 1864 Vilayet Law, modeled in part on the *Règlement Organique* for Lebanon, it appears that Bulwer supported Fuad's measures. Davison, "Provincial Government."

174. The Sharia courts continued to function alongside the new secular court system. For the *Nizamiye* courts, see Avi Rubin, *Ottoman Nizamiye Courts: Law and Modernity* (New York: Palgrave Macmillan, 2011).
175. Quoted in Davison, *Reform in the Ottoman Empire*, 157; Young, *Course de Droit*, 1:36–37. See the *Teşkil-i Vilayet Nizamnamesi* for Danube, in Düster, 1282, 517–36; de Testa, *Recueil*, 7:469–84; for general law, *Düstur* (Istanbul, 1289), 608–24; Aristarchi, *Legislation ottoman*, 2:273–95; and Davison, *Reform*, 136–71.
176. Benton, *The Search for Sovereignty*.
177. For example, [A.C. Lyall,] "Frontiers and Protectorates," *The Nineteenth Century* 174 (August 1891): 312–28; Halford J. Mackinder, "The Geographical Pivot of History," *Geographical Journal* 23, no. 4 (April 1904): 421–37.
178. For example, Babanzâde İsmail Hakkı, *Hukuk-ı Esasiye* (Ankara: Erguvani, 2014), 159.
179. Furat Andič and Suphan Andič, *The Last of the Ottoman Grandees: The Life and the Political Testament of Ali Paşa* (Istanbul: Isis, 1996), 35; *La Revue de Paris*, 1910.

2. Taming Autonomy Through Law

1. As a result of the Russo-Ottoman War of 1877–1878 and the Treaty of Berlin, Bulgaria was also divided into two principalities, both with varying degrees of autonomy—the Habsburg monarchy occupied Bosnia and Herzegovina, and the six Eastern provinces were extended the possibility of a future autonomous administrative arrangement. On demographic changes in the aftermath of 1878, see Cem Bahar, *Osmanli Imparatorlugu'nun ve Türkiye'nin nüfusu, 1500–1927* (Ankara: T. C. Başbakanlık Devlet İstatistik Enstitüsü, 1996); Vladimir Hamad-Troyansky, *Empire of Refugees North Caucasian Muslims and the Late Ottoman State* (Stanford: Stanford University Press, 2024).
2. Youssef Ben Ismail, "Sovereignty Across Empires: France, the Ottoman Empire, and the Imperial Struggle Over Tunis (ca. 1830–1920)," PhD diss., Harvard University, 2021; Mary Dewhurst Lewis, *Divided Rule: Sovereignty and Empire in French Tunisia, 1881–1938* (Berkeley: University of California Press, 2013).
3. Michael Christopher Low, *Imperial Mecca: Ottoman Arabia and the Indian Ocean Hajj* (New York: Columbia University Press, 2020); Low, "Ottoman Infrastructures of the Saudi Hydro-State: The Technopolitics of Pilgrimage and Potable Water in the Hijaz," *Comparative Studies in Society and History* 57, no. 4 (October 2015): 942–74; Mostafa Minawi, *The Ottoman Scramble for Africa: Empire and Diplomacy in the Sahara and the Hijaz* (Stanford: Stanford University Press, 2016); Minawi, "Telegraphs and Territoriality in Ottoman

Africa and Arabia During the Age of High Imperialism," *Journal of Balkan and Near Eastern Studies*, 18 (2016): 576–87; Benjamin Fortna, *Imperial Classroom: Islam, the State, and Education in the Late Ottoman Empire* (New York: Oxford University Press, 2002).

4. Başbakanlık Osmanlı Arşivi (hereafter BOA), DH. SAİD 183, "İbrahim Hakkı." Hakkı Paşa had a long and varied career in the Ottoman civil service during the Hamidian and Young Turk period. He worked in the Palace Secretariat (*mabeyn*) for Abdülhamid as a translator, where, according to Carter Findley, he translated Sherlock Holmes stories for the sultan. Afterward he taught constitutional law and later administrative and international law at the Law Faculty in Istanbul. During this time he wrote extensively on international law and produced numerous international law textbooks for pedagogical use—according to Findley, nonspecialists broadly read his textbooks as well. Hakkı was appointed as legal advisor at the Foreign Ministry at the same time as Gabriel Noradounghian, both eventually serving as grand vizier. During the CUP period, Hakkı obtained a number of ministerial posts including education and interior. His last posting was ambassador to Berlin. Following Brest-Litovsk, he negotiated with Trotsky for the return of territories lost to Russia in 1878, the so-called three provinces (*Elviye-i Selase*)—Kars, Ardahan, and Batum. Carter Findley, *Ottoman Civil Officialdom: A Social History* (Princeton: Princeton University Press, 1989), chap. 5; M. K. İnal, *Osmanlı Devrinde son Sadriazamlar* (Istanbul: Milli Eğitim Basımevi, 1965), 3:1763–1804; Ali Çankaya, *Mülkiye tarihi ve mülkiyeliler* (Ankara 1954), 54–58; F. Ahmad, "Ibrāhīm Ḥaḳḳī Pasha," *Encyclopaedia of Islam, Second Edition*, Brill Online, 2013. For his legal writing, see *Hukuk-i düvel* [International law] (Darülhilâfe [Istanbul]: Matbaa ve Kütübhane-yi Cihan, 1327 [1911]); *Medhal-i hukuk-i beyneddüvel* [Principles of international law] and *Tarih-i hukuk-i beyneddüvel* [History of international law] (Istanbul: Karabet ve Kasbar, 1303 [1885–86]). On negotiating the return of the "three provinces" to the Ottoman Empire, see Michael Reynolds, *Shattering Empires: The Clash and Collapse of the Ottoman and Russian Empires 1908–1918* (Cambridge: Cambridge University Press, 2011), chap.6.

5. Outside the Great Powers, few states in the nineteenth-century Eurocentric international order gained full sovereignty in international relations. And yet the Ottoman Empire, China, and Mexico, among other states at the boundaries of the international order whose sovereignty was limited in various ways by the Great Powers, are often treated as deficient or failing to meet the proper threshold of sovereignty. Gerry Simpson, *Great Powers and Outlaw States: Unequal Sovereigns in the International Legal Order* (Cambridge: Cambridge University Press, 2004), chap. 8.

6. Ozan Ozavci, *Dangerous Gifts: Imperialism, Security, and Civil Wars in the Levant, 1798–1864* (Oxford: Oxford University Press, 2021); Umut Özsu, "The

Ottoman Empire, the Origins of Extraterritoriality, and International Legal Theory," in *The Oxford Handbook of the Theory of International Law*, ed. Florian Hoffmann and Anne Orford (Oxford: Oxford University Press, 2016).

7. On non-Europeans, see Arnulf Becker Lorca, *Mestizo International Law: A Global Intellectual History 1842–1933* (Cambridge: Cambridge University Press, 2015).

8. Martti Koskenniemi, *The Gentle Civilizer of Nations: The Rise and Fall of International Law 1870–1960* (Cambridge: Cambridge University Press, 2002), chap. 2; Mark Mazower, *Governing the World: The History of an Idea* (New York: Penguin, 2012), chap. 3; Casper Sylvest, "International Law in Nineteenth-Century Britain," *British Yearbook of International Law* (2005).

9. Will Hanley's study of the function of consular courts in British-occupied Egypt demonstrates the ways in which private international law, the law of personal status, was just as important as matters of diplomacy and high politics. Hanley, *Identifying with Nationality: Europeans, Ottomans, and Egyptians in Alexandria* (New York: Columbia University Press, 2017). As Samera Esmeir has argued, "International law became a new political strategy: it represented a way that the Ottoman Empire both comported itself with Europe and attempted to survive." Esmeir, "On Becoming Less of the World," *History of the* Present 8, no. 1 (Spring 2018): 88–116.

10. Mehmed Cemil (Bilsel) was a prominent Ottoman and early Republican international lawyer. He made this argument often in his published works, starting in the Second Constitutional era (1908–1913) and extending into the 1940s. See Mehmed Cemil (Bilsel), *Lozan*, vol. 1 (Istanbul: Ahmed İhsan ve Şurekası, 1933).

11. Foreign limitations on finances and revenue management were just as important as European imposed autonomy and the Capitulations, but it is not possible to cover the topic fully here. Briefly, in 1881 a handful of European representatives controlled sovereign debt collection on behalf of the empire's creditors in the form of the Ottoman Public Debt Administration (Düyun-u umumiye-i osmaniye varidat-ı muhassasa idaresi). Through a series of monopolies on salt, tobacco, and other goods, European creditors seized revenues to repay loans before tax streams reached imperial coffers. The new headquarters of the Debt Administration, which was both larger than and operated independently of the Ottoman Treasury, dominated the horizon of the old city, dwarfing nearby imperial mosques from the era of conquest. Julia Elyachar, *On the Semicivilized: Coloniality, Finance, and Embodied Sovereignty in Cairo* (Durham: Duke University Press, 2025); Daniel A. Stolz, "'Impossible to Provide an Accurate Estimate': The Interested Calculation of the Ottoman Public Debt, 1875–1881," *British Journal for the History of Science*, vol. 55, no. 4 (2022): 477–93; Murat Birdal, *The Political Economy of Ottoman Public: Insolvency and European Financial Control in the Late Nineteenth Century* (London: Tauris, 2010); Şevket Pamuk, *Uneven Centuries: Economic Development of Turkey Since 1820* (Princeton: Princeton University Press,

2018); Ali Coskun Tunçer, *Sovereign Debt and International Financial Control: The Middle East and the Balkans, 1870–1914* (London: Palgrave Macmillan, 2015); Jamie Martin, *The Meddlers: Sovereignty, Empire, and the Birth of Global Economic Governance* (Cambridge, Mass.: Harvard University Press, 2022).

12. Hanley, *Identifying with Nationality*, 11–13; M. van den Boogert, *The Capitulations and the Ottoman Legal System: Qadis, Consuls and Beraths in the 18th Century* (Leiden: Brill, 2005), 1–15.

13. For other examples, see Michael Christopher Low, "Unfurling the Flag of Extraterritoriality: Autonomy, Foreign Muslims, and the Capitulations in the Ottoman Hijaz," *Journal of the Ottoman and Turkish Studies Association* 3, no. 2 (2016): 299–323; Hanley, *Identifying with Nationality*; Omar Cheta, *How Commerce Became Legal: Merchants and Market Governance in Nineteenth-Century Egypt* (Stanford: Stanford University Press, 2025); and Lilić Vladislav, "Empire of States: Law and International Order in Ottoman Europe, c. 1830–1912," PhD diss., Vanderbilt University, 2024, especially chapter on the Capitulations during the period of Serbian autonomy (1830s–1878).

14. Halil Inalcik, "İmtiyâzât," *TDV İslâm Ansiklopedisi*, vol. 22 (Ankara: Türkiye Diyanet Vakfı, 2000), 245–54; Edhem Eldem, "Capitulations and Western Trade: Western Trade in the Ottoman Empire," in *The Cambridge History of Turkey*, vol. 3, ed. Suraiya N. Faroqhi (Cambridge: Cambridge University Press, 2006); van den Boogert, *The Capitulations*; Fabiana Zarinebaf, *Mediterranean Encounters: Trade and Pluralism in Early Modern Galata* (Berkeley: University of California Press, 2018), chaps. 3–4; Natalie Rothman, *Brokering Empire: Trans-Imperial Subjects: Between Venice and Istanbul* (Ithaca: Cornell University Press, 2012); Rothman, *The Dragoman Renaissance: Diplomatic Interpreters and the Routes of Orientalism*, (Ithaca: Cornell University Press, 2021); Zülâl Muslu, "Language and Power: The Dragoman as a Link in the Chain Between the Law of Nations and the Ottoman Empire," *Journal of the History of International Law* 22, no. 1 (2020): 50–74; Feroz Ahmad, "Ottoman Perceptions of the Capitulations, 1800–1914," *Journal of Islamic Studies* 11, no. 1 (2000); Lâle Can and Michael Christopher Low, eds., *The Subjects of Ottoman International Law* (Bloomington: Indiana University Press, 2020); Umut Özsu, "Ottoman Empire," in *The Oxford Handbook of the History of International Law*, ed. Bardo Fassbender and Anne Peters (Oxford: Oxford University Press, 2012), 429–48.

15. Eldem, "Capitulations and Western Trade"; and Turan Kayaoğlu, *Legal Imperialism: Sovereignty and Extraterritoriality in Japan, the Ottoman Empire, and China* (Cambridge: Cambridge University Press, 2010). The original texts varied in length and contained a series of articles, or chapters—hence Capitulations—that dealt with issues of trade, piracy, slavery, and property.

16. See also Will Hanley, "When Did Egyptians Stop Being Ottomans? An Imperial Citizenship Case Study," in *Multilevel Citizenship*, ed. Willem Maas

(Philadelphia: University of Pennsylvania Press, 2013); Mary Dewhurst Lewis, "Geographies of Power: The Tunisian Civic Order, Jurisdictional Politics, and Imperial Rivalry in the Mediterranean, 1881–1935," *Journal of Modern History* 80, no. 4 (2008): 791–830.

17. It should be noted that apart from Hanley's book on the function of the consular courts in Egypt in the late nineteenth and early twentieth centuries, there is very little archivally grounded work on how the Capitulations operated on the ground in Istanbul or throughout the empire. We have glimpses of such cases across studies. While we know that the government tried assiduously to abrogate the Capitulations, and that many intellectuals and diplomats argued that they undermined the state, we do not yet have a monograph on the function of the Capitulations from the 1830s through the end of the First World War. One of the spectacular cases, the Joris case, covering the attempted assassination of Sultan Abdülhamid II by a protected foreigner, is one of the few that historians have covered in depth. Houssine Alloul, Edhem Eldem, and Henk de Smaele, eds., *To Kill a Sultan: A Transnational History of the Attempt on Abdülhamid II (1905)* (London: Palgrave Macmillan, 2017). Berna Kamay's dissertation, "Extradition in the Ottoman Empire: Legal Practice of the Nineteenth Century," Boğaziçi University, 2022, is a rare example of examining legal restrictions through practice.

18. Nobuyoshi Fujinami's brilliant article explains the connection between different forms of privilege. Fujinami, "Between Sovereignty and Suzerainty: History of the Ottoman Privileged Provinces," in *A World History of Suzerainty: A Modern History of East and West Asia and Translated Concepts*, ed. Takashi Okamoto (Tokyo: Toyo Bunko, 2019), 42–43; Oliver Bouquet, "Non-Muslim Ctizens as Foreigners Within: How 'Ecnebi' Became 'Yabanci' from the Ottoman Empire to the Turkish Republic," *Middle Eastern Studies* 53, no. 3 (May 2017): 486–99.

19. Among the states that obtained capitulatory privileges before the nineteenth century were the Genoese community of Galata, the Venetian Republic, France, England, and the Dutch Republic. Van den Boogert, *The Capitulations*, 7, notes that there was a massive uptick in the number of states and leaders that requested and received *ahdnames*—privileges from the sultan—including the Habsburg emperor, the king of Sweden, the Kingdom of the Two Sicilies, Tuscany, the king of Denmark, Prussia, Russia, and Spain. By the nineteenth century, nineteen states held capitulatory rights in the Ottoman Empire. In the early modern period, a relatively small number of merchants obtained these privileges form the sultan.

20. Paul Pradier-Fodéré, *Traité de droit international public européen et américain, suivant les progrès de la science et de la pratique contemporaine*, (Paris: G. Pédone-Lauriel, 1885–1906) 2:689–91.

21. Ottoman international lawyers working in the Office of Legal Consul frequently cited Pradier-Fodéré's works, especially his eight-volume *Traité de droit international*, which was one of the many works on European international law in the Foreign Ministry's law library. BOA, HR.HMŞ.IŞO 109/16 28 Mayıs 1327 (June 11, 1911).

22. "Bu kapitülasıyonların şekli ferman şeklindedir, yalınız bir taraf söyliyor. Ma'lumdur ki muahedelerde ta'ahhüd olunan şeyler iki kişini tarafından söylenilir. İki hümkümdar tarafından imza olunur. Halbuki bunda yalnız bir hükümdarı hikaye ediyor, yukarıdan aşağıya Fransa'nın şimdiye kadar aldığı kaptipolasyonlardan bahs olunuyor, 'ahd ediliyor, fakat buna karşı diğer taraf için bir şey söylenmiyor. Mesela Fransa'da biz ne mu'amele göreceğiz, ona dair hiç bir hüküm, yok! İşte kaptülasıyonların şekli böyledir. Diğer taraftan mukabilinde hiç bir şey aranmayan bir ta'ahüddür." İbrahim Hakkı Paşa, "Kapitülasyonlar," part 2, *İlm-i Hukuk* 14:1–12. Hakkı Paşa's argument that the early modern Capitulations were not treaties has been demonstrated in scholarship. Van den Boogert—who has examined the texts of the Capitulations alongside on-the-ground practices in the late eighteenth century—has shown that even in this late period, foreigners were not separate from the Ottoman legal system but were instead subject to it. Van den Boogert has also cast doubt on the degree to which the pre-nineteenth-century Capitulations should be seen as part of the framework of international law.

23. İbrahim Hakkı Paşa, "Kapitülasyonlar," part 3, *Ilm-i Hukuk,* 15:162. "Bundan sonra Ruslar için galibiyeti temin etmiş ve ikinci Katrinen zamanındaki (188) hicri ve (1774) miladı Kaynarca muahedesi cism-i devletde acı paralar açmış ve devlet için birçok mesail-i müessifeyi şamil olduğu halde vücud bulmuştur. Bu tarihe kadar Rusya tebaasının hiç bir imtiyazı yok idi. Bu muahid mucince Rusya tebası en ziyade nail müsaade millet muamelesi görecek, diğerlerinin imtiyazından istifade edecekdi. Keza Rus raiyet üzerine Rusya'nın hakk-ı himayesi tasdik olunuyordu."

24. Gabriel Noradounghian, *Recueil d'actes internationaux de l'Empire ottoman: Traités, conventions, arrangements, déclarations, protocoles, procès verbaux, firmans, berats, lettres patentes et autres documents relatifs au droit public extérieur de la Turquie*, 2, no. 25–26 (Paris: F. Pichon, 1897–1903): 79–86.

25. Lewis Hertslet, *Hertslet's Commercial Treaties* (London: Henry Butterworth, 1840), 5:506–35.

26. İbrahim Hakkı Paşa, "Kapitülasyonlar," İlm-i Hukuk, 15:167–68: "İngiltere müstemlekatından ayrılmış bizden yirmi bin kilometere mesafede yeni teessüs etmiş bir hükumet, devletin ne mecburiyetle böyle münasebetsiz bir muahedeyi akd ettdiğini akıllar tayinden aciz kalır. Bu muahede bugün yapılsa bir takım sebebler bulunabilir. Hal-i hazırda Amerika büyük bir devletdir. Büyük bir donanmaya malik, İspanya'yı mağlub etmiş. Müstemlekatı çok uzak yerde

olmağla daber hatırı sayılır bir devletdir. Fakat hin akd-i muahede de bu sebeblerin hiç yeri yok, hülasa bu muahede abes bir şeydir."

27. İbrahim Hakkı Paşa, *Ilm-i Hukuk*, 15: 169: "Vakia evvel emirde bu imtiyazatın virilmesi gayet tereddüdle vücududur olmuş ise de şurası unudulmamalıdır ki bu tereddüd imtiyazatın hukuk-i hakimiyeti tahdid etmekde bulunmasından dolayı değil mücerred falan düşmanımızdır ne için imtiyaz verelim; gelmesinler fikriyledir."

28. İbrahim Hakkı, *İlm-i Hukuk*, 15:167: "Mesela Çin, Japonya, Liberya, hükumetleri bizimle tesis münasebat etmek istiyorlar. Peka'la, gelsinler, hukuk-i düvel-i kava'idi dairesi dahilinde memleketimizde bulunsunlar her bir hususatda muhakem-i Osmaniyeye tabi olsunlar, bunun hilafında gelmesinler, onları davet edin mi var?"

29. Candan Badem, *The Ottoman Crimean War 1853–1856* (Leiden: Brill, 2010), 3.

30. Hertslet, *Map of Europe*, 2:1171–76.

31. İbrahim Hakkı Paşa, *İlm-i Hukuk*, part 4, 16:244.

32. İbrahim Hakkı, *İlm-i Hukuk*, 16:243."Bu muahedenin hududca tağyiratı mucib bazı ahkamı bulunmağla beraber devletimize müteallik bir iki fıkrası mühimdir. O zamana kadar Avrupa'da mevki'imiz Paris muahedesinden sonraki mevki' değil idi. Zamanımızda hukuk nokta-i nazarından Avrupalılar bir aile gibi birleşmişlerdir. Bu ailenin münasebatını tayin eden bazı kavaid-i umumiye vardır. Bunlar Avrupa ailesinden haric olanlara—mesela bugün bazı şark-ı hükumetlerine karşı—tatbik olunmaz o gibi hükumetler bu kavaid-i umumiyeden kısmen istifade ederler. O da insaniyete taalluk eden ahkamıdır. Bunlar aileden değildir diye tabi'i israsi idam olunmaz. Hiss-i insaniyet buna mani'dir. Fakat aileden haric kalan bir hükumeti Avrupalıların yekdiğerine karşı tatbik ettdikleri sair kavaidden istifade edemezler. Onlara denir ki: sizin çalınız, mevki'iniz, maiyet ve medeniyetiniz başkadır . . . Bu nokta-i nazardan o vakte kadar Devlet-i Aliye Avrupa ailesinden ve Avrupa devletlerince müesses olan kavaid-i umumiye ahkamından haric tutulurdu. Fakat Paris muahedesi böyle bir istisnaniyete nihayet vermiştir. O muahedede bir madde vardır ki—yedinci maddede Devlet-i Aliyenin tamamiyet-i mülkiye ve istiklaliyet-i aliyesi kifalet-i müştereke-i düveliye ile tasdik kılınmağla beraber Avrupa hukuk-i umumiyesinden hissedar ve hilka-i siyasiyesine dahil olmağa istihkaki—tasdik olunmuştur. Bu madde mucibince Devlet-i Aliye dahi Avrupa ailesine yani cemiyet-i düveliyeye dahil olan devletlerden madud olmuştur."

33. Johann Caspar Bluntschli, *Das moderne Völkerrecht der civilisirten Staten* (Nördlingen: Beck, 1872), 19. Mustafa Serdar Palabiyik argues that Ottoman lawyers were particularly invested in the works of Bluntschli, precisely because religion was not a barrier to civilization and inclusion in the international order. As Bluntschli himself argued, "The borders of Christendom are not the same

as the borders of international law." See Palabiyik, "International Law for Survival: Teaching International Law in the Late Ottoman Empire (1859–1922)," *Bulletin of the School of Oriental and African Studies*, University of London, 78, no. 2 (2015): 271–92; Gong, *Standard of "Civilization,"* 106–19; Hugh McKinnon Wood, "The Treaty of Paris and Turkey's Status in International Law," *American Journal of International Law* 37, no. 2 (April 1943): 262–74.

34. T. E. Hall, ed., *The European Concert in the Eastern Question: A Collection of Treaties and Other Public Acts* (Oxford: Clarendon Press, 1885), 241–59; Hakkı Paşa, *Ilm-i Hukuk*; Hariciye, *Muhadet Mecmuası*, 4:242–58; Noradounghian, *Recueil d'actes*, 3:70–79; Hertslet, *Map of Europe*, 4, no. 530: 2759–2810.

35. Özsu, "Ottoman Empire," 437–38. See Reform Edict of February 1856 (*ıslahat firmanı*) and the Treaty of Paris, Article IX, "Firman and Hatti-Sheriff," "The Treaty of Paris," in Edward Hertslet, *The Map of Europe by Treaty*, vol. 2, no. 263–64 (London, 1875), 1243–65; "Ottoman Reform Edict of 1856," Gregory Aristarchis Bey, *Législation ottomane, ou Recueil des lois, règlements, ordonnances, traités, capitulations et autres documents officiels de l'Empire ottoman*, vol. 1 (Istanbul: Nicolaïdes, 1873–1888), 31–32; Noradounghian, *Recueil d'actes*, 3:70–79; Hariciye Vekaleti, *Muahedet Mecmuası* ([Istanbul]: Hakikat Matbaası, 1294–1298 [1877–1881]), 4:242–58. Several Ottoman historians of international law have considered how the Treaty of Paris shaped Ottoman-European relations. See Umut Özsu and Thomas Skouteris, "International Legal Histories of the Ottoman Empire: An Introduction to a Symposium"; and articles in *Journal of the History of International Law/Revue d'histoire du droit international* 18 (2016), especially Berdal Aral, "An Inquiry Into the Turkish 'School' of International Law"; Will Hanley, "International Lawyers Without Public International Law: The Case of Late Ottoman Egypt." See also M. Palabıyık, "International Law for Survival: Teaching International Law in the Late Ottoman Empire (1859–1922)," *Bulletin of the School of Oriental and African Languages* 2 (2015); Samera Esmeir, "On Becoming Less of the World," *History of the Present* 1, no. 8 (2018).

36. Great Britain, *Protocols of Conferences held at Paris Relative to the General Treaty on Peace* (London: Foreign Office, 1856), 54. William Hall noted that "Turkey was then [1535] outside the pale of international law; but by the Treaty of Paris she was brought within it. On general principle the Capitulations should have been abrogated. . . . They have nevertheless been maintained." They were maintained and the Ottoman Empire's sovereignty had been attenuated by the fact that "her institutions were not in reasonable harmony with those of European countries." William Edward Hall, *A Treatise on International Law* (Oxford: Clarendon Press, 1909), 52.

37. Houchang E. Chehabi, and David Motadel, eds., *Unconquered States: Non-European Powers in the Imperial Age* (Oxford: Oxford University Press, 2024).

38. As the Nobuyoshi Fujinami has shown in "Between Sovereignty and Suzerainty," Ottoman commentators often bundled the Capitulations and the idea of autonomy together as part of the same broad problem.

39. See chapter 4.

40. For example, Meltem Toksöz, *Nomads, Migrants and Cotton in the Eastern Mediterranean: The Making of the Adana-Mersin Region* (Leiden: Brill, 2011); Nadir Özbek, "Policing the Countryside: Gendarmes of the Late 19th-Century Ottoman Empire (1876–1908)," *International Journal of Middle East Studies* 40, no. 1 (February 2008): 47–67. On Tanzimat of the sword in the Arabian Peninsula, see chapter 4.

41. "Girit vilayet nizamnamesi," *Düstur*, vol. 11289 (1872–73): 653–87; "Firman Imperial concernant la réorganisation de Crète" and "Règlement Organique," in Grégoire Aristarchi, *Législation ottomane, ou, Recueil des lois, réglements, ordonnances, traités, capitulations et autres documents officiels de l'Empire ottoman*, vol. 2 (Constantinople: Freres Nicolaïdes, 1873–1888), 169–203; Elektra Kostopoulou, "The 'Muslim Millet' of Autonomous Crete," PhD diss., Boğaziçi University, Istanbul, 2009); Uğur Zekeriya Peçe, Island and Empire: How Civil War in Crete Mobilized the Ottoman World (Stanford: Stanford University Press, 2024).

42. On the expulsion of Muslims, see Ayşe Özkan, "Kanlıca Konferansı Sonrasında Müslümanların Sırbistan'dan Çıkarılmaları ve Osmanlı Devleti'nin Sırbistan'dan Çekilişi (1862–1867)," *Gazi Akademik Bakıs Dergisi* 5, no. 9 (2011): 123–38; Lilić, "Empire of States," 52–57.

43. There were updates and additions in 1867 and 1873. For the reforms and reissue of the Provincial Law, see Hertslet, *Map of Europe*, 2, no. 458, "Turkish Reply to the Andrassy Note"; no. 459, "General Administration of the Vilayets," 2441–55; BOA, HR.SYS 250/4, "Büyük devletlerin Bosna'da bir muhtariyet tesisi projesi," 16 Rabiulahir 1293 (May 5, 1876); BOA, HR.TO 122/29 6 Şaban 1293 (August 8, 1876); BOA, HR.TO, 517/38 16 Ramazan 1293 (October 5, 1876); BOA, Y.A.HUS 526/77 "Bosna ve Hersek'e muhtariyet itası hakkında nesriyat," 18 Muharrem 1293 (February 14, 1876); BOA, Y.EE. 103/26 "Osmanlı askerinin harbler ve asilere karşı kazandığı galibiyet, kanun-ı cedidin faydaları, Düvel-i Muazzama'nın Hersek-Bosna-Bulgaristan'a muhtariyet verilmesini istediği, bunun yapılmaması durumunda Rusya tarafından bir harp açılması ihtimali olduğu, bunu önlemek için üç maddelik bir teklif yapıldığı," 11 Zilkade 1293 (November 28, 1876).

44. Hertslet, *Map of Europe*, 2, no. 472: 2516–17; BOA, HR.SYS. 250/4 "Projet de Règlement pour la Bosnie-Hercégovine."

45. Hertslet, *Map of Europe*, 4:2516; BOA, HR.SYS 250/4 Büyük devletlerin Bosna'da bir muhtariyet tesisi projesi; NA/FO/ 407/24. Derby also reiterated Britain's commitment to the protocols for the pacification of the Levant

regarding Mehmed Ali and Egyptian autonomy (1840), and the protocols for the pacification of Syria in reference to Mount Lebanon.

46. BOA, HR.TO 517/38; NAFO/ 407/24. In some cases, they claimed that Muslims were not interested in obtaining autonomy. In a letter sent to the grand vizier, one local claimed that autonomy would be absurd for Bosnia because the problem was that different Christan bands attacked each other.

47. These sessions in Istanbul started on December 11 and continued through January 20, 1877. The meeting was suspended January 25. The degree to which the ideas discussed in the sessions were carried on in 1878 at the Congress of Berlin is astonishing. For instance, there was much debate about breaking up Bulgaria into two provinces, which Britain supported, or creating a large Bulgarian principality, which the Russian delegation favored. The proceedings of the sessions were printed Noradounghian, *Recueil d'actes*, 3:400–494.

48. Noradounghian, *Recueil d'actes*, 3:448. BOA, HR.TO 517/38; NAFO424/37.

49. *Kanun-i Esasi* (Istanbul: Matbaa-i Amire, 1292/1876); Johann Strauss, "A Constitution for a Multilingual Empire: Translations of the *Kanun-i Esasi* and Other Official Texts Into Minority Languages," in *The First Ottoman Experiment in Democracy*, ed. Christoph Herzog and Malek Sharif (Würzburg: Ergon in Kommission, 2010).

50. BOA, HR.TO 517/38; BOA, YEE. 103/26.

51. Hertslet, *Map of Europe*, "Turkish Manifesto in Answer to Russian Declaration of War, Constantinople, 26 April 1877," 4:2601, doc. no. 495.

52. Muslim. Cem Behar, *Osmanlı İmparatorluğu'nun.*

53. Quoted in M. Şükrü Hanioğlu, *A Brief History of the Late Ottoman Empire* (Princeton: Princeton University Press, 2008), 118; NAFO424/37, Elliot to Derby, December 28, 1876; Noradounghian, *Recueil d'actes*, 3:509–21.

54. Milena Methodieva, *Between Empire and Nation: Muslim Reform in the Balkans* (Stanford: Stanford University Press, 2021).

55. *Muhadet Mecmuası*, 5:110–41; Noradounghian, *Recueil d'actes*, 4:175–92.

56. Hertslet, *Map of Europe*, 3:2516; Noradounghian, *Recuil d'actes*, 3: 522–25.

57. From Article 61: "The Sublime Porte undertakes to carry out, without further delay, the improvements and reforms demanded by local requirements in the provinces inhabited by the Armenians, and to guarantee their security against the Circassians and Kurds. It will periodically make known the steps taken to this effect, to the Powers, who will superintend their application." In Hertslet, *Map of Europe*, 4:2796; *Muhadet Mecmuası*, 5:139.

58. Abdülhamit II, *Siyasî Hatıratım* (Istanbul: Dergah Yayınları, 1987), 91–92. Local Kurdish tribal chiefs, from the Ottoman and Iranian sides of the border, banded together under the leadership of Sheikh Ubeydullah and rebelled against the state. They feared that Article 61 would give the territory over to Armenians. An already fraught situation grew increasingly tense. Janet Klein,

The Margins of Empire: Kurdish Militias in the Ottoman Tribal Zone (Stanford: Stanford University Press, 2011), 21.

59. Dufferin was also charged with overseeing problems related to the Greek-Ottoman Border Commission, but reforming the "Armenian provinces" consumed the bulk of his attention, as is evidenced by his private and political correspondence. Just before Dufferin's appointment to Istanbul, he served as British ambassador to Russia and there too worked on implementing the Treaty of Berlin. Consequently, when he arrived in Istanbul, he tackled the same problems, but in a different arena.

60. For discussions of Abdülhamid's handling of Ottoman foreign policy, see especially Engin Akarlı, "The Problems of External Pressures, Power Struggles, and Budgetary Deficits in Ottoman Politics Under Abdülhamid II (1876–1909)," PhD diss., Princeton University, 1976; and F.A.K. Yasamee, *Ottoman Diplomacy: Abdülhamid II and the Great Powers, 1878–1888* (Istanbul: Isis, 1996).

61. Klein, *The Margins of Empire*, 21.

62. Agatha Ramm, ed. *The Gladstone-Granville Correspondence* (New York: Cambridge University Press, 1998), no. 227: 139.

63. Ramm, no. 500: 278.

64. There were a number of ways to express the meaning of autonomy in Ottoman, including "muhtariyet" and "serbestiyet," but in exchanges with European ambassadors and in his various memoirs, Abdülhamid always used the French-derived "otonomie." See, for instance, Sultan İkinci Abdülhamid Han, ed. A. Atilla Çetin, *Devlet ve Memleket Görüşlerim* (Istanbul: Çamlıca, 2011), vol. 2, 40–47.

65. Between 1878 and 1882, the exact location and meaning of Armenia was in flux within British reform schemes. Just after the Congress of Berlin, reform efforts were focused more exclusively on the dispersed Christians of eastern Anatolia. The theory of European protection of Ottoman Christians clashed with the reality of a mixed population, and Dufferin started to redefine Armenia as a territory versus a people. For instance, in one of Lieutenant-Colonel Wilson's schemes based on the one forwarded to Dufferin for a "Constitution for the provinces inhabited by Armenians," Armenians were defined as the collection of Christian and Muslim religious communities inhabiting the area. NA/FO/424/123/No. 104, encl. 1, Wilson to Dufferin, August 11, 1881.

66. BOA, Y.PRK.TŞF. 1/46 30 Ramazan 1298 (August 26, 1881). Ottoman record of a conversation between Abdülhamid and Lord Dufferin.

67. BOA, Y.PRK.TŞF. 1/46: "Ermeniler ora halkın cümlesinden daha ziyade muameleye olmaktadır. Çünkü bunlar konsoluslar tarafından himayet görmektediler. Lakin mademki meydanda bir mesele varsa ve mademki Bab-ı Ali bu meselenin [halline] derude eylemişse binaenaleyh bir şeyi yapılmak lâzim gelür ve yapabilecek şeyi ise de otonomie tarikyle değildir. Bu 'otonomie'

kelimsinden asla hazz etmemen ve istemem ve zat-i şahanenin dahi otonomi-eye kabul buyulmamak hususunda hak-ı şahaninde musaddak ve aşkârdır."

68. BOA, Y.PRK.TŞF. 1/46. Abdülhamid II downplayed the significant uptick in communal violence. Recent work has analyzed that violence as resulting from state centralizing policing, including new methods of policing and capitalist encroachment. Mehmet Polatel, *Armenians and Land Disputes in the Ottoman Empire, 1850–1914* (Edinburgh: Edinburgh University Press, 2025); Zozan Pehlivan, *The Political Ecology of Violence: Peasants and Pastoralists in the Last Ottoman Century* (Cambridge: Cambridge University Press, 2024); Klein, *The Margins of Empire*.

69. BOA, Y.PRK.TŞF. 1/46. "Avrupaca ma'ruf bir zat."

70. Public Record Office of Northern Ireland (PRONI), D1071/H/L/1/1, Dufferin Papers, Dufferin to Granville, August 30, 1881.

71. BOA, Y.A.HUS. 169/43/1 23 Safer 1299 (January 14, 1882). Record of a meeting between Abdülhamid and Lord Dufferin prepared by (Salih) Münir: "esas-i idare dahi ya merkeziyet ya da mütevessi-yi idare usullerinden biri." Dufferin's version of this conversation is slightly different, and, though the meaning is not radically dissimilar to the Ottoman version, it may require further consideration. In other meetings with the sultan, Dufferin departed significantly at times from the dragoman record of court conversations. In this particular case, I have not seen the dragoman's translation, but in Dufferin's he indicated that it was Europe that was divided over which administrative framework was better, rather than the Ottoman Empire. See PRONI/D1071/H/L/1/1, Dufferin to Granville, January 17, 1882.

72. For recent work on "Ottoman Orientalism," see Ussama Makdisi, "Ottoman Orientalism," *American Historical Review* 107 (2002): 768–96; Selim Deringil, "They Live in a State of Nomadism and Savagery The Late Ottoman Empire and the Post-Colonial Debate," *Comparative Studies in Society and History* 45 (2003): 311–42; and Thomas Kuehn, *Empire, Islam, and Politics of Difference: Ottoman Rule in Yemen, 1849–1919* (Leiden: Brill, 2011).

73. Sultan Mahmud II (r. 1808–1839) is often considered the first of the reforming sultans. BOA, YA.HUS. 169/43, enclosure 1. "Fakat müşarileyh hazretleri bu usulü lağv ile kavanin-i cedide ve ıslahiyye vaz' te'sis buyurulmuşlar ve bilâhara defaalatlı dahi Tanzimat iyilenmiştir." *Derebeylik* is often translated in modern Turkish as feudalism, but it is better understood as a method of decentralized administration. The *derebeği*, literally "Lord of the valley," had an autonomous status within the Ottoman Empire not unlike that of Egypt. In contrast to Egypt, a derbeylik was not legally regulated by the public law of Europe. See Gabor Agoston, "A Flexible Empire: Authority and Its Limits on the Ottoman Frontiers," in *Ottoman Borderlands: Issues, Personalities and Political Changes*, ed. Kemal Karpat (Madison: University of Wisconsin Press, 2003).

74. Ekmeleddin İhsanoğlu, *Darülfünun: Osmanlı'da Kültürel Modernleşmenin Odağ ıi* (Istanbul: Research Centre for Islamic History, Art and Culture, 2010).

75. Antony Anghie, *Imperialism, Sovereignty, and the Making of International Law* (Cambridge: Cambridge University Press, 2005); Jennifer Pitts, "Empire and Legal Universalisms in the Eighteenth Century," *American Historical Review* 117, 1 (2012): 92–121, and *Boundaries of the International: Law and Empire* (Cambridge, Mass.: Harvard University Press, 2018); Mazower, *Governing the World*, chap. 3.

76. Kuneralp and Öktem list the ad hoc advisors as Émile Tarin, Louis Amiable, and Benjamin Édouard Cor, who were French. William Parnis was a British-Maltese subject, and the brothers Alfred and Karl Gescher were German. Sinan Kuneralp and Emre Öktem, eds., *Chambre des conseillers légistes de la Sublime Porte* (Istanbul: Isis Press, 2012), 10–12.

77. European lawyers who worked within the consular court system in the Ottoman Empire as well as the Mixed Courts in autonomous Egypt knew one another and often circulated between legal venues, as well as within the imperial court system of their respective empires. For instance, when the British arrested Colonel Ahmed 'Urabi in 1882, Wilfred Blunt tracked down and hired A. M. Broadley to defend him. Broadly had first worked as an assistant magistrate in India but later moved through the British Consular Court system and was defending the Bey of Tunis at the time of the 'Urabi Rebellion. He later acted as a legal advisor to the ex-khedive Ismail. There are numerable cases like this, especially of lawyers moving between consular courts in the Ottoman Empire and the Mixed Courts of Egypt. See A. M. Broadley and Frederick Villiers, *How We Defended Arabi and His Friends: A Story of Egypt and Egyptians* (London: Chapman and Hall, 1884).

78. *British Documents on Foreign Affairs*, part 1, series B, vol. 8, "The Ottoman Empire in North Africa: The Suez Canal, Red Sea, and Tunisian Problems, 1859–1882," doc. 231, p. 363.

79. For an excellent analysis of the Ottoman engagement with the Scramble for Africa, see Mostafa Minawi, *The Ottoman Scramble for Africa: Empire and Diplomacy in the Sahara and the Hijaz* (Stanford: Stanford University Press, 2016).

80. Carter Findley, *Bureaucratic Reform in the Ottoman Empire: The Sublime Porte, 1789–1922* (Princeton: Princeton University Press, 1980), 260.

81. Selim Deringil, *The Well-Protected Domains: Ideology and the Legitimation of Power in the Ottoman Empire, 1876–1909* (New York: Tauris, 1998); Thomas Kuehn, *Empire, Islam, and Politics of Difference: Ottoman Rule in Yemen, 1849–1919* (Leiden: Brill, 2011); Benjamin Fortna, *Imperial Classroom: Islam, State and Education in the Late Ottoman Empire* (Oxford: Oxford University Press, 2002); Engin Akarlı, "The Problems of External Pressures, Power Struggles, and

Budgetary Deficits in Ottoman Politics Under Abdülhamid II, 1876–1909," PhD diss., Princeton University, 1976.

82. Bab-ı Ali Hariciye Nezareti, *Salname-i Nezaret-i Hariciye*, 1:252–53. Carter Findley also dates the establishment of the office to 1882 or 1883. BOA, DH.SAID. 2/510, "Kişer"; BOA, HR.SAID 4/12 29 Cemazeyilevvel 1313 (November 17, 1895).

83. This practice was not abandoned during World War I. Throughout the entirety of the war into the early 1920s, the chief legal advisor at the İstişare Odası was Armenian, Hrant Abro Bey.

84. For instance, during the same period when there were three legal advisors, the Office of Legal Council had nearly fifty *muavin* listed on the books. Sinan Kuneralp notes that these figures were inflated and instead that the number of staff hovered around eight assistants. In any case, by the period leading up to World War I, the Hamidian era numbers dropped to about eight *muavin*, which is still a significant number of staff for the office and tells us something of its importance. See Kuneralp, *Chambre des conseillers*, 10–12; Bab-ı Ali Hariciye Nezareti, *Salname-i Nezaret-i Hariciye* (1320/1902), 220–22.

85. This observation is borne out through an examination of employment register (*sicil-i ahval*) as well as documents detailing the inner workings of the Office of Legal Counsel.

86. İhsanoğlu, *Darülfünun*; Murteza Bedir, "Fikh to Law: Secularization Through Curriculum," *Islamic Law and Society*, 11, 3 (2004): 378–401.

87. Raymond H. Kévorkian, "Gabriel Noradounghian (1852–1936): Extraits des memoires recuillies par Aram Andonian," *Revue d'histoire arménienne contemporaine*, vol. 1 (1995). The manuscript of Noradounghian's memoirs has never been located. His private secretary, Aram Andonian, recorded fragments of the text, which are now housed in the Nubar Library and Archive in Paris.

88. BOA, DH.SAİD 81/238, "Noradunkyan, Gabriel." See also Y. G. Çark, *Türk Devlet Hizmetinde Ermeniler, 1453–1953* (Istanbul: Yeni Matbaa, 1953). Noradounghian was elected to the Institut de Droit International in 1922. Peter Macalister-Smith, "Bio-Bibliographical Key to the Membership of the Institut de Droit International, 1873–2001," *Journal of the History of International Law* 5 (2003): 77–159.

89. Kuneralp notes that the brothers Alfred and Carl Gescher both worked as legal advisors, but that it is not clear which legal opinions where authored by which brother as they never used their first names. Moreover, Alfred appears to have been appointed as the German representative on the Ottoman Public Debt Administration. I have found far more evidence linking Carl Gescher to Office of Legal Counsel than Alfred. See Kuneralp, *Chambre des conseillers*, 11.

90. Carl Gescher, "Egypten," *Jahrbuch der Internationalen Vereinigung für vergleichende Rechtswissenschaft und Volkswirtschaftslehre zu Berlin Jahrbuch der Internationalen*, vol. 8 (1904): 1489–1505.

91. R. H. Kévorkian, *Revue d'histoire arménienne*, 16.

92. BOA, I.HR. 354/23, "Bab-ı Ali hukuk müşavirliği'ne mabeyn mütercimlerinden Hakkı Bey'in tayini," 8 Şubat 1312 (February 4, 1895); M. K. İnal, *Osmanlı Devrinde son Sadriazamlar* (Istanbul: Milli Eğitim Basımevi, 1965), 3:1763–1804; Ali Çankaya, *Mülkiye Tarihi ve Mülkiyeliler* (Ankara 1954), 54–58; F. Ahmad, "Ibrāhīm Ḥaḳḳī Pasha," *Encyclopaedia of Islam, Second Edition* (Brill Online, 2013).

93. Lâle Can, Spiritual Subjects: Central Asian Pilgrims and the Ottoman Hajj at the End of Empire (Stanford: Stanford University Press, 2020), chap. 2; Low, *Imperial Mecca*; Hanley, *Identifying with Nationality*.

94. İbrahim Hakkı Paşa's chief international law works include *Tarih-i Hukuk-i Beyn'ed-düvel* (Istanbul: Karabet ve Kasbar, 1303 [1885–1886]); *Medhal-ı Hukuk-i Beyn'ed-düvel* (Istanbul: Karabet ve Kasbar, 1303 [1885–1886]); *Hukuk-i düvel* (Darülhilfe: Matbaa ve Kütübhane-yi Cihan, 1327 [1911]); Muhammed Tatlısu, "Kitapçı Karabet Efendi'nin Osmanlı Matbuatına Katkıları Üzerine Bir Methal," *YILLIK: Annual of Istanbul Studies* 3(2021): 123–48. I am grateful to Muhammad Tatlısu for sharing the Karabet catalog with me, which showcases İbrahim Hakkı's works on law and Islam. *Karabet Kitabhânesi Esâmî-i Kütübü (Birinci Defter)* (Istanbul: Karabet Matbaası, 1308 [1891]), 8–9, 17–18.

95. Noradounghian, *Recueil d'actes*, vol. 1, preface.

96. Feodor Martens for Russia, M. de Clercq for France, Neumann for the Habsburg Empire, and Hertslet's collection for the UK.

97. Noradounghian, *Recueil d'actes*, vol. 1, preface.

98. İbrahim Hakkı Paşa, *Tarih-i Beyneddüvel*, 1:29.

99. For example, İbrahim Hakkı Paşa, *Tarih-i Hukuk-i Beyned-düvel*, 29. On the Islamic Law of Nations, see Majid Khadduri, *The Islamic Law of Nations: Shaybani's Siyar* (Baltimore: Johns Hopkins University Press, 2002).

100. Mustafa Serdar Palabıyık, "International Law for Survival: Teaching International Law in the Late Ottoman Empire (1859–1922)," *Bulletin of the School of Oriental and African Languages* 78, no. 2 (2015), 271–91; Berdal Aral, "The Ottoman 'School' of International Law as Featured in Its Textbooks," *Journal of the History of International Law/Revue d'histoire du droit international*, vol. 18 (2016).

101. "Menafinden hissedar-ı menfaat olmak üzere Avrupa heyet-i düvelisi miyanına duhulü ve saltanat-i seniye'ye ait her bir taaruz ve tecavüz bad'ema menfi-yi umumiyece haiz-i ehemmiyet add olunması." İbrahim Hakkı Paşa, *Tarih-i Hukuk-i Beyneddüvel*, 187.

102. İbrahim Hakkı Paşa, *Medhal-i Hukuk-i Beyndüvel*, "The Concept of Permanent Peace," part 3.

103. İbrahim Hakkı (Paşa), *Mukaddime-i İlm-i Hukuk* (Istanbul: Karabet, 1319/1902), 34–35.

104. Ottoman Archives, Istanbul, Başbakanlık Osmanlı Arşivleri (BOA), HR .BOA, HMŞ.IŞO 109/13. Aimee Genell, "The Well-defended Domains: Eurocentric International Law and the Making of the Ottoman Office of Legal Counsel," *Journal of Ottoman and Turkish Studies*, 3, 2 (Nov. 2016): 255–75.

105. BOA, HR.HMŞ.IŞO 167/27. The lawyers rejected Tunis's accession to the International Telegraph Convention, because like Egypt, India, and Canada, it had no "political character."

106. BOA, HR.HMŞ.IŞO 52/23 ; BOA, HR.HMŞ.IŞO 52/1. The lawyers attempted to align Egyptian and Ottoman legal jurisdiction and customs.

107. BOA, HR.HMŞ.IŞO 52/21; BOA, HR.HMŞ.IŞO 175/6; BOA, HR.HMŞ. IŞO 52/22; BOA, HR.HMŞ.IŞO 169/28.

108. BOA, HR.HMŞ.IŞO 56/16.

109. BOA, HR.HMŞ.IŞO 174/7. HR.HMŞ.IŞO 218/35 3 HR.HMŞ.IŞO 52/20 8 Nisan 1328 (1904).

110. BOA, HR.HMŞ.IŞO BOA, HR.HMŞ.IŞO 52/20.

111. BOA, HR.HMŞ.IŞO 94/20.

112. *Düstur*, vol .1, "Vilayet Nizamnamesi" (1864), 517–78; *Takvim-i Vekayi*, no. 773; Grégoire Aristarchi Bey, *Législation ottomane*, 2:273.

113. Selim Deringil, *The Well-Protected Domains: Ideology and the Legitimation of Power in the Ottoman Empire, 1876–1909* (London: Tauris, 1999).

114. Devlet-i Aliye, *Salname-yi Devlet-i Aliye-yi Osmaniye* (İstanbul: Matbaa-yı Amire, 1847); Devlet-i Aliye, *Salname-yi Devlet-i Aliye-yi Osmaniye* (İstanbul: Matbaa-yı Amire, 1864); Devlet-i Aliye, *Salname-yi Devlet-i Aliye-yi Osmaniye* (İstanbul: Matbaa-yı Amire, 1881).

115. Aristarchi Bey, *Législation ottomane.*

116. Strauss, "A Constitution for a Multilingual Empire," 27–28.

117. Aristarchi Bey, *Législation ottomane*, vol. 1, xvi–xvii.

118. "Birinci madde: Devlet-i Osmaniye memalik ve kıtaat-ı hazırayı ve eyalet-i mümtaze-yi muhtevi ve yekvücud olmakla hiç bir zamanda hiç bir sebebile tefrik kabul etmez." *Kanun-i Esasi* (Istanbul: Matbaa-i Amire, 1292/1876). As mentioned, the expression "eyalet-i mümtaze" was translated as "autonomous province" (τὰς προνομιούχους Ἐπαρχίας) in the official Greek version of the First Ottoman Constitution of 1876, and as *al-iyalat al-mumtaza* in the Arabic edition. Stanford University, Hoover Institution Archives, Hidayet Dağdeviren Collection, Box 22/9, *Tarjamat al-khatt al-sharif al-sultani wal-qanun al-asasi* (Istanbul: Al-Jawa'ib Press, 1293/1876); Θωμανικόν Σύνταγμα Ανακηρυχθέν τη 7 Ζιλχιτζέ 1293 (11/23 Δεκέμβριος 1876). Johann Strauss, in "A Constitution for a Multilingual Empire," has examined the

1876 Constitution across the empire's languages and shown meaningful differences between languages.

119. "Ve eyalet-i mümtazenin serait-i imtiyaziyelerine tevfikan icra-yi tevcihat," *Kanun-i Esasi*, article 7.

120. Hanioğlu, *Short History*, chap. 5; Aylin Koçunyan, *Negotiating the Ottoman Constitution, 1839–1876* (Louvain: Peeters, 2018); Robert Devereux, *The First Ottoman Constitutional Period: A Study of the Midhat Constitution and Parliament* (Baltimore: Johns Hopkins Press, 1963).

121. The longest-serving director of the office noted that it was established in 1297 (1879/1880), and historians have found records bearing the name of the Office from the late 1870s. Bab-ı Ali Hariciye Nezareti, *Salname-i Nezaret-i Hariciye*, 1:252–53; 1881; İnal, "Kendime dair." Eşrefoğlu, "Mümtaze Kalemi," 192, has located Bulgarian documents titled with a handwritten title, "Vilayat-ı Mümtaze ve Muhtare Kalemi," dated 1879 and 1880.

122. İbnülemin Mahmut Kemal İnal, "Kendime dair" *Son Asır Türk Şairleri* (İstanbul: Millu Eğitim Basımevi, 1970), vol. 4 (Ş–Z): 2155; Quoted in Findley, *Bureaucratic Reform*. On İbnülemin Mahmud Kemal İnal, see Syed Tanvir Wasti, "İbnülemin Mahmud Kemal İnal—the Epitome of Late Ottoman Culture," *Middle Eastern Studies* 58, no. 1 (2022): 19–31; Dursun Gürlek, *İbnülemin Mahmud Kemal İnal: Cumhuriyet Devrinde Bir Osmanlı Efendisi*, vol. 1 (Istanbul: Kubbealtı, 2017); Hüseyin Vassaf, *Bir Eski Zaman Efendisi İbnülemin Mahmut Kemal Kemâlü'l-Kemâl* (Istanbul: Dergâh Yayınları, 2012); "İbnülemin Mahmud Kemal," *TDV İslam Ansiklopedisi* (Ankara: Türkiye Diyanet Vakfı, 2000), 21: 249. BOA, BEO, 16/1164, "Vilayet-i Mümtaze Kalemi hulefasından Mahmud Kemal Bey'in telif ettigi Say-ı Beser adlı risalenin incelenerek tabına müsaade olunması. (Maarif)."

123. The exceptions are all Turkish legal and archival historians: Eşrefoğlu "Mümtaze Kalemi"; Ekinci, "Osmanlı İdaresinde"; Ceylan, *Osmanlı Taşra İdarî*.

124. In addition to explaining how to read documents from this office, Eşrefoğlu offers an exceptionally detailed explanation of how the office functioned on a bureaucratic level. E. Eşrefoğlu, "Mümtaze Kalemi ve Bulgaristan Belgeleri," *Güneydoğu Avrupa Araştırmaları Dergisi* (1978). The first mention of the Office of Privileged Provinces appeared in the imperial yearbook, or *salmane*, of 1881; *Salname* 1881; İnal, "Kendime dair"; Ayhan Ceylan, *Osmanlı Taşra İdarî Tarzı Olarak Eyâlet-i Mümtâze ve Mısır Uygulaması* (Istanbul: Kitabevi, 2014); Ekrem Buğra Ekinci, "Osmanlı İdaresinde Adem-i Merkeziyet ve İmtiyazlı Eyâletler," *Türk Hukuk Tarihi Araştırmaları* 6 (2008): 47–49.

125. "Evrak Odası'ndaki Eyaleti Mümtaze ve Muhtariye'ye ait tezkereler." A.MTZ.(05) 37/25 (15 R. 1337); BOA, DH.D 187/1 9 Rabiulevvel 1332 (February 5, 1915).

126. BOA, İ.MTZ (05) "Mehmed Ali Paşa'nın mısır Valiliğ ı görevine tayinden itbaren Mısır vilayeti eski hidivler ile yeni hidive verilen imtiyazlara ve diğer hususlara dair gönderilen bütün hatt-ı hümayyun ve emr-ialilerin birer suretunun çikarılarak arz ve takdimi fermanına dair." 7 Zilkade 1298 (November 1, 1881).

127. See chapter 1. Broadly, this official was an Istanbul-based representative of any provincial governor. The agent not only represented provincial interests at the Sublime Porte but also provided vital information for provincial governors. Mehmet Canatar, "Kethüda," in *İslâm Ansiklopedisi* (Istanbul: Türkiye Diyanet Vakfı, 1998–2016), vol. 25, 332–224; Findley, *Bureaucratic Reform*, 180–81, 195.

128. BOA, Y.A.HUS. 202 "Hidiv Ismail Pasa'nın Mısır ıslahatına dair tanzim ettigi layıha suretinin Londra veya Paris Sefaretleri marifetiyle istihsali"; BOA, İ.MTZ (05) 19 Zilhicce 1298 (December 12, 1881); İ.MTZ (05) 22/105; İ.MTZ (05) 22/1009; İ.MTZ (05) 22/1015; İ.MTZ (05); 23/1087; İ.MTZ (05), "Mısır'da çikan olayların zor kullanılmaden önlenmesi padışahı memnun ettiğ ınden padışahın memnun oldüğ ü hususunda Mısır hidiviyeti'ne çekilecek telegrafnameye dair," 19 Zilhicce 1298 (December 12, 1881).

129. Genell, "Autonomous Provinces," 540.

130. Fedor Martens, *Traité de droit international, Chevalier-Marescq.* (Paris, 1883–1887), 331: "Certain parts of these immediate possessions are subject to an exceptional regime that stems either from privileges granted to them ab antiquo by the Porte (the Mount Athos peninsula and the vilayets of Hedjâz and Tripoli), or from agreements concluded with the Powers (the three vilayets of Macedonia), or finally from a certain reluctance to assert its authority there. In this latter regard, we must mention Upper Albania and a large part of Kurdistan, Mesopotamia, and Arabia, regions whose mainly Muslim and nomadic populations recognize no law other than their traditions." A. Heidborn, *Manuel de droit public et administratif de l'Empire ottoman par* (Vienna: C. W. Stern, 1909–1912), 154.

131. İbrahim Hakkı Paşa, *Hukuk-i İdare* (Dersaadet: Karabet Matbuasim 1307 (1891), 3–15.

132. Hakkı Paşa, *Hukuk-i İdare*, 55.

133. Hakkı Paşa, *Hukuk-i İdare*, 121.

134. See chapter 1. It should be noted that in the early period of expansion, the empire often retained local rulers in exchange for a tribute and soldiers, which Colin Imber has pointed out was always less secure than annexing a territory outright. Imber, *The Ottoman Empire* (London: Palgrave, 2009), 167; Gábor Agoston, "A Flexible Empire: Authority and Its Limits on the Ottoman Frontiers," in *Ottoman Borderlands: Issues, Personalities and Political Changes*, ed. K. Karpat (Madison: University of Wisconsin Press, 2003),

16–17; İnalcik, *An Economic and Social History*, 84–88; Ekinci, "Osmanlı İdaresinde," 30.

135. *İlm-i Hukuk*; Babanzade, *Hukuk-i Esasiye* (Istanbul: Erguvani, 2014).

136. Parties and papers represented all the major languages of the empire, including Ottoman Turkish, Greek, Armenian, Ladino, and Arabic. Some of the newspapers operated in exile in Cairo, Geneva, and Paris before the 1908 Revolution. Tarık Zafer, *Tunaya, Türkiye'de Siyasal Partiler* (Istanbul: Hürriyet Vakfı Yayınları, 1984), vol. 1.

137. Among the graduates of the Law Faculty (*Hukuk-i Mektub*) who went on to have careers in journalism and politics were Krikor Zohrab, Shukri al-Asali, İsmail Kemal Bey, Celal Nuri, Ahmed Emin (Yalman), Yunus Nadi (Abalıoğlu), David Ben-Gurion, and Yitzhak Ben-Zvi.

138. *İlm-i Hukuk ve Mukayese-i Kavanin Mecmuası* (İstanbul: Hilal Matbaası, 1909–1910).

3. Ottoman Sovereignty in Egypt

1. National Archives (hereafter NA), Granville to Dufferin, July 11, 1882. The assault would unleash one of the longest military occupations in modern Middle Eastern history. Britain's permanent military occupation of Egypt has been surpassed only by Israel's occupation of Gaza, the West Bank, and the Golan Heights.

2. Charles Stubbs, *The Rights and Duties of Suzerain and Vassal States* (London: Pewtress, 1882); Sir Robert Phillimore, *Commentaries Upon International Law* (Philadelphia: T. & J. W. Johnson, 1854–1857), 113–14.

3. John Westlake, *International Law* (Cambridge: Cambridge University Press, 1904), 26–27.

4. For example, M. F. Martens, "La question Égyptian et le droit international," *Révue de droit international et de législation comparée* 14 (1882): 355–401; Frederick Edwin Smith, *International Law* (London: Dent, 1911), 29; Aimee M. Genell, "Autonomous Provinces and the Problem of 'Semi-Sovereignty' in European International Law," *Journal of Balkan and Near Eastern Studies* 18, no. 6 (2016): 533–49.

5. Such texts started to proliferate in the 1880s, coincident with the British occupation of Egypt, and continued unabated through the 1920s. Alfred Milner, *England in Egypt* (London: Arnold, 1894); Wilfrid Scawen Blunt, *The Future of Islam* (London: Kegan Paul, 1882); Valentine Chirol, "Pan-Islamism," in *Proceedings of the Central Asian Society* (London: Central Asian Society, 1906); Chirol, *The Egyptian Problem* (London: Macmillan, 1920); Evelyn Baring Cromer, *Modern Egypt* (New York: Macmillan, 1916).

6. Orhan Pamuk, *A Monetary History*, 16; Fleisher, *Bureaucrat and Intellectual*, 279–83; Oğuz Tekin, "Sikke," *TDV İslâm Ansiklopedisi İstanbul*, vol. 37 (Istanbul: TDV İslâm Araştırmaları Merkezi, 2009), 179–84.
7. Milner, *England in Egypt*; Historical accounts of late Ottoman and British-occupied Egypt have been dominated by nationalist concerns and have projected the nation-state backward in time. Ottoman historians, especially Khaled Fahmy, Jane Hathaway, and Ehud Tolendo, have sought to redress these arguments by putting Egypt back in the Ottoman context. Khaled Fahmy, *All the Pasha's Men: Mehmed Ali, His Army and the Making of Modern Egypt* (Cairo: AUC Press, 2002); Jane Hathaway, *The Politics of Households in Ottoman Egypt: The Rise of Qazdağlıs* (Cambridge: Cambridge University Press, 1997); Ehud Toledano, *State and Society in Mid-Nineteenth Century Egypt* (Cambridge: Cambridge University Press, 1990); Mikhail, *Nature and Empire.*
8. For example, PCIJ ser A/B, "Lightouses in Crete and Samos," no. 71, 103; Giovanni Distefano, "The Pertinacious Sovereignty: Traditional Territorial Regimes," in *Statehood, Territory, and International Spaces* (Leiden: Brill, 2024).
9. Comparing the Habsburg occupation of Bosnia-Herzegovina (1878–1908) to the British occupation of Egypt is especially productive. While correspondence and issues related to Bosnia would be transferred to the Ottoman Office of Privileged Provinces and Bosnia itself recategorized by the Foreign Ministry as autonomous, the Habsburg occupation was not nearly as constrained as the British were in Egypt. Greble, *Muslims and the Making of the Modern Europe*; Leyla Amzi-Erdoğdular, *The Afterlife of Ottoman Europe: Muslims in Habsburg Bosnia Herzegovina* (Stanford: Stanford University Press, 2024); Jared Manasek, "Empire Displaced: Ottoman-Habsburg Forced Migration and the Near Eastern Crisis, 1875–1878," PhD diss., Columbia University, 2013.
10. See Will Hanley, *Identifying with Nationality: Europeans, Ottomans, and Egyptians in Alexandria, Columbia Studies in International Global History* (New York: Columbia University Press, 2017); Léon Lamouche, *L'organisation militaire de l'Empire Ottoman* (Paris: Librairie militaire de L. Baudoin, 1895).
11. "Khedive" is an older Persian title for "lord" or "prince" versus sultan, which is from the Arabic root *sulta*, meaning power or authority. Sultan has the meaning in Arabic of ruler or bearer of power/authority. Nubar Paşa negotiated the title "khedive" on behalf of 'Ismail in Istanbul in 1867. The ferman changed 'Ismail's title from governor (*vali*) to prince. The same ferman also changed the rules of succession to primogeniture—this is the ferman, then, that barred Said Halim Paşa, the grand vizier at the outbreak of the war, from assuming the khedivate. See Government of Egypt, *Recueil de firmans impériaux ottomans addresses aux valis et aux khedives d'Égypte* (Cairo: L'institut Français d'archéologie orientale du Caire, 1934), p. 301, no. 936, 5 Sefer 1284 [8 June 1867]. See also Gabriel Noradounghian, *Recueil d'actes internationaux de*

l'Empire Ottoman (Paris: F. Pichon, 1897–1903), 3:261; Edward Dicey, *The Story of the Khedivate* (London: Rivingtons, 1902); P. J. Vatikiotis, "Khidīw," in *Encyclopaedia of Islam, Second Edition* (Brill Online, 2013).

12. [1882 C.3230] Egypt No. 5 (1882), correspondence respecting the affairs of Egypt, Granville to Malet, January 6, 1882, 45; Sinan Kuneralp, *Ottoman Diplomatic Documents on "the Eastern Question": Egypt from Ismail Pasha's abdication to Hasan Fehmi Pasha's mission to London, 1879–1885*, no. 121, Asim Paşa to Esad (Paris) and Musurus Paşa (London), January 13, 1882 (Istanbul: Isis, 2011), 91–92.
13. BOA, Y.PRK.M, 1/59. "Fransa ve İngiltere devletleri diyar-ı Mısriyye üzerine istila için fevkalade çalışmakta ve devlet-i aliye'ye celb-i mazarrat etmek bahisinde himemat-i kamilelerini sarf ederek ümmet-i islamiyyenin cemiyetini tefrik ve tahrik edebilmeceğe aktar-ı Arab ve Acemde bezl-i nakdine-yi cehd ve iktidar ile ellerinden geldiği kadar ikad-i şerare-i fesadı irtikab eylemektedirler. . . . Bu layiha ile bizim devlet-i aliye'den ayrılmaklığımızı ve fi ma ba'd bu iki devlete tabii Olmaklığımızı ilan ederler."
14. Kuneralp, *Ottoman Diplomatic Documents*, 85–121; BOA, İMTZ(05), 22/989.
15. Kuneralp, *Ottoman Diplomatic Documents*, no. 131, Şakir to Asim Paşa, January 16, 1882, 97.
16. NA, /FO/407/19, Egypt, Thornton to Granville, February 7, 1882.
17. House of Commons, 1882, vol. 226, c. 637, February 14, 1882.
18. NA/FO/407/19. Egypt. Tenterden to Granville, February 8, 1882.
19. NA/WO/33/40. Secretary of State for War, A. Alison to B. Seymour, July 16, 1882.
20. NA/CAB/37. General Mediterranean Telegrams, August 21, 1882, to Adm. Seymour, Port Said.
21. Kuneralp, *Ottoman Diplomatic Documents*, no. 484, Musurus to Said, July 30, 1882, 284.
22. BOA, YEE, 116/2/enclosure 2. "Bu babdaki harekatın serapa fuzüliliktir. Mısır kıt'ası ecza-yı Memalik-i Osmaniye'dendir. Zat-ı şahanemden başka ferd-i vahidin ani muhafazaya dahil yoktur ve kit'a-i mezkurede mütevattan olanların cümlesine gerek şer'an ve gerek örfen taht-ı itaat-ı Padişahenmde olması vacibdir."
23. NA/CAB 37/9/83, W. E. Gladstone, September 18, 1882.
24. House of Commons, Cmd. 3529. Egypt. No. 6 (1883), "Further Correspondence Respecting Reorganization in Egypt," Dufferin to Granville, February 6, 1883.
25. Public Record Office of Northern Ireland (PRONI)/D10171/H/L/1/4, Granville to Dufferin, September 15, 1882.
26. BOA, Y.A.HUS, 171/127. 23 Zilhicce 1299 (November 5, 1882)
27. PRONI/D10171/H/L/1/4/203. Granville to Dufferin, November 3, 1882.
28. BOA, Y.E.E., 128/131, ". . . çakerleridemedenki hak-i pay-i şahaneye sidk-i ubudiyeti berkemal olup hukuk-i sultanat-ı seniye-ye mufazayle beraber Mısır içine bir esas-ı ıslahat-ı vaz etmeye çalışmaktır."

29. BOA, Y.EE, 4/59, reproduced in Sultan İkinci Abdülhamid Han, Devlet ve Memleket Görüşlerim, ed. A. Atilla Çetin (İstanbul: Çamlıca, 2011), 2:241. Chris Low reproduces the text more fully and shows that the report's author, Ahmed Midhat Efendi, connected autonomy schemes to British plots to transfer the caliphate to Egypt. Michael Christoher Low, *Imperial Mecca: Ottoman Arabia and the Indian Ocean Hajj* (New York: Columbia University Press, 2020), 85.

30. Mahmud Muhtar, Ahmed's son, appears to have originated the idea that Ahmed was in exile. See *Evénements d'Orient* (Paris: R. Chapelot, 1908); also Rifat Uçarol, *Bir Osmanlı Paşası ve Dönemi: Gazi Ahmet Muhtar Paşa (askerî ve siyasî hayatı)* (Istanbul: Milliyet Yayınları, 1976). More recently, Maurus Reinkowski has recapitulated the idea that Ahmed Muhtar Paşa was in an "honorary exile" and at best a symbol of Ottoman "suzerainty." See Reinkowski, "Hapless Imperialists and Resentful Nationalists: Trajectories of Radicalization in the Late Ottoman Empire," in *Helpless Imperialists: Imperial Failure, Fear and Radicalization* (Göttingen: Vandenhoeck & Ruprecht, 2012).

31. Oded Peri has written about the Ottoman presence in occupied Egypt in symbolic terms. In an article largely about Gazi Ahmet Muhtar Paşa, Abdülhamid's Ottoman high commissioner in Egypt from 1885 to 1908, he argued that things such as the sultan's seal *(tuğra)* on coinage struck in Egypt, the Ottoman flag, saying Friday prayers in the name of the sultan, or the presence of the Ottoman high commissioner in Cairo had symbolic value in Egypt and represented the legitimacy of the sultan. Peri, "Ottoman Symbolism in British-Occupied Egypt, 1882–1909," *Middle Eastern Studies* 41, no. 1 (January 2005): 103–20; Selim Deringil, "Gazi Ahmed Mukhtar Pasha and the British Occupation of Egypt," *Al-Abhath*, vol. 34 (1986). Süleyman Kızıltoprak has argued that Egypt was indeed extremely important to the Ottoman state, in *Mısır'da İngiliz İşgalı: Osmanlı'nın Diplomasi Savaşı (1882–1887)* (Istanbul: Tarih Vakfı Yayınları, 2010).

32. Feroz Ahmad's biographical sketch in the *Encyclopedia of Islam* and İnal's biographical entry in *Son Sadriazamlar* are largely taken from Ahmed Muhtar Paşa's *Sicil-i Ahval* record. It is worth pointing out because neither İnal nor Ahmad dwells much on Muhtar Paşa's time in Egypt. BOA, DH.SAID. 22/91.

33. Meltem Toksöz, *Nomads, Migrants and Cotton in the Eastern Mediterranean: The Making of the Adana-Mersin Region* (Leiden: Brill, 2011); Yonca Köksal, "Coercion and Mediation: Centralization and Sedentarization of Tribes in the Ottoman Empire," *Middle Eastern Studies*. 42, no. 3 (May 2006): 469–91; Andrew Gould, "Lords or Bandits: The Derebeys of Cilicia," *International Journal of Middle East Studies* 7 (1976); Nadir Özbek, "Policing the Countryside: Gendarmes of the Late 19th-Century Ottoman Empire (1876–1908)," *International Journal of Middle East Studies* 40, no. 1 (February 2008): 47–67.

34. Thomas Kuehn argues that there were clear limits to Muhtar Paşa's centralizing impulses in Yemen. He notes that Muhtar Paşa was instructed by Istanbul to take local opinions into consideration and to place various limitations on direct control from the imperial center. Kuehn, *Empire, Islam, and Politics of Difference* (Leiden: Brill, 2011), 43 and chaps. 2–3.

35. BOA, Y.EE., 147/57; BOA, A)MKT.MHM.485/79 (Monastir); BOA, Y.EE., 42/240 (Kozan); BOA, Y.EE, 76/58, "Gazi Ahmed Muhtar Pasa'dan Mabeyne gelen telgrafta Hıstiyanların düsman tarafına kaymaları sebebiyle Erzurum'un örf-i askeri altına alınmasına dair"; BOA, A.MKT.MHM.485/79 7 Safer 1297 (January, 15, 1880). BOA, A.MKT.MHM.485/90, "Arnavutlar'ın ıslah ve idareleri hakkında Manastır Valisi Ahmed Muhtar Pasa'nın tavsiyeleri."

36. "Ahmed Mukhtar Pasha," *New York Times*, November 29, 1879.

37. Sir Drummond-Wolff, *Rambling Recollections* (London: Macmillan, 1908), 2:299.

38. Abbas Hilmi II, *The Last Khedive: Memoires of Abbas Hilmi II* (London: Garnet Press, 1998), chap. 6.

39. Eve Troutt Powell, *A Different Shade of Colonialism*, chap.1. See also Martin Daley and P. M. Holt, *History of Sudan: From the Coming of Islam to the Present Day* (London: Longman, 1988); Khaled Fahmy, *All the Pasha's Men: Mehmed Ali, His Army, and the Making of Modern Egypt* (Cairo: American University Press, 2002); Heather Sharkey, *Living with Colonialism: Nationalism and Culture in the Anglo-Egyptian Sudan* (Berkeley: University of California Press, 2003); Hassan Ahmed Ibrahim, "The Egyptian Empire, 1805–1885," in *The Cambridge History of Egypt* (Cambridge: Cambridge University Press, 1998), vol. 2.

40. The campaign reclaimed the province of Hijaz and thus the Holy Cities for the Ottoman sultan. Mehmed Ali's son Ibrahim was made vali of the Hijaz as a result of the campaign.

41. Many historians of Sudan characterize the period between 1820 and the Mahdist Revolt of 1881–1885 as the "Turco-Egyptian" regime. Powell, *A Different Shade of Colonialism*; Sharkey, *Living with Colonialism*.

42. "Egypt conquered Sudan, for example, long before achieving independence from the Ottoman Empire. Because of the relationship with Istanbul and the fact that the language spoken by Egypt's administrators and generals was Turkish, the administration of the 'Egyptian Sudan' region was known for generations as the 'Turkiya.'" Powell, *A Different Shade of Colonialism*, 39.

43. H.C.G. Matthew, *Gladstone, 1809–1898* (1997); J. Marlowe, *Mission to Khartoum* (1969).

44. The Mahdi ("the guided one") is an eschatological figure in Islam, whose rule on earth is supposed to presage the day of the resurrection. Both British and Ottoman documents from 1881 and beyond mention the growing unrest in Sudan simultaneous to events in Cairo and Alexandria.

45. Even though the last quarter of the nineteenth century in many ways belonged to surveyors, border commissions, and mapmakers, the boundary between Egypt and Sudan was somewhat flexible. This reality is especially clear in Foreign Office discussions concerning the evacuation of Egyptian garrisons. British officers wrote about the southern boundary of Egypt in terms of defensible positions, not straight lines on a map. Şükrü Hanioğlu also writes about the word *hıtta* in Ottoman as referring to territories "with vague boundaries," mentioning Tunis and Libya. Egypt and Hijaz are often referred to Ottoman documents as well as *hıtta*—as in the "region" or "lands" of Egypt. See Hanioğlu, *A Brief History of the Late Ottoman Empire* (Princeton: Princeton University Press, 2008), 9.

46. In British documents, the Mahdist state is referred to as the Khalifat and its leader the Khalifa, or successor. Muhammad Ahmed al-Mahdi died in 1885 and was succeeded by al-Khalifa (the successor) Abdullahi. Sharkey, *Living with Colonialism,* 4–5.

47. BOA, I.MTZ.(05) 24/1166 12 Cemaziyelahir 1301 (April 9, 1884).

48. Kuneralp, *Ottoman Diplomatic Documents*, no. 676, Musurus to Arafi Paşa, February 6, 1884, 383–89.

49. The Egyptian tribute serviced the Ottoman debt. Abbas Hilmi II's ferman of investiture stipulated that the tribute should be set at £T750,000 per annum. See Government of Egypt, *Recueil de firmans impériaux ottomans addresses aux valis et aux khedives d'Égypte* (Cairo: L'institut Français d'archéologie orientale du Caire, 1934), 340–42, no. 1060, 27 Shaban 1309 [March 27, 1892]. After the loss of the Red Sea ports, Zeyla and Massawa, the tribute was reduced to around £T665,000 annually and remained at this rate for the duration of the occupation. NA/ FO 141/822/ EGYPT AND SOUDAN "Minuet by Cecil Hurst on Egyptian Tribute Loans." Şevket Pamuk, *A Monetary History of the Ottoman Empire* (Cambridge: Cambridge University Press, 2004), chaps. 6 and 11; Roger Owen, *The Middle East in the World Economy, 1800–1914* (London: Tauris, 1993) chaps. 2 and 9; Suraiya Faroqui, ed., *An Economic and Social History of the Ottoman Empire: 1600–1914* (Cambridge: Cambridge University Press, 1997), part 5.

50. In an article largely about Gazi Ahmet Muhtar Paşa, Abdülhamid's Ottoman high commissioner in Egypt from 1885 to 1908, he argued that things such as the sultan's seal (*tuğra*) on coinage struck in Egypt, the Ottoman flag, saying Friday prayers in the name of the Sultan, or the presence of the Ottoman high commissioner in Cairo had symbolic value in Egypt and represented the legitimacy of the sultan. Peri, "Ottoman Symbolism in British-Occupied Egypt, 1882–1909," *Middle Eastern Studies* 41, no. 1 (January 2005): 103–20. See also Selim Deringil, "Gazi Ahmed Mukhtar Pasha and the British Occupation of Egypt," *Al-Abhath*, vol. 34 (1986).

51. Kuneralp, *Ottoman Diplomatic Documents*, Musurus to Arifi Paşa, February 6, 1884, and Arifi Paşa to Musurus Paşa, February 19, 1884.

52. For instance, Abdülhamid II referred to 'Urabi as another "Mehmed Ali" during the 'Urabi crisis. From the Ottoman perspective, 'Urabi produced a crisis, not a revolution, as the events are cast in Egyptian national histories. Selim Deringil, "The Ottoman Response to the Egyptian Crisis of 1881–82," *Middle Eastern Studies* 24, no. 1 (January 1988).

53. Jane Burbank and Fred Cooper have recently termed this the "repertoires of empire," in *Empires in World History: Power and the Politics of Difference* (Princeton: Princeton University Press, 2011).

54. Imperial historians have long emphasized the variability of British imperial control, which was never so simple as "direct" versus "indirect" rule. It is important to point out that British strategic relationships with, say, the sultan of Zanzibar as a protectorate or the princely states of India, while on the surface analogous to the British position in Egypt, was radically different. As I have pointed out, the Convention of London in 1840 and the ferman of 1841 guaranteed Egypt's position as an Ottoman province, as well as European rights there, by international treaty. Egypt had an international status that Zanzibar and the princely states did not, and it mattered.

55. During the 'Urabi crisis, Britain insisted the invasion of Egypt was carried out to reestablish law and order and good government but was also a friendly action to restore the prestige of the khedive.

56. Kuneralp, *Ottoman Diplomatic Documents*, no. 676, Musurus to Arifi Paşa, February 6, 1884, 383–89.

57. The Ottomans regularly incorporated troublesome figures into the structure of imperial governance. Abdülhamid even invited Colonel 'Urabi to Istanbul to become one of the "high state officials and dignitaries." See Karen Barkey, *Bandits and Bureaucrats: The Ottoman Route to State Centralization* (Ithaca: Cornell University Press, 1996). The Foreign Ministry responded two weeks later to Musurus's suggestions and argued that for the time being the most important thing was to maintain the sovereign rights of the sultan over Egypt. Kuneralp, *Ottoman Diplomatic Documents*, no. 684, Arifi Paşa to Musurus Paşa, February 19, 1884, 392–94.

58. Much has been written on Abdülhamid II's turn toward the caliphate and Islam as legitimizing mechanisms for the empire following the territorial losses in the Balkans after Berlin in 1878, as well as British plans to establish a rival caliphate to the Ottomans. Selim Deringil, *The Well-Protected Domains* (London: Tauris, 1998).

59. In another instance, the Ottomans protested various British leases of Ottoman territory in Sudan, including in 1894 when Great Britain tried to give a lease of the Equatorial province and that of Bahr el-Ghazal to the State of Congo.

As noted earlier, the Ottoman ambassadors in France and London, as well the grand vizier, made every effort to maintain Ottoman territorial claims to Sudan. In another example, the Institut de Droit International, which viewed international law as a tool to ameliorate international relations and publicized codification efforts, sent the Ottoman Foreign Ministry a proposal for the administration of Congo. Said Paşa, the grand vizier, was addressed as one of the representatives of the "principle states of Europe and America" and of the civilized world. BOA, HR.HMŞ.IŞO 166/21/ Institut de Droit International to Said Paşa 2 Muharrem, 1301 (October 21, 1889).

60. Martin Daley notes that the Condominium was not a haphazard decision following the battle of Omdurman; rather, Cromer and the Foreign Office had been in conversation for several years about what to do with Sudan. This is completely accurate. Daley cites a series of conversations between Cairo and London from the British decision to launch the campaign against the Mahdist state in 1896, but these conversations began the day Gladstone became the "Murderer of Gordon," in other words, with the fall of Khartoum. Daley, *Empire on the Nile: The Anglo-Egyptian Sudan, 1898–1934* (Cambridge: Cambridge University Press, 1986), 11.

61. NA/FO 633/6/no. 40, Lord Cromer, Letters to Secretaries of State 1883–1905, Evelyn Baring to Lord Granville, April 3, 1885, 43–50.

62. NA/FO 633/6/no. 40, 48.

63. NA/FO 633/6/no. 40, 48.

64. In much of the older diplomatic history, the Ottomans refused to ratify the agreement due to Russian and French pressure. At the same time, imperial historians have argued that through this agreement, Abdülhamid "recognized" the British position in Egypt. The agreement again was never ratified, and the Ottomans did not recognize the occupation. Moreover, Süleyman Kızıltoprak categorized Ottoman negotiations with Europe over Egypt as "diplomatic warfare"—especially during the Drummond-Wolff period. Kızıltoprak has rightly noted that Egypt was a critical province for the Ottoman Empire and not one it just let go of in 1882 when the British arrived in Cairo. Kızıltoprak, *Mısır'da İngiliz İşgali: Osmanlı'nın Diplomasi Savaşı (1882–1887)* [The British occupation of Egypt: The Ottoman diplomatic war] (Istanbul: Tarih Vakfı, 2010). BOA, Y.A.HUS.505/58/15 Cemaziyelahir 1324. Among the files contained here is a statement by Cromer that Muhtar's mission should have been considered terminated with the end of the "Wolff Convention," and that he regards the "the Khedive as the only legal representative of the Sultan in Egypt."

65. BOA, Y.PRK.BŞK 202/19 6 Şaban 1304 (April 30, 1887).

66. NA/FO 633/5/ Letters from Lord Cromer 1883–1895, Baring to Chermside, January 25, 1885.

67. Terje Tvedt, *The River Nile in the Age of the British: Political Ecology and the Quest for Economic Power* (London: Tauris, 2003).

68. Many controversies surrounded the Battle of Omdurman. Chief among them was Kitchener's decision to raze the Muhammad Ahmed al-Madi's tomb in Omdurman, which had become a Sufi shrine, and to dispose of his body. Kitchener was given the Mahdi's skull, which, along with the destruction of his tomb and desecration of his body, caused a small scandal in Parliament. Kitchener claimed that he thought it was "desirable on political grounds to destroy" the tomb as a site of pilgrimage. M. W. Daley, *Empire on the Nile: The Anglo-Egyptian Sudan, 1898–1934* (Cambridge: Cambridge: University Press, 1986); Winston Churchill, *The River War: An Account of the Reconquest of the Sudan* (New York: Dover, 2006).

69. NA/FO 93/32/27.

70. For instance, in Daley's excellent book on the administration of Sudan, when writing about the origins of the Condominium idea, he acknowledges the potential Ottoman problem but really casts joint administration as an answer to Europe and the Egyptian government. He writes, "Cromer therefore set himself the task of devising a solution that might win the acquiescence of the Egyptian government and avoid stating openly that Soudan is to be administered direct by England." Daley, *Empire on the Nile: The Anglo-Egyptian Sudan, 1898–1934* (Cambridge: Cambridge University Press, 1986), 12.

71. Daley, *Empire*, 111–12. He continued, "It will be seen that an arrangement was made which elsewhere might perhaps have been considered as too anomalous to stand the wear and tear of daily political existence. In Egypt, it was merely thought that one more paradox had been added to the goodly array of paradoxical creations with which the political institutions of the country already teemed."

72. NA/FO 78/4957, Cromer Memorandum to Salisbury, November 10, 1898. The Fashoda incident was the Anglo-French confrontation in Sudan over the territory of Fashoda. A French expeditionary force led by General Marchand intended to establish a protectorate. On the heels of the battle of Omdurman, Kitchener was sent to Fashoda with gunboats and raised the Egyptian/Ottoman flag. The episode was resolved through diplomacy, and Marchand and his French forces withdrew. The fact that Kitchener appealed to Egyptian/Ottoman rights in Fashoda was a significant factor in Foreign Office justifications for the reconquest of Sudan.

73. Ottoman legal advisors at the Bab-ı Ali scrutinized every commercial and customs agreement signed by the khedive to ensure that political matters remained in the hands of Istanbul. See chapter 2 in this volume.

74. See Government of Egypt, *Recueil de firmans impériaux ottomans addresses aux valis et aux khedives d'Égypte* (Cairo: L'institut Français d'archéologie orientale

du Caire, 1934), 340–42, no. 1060, 27 Shaban 1309 [March 27, 1892]. See also Noradounghian, *Recueil d'Actes*, vol. 4. Noradounghian was an Ottoman legal advisor at the Bab-i Ali for many years before becoming the first Armenian grand vizier in the history of the empire. BOA, DH.SAİD 81/238 "Noradunkyan, Gabriel." His *Recueil d'Actes Internationaux* might be seen in parallel with Sir Edward Hertslet's *The Map of Europe by Treaty: Showing the various Political and Territorial Changes* (1875–1891). Hertslet was the librarian at the Foreign Office, as was his father, and was often called on to provide historical analysis for British foreign policy decisions. Much of his four-volume collection of treaties dealt with "Eastern Question" diplomacy. I would argue that it is possible to read Noradounghian's *Recueil d'Actes* as a response to Hertslet. See also Y. G. Çark, *Türk Devlet Hizmetinde Ermeniler, 1453–1953* [Armenians in the Turkish Civil Service] (Yeni Matbaa, 1953). Noradounghian was elected to the Institut de Droit International in 1922. See Peter Macalister-Smith, "Bio-Bibliographical Key to the Membership of the Institut de Droit International, 1873–2001," *Journal of the History of International Law* 5 (2003): 77–159.

75. NA/ FO 78/4957, Cromer Memorandum to Salisbury, November 10, 1898.
76. Cromer, *Modern Egypt*, 2:114.
77. NA/F0407/150, Cromer's speech to sheikhs and notables of Sudan.
78. NA/FO 93/32/27, "January 19, 1899.
79. A sirdar, or serdar in Turkish, is from Persian and means "military chief" or "commander." From *sir*, headman, or commander, thus *sirdar* the one bearing command. The term was widely employed in British India.
80. BOA, AMTZ(05) 14-B/ 79 "Sudan'in merkezi olan Hartum'un Ingilizler tarfindan işgali,"5 Cemaziyelevvel 1316 (September 21, 1898).
81. BOA, Y.A. HUS.392/ 83/ 28 Şaban, 1316 (October 11, 1889). Muhtar Paşa sent word of Lord Cromer's speech to the "Bedouin Arabs."
82. NA/F0407/150, no. 39, Salisbury to Cromer, January 18, 1899.
83. BOA, I.MTZ.(05) 32/1867. The folder contains a number of documents related to the Condominium dating back to 1899.
84. NA/F0407/150, no. 68, O'Connor to Salisbury, January 29, 1899. See John Burman, *Britain's Relations with the Ottoman Empire During the Embassy of Sir Nicholas O'Connor to the Porte, 1898*–1908 (Istanbul: Isis, 2010).
85. While Abdülhamid was and continues to be known for having revived the Ottoman claim to the caliphate and for emphasizing the role of Islam in the empire, it was the British in Sudan who were more concerned with the fact that the Mahdi's rebellion was expressed in Islamic terms. While the Ottomans viewed Sudan as a potential route back into Egypt, territorial claims there were not as important as they were in Egypt.
86. NA/F0407/150, no. 83, Salisbury to O'Connor, February 3, 1899.
87. NA/F0407/150, no. 119, Salisbury to O'Connor, February 22, 1899.

88. It should be noted that the reconquest of the Sudan happened alongside the Cretan uprising and that the Great Powers had imposed the establishment of an autonomous Crete in November 1898. Ottoman garrisons were allowed to remain, and the territory was guaranteed under Ottoman "suzerainty." Crete, like Egypt, was viewed as more important than Sudan.

89. "L'Égypte est la terre classique du droit international." Jules Cocheris, *Situation internationale de l'Egypte et du Soudan (juridique et politique)* (Paris: Plon-Nourrit, 1903), preface.

90. M. F. Lindley, *The Acquisition and Government of Backward Territory in International Law: Being a Treatise on the Law and Practice Relating to Colonial Expansion* (London: Longmans, 1926); Sir Alfred Lyall, "Frontiers and Protectorates," in *The Nineteenth Century*, vol. 30 (1891): 312–29.

91. The French critiques of the Anglo-Egyptian Condominium anticipated in some cases Carl Schmitt's critique of the post–World War I order. Carl Schmitt, *Nomos of the Earth in the International Law of the Jus Publicum Europaeum* (New York: Telos, 2006).

92. John Westlake, *International Law*, vol. 1, *Peace* (Cambridge: Cambridge University Press, 1904), 128.

93. Positivist international lawyers like Lassa Oppenheim outlined a fairly explicit standard concerning reciprocity. See Oppenheim, *International Law: A Treatise* (London: Longmans, 1905), 157; Oppenheim, "The Science of International Law: Its Task and Method," *American Journal of International Law* 2 (1908): 313–56; Gerrit W. Gong, *The Standards of "Civilization" in International Society* (Oxford: Clarendon Press, 1984); and Gong, *The Gentle Civilizer of Nations: The Rise and Fall of International Law 1870–1960* (2002): 134–35. The analogy between Tunis and Egypt only went so far because of Egypt's guaranteed international legal status: "Despite the dialectics of the publicists across the Channel (d'outre-Manche), it would be good to recognize that the juridical analogy between the two cases was only in appearance." Egypt's international status was distinct from Tunis's, and the khedive could not be compared to the Bey of Tunis because of the fermans.

94. Franz Clément Despagnet, "Égypte et Grande-Bretagne," *Revue générale de droit international public*, vol. 6 (1899): 171–72. Although it must be said that the reverse appears true—the Condominium shocked the diplomats, not the lawyers.

95. Despagnet, 172–174, 185; M. P. Hornik, "The Anglo-Belgian Agreement of 12 May, 1894," *English Historical Review* 57, no. 226 (April 1942): 227–43.

96. Despagnet, 191. On the Berlin West Africa conference, see Minowi, "Lines in the Sand," chap. 1; Selim Deringil, "Les Ottomans et le partage de l'Afrique, 1880–1900," in *The Ottomans, the Turks and World Power Politics: Collected Essays* (Istanbul: Isis, 2000); and Ahmet Kavas, *Osmanlı-Afrika İlişkileri* (Istanbul: Kitabevi, 2011).

97. Despagnet, "Égypte et Grande-Bretagne," 191.

98. Georges Blanchard, "Le Problème de la souveraineté au Soudan nilotique," *Revue générale de droit international public* (*RGDIP*), vol. 10 (1903): 169–201. Blanchard earlier wrote another piece for *RGDIP* on Fashoda, which is recapitulated in part in the essay on sovereignty in Nilotic Sudan. Blanchard, "L'affaire Fachoda et de droit international," *RGDIP*, vol. 6 (1899): 390–427.

99. Blanchard, "Le Problème de la souveraineté," 171.

100. Blanchard, 172.

101. Blanchard, 177.

102. Blanchard, 178.

103. On the problem of the use of "sovereignty" versus "suzerainty" in European documents related to Egypt, see chapters 1, 2, and 6.

104. Blanchard, 178.

105. Suraiya Faroqhi, "Mühimme Defterleri," *Encyclopedia of Islam*, 2nd ed., vol. 7, 470–72.

106. Blanchard, "Le Problème de la souveraineté," 178.

107. Martii Koskenniemi, *The Gentle Civilizer of Nations: The Rise and Fall of International Law 1870–1960*, (Cambridge: Cambridge University Press, 2001), chap 2.

108. Mostafa Minawi, *The Ottoman Scramble for Africa: Empire and Diplomacy in the Sahara and the Hijaz* (Stanford: Stanford University Press, 2016); Haniğolu, *A Brief History*, introduction.

109. Blanchard, "Le Problème de la souveraineté," 178.

110. Jules Cocheris, *Situation internationale de l'Egypte et du Soudan (juridique et politique)* (Paris: Plon-Nourrit, 1903), 4.

111. Ottoman legal advisors at the Foreign Ministry, and by extension the Ottoman diplomatic core, maintained the same line of argumentation as European positivist international lawyers—the treaties mattered.

112. "The question of Egypt, that essential problem of international law, has been so often neglected and confused by the authors, that even from an essentially theoretical point of view, agreement is far from being complete in doctrine. A large number of jurists, Klüber, Heffter, Wheaton, G-F. de Martens, Fedor Martens, Calvo, Pradier-Fodéré, Despagnet, Heilborn, Funck-Bretano, Sorel, etc. concede a category of states which they qualify as semisovereign, among which they classify Egypt." Cocheris, *Situation internationale*, 4.

113. Cocheris was attacking a category that existed in many later nineteenth-century international law treatises and textbooks—the "vassal-state." International lawyers divided the world into the subjects and objects of the discipline on the basis of "civilization." Despite appearances, and

counter to the arguments of some contemporary legal theorists, this model of international law was not so clearly divided between "the West and the rest." There were numerous ambiguities surrounding political entities that were non-Christian, non-European, and independent of direct European control. Such states resisted easy classification by lawyers and defied their civilizational theories of international relations. Lawyers argued that states like the Ottoman Empire, China, Japan, and Persia possessed elements of "civilized" governance and categorized them on a scale between Europe and so-called uncivilized societies. International law treatises variously identified such states as semicivilized or semisovereign states. At the beginning of almost all international law texts of the period, there was a boilerplate schematic of types of states arranged in "civilizational" order. The so-called semisovereign states—the Ottoman Empire, China, Japan, and Persia—were situated, as a matter of course, below European states in the hierarchical arrangement of sovereign forms. Cocheris appears to have no problem imagining the Ottoman Empire as a sovereign state, which is at odds with the view of nearly all his contemporaries.

114. Cocheris, *Situation internationale*, 507. On French negotiation related to the Capitulations in Tunis, see Mary Dewhurst Lewis, "Geographies of Power: The Tunisian Civic Order, Jurisdictional Politics, and Imperial Rivalry in the Mediterranean, 1881–1935," *Journal of Modern History* 80 (December 2008): 791–830. See also Paul Cambon, *Correspondance, 1870–1924* (Paris: B. Grasset, 1940–1946), vol. 1, "Le protectorat tunisien; La régence en Espagne; La Turquie d'Abdul Hamid."

115. Cocheris noted, "There was a dangerous gap between appearance and reality that was created; different types of annexation were treated differently and their consequences varied." Koskenniemi, *The Gentle Civilizer of Nations*, 151–52. See also Mark Mazower, *Governing the World: The History of an Idea, 1815–Present* (New York: Penguin Books, 2013).

116. Fujinami, "Between Sovereignty and Suzerainty."

117. In *History of the Law of Nations in Europe and America* (New York: Gould, Banks, 1846), 71, Wheaton categorized Wallachia and Moldavia and Serbia as "vassal states" rather than "subject provinces" under the suzerainty of the Ottoman sultan. In *Elements of International Law*, Ottoman lawyers would follow this model of deep diplomatic history—"Relations of the Ottoman Empire with the Other European States," 555–85.

118. The preferred Ottoman term, *şibh-i sultanat*, is closer in meaning to "quasi-sovereign," or even resembling sovereignty, whereas the term employed in French and German is closer to the English term "half-sovereign."

119. Wheaton, *History of the Law of Nations*, 71.

120. To explain autonomous provinces, European lawyers often quoted Edmund Burke's speech on "Conciliation with America" to show the relationship between the Ottoman imperial center and the provinces: "Nature has said it, the Turk cannot govern Egypt, and Nature has said it, the Turk cannot govern Egypt, and Arabia, and Curdistan [*sic*], as he governs Thrace; nor has he the same dominion in Crimea, which he has at Brusa and Smyrna. Despotism itself is obliged to truck and huckster. The sultan gets such obedience as he can. He governs with a loose rein, that he may govern at all; and the whole force and vigor of his authority in his centre, is derived from a prudent relaxation in all his borders." Edmund Burke, "Speech of Edmund Burke, esq., on Moving his Resolutions for Conciliation with the Colonies," March 22, 1775 (London; J. Dodsley, 1775), 32.

121. Edwin de Witt Dickenson, *The Equality of States in International Law* (Cambridge, Mass.: Harvard University Press, 1920), chapter on "limitations on external sovereignty."

122. The idea that the autonomous provinces were nominally Ottoman is prevalent in the historiography on Serbia, Romania, Bulgaria, Egypt, Tunis, and Crete. For instance, Egypt is rarely discussed as an Ottoman province after the beginning of the British occupation in 1882, and very few scholarly works have used Ottoman archival sources for this period. There are a few recent and important exceptions to this trend, whose work I will engage. Each insists that late Ottoman Egypt cannot be understood without the Ottoman political context. They include Adam Mestyan, *Arab Patriotism: The Ideology and Culture of Power in Late Ottoman Egypt* (Princeton: Princeton University Press, 2017); Matthew H. Ellis, *Desert Borderland: The Making of Modern Egypt and Libya* (Stanford: Stanford University Press, 2018); and Hanley, *Identifying with Nationality: Europeans, Ottomans, and Egyptians in Alexandria* (2017). Khaled Fahmy's discussion of the problem of "colonial medicine" in nineteenth-century Egypt, in *In Quest of Justice: Islamic Law and Forensic Medicine in Modern Egypt* (Berkeley: University of California Press, 2018), 15–21, maps onto many of my concerns as far as how the fact of Ottoman sovereignty mattered. There are only a handful of significant articles in English and one recent book in Turkish devoted to the Ottoman response to the British occupation of Egypt: Süleyman Kızıltoprak, *Mısır'da Ingiliz Işğali: Osmanlı'nın Diplomasi Savaşi (1882–1887)* [The British occupation of Egypt: the Ottoman war of diplomacy] (Istanbul: Tarih Vakfi Yayinlari, 2010); Selim Deringil, "The Ottoman Response to the Egyptian Crisis of 1881–82," *Middle Eastern Studies* 24, 1 (January 1988), and "Gazi Ahmed Mukhtar Pasha and the British Occupation of Egypt," *Al-Abhath*, vol. 34 (1986); Oded Peri, "Ottoman Symbolism in British-Occupied Egypt, 1882–1909," *Middle Eastern Studies* 41, no. 1 (January 2005): 103–20; and

Ekmeleddin İhsanoğlu, *Mısır'da Türkler ve Kültürel Mirasları* (Istanbul: Islam Tarih ve Kültür Araştırma Merkezi, 2006).

123. Lâle Can and Aimee M. Genell, "On Empire and Exception: Genealogies of Sovereignty in the Ottoman World," *Comparative Studies in South Asia, Africa and the Middle East* 40, no. 3 (2020): 468–73; Ayhan Ceylan, *Osmanlı Taşra İdarî Tarzı Olarak Eyâlet-i Mümtâze ve Mısır Uygulaması* [Exceptional provinces as a style of Ottoman provincial administration and its application in Egypt] (İstanbul: Kitabevi, 2014).

124. Furat Andič and Suphan Andič, *The Last of the Ottoman Grandees: The Life and the Political Testament of Ali Paşa* (Istanbul: İsis, 1996), 35–36.

125. Cromer's comment was made in regard to settling the 1904 *entente cordiale*, but the idea of navigating a tight space between law and diplomacy pervades Cromer's correspondence with the Foreign Office on all Egyptian matters. NA/FO 633/6, Letters to Secretaries of State 1883–1905, no. 5 Cromer to Lansdowne, November 1, 1903.

126. BOA, HR.HMŞ.IŞO, 52/20 "Ingiltere ve Fransa arasında Afrika hakkında yapılan 1904 mukavelenamesi." This is a rather large file with documents extending well beyond the date of 1904.

127. Léon Ostrorog was the chief legal advisor at the Foreign Ministry following the Young Turk Revolution until the outbreak of World War I. At the outset of the war he switched sides, so to speak, and worked as a legal advisor to Vickers Limited, where it appears he provided the company with information on Ottoman naval power. In 1918 he authored a memorandum on Ottoman legal claims to the caliphate, which was broadly circulated within the Foreign Office. At the Paris Peace Conference, he served as a legal advisor to the Polish delegation. (Ostrorog was from an old Polish *Istanbullu* family, which had arrived after the last partition of Poland in 1795. The family owned a large seaside mansion, a yalı, on the Bosporus.) After World War I he taught Islamic law at University College London and authored an analysis of the legal aspects of the abolition of the Caliphate in 1924. See Léon Ostrorog, *The Angora Reform* (London: University of London, 1927). See also NA/FO/141/786, no. 7530, An Essay by Count Léon Ostrorog, "The British and the Mohammedans." Ostrorog also participated in a Committee of Union and Progress conference on the "renaissance of Japan" in 1911. See Cemil Aydın, *The Politics of Anti-Westernism in Asia: Visions of World Order in Pan-Islamic and Pan-Asian Thought on Anti-Westernism in Asia and Middle East* (New York: Columbia University Press, 2007), 78–82.

128. Mustafa Aksakal, "Not 'by Those Old Books of International Law, but Only by War': Ottoman Intellectuals on the Eve of the Great War," *Diplomacy and Statecraft*. 15, no. 3 (2004), 507–44.

129. Grégoire Sarkissian, *Le Soudan égyptien: étude de droit international public* (Paris: É. Larose, 1913).

4. Egypt on the Gulf

1. *Times of London* (February 16, 1913).
2. Noradounghian's treaty collection was well reviewed across Europe as an indispensable guide to the complex legal landscape in the Ottoman Empire. M. Kebengy, "Gabriel Effendi Noradounghian Recueil d' actes internationaux de l'empire ottoman," *Revue de droit international et de législation compare*, 2e series, tome III (1901): 95–97; G. Fr. Hertzberg, "Review of Gabrial Noradungian's Recueil d'actes internationaux de l'empire Ottoman," *Historische Zeitschrift* 85, no. 1 (1900): 148–49.
3. This number is based on the first British census and is estimated to be far too low. For population statistics in Egypt, see Justin A. McCarthy, "Nineteenth-Century Egyptian Population," *Middle Eastern Studies* 12, no. 3 (October 1976): 1–39; Kenneth M. Cuno and Michael J. Reimer Cuno, "The Census Registers of Nineteenth-Century Egypt: A New Source for Social Historians," *British Journal of Middle Eastern Studies* 24, no. 2 (November 1997): 193–216. On Kuwait, see Jill Crystal, *Oil and Politics in the Gulf Rulers and Merchants in Kuwait and Qatar* (Cambridge: Cambridge University Press, 1990), 19, 14; J. G. Lorimer, *Gazetteer of the Persian Gulf, 'Oman, and Central Arabia*, vol. 21051 (Calcutta: Superintendent Government Printing, India, 1908–15); Ottoman Foreign Ministry, *Kuveyt Meselesi* (Istanbul: Matbaa-yi Amire, 1917).
4. After 1878 the Ottoman Empire either debated or accepted exceptional status for several provinces, recategorized or reaffirmed some provinces as exceptional, or preemptively extended autonomy to prevent European inclusions into domestic affairs. Some cases worked in Ottoman favor, whereas others clearly worked in favor of the European powers. For example, Eastern Rumelia was created as an autonomous province at the Congress of Berlin (1878), while the Ottoman government recategorized Bosnia-Herzegovina as "exceptional" with the onset of the permanent Habsburg military occupation. Though that occupation ultimately led to Habsburg annexation in 1908, and we often think of Bosnia as outside of the Ottoman imperial and legal framework after Berlin, the reality is that Ottoman lawyers treated Bosnia like another Egypt and worked hard to maintain imperial claims to sovereignty. In other cases, like Yemen, where the central state extended autonomy to the province without Great Power intervention, the province remained under the

sovereignty of the sultan. Indeed, Yemen has the distinction of being the last of the Arab provinces to split with the new Turkey in 1923. Thomas Kuehn, *Empire, Islam, and Politics of Difference: Ottoman Rule in Yemen, 1849–1919* (Leiden: Brill, 2011). Other cases include, among others, Bulgaria, Libya, Tunis, Cyprus, Macedonia (Salonica, Monastir, and Kosovo), Mecca, Jerusalem, the Arab provinces, and the six eastern provinces designated by the Great Powers as "Armenia."

5. Giancarlo Casale, *The Ottoman Age of Exploration* (Oxford: Oxford University Press, 2010).
6. J. Crystal, *Oil and Politics in the Gulf,* 18–19.
7. For Mildhat Paşa's experiments in Tuna, see Milen Petrov, "Everyday Forms of Compliance: Subaltern Commentaries on Ottoman Reform, 1864–1868," *Comparative Studies in Society and History* 46, no. 4 (October 2004): 730–59. Midhat's provincial experiments were instrumental in crafting the Vilayet Law (*Teşkil-i Vilayet Nizamnamesi*) of 1864; M. Safa Saraçoğlu, *Nineteenth-Century Local Governance in Ottoman Bulgaria: Politics in Provincial Councils* (Edinburgh: Edinburgh University Press, 2018). See also chapter 1 in this volume.
8. Ali Haydar Mithat, Osman Selim Kocahanoğlu, *Midhat Paşa'nın hatıraları*, 2 vols. (Istanbul: Temel Yayınları, 1997); Ali Haydar Mithat, *The Life of Midhat Pasha: A Record of His Services, Political Reforms, Banishment, and Judicial Murder* (London: Murray, 1902); Roderick Davison, "Midhat Pasha," in *Encyclopedia of Islam*, new ed., vol. 6, ed. C. E. Bosworth et al. (Leiden: Brill, 1991); Gabor Agoston and Bruce Masters, eds.,"Midhat Midhat Pasha (Ahmet Şefik Midhat Pasha, Ahmed)," *Encyclopedia of the Ottoman Empire* (New York: Facts on File, 2009); Frederick F. Anscombe, *The Ottoman Gulf: The Creation of Kuwait, Saudi Arabia, and Qatar, 1870–1914* (New York: Columbia University Press, 1997).
9. Gökhan Çetinsaya, *The Ottoman Administration of Iraq, 1890–1908* (London: Routledge, 2011), 9.
10. Midhat published the newspaper *Tuna* (Danube) in Niş and *al-Zawra* (*Bend*—a name for Baghdad) in Ottoman-Turkish and Arabic in Baghdad. See Çetinsaya *The Ottoman Administration of Iraq*, 10.
11. *Düstur,* vol.1, "Vilayet Nizamnamesi" (1864), 517–78; *Takvim-i Vekayi*, no. 773; Grégoire Aristarchi Bey, *Législation ottomane*, 2:273.
12. Cevat Ekinci, *Osmanlı Döneminde Irak: Plan, Fotoğraf ve Belgelerler* (Ankara: T.C. Başbakanlık Devlet Arşivleri Genel Müdürlüğ ü, 2006); Ottoman Foreign Ministry, *Kuveyt Meselesi*; Ottoman Empire, *Salname-i Basra* ([Basra]: Vilayet Matbuasi, 1311 (1895/1896); E. Segal, "Rulers and Merchants in Pre-oil Kuwait: The Significance of Palm Dates," *British Journal of Middle Eastern Studies* 41, no. 2 (2014), 174.

13. Başbakanlık Osmanlı Arşivi (hereafter BOA), İ.DUİT 137/27 26 Zilhicce 1286 (March 29, 1870).
14. Anscombe, *The Ottoman Gulf*, 21–22; Camille Cole, "Empire on Edge: Land, Law, and Capital in Gilded Age Basra, 1884–1914," Ph.D. diss., Yale University, 2020.
15. Anscombe, *The Ottoman Gulf*, 21–22.
16. Cole, "Empire on Edge," 267.
17. Fahad Ahmad Bishara, Bernard Haykel, "The Economic Transformation of the Gulf," in *The Emergence of the Gulf States: Studies in Modern History*, ed. J. E. Peterson (London: Bloomsbury Academic, 2016), 45.
18. Farah Al-Nakib, *Kuwait Transformed: A History of Oil and Urban Life* (Stanford: Stanford University Press, 2016), 30–32.
19. Crystal, *Oil and Politics in the Gulf*, 23; Lorimer, *Gazeteer*; Anscombe, *The Ottoman Gulf*; Cole, "Empire on Edge."
20. While Mubarak held his brothers' families hostage, his nephews fled Kuwait and immediately appealed to the sultan to reject their uncle's claim. On the ground, Kuwaitis proved relatively easy to placate with Mubarak's usurpation of power; Istanbul officialdom proved less easy to assuage. The world in which Midhat managed to formalize lapsed Ottoman sovereignty in Kuwait for little cost and no governing responsibilities was dramatically changed. Officials at the highest levels of the empire debated how the state should respond. While there was a range of proposals, they oscillated between armed conquest and local accommodation. The idea of military intervention followed by the absorption of Kuwait into a neighboring province was returned to repeatedly, well into the early twentieth century. Some members of the Council of Ministers argued that Mubarak had presented the state with a unique opportunity to extend actual Ottoman control to the prosperous port town. At the other end of the spectrum, officials argued that Ottoman influence in Kuwait could be increased slowly over time by accepting Mubarak's claim to lead the kaza. The authors of those proposals feared that altering Kuwait's legal-administrative status would open the door to unwelcome international questions. What is striking is how closely these debates hewed to the lines of argumentation articulated concerning Ottoman military intervention in Egypt in 1882. The second option ultimately won out. In September 1897, over a year after the murders, Mubarak was confirmed as the new kaymakam of Kuwait. Anscombe, *The Ottoman Gulf*, chapters 5 and 6.
21. Anscombe, *The Ottoman Gulf*, 114–15; BOA, HR.HMŞ.IŞO 204/51, 28 Şaban 1330 (August 12, 1912); BOA, HR.HMŞ.IŞO 204/53 28 Şaban 1330 (August 12, 1912); BOA, HR.HMŞ.IŞO, 204/62 8 Recep 1330 (June 23, 1912); BOA, HR .HMŞ.IŞO 204/70 14 Recep 1330 (June 29, 1912).
22. BOA/HR.SYS.104/28-32; Cole, "Empire on Edge," 275.

23. Babanzade İsmail Hakkı, "Basra'nın ehemmiyet-i sisasiyesi", *Tanin*, 28 Kanun-i evvel 1910 (December 28, 1910).

24. British officials were aware of the local drama, from the family lawsuits to regional rivalries. NA/FO/406/ Herbert to Salisbury, July 6, 1896, no. 1, Memorandum by Mr. Stavrides.

25. NA 406/14/No. 71, enclosure 3.

26. NA FO 406/14/no. 52 India Office to Foreign Office explaining what happened February 14, 1899; Affairs of Kuwait: Correspondence Part 1, 1896–1899, enclosure 6, 42, governor of India to Hamilton, January 18, 1899, "You should enter into Secret Agreement with him on model of Agreement with Muscat, 20th March, 1891, but in more precise terms . . . Sheikh, heirs, and successors. You may also assure him of our good offices as long as he adheres to the agreement."

27. Two of his brothers refused to sign the 1899 agreement because Britain would not explicitly commit to protecting the family properties at Fao. NA FO 406/14 Affairs of Kuwait No. 52, India Office to Foreign Office.

28. NA FO 406/14 Affairs of Kuwait: Correspondence Part 1, 1896–1899, No. 42, India Office to Foreign Office, January 24, 1899.

29. Quoted in Briton Cooper Busch, *Britain and the Persian Gulf, 1894–1914* (Berkeley: University of California Press, 1967), 108.

30. British Library, India Office Records (IOR) /R/15/5/61 "File XXII/5 Distinctive Flag for Kuwait" [7r] (13/114); BOA, HR.SYS. 104/40.

31. Busch, *Britain and the Persian Gulf*, 311–12; FO 424/219 Knox to Cox, July 8, 1908.

32. Babanzade İsmail Hakkı, *Irak Mektupları* ([Istanbul]: Kanaat Kütüphanesi, 1329 [1913]); "Bir Fincan Suda Fırtına Koparmak," *Mizan Gazetesi*, 18 Şaban 1326 (September 15, 1908), 203; BOA, HR.SYS 104/39; BOA, DH.SFR 426/44, "Kuveyt Meselesi'ne dair Necid Mutasarrıfı Sami Bey'in raporu."

33. Crystal, *Oil and Politics in the Gulf*, 24.

34. Babanzade İsmail Hakkı was born in Baghdad in 1876, the tumultuous year in which Abdülhamid II assumed the throne. He was trained at Galatasaray High School, followed by the Mülkiye, the school for civil service in Istanbul. He was an expert in constitutional and international law, but when the Young Turk Revolution broke out in 1908, he started his career in journalism and entered Parliament as the deputy for Baghdad. Ali Çankaya, *Yeni Mülkiye Tarihi ve Mülkiyeliler*, vol. 1 (Ankara: Mars Matbaası, 1968–69).

35. Babanzade İsmail Hakkı, *Tanin Yazıları-Meşrutiyetin Birikimi*, vol. 2 (Istanbul: Ötüken Neşriyat, 2020); Babanzade İsmail Hakkı, *Irak Mektupları* [Istanbul]: Kanaat Kütüphanesi, 1329 [1913].

36. *Tanin*, December 28, 1910.

37. It should be noted that the Iraq Letters were republished as a stand-alone volume in the aftermath of the Balkan Wars, *Irak Mektupları*.
38. The idea that Britain and the other powers were abandoning international law was a pervasive theme in the writings of Hüseyin Cahid and Babanzade İsmail Hakkı during the war in Libya and the Balkan Wars.
39. Camille Cole, "Nafia for the Tigris: The Privy Purse and the Infrastructure of Development in Late Ottoman Iraq, 1882–1914," *History of Science* (March 2021); Hasan Kayalı, *Arabs and Young Turks*, chap. 3; Hüseyin Cahid (Yalçın), "Siyasat: Kuveyt," *Tanin*, February 3, 1911.
40. "Kuvyet ahiden ve hukukan Osmanlı arzisi olduğu gibi elyevm Osmanlı sancağı altında yaşamaktadır." Hüseyin Cahid (Yalçın), "Siyasat: Kuveyt," *Tanin*; BOA, HR.SYS. 104/8, "Hüseyin Cahid'in 'Kuveyt' baslıklı Tanin'de nesredilen bir makalesi."
41. See, for example, "Turkey and the Persian Gulf," *The Times of London*, January 28, 1911, 7. Hüseyin Cahid (Yalçın) responded directly to this piece in the pages of *Tanin*: Hüseyin Cahid (Yalçın), "Türkiye ve İngiltere," *Tanin* [21, kanun-ı sani, 1911].
42. NA/FO/ FO 406/14. Lowthar to Grey, Pera February 21, 1911. The articles in *Tanin* revived the old debate on sovereignty and control in Kuwait. Unlike earlier iterations of this conversation, British officials manufactured new criteria for sovereignty. In the same way that the CUP wanted Ottoman sovereignty to have the teeth of state policing power, the British began to argue that this was precisely what was missing from the Ottoman claim to Kuwait: "Turkey can point to no real act of sovereignty in Koweit [*sic*], e.g., levying of taxes or direct administration in any form, I have alluded to the intention of some members of the committee to invite England to refer the matter to arbitration. Ismail Hakki Bey has laid great store by the argument that Sheikh Mubarak has accepted the exclusively Ottoman title Pasha. It may be well to remember that Prince Ferdinand also accepted the title of pasha, as Vali of Eastern Rumelia, where there were no Ottoman police, gendarmerie, or customs. The Turkish claim to Koweit, Katar, Debei [*sic*] &c., on the grounds that such places acknowledged Ottoman sovereignty or suzerainty in the 16th century is of course preposterous."
43. Mostafa Minawi, *The Ottoman Scramble for Africa: Empire and Diplomacy in the Sahara and the Hijaz* (Stanford: Stanford University Press, 2016); and "Telegraphs and Territoriality in Ottoman Africa and Arabia During the Age of High Imperialism," *Journal of Balkan and Near Eastern Studies* 18 (2016): 576–87; Christopher Michael Low, *Imperial Mecca: Ottoman Arabia and the Indian Ocean Hajj* (New York: Columbia University Press, 2020); and "Ottoman Infrastructures of the Saudi Hydro-State: The Technopolitics of Pilgrimage

and Potable Water in the Hijaz," *Comparative Studies in Society and History* 57, no. 4 (October 2015): 942–74.

44. In a way, this was no different from the work he did as the chief legal advisor.

45. BOA, HR.SYS 104/38 [1912]; BOA, HR.SYS. 104/38104/43 [5/16/1913]; FO 424/237, Mallet to Grey, March 26, 1913, enclosure "Koweit Draft Agreement."

46. FO424/238 no. 144, Grey to Lowthar, May 8, 1913.

47. IOR/L/PS/11/56, P 2323/1913; İOR/L/PS/11/54, P 2027/1913; BOA, HR.SYS./4 1916; BOA, HR.SYS./2.

48. IOR/L/PS/18/B381/1. No. 1, "Anglo-Turkish Agreement. Collection of documents signed on July 29, 1913"; IOR/L/PS/11/53, P 1837/1913.

49. Tarık Zafer Tunaya, *Türkieye'de Siyasal Partiler*, vol. 1: *İkinci Meşrutiyet Dönemi, 1908–1918* (Istanbul: Hürriyet Vakfı Yayınları, 1988), 19–127.

50. Nader Sohrabi, *Revolution and Constitutionalism in the Ottoman Empire and Iran* (New York: Cambridge University Press, 2011); Sohrabi, "Historicizing Revolutions: Constitutional Revolutions in the Ottoman Empire, Iran, and Russia, 1905–1908," *American Journal of Sociology* 100, no. 6 (May 1995): 1383–1447; Sohrabi, "Global Waves, Local Actors: What the Young Turks Knew About the Other Revolutions and Why it Mattered," *Comparative Studies in Society and History* 44, no. 1 (January 2002): 45–79; Bedross der Matossian, *Shattered Dreams of Revolution: From Liberty to Violence in the Late Ottoman Empire* (Stanford: Stanford University Press, 2014), chap. 2; Sükrü Hanioğlu, *The Young Turks in Opposition* (New York: Oxford University Press, 1995); and Hanioğlu, *Preparation for a Revolution: The Young Turks, 1902–1908* (New York: Oxford University Press, 2000).

51. Ali Birinci, *Hürriyet ve İtilaf Fırkası* (İstanbul: Dergâh, 1990); Christine Philliou, *Turkey: A Past Against History* (Berkeley: University of California Press, 2021), chap. 2.

52. Hanioğlu, *Preparation for a Revolution*; Sohrabi, *Revolution and Constitutionalism*, 56–66; Ahmet Behevi Kuran, *İnkılâp Tarihimiz ve İttihad ve Terakki* (Istanbul: Tan Matbaası, 1948).

53. Kayalı, *Arabs and Young Turks*.

54. Cenk Reyhan, *Osmanlı'da İki Tarz-ı İdare: Merkeziyetçilik—Adem-i Merkeziyetçilik* (Ankara: İmge Yayınları, 2007). Nobuyoshi Fujinami has argued that while the Second Constitutional period is characterized as a fight that pitted CUP centralizers against usually non-Muslim decentralizers, the reality was more complex—especially the thought of Prince Sabahadin. Fujinami, "Decentralizing Centralists, or the Political Language on Provincial Administration in the Second Ottoman Constitutional Period," *Middle Eastern Studies* 49, no. 6 (2013): 880–900.

55. A founding member of Wilsonian Principles Society and supporter of the controversial Friends of England Society (İngiliz Mühipler Cemiyeti), Ali Kemal later favored a British mandate for the empire and cooperated with the Allied occupation in Istanbul. While he is still viewed as a traitor to the Republic of Turkey, in many ways his actions and political arguments were very much in line with a particular strand of late Ottoman diplomacy that saw European cooperation as the best route to safeguard the state in international politics. Faruk Gezgin, *Ali Kemal: Bir Muhalifin Hikâyesi* (Istanbul: Isis, 2010); Ali Kemal, *Ömrüm* (Istanbul: Isis, 1985); İbnülemin Mahmut Kemal İnal, *Son Asır Türk Şairleri* (Istanbul: Millu Eğitim Basımevi, 1970); Tarık Zafer Tunaya, *Türkiye'de Siyasal Partiler* (Istanbul, 1984), vols. 1 and 2.

56. Ali Kemal, "Teşebbüs-i Şahsi, Tevsi'-i Mezuniyet, Adem-i Merkeziyet," *İkdam* (5 Eylül, 1908/1324); Ali Kemal, "Sabahaddin Beyefendi," *İkdam* (2 Eylül, 1908/1324).

57. Bedross der Matossian, *Shattered Dreams of Revolution: From Liberty to Violence in the Late Ottoman Empire* (Stanford: Stanford University Press, 2014), chap. 2; Kayalı discusses the Ottoman idea of *tevsi'-i mezuniyet* (decentralized administration) as "the extension of the administrative prerogatives of local officials," p. 141. His work deals with the reception and participation of Ottomans in the Arab provinces, including Egypt, after the Young Turks assumed power. Hasan Kayalı, *Arabs and Young Turks*.

58. "Zaten Kanada'nın, Avusturalya'nın muhtariyet-i idareleri tamdır, merkeziyet, adem-i merkeziyete tatbik olunamaz!"

59. Ali Kemal, "Teşebbüs-i Şahsi, Tevsi'-i Mezuniyet, Adem-i Merkeziyet," *İkdam* (5 Eylül, 1908).

60. Prince Sabahaddin, too, had elevated Midhat Paşa, arguing that "the architect of our constitution" was also the inventor of Ottoman decentralization. Devolution had worked in Bulgaria (Tuna) and Baghdad because Midhat Paşa, "with the support of the center, had also been given free rein." The success of this project was evidenced by the fact that experiments in Bulgaria functioned as an administrative model for the entire empire.

61. "Prens Sabahaddin Bey Efendi'nin nutku," *Hukuk-Umumiye*, September 18, 1908.

62. "Hıristiyan vatandaşlarımıza karş ı müslümanlarla samimi bir ittihadın lüzumunu, yani Rum, Ermeni, Bulgar . . . ilh. cins ve mezhebi farkı gözetilmeksizin Osmanlılığ ı teşkil eden anasırdan hiçbirinin muhtariyet-i idare veya istiklal-i siyasi takib eylememeleri lüzum-ı kat'isini izhar eylemek." M. Sabahaddin, *Teşebbüs-i Şahsi ve Tevsi-i Mezuniyet Hakkında İkinci Bir İzah* (Istanbul: Mahmud Bey Matbaası, 1324/1908), 6.

63. Ali Kemal, "Teşebbüs-i Şahsi, Tevsi'-i Mezuniyet, Adem-i Merkeziyet," *İkdam*, no. 5130 (5 Eylül, 1908/1324), 1; Ali Kemal, "Sabahaddin Beyefendi," *İkdam* (2 Eylül 1908/1324).
64. "Vilayatın usûl-i idare-yi tevsi-yi mezuniyet," article 108. *Kanun-i Esasi* (Dersaadet: Mahmud Bey Matbuası, 1908), 29–31.
65. Hüseyn Cahid, "Adem-i Merkeziyet," *Tanin* (4 Eylül 1908/1324) and *Tanin* (19 Eylül 1908/1324).
66. "Adem-i merkeziyet, tabirinin muhtariyet idare tarzında anlaş ılmasına sebeb de programa suret-i mahsusada idhal edilmiş olmuştur." Hüseyn Cahid, "Adem-i Merkeziyet," *Tanin* (19 Eylül 1908/1324).
67. Bedross der Matossian's study of the ethnic press gets at the daunting complexity of the various and competing visions for the state among Ottoman religious and ethnic minorities. Through an examination of the Armenian, Arabic, Hebrew, and Ottoman Turkish press, he shows how communities within the empire were divided among themselves about the meaning of the revolution. Bedross der Matossian, *Shattered Dreams of Revolution: From Liberty to Violence in the Late Ottoman Empire* (Stanford: Stanford University Press, 2014), chap. 2.
68. James Talon, "Ottoman Anti-Insurrectionary Operations in Yemen and Albania, 1910–1912: The End of Ottomanism and the Beginning of an Age of Violence," in *Empire, Ideology, Mass Violence: The Long 20th Century in Comparative Perspective*, ed. Tobias Hof (Munich: Herbert Utz Verlag, 2016), 45–71; Bilgin Çelik, *İttihatçılar ve Arnavutlar: II. Meşrutiyet Döneminde Arnavut Ulusçuluğu ve Arnavutluk Sorunu* (Istanbul: Büke Kitapları Yayınları, 2004).
69. Nadir Sohrabi develops a theory of the "reluctant nationalist" by tracing autonomist demands over the course of the revolution, in order to explain that the final autonomy demands were significantly less expansive than demands earlier in the period. Sohrabi, "Reluctant Nationalists, Imperial Nation-State, and Neo-Ottomanism: Turks, Albanians, and the Antinomies of the End of Empire," *Social Science History* 42 (Winter 2018): 835–70.
70. Hanioğlu, 2001, 15.
71. İsmail Kemal—like so many other Ottomans who resented the CUP's centralization policies—maintained that Albanians had understood "union" as the association of nationalities to strengthen the empire by "guaranteeing to each its national existence," but the CUP "only thought of uniting all the different races by forcing them to deny their origin." He later was Albania's first prime minister. Ismail Kemal, *The Memoires of Ismail Kemal Bey* (London: Constable, 1920), 366.
72. Çelik, *İttihatçılari*; Sohrabi, "Reluctant Nationalists," 853.

73. "Denilebilir ki mademki Osmanlılar, muhtelif ırklardan mürekkebedir, (varsınlar) bunlar adem-i mekeziyt esasına göre bir muhtariyet-i idareye malik olsunlar, bundan ne çıkar? Tarihin şehadetini unutmuş olsa eden belki bu mütala'aya biraz aldanabilirdik. Fakat şimdiye kadar vatandan ne kadar parça koymuşsa hepsi idare-i mümtaze, vilayet-i muhtara şeklinde başlamış nihayet istiklâli kesp ederek bizden ayrılmıştır. Binâenaleyh bizim Arnavutluğu verilen imtiyaz-i diğer taraflara da teşmil ederek adem-i merkeziyet-i esasini tatbik-i (itişimiz) kendi elimizle memleketimizi parçalamak olacaktır." Hüsayn Cahid (Yalçın), "Arnavudluk Meselesi," *Tanin*, no. 1426 (29 Ağustos 29 1912).

74. Kemal, *The Memoires of Ismail Kemal Bey*, 366.

75. Sohrabi, "Reluctant Nationalists," 860.

76. Bosnia and Herzegovina did not have the same status as Egypt, where the province's autonomy was guaranteed in the internal legislation and by treaty, but still counted the territory as autonomous after the onset of the Austro-Hungarian occupation in 1878. From a bureaucratic perspective, the state recategorized Bosnia and Herzegovina and placed all correspondence, problems, and issues that arose during the occupation in the Office of Privileged and Autonomous Provinces. As in Egypt and the other autonomous provinces, the Foreign Ministry's Office of Legal Counsel played a significant role in adjudicating legal crises and questions of private international law that arose in the province. Leyla Amzi-Erdoğdular, *The Afterlife of Ottoman Europe: Muslims in Habsburg Bosnia Herzegovina* (Stanford: Stanford University Press, 2024), 46. Emily Greble shows how ideas about Ottoman autonomy were reconfigured on the ground in Bosnia between the Balkan Wars and the making of Yugoslavia. Greble, *Muslims and the Making of Modern Europe* (Oxford: Oxford University Press, 2021), chap. 3; Milena B. Methodieva, *Between Empire and Nation: Muslim Reforms in the Balkans* (Stanford: Stanford University Press, 2021).

77. Y. Doğan Çetinkaya, *The Young Turks and the Boycott Movement: Nationalism, Protest and the Working Classes in the Formation of Modern Turkey* (London: Tauris, 2014).

78. Edin Hajdarpasic, *Whose Bosnia? Nationalism and Political Imagination in the Balkans, 1840–1914* (Ithaca: Cornell University Press, 2015).

79. Uğur Peçe demonstrates that Crete's declaration of enosis with Greece sparked a massive debate in the Istanbul press—in Ottoman, Greek, and Ladino—as well as a protest movement in the capital and provinces that simmered through the lead-up to World War I. Uğur Zekeriya Peçe, *Island and Empire: How Civil War in Crete Mobilized the Ottoman World* (Stanford: Stanford University Press, 2024), chap. 4; Mustafa Aksakal, *The War That Made the Middle East: World

War I and the End of the Ottoman Empire (Princeton: Princeton University Press, 2025).

80. "Girit Mesekesi," *Tanin* (24 Kanun-i evvel 1324/1909).

81. "O tarihte Girit Hristiyan ahalisi arasında bir ihtilal, ıslahat komitesi teşekkül eyledi. Bu komite Milli Meclisler topladı ve Düvel-i Muazzama memurin-i siyasiyesine verilmek üzere bir arzuhal kabul ettirdi. İ şte bu dakikadan itibaren ahalinin ekseriyetinin şiddetli arzusu kendilerinin tabir-i veçhile 'Osmanlı idaresi altında muhtariyet' kelimelerinde toplanmıştır." *Girit Meselesi Nasıl Hal Edilmeli?* (Dersaadet: Tanin Matbaası, 1326/1910).

82. Eşrefoğlu, "Mümtaze Kalemi ve Bulgaristan Belgeleri," *Güneydoğu Avrupa Araştırmaları Dergisi* (1978), 200–202.

83. Louis Fishman, "The Emergence of a 'Jewish' Question in Istanbul 1908–1914: Zionism, Anti-Semitism, and the 1911 Ottoman Parliament Debate on Zionism," in *Late Ottoman Palestine: The Period of Young Turk Rule*, ed. Yuval Ben-Bassat and Eyal Ginio (London: Tauris, 2011); Michelle Campos, *Ottoman Brothers: Muslims, Christians, and Jews in Early Twentieth-Century Palestine* (Stanford: Stanford University Press, 2010); Julia Phillips Cohen, *Becoming Ottomans: Sephardi Jews and Imperial Citizenship in the Modern Era* (Oxford: Oxford University Press, 2016); Rashid Khalidi, *Palestinian Identity: The Construction of Modern National Consciousness* (New York: Columbia University Press, 1997), chap. 2; Camille Lyans Cole, "Precarious Empires: A Social and Environmental History of Steam Navigation on the Tigris," *Journal of Social History* 50, no. 1 (Fall 2016): 74–101.

84. Arkalı, *The Long Peace*; Der Matossian, *Shattered Dreams*, 67–69; Kayalı, *Arabs and Young Turks*.

85. Abdurrahman Atçıl, "Decentralization, Imperialism, and Ottoman Sovereignty in the Arab Lands Before 1914: Shakīb Arslān's Polemic against the Decentralization Party," *Welt des Islams* 53 (2013): 26–49.

86. John Willis, *Unmaking North and South: Cartographies of the Yemeni Past* (New York: Columbia University Press, 2013); Caesar E. Farah, *The Sultan's Yemen: 19th-Century Challenges to Ottoman Rule* (London: Tauris, 2002). For Jerusalem, see Butrus Abu Maneh, "The Rise of the Sanjak of Jerusalem in the Late 19th Century," in *The Palestinians and the Middle East Conflict*, ed. Gabriel Ben-Dor (Ramat Gan: Turtledove Press, 1978); Alexander Schölch, *Palestine in Transformation, 1856–1882: Studies in Social, Economic and Political Development* (Washington, DC: Institute for Palestine Studies, 1993). For Mecca, see Low, *Imperial Mecca*. For the creation of the *Mutasarrifate* in Benghazi, see Michel F. le Gall, "Pashas, Bedouins and Notables: Ottoman Administration in Tripoli and Benghazi 1881–1902," PhD diss., Princeton University, 1986; Matthew H. Ellis, *Desert Borderland:*

The Making of Modern Egypt and Libya (Stanford: Stanford University Press, 2018).

87. Thomas Kühn has shown that Ottoman policymakers in Istanbul and Yemen debated the options for bringing Imam Yahya and the Zaidis under imperial control and looked explicitly at the Anglo-Egyptian Condominium in Sudan, the Indian princely states, and Aden Protectorate as models. The final agreement amalgamated versions of these systems with existing models of Ottoman autonomy. Autonomy was designed to protect Yemen from outside interference, but, like Kuwait, the model was distinct from nineteenth-century autonomous provinces. Thomas Kuehn, *Empire, Islam, and Politics of Difference Ottoman Rule in Yemen, 1849–1919* (Leiden: Brill, 2011).

88. Thomas Kuehn, "'We Know Nothing About Yemen!' Ottoman Imperial Governance in Southwest Arabia and the Politics of Knowledge Production, 1871–1914," *Journal of Arabian Studies* 8, no. 1 (2018): 5–24; and "Shaping and Reshaping Colonial Ottomanism: Contesting Boundaries of Difference and Integration in Ottoman Yemen, 1872–1919," *Comparative Studies of South Asia, Africa and the Middle East* 27, no. 2 (2007): 315–31.

89. IOR/L/PS/11/56, P 2323/1913; IOR/L/PS/10/385, "Copy of the treaty between Bin Saud and the Turkish Government, dated 15 May 1914." For the Ottoman text, see Ottoman Foreign Ministry, *Kuveyt Meselesi* (Istanbul: Matbaa-yi Amire, 1917).

90. NA/FO/407/177, no. 135, Tewfik Pasha to Sir Edward Grey, October 1, 1911. Aksakal and Genell "Salvation Through War"; Stefen Hock, "Waking Us from This Endless Slumber": The Ottoman–Italian War and North Africa in the Ottoman Twentieth Century," *War in History* 26, no. 2 (2019): 204–26.

91. "Trablusgarb ve Bingazi kıtalarına tam muhtariyet tanıyan ferman-ı ali ile aynı husustaki kanunun suretleri." "Ferman-i Ali Suretidir," *Takvim-i Vekayi* [7 Zil. 1330]; BOA, HMŞ.İ ŞO 116/10, Imperial ferman extending autonomy to Libya. BOA, A.DVN.MKL /52/33 [1330 Za. 6].

92. For Kieser and other historians, the 1914 Reform Agreement, which was canceled in December 1914, was critical to justifying and instigating the genocide. Hans-Lukas Kieser, Mehmet Polatel, and Thomas Schmutz, "Reform or Cataclysm? The Agreement of 8 February 1914 Regarding the Ottoman Eastern Provinces," *Journal of Genocide Research* 17, no. 3 (2015): 285–304; Michael Reynolds, *Shattering Empires: The Clash and Collapse of the Ottoman and Russian Empires, 1908–1918* (Cambridge: Cambridge University Press, 2011); Peter Holquist, "The Politics and Practice of the Russian Occupation of Armenia, 1915–February 1917," in *A Question of Genocide: Armenians and Turks at the End of the Ottoman Empire*, ed. Ronald Grigor Suny, Fatma Muge Gogek, and Norman M. Naimark (Oxford: Oxford University Press, 2015).

93. Bedross Der Matossian, *The Horrors of Adana: Revolution and Violence in the Early Twentieth Century* (Stanford: Stanford University Press, 2022).

94. André Nicolayévitch Mandelstam, *Le Sort de l'Empire ottoman* (Paris: Payot, 1917).

95. Hülya Adak, "The Legacy of André Nikolaievitch Mandelstam (1869–1949) and the Early History of Human Rights," *Zeitschrift für Religions- und Geistesgeschichte* 70, no. 2 (2018): 117–30; Helmut Aust, "From Diplomat to Academic Activist: André Mandelstam and the History of Human Rights," *European Journal of International Law* 25, no. 4 (November 2014): 1105–21; *The History of International Law in Russia, 1647–1917: A Bio-Bibliographical Study*; "André Mandelstam and the Internationalization of Human Rights (1869–1949)," in *Revisiting the Origins of Human Rights*, ed. P. Slotte and M. Halme-Tuomisaari (Cambridge: Cambridge University Press, 2015), 239–66.

96. André Nicolayévitch Mandelstam, *La justice ottomane: dans ses rapports avec les puissances étrangères* (Paris: A. Pedone, 1911).

97. Erzurum, Van, Bitlis, Diyarbakir, Harput (Elaziğ), and Sivas. Kiser et al., "Reform or Cataclysm?," 1.

98. Mandelstam reproduced the entire program for the Armenian Reform Agreement in *Le sort*, 218–22.

99. Mandelstam *Le sort*, 221; Vladimir Hamed-Troyansky, *Empire of Refugees North Caucasian Muslims and the Late Ottoman State* (Stanford: Stanford University Press, 2024), chap. 4.

100. Mandelstam, *Le sort*, 222.

101. Mandelstam, *Le sort*, 227.

102. Mandelstam, *Le sort*, 229.

103. Mandelstam, *Le sort*, 230.

104. Mandelstam, *Le sort*, 230 and note.

105. Taner Akçam, *The Young Turks' Crime against Humanity: The Armenian Genocide and Ethnic Cleansing in the Ottoman Empire* (Princeton: Princeton University Press, 2012); Bedross der Matossian, "Explaining the Unexplainable: Recent Trends in the Armenian Genocide Historiography," *Journal of Levantine Studies* 5, no. 2 (Winter 2015): 143–66; Kévorkian, *The Armenian Genocide* (London: Tauris), 171.

5. Woodrow Wilson in the Ottoman Empire

1. Woodrow Wilson, "Address to the Joint Session of Congress on the Conditions of Peace," January 8, 1918, Yale University, *The Avalon Project: Documents in Law, History and Diplomacy*, http://avalon.law.yale.edu/20th_century/wilson14.asp. See also U.S. Department of State, *Foreign Relations of the*

United States, Inquiry Document no. 887, "The Present Situation: The War Aims and Peace Terms It Suggests," December 22, 1917.

2. *Meclis-i Mebusan Zabıt Ceridesi*, IIIüncü devre, 5inci ictima senesi, 4üncü inikad, 19 Teşrin-i evvel 19, 1334 (October 19, 1918), 29.
3. Başbakanlık Osmanlı Arşivi (hereafter BOA), HR/MA, 1228/1, 19 Teşrin-i evvel 1918 (October 19, 1918). Reproduced in Başbakanlık Osmanlı Arşivleri, *Osmanlı Belgelerinde Birinci Dünya Harbi* (Istanbul: Başbakanlık Osmanlı Arşivleri, 2013), vol. 2, 261–62.
4. For Cemal Paşa's wartime activities in Syria, see Talha Çicek, *War and State Formation in Syria: Cemal Pasha's Governorate During World War I, 1914–1917* (New York: Routledge, 2014); Selim Deringil, *The Ottoman Twilight in the Arab Lands: Turkish Memoirs and Testimonies of the Great War* (Cambridge: Cambridge University Press, 2019).
5. Historians of the Ottoman Empire, the United States, and Europe have largely agreed that Wilson's twelfth point signaled Ottoman demise. For instance, Şükrü Hanioğu' notes, "A second blow came when Woodrow Wilson outlined his famous Fourteen Points in a speech delivered to the American congress in January 1918: the American president called for the empire to be dismembered along ethnic lines." M. Şükrü Hanıoğlu, *Atatürk: An Intellectual Biography* (Princeton: Princeton University Press, 2011), 86.
6. Erez Manela, *The Wilsonian Moment: Self-Determination and the International Origins of Anticolonial Nationalism* (New York: Oxford University Press, 2007). Nicole Phelps examined this question with respect to the defeated Habsburg Empire. She notes that "Wilson did not commit to either the break-up of the empire or the recognition of national governments to replace the empire." See Phelps, *U.S.-Habsburg Relations from 1815 to the Paris Peace Conference: Sovereignty Transformed* (Cambridge: Cambridge University Press, 2013), chap. 6. Wilson's tenth point, relative to the Habsburg Empire, used similar language on the future disposition of that empire.
7. Mehmet Şahingöz and Vahdet Keleşyılmaz, "Milli Mücadele Dönemi Türk Basınında Wilson Presipleri," *Atatürk Araştırma Mekezi Dergesi* 7, no. 35 (July/Temmuz 1996): 357–78; Mine Erol, *Türkiye'de Amerikan Mandası Meselesi 1919–1920* (Giresun: İleri Basımevi, 1972); George Sellers Harris and Bilge Criss, eds., *Studies in Atatürk's Turkey: The American Dimension* (Leiden: Brill, 2009); Cemil Aydın, *The Politics of Anti-Westernism in Asia: Visions of World Order in Pan-Islamic and Pan-Asian Thought* (New York: Columbia University Press, 2007), 128–41.
8. Leonard V. Smith, *Sovereignty at the Paris Peace Conference* (Oxford: Oxford University Press, 1918).
9. Fahreddin Paşa refused to surrender Medina to the Sharifian army. He was not removed from the holy city until January 9, 1919. Tanvir Wasti, "The

Defense of Medina, 1916–19," *Middle Eastern Studies* 27, no. 4 (1991): 642–65; Feridun Kandemir, *Fahreddin Paşa'nın Medine Müdafaası: Paygamberimizin Gölgesinde Son Türkler* (Istanbul: Yağmur, 2018).

10. Some historians of the Middle East, as well as former Ottoman subjects, viewed the First World War as part of the longer "ten-year war" (*on yıllık harb*), which included the Balkan Wars of 1912–13, the First World War, as well as the War of Independence (1919–1922). While this remains a useful framework for understanding the pace of unremitting crises in the Ottoman Empire, there is a tendency to disaggregate the early period of the Armistice from the later war between Greece and the nationalist forces based in Ankara under Mustafa Kemal. Robert Gerwarth and others have shown, too, that the Armistice was a period of extreme volatility and violence throughout Eastern Europe and the former Ottoman lands. For the "ten-year war" idea, see Zafer Toprak, "Cihan Harbı'nin Provası Balkan Harbi," *Toplumsal Tarih* 104 (August 2002): 45–46; İzzeddin Çalışlar, *On Yıllık Savaş: Orgeneral İzettin Çalışların Günlüğu* (Istanbul: Yapı Kredi, 1997); Yücel Yanıkdağ, *Healing the Nation: Prisoners of War, Medicine and Nationalism in Turkey, 1914–1939* (Edinburgh: Edinburgh University Press, 2013); Ryan Gingeras, *Fall of the Sultanate: The Great War and the End of the Ottoman Empire* (Oxford: Oxford University Press, 2016); Yiğit Akin, *When the War Came Home: The Ottomans' Great War and the Devastation of an Empire* (Stanford: Stanford University Press, 2018); Robert Gerwarth, *The Vanquished: Why the First World War Failed to End* (New York: Farrar, Straus and Giroux, 2016); and Robert Gerwarth and Erez Manela, eds., *Empires at War 1911–1923* (Oxford: Oxford University Press, 2014).

11. Timothy Mitchell has argued that the genealogy of self-determination can be traced not to Wilson, but rather to theorists of empire in the white settler colonies of the British Empire. See Mitchell, *Carbon Democracy: Political Power in the Age of Oil* (London: Verso, 2011), chap. 3. See also Joseph Massad, "Against Self-Determination," *Humanity Journal: An International Journal of Human Rights, Humanitarianism, and Development* 9, no. 2 (Summer 2018); Mark Mazower, "Jan Smuts and Imperial Internationalism," in *No Enchanted Palace: The End of Empire and the Ideological Origins of the United Nations* (Princeton: Princeton University Press, 2008); and Susan Pedersen, *The Guardians: The League of Nations and the Crisis of Empire* (Oxford: Oxford University Press, 2015).

12. The meaning of autonomy within the Ottoman system played a significant role in historiographical debates on the development of Arab nationalism. See Rashid Khalidi et al., eds., *The Origins of Arab Nationalism* (New York: Columbia University Press, 1991).

13. Mustafa Aksakal, *The Ottoman Road to War* (Cambridge: Cambridge University Press, 2008).

14. Mustafa Aksakal argues that the CUP viewed the war as an existential crisis, but also as an opportunity. Most important, the state needed a Great Power alliance with teeth. The old Great Power guarantees to protect the "territorial integrity" of the Ottoman domains could no longer be trusted. In addition to abrogating the Capitulations and the international status of the *eyalet-i mümtaze*, the government sought to reclaim territory lost in the Libyan and Balkan Wars. Aksakal, "Not 'by Those Old Books of International Law, but Only by War'": Ottoman Intellectuals on the Eve of the Great War," *Diplomacy and Statecraft* 15, no. 3 (2004): 507–44; *The Ottoman Road to War*; and "The Ottoman Empire," in *Empires at War*; Mustafa Aksakal and Aimee M. Genell, "Salvation through War? The Ottoman Search for Sovereignty in 1914," in *The Justification of War and International Order: From the Past to the Present*, ed. Lothar Brock and Hendrik Simon (Oxford: Oxford University Press, 2021). See also Şükrü Hanioğlu, *A Late History of the Ottoman Empire* (Princeton: Princeton University Press, 2008); and Mehmet Said Halim Pasha, "Pourquoi la Turquie participa à la Guerre mondiale?" in *L'Empire Ottoman et la guerre mondiale* (Istanbul: Isis, 2000).

15. Mustafa Aksakal, *The War That Made the Middle East: World War I and the End of the Ottoman Empire* (Princeton: Princeton University Press, 2026), chap. 1; Akin, *When the War Came Home*, 74–77; Muhammet Emin Külünk, *Kapitülasyonların Kaldırılması 1914* (Istanbul: Yeditepe, 2011), chap. 6; Hanioğlu, *A Brief History of the Late Ottoman Empire*, 180; Feroz Ahmad, "Ottoman Perceptions of the Capitulations, 1800–1814," *Journal of Islamic Studies* 11, no. 1 (January 2000): 1–20.

16. Rüstem to Morganthau, September 9, 1914, and Morganthau to State Department, September 10, 1914. U.S. Department of State, *Foreign Relations of the United States with the Address of the President to Congress December 8, 1914* (Washington, D.C.: United States Government Printing Office, 1922), 1090–91.

17. Stanford University, Hoover Institution Archives, Hidayet Dağdeviren Collection (herafter Hoover/ Hidayet Dağdeviren), box 14/1, "The scourge of capitulations has been lifted!" (pamphlet, 1908).

18. BOA, HR.SYS. 2094/8/no. 12666/435, Mahmud Muhtar Paşa to Said Halim Paşa, October 3, 1914.

19. See chapter 4. Due to the war, the Armenian Reform Agreement was never implemented. The wartime government canceled the agreement only three days before Britain dissolved Egypt's special status as an Ottoman autonomous province and incorporated it into the British Empire as a protectorate. British officials justified the seizure, arguing that the "party-of-war," led by Enver Paşa, hijacked the Ottoman Cabinet. See chapter 6. On the reform agreement and its termination, see Hans-Lukas Kieser, Mehmet Polatel, and Tomas Scmutz, "Reform or Cataclysm? The Agreement of 8 February 1914 Regarding the Ottoman Eastern

Provinces," *Journal of Genocide Research* 17, no. 3 (2015): 285–304; Ozan Ozavci, "Honour and Shame: The Diaries of a Unionist and the 'Armenian Question,'" in *End of the Ottomans: The Genocide of 1915 and the Politics of Turkish Nationalism*, ed. Hans-Lukas Kieser et al. (London: Tauris, 2019), 193–220.

20. Cemal Paşa, "Ermeni Meselesi," in *Hatırat: 1913–1919* (Dersaadet: [Ahmed Ihsan ve Şürekası Matbaası], 1339/1922), 244. As Ümit Kürt has noted, Cemal Paşa's role in the Armenian genocide has long been a source of contention. Kürt, "A Rescuer, an Enigma and a Génocidaire," in *The End of the Ottomans*, ed. Keiser et al.; see also Djemal Pasha, *Memoirs of a Turkish Statesman, 1913–1919* (London: Hutchinson, 1922), 249-50; and Ahmed Djemal Pascha, *Erinnerungen eines Türkischen Staatsmannes* (Munich: Drei Masken Verlag, 1922). The German, Ottoman, and English editions of Cemal Paşa's memoirs are remarkably consistent across languages in many parts of the book but wildly divergent in others, especially in terms of the documents included. Çicek, *War and State Formation*, chaps. 1–2; and Yusuf Hikmet Bayur, *Türk İnkilabı Tarihi* (Ankara: Türk Tarih Kurumu, 1983), vol. 3, part 3, p. 12.

21. "Eyalet-i mümtazenin en vasi'-i numûnelerinden birini teşkil eden Mısır'ın İngilizler tarafından işgali müşkilat ile mi vuku buldu?" Cemal Paşa, *Hâtırat*, 244–45.

22. Talha Çicek argues that Cemal Paşa tried to bolster Ottoman control in the Arab provinces through a policy of eradicating local particularities. In addition to crushing Arabists seeking administrative decentralization, Cemal deported enemy foreigners and seized their property, shut down Zionist organizations—arguing they operated as a state within a state—and abrogated the privileges of Jewish colonies in Palestine. As we will see, he also canceled Mount Lebanon's special status. Çiçek, *War and State Formation*, chaps. 1–2.

23. On the question of Arab decentralists, particularly the claims of the Ottoman Administrative Decentralization Party, see chapter 4. For Arabism in Ottoman politics during the Second Constitutional era, especially the *hizb al-lamarkaziyya al-idariyya al-'Uthmani* (Ottoman Administrative Decentralization Party), see Hassan Saab, *The Arab Federalists of the Ottoman Empire* (Amsterdam: Djambatan, 1958); Eliezer Tauber, *Arab Movements in World War I* (New York: Frank Cass, 1993); Mahmoud Haddad, "The Ideas of Amir Shakib Arslan: Before and After the Collapse of the Ottoman Empire," in *Views from the Edge: Essays in Honor of Richard Bulliet* (New York: Columbia University Press, 2004); and Kayalı, *Arabs and Young Turks*. Similarly, Hanna Batatu argued that prewar Iraqi elites' demands for autonomy were linked to preserving privileges, in *The Old Social Classes and the Revolutionary Movement in Iraq* (Princeton: Princeton University Press, 1978), 171–73. See also Beshara Doumani, *Rediscovering Palestine: Merchants and Peasants in Jabal Nablus, 1700–1900* (Berkeley: University of California Press, 1995), chap. 1; Rashid Khalidi,

British Policy Towards Syria & Palestine, 1906–1914 (London: Ithaca Press, 1980), chap. 5. Elizabeth Thompson has shown how crucial Administrative Decentralization Party was in establishing the short-lived constitutional regime in Syria between 1919 and 1920. Thompson, *How the West Stole Democracy from the Arabs: The Syrian Congress of 1920 and the Destruction of its Historic Liberal-Islamic Alliance* (New York: Atlantic, 2020), chap. 3.

24. The resolutions adopted by the conference were published in Cairo along with the proceedings. High Committee of the Decentralization Party in Egypt, *Al-Mu'tamar al-'Arabi al-Awwal* (Cairo: Al-Bustour, 1331/1913). For the French translation of the resolution, 132–34; for the Arabic text, 114–21. For the Ottoman Administrative Decentralization Party's "Party statement and political program" from 1913 see Hoover/Hidayet Dağdeviren, box 18/11–12, al-lajna al-ulya li-lamarkaziyya al-idariyya al-Uthmani "Bayan al-hizb wa-barnamajahu al-siyasi" (Cairo: Al-Manar Press in Egypt, 1913); Hasan Kayalı, *Arabs and Young Turks: Ottomanism, Arabism, and Islamism in the Ottoman Empire, 1908–1918* (Berkeley: University of California Press, 1997, chap. 4.

25. Cemal Paşa, *Memoirs*, 323; "Arap İhtilali," *Hatırat*, 163–235.

26. Aksakal, *The War That Made the Middle East: World War I and the End of the Ottoman Empire* (Princeton: Princeton University Press, 2026), chap. 2; Çiçek, *War and State Formation*, chap. 1.

27. The volume was of the genre of dueling war crimes reports issued by the Entente and Central Powers—not least because it was published in French, Arabic, and Ottoman Turkish. Cemal Paşa discusses the text in his memoir as the "Red Book" and republishes several of the seized documents there. Dördüncü Ordu-yu Hümâyun, *Aliye-i Divan-ı Harb-i Örfisinde Tetkik Olunan Mesele-i Siyasiye Hakkında İzahat* (Dersaadet: Tanin Matbaası, 1332); Commandement de la IVme Armée, *La verité sur la question syrienne* (Stamboul: Imprimerie Tanine, 1916); *Idahat an al-masa'il al-siyasiyya allati jarrat tadqiquha bi-diwan al-harb al-urfi al-mutashakkil bi-ali* (Istanbul: Mata'at Tanin, 1334 [1916]).

28. "Yani Suriye'nin muhtar bir prensliğe kalbi ile Müslüman bir prens tarafından idare-yi ciheti tercih edeceğe benziyor." *Aliye-i Divan-ı Harb-i Örfisinde*, 52–53.

29. Cemal Paşa reproduced the document in both his postwar memoir and the wartime trove of documents. Cemal Paşa, *Hatirat*, 209; *Aliye-i Divan-ı Harb-i Örfisinde*, 37.

30. *Aliye-i Divan-ı Harb-i Örfisinde*, 38–39.

31. Mostafa Minawi, *Losing Istanbul: Arab-Ottoman Imperialists and the End of Empire* (Stanford: Stanford University Press, 2022), 194.

32. *Aliye-i Divan-ı Harb-i Örfisinde*, 38–39; Stacy Fahrenthold, "Transnational Modes and Media: The Syrian Press in the Mahjar and Emigrant Activism

During World War I," *Mashriq & Mahjar: Journal of Middle East and North African Migration Studies* 1, no. 1 (2013): 34–63.

33. "Hilafeti Mısır'da İngiltere himayesinde tesis ve hidiviyeni hilafete kalb etmek." *Aliye-i Divan-ı Harb-i Örfisinde*, 5.

34. As Talha Çiçek has argued, Cemal hanged the Arabists "because they called for the decentralization of the empire and had connections with the Great Powers." Çiçek, *War and State Formation*, 46.

35. Çiçek, 94.

36. Çiçek, chap. 2; Engin Akarlı, *The Long Peace: Ottoman Lebanon, 1861–1920* (Berkeley: University of California Press, 1993).

37. BOA, DH.ŞFR 494/90 12 Teşrin-i evvel 1331 (October 25, 1915). Quoted in Çiçek, *War and State Formation*, 96–97.

38. The *Règlement Organique*, which had governed Lebanon's status since 1861 (it was amended in1864), was revoked on July 11, 1915. In addition to a nonlocal Christian governor, appointed by the sultan and approved by Europe, Mount Lebanon had had broad local control over its internal administration. See Akarlı, *The Long Peace*; and Çiçek, *War and State Formation*, 96–99.

39. BOA, HR.HMŞ.İ ŞO. 65/20 İbrahim Hakkı Paşa to Gottleib von Jagow, 17 Teşrin-i evvel 1332 (October 14, 1916).

40. BOA, HR.HMŞ.İ ŞO. 65/20.

41. BOA, HR.HMŞ.İ ŞO. 65/20.

42. "Bab-ı Ali'nin Muhim bir Notası" *İkdam*, no. 8094 20 Teşrin-i evvel 1332 (November 2, 1916). The subhead reads: "The Imperial Government considers the Treaties of Paris and Berlin null and void and has revoked Mount Lebanon's privileges" (*Lübnan imtiyazatının teyid ilgası*).

43. "Bab-ı âli tarafından serd ve dermeyan edilen delail, hiçbir kimesnenin—bu, velev Rus hukuk-i düvel muallimi Martens olsun—redd edemeyeceği mertebede metin, resin, hatta ahenindir. Zaten şimdiye kadar Avrupa'nın en tarafkir ve sıfat-ı resmiyesi haiz-i hukuk-i düvel muallim ve müşavirleri bile aleyhimizde tatbik edilegelmekte olan desatir-i hukukiyenin ne derecelerde gidarane olduğunu ketm edemiyorlardı. Devlet ve milletimiz aleyhindeki entrikaları ile İgnatievlere halef olmak isteyen [Mandelstam] bile uhud-i kadimenin haksız olduğunu söyleşdi." *İkdam*, no. 8094.

44. Though Mandelstam had left Istanbul in 1914, he managed to get a copy of the newspaper, which he translated and reproduced in his wartime legal treatise on humanitarian intervention, *The Fate of the Ottoman Empire*. He translated the note that canceled Mount Lebanon's autonomy and did not reproduce the CUP's new vision of international law, nor the dig directed against him. André Nicolayévitch Mandelstam, *Le Sort de l'Empire ottoman* (Paris: Payot, 1917), 402–4.

45. Akin, *When the War Came Home*, chap. 4; Melanie S. Tanielian, *The Charity of War: Famine, Humanitarian Aid and World War I in the Middle East* (Stanford: Stanford University Press, 2017).

46. Mustafa Aksakal, "Holy War Made in Germany? Ottoman Origins of the 1914 Jihad," *War in History* 18, no. 2 (April 2011): 184–99; Cemil Aydın, *The Idea of the Muslim World: A Global Intellectual History* (Cambridge: Harvard University Press, 2017); Erik-Jan Zürcher, ed., *Jihad and Islam in World War I: Studies on the Ottoman Jihad on the Centenary of Snouk Hurgronje's "Holy War Made in Germany"* (Leiden: University of Leiden Press, 2016); Bruce Westrate, *The Arab Bureau: British Policy in the Middle East, 1916–1920* (University Park: Penn State University Press, 1992); Avni Ozcan, *Pan-Islamism: Indian Muslims, the Ottomans and Britain* (Leiden: Brill, 1997).

47. Jonathan Schneer, *The Balfour Declaration: The Origins of the Arab-Israeli Conflict* (New York: Random House, 2010); Abigail Jacobson, *From Empire to Empire: Jerusalem Between Ottoman and British Rule* (Syracuse: Syracuse University Press, 2011).

48. Max Reibman, "The Case of William Yale: Cairo's Syrians and the Arab Origins of American Influence in the Post-Ottoman Middle East, 1917–19," *Journal of Middle East Studies* 46 (2014): 681–702; Schneer, *The Balfour Declaration.*

49. Çiçek, *War and State Formation*, 63–65.

50. Hanioğlu, *A Brief History*, 178–79.

51. Bab-ı Ali, Hariciye Nezareti, *Kuveyt Meselesi* (Istanbul: Istanbul: Matbaa-yi Amire, 1334 [1917/1918]); Mehmed Nabi and Rumbeyoğlu Fahreddin, *Necd kit'ası Meselesi* (Istanbul: Matbaa-yı Amire, 1334 [1918]); Ragib Raif and Ahmed Rauf, *Mısır Meselesi* (Istanbul: Bab–ı Ali, Hariciye Nezareti, 1334 [1918]).

52. See chapter 4. It is striking to note, too, that all these cases are the precise issues for which Arab decentralists and other opposition figures criticized the CUP.

53. BOA, HR.HMŞ.IŞO 50/13-4, "The Ottoman Empire's legal rights over Kuwait," 27 Mart 1327 (April 9, 1911); BOA, HR.HMŞ.IŞO 50/16, "Legal assessment of the agreement between Britian and the Sheikh of Dubai," 23 Haziran 1327 (July 6, 1911); BOA, HR.HMŞ.IŞO 50/115, "Ottoman influence over Muscat," 4 Mart 1329 (March 17, 1913); BOA, HR.HMŞ.IŞO 50/11-12, "The Ottoman Empire's legal claim to the Shatt al-Arab," 13 Teşrin-i sani 1330 (November 26, 1914); BOA, HR.HMŞ.IŞO 50/10, "The Ottoman Empire's legal rights over the Bahrain Islands," 19 Kanun-i sani 1331 (February 1, 1916); BOA, HR.HMŞ.IŞO 50/17, "The Ottoman Empire's legal rights over the Kazima region located between Faw and Kuwait on the western shores of the Persian Kuwait," 16 Mart 1327 (March 29, 1916); BOA, HR

.HMŞ.IŞO 50/8, "Ottoman legal claims over the Arabian Peninsula," 29 Mayis 1333 (May 29, 1917).

54. BOA, HR.HMŞ.IŞO 50/8, "Maskat."

55. BOA, HR.SYS 89/17. This file contains the correspondence between Hakkı Paşa and Istanbul, during the negotiations over Kuweit; BOA, MV, 1233/30 [1332 Ra. 5]; BOA, MV 1233/95; BOA, HR.HMŞ.IŞO 50/8; BOA, HR .HMŞ.IŞO 50/13-4; Bab-ı Ali, *Kuveyt Meselesi*.

56. Ragıb Raif and Rauf Amhed, *Mısır Meselesi*, 176, cast the so-called reconquest of Sudan as a conquest plain and simple. They argued that Britain had illegally treated Ottoman Sudan as *terra nullius* (*sahibsiz*).

57. Raif and Rauf, *Mısır Meselesi*, chapters 1 and 2.

58. For example, they consulted Henry Bonfils (*Bonfis* in Ottoman), *Manuel de droit international public* (Paris: Arthur Rousseau, 1898); works by F. M. de Martens; as well as Jules Cocheris, *Situation internationale de l'Egypte et du Soudan* (Paris: Plon-Nourrit, 1903). Raif and Rauf, *Mısır Meselesi*, 176–78.

59. Raif and Rauf, *Mısır Meselesi*, 179, "Maamafih her ne suretiyle olursa olsun bir asırda tahdis ve inkişaf eden usul-ü idare suret-i tabiyede bir (vilayet-i mümtaze) vucuda getirmiş olduğundan vesait hukukiye-yi hazıranın o kita-yı nazardan telâkisi hakaik ahvala daha muvafık olur itikadındayız."

60. BOA, HMŞ.IŞO 233/2 (January 1, 1917). There is another copy of the map in BOA, HRT 656 "Eyalet-i Mümtaze ve Mülhakatı." This map is distinct from the "missing map" issued with the first ferman but is striking to see alongside it. See Matthew Ellis, *Desert Borderland: The Making of Modern Egypt and Libya* (Stanford: Stanford University Press, 2018), introduction.

61. The Ottoman Empire regained the "three provinces" (*Elviye-i Selase*)—Ardahan, Batum, and Kars—lost to Russia in 1878. The peace negotiations on the return of the provinces to the Ottoman Empire lasted from December 9, 1917, until March 3, 1918. Reynolds, *Shattering Empires*, chap. 6; Hans-Lukas Kieser, *Talaat Pasha: Father of Modern Turkey, Architect of Genocide* (Princeton: Princeton University Press, 2018), chap. 6.

62. Brief descriptions of Wilson's January 8 speech first appeared on January 9 and 13, followed by a more sustained analysis the next day. For example, "Wilson'un Yeni bir Beyannamesi," *Vakit*, 9 Kanun-i sani 1334 (January 9, 1918), p. 2; "Wilson'un Beyannamesi Münasebetiyle," *Tanin*, 13 Kanun-i sani 1334 (January 13, 1918), p. 2; "Wilson Nutukuna Dair" and "Amerika'nın Yardimi: Ittilafin Son Umudu," *İkdam*, 13 Kanun-i sani 1334 (January, 13 1918); "Wilson Amerika'nın Harb Gayelerini Söylüyor," *Ati*, 14 Kanun-i sani 1334 (January, 14, 1918); "Amerika Reis Cumhuru Wilson'un Nutku—Sulh Umumi İ çin On Dort Şart!" *İkdam*, 14 Kanun-i sani 1334 (January 14, 1918); "Wilson'un Sulh Şartları," *Tanin*, 14 Kanun-i sani 1334, pp. 1–2; "Wilson'un Yeni Şerait Sulhiyeden bahis yeni Hutbesi," *Tesvir-i Efkar*, 14 Kanun-i sani 1334;

"Wilson'un Yeni Nutku," *Vakit*, 14 Kanun-i sani 1334 (January 14, 1918); "Wilson'un Sulh Şeraiti," *Vakit*, 14 Kanun-i sani 1334. Ottoman translations of the 14 Points varied quite substantially. When Istanbul newspapers first published the contents of Wilson's speech to Congress, each newspaper produced different translations, although the overall general meaning was the same.

63. Ahmed Emin, "Wilson'un Sulh Şeraiti," *Vakit*, 14 Kanun-i sani 1334 (January 14, 1918).

64. "Loyd Georg'un Bayanati," *Vakit*, 9 Kanun-i sani 1334 (January 9, 1918), p. 2.

65. Ahmed Emin (Yalman), "Itilaf'in Sulh Şatları," *Vakit*, 10 Kanun-i sani 1334 (January 10, 1918). David Lloyd George claimed that Britain fought to defend "the violated public law of Europe" and "treaty obligations." He noted too that "Arabia, Armenia, Mesopotamia, Syria, and Palestine are, in our judgment, entitled to a recognition of their separate national conditions." Ahmed Emin insisted the speech offered nothing new. For Lloyd George's speech see "Address of the British Prime Minister (Lloyd George) before the Trade Union Conference at London, January 5, 1918," *State Department, Papers Relating to the Foreign Relations of the United States, 1918: Supplement 1: The World War*, vol. 1 (Washington, D.C.: General Printing Office, 1918), 4–12.

66. Fahri Belen, *Birinci Cihan Harbinde Türk Harbi* (Ankara: Gunkur Basımevi, 1967), vol. 5, "1918 Yılı Hareketleri," 207; Erik Zürcher, *The Young Turk Legacy and Nation Building from the Ottoman Empire to Atatürk's Turkey* (London: Tauris, 2010), 189; Gwynne Dyer, "The Turkish Armistice of 1918: 1—The Decision for a Separate Peace, Autumn 1918," *Middle East Studies* 8, no. 2 (1972): 143–78.

67. Erez Manela has reframed the period between Wilson's Speech and the bitter disappointments that emerged out of the Paris Peace Conference as "the Wilsonian Moment." During this period of uncertainty, Wilson's ideas—embedded within the 14 Points—triggered broad support in Europe, but especially across the colonial world. Manela, *The Wilsonian Moment*.

68. Wilson, "Address to the Joint Session of Congress," January 8, 1918. See also U.S. Department of State, "The Present Situation."

69. NA/FO/371/3448, October 4, 1919, reproduced in Dyer, "The Turkish Armistice of 1918," 153.

70. Belen, *Birinci Cihan*, 209; Zürcher, *The Young Turk Legacy*, 189–90; Charles Vere Ferrers Townshend, *My Campaign* (New York: McCann, 1920), 277.

71. The siege ended with what was at the time the largest British surrender: Thirteen thousand British and Indian troops surrendered to Ottoman forces after the 147-day siege. Eugene Rogan, *The Fall of the Ottomans: The Great War in the Middle East* (New York: Basic Books, 2015), chap. 10; *Kûtü'l Amâre Zaferi'nin zss. yılı Münasebetiyle I. Dünya Savaşı'nda Irak*, ed. Orhan Neçare (Ankara: Atatürk Araştırma Merkezi, 2016).

72. Belen, *Birinci Cihan Harbinde*, 5:208; Townshend, *My Campaign*, 277.

73. Rauf Orbay, *Cehennem Değirmeni: Siyasi Hatıralarım* (Istanbul: Emre Yayınları, [2004]), 1:145; Townshend, *My Campaign*, 286.

74. BOA, HR.HMŞ.İ ŞO 214/14, 15 Muharram 1337 (October 21, 1918). There is a clean, copied out version of the actual text, along with a printed copy, which suggests it may have been widely distributed.

75. NA/FO/608/277/212, "Ottoman Peace Delegation"; NA/FO/608/117/341, "Draft Treaty with Turkey"; George Harris, *Atatürk's Diplomats and Their Brief Biographies* (Istanbul: Isis, 2010), 289–92.

76. For example, in translating Wilson's Article 12, Mehmed Münir simplified the language and omitted reference to the "security of life" and "absolutely unmolested" development. This kind of vague, unenforceable language sounded too much like Tanzimat-era European restrictions on Ottoman sovereignty. The Ottoman translation of Article 12 reads: "The Turkish portions of the Ottoman Empire require the security of complete sovereignty, but the other nationalities that are at present under Turkish rule should be allowed the possibility of an autonomous development, and the Dardanelles should be open to the commerce and ships of all nations under international guarantees."

77. BOA, HR.HMŞ.İ ŞO 214/14.

78. BOA, HR.HMŞ.İ ŞO 214/14.

79. NA/WO 106/1433.

80. BOA, HR/MA, 1228/1, 19 Teşrin-i evvel 1918 (October 19, 1918).

81. No doubt he was concerned about the way in which Ottoman support for autonomous provinces was described in territorial and geographic terms and linked to population.

82. *Meclis-i Mebusan Zabıt Ceridesi*, IIIüncü devre, 5inci ictima senesi, 4üncü inikad, 19 Teşrin-i evvel 1334 (October 19, 1918), 30–31. The enthusiasm for Wilson's 14 Points in the Ottoman Empire was not confined to the government.

83. Orhan Koloğlu, *Mondron'tan Mudabya'ya: Osmanlı'da Son Tartışmalar* (Istanbul: Doğan Kitap, 2008); Erol Baykal, *The Ottoman Press (1908–1923)* (Leiden: Brill, 2019); Ahmet Emin (Yalman), *Yakın Tarihte Gördüklerim ve Geçirdiklerim* (Rey Yayınları, 1970–1971), vol. 1–2; Nur Bilge Criss, *Istanbul Under Allied Occupation 1918–1923* (Leiden: Brill, 1999).

84. Tarık Zafer Tunaya, *Türkiye'de Siyasal Partiler* (Istanbul: Hürriyet Vakfı Yayınları, 1984), vol. 2, 255–63. Ali Kemal was one of the key opposition figures in Istanbul throughout the Armistice. He was a founding member of the society as well as the Friends of England Society (*İngiliz Mühipler Cemiyeti*) and was fully committed to cooperating with the Allied occupation in Istanbul. He favored a British mandate for the empire and was deeply critical of Mustafa Kemal and the national movement. He paid with his life for these ideas and for being on the losing side—he was lynched en route

to Ankara to be tried for treason in 1922. See Faruk Gezgin, *Ali Kemal: Bir Muhalifin Hikâyesi* (Istanbul: Isis, 2010). On Refik Halit (Karay), see Christine M. Philliou, *Turkey: A Past Against History* (Oakland: University of California Press, 2021).

85. Akin, *When the War Came Home*, chap. 5; Hasan Kayalı, *Imperial Resilience: The Great War's End, Ottoman Longevity, and Incidental Nations* (Oakland: University of California Press, 2021).

86. As Christine Philliou has argued, the debates that raged between the CUP and opposition between 1908 and 1913 reappeared in this period of flux and confusion. Using the writer and exile Rakik Halit (Karay) as a case study, Philliou examines the meaning of opposition (*muhalefet*) from the late empire into the early Republic, which has had a lasting effect on the politics of modern Turkey. Philliou, *Turkey*.

87. The declaration was sent to Wilson, Clemenceau, Lloyd George, and the Ottoman Foreign Ministry. Erol, *Türkiye'de Amerikan Mandası*, 28; Şahingöz and Keleşyılmaz, "Milli Mücadele," 362.

88. Erol, *Türkiye'de Amerikan Mandası*, 30–31, 115, 117–18. Manuscripts and Archives, Yale University/Edward Mandell House Papers (MS 466), box 207, "Letter from the founders of the Turkish Wilsonian League to President Wilson, December 5, 1918."

89. Sati al-Husri, "Sabahaddin Bey: Fikrileri ve Muarızları—1," *Vakit* 27 Teşrin-i evvel, 1334 (October 27, 1918); and "Sabahaddin Bey: Fikrileri ve Muarızları—2," 29 *Vakit* Teşrin-i evvel, 1334 (October 29, 1918).

90. William Cleveland, *The Making of an Arab Nationalist* (Princeton: Princeton University Press, 1971), 42–46.

91. Sati al-Husri, "Sabahaddin Bey: Fikrileri ve Muarızları—1."

92. Sati al-Husri, "Sabahattin Bey: Fikrileri ve Muarızları—1."

93. Sati al-Husri, "Sabahaddin Bey: Fikrileri ve Muarızları—2."

94. Sati al-Husri, "Sabahhadin-2"; Cleveland, *The Making of an Arab Nationalist*, 46.

95. Ziya Gökalp, "Milliyetçilik ve Beynelmileliyetilik," *Yeni Mecmua*, 14 Mart, 1918, 162–64.

96. Halide Edib, "Suriye'deki Türkler," *Vakit*, 10 Teşrin-i evvel 1334 (October 10, 1918). On Halide Edib's wartime activities, see Karnig Panian *Goodbye, Antoura: A Memoir of the Armenian Genocide* (Stanford: Stanford University Press, 2015); Keith David Watenpaugh, *Bread From Stones: The Middle East and the Making of Modern Humanitarianism* (Oakland: University of California Press, 2015); and Watenpaugh, "The League of Nations' Rescue of Armenian Genocide Survivors and the Making of Modern Humanitarianism, 1920–1927," *American Historical Review* 115, no. 5 (December 2010).

97. Edib, "Suriye'deki Türkler."

98. Eleutherios Venizelos, *Greece Before the Peace Congress of 1919* (New York: American Hellenic Society, 1919), 15–17. A copy was included with a series of other texts on the future of the Ottoman Empire. Library of Congress, Manuscripts and Archives (LOC), Woodrow Wilson Papers/Reel 461–6G.

99. A handful of pamphlets and letters produced by the Ottoman Liberal Party can be found in the papers of General Bliss, the American military representative to the Supreme War Council during the Peace Conference. LOC/MSS13037/Tasker Howard Bliss Papers, box 354, file "Turkish Empire April 1918–August 1919. A. Réchid (Ahmed Reşid Bey), *An Open Letter to M. W. Wilson President of the United States of America* (Geneva: Imprimerie de La Suisse, 1919), 10.

100. Ahmed Reşid (Rey) wrote about the preparing for the Paris Peace Conference and the disappointment that followed when the Allied powers refused to implement "Wilsonian principles" in the Ottoman Empire. Ahmet Reşit Rey, *Imparatoluğun Son Döneminde: Gördüklerim Yaptıklarım (1890–1922)* (Istanbul: Türkiye Bankası Kültür Yayınları, 2007).

101. "Manda, Himaye, Istiklal," *Büyük Mecmua*, 19 Haziran 1335 (June 19, 1919), 148.

102. LOC/MSS13037/Bliss Papers, box 354, file "Turkish Empire April 1918–August 1919, pamphlet "Ligue pour la defense des droits des Ottomans."

103. "Petition to Wilson," Tarık Zafer Tunaya, *Türkiye'de Siyasal Partiler* (Istanbul: Hürriyet Vakfi Yayınları, 1984), vol. 2, 257–59; Stanford Shaw, *From Empire to Republic: The Turkish War of National Liberation, 1918–1923: A Documentary Study* (Ankara: Türk Tarih Kurumu, 2000), vol. 1, 190–92; "Wilson Pensipleri Cemiyeti," *Sabah*, 6 Kanun-i evvel 1334 (December 6, 1918).

104. Ahmed Emin, "Bir İzah," *Vakit*, 7 Kanun-i evvel 1334 (December 7, 1918).

105. Oberlin College Archives, Henry Churchill King Papers, King-Crane Commission: Reports and Correspondence, 1918–19/RG 2/6, box 123, folder 3, Report from Ahmed Emin to the commission, August 15, 1919.

106. Ahmed Emin (Yalman), *Turkey in My Time* (Norman: University of Oklahoma Press, 1956).

107. Mustafa Kemal, *Nutuk* (Ankara: Türk Tayyare Cemiyeti, 1927); and *A Speech Delivered by Ghazi Mutapha Kemal, President of the Turkish Republic, October 1927* (Leipzig: Koehler, 1927).

108. Refik Halit (Karay), *Minelbab İlelmihrab* (Istanbul: İnkilap, 2015); Ahmed Emin (Yalman), *Turkey in World War* (New Haven: Yale University Press, 1930); Halide Edib (Adıvar), *The Turkish Ordeal: Being the Further Memoirs of Halide Edib* (London: John Murray, 1928); Celal Nuri İleri, *Turk Inkilabi* (Istanbul: Kaknus Yayinlari, 2000).

109. U.S. Department of State, "The Present Situation," 52–53. See also Neil Smith, *American Empire: Roosevelt's Geographer and the Prelude to Globalization* (Berkeley: University of California, 2003), chap. 5.

110. LOC/MSS.10744, box 38, The Inquiry, Special Reports on Countries, Peoples, and Regions, 1917–1919. Several special reports analyzed the application of autonomy in the Ottoman Empire. Among these texts are Harvey Porter, "Outline of the History and Ethnology of the Turkish Empire" and "Religious Conditions in the Turkish Empire"; Dana Munro, "Turkey in Asia"; W. L. Westerman, "Just and Practical Boundaries for Subdivisions of the Turkish Empire" and "Historical Sketch of the Turkish Empire"; American Committee for Armenian and Syrian Relief, "Turkish Survey Recommendations for Political Reconstruction"; S. T. Dutton, "A Proposal to Erect That Portion of the Ottoman Empire" and "Proposal for the Federation of Turkish Provinces"; and Arrigo Cavaglieri, "The Doctrine of the Succession of State to State and Its Legal Value."

111. LOC/MSS10744, box 38, William W. Peet, "The Working of the Turkish Government."

6. Mandate Variations

1. For example, George Louis Beer's book on the Peace Conference contains a large section on Egypt and legal work necessary for the protectorate there. He also drafted the articles related to recognition of the British protectorate in Egypt for all the peace treaties concluding World War I. Beer, *African Questions at the Paris Peace Conference, with Papers on Egypt, Mesopotamia, and the Colonial Settlement* (New York: Macmillan, 1923); Vernon O'Rourke, *The Juristic Status of Egypt and the Sudan* (Baltimore: Johns Hopkins Press, 1935); Malcolm McIlwraith, "The Declaration of a Protectorate in Egypt and Its Legal Effects," *Journal of the Society of Comparative Legislation* 17, no. 1/2 (1917): 238–59; and "Legal War Work in Egypt," in *Problems of the War* (1917), 3:71–90; and Valentine Chirol, *The Egyptian Problem* (London: Macmillan, 1920). The 1914 protectorate appears as a major issue in many postwar memoirs of British officials stationed in Cairo during and after the war, such as Ronald Storrs, *Orientations* (London: Ivor Nicholson & Watson, 1937). On the Ottoman side, see Rağib Raif and Ahmed Rauf, *Mısır Meselesi* (Istanbul: Bab-ı Ali, Hariciye Nezareti, 1334 [1915]); and Süleyman Kani Irtem, *Osmanlı Devleti'nin Mısır Yemen Hicaz Meselesi* (Istanbul: Temel Yayınları, 1999). Though the 1919 Revolution in Egypt was framed in different ways at the time and since, one of the most important arguments emanating from

Cairo and Paris was that the British established an "illegal protectorate." *Egyptian Delegation to the Peace Conference, Collection of Official Correspondence from November 11, 1918, to July 14, 1919* (Paris: The Delegation, 1919).

2. See Aksakal, *The Ottoman Road to War* (Cambridge: Cambridge University Press, 2008), chaps. 5–6; Limon von Sanders, *Five Years in Turkey* (Annapolis: United States Naval Institute, 1927). Von Sanders claimed that he argued against an attack on Egypt as it would be impossible to take the territory from the British. He notes that Bethmann-Hollweg requested that he put aside his doubts and support the German plan for an Ottoman expedition to Egypt, stating (p. 27) that "an undertaking against Egypt is of great importance."
3. The Ottoman Empire signed an alliance with Germany on August 2, 1914, and the next day announced armed neutrality. Ş ükrü Hanioğlu, *A Late History of the Ottoman Empire* (Princeton: Princeton University Press, 2008); Aksakal, *The Ottoman Road to War*, intro.; Mehmet Said Halim Pasha, *L'Empire ottoman et la guerre mondiale* (Istanbul: Isis, 2000), "Pourquoi la Turquie participa à la Guerre mondiale?"; Michael Reynolds *Shattering Empires: The Clash and Collapse of the Ottoman and Russian Empires, 1908–1918* (Cambridge: Cambridge University Press, 2011), introduction and chap. 4.
4. Hanioğlu, *A Late History*, 177–83.
5. [cd. 7628] No. 13 (1914), Sir Edward Grey to Mr. Beaumont, August 7, 1914; Stanford Shaw, *The Ottoman Empire in World War I* (Ankara: Türk Tarih Kurumu, 2008), vol. 2: *1914–1916*.
6. "Resolution taken to assure the defense of Egypt in the war between Germany and Great Britain," *Journal Official du Gouvernement Égyptien*, no. 98, August 6, 1914. This document alarmed the Ottoman Foreign Ministry, and the *Journal Official* was translated for the Ottoman Cabinet. BOA, HR.SYS.2348/6/no number, "Ingiltere ile Almanya arasındaki muharbere-yi hazıra esnasında Mısır'ın müdafaası için meclis-i nazar tarafından ittihaz olunan mukarrerat."
7. Abbas Hilmi II, *The Last Khedive: Memoires of Abbas Hilmi II* (London: Garnet Press, 1998), 341.
8. Aksakal, *The Ottoman Road to War*, 137–41.
9. Said Halim Paşa (1865–1921) was an Egyptian prince and the grandson of Mehmed Ali. He lost his claim to the Khedivate during the reign of Ismail (r. 1863–1879), who negotiated a new law of khedival succession. At the beginning of the 'Urabi Revolution, the French and British considered replacing the Tewfik with Said Halim. He was born in Cairo and resided there in exile for an extended period during the reign of Abdülhmaid II, returning to Istanbul during the Second Constitutional era. He was the grand vizier through much of the war and was later assassinated in Rome by Arshavir Shiragian for his role in the Armenian genocide. See Mehmet Said Halim Pasha, *L'Empire*

ottoman et la guerre mondiale (Istanbul: İsis, 2000); M. K. İnal, *Osmanlı Devrinde Son Sadriazamlar* (Istanbul: Milli Eğitim Basımevi, 1965), 3: 1893–1932; Ahmet Şeyhun, *Said Halim Pasha: Ottoman Statesmen and Islamist Thinker* (Istanbul: İsis, 2003); Tanvir Wasti, "Said Halim Pasha—Philosopher Prince," *Middle Eastern Studies* 44, no. 1 (January 2008): 85–104; and M. Hanefi Boston, *Bir Islâmcı Düş ünür: Said Halim Paşa* (Istanbul: İrfan Yayınevi, 1992). Said Halim sent the note to German and the Habsburg ambassadors on the same day that the SMS *Goeben* and SMS *Breslau* arrived at the Dardanelles and requested permission to continue to Istanbul, where they arrived four days later.

10. Said Halim removed the next line of text from his letter: "so that I might ask the Egyptian Government to repeal the said decree." BOA, HR.SYS.2348/6/no. 53739/126, Said Halim Paşa to Hans Frieiherr von Wangenheim (German ambassador in Istanbul) and Wangenheim German and Johann Markgraf von Pallavicini (Habsburg ambassador in Istanbul). A note to the same effect arrived three days later from Pallavicini on behalf of the Habsburg Empire.
11. The Ottoman ambassador in Berlin, Muhtar Paşa, who pressed for Ottoman intervention in the war from the July Crisis, sent a note to Said Halim Paşa stating that, according to unverified reports, Britain declared a protectorate in Egypt. He argued that if the rumor was true, the Ottomans should seize the opportunity to strengthen their claim to Egypt and enhance their prestige in the "Islamic world." See *Ottoman Diplomatic Documents on the Origins of World War I: From the July Crisis to Turkey's Entry Into the War July–December, 1914* (Istanbul: Isis, 2012), no. 337, Muhtar Paşa to Said Halim, August 20, 1914, 161; Mahmud Muhtar Paşa, *La Turquie, l'Allemagne et l'Europe depuis le Traité de Berlin jusqu'à la guerre mondiale* (Paris: Berger-Levrault, 1924).
12. BOA, HR.SYS 2348/6, Wangenheim to Said Halim Paşa, August 26, 1914.
13. See *Ottoman Diplomatic Documents on the Origins of World War I: From the July Crisis to Turkey's Entry Into the War July–December, 1914* (Istanbul: Isis, 2012); Şeyhun, *Said Halim Pasha*, 110; Mehmed Cavid, "Birinci Dünya Harbine Türkiye'nin Girmesi, Maliye Nazrı Cavid Bey'in Notları," *Tanin*, August 3, 1943–June 22, 1946.
14. BOA, HR.SYS.2348/6/no. 1780, Wangenheim to Said Halim Paşa, September 11, 1914. A note to the same effect arrived three days later from Pallavicini, on behalf of the Habsburg Empire. See BOA, HR.SYS.2348/6/ no. 753, Pallavicini to Said Halim Paşa, September 14, 1914.
15. Aksakal, *Road to War*, 134.
16. Periodically the Foreign Office accused Enver Paşa and the "military party" of preparing a campaign against Britain in Egypt and warned the Said Halim and Ottoman ambassadors that armed neutralization posed a threat to Egypt's political status. For example, in one of many episodes, the British ambassador to the Ottoman Empire, Louis Mallet, linked Ottoman mobilization in Syria to a plan

to attack Egypt, based in part on articles published in *Tanin*. BOA, HR.SYS.4/5, "Ingiltere Sefareti'nin Tanin'de neşredilen mısır'la ilgili paragrapha dair açıklama isteğine verilen cevap," Said Halim Paşa to L. Mallet, October 8, 1914. Mallet wrote to Grey that "I think that it would be right to remind the Grand Vizier that have always made it perfectly clear that undertaking not to change the status of Egypt was conditioned on Turkey maintaining strict neutrality." [Cd. 7628] No. 13 (1914), "Correspondence Respecting Events Leading to the Rupture of Relations with Turkey," no. 117, Mallet to Grey, October 12, 1914.

17. Feroz Ahmad, "The Late Ottoman Empire," in *The Great Powers and the End of the Ottoman Empire*, ed. Marian Kent (London: Frank Cass, 1996); Mustafa Aksakal, "Not 'by Those Old Books of International Law, but Only by War": Ottoman Intellectuals on the Eve of the Great War," *Diplomacy and Statecraft* 15, no. 3 (2004): 507–44.
18. Mahmud Muhtar Paşa had served in the Balkan Wars and the Ottoman Cabinet before being posted to Berlin. He was the son of Ahmed Muhtar Paşa, the longstanding Ottoman special commissioner in Egypt, who represented the sultan in Cairo as long as Cromer served his masters in London.
19. BOA, HR.SYS. 2094/8, no. 12673/440, Mahmud Muhtar Paşa to Said Halim Paşa, (October 5, 1914); Mehmet Said Halim Pasha, *L'Empire ottoman et la guerre mondiale* (Istanbul: Isis, 2000), "Why We Participated in the War?"
20. BOA, HR.SYS. 2094/8, no. 12666/435, Mahmud Muhtar Paşa to Said Halim Paşa, (October 3, 1914). Muhtar Paşa continued, arguing that the Tripolitanian war—the war between the Ottoman Empire and Italy in Libya (1911–1912)—was the beginning of the current war, just as the battle of Sedan had been the beginning of the events leading to San Stefano and the Congress of Berlin (1878). Berlin inaugurated the first major Ottoman territorial loss since 1856 when the Powers agreed to maintain the territorial integrity of the Ottoman Empire in the Treaty of Paris following the Crimean War.
21. Reynolds *Shattering Empires*.
22. George Lloyd, *Egypt Since Cromer* (London: Macmillan, 1933–34). After serving as the governor of Bombay from December 1918, Lloyd followed Allenby as the British high commissioner in Egypt, where he remained until 1929. His two-volume administrative history of Egypt has been interpreted as a justification for his not implementing Foreign Office policy in Egypt as instructed during his tenure as high commissioner. He thought that the protectorate had been a mistake and independence, subject to the four reservations in 1922, an even greater error. Like those in the British government who had demanded the annexation of Egypt during the occupation, Lloyd argued that the "independence"—much like occupation—left Egypt outside of benevolent Colonial Office oversight, which would have assured good administration and more complete imperial control. Like many of the British critics of occupation,

he did not believe that Egypt was prepared for self-government and instead required, in the words of Cromer, "honest, just, and orderly administration."

23. Ronald Storrs argued later that "neither Turkey not the rest of the World could imagine that the Occupying Power, if attacked by the Suzerain, would any longer tolerate suzerainty that had been but a figure of speech for the past half century. The only question was, what form of government should replace the forfeited suzerainty. The uncertainty of Occupation, with its remote hopes and hypothetical fears, must obviously be abolished." But this was not a legal argument and was a position that would be difficult to sustain after the war. Storrs, *Orientations*, 150.

24. In Sir Edward Grey's memoirs, he argues that the decision to establish a protectorate in Egypt was the best solution at the time, given the circumstances, because of Egypt's status as an Ottoman province: "The status of Egypt in relation to Turkey, had not, so far as international law was concerned, been effected by the British occupation. Technically Egyptians became enemy subjects after the entry of Turkey into the war against us. Something had to be done to prevent legal complications." Viscount Grey of Fallodon, *Twenty-Five Years* (New York: Frederick A. Stokes, 1925), 2:176–77.

25. The Foreign Office also feared that going to war against the Ottoman Empire might incite rebellion among Britain's Muslim subjects more broadly and in Egypt most acutely. While Kaiser Wilhelm's pan-Islamic revolution never materialized, British delay and caution with respect to the future of Egypt should be seen against this possibility. Storrs's description of waiting for the Ottomans to enter the war while stationed in Cairo is striking for the fact that he argues that the possibility was the most important fact of those days over whatever was happening on the Western Front: "The horrors of Louvain and other atrocities certainly lost nothing in Allied accounts, but though brutal facts, they meant less to us than the more immediate fear of Turkey joining the Central Powers. Time-space is a natural statute of limitations, and news must be sensational indeed to survive transmission over a month from the Antipodes." Storrs, *Orientations*, 143.

26. Even after independence and Lausanne, where the Ottoman/Republican state relinquished legal claims to Egypt and Sudan, problems related to Ottoman sovereignty in Egypt persisted through a series of measures in the 1930s stemming from the Anglo-Egyptian Treaty of Alliance in 1936. The treaty opened the way to the Montreux conference of April 12–May 8, 1937, which set the date to abolish the Capitulations, only twenty-three years after the Ottomans had done so and a full fourteen years after the Ottoman state had ceased to exist. Iraq, too, invited Egypt to join the League of Nations in February 1937, and the Republic of Turkey, itself a new member of the League, proposed that an extraordinary session should be held for the purpose. On May 26, the Assembly of the League of Nations unanimously recommended Egypt as a

League member. As one legal commentator noted, "Thus culminated the long progression of events which began with the establishment of Egypt's special status within the Ottoman Empire in the middle of the nineteenth century." Manley O. Hudson, "Admission of Egypt to Membership in the League of Nations," *American Journal of International Law* 31, no. 4 (October 1937): 681–83. The mixed courts were not disbanded until 1949. See Joel Benin, "Egypt: Society and Economy, 1923–1952," *The Cambridge History of Egypt*, vol. 2 (Cambridge: Cambridge University Press, 1998).

27. The exchange between Cairo and London on the best policy to follow in Egypt between July and December 1914 is reproduced in several places, including the Milne Cheetham papers, the Wingate papers, and the Grey Papers.

28. NA/FO/800/48/229 Sir Edward Grey Papers, Grey to Cheethem, August 12, 1914.:

29. NA/FO/407/183, Cheetham to Grey, August 14, 1914.

30. Sudan Archives, Durham, hereafter SAD/164/6/95-97, Wingate Papers, no. 139, Cheetham to Grey, September 10, 1914.

31. NA/FO/407/183, no. 7, Cheetham to Grey, September 1, 1914.

32. NA/FO/407/183. Enclosure, Ronald Storrs, Oriental Secretary, "Note respecting the state of public opinion in Egypt," August 31, 1914. The quotes around the expression and words "sense of nationality," "autonomy," and "independence" were Storrs's. He reproduced the note in his memoir after the war to show that Britain was concerned about the effect of war between the British and Ottoman Empires on the Muslim subjects of the British Empire: "I have said that our major preoccupation was the threat of Turkey on the Canal; less for its military effect than for the repercussion upon a Moslem Egypt." *Orientations*, 145.

33. Storrs did not elucidate the content of "independence" nor "autonomy," nor link these words to their Arabic or Ottoman counterparts (*hukm dhati, muhtariyet*, or *ötonomie*), but by this stage officials in Cairo, particularly those around Kitchener, were well aware of Arab demands for autonomy within the Ottoman Empire, especially in Syria, as well autonomy as an actual administrative category of province within the empire. See Rashid Khalidi, *British Policy Towards Syria & Palestine, 1906–1914* (London: Ithaca Press, 1980).

34. NA/FO/407/183, No. 8, Cheetham to Grey, September 7, 1914.

35. NA/FO/407/183, No. 5, Cheetham to Grey, September 10, 1914.

36. Sa'd Zaghlul and the Wafd would later argue that ending Ottoman sovereignty in Egypt could only mean that it reverted to Egypt. This is one of the key arguments that the Wafd presented in Paris.

37. Çubuklu Palace, or Hıdıv Kasrı. The distinguishing feature of the palace is a large tower overlooking the Bosporus. Abdülhamid II ordered that it be

reduced in height from the planned size because it would be taller than some of the minarets attached to imperial mosques in Istanbul. The family of Mehmed Ali, the Kavalalı dynasty, especially the khedives, built numerous seaside mansions (*yalı*) on the Bosporus, hospitals, Sufi lodges, and schools, along with large residential structures in the European quarter of Istanbul. The bulk of these structures were constructed during the later part of the nineteenth and the early twentieth centuries during the British occupation of Egypt. The Kavalalı family constructed some of the best extant examples of art nouveau–Jungendstil architecture in Istanbul. *Nıl Kıyısından Boğaziçi'ne Kavalalı Mehmed Ali Paşa Handedanı'nın İstanbul'daki İzleri* (Istanbul: İstanbul Araştırmaları Enstitüsü, 2011); Ünver Oral, *Yazı ve Resimlerde Beykoz* (Istanbul, 2007).

38. Three days before Archduke Ferdinand was killed in Sarajevo, Abbas himself was the object of an attempted assassination in Istanbul after leaving a meeting at the Bab-ı Ali with his uncle, Grand Vizier Said Halim Paşa. Abbas recovered from his wounds through September and remained in Istanbul. He alleged that the assassination attempt was the work of Egyptian nationalists directed by the Committee of Union and Progress, and Said Halim Paşa in particular. Abbas believed, mistakenly, that Said Halim wished to claim to the khedivate. Various British Foreign Office officials also maintained this line of argumentation, including Milne Cheetham and Ronald Storrs. See Abbas Hilmi II, *The Last Khedive: Memoires of Abbas Hilmi II* (London: Garnet Press, 1998); Storrs, *Orientations*.

39. Abbas Hilmi II had never been as pliable as Tewfik and had been at odds with British representatives in Egypt throughout his tenure as khedive. He overtly supported Mustafa Kamil, who was anti-British and appealed to Pan-Islam and supported Ottoman rights in Egypt, as well as the Nationalist Party (Hizb al-Watani). Abbas's presence in Istanbul through the July Crisis also made it easy for the Foreign Office to cast suspicion on his character and to question his relationship with the Ottoman Cabinet. The grand vizier, Said Halim, was his uncle and one of the leading members of the Committee of Union of Progress. Once the protectorate was declared and he was deposed, the British justified the deposition on the basis that he had thrown in his lot with the Ottoman Empire. For Abbas's troubled past with the British, see Afaf Lutfi Al-Sayyid, *Egypt and Cromer: A Study in Anglo-Egyptian Relations* (New York: Praeger, 1968), chap. 6; Jeffrey Collins, *The Egyptian Elite Under Cromer, 1882–1907* (Berlin: Klaus Schwarz, 1984), chaps. 6–7; Evelyn Baring, *Abbas II* (London: Macmillan, 1915); Şeyhun, *Said Halim Pasha*; Abbas Hilmi II, *The Last Khedive*.

40. NA/FO/48/220, Cheetham to Tyrell (for Kitchener), July 9, 1914.

41. Abbas Hilmi II, *The Last Khedive*, 307; Sudan Archive, Durham (SAD)/HIL/81–HIL/85.

42. The Egyptian government issued a proclamation on August 6 for the defense of Egypt, after discussions on August 5; *Journal Official du Gouvernement Égyptien*, August 6, 1914, no. 98, "Resolution taken to assure the defense of Egypt in the war between Germany and Great Britain."
43. SAD/HIL/81/1-25, Abbas Hilmi II papers, Rushdi Paşa to Abbas Hilmi, August 5, 1914. Reproduced in Abbas Hilmi II, *The Last Khedive*, 338.
44. Rushdi Paşa to Abbas Hilmi, August 7, 1914. Reproduced in Abbas Hilmi II, *The Last Khedive*, 340.
45. NA/FO/407/183, no. 9, Cheetham to Grey, September 24, 1914.
46. SAD/HIL/84/1-74 1914/, Dispatches from Regent (Rushdi Paşa) to Khedive at Constantinople, Rushdi to Muhib Paşa, September 6, 1914
47. SAD/164/6/95-97, Wingate Papers, "Notes on the Question of Succession," no. 226, Grey to Cheetham, September 26, 1914, "Appointment of Prince Hussain as Khedive approved." NA/FO/407/183, no. 11, Grey to Cheetham, September 27, 1914.
48. NA/FO/407/183, no. 17, Cheetham to Grey, October 12, 1914. The section on internal administration did not differ significantly from the final draft issued to Prince, then "Sultan," Hussein: "In the field of internal administration I am to remind your Highness that, in consonance with the traditions of British policy, it has been the aim of His Majesty's Government, while working through and in closest association with the constituted Egyptian authorities, to secure religious and personal freedom, to promote the spread of education, to further the development of the natural resources of the country, and in such measure as the degree of enlightenment of public opinion may permit, to associate the governed in the task of government. Not only is it the intention of His Majesty's Government to remain faithful to such policy, but they are convinced that the clearer definition of Great Britain's position in the country will remove misunderstandings which in the past retarded the progress of reform."
49. NA/FO/407/183, no. 29, Cheetham to Grey, October 30, 1914.
50. This change is striking, for from Cromer to Milner to other commentators during the occupation who favored annexation, the things that hindered progress in Egypt were institutions linked to Ottoman sovereignty, in particular the Capitulations and other European privileges. The original phrase "but they are convinced that the clearer definition of Great Britain's position in the country will remove misunderstandings which in the past retarded the progress of reform" was changed in the final text to "but they are convinced that the clearer definition of Great Britain's position in the country will accelerate progress towards self-government."
51. NA/FO/407/183, no. 29, Cheetham to Grey, October 30, 1914.
52. NA/FO/407/183, no. 36, Grey to Cheethem, November 1, 1914. Martial law was proclaimed on November 2, 1914.

53. BOA, HR.SYS.2404/14, November 5, 1914.

54. "Khedive" is an older Persian title for "lord" or "prince" versus sultan, which is from the Arabic root *sulta*, meaning power or authority. *Sultan* has the meaning in Arabic of ruler, bearer of power/authority. Gabriel Noradounghian, *Recueil d'Actes Internationaux de l'Empire Ottoman* (Paris: F. Pichon, 1897–1903), 3:261.

55. "Prince Husayn has, at more than one interview, reiterated his opinion that Egypt should be transformed into a Kingdom under an Egyptian King. He has compared the extent and wealth of this country with that of the Balkan Kingdoms, and laid stress upon the very great satisfaction which such a transformation would give to Egyptians of all classes." Middle East Center, St. Anthony's College, Oxford/GB165-0055/ File 4, Cheetham papers, Cheetham to Tyrrell, November 10, 1914, enclosure note by Ronald Storrs.

56. Grey eventually approved of the title "sultan" but instructed Cheetham to exclude any reference to Sudan.

57. MEC/GB165-0055/4.

58. There was always a large group of colonial administrators, journalists, lawyers, and commentators in Britain who favored annexation over occupation. The war provided a crisis serious enough to challenge the longstanding Foreign Office policy of managing Ottoman weakness through administrative solutions, whether directed by the British themselves—as in the case of Egypt—or by other European powers through permanent military occupation or through the intervention of international commissions as in Macedonia or other international agreements on administrative reform, such as in Eastern Anatolia.

59. SAD/164/6/95-97, Wingate papers, no. 334, Grey to Cheetham, November 13, 1914.

60. NA/FO/407/183, no. 45, Grey to Cheetham, November 17, 1914.

61. SAD/164/6/95-97, Wingate papers, no. 350, Grey to Bertie, November 17, 1914.

62. SAD/164/6/95-97, Wingate papers, no. 274, Cheetham to Grey, November 18, 1914, in "Notes on the question of succession." Storrs's version of events is even more dramatic. He reported that Cheetham wrote to him, "By the time you get this, it is possible the political status of Egypt will have been decided and announced. I am anti-Annexation and pro-Protectorate. It is too late, even in the twentieth century to denationalize or attempt to absorb races; and even if it were practicable elsewhere, the Nile Mud, which has absorbed Hebrews, Persians, Greeks, Romans and Turks so completely as to efface every trace of them, is not a suitable medium for any such experiment." Storrs, *Orientations*, 151. Cheetham's analysis of governance under occupation is significant and fits in with longstanding Foreign Office attitudes toward administrative ideas in the Near East.

63. NA/FO/407/183, no. 52, Bertie to Grey, November 19, 1914; NA/FO/407/183, no 16, Cheetham to Grey, October 12, 1914. See Renzi, "Great Britain, Russia, and the Straits, 1914–1915," *Journal of Modern History* 42, no. 1 (March 1970): 1–20, especially p. 6.

64. NA/FO/800/48/259, Grey papers, Grey to Cheetham and Wingate, November 18, 1914.

65. NA/FO/407/183, no. 59, Grey to Cheetham, November 25, 1914.

66. NA/FO/407/183, no. 65, Grey to Cheetham, December 1, 1914.

67. SAD/164/6/95-97, Wingate papers, no. 306, Cheetham to Grey, December 8, 1914.

68. NA/FO/407/183, no. 86, Cheetham to Grey, December 21, 1914, three enclosures.

69. The Foreign Office appointed Sir Henry McMahon as first high commissioner for Egypt, where he remained through the end of 1916. Reginald Wingate, who previously held the post of sidar in Sudan, later replaced him.

70. Sir Malcolm McIlwraith, "The Declaration of a Protectorate in Egypt and Its Legal Effects," *Journal of the Society of Comparative Legislation* 17, no. 1/2 (1917): 238–59.

71. Rashid Khalidi's text is an exception: *British Policy Towards Syria & Palestine, 1906–1914: A Study of the Antecedents of the Hussein-the McMahon Correspondence, the Sykes-Picot Agreement, and the Balfour Declaration* (London: Ithaca Press, 1980). See also Aaron Klieman, *Foundations of British Policy in the Arab World: The Cairo Conference of 1921* (Baltimore: John Hopkins University Press, 1970); Elizabeth Monroe, *Britain's Moment in the Middle East* (London: Chatto & Windus, 1963).

72. The fact that British and French wartime planning depended on Ottoman defeat may seem too obvious a point to make explicitly, but the bulk of books and articles on British policy in the Near East, and later the Middle East, treat the Ottoman Empire as an unimportant factor in postwar outcomes. Postwar planners were exceedingly aware that without a decisive Ottoman and German defeat, their schemes would amount to nothing.

73. NA/CAB 27/12, "Report of the Egyptian Administration Committee."

74. Klieman, *Foundations*, 4–7; Monroe, *Britain's Moment in the Middle East*, chap. 1. For the report, see British National Archives, NA/WO/106/6286 and CAB 27/1, "British Desiderata in Turkey in Asia." The bulk of the Cabinet paper is reproduced in J. C. Hurewitz, *The Middle East and North Africa in World Politics* (New Haven: Yale University Press, 1975), 2, no. 12: 26–46. G. P. Gooch and H. Temperley, eds., *British Documents on the Origins of the War, 1898–1914*, vol. 13 (1926–38).

75. Klieman, *Foundations*, 4.

76. NA/CAB 27/1, "British Desiderata in Turkey in Asia." Britain already had strategic interests in these Ottoman provinces, dating from well before the war.

77. NA/WO/106/6286 and NA/CAB 27/1.

78. NA/CAB 27/1.

79. NA/CAB 27/1.

80. NA/WO/106/6286, "British Desiderata in Turkey: Report, Proceedings and Appendices," 67–68.

81. See chapters 5 and 7. The Hürriyet ve İtilaf Fırkası was the CUP's only significant political competitor between 1908 and the Bab-ı Ali Coup of January 1913. As we will see, this party reemerged during the Armistice period (*mütareke*) and controlled the Istanbul government for much of the Allied occupation of Istanbul.

82. NA/CAB 27/1; Parliamentary Archives, LG/F/26/2, Maurice Hankey to Lloyd George, October 12, 1922.

83. The British were well aware of Arab demands for greater autonomy within the Ottoman Empire during the Second Constitutional era. See Rashid Khalidi, *British Policy*, chap. 5; and his "Ottomanism and Arabism in in Syria Before 1914: A Reassessment," in *The Origins of Arab Nationalism*, ed. Lisa Anderson et al.

84. IOR/L/PS/11/128, P 4340/1917; 4384 Turkish Military Plans, Berne 24/10/17 recd 27/10/17, and 4384 Report from Agent 94, September 8, 1917.

85. In the twenty-odd volumes containing documents related to Lord Milner's mission to Cairo in 1919 and 1920, there are hundreds of telegrams from various groups and unions denouncing the "illegal protectorate." For example, a group of students in Cairo sent Lord Milner a telegram for the anniversary of the protectorate: "Lord Milner, Engineering students on strike protest against forced illegal protectorate in interests of friendship pray this may be the last anniversary." NA/FO848/12, Milner Mission, Public Opinion.

86. NA/FO848/12, 12.

87. NA/FO848/12, 13.

88. NA/FO848/12, 20–21.

89. "Report presented in Arabic, with a French Translation to the British High Commissioner on March 30, 1919," in *Egyptian Delegation to the Peace Conference*, 35. Like members of the Wafd argued in Paris, Egyptian nationalists who were willing to meet with the Milner Mission continued to maintain that Egyptian autonomy was won by Mehmed Ali. Rennell Rodd met with Mahmoud Pasha Soliman at Luxor, who insisted, "Egypt must have complete independence. The people of Egypt had won it by arms in 1841. There remained only a shadow nexus with Turkey but that had had no importance

in their eyes." Rodd replied that he "was not prepared to admit that Turkish sovereignty was a mere fiction as he seemed to imply and that Egypt had ever since been independent in the accepted sense of the word. The question was what he meant by independence. He said he meant just the same conditions that were enjoyed by Servia [*sic*] and Greece and other such countries. Egypt was in a higher state of civilization than these countries and once she also had her independence she would go ahead as rapidly as Japan had done in recent years." NA/FO848/8, visit of Sir Rennell Rodd to Mahmoud Paşa Soliman at Luxor, 144.

90. NA/FO608/213, Allenby to Balfour, April 4, 1919.
91. Rennell Rodd, John Maxwell, Sir Cecil Hurst, John Spender, Sir Owen Thomas, and A. T. Loyd.
92. McIntyre, *Boycott of the Milner Mission* (New York: Peter Lang, 1985), 35.
93. NA/FO/848/8, Milner Mission, "Note on the Arabic translation of the word protectorate," Rennell Rodd, October 21, 1919.
94. NA/FO 848/3, Milner Mission, "Record of conversations held with various people of authority in Egypt," conversation between Brigadier General Sir Owen Thomas and Delabor Bey and Saddik Sahmy.
95. NA/FO/848/8, Milner Mission, "The Veiled Protectorate."
96. *In foro demestico* is a legal expression meaning "in a domestic court" versus a foreign court. Emphasis in original. NA/FO/848/8, Milner Mission, "The Veiled Protectorate."
97. Lord Milner, *England in Egypt* (London: Edward Arnold, 1909).
98. Great Britain, *Lausanne Conference on Near Eastern Affairs 1922–1923: Records of Proceedings and Draft Terms of Peace* [Turkey no. 1 (1923); Cmd. 1814] (London: HMSO, 1923), 190.
99. H. W. Temperley, *History of the Peace Conference*, vol. 5, *Economic Reconstruction and Protection of Minorities*, chap. 2 (London: H. Frowde, 1920–1924); Umut Özsu, *Formalizing Displacement: International Law and Population Transfers* (Oxford: Oxford University Press, 2015), 21–50. For the perhaps astonishing accuracy of these claims, see Laura Robson's excellent article "Capitulation Redux: The Imperial Genealogy of the Post-WWI 'Minority' Regime," *American Historical Review* 126, no. 3 (September 2021): 978–1000.
100. Mustafa Aksakal et al., "The Ottoman Empire," in *The Edinburgh Companion to First World War Periodicals*, ed. Marysa Demoor, Cedric Van Dijck, and Birgit Van Puymbroeck (Edinburgh: Edinburgh University Press, 2023); Erol A. F. Baykal, *The Ottoman Press, 1908–1923* (Leiden: Brill, 2019); Orhan Koloğlu, *Osmanlı'da son Tartışmalar: Mondros'tan Mudanya'ya* (Istanbul: Doğan Kitap, 2008).
101. On the Capitulations, see chapter 2. Also see Lâle Can and Aimee M. Genell, "On Empire and Exception: Genealogies of Sovereignty in the

Ottoman World," *Comparative Studies in South Asia, Africa and the Middle East* (2020) 40 (3): 468–73; Ayhan Ceylan, *Osmanlı Taşra İdarî Tarzı Olarak Eyâlet-i Mümtâze ve Mısır Uygulaması* [Exceptional provinces as a style of Ottoman provincial administration and its spplication in Egypt] (Kitabevi, 2014); and Nobuyoshi Fujinami, "Between Sovereignty and Suzerainty: History of the Ottoman Privileged Provinces," in *A World History of Suzerainty: A Modern History of East and West Asia and Translated Concepts*, ed. Okamoto Takashi (Tokyo: Toyo Bunko, 2019).

102. Lerna Ekmekcioğlu has shown how elite understandings of non-Muslim privileges during the Ottoman era fundamentally shaped constructions of citizenship during the early Turkish Republic. She persuasively argues that Republican formulations of citizenship excluded non-Muslims from full citizenship while paradoxically assimilating them through compulsion into the new state. See Ekmekcioğlu, "Republic of Paradox: The League of Nations Minority Protection Regime and the New Turkey's Step-Citizens," *International Journal of Middle East Studies* 46 (2014): 675–79.
103. For Armenian efforts to establish an autonomous province in the new Turkey, see Lerna Ekmekçioğlu, "Republic of Paradox"; Ercan Karakoç, "Osmanlı Hariciyesinde Bir Ermeni Nazır: Gabriyel Noradunkyan Efendi," *Uluslararası İlişkiler Dergisi* 7, no. 25 (Bahar, 2010): 157–77.
104. Mustafa Aksakal and Aimee M. Genell, "Salvation Through War? The Ottoman Search for Sovereignty in 1914," in *The Justification of War and International Order: From the Past to the Present*, ed. Lothar Brock and Hendrik Simon (Oxford: Oxford University Press, 2021).
105. Mehmed Münir served the Turkish state in several crucial roles and was perhaps one of the most important legal mediators between the republic and postwar European states. He spent years in Europe as a Turkish observer at the League of Nations, where, among other things, he attempted to negotiate the return of Mosul to Turkey, based on the armistice lines of 1918 and the National Pact (Misak-i Milli) of 1920. He defended the republic's treatment of Greek minorities after the population exchange. In the early 1920s, he traveled between Geneva and Paris to settle the Ottoman debt. See United Nations Archives Geneva/League of Nations (UNAG/LN)/C.783.1925.I, "Frontier Between Turkey and Iraq" and "The Greek Minority in Constantinople and the Turkish Minority in Western Thrace."
106. Emery Kelèn and Aloïs Derso, *Guignol à Lausanne* (Lausanne: A. Marsens, 1923); Emery Kelèn, *Peace in Their Time: Men Who Led Us In and Out of War, 1914–1945* (London: Victor Gollancz, 1964.)
107. Reynolds, *Shattering Empires*.
108. Newspapers across the political spectrum weighed in on the question of minority rights during the early Armistice period, many of which argued

that legal privileges tied to religion were inimical to modern ideas of citizenship. See, for example, Abdurrahman Şeref, "İmtiyazat-i Mezhebiye," *Sabah*, 9 teşrin-i evvel [October], 1918.

109. Cemal Paşa, *Hâtırat: 1913–1919* (Dersaadet: [Ahmed Ihsan ve Ş ürekası Matbaası,] 1339/1922), 237.
110. BOA, HR.HMŞ .İ ŞO 214/14 15 M 1337 (October, 21 1918).
111. BOA, HR.HMŞ .İ ŞO, 214/14.
112. Ekmekçioğlu, "Republic of Paradox."
113. Karakoç, "Osmanlı Hariciyesinde," 171–72; Bilal N. Şimşir, *Lozan Telgrafları* (Ankara: TTK Yayınları, 1990), 192.
114. UNAG/LN/R1617/41/23457/807, "Protection of Minorities in Turkey," Mr. Colban, "Record of conversation with M. M. Gabriel Noradounghian and Mikael Papadjanian of the Armenian Delegation on the question of the protection of minorities in the Ottoman Empire, particularly Armenians," September 14, 1922. Erik Colban was a Norwegian international lawyer who was the first director of the Minorities Section at the League of Nations.
115. "Je crois au contraire que ce serait un danger pour les Armeniens parce que les Turcs y verraient le signe et la menace d'un nouveau partage de leur territoire national."
116. *Lozan Telegraf.* In the days leading up to Lausanne, Refet Bele gave an interview to the *Manchester Guardian* where he noted: "Mosul is Turkish and we want it back. Here is England's opportunity. She could win our friendship with one strike if she gave Mosul to us without bargaining. And if she were to give us Mesopotamia as well she would win not only our friendship but that of all Islam."
117. Aimee M. Genell, "The End of Egypt's Occupation: Ottoman Sovereignty and the British Declaration of Protection," in *Beyond Versailles: Sovereignty, Legitimacy, and the Formation of New Politics After the Great War*, ed. Roberta Pergher and Marcus Payk (Bloomington: University of Indiana, 2019).
118. Great Britain. CMD 1814, *Lausanne Conference on Near Eastern Affairs: Recordings of the Proceedings* (London: HMO, 1923).
119. Ahmed Reshid, "Les droits minoritaires en Turquie dans le passé et le présent," *Revue générale de droit international public* (1935): 293–341; Ahmed Réchid [Ahmed Reşid], "L'Islam et le droit des gens," *Collected Courses of the Hague Academy of International Law/ Recueil des Cours* 60 (1937): 371–506; BOA, HR.SAID 19/21; Bab-ı Ali Hariciye Nezareti, *Salname-i Nezaret-i Hariciye* (1306/1899).
120. Ahmed Reşid, "Kapitülasyonlar," *Dârülfünûn Hukuk Fakültesi Mecmuası* 6/37 (1928): 1–38; "Kuvve-i Müessese Nazariyyesi," *Dârülfünûn Hukuk Fakültesi*

Mecmuası 6, no. 38 (1928): 1299–328; *Hukuku umumiyei düvel* (Istanbul: Arkadaş Matbaası, 1928).

Conclusion

1. The *Safahat* (Pages) consisted of seven volumes published between 1911 and 1933, the last being *Gölgeler* (The Book of shadows), published in exile in Egypt. The poems were often somewhat autobiographical and contained stories about his experiences and travels. For example, "Berlin Hâtıraları" (Berlin recollections) and "Necid Çöllerinden Medine'ye" (From the deserts of Nejd to Medina) were based on his Teşkilat-i Mahsusa missions. Mehmet Akif Ersoy, *Safahat*, vol. 5, *Hâtıralar* (Istanbul: Dergah Yayinlari, 2010)
2. Benjamin Fortna, *The Circassian: A Life of Eşref Bey, Late Ottoman Insurgent and Special Agent* (New York: Oxford, 2016), 174–75; Brett Wilson, *Translating the Qur'an in the Age of Nationalism: Print Culture and Modern Islam in Turkey* (New York: Oxford, 2014), 176–80; Ertuğrul Düzdağ and M. Orhan Okay, "Mehmed Akif Ersoy," in *Türk Diyanet Vakfı İslam Ansiklopedisi*, 28:432–34.
3. In the same sermon, he also cast his patron, Abbas Halim Paşa, as "one of the most self-sacrificing and virtuous men of the Islamic world (*alem-i İslam*)." Mehmed Akif (Ersoy), "Nasrallah Kürsüsü'nden," (Anadolu'da) *Sebilülrreşad*, 25 teşrin-i sani 1226 [1920], no. 464, p. 2.
4. To this day, Ersoy's poem hangs in most every classroom across Turkey.
5. The first article of the 1921 national constitution stated that "sovereignty resided in the people, without conditions." T.B.M.M., "Teşkilâti-i Esasiye Kanunu," *Ceride-i Resmiye*, no. 1, 7 Şubat 1337 [February 7, 1921]: 196–99.
6. Wilson, *Translating the Qur'an*, 178.
7. Wilson, chap. 7.
8. Halil Halid wrote in English and Ottoman Turkish and published in London, Istanbul, and Cairo. See his *Diary of a Turk* (London: Adam and Charles Black, 1903); *Study in English Turcophobia* (London: The Pan-Islamic Society, [1904]); *The Crescent Versus the Cross* (London: Luzac, 1907); *Türk ve Arap* [Turk and Arab] (İstanbul: Kapı Yayınları, 2016), originally published in Cairo in 1912; *Türk Hakimiyeti ve İngiliz Cihangirliği* [Turkish sovereignty and English imperialism] (Istanbul: Yeni Matbaa, 1341 [1925]); and *The Turcophobia of the English Imperialists* (N.p., 1919).
9. Ahmet Hamdi Tanpinar. *Beş Şehir: Istanbul, Bursa, Konya, Erzurum, Ankara* [Five cities] (Istanbul: Dergah Yayınları, 2004), 122.
10. The Kavalalı were major architectural patrons in Cairo too. While at times they borrowed from styles popular in Istanbul—especially the yalıs that linked

the Bosporus—and Mehmed Ali's Ottoman-style mosque in the Citadel in Cairo and the sabil, for the most part they used a local vernacular, particularly when building monumental constructions such as the Khedive Abbas Hilmi II's patronage of the al-Rifa'i Mosque (b. 1869–1912), which was built in neo-Mamluk style and faces the fourteenth-century Mosque of Sultan Hassan. See Khaled Fahmy, *All the Pasha's Men: Mehmed Ali, His Army and the Making of Modern Egypt* (Cairo: The American University in Cairo, 1997); Agnieszka Dobrowlska and Khaled Fahmy, *Muhammad 'Ali and His Sabil* (Cairo: American University in Cairo Press, 2005); Nebahat Avcioğlu and Mercedes Volait, "*Jeux de miroir*: Architecture of Istanbul and Cairo from Empire to Modernism," in *A Companion to Islamic Art and Architecture*, ed. Finbarr Barry Flood and Gülru Necipoğlu (London: Wiley Blackwell, 2017), 1122–49; and Klaus Kreiser, "Public Monuments in Turkey and Egypt, 1840–1916," *Muqarnas, An Annual on the Visual Culture of the Islamic World* 14 (1997): 103–17.

11. Quoted in M. Baba Tanman, "The Social and Cultural Impact of the Kavalalı Mehmed Ali Paşa Synasty on Istanbul," in *Nil Kıyısından Boğaziçi'ne: Kavalalı Mehmed Ali Paşa Hanedanı'nın İstanbul'daki İzleri* (Istanbul: İstanbul Araştırmaları Enstitüsü, 2011), 43; Ahmed Cevdet Paşa, *Marûzat* (Istanbul: Çağri, 1980), 7–8: "El-hâsil, Mısır döküntüleri Istanbul ahâlisinin ahlâkını bozmağla devlet ü millete azîm zararları dokundu."

12. The first such structure was Beykoz Palace, a gift from Mehmed Ali Paşa to Sultan Abdülmecid. Construction started in 1845 but didn't finish until 1855, after Mehmed Ali had died. Sinan Kuneralp, ed. *Nıl Kıyısından Boğaziçi'ne Kavalalı Mehmed Ali Paşa Handedanı'nın İstanbul'daki İzleri=From the Shores of the Nile to the Bosphorus: Traces of Kavalalı Mehmed Ali Pasha Dynasty in Istanbul* (Istanbul: İstanbul Araştırmaları Enstitüsü, 2011), 144–48; Heath Lowry and İsmail E. Erünsal, *Remembering One's Roots: Mehmed Ali Paşa of Egypt's Links to the Macedonian Town of Kavala Architectural Monuments, Inscriptions & Documents* (Istanbul: Bahçeşehir University, 2011).

13. Ilham Khuri-Makdissi. *The Eastern Mediterranean and the Making of Global Radicalism, 1860–1914* (Berkeley: University of California Press, 2010); Julia Ann Clancy-Smith, *Mediterraneans: North Africa and Europe in the Age of Migration, 1800–1900* (Berkeley: University of California Press, 2011); Jens Hanssen, *Fin de Siècle Beirut: The Making of an Ottoman Provincial Capital* (Oxford: Oxford University Press, 2005); C. A. Bayly, *Modernity and Culture: From the Mediterranean to the Indian Ocean* (New York: Columbia University Press, 2002); Leila Tarazi Fawaz. *Merchants and Migrants in Nineteenth Century Beirut* (Cambridge: Harvard University Press, 1983); Joel Beinin and Zachary Lockman, *Workers on the Nile: Nationalism, Communism, Islam, and the Egyptian Working Class, 1882–1954* (Princeton: Princeton University Press, 1988).

14. Christopher Michael Low, "Ottoman Infrastructures of the Saudi Hydro-State: The Technopolitics of Pilgrimage and Potable Water in the Hijaz," *Comparative Studies in Society and History* 57, no. 4 (2015): 942–74; Venetia Porter, ed., *Hajj: Journey to the Heart of Islam* (Cambridge, Mass.: Harvard University Press, 2012).

15. The Mixed Courts adjudicated civil cases between Europeans and Ottomans subjects and were staffed by European and Ottoman/Egyptian judges. The language of the court was French. The Commission of the Public Debt was staffed by British, French, German, Austrian, Italian, and Russian commissioners and oversaw control Egyptian finances, the supervision of Egyptian debt by European lenders.

16. Mehmet Akif (Ersoy), who produced the first modern Turkish translation of the Qur'an, worked largely in Cairo. See Brett Wilson, "The First Translations of the Qur'an in Modern Turkey (1924–1938)," *International Journal of Middle East Studies* 41, no. 3 (2009): 419–35.

17. Quincy Wright, "Sovereignty of the Mandates," *American Journal of International Law*, 17, 4(1923): 691–703; *Mandates Under the League of Nations* (New York: Greenwood Press, 1930). As Susan Pedersen has shown, this question provoked intense debate among League officials through the end of the organization. Susan Pedersen, *The Guardians: The League of Nations and the Crisis of Empire* (New York: Oxford University Press, 2015), chapter 7.

18. Manley O. Hudson, "Admission of Egypt to Membership in the League of Nations," *American Journal of International Law* 31, no. 4 (October 1937): 681–83. The mixed courts were not disbanded until 1949. See Joel Benin, "Egypt: Society and Economy, 1923–1952," in *Cambridge History of Egypt*, vol. 2.

19. Mustafa Kemal (Atatürk), *Nutuk: Gazi Mustafa Kemal tarafından*, trans. with Mustafa Aksakal (Ankara: n.p., 1927), 494.

20. This is one more reason to take Richard Bulliet's question, "What went right?" versus "What went wrong?" more seriously in comparisons between modern Turkey and modern Arab states. The Republic of Turkey had a functional and long-existing bureaucracy, among other assets. Bulliet, *The Case for Islamo-Christian Civilization* (New York: Columbia University Press, 2006).

21. The original sign in the old Büyük Meclis in Ankara, before its present location, read "Hakimiyet milletindir." Today it reads "Egemenlik, kayitsiz, sartsiz milletindir!"

Index

Printed and bound by CPI Group (UK) Ltd, Croydon, CR0 4YY

16/09/2026

14963454-0004